OFFICE HOURS: DAY AND NIGHT
The Autobiography of Janet Travell, M.D.

An NAL Book
The World Publishing Company
New York and Cleveland

Acknowledgment is gratefully made for permission to quote from the following sources: Ernest Fleischer, "A Fable for Curriculum Makers: Gulliver Also Ran," *Junior College Journal,* Vol. 33, pp. 13–15. Copyright 1962 by Ernest Fleischer; used by permission of Ernest Fleischer and the American Association of Junior Colleges, Washington, D.C. John F. Kennedy, "To an Unknown Youth Somewhere in America. How to Prepare for the Presidency," *Parade Magazine,* Sept. 23, 1962, pp. 6–7. Copyright 1962 by Parade Publications, Inc., New York, and used by permission. Virginia Powell, "Are the Children of Women Doctors Neglected?" *Westchester Medical Bulletin,* Vol. 17, pp. 32, 39. Copyright 1949 by the Westchester County Medical Association, Purchase, N. Y., and used by permission. Janet G. Travell and David D. Lewis, "Fit to Be President," *Sports Illustrated,* April 3, 1961, pp. 8–9. Copyright 1961 by Time, Inc., New York, and used by permission.

First Printing   November 1968

Published by The New American Library, Inc.
in association with The World Publishing Company
2231 West 110th Street, Cleveland, Ohio 44102
Library of Congress Catalog Card Number: 68-57422
Printed in the United States of America

TO JACK, my husband,
with love and appreciation for his words,
"Writing a book excuses everything."

OFFICE HOURS:
DAY AND NIGHT

Contents

Author's Note

Our second grandson was six and in first grade when my husband and I visited the family for Christmas, 1963. A girl in second grade came by to see him and after she was introduced to Mrs. Powell, alias Dr. Travell, I overheard them talking.

"She's my Grandma and she's the doctor for the President," Gordon explained proudly.

"Oh, we studied all about her in school last year," was the nonchalant reply.

It startled me that I was being taught as an object of history to first-graders; I felt more a part of the living future than of the historical past. What bare facts about me did the teacher have, I wondered, with which to kindle the imagination of youngsters?

True, I had studied hard and become a doctor, I had been the first woman to serve as Personal Physician to the President at the White House, and I had brought back the rocking chair. I had children and grandchildren. I still enjoyed tennis and an active life. But how had it all come about? What inner drives and forces of circumstance had molded me? Where did I acquire my energy? Had the rewards outweighed the regrets and personal sacrifices of my demanding profession? No written record was accessible to provide the answers.

The first purpose in writing this book, then, was to uncover in my unique upbringing, my education, and home life the solutions to those perplexing questions and, through personal recollections, to disclose the fruits of my search.

In that filtering of experience I hoped to inform young people about the profession of medicine—either to attract them toward it or to repel them from it. As one of my Wellesley College classmates who became a schoolteacher said, "If I can not be an example, at least I can be a warning."

If I could mirror my life as a wife, a mother, and a physician, I might provide some needed guidelines for the wise choice of a career.

This book is a story of dreams come true. I have written it not because of misfortune or controversy, but to share the good things that have been mine. In doing so, I have tried through first-hand data to sketch human portraits of some people with whom I have traveled on the journey of life.

I have lived in a very special world—a world of love and security; beauty and serenity; opportunity, adventure, and variety; challenge and achievement; and the appreciation of my peers. I have had a sufficiency of everything that I desired and a surfeit of nothing.

I can say this in spite of having lived through two World Wars and the Korean and Vietnam wars, the financial crash of 1929, and the economic depression of the Thirties. In those years, pessimists were trumpeting that there would be no future world for their children, and the birth rate in this country fell.

Now, even as then, children have a future. I believe that the coming generations will find their existence in this universe to be as vivid and satisfying as mine has been. The resources that are built within each person during growth—by family, teachers, and friends—can enable mankind to surmount change and to survive in a milieu which we can not now envision.

I have faith that young people will create a better world while they are forcing change. Apathy—indifference due to the feeling that nothing can be done about a problem—tends to characterize their elders and deters action for progress. It is my dream that this autobiography will stir older generations to a more actively enthusiastic outlook. In a poem I advise them to:

KEEP RIDING THOSE TROLLEYS

Most people live in the valleys,
But some withdraw to mountaintops
And leave below in dim alleys
Shadows of strangers, neighbors, cops.

Below, men arm for their rallies,
Seek shelter in gutters of blood.
Still, hate with love never tallies;
Strong souls with lost ones tramp through mud.

Aloft, their shelters are gullies
Rain-made on wind-shaven summit.
No hullabaloo there sullies
Echoes of rocks as they plummet.

To dwell above all man's follies
Is cowardly resignation.
Better to climb on life's trolleys
With hope and high destination.

Janet Travell, M.D.

Acknowledgments

First, I thank Robert A. Gutwillig, my editor, for persuading me to undertake my autobiography, and for encouraging me to write it in my own way and at my own pace. Without him, this book would not have been written.

I wish to thank those people who have given me permission to quote their letters: former White House Physicians Vice Admiral Joel T. Boone and Major General Wallace H. Graham; Senator Barry Goldwater and Representative William S. Moorhead, Congress of the United States; Dr. Edward Tolstoi and Dr. Myron August; Ernest W. Rose, Sr.; Mrs. Lola G. McGillivray for a poem written by her father, Charles M. French; my husband's sister, Dorothy Powell Moore; Captain Vinicio Pinci, our son-in-law; and our daughters, Janet Pinci and Virginia Street.

For permission to publish their poems, I express further appreciation to our two daughters; and also to our son-in-law Edward H. Street and to our grandson Richard McAlee.

I extend thanks to Frederick K. Trask, Jr., Chairman of the Executive Committee of the Society of the New York Hospital, for permission to quote President John F. Kennedy's filmed greetings to that hospital's Fund for Medical Progress Dinner on December 7, 1961.

For the historical background of laws that established the post of White House Physician, I express appreciation to Hon. Lewis Deschler, Parliamentarian of the U.S. House of Representatives.

For data concerning my family, I am indebted to my sister, Virginia Travell Weeks; my brothers, Clark Travell and Talcott Bates; and my first cousin, the late Margaret Travell Bennett. For reminiscences about my father I am grateful to my father's and my friends Boyd Lewis, William Earl Bradley, and Dr. Harry Gold. I thank Mr. and Mrs. Franz T. Stone, and also Dr. Rudolf W. Hack, for their letters from my father.

For information about my husband's family, I am indebted to Dorothy, his sister, and to his first cousins Edgar and Eric Norfleet.

I am most grateful to my mother and father for having preserved many of my early sayings, school notebooks, and my letters, as well as our family mementos and documents.

My deepest gratitude goes to Jack, my husband, for his inexhaustible good humor in finding material that was lost in my mysterious filing system, for tireless proofreading of manuscript and galleys, and for his sense of proportion in criticism. Without him, this book would never have come to fruition.

List of
Author's Poems

CHAPTER 1

The Discipline
of Disability

In April, 1955, at our home in Pelham, New York, I lay flat on my back with my neck held rigid in a steel collar. Chin braced high, I slept in the collar, ate in the collar, and in fact, wore it twenty-four hours a day. I could not lie on either my right or left side without pain, and my eyes traveled over only a small territory of ceiling that had no horizon. Time seemed to stand still.

My left arm was partially paralyzed. When I raised it, my elbow and wrist flopped unexpectedly and my hand sometimes hit me in the face. The end of my left thumb lacked sensation. Patches of skin on my left arm were disagreeably numb and at the same time burning and prickling. Wearing the collar was no hardship because without it I suffered severe pain and with it, if I did not move, I was relatively comfortable.

The diagnosis was clear: acute rupture of an intervertebral disk in the neck with compression of the sixth cervical, spinal nerve root that supplied certain muscles and skin areas of my left arm. I knew the nature of the trouble myself when it happened, as I awkwardly tried to shut our wide car door, in Pelham on April Fool's Day of all days!

My husband was driving the car, and I was late. As I hurriedly jumped in and sat on the seat beside him, the lower corner of the open door stuck in soft dirt banked above the curb. First I pulled at the door with my right hand and then for greater strength I reached across with my left arm and gave a great tug on the handle. A sharp pain enveloped me. I said, "Jack, I hurt my neck. I don't believe I can close that door."

1

As the symptoms developed, I went to bed at home, and I telephoned Dr. Nelson W. Cornell at his office in New York. He was a friend of nearly thirty years. We had worked together in the old New York Hospital on West 16th Street where I interned. There I had acquired first-hand knowledge of his competence in orthopedic surgery and of his intuitive consideration for sick people.

"Pete, I think I have an acute cervical disk. Can you stop and see me on your way home tonight?"

Fortunately for me, he was our neighbor in Pelham.

"Yes, and I'll bring you out a collar," he said.

I felt reassured that I had reached him and that help was on the way. Sometimes, the sudden rupture of an intervertebral disk requires emergency surgery in order to prevent further and perhaps permanent nerve damage. In any case, the course of recovery was likely to be slow. Exactly how long I would be disabled I knew that no one could predict. Weeks? Months? Even years? I would not waste Pete's time by raising the question.

On a bedside table at my right, a radio and telephone provided me with the means of communication with the outside world. I became acquainted with the all-night radio programs and broadcasters. I tried to keep in touch with my research team at the medical school and with my patients through my secretary in the office at 9 West 16th Street. For the moment, they were part of another existence. It was a shock to everyone that so durable and active a person as I had been could have vanished suddenly from the scene.

The house was very quiet. Our two daughters, Janet and Virginia, were away in college and both were married. Evenings, my husband would read aloud to me, and I marveled that his soothing and expressive voice held out so long. His patience was unlimited.

For the most part our diet of reading matter was light. It included, I remember, Harry Golden's *Only in America* and Patrick Dennis's *Auntie Mame.* We reread Mark Twain's *Innocents Abroad* and *Joan of Arc,* some of O. Henry's stories, Stephen Leacock's essays, and David Grayson's *Adventures in Understanding.* Cornelia Otis Skinner and Emily Kimbrough's *Our Hearts Were Young and Gay* revived my own excursions to Europe in 1922 and 1926. One heavier item in our diet that I recall Jack's reading was Gunnar Myrdal's *An American Dilemma,* which the author had given me in 1954. Sometimes we read poetry; Jack and I both enjoyed Joyce Kilmer's verse. Detective stories we ran through too fast. Erle Stanley Gardner's Perry Mason mysteries were our favorites, but we liked the continued serials in the *Saturday Evening Post* that left us dangling in suspense. The short stories and reviews in the *Atlantic Monthly* were a constant source of entertainment, and we went back through issues that we had not had time to read. I still have on my bookshelf the January, 1954, number of this magazine that contains an article by Senator John F. Kennedy on "New England and the South, The Struggle for Industry."

During this period, my father, Dr. Willard Travell, spent the nights at our house. Then eighty-five, he was actively practicing medicine, and still playing tennis and commuting by train and subway between the office and the three places that he called home; one was with us in Westchester County, one with my sister, Dr. Virginia Travell Weeks, a pediatrician in Brooklyn Heights, and one with my brother, Clark Travell, in Wilton, Connecticut. A pioneer in physical medicine, my father was especially skilled in the treatment of musculoskeletal and neurological pain, and he helped me greatly at the onset of this painful attack by injecting procaine (Novocaine) into the tightened muscles of my neck.

Mine was mainly a waiting period, however. Given time, the gelatinous material that is extruded from a ruptured intervertebral disk should shrink and the pressure created on the nerve root be relieved. The two keys to recovery without surgery were immobilization of the spine and muscular relaxation. Tension would shorten the long spinal muscles that pull the vertebrae closer together, and so would increase the pinch on the weakened disk and on the injured swollen nerve fibers.

I forced myself to concentrate on how to relax. I let my thoughts roam over my happy, adventurous, and rewarding lifetime of over fifty years. I pondered on this crippling kind of illness that represented a new experience for me; as a physician, I had much to learn from it of a constructive nature. I could wait for the outcome, patiently, as many had waited before me.

About a week after my neck strain, as I lay in bed at home, Dr. Ephraim Shorr telephoned from the New York Hospital–Cornell Medical Center, where I was also on the medical staff. He asked me to see a patient of his who was suffering from a complicated low back problem.

"Eph, I would be happy to, if I could, but I can't," I told him.

"This is a very special person, a wonderful young man, Jack Kennedy from Massachusetts. I have known him for years. He is on leave now from the United States Senate, and he can't carry on. He is in the Hospital for Special Surgery for a checkup after a spine fusion there about six months ago. It didn't help him as we hoped it would."

His words were quick and urgent, and his voice was almost pleading.

"But Eph," I interrupted, "it wouldn't matter who he is or what the trouble is, I couldn't see him now. You don't know what has happened to me."

I explained my situation. The natural question followed.

"When do you think you *will* be able to see him?"

"I just can't say, I'm sorry," I replied.

I could hear Eph sigh at the other end of the line. There was a long pause before he said slowly, "Very well. We will send him back to Florida, and when you are better he will come to New York to see you."

I agreed, wondering about *my* future, not knowing that history had tapped me on the shoulder.

People in pain spend lonely hours. Ordinary conversation often fatigues them, and this was particularly true in my case. The steel collar, that braced my lower jaw against my breastbone, prevented the hinged jawbone from descending. To open my mouth I had to raise the upper jaw and with it the whole top of my head, by tilting my skull backward. Talking and chewing required a completely new coordination of movement of the neck muscles that pivot the head on the upper end of the spine. This effort was tiring and painful. I preferred to sip liquids through a tube and not to speak.

Friends who came often and made no demands of me were Dee and Zella du Vigneaud and Boyd and Hazel Lewis. I would listen to their banter with Jack until I could not refrain from laughing—and that hurt, too. Writing and even reading were virtually impossible since I could not hold my arms up for any length of time. My resource was meditation.

My thoughts floated like clouds in the sky, sometimes lofty and changing shape slowly, sometimes racing in opposite directions at the same time according to the levels of consciousness. Having nothing to do but think was a rare and not unwelcome event for me.

I gave little thought to another patient who was at the same time confined to inactivity by disability, Jack Kennedy, the Junior Senator from Massachusetts. Crutches enabled him then to move slowly and painfully from his bed to a table on the lawn of his father's Palm Beach home by the ocean. Overriding his illness, pain, and discouragement, he kept busy painting the portrait of courage. His pen sketched the lives of men who fought for principle in the national interest and who surmounted obstacles against hopeless odds. Their triumphs, which he portrayed in his book *Profiles in Courage,* soon won acclaim.

Meanwhile, my own recovery from disability progressed faster than anticipated. My first excursion from home was on April 11 for X-rays of my neck and a complete examination by a neurologist. Those had been delayed because in Pete Cornell's clinical judgment the benefits of immobilization and bed-rest outweighed any new information to be gained immediately by these additional examinations. I have a conviction that the surprising speed with which my mechanical type of pain was alleviated was in large part due to Pete's wisdom and my good fortune in being confined at home rather than having been transported at a critical stage by car or ambulance to the hospital.

Within a few weeks, I graduated from my hard steel collar to a leather one with soft rolled edges. Wrapped in a silk scarf, it brought me comfort for many months, particularly in checking the whipping motion of the head and neck whenever I rode in a car. However, even with the support of the collar, for a long time I had to ride lying flat on the back seat while Jack and I commuted forty miles round trip between Pelham and the hospital and our offices in New York.

On April 25, I had lunch with Dr. Ephraim Shorr in the student cafeteria of Cornell University Medical College. We spoke about Jack Kennedy in Florida. Eph said that Dr. Philip D. Wilson, his orthopedic surgeon at the Hospital for Special Surgery, whom I knew well, was enthusiastic about my seeing the Senator; all his records would be available to me. I gave a few scheduled lectures in pharmacology to the second-year medical students. For these I was vain enough to remove the collar, but my impression is that the lectures were not improved by my pride.

By mid-May, I was seeing patients, although I was not working full time. I was looking forward to spending the long Memorial Day weekend at our isolated farm in the Berkshire Hills of western Massachusetts. The great hedge of purple lilacs around the old farmhouse would be in full bloom and their fragrance would perfume the mountain air. The change and rest would do me good. We might even stay until the time came to drive to Wellesley College near Boston, where our older daughter, Janet, would receive her B.A. degree on June 13. My husband and I had arranged to take the entire month of June for our vacation, and both our daughters were to join us at the farm.

On May 24, Eph Shorr telephoned again and then he made an appointment for Senator Jack Kennedy to see me in my 9 West 16th Street office at 1:30 P.M. on Thursday, May 26. Eph would come with him. The Senator called from Washington and spoke with me directly. I cleared my calendar of other work for the length of time that I thought the Senator's medical problem might need. On this visit and on subsequent ones, I made sure that he encountered no other patient in my office.

At our first meeting, the thin young Senator on crutches could barely navigate the few steps down from the sidewalk into my ground-floor office. Left-sided pain in his back and leg made it almost impossible for him to bear weight on that foot, and a stiff right knee since a football injury in his youth made it difficult for him to step up or down with his weight on the right leg, because that required bending the right knee. He had come with Dr. Shorr by taxi, and the taxi driver helped him down the steps.

Three days earlier on May 23, 1955, Washington newspapers had headlined the return of John F. Kennedy to the United States Senate after seven months of convalescence from back surgery. That Monday at National Airport, reporters welcomed him "looking tan and fit" and walking without crutches as he and his wife, Jacqueline, deplaned from their flight from West Palm Beach. It must have taken tremendous grit for him to create that effect of health.

He and I and Eph talked. Senator Kennedy seemed tired and discouraged. He listened intently, but he answered my questions briefly, almost reluctantly, as if he were retelling a boring story. He looked thin; his weight of about 155 pounds did not adequately cover his generous frame and stature of six feet. In spite of his Florida suntan, I thought that he appeared pale and anemic, and that indeed proved to be the case. He moved guardedly. He turned his body in one piece when he wanted to face me or Dr. Shorr; Eph and I sat on opposite sides of a wide desk, while his chair was placed at one end. Not only the motion of his back, but also the rotation of his neck was restricted. When I examined him, the reality of his ordeal was brought home to me by the callus under each armpit toward the shoulder blade where the skin had borne his weight on crutches for so long.

I explained my findings and outlined a general plan of management. That day I was able to demonstrate the role that residual muscle spasm may play in longstanding pain and stiffness of a joint after injury; the range of motion at his right knee was increased at once by my brief and simple treatment of the knee muscles that were in spasm. The wisest course would be for me to admit him to the New York Hospital for intensive treatment and some additional tests.

The Senator sat in an old-style, North Carolina porch rocker with woven cane seat and back. The office was quiet and unhurried. He asked a few questions, always to the point. How long would the improvement in the motion of his knee last? He was understandably skeptical. He was not prepared to accept readily one more doctor and another kind of treatment. Seven months earlier he had undergone a lumbar spine fusion, after which a local infection had developed, and about four months later the metal fusion plate had been removed in a second operation. His crutches had been a familiar sight in the Senate during the summer of a year ago, and now he was still obliged to use them. Could he face another hospital?

He had come to see me because of his stubborn hope for better health and respite from pain, and because of his respect and regard for Dr.

Ephraim Shorr, who, as Chief of the Endocrinology Service at the New York Hospital–Cornell Medical Center, had successfully managed his adrenal insufficiency in collaboration with Dr. Sara Jordan of Boston.

It was decided. He would enter the New York Hospital as soon as possible. I telephoned the hospital admitting office. A room was available on the fifteenth floor of the Baker Pavilion, Room 1502. He would go there directly.

On leaving my office with Dr. Shorr, he asked as an afterthought, "Will there be a television in the room?"

I made certain that the hospital would have a TV set ready for him.

I took with me to the New York Hospital and installed in his room, too, the rocking chair that he had been sitting in and had commented on. It was bulky and high backed, but by knocking off the rockers I could fit it inside my two-door sedan, the car with the extra-wide, heavy door that had been the cause of my neck injury two months earlier. I parked my car at the delivery entrance to the hospital and transported the rocking chair up in the freight and food elevator. The nurses thought it funny to see the chair coming down the hall with the loose rockers, a leather cushion, a sloped footstool, and my medical bag on top, all stacked on the chair's seat.

Senator Kennedy remained in the New York Hospital under my care for a week. Sorensen recorded his return to the United States Senate on June 1.[1] The Senator's thirty-eighth birthday fell on Sunday, May 29, and he went out of the hospital for the day on a pass. The Senate had recessed over the Memorial Day weekend, from 10:30 A.M. on Friday, May 27, until noon on Tuesday, May 31. No notice was taken by the press of Senator John F. Kennedy's whereabouts during that holiday period.

When Senator Kennedy could leave his demanding duties in the Congress, other visits to my New York office followed. Before the year was out, I would sit at the table in Palm Beach where he wrote *Profiles in Courage* and I would view the ocean surf from that same lawn under the sloping palms in the company of a revitalized John F. Kennedy. We had started a long journey together.

[1] Theodore C. Sorensen, *Kennedy* (New York, Harper & Row, 1965), p. 68.

CHAPTER 2

Early Conditioning
of Behavior

My birthplace was a house at 17 East 12th Street in the city of New York; the date was December 17, 1901, and the hour was 1:45 A.M. The next winter my parents moved to an old brownstone house with a high stoop at 27 East 11th Street, and that was my home for fifteen or sixteen years. The front of the four-story building was eventually covered to the roof by a giant wisteria vine that my mother planted about 1902. From inside the house it framed the windows in green leaves, and sometimes its lavender blooms hung against the city skyline.

Under the front stoop was an iron grill door that had six or eight inches of clearance between its bottom edge and the cement floor. At an age when I could only creep, I crawled out under this gate unobserved and inch-wormed my way on the sidewalk around the corner to University Place. There I was recognized and brought home by the owner of a nearby cleaning and tailoring establishment, Pomeranz and Goldfein, which our household patronized. In later years, the tailor used to tell me about my early escapade in exploration.

My earliest recollection is an event that occurred in the summer of 1903 when I was about twenty months old. That age must be correct because 1903 was the last summer that my family spent at Elm Hill, the Travell farm near Troy, New York. I am certain that I do remember it because it was a happening that I never heard my parents describe, and because it arouses a series of emotions that I can still feel.

I was walking with my father and other grown-ups on a dirt road at Elm

Hill. We came to some baby goats in a pasture; they are shining white in my memory. I wanted one badly. The farmer said, "You can have one if you can catch it."

I crawled under the wire fence and stumbled after the lively little kids, this way and that, falling as I reached for them. Frustration and anger rekindle as I think of it. I would not give up the chase, nor would I come out of the field; my mother used to say that I was the most stubborn child she ever knew.

I must have at first entertained and then exasperated those grown-ups. Finally, the farmer called to me, "Come out, and I will send you one to New York."

Satisfied, I crawled back onto the road. I have a visual flash of reaching up to hold my father's large hand—he seemed to be all hand—and of walking along contentedly.

Time passed in the city and my baby goat did not arrive. After what seemed to me a long wait, one day I asked my father, "Will my baby goat come for Christmas?"

He laughed and said, "Haven't you forgotten that? The farmer was only joking."

The sense of disappointment and injustice remained with me and made me wary of people's promises. And when I thought later how this light-hearted deception had hurt me, I vowed never to make a promise that I could not keep, above all to a child.

My next recollection is of a Christmas Eve at 27 East 11th Street when I had just had my third birthday. The occasion stands out in my memory, perhaps because it represented another kind of disillusionment. I had been put to bed and supposedly I was sound asleep, but I was awake and listening for Santa Claus and his reindeer. When I heard a noise, I tiptoed to the open living room door. There by the fireplace my mother and father were gaily filling our stockings and arranging packages under the tree. Unnoticed, I watched in surprise. Silently I returned to my cot. I was not disenchanted but excited by my discovery. Now I, too, could pretend to believe in Santa Claus. I kept my secret and played the game well.

When I became a parent and our daughter Janet was five years old and Virginia was three, Janet furtively raised the question of Santa Claus and her younger sister, who had not yet been exposed to nursery school. Shortly before Christmas, this conversation took place: "Mummy, what are we going to do about Ginia?"

"What do you mean, Janet?"

"I mean about Santa Claus."

"I don't understand."

"Come on, Mummy, you know Santa Claus isn't real."

"But Janet, Santa Claus is real." I was thinking of the Spirit of Christmas and stalling for time.

"Oh, Mummy, you know that Santa Claus is just a personification."

"Janet, you don't even know what that word means."

"Yes I do, too."

"What does it mean?"

"Well, there's Uncle Sam, he's a personification."

Janet won the argument. We decided to wait another year to let Virginia in on the secret of Santa Claus.

As the years passed, on Christmas Eve my husband used to read aloud not only Clement C. Moore's classic poem, " 'Twas the Night Before Christmas," but also Francis Pharcellous Church's lyric prose that answered a little girl's question in the *New York Sun* of September 21, 1897. She asked, "Please tell me the truth, is there a Santa Claus?"

"Yes, Virginia, there is a Santa Claus. He exists as certainly as love and generosity and devotion exist, and you know that they abound and give to your life its highest beauty and joy. Alas, how dreary would be the world if there were no Santa Claus! It would be as dreary as if there were no Virginias. There would be no childlike faith then, no poetry, no romance to make tolerable this existence. . . .

"Not believe in Santa Claus! You might as well not believe in fairies! You might get your papa to hire men to watch in all the chimneys on Christmas Eve to catch Santa Claus, but even if they did not see Santa Claus coming down, what would that prove? Nobody sees Santa Claus, but that is no sign that there is no Santa Claus. The most real things in the world are those that neither children nor men can see. . . .

"No Santa Claus! Thank God he lives, and he lives forever. A thousand years from now, Virginia, nay, ten thousand times ten years from now, he will continue to make glad the heart of childhood."

On that Christmas Eve when I was only three, like Janet I recognized that Santa Claus was the personification of loving parents, and I accepted my mother and father in Santa Claus's place.

One day lightning struck our house at 27 East 11th Street. I was quite small and I was standing alone on the long staircase that rose from the main floor. Suddenly a huge ball of brilliant light appeared beside me; it traveled down the banister at tremendous speed. That seemed natural since I often slid down the banister myself, and its mahogany rail was grooved by the buckles and buttons of my clothes. I was enthralled by the wondrous sight, and when my parents returned home, excitedly I described what I had seen. They did not believe me. Later, my father discovered that the gutters of the roof and the drainpipe at the rear of the house had been melted by the lightning bolt, and I was cleared of fantasy.

I was fortunate in that my mother and father had already taught me to love a storm. Through the open triangle of a tent flap at night, or from a wind-swept porch, or walking together in the rain, we would watch for crooked lightning flashes and would gauge their distance by counting off the seconds, "One thousand one, one thousand two, one thousand . . ." until the thunder reached us. More than once, lightning struck so close that its sharp crack merged with the thunder instantly. I do not recall that these things ever startled me, even recently in the spring of 1964 when the plane in which I was flying with Mrs. Lyndon Johnson from Washington to Cleveland was struck by lightning.

The heritage to brave the challenge of the storm with delight and awe is a legacy which my husband and I unconsciously passed on to our own children in their infancy.

On a sultry summer afternoon when Janet was two and a half years old and Virginia sixteen months old, I stood on the rear terrace of our house at Hartsdale wondering how far into the woods Sigrid, their nurse, had taken them. A black cloud hung overhead and an ominous stillness of the air heralded a violent thunderstorm. Then I saw them. Sigrid was running for home with both children crowded into a wicker stroller that bumped along the dirt path. As they reached the edge of the woods beyond our lawn, a jagged fork of lightning split directly over them and seared a tall oak fifty feet away. It became a standing skeleton of the tree that had borne the brunt of the storm and had probably saved their lives. Sigrid's face was white when she reached the terrace, but Janet and Virginia were laughing and clapping and shouting, "More, more." They loved the thunder as a bird dog does the crack of a gun over its head.

Now our grandchildren have inherited the same legacy. I have seen them run out to dance on the grass in the rain and watch for lightning flashes.

On a sunny Saturday when I was nine, our Irish maid and I walked down Fifth Avenue to Washington Square. There I liked to play in the park to the east of the Washington arch. A fire broke out in the upper floors of a high loft building on Washington Place nearby, just beyond the New York University Law School which fronted on the east side of the Square. With bells ringing, fire engines rushed from all sides and we ran to the edge of the sidewalk for a better view. A large crowd gathered rapidly in the park behind us and we were wedged in place. It was exciting, like a Fire Department parade.

Smoke was pouring from several windows eight or nine stories up. Occasionally a person appeared at a neighboring window and then withdrew. Firemen in their black waterproof hats and long rubber coats were setting up ladders that reached a pathetically short distance up the tall building. The smoke grew blacker and more dense and enveloped more windows. More people appeared at open windows, leaning far out and looking down. A net was spread below them. A hush came over the crowd.

Suddenly a woman crawled out onto a window ledge, hung by her arms for a breathless span of time and let go. The loud thud when she hit the pavement not more than a couple of hundred feet from me still sounds in my ears. Then the earth-shaking thuds came rapidly as more and more bodies fell from that great height. I remember no other sounds, no screams from above, no moans below. Silent, too, were the crowd, the fire engines' bells, and their water hoses.

I watched in fascination. Why did the bodies turn end over end as they fell, slowly at first and then faster and faster? Why did their arms and legs flap about like a rag doll's tossed into the air? Did their long ballooning skirts act like umbrellas to flip them over? Or were their heads heavier than their feet? Was that what started them spinning when they dropped feet first from the window ledges? But *I* didn't spin end over end when I jumped feet first from a high beam into a haymow. Long afterward, I would gaze up at a tall building or wake at night wondering about the answers.

The holocaust that I had witnessed on March 25, 1911, was the Triangle Shirtwaist Company fire. With smashed bodies it paved the way for new labor legislation to protect factory workers against the terrible hazards of fire. In that conflagration, 146 seamstresses and sewing machine operators lost their lives, most of them in desperate leaps. The floor of the sweatshop was littered with piles of cloth cuttings and the doors to the fire exit stairways were locked. Most of the women preferred any death to that in the inferno of the factory. Not one was saved by the firemen's nets; even the sidewalks were broken by the impact of falling bodies.

That experience should have imprinted deep scars within me, but I judge that if it did, they healed. I seem never to have identified myself with the victims, perhaps because curiosity and a habit of observation prevailed over imagination and emotion.

I might well have acquired a fear of high places, but I continued to jump merrily from cross-beams under barn roofs into low haymows. Sure-footed, I climbed the tallest trees and at their very tops I swayed with the wind on thin branches; the wind sighs only in tall trees.

On July 25, 1911, four months after the Triangle Shirtwaist Company fire, I wrote a letter from Sheffield, Massachusetts, to my father in New York that expressed my joy in high summits even then:

Today Sophie and Tillie and I went for a long walk. We went around a big hill. There were birch trees about one foot around, and lots of oaks and pine trees on the hill. Back of the hill there was a mountain. We wanted to climb it, but Sophie said she wants to climb it when mother is along. It is all covered with steep rocks. I think it will be very hard to climb.

I know now that there was no "mountain" within walking distance of our rented house in the Housatonic River valley.

As I grew older, I climbed not hills, but mountains. I scaled cliffs with sheer faces, Skytop at Lake Mohonk in the Shawangunk Mountains and peaks in the Colorado Rockies. At Lake Mohonk, too, in my teens I used to jump from a second-story balcony to the ground because that was the shortest route from our wing of the big hotel to the swimming area of the lake. When another girl of my age, Carol Rhodes, followed me off the balcony, she unfortunately sprained her ankle.

During my first year in medical school, when I took an unpublicized week off from classes to enjoy the Dartmouth Winter Carnival at Hanover, I skied off the old Dartmouth ski jump three times. Looking down a thousand feet of rutted icy runway to the jump itself, I stood for a long while at the top before I took off, but when I reached the bottom, I could hardly wait to climb back and try it again. The sensation must be akin to a bird's in the air. After the Carnival had ended and the visitors departed, my escort was reprimanded by the college Athletic Association for letting me risk my limbs and life on that ski jump.

Fire I always held in great respect, but happy days of camping with the family in the Adirondacks in my childhood taught me the beauty of fire. At night, I loved to watch flames and sparks shooting skyward from bonfires. At home, my evening luxury is still to meditate beside an open fire in the fireplace; the crackling of the burning wood interrupts my train of thought and rests me, like the sound of the ocean surf.

In 1957—I remember the setting well—John F. Kennedy, then the Junior Senator from Massachusetts, mentioned to me the personal problems that a mutual acquaintance had laid at his doorstep. It occurred to me that the Senator had enough problems of his own and I remarked, somewhat out of context, "At least, I never brought you any of my troubles."

"You don't have any," he challenged.

"Oh yes, I do," I contradicted.

"What are they?" he pressed.

I had to pause to think of one, and finally I said, "Sometimes I get tired."

"What do you do then?" he queried.

"I go home and lie on the floor by the fire and my husband reads to me," I said. That closed the subject for about two years.

Then after that long interval, late on one of my long working days he studied me quizzically. At length he asked, "What are you going to do now, go home and lie on the floor by the fire?"

I thought to myself that I must look very tired indeed.

In 1964, my husband and I spent the Fourth of July at Nags Head with our daughter Virginia, her two children, Gordon and Janet, and several of their young North Carolina cousins. We stayed in old-fashioned, ocean-front cottages far from the village, where there were long stretches of uninhabited beach to the north and the south of us. Evenings, we built great fires of driftwood on the sand.

Seven months after the heartbreak of President Kennedy's assassination and the strains of the ensuing transition at the White House, on that wide windy beach under the stars the beauty of the firelight brought me peace and illuminated the continuity of life. There at Nags Head with the children I wrote a poem:

FOURTH OF JULY 1964
ON THE OUTER BANKS OF NORTH CAROLINA

Wrecked ships yield bleached logs,
Beach fires blaze and burst the dark.
Flames play they're leap frogs,
Disappear in sprays of spark,
Night gay, free from fogs.

Sparks play they're fireflies
Myriad as the host of stars
Winging in the skies.
Stars look down on burning spars,
Fire flares and dies.

Coals breathe the night breeze,
Spout out flames as whales do streams
Of water to tease
One another, spinning dreams
About birds and bees.

Waves play seek-and-hide,
Chase along the slanted beach.
Motion of the tide
Stills the sound of human speech,
Trouble sets aside.

Sparklers in their hands,
Children, pixies of the night,
Swing their fairy wands,
Dance until the circling light
Fades on lonely sands.

CHAPTER 3

My Civilized Mother

Janet Elizabeth Davidson was twenty-eight when on June 29, 1899, she married my father, Dr. Willard Travell, at her home, 216 Lancaster Street, in Albany, New York, and they settled in New York City. My mother was beautiful. She wore her soft, brown hair then in the high pompadour of the Gibson Girl, but as I first remember her it was parted in the middle and piled on the back of her head. Her skin was fair and freckled. Her brown eyes were always smiling above her delicately pointed nose that tilted up ever so slightly at its tip.

I admired her nose very much. Mine broadened at its upturned end like my father's and I thought it ugly. When I was little my mother would console me by saying, "Never mind, if you pull down on your nose often, maybe it will straighten as it grows."

I pulled and pullled on my nose surreptitiously in the dark at night, but its shape never improved.

In our Wellesley 1922 *Legenda* at graduation, my classmates voted me "the girl with the funniest nose." I was more insulted about my nose than complimented by their listing me as the "best athlete" (vote tied with Helen Forbush) or the faculty's naming me the "most intelligent" (vote tied with Muriel Morris).

My mother was graceful and petite, only five feet four inches tall, but her softly spoken words always commanded attention. At her dinner parties in the shaded candlelight my father loved to see her in jewels, about which she cared nothing, but he gave them to her and she wore them to please him. Sometimes when they had company, after I had been put to bed I would steal down two flights to the dining room on the ground floor of 27 East 11th Street. I would hide in a dim corner of the staircase where I could watch my mother. In her white evening dress with big, puffy sleeves, she made me think of the white lily that she said my beautiful soul would look like if I were a good little girl. Only I told her, "No, I'd rather have it look like a white rabbit."

My mother was born on December 29, 1870, in Albany and she was graduated from the Albany High School in 1888. She grew up in a well-organized home of fixed routine and social graces. When my sister and I, as small children, visited our grandparents in Albany, we were always washed and freshly dressed, and meals were served punctually on the minute. Tea was a daily institution. My grandfather, at the same hour each day, went to and from the Mechanics and Farmers Bank of Albany where he was Cashier for thirty-two years, took a five-mile walk for exercise, and made entries in a notebook of all cash expenditures, no matter how small. He had no charge accounts and often remarked that if he were to drop dead at any moment, he would not owe a penny. He was brought up in the Dutch Reformed Church. I remember him as tall and handsome, honest, intelligent, methodical, industrious and thrifty, kindly and strict.

George Graham Davidson, my grandfather, was proud of his ancestry from the great Clan Chattan in the Highlands of Scotland. He used to quote Sir Walter Scott, who wrote, "Every Scottishman has a pedigree. It is a national prerogative as inalienable as his poverty." His pedigree was a life-long interest of my grandfather's, and shortly before he died at eighty-six on January 12, 1928, my mother helped him publish *The Davidson Genealogy*. He described his family as "plain, honest, Scotch people, and though none of them acquired wealth or official position until comparatively recent years, they had what was better still, the respect of the people among whom they lived." [1]

Although extremely conservative in many ways, my grandfather Davidson was ahead of his times in that he sent not only both his sons, but his two daughters to college. That was an era when attendance at a "finishing school" was considered a suitable education for a young lady. He himself had had to go to work when he was not quite fourteen to help support his widowed mother and his three sisters.

When he wrote about his own father, George Davidson, who was born in Inverness, Scotland, in 1795, he might have been describing himself: "Although not highly educated in the common acceptation of the term,

[1] George G. Davidson, *The Davidson Genealogy* (New York, Tobias A. Wright, 1927), p. 3.

having been obliged to work from an early age, he made up for the want of a thorough education by the most extensive reading. . . . I may truly say that it would have been rare to find a better read or more entertaining man in conversation." [2] My grandfather's library was a favorite haunt of mine. It was an inside room without windows, lighted by a gas chandelier, and its walls were covered with books from its carpeted floor to the ceiling. A movable wall ladder may have enhanced my sense of adventure there. Each year, in 1912, 1913, and 1914, my grandfather sent me by express a steamer trunk full of books for my summer reading at our farm in Sheffield. When I was twelve, I had read all of Sir Walter Scott's novels and most of the books about bonnie Scotland in his Albany library. I grew up with the legends of Scotland's battles with England, from

> Scots! wha hae wi' Wallace bled,
> Scots! wham Bruce has aften led,
> Welcome to your gory bed,
> Or to victory! [3]

to Mary Stuart, the romantic last Queen of the Scots, who, dressed in chain mail beneath her velvet, led her troops in the field. In much the same way, my husband grew up in the South with the War Between the States. I had felt no personal involvement in the Civil War.

Grandpa Davidson's chief pleasure was reading. He longed for the education that he had missed, and in addition he must have acquired a special feeling for books from his father, who was a printer. In about 1815, George Davidson had worked for James Ballantine and Company in Edinburgh, then at the height of their fame as printers of the Waverly Novels. Later he worked in the University Printing Office in Glasgow, and in 1818 he took with him to Niagara, Canada, via Quebec, "the complete outfit of a printing establishment." Five years later, he moved to Albany, New York. His outlook on life was mirrored in the newspaper obituary of his fifteen-year-old son, Roderick, who was drowned in 1840, a year before my grandfather Davidson was born:

From the *Albany Bee*

The funeral of Roderick Davidson was . . . numerously attended by a large number of printers of this city and citizens generally.

In speaking of Mr. Davidson we can only say that he was a young man of great worth. Among the great number who learn the printing business, he was like an oasis in the desert. He was one in a thou-

[2] *Ibid.*, p. 14.
[3] Robert Burns, "Robert Bruce's March to Bannockburn," Verse 1.

sand; ready and skillful in his business, for one of his age; inoffensive in his character and demeanor; a correct exemplary young man.[4]

My grandfather expected his children and grandchildren to be always correct and exemplary. In January, 1908, when I was just six years old, he wrote me a letter, addressing me by the nickname given me by my older sister who could not pronounce *baby:*

My Dear Little Bobby:—
    I thank you very much for your nice little letter for it is not often that I get one from you. It was a very good letter and you must be getting to be a very good scholar. Are you liking your school and do you mind well in school? I hope that you do. . . . Be a good girl and remember there is nothing that you can do that will please grandpa more than to be a good girl and to always mind Mamma and Papa.
                    Your affectionate grandfather,
                    G G Davidson

In June of 1926, my mother and I retraced the trip that she and her father had taken about thirty years earlier to assemble data for *The Davidson Genealogy.* We traveled by boat from Quebec to Glasgow, then up the west coast to the Isle of Skye and across Scotland to the town of Inverness in the north. We inspected the family tombstones in the Inverness cemetery. Of greater interest to me, I must confess, was Cawdor Castle where scenes from *Macbeth* were sketched in black on its white bedroom walls. And I have nowhere else seen such large roses as were in bloom in the foggy Highlands of Scotland.

My grandfather was twenty-seven when he married Julia Elizabeth Griswold, a bride of nineteen, on August 4, 1868, in Delhi, New York. She was the one who gave my mother insight into the imaginative world of art and music and imbued her with strong spiritual values. All her grandchildren loved Grandma Davidson.

Her family background was quite different from her husband's. Her ancestors included many distinguished men of government and of the church. My grandfather traced her genealogy as far back as the twelfth century to Sir Launcelot Griswold of Cambridgeshire, England, who was a member of the House of Commons. In 1639, her great-great-great-great-great-great-grandfather, Edward Griswold of Malvern Hall, Warwickshire, England, arrived in Massachusetts with a company of Pilgrims; he joined his brother, Matthew, who had come to America about nine years earlier with another band of Pilgrims in search of freedom to worship and to dissent. Edward settled at Windsor and Matthew at Saybrook, both in Connecticut. The

[4] Davidson, *op. cit.,* p. 41.

Connecticut records show that Windsor was the first settlement made by white men in that state. One of Matthew's lineal descendants, also Matthew Griswold, was Governor of Connecticut from 1784 to 1786, and his son, Roger, likewise became Governor of that state. My grandfather lists three ministers of the gospel among our Griswold forebears and two bishops.

One was the controversial Alexander Viets Griswold, who was born in 1776 in Simsbury, Connecticut, and who was the first Protestant Episcopal Bishop of Massachusetts from 1811 to 1843.[5] He helped organize that large diocese; it comprised Massachusetts, Rhode Island, Vermont, New Hampshire, and part of Maine. As a young minister and as bishop, he traveled through Great Barrington and Sheffield in the Berkshire Hills of Massachusetts where I spent many happy summers. He differed from contemporary Episcopal theologians on issues that grew out of the Protestant Reformation; for instance, he advocated changes in the Liturgy of the Church as directed in the prayer book. He had learned to read fluently when he was three years old and he became a cogent and prolific writer in defense of his original thinking.

My grandmother's younger brother, Sheldon Munson Griswold, was consecrated the first Protestant Episcopal Bishop of Salina, Kansas, on his forty-second birthday, January 8, 1903, and he became Suffragan Bishop of Chicago in 1917. Uncle Sheldon, as we called him, survived my grandmother by many years and he read her funeral service at Albany, New York, on September 29, 1919. He had also performed the marriage ceremony for my mother and father, baptized me into the Episcopal Church at Grace Church Chapel, New York, on January 10, 1903, when he had just become Bishop of Salina, and he came from Chicago to marry my husband and me in the Church of the Ascension on June 6, 1929. He died in 1930. He was an imposing man with a rich speaking and singing voice. I remember hearing him preach one Sunday in Trinity Church at the foot of Wall Street and in the hymns and responses his resonant tones could be heard above the choir and the congregation. Spiritual force emanated from him as naturally and as constantly as the beauty of his speech and the elegance of his manner.

Uncle Sheldon's wit and humor matched his grace and dignity. One year when I visited him and Aunt Kate in Evanston, in his round collar and clerical attire he drove me in his car to the University Club of Chicago for lunch. He told me with glee that on his last trip to the city he had been stopped for speeding. The policeman had walked over to his car and said,

[5] John S. Stone, *Memoirs of Alexander Viets Griswold,* abridged by Dudley A. Tyng (New York, Protestant Episcopal Society for the Promotion of Evangelical Knowledge, 1854).

"Oh, I beg your pardon, Fayther. Let me warn ye to be more careful, there's a Protestant cop in the next block." Uncle Sheldon taught me several mathematically complex games of solitaire that I have enjoyed playing throughout the years. My mother played solitaire, too, and I think that we never used to cheat ourselves. Uncle Sheldon loved to fish—he brought my husband a fishing rod as a wedding gift—and at his summer camp at Sault Sainte Marie on Lake Superior, Canada, I pursued that pastime with him. None of my Davidson or Griswold relatives were athletic in the sense that they participated in competitive sports, but they were vigorous and long-lived. The formal ritual of the High Episcopal Church appealed to Uncle Sheldon, and at my wedding when he blessed us he looped his bishop's stole in a knot around Jack's and my hands. Later he laughed and said that any minister could have married us, but that when he tied that knot, the marriage vows never came untied. At our bridal party the night before the ceremony he gave us a toast: "To John and Janet, prosperity and posterity!" All the good things in life that he wanted for us have come true.

When my mother became the wife of a New York physician, a busy general practitioner with his office in the home, the pattern of her life must have changed radically from that of her maiden years. The clock could no longer inflexibly control the day's activities, as it did in my grandparents' home in Albany and even at the farm when they came to visit us in the summer. My hostility toward clocks probably began then. Years later, it took the form of this poem that I wrote in January, 1965:

THE CLOCK GOD
A LAMENT

The time of my life is ruled by a clock
Authoritarian as a traffic cop.
The moving hands direct the pace. "Tick, tock,
Tick, tock," counts down the race . . . Oh, stop!
Delay! Alas, we can not stop the clock.
The future's hours are not ours to unlock.

We bow to the Clock God, image enshrined
In every home on mantel, table, wall,
Atop of buildings, billboards to remind
Us fools: "Jump, run, obey the Clock God's call."
The clock face grins but it is deaf and blind.
Not mute, its voice repeats alarms unkind.

The calendar is its high priest supreme.
Each day we're boxed in little squares of time.
Their prison walls shut out the right to dream,

To seek the truth in beauty. The gods chime;
We see the calendar and clock, a team,
Drag past the days, months, years of life's mainstream.

My father had a refreshing unconcern for the clock. My mother was imperturbable and she apparently adapted herself completely to his informal habit of activity unusual to the hour and the place, but my Davidson grandparents must have regarded his demeanor as not always exemplary and correct. When I was six months old, my mother made the following notation about my father in my Baby Book that she kept for me: "July 4, 1902. At Albany. Her father comes up from New York to celebrate, and awakens her at 3 A.M. with giant firecrackers."

In defense of my father I should say that he was a teetotaler and also that our bedroom in the house at Albany had a screened fireplace. Furthermore, his freedom from feeling time-bound did not keep him from meeting the responsibilities of scheduled appointments and deadlines. Dr. Harry Gold, the cardiologist, in 1950 inscribed a copy of his book, *Quinidine in Disorders of the Heart,* as follows: "For Dr. Willard Travell. His balance between work and play is an inspiration to all who would wish to live well."

Virginia, my sister, was twenty months older than I, and my mother loved her two babies. The diaries that my mother kept of our doings and sayings for several years, written in her even, flowing hand, are a remarkable record of her own insight into the behavior and needs of her children. Her notes show her concern about the effect that our moving into a new house had on me when I was ten months old. She wrote in my Baby Book in late November, 1902:

> October 1st 1902 the lease was signed for the house at 27 East 11th Street. November first was the date set for chaos—and a most upsetting time it was! From Bobby's point of view the months of October and November have no pleasures to record. Moreover she was under a great mental strain and at a period of very rapid development. She was acquiring teeth and learning to walk with amazing rapidity—yet was an object of small attention. Doubtless she would not have escaped utter obliteration had it not been for her grandmother who did not forget her and tided her over this time of adversity.
>
> Dec. 3, 1902. Bobby, Virginia, mother and grandmother go to Albany for a much-needed change. Bobby goes to recuperate from the moving process.

I wonder how many mothers find time during "chaos" to write so thoughtfully in the Baby Book of a one-year-old.

> Jan. 10, 1903. We are all installed in our new home for the winter. Bobby takes her daily nap in the garden in her carriage to the horror

and consternation of the neighbors. [My adaptation to the cold began young.]

She is fast mastering the English language, having already quite a vocabulary.

The baby is such a little tot to be running around that she looks like some big French doll that has escaped from a shop window. [I was twelve months old.]

In June, six months later, when I was eighteen months old, she continued: "She can dance like an Indian and is as lively as a cricket and as full of mischief as a monkey."

A year later, my mother's notes again indicate my early aptitude for physical activity: "May 1904. She has a way of 'jumping' her clothes off—after they are unbuttoned—quite a violent form of exercise—but no exercise is too violent for that indefatigable little curmudgeon."

My mother's notations reveal how she fostered learning and creativity. "Jan. 1906 Bobby aged 4, full of 'Magination and Pertend'. Busy making the sweetest pictures—pasting a scrap book at her new desk—accumulating picture postal cards for an album—learning to spell on the board, first word 'Light'—blowing soap bubbles with new outfit—helping mother receive Fridays—learning Neidlinger Songs [6]—stringing beads—dressing up pins, all named."

A year and a half later, on July 4, 1907, my mother wrote down a story as I told it: "One day while I was thinking I forgot my treasure words. One day at the seashore I saw a crab walking along on the sand and I did not forget my treasure words then. I remembered that I had them still in my mind. I said to myself—there is a precious crab—I will pick it up. Instead it walked away but I found so many jelly fish and star fish that I did not know what to do with them—and I walked home with them, my treasure pets."

"Bobby's wishes for Christmas 1907: 'A real fairyland and the way to it. A sunny window in everyone's closet (as a preventive against moths). A quintillian dollars in everyone's pocketbook Christmas morning—rich and poor—and a hundred dollars in every doll's pocketbook.' " My imagination had a practical slant even then.

My father's medical office and my mother's household were staffed to meet the variety of their professional and social activities, as well as the nursing care of two small babies in the city. In November, 1902, when we had just moved into the house at 27 East 11th Street, my mother described in my Baby Book our wonderful new man-of-all-work, Coleman. "Coleman began a period of long service as general indispensable—a combination of

[6] W. H. Neidlinger, *Small Songs for Small Singers,* with pictures by Walter Bobbett (New York, G. Schirmer, 1896).

butler, office boy, cook, gardener, furnace man, parlor maid, rug-beater, window cleaner, painter, decorator—altogether the *sine qua non* of the household. Bobby and Coleman soon became fast friends." In the spring of 1903, a domestic crisis arose.

> During the month of March we were under the dominion of foreign nationalities—Svea, Swedish race, Lisa, German race, Coleman, African race. These three did not amalgamate, so we have fallen back on Erin and now have Delia and Annie (of the same race but different brogues) and Coleman remains no matter who comes or goes. Whatever the kitchen contingent, Bobby is always a favorite with all of them. Her fun and frolic bring everyone to her feet.

My mother's closest friend then was Harriet Burton, whose grandmother, Christina Andrews Davidson, was my grandfather's first cousin. On the day of my birth at the 12th Street house Cousin Harriet was my "first caller with a great bunch of flowers by way of greeting." Nearly four years later on October 25, 1905, Ginny and I were flower girls at her wedding when she married James Lees Laidlaw in our home at 27 East 11th Street. My only image of that event is my white dress trimmed with lace and long pink ribbons that served as reins while I pretended to be a galloping horse driven by a wedding guest.

One Sunday, my parents had taken Jim Laidlaw and Harriet Burton for a drive through Van Cortlandt Park in the Bronx in my father's new horseless carriage, a 1902 Model A Cadillac. Like a buggy, it had no top, and two unsociable seats in back faced each other on either side of a door above the steps at the rear. Like a bicycle, the wheels were chain-driven, but the car's only brake operated through the chain mechanism. Going down a long hill in Van Cortlandt Park that day, the chain broke, the brakes failed and after a hazardous roller coaster ride the Model A coasted to a stop. My mother and father walked back up the dusty road, hunting for the chain, and by the time they returned to the car with it, Cousin Harriet and Cousin Jimmie had become engaged.

People thought it outrageous that my parents, in dusters and goggles, proudly drove their two small daughters up Fifth Avenue in such a dangerous, speedy vehicle. Its noise and strange look frightened the horses on the city streets. My husband says that in those years when he was a small boy on a farm in eastern North Carolina, he would run a quarter of a mile across the fields to the main road just to see one of those contraptions go by; he could hear it coming long enough in advance to get there. The Cadillac survived until my father had driven it about five hundred miles in six months, a lot of mileage; then its one cylinder, located horizontally under the floor boards in back, overheated and "froze." No one had told him to put oil in it, he said. That ended our automobiling until my mother acquired a 1914 Model T Ford for the farm.

In New York my mother was separated geographically from her two brothers. They were younger than she and both were graduated from Williams College—George Graham Davidson, Jr., in 1895 and Alexander in 1897. Both then obtained LL.D. degrees from the University of Buffalo Law School, married and settled in Buffalo, New York. Their sister Elizabeth died of typhoid fever the same year that my mother and father were married. Our Davidson relatives seldom came to New York to visit us, but we all gathered on holidays in the old Albany home with my grandparents. On winter vacations from school, Ginny and I played there with Celestia and Graham, cousins of our own age; Jerome and Billy were several years younger.

My mother's college friends came to visit her and to see New York— she was one of a hundred and sixteen girls in the graduating class of 1892 at Wellesley College. Other classmates lived in the city—Florence Wilkinson (Mrs. Wilfrid Evans), some of whose books of poetry I still have, and Nan Winegar, the painter. My mother soon attracted talented women around her who were vitally concerned with the artistic, literary, and civic activities of the times. They gathered informally for tea on my mother's day "at home" or on Harriet Laidlaw's "Thursdays" in her spacious house at 60 East 66th Street, where my mother "poured" for her regularly. My cousin Harriet had graduated from Barnard College and was the focus for another intellectual group with overlapping viewpoints. Another Barnard graduate, Edith Talcott, who married my father's friend Roswell Bates in 1909, became a close friend of my mother's. In 1930, after my mother's death, she was to become my father's second wife.

At an early age I became an active participant in the art work of my mother's friends. She made this notation in June, 1907, when I was five: "At Mrs. Dewey's studio . . . Bobby is devoted to the weasel (easel) and to squeezing the paint." When I was older, we used to call on Alphaeus P. Cole, the portrait painter, and his wife, who was a sculptor, and I took lessons from her in modeling clay. The oversized likeness of a human ear that I made in plaster lay around our house for years.

We often visited the sculpture studio of Clara Hill where she created the bas-relief of "The Woman Physician" for the Woman's Medical College of Pennsylvania. It was presented to the medical school in 1916 by an alumna, Dr. Rosalie Slaughter Morton, who was an associate of my father's in New York. On many afternoons after school, I posed for Clara Hill as she worked on various figures in that bas-relief, while my mother drank tea and offered criticism. I still treasure a small statuette that Clara Hill made of me when I was about twelve years old. But we had known her for a long time then. Under date of June, 1907, my mother made an entry in my Baby Book that "Clara Hill taught Bobby a poem." Apparently I replied in kind, and my mother recorded: "Bobby July 7, 1907. 'Do you want to hear a song about the truth?' She sang—

> 'Sweet and low, sweet and low
> Love the truth, as daisies blow.

You know, I really like the truth. Every poem that I write, it shall be a nice one.' "

After my mother's death, among her papers I found a poem about a flower that I had written on a child's wide-ruled pad in my careful large script, when I was about seven years old:

THE LAZY POSY

There happened to be a little Posy, asleep in a little brown room; she did nothing but sleep, which was wrong.

The Grass saw this, and they said, "We must wake the Posy." So they went to her and said: "Little Posy *please* wake up for to-morrow is Mayday." But still she slept on.

When the Robins saw the Posy was still asleep, they went to her and said, *"Please* wake up for to-morrow is Mayday." But she did not wake.

The Spring, who had crept from behind a mountain so softly nobody noticed him, said, "I will wake her."

So he went and gave her rain and sunshine, and the Posy awoke; and she was the prettiest flower on the hill.

Janet Travell

My mother was an accomplished pianist. She had an upright piano in our second-floor sitting room, which opened through French doors into the glassed-in, unheated, back extension room that was my sister's and my bedroom for as long as we lived in that house at 27 East 11th Street. When we went to bed at night, our mother used to play for us—Chopin, Mendelssohn, Bach, and Mozart—and she used to sing us lullabies in her pleasant soft voice—German *Lieder,* French songs, "Sail, baby, sail, out upon the sea, only don't forget to come back again to me," "One, two, three, the riddle tell to me: The moon afloat is the silver boat, and the sunset is the sea," "Winkin', blinkin', niddy nod, Father is fishing off Cape Cod," and always at the end we sang in chorus:

> Jesus tender Shepherd hear us,
> Bless Thy little lamb tonight.
> Through the darkness be Thou near us,
> Keep me safe till morning light.

Often on Sunday evening, my mother played the piano at the Henry Street Settlement House on the Lower East Side and accompanied the girls in hymn singing. At an early age my sister and I took piano lessons from Miss Frances de Villa Ball, and her pupils sometimes held recitals in my mother's drawing room, with neatly printed programs. A Steinway grand piano in the big room downstairs was my mother's special pride, partly because Mabel Wagnalls (Mrs. R. J. Jones), a concert pianist and author of books on music, helped her select it. I heard Mabell, as I called her, play that piano many times in our home. It accompanied my husband and me when we moved to Washington in 1961.

Mabel Wagnalls introduced O. Henry to my mother in New York, following a correspondence during the years 1903 to 1907 that was published in *Letters to Lithopolis, From O. Henry to Mabel Wagnalls*.[7] In the preface to that limited edition, Mabel Wagnalls described O. Henry's earnestness "as an occasional caller in our New York home," where he left

> the memory of a quiet, serious, hard-working author; one whom I felt was predestined to fame though he had slight regard for the author-craft. . . . I told him how his first letter reached me when I was up in an attic trying to imagine myself a poor starving poet. I can hear yet his prompt and serious reply. "That is something you cannot imagine. No one who has not known it can imagine the misery of poverty." His voice became almost tragic. "Poverty is so terrible and so common, we should all do more than we do—much more—to relieve it."
>
> Though making a social call, O. Henry was just then deeply solemn and earnest. Was he ever jocose in his talk as in his writings? I never found him so.

Some of O. Henry's best stories tell of hairbreadth escapes from the catastrophe of going broke. My mother had never been poor but her father had, and she did much in a personal way to alleviate that hardship. She always had an extra bed and plenty of food—she loved to cook—for a friend who was hard up and lonely in the midst of the preoccupied city populace.

O. Henry inscribed one of his books as follows: "To Miss Mabel Wag-

[7] (Doubleday, Page & Company, Garden City, N. Y., and Toronto, 1922.)

nalls—with pleasant recollections of a certain little tea party where there were such nice cakes and kind hospitality to a timid stranger. O. Henry."

She wrote, "That describes him. To life and the whole world he carried the air of a timid stranger."

Excerpts from his letters to her were in sharp contrast to their conversations. On June 25, 1903, he wrote her:

> Am I interested in music? . . . Why, certainly—interested, but not implicated. I once was reputed to know something about printed music, but I acquired the distinction by fraud. I gained it by being able to stand at the piano and turn the music exactly at the proper time for a certain young lady, who aggravated the ivory frequently. No one ever found out that she gave me the signal by moving her right ear, a singularly enviable accomplishment that she possessed. I may say that I had an ear for music, but it did not belong to me.

And in a later letter to Lithopolis, O. Henry wrote my mother's friend, the talented pianist, "Of course I'm not saying anything against the piano. Before the pianola was invented, the piano was a real joy and convenience in homes where nobody could play it—they're so handy to pile old magazines on."

Now, Mabel Wagnall's choice of a Steinway piano sometimes supports my accumulated medical journals in Washington.

My father did not share all my mother's literary interests. He felt about authors much as O. Henry put it in writing to Mabel Wagnalls: "I have much more respect for a man who brands cattle than for one who writes pieces for the printer. . . . It doesn't seem quite like a man's work."

When Sinclair Lewis came to our home once, not long after his *Main Street* became a best seller, my father asked him, "Mr. Lewis, what do you do for a living?"

My father was not impressed by the reply, "I'm a writer." He used to say—and probably told Sinclair Lewis—that he never read a novel unless it had been out five years and people were still talking about it. My father was essentially a man of action.

In the world of art and letters that meant so much to my mother, my father held in esteem those creative people who turned out a tangible product, such as a book or magazine or newspaper, a building or a marble or bronze ornament. Thus, he had a high regard for such friends as Harvey Wiley Corbett, the architect who later introduced us to the Gipsy Trail Club at Carmel, New York; Ray Brown, the magazine editor; Carr V. Van Anda of *The New York Times;* and Edward Field Sanford, the architectural sculptor whose bas-reliefs of wild animals beautify the façade of the New York State Roosevelt Memorial wing of the Museum of Natural History on

Central Park in New York City. My father mistrusted most actors, musicians, dancers—those in the performing arts—and he seldom attended the theater or opera, except the plays of the Amateur Comedy Club, of which he and my mother were members. Mabel Wagnalls, though pianist and author, had special status with him, perhaps because her husband's firm was concerned with building the Bear Mountain Bridge across the Hudson River.

My mother unobtrusively befriended a number of artists, although she had no large means at her disposal. Queena Mario, prima donna of the Metropolitan Opera Company and director of the Opera Workshop at the Juilliard School of Music, told me that my mother had encouraged her to study singing and had helped pay for her first voice lessons when she was a girl living in Plainfield, New Jersey, where my Uncle Winthrop Travell was principal of the high school. Years later, it was natural for me to ask Queena Mario's advice when our daughter, Janet, showed a serious interest in a professional career as a singer.

My mother was prudent and frugal, my father adventurous and inclined toward extravagance. She made every penny go a long way, but she was never stingy. She took charge of the family business affairs, for which my father had little time or interest. He told me that from his first year of medical practice they saved half his annual income, whatever it was. My mother invested it wisely, some of it in New York real estate. She knew also how to *spend* money wisely, often for abstract values, such as education, travel, and recreation. She carried her share of responsibility and was always busy in a constructive way. Her hands were never idle. She sewed for herself and her two daughters, knitted for the Red Cross, built bookshelves, framed pictures, upholstered her furniture, and made such things as drapes, cushions, and bedspreads for her home. My father had a lathe, a large vise, and complete carpenter's tools in the basement, and my mother put them to good use. She constantly answered the telephone for her husband's patients in "off hours"; she gave sympathy and encouragement to many. She never put out her light at night until she had finished the newspapers and had indulged in some more literary reading matter, often making notes for future reference—a habit that she may have developed when she served as editor of the *Wellesley Magazine* from 1890 to 1892.

A deep concern for human welfare and for better government strongly motivated my mother. She was a member of the Washington Square Association and later, after we moved in 1919 to a house at 40 Fifth Avenue, a member of the Fifth Avenue Association. She worked for the beautification and preservation of that historical part of the city. The great wisteria vine on the front of our house at 27 East 11th Street was symbolic of that facet of her character. She contributed her time to the League of Women Voters, the Citizens' Union, the nonpartisan publication known as the *Voters Directory,* and to the New York Wellesley Club. She belonged to no strictly social club. She worked for the League of Nations, and during World War I she supported the controversial Free Speech Forums initiated by Dr. Percy Stickney Grant, Rector of the Church of the Ascension where I had attended Sunday School and had been confirmed.

A burning issue of those days was whether women in the United States should have the right to vote. My mother was a member of the Woman Suffrage Party, the Equal Franchise Society, and the Collegiate Suffrage League. On May 5, 1912, the *New York Tribune* reported:

> Militant suffragism turned out in New York yesterday afternoon and without any hurling of cobblestones or mobbing of police demonstrated its strength in a wonderfully efficient manner. Last year there were but 3000 marchers and a thin rank of curiosity seekers stood upon the curbs and made comments. This year there were 20,000 in line and 500,000 watching. . . . This year the crowds were there to cheer and encourage.
>
> Nearly a thousand men of the New York State League for Equal Suffrage took part in the parade yesterday. James Lees Laidlaw, chairman of the league, said, "We are marching to give political support to the women and moral support to the men." [8]

Cousin Harriet and Cousin Jimmie were among the most active leaders in the cause of woman suffrage and my mother joined them in that effort until the Federal Suffrage Constitutional Amendment of 1920 ratified that goal for the nation.

[8] *James Lees Laidlaw 1868–1932,* Harriet Burton Laidlaw, ed. (privately printed, 1932), p. 93.

CHAPTER 4

Roughing It for Pleasure

Camping runs in some families but my mother's was not one of them. Willard Travell and his three brothers initiated her, however, into the many ways of roughing it, and her hardiness eventually matched theirs.

The first two summers after I was born my civilized mother and her two babies "vacationed" with her in-laws at Elm Hill near Troy, New York, the farm to which my grandfather Travell had retired because of ill health. The living facilities there were primitive; water for the house was carried from the hand pump of a well at the back porch and there was an outhouse, of course. When I was six months old, my mother wrote in my Baby Book: "July 8, 1902. [From Albany] we go to Elm Hill, with hammocks, baby carriage, cart, chair, bicycle, and other fixtures appertaining to a baby plant. We all remain at the Farm until Aug. 4—during which time baby becomes familiar with farm sights and sounds. She lives outdoors—sleeping in her carriage, and when awake, sitting and sometimes *standing* in it. She likes to watch the dogs and chickens and ducks and especially enjoys the hammock." I still love a hammock for its motion and the view of treetops and clouds that it provides.

Life at Elm Hill then must have been a merry-go-round of activity with five young cousins close in age: Virginia and I; Arthur Travell, my Uncle Warren and Aunt Minnie's son; and Marge and Winthrop Travell, children of my Uncle Winthrop and Aunt Belle. It was a congenial family group; Aunt Belle and Aunt Minnie were sisters. Winifred, my Uncle Howard and Aunt Anna's daughter, was several years younger than I and they seldom

31

joined us on our summer outings. When my Travell grandparents died within a few months of each other in the autumn and winter of 1903 to 1904, the joint families of Wint, Will, and Warren sought other pastures for roughing it. Each summer found us in a different locale, the Adirondack or Catskill Mountains perhaps, or the Delaware Water Gap or the Berkshire Hills.

In 1908 when I was six and a half years old, the choice was a wild region of Nova Scotia about twenty miles south of the Bay of Fundy. My mother's almost daily letters to my father during that July reveal her serenity under stress and the younger generation's natural aptitude for outdoor living. The camp consisted of a central dining hall and a group of extremely rustic cottages spread out along the shore of a lake. My mother's first letter gave this description:

> Our house is cool and comfortable. It's like one room because the partitions are only halfway up to the ceilings. Bobby calls the house The Hut. It has only one floor but a fine high gable under the roof. All around is open with few trees so that we have the feeling of being out in the open country. Our porch looks right over the Lake or one small corner of it. It is a most irregular Lake like a labyrinth full of rocks and islands. We have a lovely place for swimming—the best yet. . . . There are no mountains or hills. . . . We seldom see any of the occupants of the other cottages . . . but perhaps we shall get better acquainted with them before the summer is over—too well perhaps.

I remember the interior of The Hut clearly. The front door opened into a long and narrow living room that was not much more than a wide hall between two bedrooms on each side. I could climb onto the head of my iron bedstead and look over the partition into the next bedroom; we could talk from one room to another. At the far end of the center room a stone fireplace and chimney rose to the peaked roof, with great logs of firewood piled on each side. About sunrise one morning, my cousin Marge, who was seven, opened the front door to peek out. A large brown bear outside may have mistaken the dark opening for a cave and it followed Marge inside. Screaming, she dashed back into her bedroom and slammed her door shut. The bear took to the woodpile beside the fireplace. With a terrible noise of grunting and a clatter of logs rolling down, its furry head appeared over the partition, and its eyes looked straight into mine where I lay in a double bed with my sister. Virginia pulled the pillow over her face, but before I became frightened a man rushed in and corralled the bear. It was being taken to a circus.

Aunt Belle, Uncle Winthrop, Marge, and her younger brother Win, who was also called Bub, had preceded us to the cabin that we shared with them;

Uncle Winthrop taught school and could take a long summer holiday. My mother, Virginia, and I had traveled by overnight boat from New York to Boston, by another overnight boat from Boston to Yarmouth, Nova Scotia, from there by railroad northeast about seventy miles to Annapolis, and then by horse and wagon fifteen miles to South Milford. In telling about our trip, my mother gave my father some pointers for the time when he would come in August. She proceeded in the reverse direction of our route:

> When you reach Annapolis, Mr. Thomas is usually there or one of his drivers with a buckboard at the station. You get your dinner—50¢ —at the Queen Hotel. You will have time to walk around the fort. At Yarmouth if you get up early, get some breakfast at the restaurant on the pier. Then you will have until 9:30 to do the town of Yarmouth and take the train at the R.R. Station instead of the Pier. If you come to Boston by the Metropolitan Line you land at a pier very near the Yarmouth boat. You can go there and check your bags in the parcel room and have till one o'clock or later for Boston. The elevated trains run right near all the piers. If it had not been so fiendishly hot that day I should have tried to take the children somewhere. We had our luncheon in Boston which leaves only one meal for the boat—so that one does not lose much by rough sailing. [My father was notoriously seasick at the slightest excuse, yet was often in a boat.] The drive from Annapolis was very dusty but we have had some rain since, so it is not quite so bad now. I think you will like this place.

On July 7, she wrote her

> Dearest Love—
> A week today since we left home. We are now so settled that it seems almost a dream that I was at home then so hurried and tired and disagreeable. . . . Even yet I have little or no disposition to do anything but sit around. . . . We go to bed at night often with the children and I shall do so until I feel energetic. The children are almost never indoors. . . . They were in the water three times yesterday. I shall go in today—I had to fix my bathing suit before I could appear in it.

My mother never learned to breathe while she swam; she could do a breast-stroke for a few feet and then she had to touch bottom. She did not fear the water, however, and she made sure that my sister and I learned to swim when we were young. She continued, "It is hot up here, almost as hot as New York, but they say the weather is phenomenally hot. Last night Wint took us canoeing by moonlight—and it was delightful except for mosquitoes. We have some citronella—but when you come bring a bottle from the box under the bed. Horses are so cheap here that bicycles are not very desirable—the roads are heavy, sandy and dusty." The one outdoor sport in which my mother excelled was bicycling. "We are all counting on your coming to stir things up and make them interesting." My father always did.

A later letter indicated her difficulties with canoeing. "Today we had our usual swimming lesson. Afterward I took Miss Van Vliet out in the canoe. . . . When I started for home there was such a gale that I could scarcely manage. . . . I don't think much of canoes anyway. I had to almost pull my arms out to get the boat ahead by inches. However I might as well try it."

Swimming and hiking were "the greatest attractions." On July 14, my mother wrote: "We had a fine time today. Eight of us including the four children took a cross country tramp to another lake and had an all day picnic. . . . We tramped about five miles. Bobby was very game and led the way home finding the trail, which was scarcely perceptible most of the way, and never once losing the path."

On July 16:

We have had a fine clear cold day just like the Adirondacks—the kind of weather when you can walk unendingly. This morning we took a tramp and also this afternoon. . . . Bobby says to tell you "We had a lovely picnic through swamps, over mountains, rocks and steep places. I was the scout—an Indian guide. My name was Snow-in-the-Ear. Marge's name was Rain-in-the-Face. Virginia's name was Straight-to-the-Mark. I hope you'll come soon. I miss you very much."

After we had been in camp about two weeks, my mother replied to my father's letters that asked about all the things he liked to do outdoors.

We just came in from the Lake—moonlight and sunset—I paddled all the time. I will now answer your questions.

1—Baseball—no one plays baseball at all. I would not bring one.

2—Tennis—constant tennis. One grass court—not very smooth.

3—I have the fish hook book. [He made his own flies.]

4—No fishing in the Lake. All the people go off to ponds and streams, take a guide. But guides are only $2.00 a day.

5—Wint says there is no shooting of any kind.

6—I cannot get a canoe just now, but have ordered one for you.

7—Milk and eggs are abundant but the milk is not always palatable. Berries are drying up from lack of rain.

8—There are said to have been 30 deer brought to Nova Scotia from New Brunswick once upon a time. No one has ever seen any since. There is a moosehead in the office but it costs $100 to shoot one. However there is a five dollar premium on bears. There are two bear cubs in the camp—some one has them for pets.

9—I have not heard of there being any ducks. Wint says there are said to be ducks.

Please tell Dr. Koller [Karl Koller, the physician who discovered cocaine by chewing coca leaves in South America] that Mr. Thomas says he cannot promise anything at all for August. . . . He could not even promise me one room for Clara [Clara Hill, the sculptor] except he might be able to get her one in some farmhouse.

Now for my errands. Please go to Wanamakers and look at bathing suits—all black brilliantine *no color* on it Size *38 bust.* About $5.00—a little more if necessary. Then some *dark blue* brilliantine sometimes called *mohair,* it is the regular bathing suit material—1¼ yards if it is 45 inches wide or more. If it is only 36 inches wide send me two yards. Bobby's suit needs a lot of mending up. The children almost live in their bathing suits. . . . They are crazy in the water. They will be glad to have water wings. . . . When you come, buy a *gray* flannel shirt at Wanamaker's for $3.00 and bring a bright necktie to wear with it. . . . I have a good red one with me so don't bother to buy one. [My father loved bright colors and especially red.] We are glad to have a paper occasionally. Don't overexercise in the heat. [He played tennis several times a week.]

The heat spell ended. The exercise and unhurried existence restored my mother's energy and her pleasure in roughing it. Three weeks after we left New York, on July 21 her letter to my father reported:

We have spent the whole day out of doors—picking berries, tramping, canoeing and swimming. I feel fine now—and lack only you. The children tried the water wings and found them a perfect success. Virginia swims alone with them and Bobby a little too. . . . We have very uneventful but very busy days. Wint went today to Seven Mile Brook with a guide and two other men and brought back 59 trout. . . . Huckleberries and raspberries are just ripening and there are many—if one looks for them. . . . We will have another canoe when you come and take some trips. There is a big tract of country to explore. . . . The woods are wild and unsettled. . . . We shall be so glad to see you and I, most of all. I seem to be half living in another world until you come. . . . That is my focus in time. With love always, Janet.

After that summer in Nova Scotia, my mother and father took up canoeing in New York on the Hudson River. They bought a twenty-foot special Oldtown canoe that was equipped with removable side-keels and a cross-piece to hold a sail. On a Sunday we would take the Broadway sub-way for nearly an hour's ride to Dyckman Street and get the canoe from a boathouse at about 204th Street. Fastened into our life preservers, Virginia and I sat motionless on the bottom of the big canoe while they paddled and sailed it over the vast expanse of the Hudson. The ocean-going steamers and river day-liners never looked so huge as they did then from the water level. Their wash from astern could have swamped our unstable craft if it had not ridden the rough waves right. We used to navigate across the mile-wide river and picnic below the sheer forbidding cliffs of the Palisades on the New Jersey shore. On our return trip to the boathouse, bucking head-winds and the tide frequently required mighty armpower. Sometimes for diversion we paddled through Spuyten Duyvil Creek and the Harlem River around the north end of Manhattan Island and back. Now in retrospect, remembering that neither my mother nor father could swim, I am forced to conclude that those jaunts in our sailing canoe were hazardous, but at the time we thrived on their novelty and excitement.

My mother and father and their two daughters were united in their ardor for the flexible life of the vagabond and for the adventure of braving the elements and wilderness. My mother also reveled in the closeness to the beauty of nature that comes with living out of doors, and she made a game of playing house in a tent, a log cabin, or an automobile. Her metamorpho-sis to a nomad at heart seemed complete.

In 1924, when Ginny and I were in medical school, the family made a memorable summer tour of the Far West by motorized camping. On July 2, we left New York for California by train, stopping off to sight-see at Denver and Salt Lake City. Between those cities we traveled through the Rocky Mountains in the roofless observation cars of the Denver and Rio Grande Railroad. In later years, that same scenic trip in the D. & R. G.'s glassed-in Vistadome lacked the thrill of wind in your face. My Uncle Warren—inven-tor, construction engineer, geologist, and naturalist—and Aunt Minnie were living then in San Bernardino in southern California. My father and his younger brother Warren had taken many camping trips together in their bachelor days. Aunt Minnie did not like that kind of recreation, but she was gay and sociable and never wanted to miss anything. In 1921, they had camped in tents with us on Raquette Lake in the Adirondacks. In 1923, I had traveled alone to California and the three of us had camped out without overhead shelter except for the great trees of the Sequoia National Park. Perhaps I felt especially close to Uncle Warren because of his exciting knowledge of science and because his only child Arthur had died at Cornell University in the influenza epidemic of 1918. Now, in 1924, Aunt Minnie and Uncle Warren were ready to join us on our merry motor tour.

Before we arrived in "San Berdoo," arrangements were made for us to purchase there a seven-passenger special model of the "Big Six" Studebaker, which would accommodate all six of us. We named it Pegasus. Its exterior was covered with alligator leather, and the front and middle windows slid backward in grooves beside the rear window, which was set in a high square top. The straight windshield opened and tilted out to let in the breeze—and with it the dust. I remember Pegasus as an elegant vehicle—before we loaded our camping gear. On the left side the wide running board carried a spare tire and our suitcases, which were stacked within an extensible rack like a child's stair gate. Front and back fenders were piled with our bedrolls. On the luggage rack at the rear was strapped a metal trunk; it contained staple foods, our pots and pans, tin eating ware, and an iron grill with four fold-under spike legs that could be stuck into the ground anywhere. An open fire was quickly built under the grill and that served as our stove. We cooked most of our meals en route; hot chocolate and coffee were our chief beverages. Our frying pan and metal plates were often scrubbed with sand or gravel in the cold fresh running water of a stream or in the ocean. Since it never rained in California during the summer—except in the high mountains—we dispensed with tents. At night we slept under the stars. We had only to find a comfortable hollow on the ground where there were not too many stones and unroll our waterproofed blanket rolls.

The days were packed with action, not merely with sitting in an automobile. If each of us had had his way, Pegasus would have been stationary most of the time. Uncle Warren and I carried cameras and at almost every turn of the road a scenic view unfolded that seemed worth recording. My father wanted to pause and cast a fishing line in every stream and lake. Many of these spots Ginny and I thought ideal for a quick swim. Rare trees and plants and rock formations caught Uncle Warren's trained eye. California's countless mission churches were of historical interest to my mother and Aunt Minnie, as my photograph album proves. Groceries, as well as gas and oil, had to be bought each day, and afterward another edible item was always added to the list for purchase at the next roadside market. "How about those beautiful melons? Couldn't we stop and run back for a few?" Someone was forever hungry for an ice-cream cone. "That side road looked like a fine picnic spot for lunch—too bad we went by so fast." Or, "The sun will set soon and we need more time to camp than we had last night. I could have found a more comfortable bed." Our car-bound community of six soon set up a Boss System, with a new boss every hour in regular rotation. His, or her, moment-to-moment decisions were final. The Boss's popularity rating varied inversely with the number of miles traveled in the hour. In spite of the System, our journey was marked by milestones of adventure.

North of San Diego on our way from La Jolla to Mexico, the Boss let us stop at Mission Heights to admire a large purple bougainvillea vine in magnificent bloom. Close by was an ostrich farm. I saw a sign that advertised ostrich rides. We investigated. Although I was dressed to impress the Mexican border guards and not to ride a biped, the opportunity for that new experience was irresistible to me. A gigantic black and white bird, hooded, was led onto a circular track perhaps a quarter of a mile long and enclosed between high board fences. I pulled my flapper hat down tight and my tight skirt up, and I clambered aboard from a mounting block. No saddle, strap, or reins helped me retain my feathered seat. My hands grasped the base of the ostrich's wings and their soft plumes happily covered my thighs as I straddled the broad back. My feet dangled a long way from the ground. Then the hood was removed. With its "head out of the sand," the ostrich took off around the track at a run, as fast as a racehorse and as undeviating as a rocket. The bird's two-legged gait was a medley of strange movements that combined dipping, rocking, and rolling all at once. With each lunging stride its handsome tail feathers bobbed up and down and its small head oscillated forward and backward on a level with mine. Every few seconds, without slackening pace or breaking its offbeat rhythm the ostrich turned its head 180 degrees and fixed its beady eyes on mine. At the same time, its powerful beak approximated my nose with each rearward arching of its long neck. I could not lean back far enough to escape its reach and my hands were not available to defend my face from a ferocious pecking. I thought that the size of the ostrich's brain in proportion to its body's augured poorly for its good sense and I also doubted its good nature. As with so many threatened "happenings," nothing untoward came to pass, and my unscheduled ride on an African ostrich ended uneventfully when we completed the circuit of the track. Although that bird could not fly, I labeled the snapshot taken then as "The Twentieth Century in Flight."

Our finest swim was also on that lap of our travels. At La Jolla, Ginny and I rode the surf into the deep caves that the ocean had worn in the high overhanging bluffs. A school of mammoth goldfish was also playing there, six or eight feet beneath the surface of the water. By working hard against the buoyancy of the salt sea we could swim down among them and almost touch their darting forms. They must not have had many such visitors for they seemed not to mind our presence.

Our motorized camping trip was not a short one. After we drove from San Bernardino about a hundred miles due south to La Jolla and through Mission Beach, where on July 17 I rode the ostrich, to Tijuana, Mexico, we followed the length of California's spectacular coastline as far north as

Crescent City near the Oregon state line. Between Santa Barbara and Monterey we spent a cold, uncomfortable night sleeping on ocean sand at Pismo State Beach. At daybreak we moved on. We never tried the sand again. That day on Point Lobos, south of Carmel, while we cooked lunch beside the Devil's Cauldron we had an encounter with the Pacific Ocean. My father and Uncle Warren climbed down the steep sides of that dead-end trap in the rocky coast to get us a pail of sea water. As each towering wave surged out, large abalone were seen clinging to the lowest line of rock. Then they were quickly covered by the next inrush of tons of water. Displaying a delicate balance of boldness and discretion, our intrepid men managed to pry loose a number of those big mollusks; we still keep their pearly shells. Uncle Warren and my father got their game but they got thoroughly wet besides. Our roughing it was interrupted by a civilized visit in Oakland with my father's and Uncle Warren's first cousin, Sarah Wiswall Meyer, and we toured the San Francisco Bay area from that base. As we again proceeded northward, we planned our itinerary to arrive at a state or national park well before sunset, since darkness engulfed us suddenly, without twilight.

Our route was along the old "redwood highway," a curving road of dirt that was notched into the bluffs of the coast range above the Pacific Ocean. A new road through the redwoods was under construction. It suited us exactly that the existing one was little traveled. At one point we crossed the wide mouth of the Klamath River on a ferry that operated only during high tide. In the thick forests of the Sempervirens redwoods, at night I arranged my blankets on ground softened by layers of their springy needles. My bedpost at each corner was a tree eight or ten feet in diameter and straight as a church spire. Lying there, I looked up into a vault of cathedral woods with tops so thickly interwoven that the stars were invisible. Those massed redwoods surpassed in majesty even the gigantic sequoias that I had seen in the high Sierras the summer before.

It was in one of the California redwood reservations that my father made his most successful fishing catch. Late in the afternoon, discouraged by fruitless fly casting he walked with Ginny and me to a small lake formed by a natural dam in the mountain stream. While she and I had our afternoon swim, he prodded around the bank and flushed a frog. "I believe I'll set a line for an eel," he said. He had hardly dropped the frog bait to the bottom beneath where we were splashing and diving when he exclaimed, "I've got one already. It's very heavy—maybe a log."

I scrambled onto the bank and prepared to pounce on the eel with a towel when he flung it up out of the water; as a child, I had held many a slimy eel with a burlap bag. But that time my father dragged out a three-foot-long salmon trout. His bottom-feeding fish was the only one caught in that state park in many weeks the other campers told us. We shared it with them.

When we turned inland from the coast, Pegasus needed his wings to traverse the old road over Grants Pass in Oregon. Unguarded by any rail and one lane wide except for turnouts for passing, the road edged around such precipitous drops of hundreds of feet that my father sat on the floor of the car in back where he could not see over the side. High places always made him dizzy. On hourly shifts through those mountains Ginny and I drove that heavy car without benefit of power steering or power brakes. At Portland, Oregon, Aunt Minnie and Uncle Warren regretfully left us to return home by train.

Our next objective was Mount Hood, 11,245 feet in altitude, in the Cascade Range. We spent a night at Cloud Cap Inn at an elevation of 6,000 feet so that Ginny and I could climb the steep north side of that snow-capped peak the next day. On the drive up in the afternoon, not content with the planned ascent to the summit, she and I left the car on the lower slopes of the mountain at Mount Hood Lodge and we hiked alone the six miles and 3,200 foot rise from there to Cloud Cap Inn. On the climb to the top we were conducted by a guide. We crossed the Elliot Glacier where only a few days later other mountain climbers were killed by an avalanche of rocks that the summer heat had loosened at the glacier's head. Although not the highest mountain in the range, Mount Hood towers 8,000 feet above the plateau of the Hood River valley, and when we emerged from the thick clouds that surrounded its base, the view of Mount Rainier and other isolated snowy peaks was like the perspective from an airplane. It was quite unlike the views in the continuous massive ranges of Colorado, where a year earlier I had climbed higher mountains in the Rocky Mountain National Park from Estes and near Denver, from the Colorado Mountain Club tent camp at timberline above Silver Plume.

After the expedition up Mount Hood we camped that night about fifty miles away, close by The Dalles, beside the rapids of the Columbia River. It was dark when we got there and we had a hard time finding a space that was not cluttered with rocks. In the morning we learned that the region was infested with rattlesnakes and that we should have circled our beds on the ground with manila rope to keep out the snakes. Providence had cared for us once more. Testing fate again, we climbed out onto rocks in the rushing water to watch Indians spear the salmon as they leapt upstream toward their spawning grounds. Standing in the midst of the tumbling rapids, I seemed to be a part of their great power. I can still feel the wet spray and hear the steady roar as the white water poured down against the rocks. I was less intimately stirred by the high, straight waterfalls that we saw from the distance of the highway, like a painting or a picture, where mountain streams cascaded over cliffs into the broad Columbia River west of The Dalles.

From there we drove south and crossed a stretch of two hundred more miles of mountains to reach Crater Lake National Park. My mother, father, Ginny, and I hiked a thousand feet down—and up—the trail that looped against the steep volcanic rim of the lake, the surface of which is more than a mile above sea level. We rented a boat, picnicked on the less rugged of the two islands, and swam in the incredibly clear violet-blue water. A silver coin thrown on the rocky bottom near the shore could be clearly seen twenty or thirty feet under water. The rare transparency and indigo of the lake are said to be due to its depth of 2,000 feet, within a palisade setting.

Our next destination was Reno, Nevada, where on August 8 my father took the train back to New York and my mother, Ginny, and I visited friends who lived in that city. It was my first introduction to the pastel colors of the desert in bloom framed by the pale blues of the distant Nevada mountain ranges. Two girls from Reno joined us on our further camping tour of Lake Tahoe and Yosemite. The first night out from Reno, on August 11, our now feminine contingent made camp near Coleville, California, and according to my camera our larder was invaded by sheep. We entered Yosemite National Park over the high mountains to the east by way of Mono Lake and Lee Vining Pass. It was a rugged trip that was complicated by broken gears in Pegasus's differential and we were happy to spend a few days in Park cabins on the floor of the Yosemite valley. There wild deer ate bread and lettuce from our hands and bear raided our camp garbage.

From Yosemite we returned to Oakland. Roughing it, we had covered more than three thousand miles in exactly one month. We shipped Pegasus in a crate by steamer, via the Panama Canal, from San Francisco to New York, where more adventures were in store for that indefatigable vehicle. We ladies still had four thousand miles to go. On August 18 we left by train for Seattle, Vancouver, Lake Louise in the Canadian Rocky Mountains, and Port Arthur on Lake Superior. We went by boat across that Great Lake to Sault Sainte Marie where we visited Uncle Sheldon and Aunt Kate Griswold at their lakeshore cottage. By train again, we proceeded to Buffalo to see our Davidson relatives, my mother's two brothers and their families. At long last on Monday, September 8, we were home in the familiar canyons of Manhattan Island. Ginny and I were just in time for the opening of medical school.

I loved every moment of that summer's ten thousand miles of wandering. As our family together surmounted obstacles without mishap, we grew in endurance, resourcefulness, curiosity, and knowledge. I came to know at first hand the vast territory of the United States and to feel that it belonged to me. With pride of ownership comes a feeling of responsibility.

Yet our roughing it for pleasure would have left me dissatisfied and restless had I not had roots that pulled me home. A nomad existence was acceptable to me only so long as work and home and love were waiting for me at the other end of the trail. To the vagabond who lacks a roof of his own, sleeping under the sky means enforced loneliness, not elected solitude. Some of that feeling I expressed in a poem, written in retrospect:

SLEEPING UNDER STARS

Night's sounds bedevil the city,
Feed fears and speed retreat indoors.
The ambulance that reels and roars
Pursues a trail of blood. Pity
The homeless—"free," quip the witty—
The vagrants sleeping after dark
Roofless on benches in the park,
Roused by the cops' nightstick ditty.
Stars ignore the blindfold city.

Night's sounds serenade the country,
Entice me sweetly out of doors
To lay me down beside the shores
Of lakes and streams. A still sentry,
The tallest tree, guards that entry
Where under summer's stars I sleep
Secure in my own roots grown deep
In home. Though world's winds blow wintry,
Stars illumine my soul's country.

In New York we missed the country. My precocious parents, however, found ingenious ways to make roughing it accessible. The farm that they bought in 1911 in the Berkshire Hills was only a hundred and twenty-five miles from the city and it partly filled that need.

When my sister and I were in medical school, we found other hardy souls among our classmates who missed the out of doors in the city where they had come to study. Central Park was not large enough for them. With their encouragement, Ginny and I conceived the impractical idea of spending a winter holiday at our Merryfield Farm.

Mrs. Laura Merriefield had lived in the old farmhouse that was built in 1799 for about eighty years. During her lifetime, in winter the house was heated downstairs by stoves and there were no water pipes inside it to freeze. Handy hot water was provided by a "water back," a built-in chamber in the wood-burning range that was filled and emptied by a large tin dipper. My mother set about to improve the house for summer use. She put running water in the kitchen and added two bathrooms. She installed a heating coil in the firebox of the black iron range to heat the water. She removed the bricks that sealed up the front of the shallow fireplaces in the center chimney downstairs. An old crane in one fireplace and a baking oven were uncovered. A man-high heating stove and its curved pipe to the fireplace disappeared from the great hearthstone that projected into what had been the all-purpose winter living room. It became our dining room. My mother removed the partition and door that had sealed off the staircase and kept the heat in downstairs. In their place she substituted an open balustrade and graceful mahogany rail for cooler ventilation on hot summer days.

On the day after Christmas, 1923, my mother, Ginny, Pop Weeks, engineer and member of the Explorers Club who married my sister not quite two years later, I, and three of my medical-school classmates—Kay Burnet, Norm Plummer, and Irv Wright—took the New York, New Haven and Hartford morning train to Sheffield, Massachusetts. Our gear filled one end of the railroad car. There were skis, snowshoes, ice skates, winter apparel, blankets in duffel bags, and hampers and hampers of food ready to eat. Roast turkey, baked ham, boiled tongue, whole cheeses, hard-boiled eggs, canned soups, beans, and much more would provide the "specific dynamic action of protein" to protect us against the winter cold, feed fuel to our muscles, and simplify our cooking on the antique crane in the dining-room fireplace.

We drove up the hill in Mr. Warner's small truck. As we approached the old frame house, it looked small, desolate, and exposed to the weather under the great maples that no longer screened it with their leaves. In snow boots and ski clothes we made deep tracks through the unbroken snow from the road to the porch and we were soon stowing our things in the closed damp house. Speedily, everyone went to work. Wood was brought from the woodshed and fires lighted in the three fireplaces on the ground floor. Water from the spring ran all winter from an open pipe at the porch. A large galvanized pail was filled and set in one end of the five-foot-wide fireplace in the dining room. A black iron kettle full of water was hung on the swinging crane by means of an S-shaped heavy wire hook. We could not use the kitchen stove because it contained the now empty coils for heating water in the summer. The pipes in the house had been drained when it was shut in the fall.

Food was spread out in the kitchen. We learned later that this was a mistake because all of it froze solid—meat, canned goods, and even the bread. In fact, during the week that we stayed there we never got any part of the house up to freezing. I can still remember my mother walking around and holding a small room thermometer at arm's length to find the warmest spot in the room. The water in the open pail in the corner of the fireplace always showed a rim of ice on the side away from the fire. The outdoor temperature ranged from about 10 degrees above during the day to 15 or 20 degrees below zero at night. Lamps were filled with kerosene, wicks trimmed, and candles set in candlesticks. By then, water was boiling in the kettle over the roaring fire and I poured a little onto the dining-room table to wipe it clean of dust. The water froze as it spread and the lake of ice was still there when we left. Lacking electricity, we had no way of warming the upstairs bedrooms. My mother occupied the least chilly bedroom downstairs; it opened off the slightly warmed dining room. She took a hot-water bag to bed with her, but by morning even that had turned to a cake of ice under her covers at the the foot of the bed. I slept on a cot in the north parlor, which boasted a fireplace. Perhaps the heat from it made me braver than the rest—the first night that we were there. The consensus was that it would be wise to sleep in our clothes but I decided to undress and put on my warm pajamas. I never took them off there and I wore them back to New York on the train.

All day long we tramped through the woods and open spaces on snow-shoes or skis. Beyond the house the groove of the dirt road was leveled by drifts. Even the fences had disappeared under the snow. At night, the stars overhead had never been so brilliant. In the silence miles away the bark of a dog or a fox echoed. Evenings, wrapped in blankets like Indians, we sat on the floor by the fire and we sang and laughed at our jokes and projected visions of what we would do after we graduated from medical school. Ginny was set on pediatrics and I on becoming a heart specialist. Irv was going to find the cure for cancer. Little did he think that after years of a career in cardiovascular disease, he would serve on President Lyndon Johnson's Commission for Heart Disease, Cancer and Stroke. Pop was a few years older than my generation. He regaled us with his adventures in the lighter-than-air world of balloons and dirigibles. He told us the tale of his flight in the International Balloon Race, when he came down prematurely in the wilds of Canada and was lost for several days. Most of the equipment and supplies in his open balloon basket had been hastily jettisoned to lighten it and to check the too rapid descent.

On the first day of January, 1924, for New Year's diversion we borrowed Mr. Woodbeck's team of horses and a hayrack on sleigh runners. Reclining on a generous padding of hay, we drove ten miles across the

Housatonic River valley through Sheffield to the Berkshire School at the foot of Mount Everett, the highest peak in the Taconic Range. We put the horses in the school's barn and parked my mother with Mrs. Buck, wife of the school principal, while we climbed about 2,000 feet up the steep "telephone trail" to the summit. At some points on the trail we had to boost each other up over sheer ice cliffs.

We were told that the temperature at the top of the mountain reached 40 degrees below zero, and I believe it. Optimistically, we had brought hamburgers to cook when we reached the summit where we could admire the view. In our knapsacks we also had canned baked beans, with kindling and paper to start the cookout. We had not figured on the icy snow, however, that was many feet deep and nearly level with the tops of the scrub pine. Our fire sank gradually into a deepening pit in the melting snow and kept putting itself out. Finally we were leaning way down into the pit to reach the food. We never managed to cook the hamburgers but we did thaw the rolls and beans enough to eat them, while at the same time we warmed our hands and faces over the scanty coals.

As we finished that chilly picnic on the mountain, my mother suddenly appeared over the top of the telephone trail, beaming like the cat that swallowed the canary. It looked odd to see her standing there wearing a dress and full-length fur-trimmed wool coat and a fur hat—I can not remember ever seeing my mother in slacks or any kind of pants. She had climbed the steep way alone, she said, because she didn't want to slow us up. She knew her own pace.

Marvelous to relate, not one of us caught pneumonia or even the "sniffles." We did not seem to mind the severe cold, but we were dressed for it. Years later, when my husband saw a snapshot of me taken then outside the house, he remarked, "I didn't know you were ever that fat."

Indignantly I enumerated the layers of clothing that I had on over my flannel pajamas.

CHAPTER 5

Merryfield Farm

Merryfield Farm was my mother's creation. It gave her the fullest expression of her personality during the latter part of her life, and it was a lifeline that she wove for the family. It drew us back year after year and pulled us together, one generation to another, like and unlike. The forces with which she endowed the farm continued to renew our physical and spiritual strengths. My mother quoted a verse that she may have written about her haven for restless travelers on earth:

> Come share our rest where none molest,
> And none can make afraid,
> With Peace that sits as Friendship's guest,
> Beneath the homestead's shade.

My mother knew the Berkshire Hills from the 1890's when her father rented a dark red clapboard house on the main street of Stockbridge, Massachusetts, across from the Red Lion Inn. She used to tell me how she and her Wellesley friends would bicycle together around the Stockbridge Bowl, pedaling or coasting abreast while they all held hands, not touching the handlebars. I myself never learned to balance that well on a bicycle. In 1911 when I was nine, she and my father in their turn rented an old white frame house for the summer in the elm-shaded village of Sheffield on the Housatonic River fourteen miles south of Stockbridge. Located at the north end of the little town's one street, the house was—and still is—approached by a long driveway with a double row of large hydrangea shrubs.

In the rear there was a dirt tennis court that we kept in constant use except when the river-bottom fog blanketed the low land. Our place bordered on muddy Schenob Brook, a hideout for frogs, a home for mosquitoes, and our fishing ground for eels. I thought it a paradise. My respectable grandfather and grandmother Davidson came from Albany to spend the summer with us. He had retired from the bank the year before, "having acquired a sufficient competency." He was horrified when he saw me walking barefoot down the village street or sitting astride the horse that pulled the garbage collector's wagon from back door to back door of those well-kept old New England homes.

Sheffield then had a population of about five hundred, not counting the summer residents. Privacy was in short supply, and my mother longed for the hills that she loved. That summer she consulted real-estate agents in search of a farm to buy. Her criteria were two: a mountain view and a dependable spring. She found both in a 120-acre farm about four miles from Sheffield at an altitude of 1,100 feet on a windswept ridge across the valley from the Taconic Mountain Range. On the "under mountain" road the sun set early, but from our hill sunset colors lingered behind the distant mountain skyline far into the twilight. We have blessed the hill often for the years of isolation and independence that it ensured us in an age of intrusion. Our nearest neighbor was about a mile away in one direction and half a mile in the other. In heavy rains the steep road made Crow Hill's rutted dirt impassable to a car without chains. Merryfield Farm was so inaccessible then that some of our city friends referred to it derogatively as the Mountain Goat Estate.

During the century since the farmhouse had been built the spring had not gone dry. It was located on the ridge higher than the house—my father and I surveyed its elevation together—so that we could install a water storage tank in the attic that filled by gravity flow. In the absence of electricity to operate a pump, that was the only way to obtain all the conveniences of indoor plumbing. My mother could do without electric lights, and without the electric iron, vacuum cleaner, washing machine—it had no wringer or dryer—electric toaster, and electric hair curler that she had in New York. But even after ten summers of roughing it my mother was still sufficiently civilized to want hot and cold running water in the house that was to be her permanent vacation home.

My father's sole criterion for a summer place was that it should be a farm. When he was fifteen, between high school and college he spent a year working on his father's farm, Elm Hill, and he called it perhaps the most valuable single year of his life. Brush Hill, the long ridge on which Merryfield Farm was located, comprised several thousand acres of cleared land

and woodland and we were the only summer residents—"city folk"—in the area. We were proud to be accepted into that stable community of productive New England farmers. When we took title to the place in the summer of 1912, Mrs. Laura Merriefield moved to her smaller dairy farm at the foot of Crow Hill and lived with her nephew, Roy Orcutt. He continued to work our fields to obtain feed for the cows that moved down with her. For us he planted several acres of our farm to potatoes and golden bantam corn and he started our large vegetable garden before we arrived for the summer. My father, mother, sister Ginny, and I, with the help of visiting cousins and friends, carried on the continuous job of planting, weeding, and hoeing our edible crops.

My mother purchased the farm complete with the old furniture in the 1799 house, with ice in the sawdust-filled icehouse, hens and a rooster in the chickenhouse, young pigs in the pen for our garbage disposal, farming tools in the workshed that had once been a blacksmith's shop, and best of all, a general utility mare in the pasture. Maggie's harness and draft collar hung in the horse barn, and there was even an English saddle. Working as a farmhorse, Maggie pulled the garden cultivator, a stone boat, and the buckboard wagon. Hitched to the light, topless buggy or to the two-seater surrey with isinglass curtains rolled under its top, she provided us with essential transportation to town. My grandfather Davidson liked to drive Maggie stylishly to Sheffield in the valley or occasionally over the hill six miles to Great Barrington. Returning, the rest of us got out and walked up the quarter-mile-long Crow Hill to lighten her load. She would really breathe a "Thank you, Ma'am," as she stopped and the surrey rested on the short leveled stretches beyond the steepest pitches of the road.

On a farm, chores must be done whatever the weather. Each day in rain or shine, Maggie and I went to get milk from Roy Orcutt's cooler and to retrieve the mail from our R.F.D. box on the County Road at the bottom of the hill. When it rained I preferred to ride without a saddle, but then I would have to climb a fence to mount Maggie with the heavy milk pail and mail packet in my hands.

Maggie was my playmate and constant companion out of doors, especially after we acquired the Model T Ford in 1914. I thought her very pretty; I liked her horse-chestnut color, long black mane and tail, and the white star on her forehead. I brushed her and fed her and led her at dusk to the night pasture that had access to our farm pond. Neither my mother nor sister cared much for horses, so it was my pleasant duty to hitch her up and drive her when she was needed to go on errands. The great event of the week was meeting the Friday night whistling train at the Sheffield railroad station when my father came from New York for the weekend. Maggie's eyes had no need of the kerosene lantern that swung underneath the buggy but mine did. In 1913, all summer long a new cement bridge was being built on the County Road, which we traveled to the village, and we had to ford Iron Works Brook at that point. Lantern in hand, I would lead Maggie down the steep bank and wade through the rushing stream while the buggy jolted and tilted on the rocky bottom.

Maggie was a patient pet and she understood children. We could walk safely between her legs and hang around her neck. She would drag the stone boat a short distance at a time across a field while the whole family loaded it with the winter frost's fresh crop of stones. Then she would stand while we competed in throwing them off as fast as we could against the stone wall that bordered the field. It was more fun than skipping stones over the surface of a lake. When the apples ripened in our orchards I used Maggie as a tree ladder. With the reins looped over my elbow, I stood on her back and picked the fruit on the lower limbs, placing it carefully in a pau hung by a wire hook. (We never shipped a bruised or wormy apple to New York; windfalls showed up in jelly, cider, or apple vinegar.) My father at the same time, climbed to the top of the tree and picked it clean. Trees were made to be climbed, I thought, but just then I preferred an animated ladder and the challenge of my balancing act. Sometimes Maggie tired of it all and moved, leaving me dangling from whatever branches I could grab.

For seven summers until I entered Wellesley College in the fall of 1918, we enjoyed long unbroken vacations at Merryfield Farm. Ginny's and my school in New York, The Brearley, did not start until the end of September, and one wonderful brilliant autumn during the polio epidemic of 1916 we stayed until mid-October. Then my father and I picked not only the late Northern Spy apples into barrels set on the back of the buckboard, but also boxes of hickory nuts for the winter. We had extra time, too, for the fall pruning of the fruit trees—cherry, plum, apple, and pear. During those years, restrictions imposed by the First World War may have limited our travel, but the hill satisfied me and I had no desire to leave it.

It was not all work for Maggie and me. She and I often set off, destination unknown. I usually strapped a book to the saddle. We would ride first to a haunt of mine in the woods where I knew a comfortable perch in an ancient white pine that looked over the surrounding trees to Mount Everett. There I would tie Maggie so that she could nibble while I sat and read, braced in the swaying tops where the wind blew through the thick soft needles. Sometimes we went down the hill by way of the Ford's farm and called on the Orcutts or stopped at Mr. Woodbeck's place on Three Mile Pond where my father took us fishing from a rowboat. I learned to know our neighbors well and any of them would give Maggie and me a meal.

When she and I went in the other direction to the Hickey's big farm, I helped with the haying in the fields and Maggie liked the companionship of the other horses. When the hayrick was full, I sat on the high load and sometimes was allowed to drive the team to the barn while Maggie followed along behind. At another season I bound the golden oats where they lay in even rows as the mowing machine had left them. I learned to milk the cows and I became a regular volunteer hand at the afternoon milking of Mr. Hickey's large herd. There are never enough hands on a farm. We had no cows on our place and I missed them. If I had not returned home by dinner time, my mother started telephoning to find me. Her imperturbability was remarkable.

At times I rode Maggie at a slow walk through pastures, fields, and woods in search of some rare flower or shrub. Even today I can lead the way to spots where native azalea and laurel grow wild on our place, where maidenhair fern lurks, where the largest paper-white birches are found, where an isolated tamarack has survived and young chestnuts are now filling in the gaps fifty years after every parent tree was killed by the great American chestnut blight. I knew also the haunts of the high-flying butterflies, the Cloudy Swallowtail, the Monarch, and the Mourning Cloak. Maggie and I would chase a particular one that I wanted for my insect collection, galloping back and forth and round and round in a field. In my pocket I carried a wide-mouthed specimen jar that contained sodium cyanide crystals layered under cotton and wire mesh. In one hand I held the reins and in the other I waved a butterfly net on a ten-foot light bamboo pole that my father had fixed for me. I watched where the butterfly finally settled and then without alighting from my horse I eased the net down over it. One of our neighbors on the hill started a rumor that Bobby Travell was training for the circus.

Catching butterflies was not a simple pastime for me, but an education. Reference books at the farm enabled me to classify my specimens of the invertebrate Arthropoda—grasshoppers, darning needles, flies, bees, beetles, and spiders, as well as moths and butterflies. I learned to perceive what is in plain sight but not ordinarily noticed; my trained eye could spot the elusive walkingstick or a rare praying mantis where it clung motionless to the twigs that it resembled. In July, 1955 not long after I met Senator John F. Kennedy, I glanced down at the ground from the high seat of a big tractor in Waterloo, Iowa, and suddenly exclaimed to the man with whom I was talking, "Look! Just in front of your foot in the grass is a four-leaf clover." It took him a while to see it. I still have that good-luck clover pressed in the old prescription pad that I had with me in my purse. At Merryfield Farm I mounted my carefully prepared collections under glass in a tray arrangement or I framed them for wall display with the aid of a glass cutter and panes of glass, cardboard, a roll of soft cotton, and *passe partout* binding tape.

I did not merely collect specimens. I studied those creatures' habits in life. I knew where the large black and yellow spiders spun their vertical silken traps in the brush by a stone wall. I caught small molasses-spitting grasshoppers or a savage robber fly and dropped them singly against the webs to watch the spider quickly transfix its prey and bind it in a silk netting with scarcely a struggle. The spider sometimes lost the battle: the heavy furry caterpillar that I brought would thrash itself free and fall to the ground, dragging down the spider's sheer creation.

Memories stored from those childhood hours and tempered by more mature experience sparked a poem that I wrote in 1965 in Washington:

NATURE AND HUMAN NATURE

Plant your feet down deep in the soil.
Bare your feet first of man-made clods,
Learn the feel of the earth you toil
To plow, the good sod that is God's.
Destroy it not.

Raise your head up high in the trees,
Poise, peer through at the golden sheaves.
Learn the view that the bird's nest sees:
Insects for feed beneath the leaves.
Poison them not.

Plummet your weight to ocean floor,
Join the fish there that gawk at your
Tank and life line. The water's store
Of air is theirs, and not your sewer.
Befoul it not.

Turn your eyes up toward the skies,
Breathe the wind that is God's affair,
Drink of sunset before it dies;
Cumulus clouds float on clear air.
Pollute it not.

Bend yourself low and lightly tread,
Spy as the spider veils the bush,
Lies there in wait as still as dead,
Nature's cruel guerrilla ambush.
Imitate not.

The flower gardens were my mother's main recreation at the farm and Ginny was her chief helper. However, as a part-time apprentice I absorbed from her a considerable knowledge of gardening: what plants and shrubs could be layered, slipped, or best grown from seed; what season was right for transplanting each; how to handle the roots and how deep to set them; what variety of soil and how much sun each one liked; which plants would winter kill on the north side of the house. My mother passed on her love of garden beauty and her busy green thumb to both Ginny and me. Just as her wisteria vine at 27 East 11th Street had climbed to the top of the house, whatever she planted at Merryfield Farm grew like the magical beanstalk of Jack-the-Giant-Killer. Her hollyhocks by the porch shot up several feet taller than my father. Hydrangeas that she set out in the perennial border now are three times my height, and her double-petaled syringa bushes are three stories high. I have climbed out on the shingled roof to trim them back. Her old-fashioned yellow lilies and primroses even choked out the grass. With the benefit of heavy night dews and clear bright days, the hill was grass country. My father bought a gasoline lawn mower and my mother named it Nebuchadnezzar. We all took turns running after it and steering it while that high-powered King devoured grass on the expansive lawn that my mother had mapped out. In a later era, my husband and I employed our riding horses to advantage for mowing that lawn.

My father's utilitarian instincts and the number of things to be done on a farm kept him busy without his participating in my mother's gardening projects. Our wood-burning kitchen range consumed enormous quantities of fuel. Each winter on our place, selected maple and ash trees were cut in cord lengths and stacked outside the woodshed. In the summer my father and I worked many hours pulling a crosscut saw through those seasoned hardwood logs and splitting them into pieces to fit the kitchen firebox. I learned to swing an axe with the precision of a woodsman. My grandfather Davidson, always well dressed in a business suit, liked occasionally to take a little exercise with a bucksaw, cutting the smaller logs that were racked up on a small sawhorse. His regular exercise was walking, usually several miles a day. My grandmother weeded the lawn and the flowers, but she became progressively invalided by Parkinson's disease before her death in 1919.

Since my mother brought two maids from New York for the summer, keeping the house made small demands on our time. My special indoor duty was, by choice, to have the candles ready for use and the lamps filled with kerosene, their wicks trimmed and chimneys clean. My mother and Ginny used to hang wallpaper and they could do over a bedroom, including the ceiling, with amazing speed. We all helped in preparing and preserving jars and jars of fruit, vegetables, and even broilers, particularly during the war years after August 4, 1914, when Great Britain declared war on Germany. Ginny loved to cook and baked us delicious cakes. I liked to cook only out of doors and we often picnicked near the house by a large boulder against which we built a simple fireplace of stones. Evenings, wrapped in blankets we sat around our cookout fire until the dew drove us indoors. Sometimes we built a huge bonfire in the big field after dark to exchange signals with our cousins, the Laidlaws, who did likewise on their hilltop ten miles across the valley as the crow flies.

On rainy days we had time to read and to learn a variety of crafts through my mother's guiding example. We made baskets with dampened reed and raffia, creating Indian-style designs. We stenciled floral borders on cloth table covers. We made decorative objects by tooling leather, carving wood, and hammering brass. We sewed, embroidered, tatted lace, and, of course, knitted helmets, sweaters, and socks for the Red Cross and for our soldiers overseas.

Years later one of my patients told me, "You have eyes in the ends of your fingers." I thought how much medical skill I owed to my early training in manual dexterity.

My father could transform any kind of work into play and he loved games. When he came on weekends, after dinner the whole family played hearts with two packs of cards by the light of an Aladdin lamp, candles on the mantelpiece, and an open fire. He taught me the rudiments of chess. He put up posts and a tennis net across our lumpy lawn so that Ginny and I could hit balls to each other for practice; the outrageous bounces improved the coordination of eye to racket. My father was a demon at croquet, and even when he was in his eighties, he still almost always hit the post first to win the game. He taught me to shoot. I sighted down a long-barreled pistol or a .22 rifle at a printed target that he tacked up on a pear tree. When he wanted to practice shooting a moving target, he tied a stone to the end of a long string and tossed it over a high limb; then he replaced the stone with an empty soup can. I stood back from the tree and with a strong throw I launched the tin can at the end of its tether horizontally in a wide circle. While the target circled once he emptied both barrels of his shotgun at the can and we counted the number of pellets that hit it. I felt rather like William Tell's son when his father shot the apple on his head; I had equal confidence in my father's marksmanship. I became an excellent shot but I never hit, nor intended to hit, any living creature.

Ginny's and my best hours together were after we had gone to bed. We concocted fantastic stories that were undoubtedly enhanced by the fact that we slept out under the stars. In the plum orchard back of the house were hung two canvas sleeping hammocks that my mother had designed, stitched, and waterproofed for us. Each hammock was roped at its corners to four trees. Wooden crossbars at the head and foot also helped to keep the hammock flat. A square canvas fly extended from the headpiece and was tied up to the branches above. The top of the hammock was a canvas flap that hung over and snapped at one side and the foot. Those devices shed water pretty well. Rain on the hammock was a pleasant sound, like rain on a tent. Ginny and I experimented with sleeping in the soft haymow of the big barn across the road, but I do not recommend hay inside the bedclothes as a cure for insomnia. No bed suited us as well as our snug hammocks that swayed a little in the wind, that gave off the fragrance of citronella oil and brought us close to nature's night life.

Our Model T Ford extended the range of our activities at the farm. My mother, Ginny, and I drove five miles to Lake Buel to swim and sometimes to spend the night with Mrs. Merriefield's daughter Bessie, who owned a rustic cottage on the lake. We had picnics at the Laidlaws' "Summit of Echoes" where Cousin Harriet, Cousin Jimmie, and Louise lived in tents. From there we drove on through Copake, New York, and the Taconic State Park to Bash Bish Falls, where we climbed the rocky gorge and swam in the icy mountain pool under the high waterfall. We named the Ford "Ophelia Bump," and she earned her surname.

After several summers of going up and down Crow Hill, Ophelia's engine needed overhauling. By natural aptitude and under my father's tutelage, my mother had become a skilled mechanic. She and I took Ophelia apart, cleaned the carbon from her four cylinders, put in new rings, ground her valves, reset the sparkplug gaps with a thin dime, and put her back together again. That kind of experience was valuable when Ophelia went to Wellesley College with me in the fall of 1921.

Although I was only twelve when we acquired the Model T in 1914, I could not wait to drive her until I became sixteen and got a Massachusetts operator's license. Ophelia's cloth top stood seven feet from the ground and she seemed enormous to me as I peered over her steering wheel at the level dirt road on top of our hill. An "acetylene tank," bolted onto the left running board, supplied that flammable gas to the headlights. The small parking lights on each side of the windshield were kerosene lamps. At dusk, we turned them on with matches.

My mother sat beside me on the front seat and gave me driving directions. First I placed my left foot on the forward-gear pedal and blocked it at a vague mid-position that was neutral. Holding it there, I released the emergency hand brake. When that hand lever was pulled backward, it first threw the clutch into neutral and then braked the rear wheels. When it was moved into the forward position, the car was thrown into high gear unless the foot pedal held it in neutral. With my foot still balancing on the pedal, my right hand pulled the throttle toward me to give her gas—the lever was located just underneath the steering wheel. Then, I pushed the forward-speed pedal hard down to the floor boards to engage the low gear. Ophelia eased into slow motion with engine racing. As I lifted my left foot off the pedal, it jumped up through neutral into high—she had only two forward speeds— and Ophelia leapt ahead swinging from side to side in the deep ruts. I hung on to the steering wheel.

To slow her down, my feet had a choice of three pedals: low gear at the left, reverse in the middle, and foot brake at the right. With her eccentric "planetary" clutch mechanism, any one of those three pedals could be used as a brake, whether Ophelia was traveling forward or backward. In indecision, however, I did nothing with my feet. I hurriedly reached for the hand throttle and pushed the lever hard forward to give her less gas—there was no foot accelerator. The cantankerous creature balked abruptly and then racked like a horse before the engine stalled. I got out and cranked her up again, being careful first to set the emergency hand brake back so that she would not creep up and run over me. On the next try I made it to the house. The only time that I felt equally strange operating a motor vehicle was when I drove a military tank "in formation" at Fort Knox Army Base in 1958.

Our daughters, Janet and Virginia, were in their early teens when they likewise learned to drive an automobile at Merryfield Farm. In a hayfield one of them would hang out the front window of our Chrysler Windsor sedan while the other practiced changing speeds—that car had three speeds and a clutch—circling in reverse and zigzagging like a cowboy on his pony cutting cattle. That training on the farm at an early age made them proficient drivers. As soon as Janet became sixteen, when she was a high-school senior at Pelham, she obtained a New York State junior operator's license. Promptly she and Virginia set off for a ride. They crossed the Boston Post Road in Westchester County's Pelham Manor and were attracted by a dirt road that turned off toward Long Island Sound. Imbued with Merryfield Farm's spirit of adventure, they followed it. The road became poorer and narrower. Around a bend, riders on horseback suddenly met them and threatened to have them arrested for trespassing on a bridle path. Janet was stuck; she could not back out, nor could she drive forward. With ingenuity she worked the car through bushes and a fence, off the trail, and into a field. Feeling entirely at home then, she took off cross country in the Chrysler, heading in the general direction of the Post Road. When they reached that main highway the approach to it was down a steep grassy bank. The under part of the car hung up on a hidden culvert at the bottom and they were stuck again. Their SOS from the nearest telephone booth to our understanding Pelham mechanic brought a tow car. Neither a police summons nor damage to the Chrysler resulted, and the girls' respect and regard for a paved road increased notably.

The summer of 1942 found me with Janet and Virginia in Sheffield and the United States again at war with Germany. The girls were eight and seven that year. The three decades between the outbreak of World War I and the end of World War II had made little change in the way of life at Merryfield Farm, except perhaps to increase its isolation. The Hickeys' big barns and house down the dirt road to the south had burned one windy March day in 1922. The ruins still marked the spot where I had spent busy hours as a child, and their fields were vacant of cows and horses. After the fire the Hickey family took refuge for a short while in our empty house and then moved to Great Barrington. The distance to our nearest neighbor had become about a mile in *both* directions. We were without a telephone in 1942. During the previous winter, after the attack on Pearl Harbor, while our house was unoccupied and telephone service discontinued, the New England Telephone and Telegraph Company had removed the instrument to meet war shortages and we could not get it reinstated. When someone sent us a telegram then, Western Union mailed us a notice by Rural Free Delivery to pick up a message at the Sheffield railroad station.

Gasoline was rationed and pleasure driving banned. Our big Chrysler New Yorker stood idle except for two essential trips each week. On Fridays we marketed for food, bought a block of ice at Mr. Tyrell's coal and ice yard, and met Jack, my husband, on the afternoon special weekend train from New York. On Sunday nights we drove him down to the railroad station again and ate ice-cream cones in the drugstore. Our newspapers were slow in coming by mail and we eagerly asked Jack on those weekends what was the latest news of the war. The report was always the same: the German army was besieging Stalingrad deep inside Russia. The farm was an oasis of peace and time seemed to stand still.

In those thirty years between wars, of course some changes had taken place at Merryfield Farm. There was a new generation of children to play croquet with "Gran" and to chase the Queen of Spades with the Jack of Diamonds in a family game of hearts. Wood was needed only for the fireplaces and no longer for cooking because my mother had installed kerosene burners in the firebox of the kitchen range before she died in October, 1928. Shrubs and trees were encroaching on our mountain view; Jack, my father, and I tackled them constantly with clippers and axes. Our two hay barns had deteriorated and we pulled them down. The canvas sleeping hammocks had worn out and the second generation of children slept on the big open porch that my mother had added or in a tent on the lawn. A badminton court had replaced the old tennis net. Our girls caught their butterflies with a net on a pole of regulation length. They discovered that black salamanders lived underneath rocks in the brook in the ravine, and they caught orange ones in the pine woods. Salamander hunts with their Daddy took the place of Ginny's and my eel fishing or eel spearing night expeditions with our father. The days of Maggie's transportation were over and we had not yet acquired riding horses for the girls at the farm. We depended on our feet and on our bicycles. Bicycling down Crow Hill and up again, however, was not to be undertaken lightly. We preferred each day to hike the two miles round trip to Roy Orcutt's for our milk and for the mail in our R.F.D. box on the County Road. Dorothy Moore, Jack's sister from Charlotte, North Carolina, spent four weeks with us that summer of 1942 and the children, she, and I usually walked down together. We would stop at the bottom and all get wet in Iron Works Brook, but we were hot again by the time we had climbed back up the hill. Our pail of milk often soured after an afternoon's thunderstorm.

The most exciting difference in our activities was the bicycling. One morning Janet, Virginia, and I set off on our bicycles for a trip to Sheffield. We rode single file down Crow Hill. I went first on my come-apart paratrooper's bike that would fit in the trunk of a car, Janet came next on a small red one with a coaster brake, and Virginia was last on a diminutive French blue bicycle with a hand brake. As we reached the steepest part of the hill, I looked around. Janet was one "Thank you, Ma'am" behind me, but Virginia was not in sight.

"Janet, what happened to Ginia?" I called.

Janet looked back over her shoulder, still riding. "I don't know, Mummy. She was there a minute ago."

We got off and walked back up the rough road, calling constantly. There was no answer and no trace of the little blue bike. Then I heard a moan from one side of the road. Hidden by ferns Virginia lay in the bottom of the drainage ditch with her head wedged between two rocks. Janet and I freed her and she sat up. A deep cut along the hard edge of her chin was bleeding profusely. Mud and blood covered her features. I examined her quickly. Except for the laceration on her chin and her loss of face, she was not hurt. She told us that the front wheel had hit a stone and she had lost hold of the brake. The next thing that she remembered, she was lying head down and we were nowhere around. Her bicycle had plunged off the steep side of the road and vanished in the underbrush.

We sat in the road and held a council. We decided that Janet should ride on down the hill and try to get help at Roy Orcutt's farm. Fortunately he was there and he drove us home in his pickup truck.

Virginia's cut was full of road dirt and I gave her a booster injection of tetanus toxoid. It required stitches and I prepared to suture it. I chipped some ice from the block in the cellar, crushed it in a clean dish towel and held it against her chin for several minutes to produce refrigeration anesthesia. I cleaned the wound and swabbed it with antiseptic solution. I covered her eyes with a handkerchief.

"Ginia, don't speak, don't move your chin—you might spoil my embroidery," I warned her.

I put in several stitches. She made no move and no sound. I thought that she might have fainted and I anxiously raised one corner of the handkerchief to look at her. A very bright eye all but winked at me.

"Mummy, can I speak now?" she whispered through set teeth without moving her jaw.

"Yes, Ginia. What is it, dear?"

"Mummy, what color thread are you using?" Her interest in art was already apparent. She was disappointed that the color was black.

After Aunt Dot returned to North Carolina, undaunted by that accident we decided on a pleasure bicycling trip. In 1922, my sister and I with a Wellesley friend and her mother had bicycled for two weeks around the Brittany coast, stopping for a night or two at a time in the little French inns. I recalled our flexibility of schedule in that kind of travel, our intimate contact with the people of the country, and the pioneer fun of living out of knapsacks in all sorts of early September weather. Jack and the girls in that war year of 1942 wanted a change of scene from the hill, and my nephew Sheldon Weeks, who was ten, was with us, and he joined us on his bicycle. We arranged to stay in a farmhouse that was part of Jug End Barn, a resort hotel in the township of Egremont on the northerly ridge of the Taconic Range and fifteen miles from the farm across the Housatonic Valley. For one of the days we planned a side trip from there sixteen miles into Great Barrington and back to have lunch with friends.

Jack and I rode identical paratroopers' wheels and we carried the paraphernalia strapped on our luggage racks at the rear or piled in our handlebar baskets. On top were fastened Jack's and my tennis rackets; Jug End Barn had tennis courts as well as a large swimming pool. The three children's small bikes had baskets at the front, too, that were filled with miscellaneous items, including a large mud turtle that Virginia spotted on one of our roadside stops. Try as we would to pack that reptile firmly down in a basket, it kept crawling out and adding to the excitement. The flat macadam road was ideal for bicycling. Gasoline rationing had practically eliminated automobile traffic and we made good time. Poor little Virginia's legs were so short and the diameter of her bike's wheels so small that she had to pedal twice as fast as Jack and I did to cover the same distance. Dogs dashed out from the houses as we passed and barked at the calvalcade. Virginia's seat was so close to the ground and to those yapping jaws that her Daddy and Mummy tried to ride guard on either side of her down the middle of the road.

While we ate lunch in the main dining room of the Barn, the girls parked their turtle in a sink filled with water in the bathroom of the "Cow-pen," the large dormitory of built-in bunks for girls. The sink was no better a cage than the bicycle basket, and the turtle crawled on through the "Cow-pen" to the "Bullpen" on the other side of the Barn. Recaptured, it became a topic of general debate: "Is it a boy turtle or a girl turtle?"

Janet and Virginia kept asking that question until they found someone in the hotel who knew how to sex a turtle. It was a lady turtle with a delicately pointed tail. That afternoon, Sheldon and our girls took the turtle swimming with them in Jug End Barn's elegant pool, and a number of city weekenders scrambled out. Jack and I dropped our rackets on the tennis court just below the pool and rushed up to see what was causing the commotion. The next day at lunch, one of those apprehensive strangers sought me out and said, "When I was hiking on the mountain this morning I found a turtle and I brought it down. I thought maybe your girls would like another one."

When the time came for us to leave, a couple of days later, the turtle census in the woods there had diminished and in our bathtub it had increased. Under the stimulus of the children's quest for knowledge, kindly guests with a new zest for turtling had presented us with more live specimens, all of which journeyed back to Merryfield Farm in our bicycle baskets.

In the summer of 1942, things began to happen on our hill. Its name was changed to Hickey Hill. Although the stone foundations of the Hickey house and barns had burned, their combination garage and henhouse had been saved by throwing road mud against it. Brush had grown up around them. The war kept the Weekses from sharing Merryfield Farm with us, except for Sheldon's short visit. Ginny and her four children spent that summer in a cottage on Lake Ontario to be with her engineer husband, Harold "Pop" Weeks, who was engaged in building a war production plant on the Niagara River. Jack's sister Dorothy and I on those chilly late August evenings would walk up the dirt road under the brilliant stars to the Hickey's elevation and would view from there the lights of Sheffield and the auto headlights blinking miles below in the valley. On a rare night, red and yellow and green streamers of the aurora borealis lit the dome of the sky like giant fireworks. When peaceful little Sheffield had a practice blackout against air attacks, we blew out our candles and kerosene lamps and went

outside; the stars overhead did not change. We loved the solitude and simplicity of living. War was far away.

One day an investigator came from town and asked me, "Have you
noticed anything going on at the Hickey farm? We have reason to believe a
German spy is using the old garage to send signals. Smoke was seen coming
out of the chimney."

We had observed nothing unusual but the questions gave us an eerie
feeling. With heightened curiosity we continued our solitary strolls but
stayed closer to home. Once we passed a stranger, an uncommunicative
blond young man. Not until the following summer did we learn that he was
Tilo Kaufmann, the supposed "German spy," but actually a paratrooper
on leave from his U.S. Army base in Florida. His German mother, Erna
Kaufmann, had made a quick purchase of the Hickey farm—she loved its
mountain view—and she had returned at once to Florida. At the site of the
Hickey garage where he was camping out, Tilo eventually built a hand-
crafted fieldstone house for his mother. It, too, was to burn down one wintry night in 1953.

Other new neighbors came to the hill. Karl and Margrit Suter of Swiss
origin put their hearts, as well as brains and money, into that American soil.
Tilo's brother, Hans Kaufmann, moved with his family into an old farmhouse to operate the Suter's large tract of farmland that adjoined Erna's to
the south. A transformation took place in the hill's traditional methods of
New England farming. The latest mechanized equipment appeared. Bull-
dozers pushed huge boulders to the edges of cultivated fields and cleared
other fields that had grown up to hardhack and trees. Tractors and trucks
drove past our house, hauling fertilizer at one season and neat rectangular
bales of hay at another. Milking the cows and handling the milk were done
by machine. The milk output of the herd was scientifically increased.
Fences, a big silo, and barns were constructed. Red geraniums appeared in
Hans and Eileen Kaufmann's first- and second-story window boxes.

After the war, when Virginia and Janet were twelve and thirteen, they
had no difficulty in persuading me that they should have riding horses at
Merryfield Farm. From 1947 to 1951, for five summers Jack and I rented
two horses for them and sometimes also a successor to Maggie for me.
Each year the girls graduated to livelier mounts. The horses were almost a
full-time project; we fenced pastures, built gates, cleared riding trails
through the woods and gave each one a name. There was Ice House Road,
Pond Shore Drive, Deer Run, Horseshoe, Texas Trail, and Regent Street.
When Janet was in college and married, we bought Virginia a thoroughbred
racehorse, Carter Road, from Frank Retzel at the Great Barrington County
fairgrounds. The next year he found for me an amiable pretzel-colored,

nosy horse; we called him Retzel-Pretzel, Retz for short. In the winters Hans Kaufmann, and when he moved away, Henry Eggenberger kept them for us in a pasture and an open shed with the cows. By Christmas the horses looked like shaggy bears and their coats were so thick that the snow did not melt on their backs.

Our "horse crazy" daughters had put their horse-loving mother back in the saddle. Those were golden days and moonlit nights. On the Labor Day weekend of 1953, while we were in process of closing our house for the winter, Virginia and I took a last ride around the big fields, past the farm pond and along the pine woods trail that was Pond Shore Extension. She would return to Cornell University as a sophomore that fall and in June she would be married. As our horses cantered slowly on the familiar packed dirt, I fixed my mind's eye on the early autumn scenes around me and I wrote in my head then:

SADNESS OF ENDING

> There's a redness on the apple
> And burnt brown upon the tassel,
> There's a coldness in the night wind
> Tells of summer's end.
>
> Drought-dried leaves now blow and spiral,
> Pile in heaps for snowy burial.
> Flocks of grackle in migration
> Stipple black the sun.
>
> Creatures seek their own survival,
> Humans rush to pack and travel,
> Rush to leave the season's new friends,
> As the summer ends.
>
> Not for us to make disposal,
> We're awaiting God's appraisal.
> Who'll return to nest in shut homes
> When the summer comes?

I could see the future catching up with me, no matter how fast we rode.

It may have been the trail riding, or perhaps our vacation life without clocks, or even the superb view of the sunset mountains that attracted Dee and Zella du Vigneaud in 1950 to buy a piece of woodland on the north side of our farm. Until then we could not see the smoke from our nearest neighbor's chimney. That fall at "Birchshire," the du Vigneauds drilled a deep well and dug foundations for their house, which was completed the following summer. Before he was a biochemist, Dee had been a stunt rider in the cavalry—top man in the human pyramid on horseback—and he bought an energetic Western cow pony that could "turn on a dime," Sunny, for their daughter Marilyn. She and Virginia were the same age and close friends. They had to learn the limit of their horses' capacity to explore the countryside. On one excursion Virginia and Marilyn turned back with difficulty when they tried to ride Carter and Sunny on the Appalachian Trail for hikers over steep and rocky North Mountain. Evenings on the hill, with a "Hi, neighbor!" du Vigneauds and Powells and Weekses would walk each other back and forth on the dirt road between the two houses. Dee and Jack in their black wool berets could yodel to the moon and test the hills for echoes to their hearts' content.

A milestone of progress came to Merryfield Farm with the advent of the du Vigneauds to the hill: *electricity* in our one-hundred-and-fifty-year-old house. They needed electricity to build, and in August, 1950, I signed a contract to share with them the cost of putting in poles and bringing the line a mile, from Hans Kaufmann's farm on the other side of the hill in Mill River. My sister and I had inherited Merryfield Farm in 1928 and we owned it jointly, but Ginny was in Europe that summer and I made the decision, knowing well that none of the Weeks family wanted electricity in the house. I had only four outlets installed: a light in the upstairs hall bathroom, an outlet in the woodshed for my father's electric saw, a double unit in the wall that faced both kitchen and dining room for Jack's electric toaster, and another outlet in the kitchen for the refrigerator that I considered a necessity. When my Weeks relatives returned to the farm in September, they resented the threat of change to our way of living there.

My father soon ran an extension cord from the bathroom through the hall into his bedroom and hooked up his electric blanket. Ginny said, "That's a fine idea. I could have my electric blanket, too."

She followed suit with a longer extension cord from the bathroom across the house to her bedroom at the front. My nephew Willard, a senior at Amherst College, remarked that if only he had an electric light in his room he could study at the farm instead of going back to Brooklyn Heights where they lived. He ran his extension cord from the woodshed outlet up the back stairs, through the attic over the kitchen and into his bedroom in the main part of the house. Before long we could not walk, either upstairs or down, without danger of tripping over the crop of wires. Before Jack and I arrived at the farm the following summer, my sister had installed an electric outlet in every room in the house.

We did not let progress destroy the spirit of Merryfield Farm. After dinner we sat in half-darkness on our open porch that faced the mountains. It was still lighted at intervals by the identical candle-powered Japanese

lanterns that Ginny and I had hung there during our childhood. The new
generation of girls, Ginger and Elinor Weeks and our Janet and Ginia, had
better singing voices than Ginny and I did, and our new hill neighbors
joined us in songs of many nations and many wars, from the Civil War
marching song, "Hay foot, straw foot, belly full of green peas, right—right
—right," to "Those caissons go rolling along."

Nor did the obstacle nature of the road up Crow Hill change, and we
were grateful for its continued protection. In wet weather and spring thaws,
cars still got stuck in the mud. When it was announced on November 2,
1955, that Dee had been awarded the Nobel prize in chemistry, a reporter
for *The Berkshire Evening Eagle* interviewed Sheffield sources and stated:

> Francis M. Kersey, in whose market Dr. and Mrs. du Vigneaud shop
> said, "Couldn't have happened to a nicer man. . . . An expert on
> steak, too." To Mrs. Erna Kaufmann, the du Vigneauds are "the nicest
> of neighbors. . . . Mrs. du Vigneaud always has time to ride and
> work with the doctor. . . . He was up just a week ago to shut off
> the water and close up the house," Mrs. Kaufmann said, "and had to
> call for help when he got mired in the mud on our steep road. I tried
> to pull him out, got stuck myself, and we both had to be rescued by
> my son, Hans." . . . The du Vigneauds came to Sheffield because of
> friendship with Dr. Willard Travell and his daughters, according to
> Fire Chief Frank A. Percy. Dr. Travell, who also has a home on
> Hickey Hill, is in his 80s and practices in New York City.

My mother's great-grandchildren now are beneficiaries of her vision for
Merryfield Farm, and they love it as I did. On a July weekend in 1957,
Janet's small son Richie and I together reveled in the luxurious daisies,
tawny hawkweed, black-eyed Susans, and yellow buttercups of our hayfields and the road's open spaces. At the house I wrapped my armload of
wildflowers in wet newspaper for the hot ride to New York. I tucked them
in a corner of the car away from Richie's feet. He liked flowers, but he was
too tired then to cherish them on the long trip to the city. As the engine
hummed along the highway in a hiatus of time, I scribbled while the miles
passed:

WILDFLOWERS FROM THE FARM
or
WHEELS OF TIME

> To you, they're just some country flowers,
> White-rimmed daisies, black-eyed Susans,
> Crowded in vases, faded from hours
> In city-bound hot caravans.

To me, they're dust of dancing sunbeams
Lighting hayfields, daytime's fireflies
Brightening roadsides, summertime's dreams—
"He loves me . . . not,"—so fraught with sighs.

I see myself wear on my hair
Stiff-stemmed daisy crowns, sweet masses
Of petals bobbing as my bare
Feet run, toes tangled with grasses.

Another child in glee runs wild
Plucking the gold and orange flowers.
Bright hayfields claim our daughter's child
While faded flowers turn back the hours.

In the summer of 1928, my mother ordered four thousand red-pine four-year transplants from the State of Massachusetts for spring delivery. She selected a spot for them, an old apple orchard on our high land that was filling in with young birch and alder, sweet fern, blackberry bushes, and hardhack. She had previously planted one small gone-to-seed hayfield with two-year seedlings of Austrian pine, but most of them did not survive the overgrowth of brush. With those larger plants of faster growing red pine she foresaw a great fragrant forest on our hill top.

That October my mother died suddenly. In April, 1929, when the shipment of trees arrived at the Sheffield railroad station, my father, handsome Jack Powell—he and I were to be married in June—and I drove to Merryfield Farm to plant them. We slept in the cold, shut house. Over the long weekend we worked for three full days in the field. With the assistance of Roy Orcutt and his boy we set out all four thousand of those little pine trees. The ground was white with fresh snow, and that was a great help to us. To mark off the rows for planting all we had to do was to walk the lines in the snow, as straight as we could. We used an assembly-line system. One person made a deep cut in the thawed earth with a one-sided adz. The next person dragged along a basket of manure and threw some into the hole. The third in line carried a bundle of trees and handed them singly to the "planter." He, or she, then tucked the roots into the slit in the ground to exactly the right depth and stamped the dirt hard against them. The fifth person rested, ran, and fetched. We rotated jobs. Walking right along down the rows we could plant about four trees a minute that way, or 240 per hour. We kept at the task and in about eighteen hours of work spread over the three days we planted all the trees except for a few that Roy took down the hill to set out on either side of his driveway. All of them thrived.

My mother would have been proud of us and prouder still of the majestic forest that stands now as she designed it. We often walk on the soft pine needles or ride on horseback between the long rows and we look up into the vaulted tops high overhead, so thick the sun does not penetrate them. In the summer it is always cool there and the wind sings. Jack calls it "Our Cathedral."

CHAPTER 6

School Days

In the autumn of 1911, at the same time that my family bought Merryfield Farm as a summer home, I entered Class II at The Brearley School. For three years I had attended a small private school at 27 West 11th Street, and I was nine years old. My letters to my father and mother from 1909 on were written with an ease of expression and a flow of ideas that show how far my education had advanced when I started at The Brearley:

June 11, 1909

My Dear Mother.

I have a beautiful plan in my head, and that is if grandpa could have a vacation until the first of September. He could go to the country with us and Sophie as well. Would not that be nice? . . . Sophie cooks beautiful asparagus. Better than Katie [*our* cook in New York]. Do not tell her so. . . . I thank you very much for your kind letter. Are the cat and bird well? Is the bird safe from kitty? Do the bird every day. [Cleaning its cage was ordinarily my job.] . . . I am wearing my hair like Virginia to-day, and not my hair braided any more. It is very becoming to me. . . . I hope that you and father are very well and happy.

From the house in the village of Sheffield two years later,

July 18, 1911

Dear Mother and Father;

I wish I was with you. It rained almost all day yesterday. It was very dry. Some of the sweet-peas dried up. We transplanted beats yes-

terday before it rained. . . . When are you coming home, or aren't
you thinking about coming home yet? [Home was where *I* was.] We
have not found any more turtles yet, because we have not had any
walks but one, and then we went way up on a hill, where there were
deep ravines of rock, where the water probly flows in the spring when
there are heavy rains. There was a pretty view. To-day I climbed high
in a willow tree, there was a nice view from there two. With love

your Bobby.

At The Brearley I progressed straight through seven classes and was
graduated at sixteen from Class VIII, preparatory to entering Wellesley
College. The Brearley was a day school in a big city. My free hours at home
were endlessly exciting and it is not strange that my recollections of the
extracurricular activities during seven years at the school have largely
faded. My courses and my teachers are vivid in my memory.

When I entered The Brearley I was already saying that I wanted to be a
doctor and I devoured the work. The process of learning fascinated me
then, as it still does. Solving the unknowns of an algebraic equation was an
exciting experience under the imaginative direction of Miss Arnold and it
satisfied my need for tangible accomplishment. Science, as taught by Miss
Littell, was pure joy and I was allowed to assist her in small ways. One of
my privileges was to supply the class with earthworms for dissection. Those
I dug in our backyard at 27 East 11th Street. In one corner nightcrawlers
could always be found deep in the moist dirt around a sunken tub of water
that a snapping turtle inhabited; the turtle was a former resident of Schenob
Brook in Sheffield.

I was fortunate in being exposed at an early age to Miss Littell's wisdom. A tribute written by another Brearley teacher matches my memory
of her:

> She never taught by textbook and laboratory manual but insisted that
> all her students see for themselves, through the microscope or dissec-
> tion, the phenomena that they were studying. . . . As a scientist she
> learned to question and test any proposition. . . . She knew that the
> easy answer to any question is almost never valid because it is based
> on insufficient information and inaccurate perception. . . . To young
> teachers working under her, she seemed to have confidence in our abil-
> ity to think for ourselves. She never told us things but instead, asked us
> questions.[1]

Another of my favorite subjects was Latin, which I took for several
years, as well as French. And then there was German.

[1] Katharine Van Bibber, "Elizabeth D. Littell," *The Brearley Bulletin,* Vol. 39 (Fall
1963), p. 5.

From 1914 to 1918 World War I raged in Europe, and in April, 1917, the United States declared war on Germany. War frenzy permeated the school. That September of 1917 when I entered Class VIII and became a senior in high school, German was offered in the school catalogue but no one in the class elected to take it. I believed that a knowledge of this language would be useful in the study of medicine—and indeed it was. Another individualist, Virginia Grace, joined me, and a German teacher, Miss Scott, was assigned to us. In that "Hate the Hun" era we became traitors to the United States in the eyes of our classmates, although we could not see what our learning German had to do with fighting the Prussian war machine.

Years later, I discovered that Miss Scott had been subjected to the same pressures of intolerance as Virginia Grace and I had been. She joined the Brearley faculty in 1915 and forty-eight years later she wrote: "From my earliest days there . . . I was happy to be a member of the Brearley faculty. Yet after five years of teaching German I was thinking of leaving. The first world war raised violent feelings about the 'Hun', even his language, even his music. . . . Colleges no longer required German for entrance, and it became a casualty." [2] She joined the English Department.

I neither liked, nor disliked The Brearley School. I was set apart in it for several reasons. The pursuit of scholarly excellence was not fashionable then, but the certainty of my purpose toward medicine and my innate curiosity drove me to study. In retrospect, the "finishing school" girls, who were not going to college, were socially more secure and they dominated our extracurricular activities. In particular, they had more dates and went to more dances and parties at each other's homes.

Although in school I took part in dramatics and athletics (basketball, volley ball, batball, and indoor baseball), I was younger and less sophisticated than most of the girls, and I was shy in a crowd. At the same time, I was exasperatingly independent. As one of a small minority who did not smoke cigarettes, I was conspicuous at the social events of our senior year. I did not seek nonconformity; smoking was simply distasteful to me. Often since, I have been thankful that I never learned to like it. But in high school nearly fifty years ago, smoking was a new status symbol and the nonsmoker was out of step with those avant-garde New York City girls.

Our *Class Book 1918* rendered the judgment of my peers. Above my graduation picture was written:

> And still they gazed and still the wonder grew,
> That one small head could carry all she knew.

[2] Margaret S. Scott, "The Fair Moment," *The Brearley Bulletin,* Vol. 39 (Fall 1963), pp. 13–14.

Below my picture the verse resumed:

> There was a girl; her name was Janet,
> Her proper sphere was not this planet.
> Her aspirations were so high,
> Her proper place was in the sky.

I concluded that I was a thoroughly obnoxious creature. On the other hand, I am reassured now to read in that *Class Book* several attributes that I was *not* awarded by my classmates; other girls were voted "teacher's pet, the worst grind, the most conceited, the most self-conscious, the most demure, and the most gullible."

None of this really bothered me because I enjoyed the close friendship of two or three girls in my class. My best friend was Evelyn Rogers; she went on to study medicine and she married a physician, Harry Inkster. Outside the school, I visited in the formal homes of Evelyn Rogers, Virginia Grace, Josephine Whitehouse, Serena Hand, Ruth McAneny, Beatrice Schurman, and others. I was a frequent guest at the Graces' waterfront estate at Point Pleasant, New Jersey. I stayed often at Mr. and Mrs. Rogers' brownstone house in the East Sixties or at their summer place, Pipestave Hill Farm, in West Newbury, Massachusetts. There, their tennis court was as nearly perfect as it could be, and a tennis teacher came to play with Evelyn, her younger sister Elinor, and me, and to give us lessons. Their enormous barn was as neat as any that I can remember. It was capped by a cupola to which one might climb for the view, but jumping into haymows was regarded as unladylike. We were allowed to feed the huge Percherons sugar. On Sunday afternoons, wrapped in dusters the family went to ride through the countryside in an open seven-passenger touring car with a cloth top. Evelyn and I usually sat on the folding seats in back, which had an unobstructed view to the side, like the end seat of an open trolley car. It tired me to sit still so long gazing at the fields and woods that we passed too fast. I would have liked to explore them. On a suitable day, we drove to the ocean where the family owned a gray, shingled beach cottage. There we picnicked and swam in the surf, but I can not remember that we stayed overnight. Evelyn's and my chief diversion was reading and we did that by the hour, each absorbed in a separate world within the pages of a book. Sometimes after dinner, in the dark, with visitors we pushed the furniture around a bedroom to make the place unfamiliar for a hide-and-seek game of "sardines"—we could really make a wreck of a room. During one of my visits to West Newbury, I wrote my mother at home: "We had the most delightful midnight repasts. I'm afraid the cook thought there were thieves in the house." Somehow, I managed to get into mischief.

Evelyn went off to boarding school during my last two years at The Brearley and then to Bryn Mawr College, but we continued to visit each other in the summers at Sheffield and West Newbury.

One of my Brearley schoolmates, Bettina Warburg, and I became friends years later, by chance. She went to The Brearley for only one year before her father, Paul M. Warburg, was appointed by President Woodrow Wilson to organize the Federal Reserve Banking System and in 1914 she moved to Washington. In Class III Bettina and I sat at adjoining desks because *T* came next to *W* in the class list; desks were paired with an aisle on each side. We were ten or eleven years old and the complete antithesis of each other. She didn't like me, and I didn't like her. I remember her then in a Buster Brown stiff white collar over a neat jumper of checked black and white wool. Her hair was bound in tightly tied up pigtails and her idol was her older brother, Jimmy. My idol was my older sister. My hair hung in curls almost to my waist and was held by a large bow on top of my head. The ribbon annoyed me and Bettina because it tended to loosen and slide down toward my neck. My dresses were girlish and gaily colored, with full skirts and flounces and ruffles. If The Brearley had required a uniform, such superficial differences would have been less important.

Bettina and I did not meet again until September, 1922, when we entered Cornell University Medical College in the same class. We eyed each other like cat and dog. It was not long, however, before I felt at ease in her magnificent home in the East Eighties and at the Warburg's wooded estate in Hartsdale, Westchester County, while she took to my family's informal outings enthusiastically. In 1931, after Jack and I were married, Betsy joined us in a motor camping trip around the entire periphery of Nova Scotia, where we pitched tents every night.

During my school days, most important to me were the serenity and security of my life at home and the companionship of my sister. A wonderful part of each day was walking to school at a fast clip with my mother and Ginny, up Fifth Avenue from 11th Street to 17 West 44th Street where The Brearley was located when I first went there. The great granite lions that guarded the New York Public Library at 42nd Street always seemed to welcome us, and I raced up and down the broad steps to greet them. Later the school moved farther uptown to Park Avenue and 61st Street, and we walked less often. Then, Ginny and I proudly rode the open upper deck of a Fifth Avenue bus—come snow, rain, or shine.

The Brearley offered scholastic opportunity and I took advantage of it. But my father, not the school, taught me how to think. Over and over, he pointed out the value of time and the importance of concentration. If I could do a piece of homework well in fifteen minutes, I should not dawdle over it for thirty. I learned to shut out extraneous matters and to accelerate the pace of my thinking. Another technique of learning that my father taught me was to focus my attention on the things that I did *not* know—new ideas, strange words, and my own mistakes.

Today, when I pick up a medical journal, I look at the table of contents and read first the article about which I am least informed, rather than one that deals with familiar material and is therefore easier to comprehend. That form of mental discipline and with it the challenge of the unknown were implanted in me at a very early age by my father.

As a corollary of this approach, I learned to distinguish readily the facts and figures that I knew "for sure" from those that I half guessed. Recognition of the uncertainty of one's knowledge is of paramount importance in the profession of medicine. The physician may not have the opportunity to correct his errors.

John Christian said that living is the art of drawing without an eraser, and so is the practice of medicine. The lessons of ignorance and pride must often be learned the hard way, by making serious mistakes. Such an experience during my senior year at the school was probably of inestimable value to me. It made a lasting impression and luckily it was a mistake that could be erased.

Brearley's academic standing was as high as that of any school in the country, and Wellesley College graciously admitted me by certificate, waiving examination. My eccentric and egocentric attitudes of sixteen convinced me that this exemption represented unfair and special privilege, particularly since my mother was a Wellesley graduate and my sister a student there. I insisted on taking the unnecessary college entrance examinations in the spring. To my dismay and discomfiture, I failed the examination in English literature and composition, and I had to repeat it during the city heat of summer. That time, I made sure to review the required reading and I passed with a satisfactory grade.

I did not accept that failure nonchalantly, however. I tried to analyze and correct the reasons for it. Although I was an avid reader of books and understood the meaning of many uncommon words, my vocabulary in actual usage was limited. I undertook to enlarge it. Whenever I heard a lecturer use a word that I never did, I wrote it on a card. I kept the list in my purse or in the drawer of my desk where it would catch my eye until I found myself spontaneously speaking those symbols that were strange to my tongue. Even now, I occasionally come across one of my compilations of unrelated words. I struggled also with the wordiness of my sentences.

Deep in my heart I knew that the one thing I could never do was to write.

Years later, I asked Dr. Herald Cox, who made the first successful vaccine against human Rocky Mountain spotted fever, what had influenced him to enter the field of higher mathematics and ultramicroscopic particle size, instead of medicine.

"I failed eighth-grade arithmetic," he replied.

Recently, I felt almost normal when I read Thomas Mann's definition of a writer: "A writer is a person for whom writing is more difficult than it is for most people."

My English compositions had a slightly mathematical, or scientific, cast. In the equivalent of ninth grade (April 8, 1915), I wrote a theme on "Footsteps:"

> Problem: to show the different kinds of footsteps belonging to different people.
>
> One person's footsteps are as different from another's as they can be. The footsteps of the very young are tottering and uncertain. They are unbalanced, and seem to need support. . . . Take the footsteps of a girl who is late to school. . . . They are light and hurried. They are quick and have a definite purpose. When a doctor is called out at night, his footsteps are resigned, though quick, and they are patient, too. But a lawyer's feet are judicial and dignified. They always look before they step, and are majestic and slow. A blacksmith's are slow, too, but because they are ponderous and heavy. They sound as though tired and clad in iron shoes, like horses. Footsteps homeward-bound are, like the blacksmiths and the horses, often tired, but they are usually glad and happy, and the people they carry are sometimes thinking of their good dinner at home. The criminal is the very opposite. His feet are guilty and sly. They must be silent and cautious. The soldiers' are loud and martial and they are measured and firm.
>
> These are only a few kinds of footsteps but they are different from each other, except that they all show that their owners are able to walk.

The common denominator of people always interested me.

In another English composition, dated April 22, 1915, and entitled, "If ——" I let my mind roam in the future, three hundred years from then:

> If it were 2215, instead of 1915, what a different place the world would be! I think that if it were then and not now, the government would provide for the beautification of the cities. People would be forced by law to have flower gardens in front of their houses, and the streets would be lined with trees. There would be no more subways, elevateds, or street cars. Automobiles would be old-fashioned, and horses would be used only for pleasure. Aeroplanes would take the place of these. We would have trucking aeroplanes, bus aeroplanes, and pleas-

ure aeroplanes. Each person would . . . [have] his own pair of wings. If one were too tired, or lazy, or fat, to fly, one might ride. We would also have no telephones. Wireless telegraphy would be used generally, but those who were able, would speak from mind to mind, without words. This would be a very great improvement. We would have a little machine to place over the mouth and nose, which would enable us to live under water. It would collect the oxygen in the water, and put it into proper breathing form. We would live in the water like fishes, if it were 2215. In school, there would be no more Latin, no more Greek. We would study more science, chemistry, and mathematics. We would learn mechanism, so that we might run our aeroplanes. Also, we would not have stiff-backed, maiden aunt chairs, but everywhere there would be comfortable, soft divans. The school walls might be opened out, especially on sticky, hot summer days. If it were then, not now.

My prophecies did not wait three hundred years to come to pass.

Brearley teachers did not allow us to suffer from monotony or boredom. In the early grades my class—twenty-six girls were graduated—was divided in small sections on the basis of ability and performance. Later we were grouped according to our goals, into college-preparatory and noncollege sections. We did not feel discriminated against because we were classified in that way, insofar as I can recall. On the contrary, it lessened the tendency of young people to acquire a sense of inferiority in the face of disproportionate competition. Work was paced as fast as we could absorb it. At the same time, the individualized teaching gave us an opportunity to develop our own aptitudes and interests. At The Brearley I think that we were relatively free from needless scholastic conformity.

The dilemma of schools now in meeting curriculum standardization while encouraging originality in the pursuit of excellence is told in a fable for curriculum makers

in Nonanthropoidia, the land of smaller animals. . . . Running, climbing, swimming and flying were to be included in the curriculum. . . . The duck was excellent in swimming, but he made only passing grades in flying, and was very poor in running. . . . He was assigned to a remedial laboratory in running . . . until his webbed feet were badly worn and he was only average in swimming. But average was acceptable and he had received a low passing grade in running. But nobody worried about the special and major talent, except, perhaps, the duck. The rabbit started at the top of the class in running but he had to make up so much work in swimming that he suffered a series of neuroses, a breakdown, and had to quit school. . . . The squirrel was excellent in climbing . . . but he still had to study flying. However, his course was altered and he was permitted to fly from the tree-top down. Others had to start from the ground up. . . . Until his studies were changed, he did attempt to fly . . . and because of this over-exertion became tired. His mid-term marks reflected this since he received a C in climbing—his major talent—a D in running and an "inc." in flying. (He stayed away from the exam.) The psychologist who interviewed him . . . said he was an atypical student who imposed negative values on himself. . . . The eagle was a good student because of his ability to run and to climb and to fly. He did not have to worry about swimming because another institution had exempted him from swimming with an acceptable grade. He was a problem, though, and was disciplined because he wanted to use his talents rather freely. For instance, in climbing he beat all the others to the top but he insisted on his own way of getting there. At the end of a year, an abnormal eel who could swim exceptionally well, could run, could climb, could fly—a little of each—had the best ratio. He was valedictorian.[3]

At The Brearley the work was hard and standards were high, but the emphasis was happily on diversity rather than on equality.

The Brearley School Song, written by Annie Winsor Allen, who taught there from 1889 to 1899, expresses the heritage for which I am deeply grateful. Its second verse rings out:

> Truth cometh not unsought for;
> The spirit's purest light
> Must burn undimmed and clearly,
> To guide our minds aright.
> So standing here together,
> Triumphant thanks we give,
> That here our spirit's flame is fired
> By Truth and Toil to live.

[3] Ernest Fleischer, "A Fable for Curriculum Makers: Gulliver Also Ran," *Junior College Journal*, Vol. XXXIII, No. 3 (1962), pp. 161–162; the article also appeared in the *West Virginia Hillbilly*, Vol. III, No. 46 (November 17, 1962).

CHAPTER 7

My Father the Magician

When I was a little girl, I decided to be a doctor like my father because he was a magician and whatever he did was wonderful. An aura of excitement and mystery surrounded him from my earliest memory to the end of his nearly ninety-two years of life. It was no accident that he set off giant firecrackers in my room at Albany on the Fourth of July when I was six months old; I think that he must have been born with a firecracker in one hand and a lighted match in the other.

His grandchildren and some of his great-grandchildren will long remember his magic. He used to count up his descendants with pride; when he died they numbered thirty. He included, of course, his second wife's children, Talcott Bates, Peggy Bates Husband, and Clark Travell, and their children. About two years after my mother's death and a year after Jack's and my wedding, when my father was sixty, he married on August 14, 1930, a New York widow, Edith Talcott Bates. He knew her through her first husband, the Reverend H. Roswell Bates, his close friend, who was just a year younger than he was. She and my mother became congenial companions with a variety of interests in common, such as the Spring Street Church, where Roswell Bates was minister until his death in 1920; the Bible and Fruit Mission; New York real estate; their farms at Westfield, New Jersey, and at Sheffield; the Philharmonic Symphony; and their children. Talcott Bates was one year old when his father died of high altitude sickness, mountain climbing in the Andes of South America. Talcott was encouraged by my father to study medicine, and when he was my stepbrother in 1935,

I taught him pharmacology at Cornell University Medical College. In 1965, he and I were on an equal footing as participants of the White House Conference on Health in Washington.

My father was a star performer at the children's birthday parties. Sometimes I acted as his assistant in the wings and in later years my brother Clark assumed that role. The performance was never the same on any two occasions, and I was as much entertained by it as were the eager youngsters who sat on the floor in a semicircle around him. I recall one party in Edith's parlor at 12 East 64th Street where he "incubated" six eggs in a small brown paper bag. If the magic succeeded, they would hatch into little fluffy chicks. Who would get them? Anticipation filled the air. He lit the candles in two silver candlesticks and placed them on the floor beneath a small mahogany table on which he set the bag of hen eggs that had been inspected by each child and then tied with a string around the top. The Wizard made a variety of magical passes over that object of every eye and he accompanied them with mystical incantations, "Hocus pocus, Ish-ke-bub, Hocus pocus alleopus, Abracadabra, Hocus pocus."

When "long enough" had elapsed for the eggs to hatch, he blew out the incubator candles and lifted the bag to his ear to listen for sounds from its interior. A bewildered expression crossed his face. He loosened the string slightly, peeked inside the bag and closed it again quickly.

"The magic is a failure—I don't know why. It never happened this way before." His voice conveyed despondency. "I could try it again," he added without enthusiasm.

The audience was hushed, and crushed.

"Come see for yourself," he told the birthday girl and he handed her the brown bag. Squeaks and squeals filled the room as out of it climbed six lively white mice that scurried to take refuge underneath the seated children.

By a ruse, he had tricked them twice and he had doubled the surprise of his magic. You never knew what to expect of my father.

In May, 1910, my father was admitted to membership in Assembly One of the Society of American Magicians. The Society's records show that he held membership number 372 in the New York chapter and that his interest in magic commenced about 1890 as an amateur when he was at Williams College. I remember going with him to that magician society's stage shows and my father's studying the magical material that members exchanged among themselves. With his expertise at sleight of hand, his Yankee ingenuity, and technical scientific knowledge, he had no difficulty in inventing his own tricks.

His fire magic would have ranked high on the professional stage. It proved particularly exciting when he performed it in the living room and bits of ignited trash hit the ceiling. The audience participated in the preparations by "laying the fire" with shredded paper, excelsior, dry pine needles, if available, or whittlings of pine wood, arranged together in a cooking pot set within a dishpan in the center of the room. My father then called for a kitchen match and struck it on the sole of his shoe. When it was burning brightly, he placed it lighted inside his mouth and owlishly closed his lips around it. Having removed the burnt match he drank a glassful of cold tap water brought by one of the spectators.

"First I swallow the fire and then I wash it down with water. I transfer the fire to the water. Now I will blow the firewater back and it will light the kindling you have laid." He rubbed his hands together briskly. He passed around for inspection a piece of narrow glass tubing that he had cut several feet long. He introduced one end into the kitchen pot. After a great preparatory huffing and puffing of his cheeks, he sipped more water and blew it through the glass tube. Almost immediately the tinder literally exploded into flames, traveling in all directions—that is, before we learned to screen it as well as possible with fine wire mesh. I never saw that trick fail and it never failed to cause a commotion.

A magician never gives away a secret; the fun is not in telling, but in knowing the facts. When my father trusted me with a secret, wild horses could not have dragged it out of me. How to keep a secret is a useful skill for a physician to acquire early in his career; it leads to protection of the patient's privacy.

In the early 1900's, my father practiced medicine in the customary cutaway coat, striped trousers, ascot tie, and, of course, a full beard and mustache. The beard was a status symbol then like the physician's gold-headed cane in the days when reassurance and understanding were his chief armament against disease. But by about 1916 my father tired of all that hair on his face and one day he told my mother that he intended to shave it off.

"Please don't do that, Willard," she begged. "I like it."

He did not answer her, but day by day he shaved off a line of hairs on each side. He and I laughed about it because mother hadn't noticed, even when he had only a little goatee left on the point of his chin. It took him a year to get rid of his beard. An old friend came by who had not seen him in more than twelve months and remarked, "Hello, you've shaved off your beard—how well you look."

My mother stared at her husband in astonishment. "Why, Willard, so you have! When did you do that?"

The wind had been taken out of her protest. Clean-shaven by a long-range ruse, he had kept silent those many months—and so had I. My father seldom became involved in a fruitless argument.

It was second nature for my father, magician and physician, to guard a secret, yet he was never secretive about his personal plans and affairs. Even when my sister and I were very young, he let us share his responsibility for making decisions. I was five years old when he wrote me a letter from New York: "August 7, 1907. My dear Bobby: What do you think of the white mice? And what do you propose to do with them? Shall I build another house and how would you have it made? You might write me full instructions so that I can have it done soon. I wish you and Virginia would each write me a good letter telling me what you do. With lots of love, Your Father, J. Willard Travell."

One effect of his magician's art was to provoke curiosity. My father encouraged questions, and I had plenty of them for him. That summer when I was five years old, my mother wrote him on August 2, 1907, from Cold Spring on the Hudson: "Bobby caught a moth miller this morning—put it under a glass and said 'Please tell me what kind of *cloth* to feed it!' "

Through my father's eyes, every living creature became a challenging mystery. He led me to wonder, to observe, and to think about what I saw. In his letter to me of August 7, 1907, from New York, he went on to answer a question of mine: "The only mosquito I have seen in the house I killed tonight and he had Sing Sing stripes on his legs, yellow & black, and on the body too, looking just as if he had on a complete new suit of clothes both coat and skin tight trousers. Under the microscope he looks like Sunday. When you catch another, borrow mother's microscope for a good look at him."

My father's rare example and wise direction made it inevitable that I should become deeply concerned with the life processes of nature. The frogs and snakes that we caught served first as our pets, but if disaster overtook them we set about dissecting them and learning anatomy and physiology. Snapping turtles provided us with hearts to study while they beat for forty-eight hours or longer in cold salt water. That fresh-water reptile, I learned, had truly emerged by evolution from the salt sea.

Home on vacation from Wellesley College in 1919, at dinner I was telling Mrs. Edith Bates about the snakes that my cousin, Arthur Travell, and I had kept as children in the Pennsylvania Pocono Mountains. My father corroborated that we had in our snake cage two wide-jawed water moccasins, baby deadly coral snakes that I found in a nest under a rock, numerous plaid garter snakes that could nip you, and pretty green grass snakes that lacked even teeth with which to bite. We exhibited them in our hands without fear but with trained skill in imitation of my father and Uncle Warren. When a big snake cannibalized a smaller one, we understood that that was nature's way. Man's indiscriminate dread of serpents may be well founded. Now microbiologists have shown that even the garter snake, harmless as far as its fangs are concerned, may be a reservoir of mosquito-borne disease. Snakes can harbor the virus of western equine encephalitis and if the reptile "carrier" is bitten by a mosquito, that insect vector may innoculate a human being with the virus.

Edith was well versed in herpetology. That evening at dinner, I discovered that she knew Dr. Raymond L. Ditmars, Curator of Reptiles at the New York Zoological Park, and she arranged for me to meet him. I wanted a closer acquaintance with some of his charges there and to talk with that distinguished expert.

I set off alone on the subway to the Bronx Zoo. Dr. Ditmars took me first into an enclosed area where huge sea turtles loafed. I sat down on the stationary shell of one that probably weighed three hundred pounds. With me on its back, it rose a few inches on its flippers and with a kind of sailor's rolling gait it lumbered across the stone floor toward a deep pool. I quickly slid off onto my feet. I had a feeling that the tortoise resented my intrusion.

Dr. Ditmars led me next along a rear corridor in the reptile house, from which solid steel doors opened into the rattlesnakes' cages. Above each door was a hinged grill, like a transom, and through it beyond the glass front I could see visitors to the Zoo watching the snakes as if hypnotized. The Curator opened one of the transoms and poked a large coiled reptile with a long pole to wake it up and make it rattle. The never-to-be-forgotten sound of those rattles was like dry shelled peas being shaken in a metal pan. The snake struck in anger at the pole only a short distance from where Dr. Ditmars's bare fingers held it. Later he showed me deep scars on his hands caused by rattlers' fangs that had brought him near death. He seemed no more concerned about those vipers than I might have been if I were chasing a mouse with a broom handle.

We moved on to cages occupied by pleasanter snakes. He brought out a friendly king snake five or six feet in length that could kill a rattler. He headed the snake into my loose coat sleeve, and it worked its way up until its head protruded above my coat collar. Finally it anchored its tail section inside my coat under my arm pit and waved its head and several feet of itself in front of my face. I took hold of its big, cold body with both hands and I bent it back and forth. Its flexible form offered no resistance to my pressure. But no matter how I moved its body, its head maintained a fixed position in space seemingly in defiance of the laws of force and gravity. The sensation of handling that pliable snake was so strange and unreal that I almost imagined it a hangover from my father's conjuring tricks.

Dr. Ditmars and I walked on into the monkey house, together with the Zoo's crowd of visitors. Surrounded by curious onlookers, a guard opened a gate and placed a young female gorilla in my arms. Her black body was covered with stiff rough hair, and she weighed about a hundred pounds, I suppose. Dr. Ditmars assured me that she was quite a pet. She draped her long arms affectionately around my neck and started chattering. Pressing her flesh was like grasping hard black India rubber. When I became a physician, I was reminded once of that gorilla when I felt the hardened muscles of a professional wrestler. Holding her was an education in the comparative anatomy of the primates. Her upper limbs were startlingly long and her torso was relatively short. I was told that the gorilla had only four lumbar vertebrae, or sometimes three, as compared with man's five. A chimpanzee was my next acquaintance. She was said to be the most intelligent of the anthropoid apes but untrustworthy, and I was not permitted to be hugged by her. The chimp is the only animal whose blood proteins we think are indistinguishable from those of man. I was surprised to see that the chimpanzee's thumb was not prehensile; but she did have a prehensile big toe, which could be apposed to her other toes and could be used for picking up small objects, like fleas. She could scratch with her fingers, too. In contrast to the gorilla, I learned that the chimpanzee usually had six lumbar vertebrae.

Those bits of anatomical information I relayed to my father whose major interest was physical medicine and the relief of pain from the skeleton and muscular framework of the body. I stowed those facts away in my mind, too, for future use. Malvina Hoffman's remarkable bronzes of one hundred and one racial types of man drew me to the Field Museum when I was attending a medical convention in Chicago. Adjoining the galleries of that "Hall of Man" I studied four "normal" skeletons on exhibition—the Negro and the white man and woman. I was astonished to observe that one skeleton had four lumbar vertebrae and one had six. Such congenital variations are infrequent in the human race and the Field Museum was appreciative when I pointed out their freak selection of exhibit material. During my practice of medicine over the years, when I have encountered such an anomaly in the number of lumbar vertebrae in patients, I have tended to classify them in my mind as descendants of the gorilla or of the chimpanzee, as the case might be.

My father looked, I thought, as a magician should look. He was six feet tall and appeared taller. His large frame carried not an extra ounce of fat. In adult life he never weighed more than one hundred and fifty pounds and in his latter years it was less. He walked silently, with a bounce in his step. He toed in like an Indian. You never heard him moving around in a house. He often surprised you when he entered the room; you were not sure how long he had been there. He was agile as a cat. He could wiggle his ears separately. When he was eighty, he could turn a full somersault like a youngster. Few opponents could throw him in a one-hand wrestle. All his movements were quick—so fast that the eye could not follow them in his magic. Yet he never seemed to hurry. His strong, square hands were never idle and they showed the wear of using tools. He never sat still unless he was listening to what you were saying. Then his deep-set hazel eyes concentrated on you with penetrating intensity—he was a remarkable listener. His words were sparse, as a rule, and he never raised his voice in anger. He had the power to hold attention and he was not afraid to let silence fill the room. You could feel his brain at work. One of his eyes was set lower than the other in his craggy cranium, and to level them he cocked his head a little, as if he were listening all the time. When he looked at you, he tilted his head down to focus through the upper part of his bifocal lenses. To see you better, sometimes, he peered above the rim of his glasses with his eyebrows raised and his forehead wrinkled. That made him look extra wise. He had a quizzical questioning expression that led you to ask yourself if you had said the right thing or done something wrong. He always expected the best of you. His smile was a wonderful thing to see, full of kindness and understanding and mischief.

His inventive imagination led him into pranks and trouble when he was a boy. He used to tell us about a terrible trick that he once played on his grandmother. He dug a pit in the garden path that she liked to walk and he filled it with mud to the level of the ground. He camouflaged that trap with leaves and dirt. As he expected, she stepped into the invisible mud pie. She did not think it funny and he miscalculated the consequences. When his father sent for him, he concealed a plate in the seat of his pants. It did not help his standing—nor his sitting, either—that the plate broke during the spanking that he received. He was locked in his room and sentenced to bread and water for three days. His younger brother Warren climbed the tree outside his second-story window and secretly brought him food, so he did not go hungry. However, I think that the punishment made him more perceptive of other people's points of view.

My father liked to match his wits not only against an audience, but also against nature's unpredictable forces. At heart he was an explorer. He had the optimism, stamina, and perseverance of the man who conquers the wilderness or icebound poles of the earth. He was never afraid of the unknown. His competitive spirit was partly explained by his having three brothers. He also shared with them, especially with Warren, scientific curiosity, resourcefulness, and a love of the outdoors.

Will and Warren in their Williams College days hiked on the slopes of Mount Greylock—altitude, 3,491 feet—the highest mountain in Massachusetts, which was about thirty miles from their home in Troy, New York, and six miles from Williamstown, Massachusetts. It is about forty miles from our Merryfield Farm. On trips to the Adirondack Mountains, my father and Uncle Warren tramped and camped and canoed for days at a time carrying their supplies in knapsacks. Their most essential pieces of equipment were the compasses that hung from their belts to map their direction and their fishing tackle to supply them with food. My father could always outwit the fish. He experimented with one kind of bait after another until he made his first catch. Then he opened the stomach of the fish and examined the contents. He would use on his hook whatever the fish had eaten—worms, hellgrammites, insects, or a small frog. One summer they took a canoe through the Fulton Chain of eight lakes; there were long portages between them. Once, Will and Warren went through the Erie Canal in a rowboat, at least until their small craft was pounded to bits by torrents of water when a sluicegate in one of the locks failed to close behind them. They escaped death by hanging onto the anchor chain at the stern of a ship that was going through the barge canal ahead of them.

Three of the Travell brothers were at Williams College at the same time. (Charles) Howard was graduated in 1889, (Ira) Winthrop in 1890, and (John) Willard in 1891. All three won Phi Beta Kappa keys. Warren (Bertram) entered Williams with the Class of 1893, but he transferred to the Rensselaer Polytechnic Institute in Troy and obtained a civil engineering degree there in 1894. Howard and Willard went to the Albany Medical College for their M.D. degrees in 1894 and 1897. Winthrop joined the rank of educators after postgraduate study in several universities. He was principal of the high school at Plainfield, New Jersey, before he became superintendent of schools, first at Morristown from 1909 to 1912 and then at Ridgewood, New Jersey, until he retired in 1931. He died on June 2, 1946. When the Ira W. Travell School in Ridgewood was dedicated in 1951, his wife, my father, sister and Pop Weeks, Jack and I, and Bob and Marge Travell Bennett with their girls attended the ceremonies. Among the tributes to Uncle Winthrop were a selection by the Travell School Orchestra and an appreciation by the President of Travell P.T.A.

Warren Travell was a mathematical genius. He could multiply in his head six or eight digits by as many digits almost before we could write the figures down on paper. It took us even longer to verify that his answer was correct. After graduating from Rensselaer Polytechnic Institute, he first supervised all the unpaved roads in the City of New York. He was instrumental in cutting down the sidewalk curbs from the height of a carriage mounting block to one more agreeable to the pedestrian who crossed the street. He worked in Thomas A. Edison's patent laboratory where he screened the new ideas that were submitted to Edison for patenting and development. One day, Edison asked him to figure out how cement should ideally be made.

My Uncle Warren tentatively said, "Mr. Edison, I suppose you would like me to start by inspecting present methods—I don't know anything about manufacturing cement."

"Young man, that's why I picked you for the job," was Edison's brusque reply. "If I ever catch you inside a cement plant, you're fired."

My Uncle Warren became the expert in cement and he moved to California to revamp according to his methods the Portland Cement Plant in Colton near San Bernardino, where he and Aunt Minnie lived for many years. He conducted me through that cement plant in 1923. He was an inventor in his own right and held many patents for the design of cranes, hoists, and aircraft. He stayed with us whenever he came to New York. One of his engineering consultant jobs was to assist in calculating the stresses and strains on the Holland Tunnel when it was built under the Hudson River.

My father was a school teacher for a while. Like his brother Warren, he had a mathematical, logical mind and he taught mathematics for two years (1891 to 1893) at Culver Military Academy in Indiana. A. Courtney Washburne was at Culver at the same time and became a lifelong friend. He settled at Pittsfield, Massachusetts, some thirty miles from Sheffield, and the younger generations carried on their friendship.

Elvira Amelia Pierce, my father's mother, who was born on July 26, 1834, at Troy, encouraged her sons in their thirst for education. Before she married Ira Rose Travell on August 8, 1859, at the age of twenty-five, she had been graduated in 1853 from the Troy Female Seminary, later the Emma Willard School. She had taught school and served as the lady principal of the Female Seminary in Poultney, Vermont. My father's enterprising father lacked the opportunity for a formal education but he and his wife were descended from the same sort of industrious, sturdy English people. Ira's great-grandfather, Circuit Travell (his mother was Martha Circuit), was born in 1776 in England at Eaton Bray, Dunstable, Bedfordshire. In about 1799, Circuit and his wife, Judith Purcell, came to America; on the passage over they had smallpox and their ship was wrecked. Their only son, John, was born in 1803 at Albany, New York. Circuit worked as a gardener on the Schoharie property of John Lansing, Jr., Chancellor of the State of New

York, and Circuit bought his own farm from him outright—without the then customary ground rent. John inherited the farm and married Celecta Rose in 1824; their third son was my father's father, Ira Rose Travell. Born on September 21, 1836, at Gilboa, New York, Ira moved to Troy where he started as a clerk in the Burton Iron Works store. He opened the first steam laundry in that city and became a successful shirt and collar manufacturer there. When his health deteriorated, he retired to Elm Hill in the little town of Johnsonville, fifteen miles to the northeast. Elm Hill was the Yates-Travell family farm where his boys helped out during the summers and where my father spent the academic year of 1886 to 1887 after high school. He was thought too young to enter college.

The achievements and activities of the Travell brothers at Williams were legendary. *The Times Record,* Troy, New York, reported on August 15, 1961:

> Dr. Willard Travell, [nearly] 92, a native Trojan, died . . . yesterday. Dr. Travell was one of four brothers. . . . They were all great walkers and while at Williams College one of their weekend pleasures was to leave Williamstown after their last class Saturday morning and walk to Troy, a matter of more than 25 miles. They would reach their home in Troy in the early evening, spend the night with their parents, have dinner on Sunday and then walk back over the mountains to Williamstown.

Those fifty-miles-a-weekend hikers did not walk for "physical fitness." It was in their genes. Their pioneering grandfather, Hiram Dwight Pierce, had twice left home to seek fortune on foot in unknown places. Born on May 25, 1810, at Copake, New York, Hiram was apprenticed to a blacksmith following his father's early death. At eighteen,

> taking his leather apron and skates he made his way to the Hudson River and skated up to Troy [about twenty miles overland and forty miles up the river]. Entering a blacksmith shop, he found the smith working alone, while several men were waiting to have their horses shod. Without wasting words he put on his leather apron and went to work. When the rush was over he asked for a job, which was granted him immediately, and at the end of a year he bought the shop.[1]

[1] *Diary of Hiram Dwight Pierce: A Forty-Niner Speaks,* Sarah Wiswall Meyer, ed. (Oakland, California, Keystone-Inglett Printing Company, October 30, 1930), pp. 1–74.

Sarah Wiswall Ostrom, who married Frederick W. Meyer, D.D.S., of Oakland, California, was Hiram Dwight Pierce's granddaughter and my father's second cousin.

Prior to the automobile and tractor, the blacksmith was a key man in a horse-powered economy. In 1859 in the South, a slave who was a blacksmith brought the fancy price of $2,100 in the market at Fayetteville, while at the same auction the overall price for Negroes averaged about $1,000.[2] In the North, my great-grandfather as a young blacksmith responded to the challenge of earning a living by that manual skill, and he did it with enterprise.

Established at Troy that way, Hiram Pierce enlarged his shop and became a wagonmaker. A religious, home-loving leader of the community, he was an elder in the Second Presbyterian Church, a Troy City Alderman—serving at the same time (in 1843) as Russell Sage—and President of the Fire Department. In 1848, the carriage shop was making a good living for Hiram, his wife, Sarah Jane Wiswall, and their seven children. However, his health was not of the best and a sea voyage was advised. Nearing thirty-nine, he joined a company of mining prospectors—he was on its executive committee—and for $150 he bought a cabin passage on a steamer leaving New York on March 8, 1849. His destination was California and its newly discovered gold fields.

With stops at Charleston, Savannah, Havana, and New Orleans, in three weeks the ship arrived at Chagres on the north coast of the Panama Isthmus. Hiram's unabridged diary, *A Forty-Niner Speaks,* describes the pleasant life on the *Falcon:* "One word about our ship. She is a fine strong Sea craft of about 700 tons. Two 250 horse power Engine. Not verry fast but verry strong. She has a crew of about 70 including Officers Seamen Engineers Cooks, Waiters, Stewards &c. We live like nabobs & do nothing but Read Smoke talk & think. To the latter I incline."

That inclination led him to make six hundred and seventy-four entries in his diary, one for each day of that journey, under most arduous circumstances. The start of his endeavor was deceptive. Twenty-two months were to pass before he saw home again, in debt and ill from dysentery, Chagres fever—a malignant form of malaria contracted on his return through Nicaragua and the Isthmus of Panama—seasickness, lack of sleep, exposure to extremes of heat and cold, and many other hardships.

En route to California, Hiram's company went up the Chagres River in small boats and then traveled on foot overland to Panama City on the Pacific. Engineers were surveying then for a railroad across the Isthmus; there was no Panama Canal. Concerning the last twenty-four hours of that first march he wrote:

[2] Guion Griffis Johnson, *Ante-bellum North Carolina* (Chapel Hill, The University of North Carolina Press, 1937), p. 476.

Wensday, 4th [April]. Arose early and started to march about 9. . . .
It was excessive warm. . . . Verry rough up & down, winding about
in the bushes. . . . On either side the copse or jungle of vines were
so thick that . . . the air could not circulate if there had ben any.
. . . I in company with 3 others halted at about 8 in the evening 6
miles from Panama. There was a tent, just started by a man who intended to accommodate travelers with coffey. I lay down in his tent
with a thin India rubber blanket under me & nothing over me. . . .
It beeing damp & cool I soon got chilly. Besides, the gravel on which
I lay prooved harder than my bones, so I got up and sat around the
fire nearly all night. At 11 a man shot a tiger near our tent. . . . I
arrived at Panama at 8 in the morning much fatigued.

Ten days later he was still in that city:

Our prospects for getting away looks verry dubious, with 2 or 3000 on
the Isthmus & not Sails arriving to take them off as fast as they arrive.
. . . I think of that Shop in Troy, & that Wife, whose likeness I look
uppon & those dear Children, & my feelings by some might not be
called manley. . . . Whatever may be the results of this enterprise, I
am sattisfide there is more folley in this world than I supposed before
leaving home.

Hiram was not idle in Panama. Another week passed: "I am quite diligent in learning Spanish & make some proficiency. . . . Mended my
clothes a pacho (a little). . . . Spent the afternoon in examining bills [for
the Company]. Tried to get work. Blacksmiths are getting $4.80 per day,
with verry little work to be done. . . . Bought ½ Bbl of pork at $25., a
Box of Tea 6 lbs at $9. Everything is extreordinary high in Panama & it
seems as though we should raise a famine." He took his turn at cooking for
his "party of 17 men, 2 Women, 1 Girl & 1 Boy." He put up a notice of
meal hours signed, "By order *Don Hiram,* Cook—Panamay, April 13th,
1849."

His inquiring mind led him to walk five miles to the ancient ruins of the
Spanish colonial city of Panama.

Friday . . Viernes . . 20th. Visited Old Panama in co. with the Dr.
& 4 others. . . . We saw the ruins of . . . several large Cathedrals
& Churches. . . . The walls are of coarse lime stone & their Morter or
Sement so strong that where walls have fallen 20 feet the masses of
stone & morter still firmly adhere together, although it is said to have
ben in ruins 300 years. . . . On some walls I saw trees of 3 feet dia-
metor, standing 12 feet from the ground with roots running down on
each side. I saw a dungeon, probably an inquisition. There is a tower
standing entire some 100 feet high with walls of 7 feet thickness. The

whole place is so overgrown with Brush, briars &c. that it is allmost impossible to get about except to follow some rude paths made as I suppose by wild animals. . . . Mr. Bell was treed by a wild boar. . . . he shot one. He shot 2 Green Snakes 9 feet long in the ruins, he allso saw a Panther. He had a tustle with an Aligator & shot one some 12 feet long. . . . As I sat in the Cathedral & reflected on the egar devotees that once throunged its broad isles, with all their Pride & Passions, that have now passed away like the waves of the Ocean . . . I was led to think that Man truely is of Small account. The evedence still exists that the city once contained a large population, from 150 to 200,000 Inhabitants. They say it was the first town built on the Pacific side of the continent, & was destroyed by the Pirates. . . . Such in brief is Old Panama. . . . We retraced our weary steps & arived home at dusk . . . feeling well paid for our toil.

Hiram had the explorer's desire to record and share what he observed of a strange nature.

After waiting five weeks in Panama, his company at last obtained passage for San Francisco on a "wretched dirty, crowded schooner." Contrary winds carried them due south as far as Atacames in Ecuador just above the equator. For periods they were becalmed, at other times tossed by violent storms. "My stomach rejects food. Our fare for breckfast Coffey & hard Bread & molasses. For dinner Pork, Corn beef, & beans or rice sometimes. Supper Bread & Sugar. Butter is served but the sight is sufficient without the smell." Hiram kept busy nursing the sick, making notes, sitting and thinking. "Monday, 21st [May]. 12th D.O. [day out]. . . . Saw some turtles 5 or 6 feet across." On the fifteenth day, the schooner dropped anchor and he went ashore at "Tecamos in Ecuador. . . . I got some dinner such as it was. It consisted of Stewed Monkey, Boiled plaintain, hard bread & peppers. I supposed the meat to be wild hog until after I had eaten. It was not the most savory dish. . . . We had oranges picked at 50 cts the hundred and picked them ourselves at 20 cts. I helped bring a bundel of Bananas to the Boat that cost 2 rials, as much as 2 could carry handily on a pole." Their harvest of hundreds of oranges probably saved them from scurvy, for they still had a long way to sail.

On July 11, Hiram recorded: "63rd D.O. There is some talk about going to the Sandwich Islands [Hawaii], as it seems impossible to get to San Francisco. [They had been blown westerly parallel with the equator for seventeen days.] Our bread is miserable and the meat seems likely to make us sick . . . & 1 quart of water per day. . . . 68th D.O. Mr. Bristol expired. . . . His request was that his body be sent home." They considered preserving it in spirits, but forty gallons would be needed and that would require "opening him up. . . . He was committed to the deep with a solemn English service. . . . 74th D.O. Coast of California in sight [Monterey]." On July 26, the seventy-eighth day at sea, that schooner anchored in San Francisco Bay. Nearly five months had elapsed since the prospectors left Troy.

Hiram and half the Company went by riverboat to Sacramento and then marched to Mormon Island. On August 3, they "walked 16 miles the first day over a verry sandy road." The next day, they "rose early and walked to the diggins." They had attained the land of great expectation, but disappointment followed fast.

> Monday, 6th. . . . All of us got much less than an ounce. It is verry much like work. . . . Tuesday, 7th, All hands went to work. We gathered less than an ounce. Potatoes are $1. a piece, onions the same. . . . Eggs $12. per dozen. . . . Axes $8. At night the Wolves & Kiotas give us plenty of music. . . . Thursday, 9th. Went out prospecting and find that every Stone & foot of Ground has ben turned over. . . . We bake pan cakes, fry pork, drink Tea or coffey & sleep on the Ground. During the day said to be as high as 130 deg. in the shade. . . . The Sun Shines with great power. . . . The nights are pleasant and fine. No dew. The diggins looks rather poor, verry few get over 1 ounce per day. . . . Saturday, 11th. We all continue digging. . . . All feeling verry tired. Newcomers are coming and going. They try the different diggins & hear great reports, & run from place to place. I would gladly warn my brethren & friends against comeing to this place of torment. Sunday, 12th. Preaching again at 4 under live oaks to a respectable and attentive congregation. In the evening we went up the river and held [another] meeting.

Hiram attended two or three services and never dug gold on Sunday. The next day: "We worked hard and got but little gold." Ten days later: "My back getting lame in consequence as I think, of getting my feet wet days & sleeping on the ground nights. . . . A Company just arrived, 31 in party overland, & lost 8 by Colera & 2 otherways. . . . Much suffering on the road."

The meager gains and unhealthy conditions drove Hiram's group to leave that location after a month. On September 6, Hiram sold their provisions and tools, hired a team and they returned to Sacramento. There they engaged passage on a small vessel. "Tide in favour but wind contrary. Made slow progress beating down the narrow river. . . . This is emphatacally the Musketoes batle ground & the man that comes off with a whole hide may be counted luckey." Owing to lack of room inside they had to sit up all night on deck. At Benicia Hiram stopped in a hotel, "hopeing once more to sleep on a bed, & truely I had a bedstead & cords under me, but there was not enough in the tick to tell what it was filled with. The fleas literally covered a person, however I managed to pass the night." On September 11, Hiram and his group located the rest of the original Company at San Francisco, "encamped in Happy Valley 1 mile east of the postoffice. . . . A meeting was held at which time a Resolution was passed that we believe the project of dredgeing for gold utterly impracticable. . . . We made a dividend of our earnings at the mines. It amounted to $39.40 each —2 oz. 9 penyweights." Gold was priced at $15.25 per ounce. On September 22, the Company agreed by "Constitutional vote" to dissolve.

Afflicted with chills and fever, "the dum Ague," Hiram remained in San Francisco. On October 10, he wrote:

> I went to the Parker House & sat by the fire & had a chill. I paid one dollar for the privilege of sleeping on a Buffalow Skin [that night], not feeling able to walk to the tent. [Another day:] The Dr. was in 2 or 3 times. He continues to give powders & I to throw them up. . . . The Dr. promised to change his medecine. I laid for 18 hours, rolled & tumbled, pained in every joint, Sleep beeing a Stranger. . . . I put a mustard paste on my Stomach & ate a little arrowroot without Seasoning, a miserable tasteless thing. . . . Mr. Eddy brought me some pears & they did me more good than anything else. I had not ate a meal in a week.

By the end of October, he decided to try again and to prospect for gold for himself.

With a friend, Hiram boarded a river vessel for Stockton. There they bought mules. On November 12, they crossed the Stanislaus River "on a flat," after having first tried to ford the river "to the great danger of drowning the mules." Obstacles and hazards did not deter Hiram.

> Tuesday, 13th. Rained all night with a cold strong wind. Mountains in sight are covered with Snow. We passed a verry uncomfortable night Sitting under our Frail shelter, which was made by tying some blankets on poles. The ground was covered with water. . . . Wensday, 14th. We found on the road an animal resembling a spider. Black & 2 or 3 inches long more poisonous than the Ratle Snake. It is called the Tarantler. . . . Friday, 16th. Roads allmost impassable. . . . At 8 this morning we started. After getting 2 miles we got stalled in the mud & the mules could not Start the wagon. So we took them off & went back to camp & made pack saddles. . . . Sunday, 18th. The dew falls like rain, & our blankets were wet. The road verry bad. We made 20 miles & encamped, after dark under a tree at Scots ranch, near the Mersais [Merced].

The next day he hiked up the river for salmon: "Shot some & got one of 20 lb. It began to rain at 9 & rained until one. I walked 10 miles to the crossing with my wet Stockins & boots & never I think was so near exhausted. Crossed the river & went 6 miles & encamped."

In the mountainous country with cold nights and sharp frosts, Hiram decided to build a house. All hands worked hard at it.

> Tuesday, 4th [December]. I had a slight chill today. Our manner of building the house was to cut the logs, get a pair of cattle & hawl them to gether, lay them up, then chop large trees & split boards part of Oak & part of Pine, for the roof & door & floors & for want of nails to put on the roof it was fixed by lashing on poles to hold the boards on. The peaks were closed with rawhides. We then put up berths & had quite a comfortable house.

They added a chimney on the outside.

Hiram was having another siege of malaria then and he "took 13 grains of calomel & followed it with quinene." Illness did not disable him. On December 14, he began to wash gold for himself. "Tuesday, 18th. Worked until 12, then had a chill, followed as usual by fever. Got 4/- [4 shillings]. . . . Tuesday, 25th. *Christmas.* I spent most of the day in diggin, though I got but $1. Took Supper of our everyday fare, fried pork & hoecake." On January 11, 1850, after a diet of fish, meat, and cooked flour for nearly two months in the wintry Sierra Nevada Mountains, a new sickness plagued him: "I fear the Scurvy. My mouth & gums are sore & teeth loose and legs sore & lame." Ten days later: "I tried digging 2 hours. I made nothing. . . . Snowed a little. I have the Symptoms of Scurvey. I have commenced eating grass." Hiram had horse sense and he recovered. Within a week he was hard at work still unlucky: "Saturday, 26th [January]. Made some $3. Felt quite smart. . . . Sunday, 27th. Quite well. . . . Monday, 28th. A fine Spring day [still January]. Dug about $7. & washed [his clothes]."

On March 1, a six-inch snowfall and frozen ground discouraged him. In February, all the prospectors had left that camp except Hiram and his friend, "Lewis a poor criple." On April 1, each of them led "a packed mule" and started through the mountains in search of unmined territory. Hiram summarized then: "I have now spent four months & one half in this place & worked hard & ben diligent & yet lack $125. of paying my board from my earnings, & live some of the time as I would hardly ask a dog to live. I leave . . . over $100. in debt."

Through the extreme heat of the California summer, Hiram tried prospecting in many locations on the rivers and mountain streams. He took a partner and they hired other men. They even built a dam and turned a stream, at a cost of $3,000. The best week's work netted him $116.63. He quit at last. On October 4, he returned to Stockton and two days later he reached San Francisco. It was a year to the month since he had left that city to prospect on his own and fifteen months since he had landed there from Panama with his Company.

The village of San Francisco, which was Mexican until 1846, had grown phenomenally under my great-grandfather's eyes. On his first visit he described it as "a miserable dusty dirty town of some 5000, out of every kind of tongue & people under Heaven." Six weeks later on his second visit he wrote:

> I think the place contains 15,000 inhabitants. . . . The Chinese with his turban, Short tunic, Black petticoat & wooden shoes. The Peruvian with his Small Steeple crowned, broad brimmed Sombraro, Sitting on the top of his head & dressed to suit. The Chillanean, the Cannacker, the Greaser, the Senoranians, the representatives of the diferent Tribes & races of Indians & in fact as much of a mixed Congregation as ever Peter preached to . . . but the Gambling houses are dooing a driving business. Here Men stake & lose their Thousands in an hour.

A year later the city had a new look:

> San Francisco contains about 25,000 inhabitants. . . . It is a place of great business & is full of life and bustle. Where a few tents stood last fall is now covered with permanent buildings. Some of them iron. Wharves are extended out ¼ of a mile. . . . The Citty is making great improovement. . . . They are digging down hills, raising Streets & planking them, & putting a plank Sewer along each side, which makes a verry good sidewalk. The gambling halls are on a princely and Magnificent Style.

On October 13, 1850, the "Brig Swift Shure" sailed from San Francisco with twenty-six cabin passengers—Hiram was one of them—and sixty-one steerage. On the twenty-fifth day out, water was rationed and "the potatoes failed." Seven of the passengers died and "were put over the side." It took thirty-seven days for the sailing vessel to reach the northerly coast of Nicaragua. In company with thirty-five, mostly on horseback, Hiram trekked across that country one hundred miles overland from Chinandega to Granada in eight days. He hired an ox cart for the trip, being carried with his baggage when he chose to ride. He described the cart as "a rude concern, without a particle of iron. The wheles are made from a log." It did not appeal to the fine carriage maker that Hiram was. At Granada the party transferred to a *bunga* with a crew of eleven for about a hundred-mile trip down Lake Nicaragua and another hundred miles on the San Juan River, through the rapids. The passengers included "2 monkeys & 6 or 8 parrots." One night the *bunga* tied up at a small jungle island, and Hiram recorded: "Our chances for sleep was like hanging on a pole & it rained." The sun was scorching. Provisions had been bought at Granada since nothing could be obtained en route. The trip took a week.

On December 5, the party disembarked at "San Wan (Grey Town)," but could not get passage on a boat to New Orleans. Finally, after two weeks, "the English Consul was waited on by a Committy to see if the Friggate could not be sent to take the American Emigrants to Chagres. On consultation they turned the Manowar into a passenger boat, & the polls were opened at 3 different places to sell tickets, & the rush commenced. Some 500 of us paid one ounce each for about 30 hours run. The Inflexible is a noble substantial war steamer of 1300 tons. . . . We passed a hard night on the deck. No provisions except such as we brought." At Chagres Hiram bought a steerage ticket for $65 on the *Crescent City,* leaving December 24 for New York. That Christmas Eve he came down with Chagres fever.

The closing entries in his diary were: "Tuesday, 7th [January, 1851]. At 3 A.M. made the lights of Never Sink [Sandy Hook]. Left 3 at the Hospital & got to hur berth at 9 A.M. Went up in carriage to Earls Hotell [New York], & felt as if at home. Wensday, 8th. Got into the Cars & at 7 P.M. joined my family with rejoicing, still weak & feeble with the Chagres fever."

Not all the Forty-Niners were as hardy and resourceful as Hiram Dwight Pierce and many did not survive to return home. After the gold rush my father's grandfather thrived in Troy for another fifteen years. He accumulated the means to help his son-in-law, Ira Rose Travell, start the steam-laundry business there. He died on May 10, 1866, three years before his grandson, John Willard Travell, was born, but the heritage of intelligence and intrepid independence that he left lives still in his great-great-great-grandchildren.

My father and his grandfather Pierce were alike in many respects. Inventive and adventurous, they were happy, never moody in temperament. In his diary as a Forty-Niner, not once did Hiram reveal self-pity, impatience, or loss of his good nature. He never swore. He accepted physical discomfort with equanimity. He took responsibility without undue regret for the decisions that he made. Eminently practical and endowed with common sense, in adversity he was not overwhelmed by discouragement. He sought the best way out. Many people relied on his judgment and he bolstered morale. When he was in California, his wife wrote him from Troy: "It almost undone the church to have you go away. . . . They were leaning on you more than on God." [3]

These facets of character Hiram Pierce shared with my father. If he had had the advantage of an education like my father's, he, too, would have made a fine physician.

Regular exercise of the right kind is necessary for health, my father believed. His choice for himself was tennis, because it was competitive, energetic, and required only an hour or so for a workout. He allotted at least one afternoon a week from his working schedule to play indoors in the winter at an armory or the old Times Square Tennis Building, and during the outdoor season at the West Side Tennis Club. He was an early member of that club when it was located on New York's upper West Side near Broadway and he followed it to Forest Hills on Long Island. He had a Class A rating there for years. Although he never had a racket until after medical school, he achieved excellent form through scientific study of the follow-through of the stroke. His wizardry displayed itself in his tennis. He could conceal the intended direction of his shots to the surprise and helplessness of an opponent. You could not anticipate by his look or movement where he would place the ball. He played a tricky game to win, but when he was caught in an unequal singles contest against a beginner, he shifted his racket to his left hand and smiled to himself about that self-imposed secret handicap.

My father kept up his tennis until he was eighty-eight, in spite of three heart attacks, each with myocardial infarction. He did not let illness disable him. In the latter years he could not cover court, but he put the ball away when it was within his reach. At his eighty-fifth birthday party in Pelham, gifts for him included a new lightweight tennis racket, a white tennis hat, and a dozen tennis balls. I gave a toast to him:

LOVE TO GRAN
NOVEMBER 5, 1955

There was a youngster of eighty-five,
Who hit a terrific backhand drive.
Tossed a ball into space
And he served up an ace,
Saying, "Gosh, but it's great to be alive!"

The large reserve of physical stamina that my father and his brothers enjoyed not only came from their forebears, but was trained and developed when they were young. Such endurance depends to a large extent on the economical use of muscular energy and that can best be learned in child-

[3] *Diary of Hiram Dwight Pierce: A Forty-Niner Speaks*, p. 6.

hood. The muscle memories that are built then are stored for a lifetime.

At an early age my sister and I were imbued with my father's enthusiasm for tennis. When Ginny and I came home in the afternoon from The Brearley School, we would hit balls to each other in our backyard at 27 East 11th Street. When he could, my father would leave his office in the house and join us. The yard was perhaps half as long as a tennis court, partly paved and partly planted, with a brick wall at the far end. The snapping turtle lived in one corner under the ailanthus tree and we had to be careful to keep the balls from getting wet in its pool. We broke so many windows in the basement and first floor of our house that my father covered it with chicken wire to the second story. When our balls were lost over the high board fence on either side of the yard, we used a homemade rope ladder with an iron hook on the end to retrieve them. We threw the hook up to latch onto the top of the fence, then one of us climbed up, sat on the fence and dropped the ladder into the neighbor's yard. Once in a while we lost a ball forever in the high gutter of a sloping roof. Even when snow covered the backyard, in boots and gloves Ginny and I practiced volleying. First, we warmed a bushel of tennis balls on the big coal range in the downstairs kitchen to increase their pressure and make them lively in the cold. We used each ball only as long as we kept it in play in the air. When it fell in the snow, it was discarded into another basket to be dried on the stove.

Ginny and I still play tennis indoors in winter and outdoors in summer, and so does my husband. Jack became a member of the West Side Tennis Club soon after we were married and he worked his way up "the ladder" as high as number 25 in Class A. I played there first as a junior member. When I was a senior at Wellesley, my father wrote me on April 14, 1922, "Yesterday . . . you were elected to membership in the West Side Tennis Club. This is Events Week." I competed in the singles of the Women's Nationals at Forest Hills, but my avidity for the study of medicine interfered with my career in tennis. Nevertheless, after Jack and I moved to Pelham in 1944 and we joined the Pelham Country Club, I surprised the local young women by winning the singles championship of the club. Jack married into a tennis-playing family, and at seventy he graciously says that tennis is better exercise for him than his first love, golf, in which he held a handicap of three.

My father had a magical way of bringing the country to us in the city. Tennis in our backyard and canoeing on the Hudson were only part of it. When Jack, my husband-to-be, first came to a black-tie dinner in our New York home at 40 Fifth Avenue—we moved there in 1919—he was startled to hear my father invite the guests afterward to go downstairs and shoot with him. He had indeed set up a shooting range in the subbasement, with a paper target stuck on a brick wall at the front, under the sidewalk. We lined up beside the coal bins. To the noise of Fifth Avenue buses, we took turns firing a long-barreled target pistol from the rear of the cellar down the eighty-foot length of the house. Although less exciting than skeet shooting at Edith Bates's Talcott Farms in Westfield or my hurling the tin can on a string for my father to pepper with gunshot at Merryfield Farm, the competition provided a country flavor to the evening's entertainment.

Fishing was within the radius of lower Fifth Avenue in my childhood. When I was two and a half years old, in the Baby Book that my father kept for me he wrote about a trip that we made on Memorial Day by ferry, five miles across New York Bay from the Battery to St. George and then by rapid transit to Silver Lake: "May 30, 1904. A picnic and fishing expedition on Staten Island composed of Warren, Minnie, Arthur, Bobby and parents—get caught in a thunderstorm, catch one fish and four eels, dig ferns, build a fire, then return weary." Ginny was visiting our Davidson grandparents in Albany, who adored her; everyone called her "Sweetie." Sometimes, our family went deep-sea fishing off the south shore of Long Island; the subway took us near the dock at Far Rockaway. Sometimes, my father took me with him when he went duck hunting in marshy Jamaica Bay. In perfect contentment I lay for hours flat beside him in a duck blind level with the surface of the water.

The pets that my father collected brought the country to our city home. In a corner of the backyard at 27 East 11th Street a great horned hoot owl lived in a large wire cage about eight feet high with perches and a roof. At night in my bed in the second-floor extension just above the cage, I could listen to the owl's "Whoo, Who Who, Who Whooooo," and imagine myself far away. Later the cage was occupied by a brood of chicks that hatched late in the season at Merryfield Farm just before we returned to the city. Another occupant for two years was a pet partridge that my father had shot through the wing. She could not fly and divided her peregrinations between the cage and our house. Once when I was away visiting, I wrote my father, "How many eggs has Partridge?" I was disappointed that her eggs never hatched. When I was nine, I wrote him in August from the village of Sheffield, "Write and tell me whether the eel got home alive [on the train to New York]." Two days later I wrote again: "Dearest Father; I just received your letter. . . . You did not say anything about the live eel. Did you get it home alive?" I intended it to keep the snapping turtle company in its tub of water.

The backyard of our house at 40 Fifth Avenue was cemented over. In the years that we lived there, when my father was preparing to go fishing we caught the bait in Washington Square. On a rainy night, under an umbrella and in raincoats, he and I walked down Fifth Avenue three blocks—not counting the alley called Washington Mews—to the park and we stepped over the low railing onto a plot of thin grimy grass. Armed with dim flashlights, we walked lightly, like Indians, to spot those city nightcrawlers that glistened in the drizzle. They lay stretched out with their tails nestling in their holes, and they would whip backward, down out of sight, if too bright a light hit them. With lightning sleight of hand, we aimed to grab the tail but the worm moved so fast that it was usually its head that we pinned against the ground. Then gently we pulled its length of five or six inches up out of its hole. Once a policeman came over to see what those two "nuts" were doing in the dark. He was inclined at first to arrest us, but my father soon had him trying his hand at the elusive worms. When he learned the difference between heads and tails and made his first catch, he was as proud as a small boy. He helped us fill our bait can.

Originality has many faces. My mother was creative in an artistic way, seeking the fresh expression of beauty through her home, her garden, her children. My father was inventive; his imagination had a utilitarian purpose. His ingenuity could fix any mechanical thing. To him, a piece of machinery was an adventure in discovery. Take it apart, see how it works, and put it together again. He used the experimental method; the hypothesis was that he could make it work better. One of the few things that ever defeated him was an old French clock with wooden works that stopped. Its parts lay scattered around our workbench for years. But then, he did not like clocks any better than I did.

With apologies to Lord Tennyson, I sketched a vignette:

TO AND FRO

The French clock stands with circling hands
That set the pendulum amoving
The time to mark from dark to dark,
A metronome for ordered living.
Swing, pendulum, swing to and fro aspiring,
Untiring, in the end unwound, run down, expiring.

My father's pockets always bulged a little with assorted nails and screws and a sturdy jackknife that was also a screwdriver. For fishing, his jackknife had a cork covering so that it floated if he dropped it in the water. Like his grandfather the blacksmith, carriage maker, and Forty-Niner, he loved working with tools. He had a complete workshop in our house. A large lathe could turn wood and metal. Chisels, planes, hammers, fret saws, rip saws, an electric soldering iron, Stillson and other wrenches, an electric drill, folding rulers, and marking pencils were handy. At one end of his workbench was fastened an electric whetstone for sharpening the tools and fixed at the other end were a vise and electric buzz saw.

For mending our antique furniture, long clamps stood in a corner of the shop. A special toolbox contained smaller clamps, a brace and bit, wood files, doweling, glue, a feather for applying it, sandpaper, and other equipment. I enjoyed assisting him in odd jobs about the house. Undoubtedly, my "know-how" in seating design got a headstart from an apprenticeship in reupholstering chairs.

As soon as the crystal radio set was invented in 1919, he put one together with earphones to divert my mother while she sat and sewed by hand. Fifteen years before the Singer Sewing Machine Company manufactured an electrified machine in 1920, my father bolted a motor to the shelf of my mother's treadle-operated machine. He disconnected the drive belt from the treadle and substituted another belt from the drive shaft of the motor. He set a switch on the shelf with two buttons, one for ON and one for OFF. The motor had only one speed and when the ON button was pushed the machine leapt into action like the Model T Ford going into high gear. It was a challenge to guide the material and stitch at that rate. I inherited that sewing machine from my mother and with my father's aid it functioned well for fifty years. He finally gave me a factory-electrified model for Christmas about 1955.

Another of my father's inventions was a three-legged wooden ladder that he made at Merryfield Farm. We still use it there. He built it so that its three fifteen-foot-long legs met together at the top like a tripod. Two legs were stable with crosspieces for steps and the third leg was hinged at the top to change the size of the triangular base and to vary the slope of the ladder. The third leg folded flat when it was stored. Our small children and large springer spaniel dog practiced climbing it while it was set up like a pyramid on the lawn. It served the double purpose of a self-supporting ladder and a jungle gym.

In the practice of medicine, with his mechanical bent it was only natural that my father was attracted to machines, especially electrical modalities. He was more than a match for the temperamental Toepler-Holtz static machine that was employed then to treat painful conditions of the muscles, nerves, and joints. The glass plates of the giant machine revolved inside a low-humidity case and they generated by friction against brushes an electrical discharge that was condensed in the Leyden jars. Starting the static machine was like cranking up the Model T; my father ran back and forth from the switch and rheostat on the wall to the machine to slide the brass rods in and out and regulate the spark-gap. On a damp day it might take several tries to get it running. My father's parlor magic after dinner sometimes included a hair-raising session with the static machine. When a lady sat on its insulated platform, connected to one pole of the wide-open spark-gap, the electrical charge flowed off her head into the air and every one of her hairs stood straight out. Ginny's hair was so long that she could sit on it and when she loosened it the static electricity caused it to rise nearly to the ceiling. Her Brearley School 1917 *Class Book* observed appropriately: "Virginia MacQueen Travell—Her hair streamed like a meteor to the troubled air."

The Toepler-Holtz machine generated enough current to operate an X-ray tube, and my father was an early exponent of Roentgen's new diagnostic apparatus. Against that strangely glowing glass tube it was a marvel to me to recognize the doorkeys and nails within his fist and to see the bones of his hand when I looked through the long black box that was the fluoroscopic screen and that made darkness for my eyes.

With the swift progress of medical knowledge, the implements of medical practice become rapidly obsolescent, and so do some physicians when they fail to update their thinking. My father dismantled his static machines when newer methods of treatment became preferable. His attitude was one of receptiveness to change. He studied medical journals constantly even in his last year of life and his techniques never hardened. His mind never became obsolete.

Thinking of my father, I wrote:

EXPLORATION IN THE ROUND

The finite circle of the skull surrounds
The brain. Inside that cranium expands
A universe infinite where resounds
Emotion's thunder, thought's lightning. The hands
That rock the mind's cradle of creation
Are dynamos [4] cerebral, in action.

A bony funnel circles close around
Each eye. Those periscopes of the brain sweep
In wide orbits the sea, the sky, the ground
Endlessly, except when the eyelids sleep.
And then, the mind's eye stores each fresh vision,
Explores the galaxies of decision.

[4] A dynamo is a machine for converting mechanical energy into electrical energy.

CHAPTER 8

College Years
at Wellesley

Wellesley was my mother's alma mater and my sister's choice, and I was proud to follow in their tradition. I never wanted to go to any other college. At The Brearley School I was the only one in my class to elect Wellesley, but being different in that respect did not disturb me. I had made up my mind about it when I was a little girl. When the time approached for me to apply for admission to college, however, I scrutinized my preference critically. I had made no mistake, I decided. Wellesley had everything that I wanted: science departments of superior reputation, a country campus with outdoor sports, the city of Boston accessible for music and the theater, and a reasonable distance to travel home on vacations.

It did not seem strange, nor did it matter to me, that I knew not a single girl who was also entering Wellesley that fall in the Class of 1922. Our number was four hundred and twenty-four in our *Freshman Portrait Directory* and four years later three hundred and ninety-two were graduated. I do not remember ever being homesick and I soon had a host of friends. Of course, my sister was only one year ahead of me, and although our dormitories were located a mile apart, Ginny had a motherly way of looking after me. She and I had more good times than most sisters do in the same college. Through the spring and fall we played tennis together several times a week, for fun and in tournaments. As partners we won the college doubles championship. Her circle of sophomore friends made her "little sister" feel at ease with them—especially Polly Snow, Ginny's roommate, Maude Ludington from Albany, Schmittie (Marion Smith), Mildred Hesse, Cathy Mitchell, Bess Rand, and Laura Johnson. They included me in their picnics at Peagan Hill, their weekends on the beach at Marblehead, and in dormitory parties when food packages arrived from home. I welcomed their friendliness and my freshman friends reciprocated by inviting them to our special events.

When I entered Wellesley at sixteen, I was in the enviable situation of knowing what I wanted to do after college. Many students had no clear idea of their educational goals. But I was able to plan my courses from the start to meet the heavy premedical science requirements. I set myself an accelerated program; each semester I carried two full courses in science—six lectures a week and laboratory sessions in addition. My "major" was chemistry and my "minor," zoology. The work was never monotonous. Exceptional teachers made the study of science a series of enterprises in exploration. Wellesley offered me all that I had hoped in the way of a creative climate for scientific thinking.

At the end of my junior year I wanted to enter medical school in the fall (1921). I had met all the premedical requirements with honors. Wellesley approved my plan to combine my senior year with the first year at Cornell University Medical College and was willing to award my diploma on that basis. However, the Cornell admissions committee in New York informed me that at nineteen I was too young for medical school. That attitude contrasts with the present trend to let competent students shorten the long period of medical education from eight years to a seven- or a six-year combined program. And Jefferson Medical College is even experimenting with a five-year program.

College was not just a stepping-stone to graduate school, however. From the start, I did not waste my opportunity to study the liberal arts. I delved into unfamiliar fields of thought seemingly unrelated to medicine. I realized that the good physician should meet his patients not in his world, but in theirs. My courses included history, philosophy, English, the Bible, economics, foreign languages, and art. During freshman year I studied Italian. That course, together with art appreciation, so enamored me of Italy that when Ginny and I were planning to tour Europe in the summer of 1922, I was insistent on spending most of the two and a half months in Italy. On April 14, 1922, my father wrote me his decision: "Dear Bob— Today Mother, Virginia and I decided that your Italian enthusiasm would give way to satisfaction in the General Tour with trips through upper Italy, Venice, Florence, etc., the Tyrol, Switzerland, Munich, the Passion Play, France, Belgium, England, with a reception at Oxford, etc. It would be a crime to contemplate spending the summer months in overheated Southern Italy—I could not bear the idea so of course you won't mention it again."

I did not bring it up. My father, with all his easy nature, had a will of iron. However, I had a long memory. My wish came true in 1956 when my husband and I spent a leisurely month on the Tyrrhenian seacoast of southern Italy, driving a small Fiat from Positano on the Amalfi Drive to out-of-the-way places.

Grades were important to me, of course, since they served as one yardstick of competence for admission to medical college. That did not determine my choice of courses, however. I took the subjects that interested me, whether they were noted for being easy or hard to pass. Some risk is involved in that approach, but it should be weighed against the detriments of deliberately limiting one's intellectual initiative during those glorious years of growth. I aimed also for the imaginative teachers, with the guidance of Ginny and her friends. They told me how the different courses were taught and I benefited, especially as a green freshman, from their knowledge and experience.

Knowing my deficiency as a writer, I applied myself energetically to the required freshman course in English composition. My grade of A for the first term delighted me. During the second semester, under the supervision of the English Department faculty several of us in the "Comp" class initiated a freshman literary magazine called *The Twig*. We published five issues. While Editor-in-chief, I acquired a large measure of respect for an editor's job. On May 4, 1919, I wrote my parents: "Did I ever tell you that I am editor-in-chief of the freshman paper, the TWIG? The only trouble is that there is an awful lot of work attached to the editing of a paper. There are hundreds of themes which have to be read, and which I must have every one of my editors read. That last is the worst. As for printing, arranging, proof-reading, editors' meetings, seeing faculty, oh my!"

A week later I wrote to reassure my alarmed physician-father that I was not neglecting my other work for the publishing business: "I have been burning the midnight oil this week, but evidently you don't understand that one girl is editor-in-chief for only *one* issue. You should have seen me leading an editors meeting last night, consisting of six girls & 2 faculty. It lasted from 7:30 till 9:45."

My own essay in an earlier issue of *The Twig* dealt with the life and character of John Masefield, Poet Laureate of England, as revealed in his writings. By my process of selection, the composition disclosed as much about my insights, I think, as about his. I wrote in *The Twig:*

Masefield's desires for a free and active life were satisfied when his father indentured him at the age of fourteen to the captain of a deep-sea-going sloop. . . . He came to love the sea in all its moods, when its great, blue-green rollers sparkled under tropic skies, and when its icy spray stung the hands and faces of the half-frozen sailors as they clung to the swaying ropes and fought the flapping sails. . . . Masefield endured such hardships that at length he left the sea and became an assistant bartender on Sixth Avenue in New York. He did not remain here long, however, for he was born a wanderer. He tramped westwards, through the country, working as a farm laborer. . . . Masefield returned to England to write. His experiences had been among the roughest . . . of men. . . . He had seen the agonies of shipwreck and knew the cold, the dreariness, and the fatigue of a sailor's life. He had lived among the poorest and most degraded in a big city, and had toiled throughout the country. . . . He had not stood at one side and watched the sufferings of others, but had felt their pain himself. . . . It's a hard life for laborers, but they live in a world of beauty, and Masefield, poet and toiler, never forgets the beauty. . . . There is, perhaps, another glory in the work of the lowest classes, which may be discovered in his writings. Men slave, uncared for, miserable in sickness, fighting desperately against the forces of nature, but it is their sublime privilege to supply the needs of an advancing civilization. If there were none to till the land in rain, in cold, in scorching heat, none to work in factories, and to give up their lives on the sea that commerce and intercourse between nations might go on, civilization would perish. . . . It is the glorious privilege of the "scum of the earth" to toil for the life of the world, both physical and intellectual. This truth Masefield has subtly woven into his writings, and by the power of the poet has made us appreciate the difficult accomplishments of the workman.

In the fall of 1918 when I entered Wellesley, the United States was fighting World War I, and by late September the country was being overwhelmed by the deadly influenza epidemic. Academic work stopped at Vassar and Smith, but at Wellesley classes continued. Students were not permitted, however, to ride in any form of public transportation or to enter any public places. The freshmen were not allowed to visit in the dormitories of the upper classes on the campus—we were all housed in the village dorms. The quarantine drew our freshman class close together.

My dormitory then was Noanett. Its large dining hall served our fifty-eight girls and two "Village Seniors," as well as students from several smaller freshman houses in the "Vill." On September 21, 1918, during "Freshman Week," I wrote to my parents:

No, studies haven't begun yet. . . . You should have seen me last night. I was helping two roommates put in extra lights in their room. One was Emmavail Luce, born in China, daughter of a professor in a large English University there—the other, Margaret Eddy, born in India, daughter of Sherwood Eddy, missionary. We climbed up mountains and mountains of tall bureaus, chairs, desks, tables, etc. and almost died of laughter. The tears fairly streamed down our faces. We changed those various lights four times, and about roused the dead in the process. One of the Village Seniors has Spanish Influenza.

With lots of love,
Bobby

A month later I was enthusiastic about the diverse people and activities in the new world of college.

October 19, 1918

Dearest Family:

All the girls in Noanett are perfectly lovely. The Freshman song leader, Margaret Eddy, lives here. . . . Today has been so thrilling!!!!! This is the anniversary of Miss Pendleton's inauguration [as President of the College], the last day of the Liberty Loan drive [for war bonds], Sophomore Serenade and today all those who made teams were announced! Oh thrills! [I made the tennis team.] . . . In the ten minutes between classes the Freshmen gathered, & sang songs & cheered to persuade people to buy bonds. We covered ourselves with glory in both the words and spirit of our songs. We are considered one of the nicest and peppiest Freshman classes that ever came to college, even though I do say so.

Like everyone else, I worked for the war effort, making surgical dressings and knitting sweaters for the Red Cross, weeding and harvesting vegetables as a "Farmerette," and doing odd jobs to help raise Wellesley's quota of $20,000 in war bonds. To earn my contribution I waited on table in Noanett while two of the waitresses were ill, I polished shoes and made up beds. I even rented out my precious bicycle.

When I arrived at Wellesley in the midst of the war fervor, I was surprised by the absence of newspapers and lack of student interest in day-to-day events. In my letter of September 21, I begged: "Please, *please* send me the *Times*. I haven't seen a paper, haven't hardly heard a word of war news this week, and if I'm going to be *at all* intelligent, I must have a paper. If I had the *New Republic* I would never have time to read much of it, but I would read the paper every day, somewhat." On September 28, I wrote, dissatisfied: "Thank you for the *New Republic*. Won't you please send me the *Times?*" I did not wait for it indefinitely: "November 14. Four of us are taking the *New York Times* together, so I see the paper every day now." But I could not accept silently the apathy toward current world news. On November 15, I wrote my parents about English composition: "We got back the big theme of the first three months, and mine was an A, the only one. It was about 'The Importance of the Newspapers.' " I must have made my point. Like my mother, I can not go to sleep, no matter how late the night is, until I have scanned the day's papers.

In the transition from high school to college, several surprises were in store for me besides the scarcity of daily news reports. I knew that there were rules about overnight chaperones and being in the dorms by 10 P.M., but life at college was more regimented than I had anticipated from attending a liberal day school and living at home in relative independence. I disliked the loud harsh bells everywhere that ordered us to get up, go to bed, and eat meals, and that announced the change of classes. Those alarms created an atmosphere of hurry and frustration; I went hungry if the dining room doors shut ten seconds before I arrived. During wartime then, the doctrine of the "clean plate" ruled, and to avoid waste the minimum amount of food was served. From Noanett I reported to my family: "You get *just* enough to eat if you don't eat between meals. You are always starving at mealtime, however. The Head of the House, Miss Snyder, was a dietician before she came here, so we are supposed to get excellently balanced food." Nearly every letter that I wrote home contained a request or thanks for some special item—molasses cookies, jelly, cocoa, cake, home-baked bread, hickory nuts and apples from Merryfield Farm. I must have devoured apples all day long. When team members were "in training" for sports, as I seemed to be most of the time, only fresh fruit might be eaten between meals. Training rules also specified that the girls must be in bed with lights out by 10 P.M. and that they might not arise before 6:30 A.M.— in case they had not done their assignments.

It surprised me how fast money disappeared. I had had little need for cash at home. My frequent letters mentioned that commodity about as often as they did food: "November 26, 1918. Today I learned that two $5 laboratory fees, one chemistry and one physics, were due, which I had forgotten. I need money urgently, since the fees were supposed to be paid today. I will need a check of at least $20, which includes $10 for the trip home." Three days later my estimated budget had increased: "I'm sorry to say that Dot had to lend me $10 for my lab fees, and I *hate* borrowing [like my grandfather Davidson]. Please send me at least $30. I ought to have extra when going home, in case of need, and I might have to spend some before then." I made abstract accountings of my deficit spending: "May 9, 1919. I will have to pay a $10 application fee for next year next week, and so will you please send me some more money? I haven't been extravagant. I had to get a new bike tire (the valve didn't leak and never-leak wouldn't help, so—) and new sneakers, and supper on the lake costs quite a little, and then a little goes to a castle in Spain, some more for a new book and paper and Thrift stamps. I really need some money, please."

My father kept me supplied with postage stamps. Once when I had spent money earmarked for my railroad ticket home, I persuaded the College Post Office to buy the stamps from me and so made up the shortage.

On December 1, 1920, I wrote my parents: "Yesterday I mailed you a letter which I found tucked away in a book. I didn't open it to see when it was written nor what it said. I trust it didn't perplex you." I must have run out of money and stamps.

Problems in higher mathematics were easy for me to solve, but I could not keep up with the pennies in my purse. On the other hand, I was meticulous about many details, like the new system for addressing letters. My father was instructed: "January 22, 1920. By the way, our address henceforth is Wellesley 81. They are using a European postal system in Boston. Please send laundry and all mail with that number," including "aero-mail." It has taken a good many years for the country to catch up with Europe's Zipcode, and with Boston.

I had not realized how important clothes can be until I went off to college. I seemed to need many things all at once. My mother sewed and sent them as fast as she could for Ginny and me to wear. Dresses, skirts, blouses, coats—most of our clothes were made at home, with the assistance sometimes of a dressmaker. We mailed our laundry to New York each week —there were no laundry facilities in the dormitories. On its return the box was likely to contain a surprise piece of wearing apparel. Once my mother sent a new-style dress with a hobble skirt and I was at a loss how to express my thanks:

February 17, 1919

Dearest Family:

I have worn my new dress twice, and I can't tell you all the compliments it has received. The length of skirt is absolutely in the latest fashion, and I'm sure it would just suit Mother who likes long skirts. No, she would surely say it made me look too old. . . . The skirt is quite narrow, which I abominate, but which is also stylish. No, it isn't really uncomfortably tight, just unexpectedly so at times, when I try to go upstairs two steps at a time, or stand in a chair. I really like it immensely,—the dress, I mean.

Although in those years we did not appear in pants even to ride a bicycle, I was accustomed to freedom of action in the cut of my skirts. A few months later, in May of 1919, I wrote with greater enthusiasm: "Dear Mother: I thank you *very* much for the perfectly darling skirt. . . . I am crazy about the pleats." For gym and all sports girls wore white middy blouses, black kerchiefs, and voluminous long bloomers of navy-blue serge. In the autumn of 1919 when I won the college tennis singles and Ginny was runner-up against me, a news picture was taken of us in that sport outfit beside the court. To our dismay it was published in a Boston paper. The caption under our photo read: "TWO WELLESLEY TENNIS EXPERTS

—Two New York girls, the Misses Virginia and Janet Travell, are making a strong bid for tennis honors. They play opposite each other in the Wellesley tournament and are considered among the best all-around athletes in the college. (Keystone View.)" Afterward Ginny wrote home: "Dear Mother and Father: Did I ever tell you about those pictures of Bob & me? The moment I set foot in Beebe [her dormitory] Miss McGregor, Head of House, told me about it, then one of the maids, then a girl who lives in Boston, and Monday Mrs. Hayward in charge of Red Cross told me what a *shame* it was that our pictures were in the paper!"

For young ladies in the New York Social Register such publicity was taboo.

In the spring of 1921, I was one of two juniors—the other was Helen Forbush—to be awarded the highest athletic honor, an Old English "W" and a sweater. That award required a total of at least 80 points. I had earned 44 points in tennis, 22 in indoor baseball, 15 in basketball and 5 in indoor gym. I made the college varsity teams in tennis and indoor baseball, in which my position was catcher. In addition, I played field hockey and rowed on crew, but not for long enough to score any points. It tires me even to think of it, now.

When I came to Wellesley as a freshman, one of my first comments in an early letter to the family was: "Most of the girls are not at all athletic, as far as I can discover." I was mistaken. Until I took standard tests of muscular strength as a part of my freshman physical examination, I had not appreciated that I was unusually strong. On September 18, 1918, I reported: "I was the strongest of the class in the muscles of my hands, arms, back, knees, etc. I could squeeze 33 when 18 was average. Average total strength is 264 and my total was 422, about twice as much as most of the girls." My father always liked excellence. I liked to please him and I was grateful for all that woodchopping at the farm.

At Wellesley it did not take me long to find congenial girls with plenty of stamina and a mutual ardor for the outdoors. On the Columbus Day weekend, the autumn brilliance of the New England foliage was magnified by reflection in the quiet waters of Lake Waban. We followed the wooded campus path along the irregular shoreline for about three miles and I was entranced by the splendor of color. My parents would understand. "Sunday. October 13, 1919. This afternoon Dotty Blossom, Carol Ingham, Mary Allen, Margaret Eddy, Betty Frost, Jo January who is one of Noanett's seniors, and I took a walk around the lake. . . . Mary and I found a tree whose branches hung about two feet above the water. With difficulty we climbed out and stayed there for about half an hour. . . . The other night we had supper on the lake—eleven of us. It was wonderful." We tied the canoes together and sang softly the songs of the First World War while we drifted across the water in the twilight.

The freshman dormitories in the village were a mile from our class-rooms on campus and from the library that overlooked the lake. It was another mile from there to the hockey field, main tennis courts, and the gym. Everyone walked or rode a bicycle. There was no other way to get there. The influenza quarantine prohibited the college students from using taxis, trolleys, or any other public transportation. My parents may have been concerned—but I doubt it—when I wrote them on November 18, 1918:

> Such beautiful weather! Pouring pitchforks! It was all day yesterday and when we awoke today, and is likely to be for some time. Yester-day we became desperate and Ginia,[1] Did [Dorothy Blossom] and I went for a delightful long walk without umbrellas for about two hours. . . . Yes, we were soaked and you are saying we might have caught cold, but we took hot baths when we got home. We waded through puddles, walked on stone walls, and had all the beautiful gray coun-try to ourselves.

I was entranced with the snow. Until then I had not had much deep snow to enjoy except at Albany during Christmas vacations from The Brearley School. At Wellesley on December 7, 1918, I wrote my imper-turbable parents: "It snowed all the night before last and day before yester-day. . . . Yesterday was marvelous, and there was a lot of snow on the ground. . . . I walked three times to campus, morning, afternoon, and evening, and went on a five-mile walk in the afternoon besides, altogether at least eleven miles. I wore my rubber boots, much to everyone's amusement, and jumped into deep drifts as often as I pleased." When my schedule al-lowed only an hour between classes at noon, I carried a "bag lunch" from Noanett.

Since indoor recreation in public places was "verboten" during the in-fluenza epidemic, several of us stirred up excitement with a Saturday out-ing.

November 9, 1918

Dear Mother and Father:

> Ten of us from Noanett hired a horse and wagon, a regular de-livery wagon which was filled with straw. [I named it the "Fool's Liv-ery."] We provided about 50 cushions, 10 blankets, and extra sweaters and coats besides what we wore, the number of which was tremendous. . . . You can gather that it is cold here. Three of us sat on the seat

[1] At Wellesley College, my sister began to sign her name as Ginie, and sometimes I called her Ginia, but usually I wrote Ginny.

and the rest in back and one rode the horse which was very fat and somewhat lazy. We took turns riding. We invented a song for each of us to the tune of "Where, oh, where are the green young freshmen? . . . Down, down in the world below." I went down on my big blue numerals [1922], and my last words were "Will you sew on my W?" . . . We went to South Natick, a cider mill, where we all had cider and bought some to bring home. Then we went to Natick where we had hot dogs, and came sailing home. All together I doubt whether it cost $5, and the fun we had was well worth it.

Those were carefree days, in spite of the mounting toll from the flu and the war. In October, 1918, my cousin, Arthur Travell, died of influenza during his sophomore year at Cornell University in Ithaca. At Wellesley, we were fortunate to have only one influenza death, although there were hundreds of cases, including myself.

Two days after our hayride, on the date that became the national holiday Armistice Day, I wrote my parents in the morning:

Peace at last!! . . . This morning at 4:30 A.M., we woke up and heard cannons going off one right after another. So we got up out of bed and piled downstairs, all shouting and talking, and making a great racket in what seemed the middle of the night. We went out on the porch and sang the Star Spangled Banner, and with difficulty persuaded ourselves to return to bed. We were all up for good at 6 A.M., and a lot of us went down to the vill, saw the flag raised, and serenaded an early train. . . . We are so happy and excited!

That evening, another letter continued:

There were cuts in classes in the afternoon, and about ⅚ of the college rushed in to Boston to celebrate. [The ban on riding in a public conveyance had been lifted.] Ginia, Dotty and I went to Natick on our bikes, and had dinner with Helen Forbush and her family. . . . We lost track of time. When we started we had 12 minutes to reach home in the vill—4 miles on bikes in pitch blackness. We just did it, and reached Noanett exhausted. Imagine—a rate of 20 miles an hour! We peddled down hill and up hill, and never stopped for breath or speech. . . . Ginia, Dotty and a lot of us are walking to Boston tomorrow! Holiday!

Concerning that hike my next letter merely said: "Ginia has told you all about our wonderful walk—20 miles. I was rather tired when I got home, but felt able to wait on table at dinner, which takes at least an hour and is hard work for the trays are very heavy. I was scarcely stiff the next day." As a substitute waitress, I earned 25 cents an hour, $3 per week, toward my war-bond pledge.

The Kaiser had abdicated on November 9, and two days later the German army surrendered, but after the cheering we still had to pay the costs of the war. At Wellesley our work for the Red Cross and the drives for Liberty Bonds continued. The students took an active interest, too, in the League of Nations and the rehabilitation of Europe. On December 7, 1918, I wrote:

Dearest Family:
    Polly Snow had dinner with me, and afterward we all went to hear Dr. Kallen, who is a representative of the League of Nations at the Peace table, or a member of Col. House's Commission. He spoke very well about the League of Nations. He explained what it had been, what it was hoped it would be, and he urged us to write our Senators and Congressmen to advocate its being formally constituted at the peace table. So *you* can do it for me, explaining that it will act for international trade on land and sea as our Interstate Commerce Commission does for trade among our states. Will you? . . . I went to a tea given by Vail [Emmavail] for the Chinese girls in college. . . .

Con molto amore a voi due,
Bobby

World War I had ended, but the folly of war was forever impressed on my consciousness.

The sociable habits of hiking, canoeing, and picnicking that I and my energetic freshman friends established in our first term stayed with us through college. Eleanor McArdle, Grace Osgood, Maddi Josephi, Emily Gordon, Cat Ashburner, and I, with others, often hiked to Natick for a supper of hot dogs and ice cream cones, or we took our food out on the lake in canoes. In the spring of my sophomore year when I lived in Cazenove Hall, Mary Hering, Class of 1920, and I on certain mornings, rain or shine, ran a mile together before breakfast. Lois Childs and Emmavail Luce and I occasionally rode the college horses on trails through the open woods. In winter, Ginny and I and our friends skated on the smooth-frozen ice of Lake Waban at night by the light of the bright stars. I skied down Tower Court Hill—a popular sport when the deep snow was well packed. On Washington's Birthday, February 22, 1922, I wrote my parents that "eight of us hiked to the Wayside Inn in a gorgeous snowstorm, and had a delicious chicken dinner." The Inn was only about thirteen miles from the campus, via Natick and the back roads. A letter written during my commencement week tells how on June 11, 1922, Jo Fleming, Wooly (Cynthia) Lamb, Class of 1924, and I spent the hottest day of the year canoeing up the Charles River from Lake Waban. We paddled twenty-five miles in eleven hours, starting at 8:30 A.M. and taking an hour and a half out for a swim.

We changed positions in the canoe "every half hour: bow——→stern——→ loaf——→repeat, so that each one paddled an hour for a half hour's rest. . . . We look like Indians now." I was so sunburned that I was scarcely presentable at graduation. The following summer I visited Wooly Lamb at Denver and learned from her about mountain climbing in the high Colorado Rockies.

My friends and Ginny's came to Merryfield Farm during the summers and to our home in New York for vacations. I became an experienced guide around town for first-time visitors to the city. We even climbed the Statue of Liberty. Those Wellesley friendships that were founded on our extracurricular activities have endured for a lifetime.

In September, 1921, I brought our seven-year-old Model T Lizzie— Ophelia Bump—from Merryfield Farm to stay on campus with me at Norumbega Hall. I was one of the few seniors to have a car at Wellesley then. Ophelia made it easy for me to get to classes, to the village, to Natick and Boston. Under the circumstances, my consistent devotion to the hardy outdoor life might well have waned that year, but it did not.

Ophelia held a warm spot in the hearts of my college friends and a large place in my correspondence with the family—Ginny was at medical school in New York that year. "May 7, 1922. Ophelia is invaluable. . . . I just took her on a Museum trip to Cambridge with a full crew." We were collecting source material for the final paper in Miss Avery's senior art course. When Ophelia parked at the curb, people in town smiled to see her name painted in our class color, purple, across the front of her brass radiator—I had repainted the rest of her standard black, like "any good-looking stove." Bystanders thought it a novelty to see me spin her engine with the crank. She started harder if the batteries were old or the weather bitter cold, as it usually was during the long winter. Spring came late and on March 17 I pictured the scene on campus: "I am gazing at a wintry world. The ground is covered with gray-white melting snow, the sky is leaden gray, the chapel is cold gray stone, the paint on the corner of the Ad Building is dirty white, and even the trees are gray, frosted with ice." Ophelia's chains had hard wear.

The Model T opened up new territory for us to explore, as far away as Mount Monadnock in New Hampshire. On a Saturday afternoon in mid-May, five of us drove to the Shattuck Inn in Jaffrey, 1,200 feet high on the slope of the mountain. My written account revives vivid memories:

We came in Ophelia without any trouble in 3½ hours including stops [about 80 miles]. She's running like a dream. . . . After dinner we went riding around a wild lake until we found a place to swim. We three in my room got up early, took Ophelia and went swimming be-

fore breakfast. After much fuss about a fire permit, we got started up
the mountain—altitude 3,100 feet. We took the steep trail up—about
two hours going at a medium rate. . . . It's a lovely rocky summit
and after lunch we lay on the rocks and read for some three hours.
. . . Sunday night we all felt gay, but about 11:30 I studied a little
for my Zoo quiz Monday morning. Our room settled to sleep about 2,
and we all rose at 4:30 A.M. The ride home was glorious especially
since we got lost in the wild back woods mountains of New Hampshire. When we passed a rare house, no one was up. There was an
early morning fog in the valleys and a sunrise. Just outside Wellesley
we had three blow-outs in succession. Two came together because
when fixing the first, we didn't discover a rip at the side in the canvas
[of the shoe]. One was in the *new front* tire. . . . The split is about 6″
long and I have an insecure blowout patch in it now so that I can't
really drive. It may go any minute. . . . I have no spare for the
front. There is a brand new *rear* tire on the rack. [Her front and back
shoes were not the same size.] . . . I want to drive down to the
shore Saturday. . . . Otherwise Ophelia is working like a charm.

We were not even late for classes. I carried a patching kit for Ophelia's
pneumatic inner tubes and blowout patches for a break in a casing. It was
only a matter of minutes for us to patch a hole, put the tire back on the rim,
and pump it up.

Ophelia's engine and delicate electrical system presented more of a
problem. Fortunately, my mother and I had overhauled her one summer at
Merryfield Farm. In addition, during junior year at Wellesley as part of my
premedical credits in physics, I had taken Miss Lucy Wilson's practical
course in automobile engineering, with a field trip to the assembly line of a
Ford factory. I was well versed in my car's idiosyncrasies.

May 12, 1922

I tried to install that device, but couldn't get the locknut off the end
of the cam shaft. I took the radiator off in the process and put on a
new hose connection because the other one leaked. Cleaned the timer
and spark plugs, and dosed the cylinders with kerosene. No. 3 simply
wouldn't run, and I finally took the coil box apart, wherein I found
some wax right on the inner contact, and the trouble was cured.

Like many enigmas of medicine, the solution to the seemingly complex
problem was simple when the cause had been pinpointed.

Ophelia was then eight years old. With her future in mind I asked my
parents: "How much is Ophelia worth? Would you like me to sell her, say,
to some junior? [To me, her worth was incalculable.] Today I overhauled
her, looking for source of trouble, and found it in the commutator wires."

Soon after our trip to Mount Monadnock, I answered my father's question as to whether my Uncle Warren could use her in California. "Ophelia is behaving most excellently, but I *don't* think she would stand a long cross-continent trip, and this is why. The crack in the water head is open, and cannot be permanently mended, I fear. She is all right around here on the level, but the water circulation is not perfect and Ophelia heats up on hills." At the farm one fall, an early freeze had caught us before we drained the water out of the cylinder head. Its cast-iron jacket cracked in a thin line. I discovered that if we plastered the crack with chewing gum while the engine was hot, the water leakage was reduced for some time. At Norumbega, when a fresh repair job was needed, we stood around Ophelia behind the dormitory and chewed packages of gum while Mac—Eleanor McArdle—led us in her song that began, "Oh, chew for Ophelia!"

That handicap would have disabled many a car, but not Ophelia.

Mac ultimately purchased Ophelia for one dollar. The old Model T flivver gave good service while Mac taught in the high school at Ridgewood, New Jersey, where my Uncle Winthrop was the Superintendent of Schools. Gertrude Joslin, another friend of ours, taught there likewise and later inherited the car. Ophelia kept going. Gertrude sent me a picture postcard of Ophelia dated September 3, 1925, with the message: "Ophelia sends her love. She has been inactive this summer because I was at camp. . . . I expect she'll go beautifully next week when I start for N.J." Ophelia's age was twelve then. As a memento for myself, I saved her big black Klaxon. When my father was advanced in years, he had that Klaxon horn on his bedside table to summon breakfast when he awoke. Ophelia's voice could be heard from top to bottom of the house.

The new horizon that I valued most at Wellesley was the larger world of diverse people. I did not limit my friendships to any small coterie or clique. I ranged widely for my friends in all the Classes, wherever I found overlapping interests. There were, for instance, my tennis pals. When a senior, I held the office of Head of Tennis in the Athletic Association. I was responsible then for selecting the freshman tennis team, presiding at meetings and participating in the activities of the A.A. board. I had won the Wellesley singles championship for three years. My last year at college I lost it to a sophomore and my doubles partner in the tournament. I served as Secretary of the Christian Association in my sophomore year and as a committee chairman and member of that organization's governing board when I was a Junior. For two weeks between my freshman and sophomore years, Ginny and I attended an intercollegiate religious conference conducted by Dr. Henry Sloane Coffin at Silver Bay on Lake George, New York. In our freshman year, the Class of 1922 had elected Dr. Coffin, Minister of New York's Madison Avenue Presbyterian Church, our honorary member.

A social group to which I belonged was the Zeta Alpha Society, and during my senior year I was its Treasurer. My mother and sister were members of that one of Wellesley's six non-national sororities. I suppose that I had an average number of dates and it was pleasant to have the Z.A. House as a place to cook Sunday morning breakfast and to entertain guests indoors. My congenial cousin, Graham Davidson, was studying aeronautical engineering at the Massachusetts Institute of Technology in Cambridge, and he came out to Wellesley for some special events. I invited two men to our Senior Prom and I filled their dance cards in advance with the most popular '22 girls. Perhaps I should say, *only* two men; my husband entertained four girls at his commencement dances in 1919 at the University of North Carolina and he booked their dance cards in the same way. To college students now, that seems a bizarre custom, but for us it ensured diversity of acquaintance.

Student attitude toward smoking differed then, too: smoking was forbidden anywhere on the Wellesley campus. In my senior year, infringement of that rule was punished by suspension from classes for two or three weeks, or with repetition of the offense a girl might be expelled from college. Some girls smoked at home and they wanted the rule modified. Under the democratic process of our Student Government Association, a referendum was submitted to the student body at the polls when officers of the college organizations were elected. With some satire our 1922 *Legenda of Wellesley College* gave the verdict:

ODE TO WELLESLEY COLLEGE
From the Anti-Tobacconist League

Oh, Wellesley, let us crack our throats
To give you praise indeed—
Because your students by a vote
Eschewed the noxious weed.
The seniors up to freshman came,
And asked them if they ought
Associate with one who smoked.
Oh, never!—Horrid thought!
Public opinion you aroused,
With questions swift and cogent;
And to the question, "Shall we smoke?"
Your righteous, thundering "NO!" sent.

The students did not always unanimously accept the disciplinary action of their student government. About an episode of indiscreet swimming at night in the fall of my senior year, I wrote my sister in New York:

> You remember the cases of swimming, Ginny? In the latest scandal, today '22, '23 and '24 held class meetings and sent in protests to the Senate [of Student Government]. Mark [Hanna] and Mid [Margaret Eddy] and I called our meeting by getting up a petition to discuss it. The A.A. Board was unanimously agreed in sending its protest. . . . Besides that, a general all-college petition has gone to the Senate concerning the severity of the penalty for the four girls—six weeks suspension and no offices or honors!—and the Senate is up in the air. There is a freshman-sophomore debate tonight: Resolved that the names, *facts* and penalties of all special cases decided by the Senate be made public. . . . And lastly, Miss Manwaring [Assistant Professor of English Composition] is getting up a petition to be signed by the faculty to ask the students to please be more quiet. This is the age of petitions and certainly of agitation and governmental revolution. The Senate and House have been calling each other bad names all year, you know, privately and officially.

Our idealistic involvement in causes and our wholehearted willingness to work for them were the same traits that college students display now. Although our goals were sometimes shortsighted, we pursued them, to the distraction of the faculty, with a tenacity that in our later years was re-labeled "motivation" or "drive." According to the circumstances, such intense dedication may be an asset or a liability. It is an essential ingredient for accomplishment in the profession of medicine.

I was experienced in circulating petitions, even concerning the academic curriculum. In January, 1922, we thought it unfair for the faculty to schedule classes on the day before midterm examinations began; it penalized those students who had to prepare for tests on the first day of the period. I said,

> We got up another petition, signed by 1,000 students (two thirds of the college), asking that the Tuesday before exams begin, on Wednesday, be free from academic appointments. Lo and behold, we got it! But you should have heard the Dean when she announced it at chapel! Sarcastic isn't the word! She ended by giving out the last hymn, "Work for the night is coming," and the whole long rest of it. . . . The choir shook with laughter all the way down the aisle.

I was never in awe of the faculty. In March of my freshman year, I wrote: "Dear Mother and Father; This morning I went to call on my faculty advisor, Miss Waite. Peter [Mary Allen] went with me. Miss Waite, the Dean, and another faculty were there. We had a delightful time. It is surprising how very charming such imposing and important personages can be. Dean Waite seemed to accredit us with as much intelligence as she had, and seemed quite interested in our opinions." I acted accordingly. I did not hesitate to ask for special permission.

As a senior, I took the course in elementary German. I had not studied that language since Brearley School and I knew that it would be difficult for me. The class procedure, I found, was for one student to read aloud her composition in German and for the others to correct it. I went to Fräulein Wipplinger, Head of the Department, and counting on her liberal European background I asked her to excuse me from attending her class.

"I could use the time to better advantage working by myself," I told her. "The errors that are read out loud are not the same as my mistakes. Anyway, you read and correct our essays. I will send mine to you on time and I will get back your comments. That is what is important. I will learn German script and write in it." That appealed to her. She agreed that my request was reasonable and with special permission I cut that class for the year. In both semesters my grade was A.

I elected advanced chemistry and advanced physics in my senior year. I wrote my father: "I am by special permission taking a course called 'Recent developments in electricity' which includes the electric disassociation theory; conduction through gasses; cathode rays, Roentgen rays; radio-activity and the electron theory. I am quite thrilled, because the course isn't logically open to me at all." I had not taken the prerequisite intermediate credits in physics. The laboratory hours conflicted with those of my organic chemistry course—no student took both at once. Miss Bragg, Head of Chemistry, solved the dilemma by giving me a key to the chemistry building and allowing me to do experiments there on my own time, often in the evening. The final examinations were scheduled at the same hour; Miss Bragg agreeably held a separate one for me. With special permission I enrolled in a graduate seminar in zoology. I had arranged a stiff schedule for myself.

My anxiety about my work was compounded when in late October, 1921, I was one of seven girls in our class who were elected to the Phi Beta Kappa Society on the basis of three years' scholastic achievement. I was surprised to be feted with orchids and parties. Ginny had a Phi Beta Kappa key, too, and I wrote the family: "I'm glad if you were pleased. I'll try not to live on my reputation for the rest of the year." Sometimes I was greeted by the snide remark, "Now that you've made Phi Bete, you won't have to do a lick of work." My reaction was the opposite. For the first time at Wellesley, that year I made "straight A."

I learned that exceptions could be made not only to academic rules, but also to social restrictions at college. When I lived on the top floor of Cazenove Hall, the house mother granted me permission to sleep on the roof. Even to go on the roof was against the rules, except in case of fire. At the end of my corridor was a ladder with a trapdoor to the roof, which had a low stone parapet. At bedtime on a clear night, I dragged my pillow and blankets up the ladder and slept on the hard brick under the stars in the crisp fresh air where I could listen to the wind. It was an exhilarating experience.

When Ophelia Bump was parked outside Norumbega Hall, I persuaded that house mother to approve as my chaperone my first cousin, Winthrop Travell, then a student at Dartmouth College. He was exactly like a brother to me, I claimed. When he came for the weekend, we set off together to see the country.

At Wellesley I learned how to balance work and play. I was not absorbed in studying to the exclusion of extracurricular activities, nor vice versa. My spare time shrank to the vanishing point, but I usually completed my assignments well ahead of time. I could discipline and command my mind. I obtained deeper satisfaction from the performance of intellectual tasks than from my energetic participation in sports, which were important to my health and a happy attitude.

When the time of 1922's Commencement finally arrived in June, the prerogatives of achievement crowned us, the outgoing senior class. We paraded in cap and gown to hoop rolling, step-singing, and academic functions. We had reached the top of the ladder in that domain. My mother's thirtieth alumnae reunion and my sister's first reunion at Wellesley were of secondary importance to me. My parents and sister came up for my gradaution.

Not long before, in May, the Cornell University Medical College in New York had accepted me for admission to the first-year class in the fall. Cornell was the only medical school to which I had applied—again I knew what I wanted. It was perhaps unwise to put all my eggs in one basket in that way, but I believed that a strong preference for a particular college weighed heavily in the decisions of an admitting committee. I relied on my expressed preference for Cornell, on my academic record, and my long, consistent interest in a medical career.

I knew how demanding was the profession of medicine; I had witnessed the tedious hours and hard work that my father gave to his medical practice, but his unfailing enthusiasm for it was contagious. He and I never discussed any special hardships or prejudices that the doctor who was a woman might encounter. I think that those were taken for granted. We also assumed that whatever the obstacles, Ginny and I would surmount them. I had confidence because he had confidence in me. Actually, in years to come I found that discrimination against me as a physician, because of my sex, was almost nonexistent.

I never wavered in my plan to study medicine, although at Wellesley I was influenced by my regard for my Uncle Warren, the engineer, to consider a career in his field. My science credits would have allowed me to switch from a premedical course to engineering until my junior year. Uncle Warren's enthusiasm for the unknown realms of mathematics, astronomy, and geology was as contagious as my father's for the conundrums of biology and human life processes. I was tender-hearted like my mother and it hurt me to see any person or creature suffer. I wondered whether that would disqualify me from a medical career. On the other hand, I loved people and their problems. I could not picture myself working in a world of inanimate objects and mathematical values. Engineering was definitely not my life work.

Non Ministrari Sed Ministrare—not to be ministered unto but to minister —is the Wellesley motto. The all-around training that I gained at college there stood me in good stead throughout my many years of "Office Hours: Day and Night."

CHAPTER 9

Home

After four restless years at Wellesley College and a student grand tour of Europe during the summer of 1922, that September in New York I suddenly realized that I had come home. I was at home with my parents and my sister in a pleasant house at 40 Fifth Avenue, at home in the city of privacy and opportunity where I had grown up, and at home in medical school, the new world of mature men and women that had been my dream for years. The doors and windows of my life were opened wide and fresh breezes blew through. My college years shrank to diminutive proportions; they seemed then like an almost wasted interlude, a time of waiting until I could embark on the real purposes of my existence.

No graduate student ever enjoyed a more favorable climate for work than Ginny and I did while we lived at home in New York and attended the old Cornell University Medical College on First Avenue at 28th Street opposite Bellevue Hospital. The long hours of indoor study were balanced by our pattern of invigorating outdoor activity. From Fifth Avenue at 10th Street Ginny and I walked together about two miles to classes, whatever the weather. We usually met to walk home after classes at five-thirty or six o'clock in winter's early darkness when the tall office buildings were still lighted. As we walked diagonally across Madison Square, the Flatiron Building loomed to the south in the wedge between Broadway and Fifth Avenue and to the east the Metropolitan Life Insurance Building topped the skyline beyond the old Madison Square Garden. Our books and notebooks were wrapped against the wet and were strapped together with leather straps. We dispensed with umbrellas. Ginny and I made better time walking in the morning than at the end of the day; then we might take the I.R.T. subway from Fourth Avenue and 28th Street to 14th Street at Union Square.

Our parents' first concern appeared to be our study of medicine. They made no social demands on our limited time. They protected us from material cares. Meals at home were scheduled to suit our needs, and my mother packed paper-bag lunches for us early in the morning. I usually ate my sandwiches while I worked at a laboratory desk or studied in the library or in the women students' small lounge. Sometimes at lunch hour, when time and weather permitted, we walked out onto an East River pier at 26th or 30th Street and watched the tide of oil-slick water slide past.

The Cornell medical school had no dormitory, no student cafeteria, and no facilities for exercise or recreation. There was no "college life" and no great feeling of class loyalty. There were no freshmen or seniors, only first- and fourth-year men and women. Medical students from out of town—both Ginny's and my friends who found living in New York unnatural—came to our home to study and laugh by our open fires. My mother fed them generously with her homecooked food.

My Class of 1926 graduated sixty-three students, nine of whom were women (14.3 percent), and Ginny's Class of 1925 contributed fifty-eight doctors with twelve women (20.7 percent). The competition to enter medical school was not as keen then as it is now, and at that time an appreciable number of qualified young men had had a medical education deferred by World War I.

Work began in the dissection room at 9 A.M. on the day that college opened. We spent every morning there until noon, six days a week for two trimesters of the first year. Anatomy was the major course that year; we had to know well the structure of the human body that is fundamental to the practice of medicine and surgery. We walked up the three flights to the anatomy lab on the top floor. The large room was well lighted by skylight, like a studio, and it was well ventilated although its atmosphere smelled mildly antiseptic. There was nothing ghoulish about it. I never had qualms about dissecting a cadaver. The techniques were not strange to me after my advanced course in comparative mammalian anatomy at Wellesley, in which I had dissected formalinized animals. The dead do not suffer.

Years later, I asked a man why he had not followed his father and grandfather in the study of medicine—his interest in it was obvious—and he replied, "I could not face the idea of the dissecting room."

The deftness of my fingers and my powers of concentration enabled me to complete our laboratory assignments way ahead of schedule. Dr.

Charles R. Stockard, Professor of Anatomy and Chairman of the Department, in his elegantly cut and stiffly starched, long, white coat hourly around the room, inspecting each student's dissection. He held great power because a failure in anatomy could mean that the student would not be promoted to the second year. At my table, he would stop and shake his head disapprovingly.

"Miss Travell, you dissect too fast. You can't have learned all that you should about the structures in that time."

"But I have, Dr. Stockard. Please let me show you."

I pointed out to him the course of nerves and blood vessels, their branches, the attachments of muscles and relations to neighboring parts, and I expounded their function and anatomical variations. He did not stump me with his questions about the assignment. Dissatisfied, he moved on to the next student while I moved over to a center free table. I looked up pertinent facts in my big anatomy textbook and sketched cross-sectional material for my notebook.

Then it occurred to me that I could train my left hand for greater dexterity. I shifted the scalpel over from my right hand. Although I dissected clumsily at first and made some bad slips of the knife, the slowed pace of my left-handed dissecting matched the average speed of the class. No one noticed my new technique. At home I practiced even eating left-handed—it prolonged our meals at first, but my family understood. Although I am truly right-handed and have a dominant right eye, my left hand can now manage a soup spoon or a syringe with facility. I am grateful to Dr. Stockard for the fringe benefits of his regimented teaching. When I learned later that he had been Professor of Military Science and Tactics at the Mississippi Agricultural and Mechanical College, I realized what I had been up against.

After Christmas that winter, I received an invitation to the annual Winter Carnival at Dartmouth College. It was irresistible. The trip to New Hampshire and the series of parties and dances would necessitate my cutting classes at the medical school for a whole week. I knew that I could never obtain special permission for such truancy. My magician father had taught me how to keep a secret and none of my classmates were aware of my plans. Then unexpectedly I found myself in a predicament. The week before I intended to vanish, Dr. Stockard stopped beside me at work and said, with the manner of one bestowing a valued gift,

"Miss Travell, how would you like to give the bone quiz next Monday?"

The "bone quiz" was an honor and special mark of his favor. For each Monday conference of that trimester, a top student was invited to lead the discussion and to quiz the class, while Dr. Stockard and other faculty members of the Department of Anatomy sat in the front row. I would not be there.

"Oh, no, Dr. Stockard. I couldn't," I gasped in dismay.

"Now, don't be nervous about it—you can do it as well as anyone else, Miss Travell."

"It isn't that. I just can't do it," I said lamely.

"Miss Travell—you mean you *won't* do it?" He could hardly believe my words.

"Yes, Dr. Stockard."

"I see," he said sarcastically and walked on.

I wondered whether the Winter Carnival would be worth his ire. Afterward, I decided that it was. Returning on the sleeper to New York Sunday night, weary from skiing and dancing, I lived the engrossing hours again and thought that they had exceeded my finest expectations. But that Monday morning I entered the anatomy lab with trepidation. Sitting on my high stool, I busied myself assiduously with the dissection as Dr. Stockard approached.

"Good morning, Miss Travell." His voice was quiet and ominous. "I see that you have been absent from class."

"Yes, Dr. Stockard."

"I hope that you weren't spending the time in bed?" He studied my face.

"No, indeed, Dr. Stockard." I made no explanation. The Sphinx had nothing on either of us.

Later, Dr. Stockard was ill for a short while and Dr. Charles Morrill, Associate Professor of Anatomy, stopped at my table. The trimester and the course were nearing their end.

"How is it that you haven't given a bone quiz this year, Miss Travell? Would you like to take the next one?"

"I would be truly delighted, Dr. Morrill."

Fate had played into my hands. On that Monday, Dr. Stockard sat in the front row while I conducted the class.

In June at the close of the medical school year, we filed into the Dean's office and were notified whether we had passed or failed each course. That was all. No grades were given out until graduation. Four years after the Dartmouth ski carnival, I learned my marks in the three courses that I had cut that week: histology 95, biochemistry 95, and anatomy 95. Dr. Stockard, in spite of his M.S., Ph.D., M.D., and Sc.D. must have been more human than I judged.

Physiology was the main course in the third trimester of our first year at medical college. In that subject, with all its mechanical apparatus and my prior training in biology by my father and at Wellesley, I felt completely at home. The eminent scientist Dr. Graham Lusk, Professor and Chairman of the Department, was an inspiring teacher, although he was so deaf that he could hardly hear himself speak. Sometimes his voice rose to a shout and sometimes its volume dropped to a hoarse whisper, but his eyes sparkled with intensity of feeling. We were spellbound by the living meaning that he gave to physiological facts and by his vision of physiological research in the future.

When the physiology class worked in sections for special experiments that ran simultaneously in our day-long laboratory sessions, I was asked to be a student assistant in the teaching. I checked apparatus for the next exercise, premedicated animals early in the morning before class, and then demonstrated the experimental techniques that I had just learned. I kept about one week ahead of my classmates in the course. They were hard critics. To teach is to learn, and my grade of 98 in physiology showed me later that I did not waste that opportunity.

That was my first taste of formal teaching. It was one career that had never interested me and it did not appeal to me then. Besides, I thought that I had no talent for it. At Wellesley, I had now and then helped a friend who was having difficulty with a science course. Emmavail Luce autographed her picture for me with the inscription, "Rescued by Bobby from the mire of Physics." Eleanor McArdle—Mac, who inherited Ophelia Bump—liked to tell how I coached her for a week when she was warned that she was failing freshman chemistry. After my tutoring—she was an apt pupil—she passed the final examination with such a high mark that she had to take an oral test to prove that she had not cheated. But at college and at medical school, even in the farthest reaches of my imagination I never pictured myself as the full-time instructor in a preclinical science department that I would become.

My Wellesley major in inorganic chemistry gave me the grounding to enjoy the intensive course in biological chemistry during my first year at Cornell medical school. Dr. Stanley R. Benedict, Chairman of the Department, who devised the quantitative procedure for sugar determination that is still in use in medical laboratories, told us how biochemistry was providing keys to many mysteries of life. The term *molecular biology* did not achieve stature until years later, but even then biochemical methods were beginning to unfold the role of the body's "internal secretions," such as insulin and the hormones of the thyroid, adrenal, "generative," and other "ductless" glands.

Dr. Benedict encouraged me to pursue a small research project in order to answer a question of mine concerning insulin, a compound discovered by Banting and Best only about three years earlier. A liberal supply of that pancreatic hormone was just becoming available for treatment and for investigation. For a while after school closed in June, 1923, pipetting and titrating chemical solutions, I sat on a high stool in the laboratory on the second floor. It overlooked First Avenue and it had no air-conditioning. In New York's humid summer heat and grime, to the roar of trucks heard through wide-open windows, Professor Benedict stood in his natty short white coat and chatted with me about medical education and my future. His dry humor broke through his strong personal reserve.

"Miss Travell, you will waste your time in clinical medicine. You should quit after the two years of basic science here and then go into laboratory research. Medical schools should offer two divergent courses, one pointed toward the practice of medicine and the other toward a career in medical science. That's where the future of medicine lies, in fundamental research—in biochemistry, of course."

I had no intention of becoming a medical school dropout.

"Dr. Benedict, I like people too much to spend my days in a laboratory. I can't see myself ever doing that." I wondered why I was doing it then, when I might be playing tennis outdoors at Forest Hills.

My chemical experiments with insulin yielded negative findings, but Dr. Benedict insisted that I publish them.[1] Dr. Jeanette Behre, Instructor in Biochemistry, helped me make them conform to the scientific style of writing. The results of my efforts were not ultimately negative, however, for she and I maintained a friendship for years. Furthermore, Dr. Benedict's words of prophecy and advice made a deep impression on me. They may have influenced me seven years later when Dr. Robert A. Hatcher offered me a full-time appointment as Instructor in Pharmacology at the Cornell University Medical College; I accepted it. I would spend some of my days in the laboratory, after all.

My introduction to pharmacology was in the first trimester of the second year. The course was imaginatively taught by Dr. Hatcher and the instructor, Dr. Harry Gold, in the old Loomis Laboratory, a ramshackle building on 26th Street near the East River. That basic science was relatively young as an independent medical discipline; in some schools pharmacology was still being taught as a subscience of physiology or biochemistry. When I asked Dr. Gold a question in a class conference, he replied: "The experiment that would answer that question has never been

[1] Janet Travell and Jeanette A. Behre, "Effect of Insulin upon the Rate of Fermentation of Glucose by Yeast," *Proceedings of the Society for Experimental Biology and Medicine*, Vol. 21 (1924), pp. 478–479.

done, so far as I know. How would you go about it? Would you like to undertake such an experiment?"

Inevitably, I became involved in another student *Arbeit*. With my three partners—we worked in groups of four—outside of class hours we learned more about the experimental method and obtained a partial answer to my question: "In a case of morphine poisoning when the drug is injected, not swallowed, why does the textbook recommend that the patient's stomach be repeatedly washed out for a period of two or three days afterward?"

Our chemical analyses of the stomach washings and of the stomach wall in a dog treated with shots of morphine suggested that the textbook was in error. Our observations were incorporated in a larger study of Dr. Hatcher's that was published in 1925, with the credit line in the text: "Experiment no. 1 was performed by four students (Misses J. Travell, Josephi, Kittredge, Burnet)." [2] Dr. Hatcher's conclusions were: "The commonly accepted view that important amounts of morphine are excreted into the stomach . . . is not supported by any evidence that we have been able to discover. . . . If gastric lavage is of value in the treatment of [injected] morphine poisoning, this value does not depend upon the removal of morphine from the stomach."

Although crystalline morphine was isolated in 1805 from opium (dried juice of the opium-poppy seed) and although its therapeutic value had been recognized for centuries, in 1923 there still existed important gaps in knowledge with respect to the fate of morphine in the living body—knowledge that was essential to its intelligent use. And that was before the drug explosion of modern times.

A few years later, I was called to see a young woman in the hospital whose pain was not relieved by very large doses of injected morphine. The house staff concluded that she was an addict. That night, in a short time, I was able to show by the same chemical quantitative method of my student pharmacology *Arbeit* that the morphine solution given her was only one-tenth of its labeled strength. She was not unusually tolerant to morphine and she was suffering real pain.

I was told that my analysis could not be correct because that lot number of morphine solution had been used on all services, medical and surgical, of the entire hospital for a month—and no one had reported that it was ineffective for relieving pain. Subsequently, the manufacturer confirmed my findings; the decimal point had been misplaced in the calculations for preparing the solution.

---

[2] Robert A. Hatcher and David Davis, "The Excretion of Morphine into the Stomach," *Journal of Pharmacology and Experimental Therapeutics,* Vol. 26 (August, 1925), p. 57.

I had become involved in *clinical* pharmacology.

While I followed my dream in the chemistry laboratory during the early summer of 1923, in my extra time I operated the Einthoven electrocardiograph that was located in the Department of Physiology. As student assistant, I had learned to run that cumbersome string-galvanometer by demonstrating it to my fellow students. That summer, by special arrangement with Dr. May Wilson I took records on children with rheumatic heart disease from her clinic. We called the record then an EKG—an ElektroKardiogram—because of its German origin, but later the abbreaviation became Anglicized. That new research tool was not mentioned in Starling's 1920 textbook, *Human Physiology,* which I used in class. Its clinical application in heart disease was not yet appreciated, but making all the parts of that electrocardiograph function together was a sufficient challenge for me.

That monster machine sprawled some ten feet long against the wall, from its carbon-arc light at one end to the camera box that was bolted to the floor at the other. The electric current generated by the beating heart was led from the body by wires to the invisible "string," a fragile gold-plated quartz fiber about 1/200th of a millimeter in diameter. The string was suspended within an electric magnet in the light beam from the carbon arc and it moved with the heart's cycle of contraction. The magnified shadow of the string was projected through a slit in the camera lens and was photographed on running paper. The spokes of a revolving wheel also flicked past the lens to mark time intervals. The timer had to be started manually by whirling it until its speed matched the vibrations of an electric tuning fork that then sustained the wheel's motion. Getting everything going together needed supernumerary eyes and hands.

While the electrocardiogram was being recorded, the light might sputter out, or the timer stop, or the string jump out of focus, or the paper jam in the camera feed, or if the subject moved suddenly the delicate string might break. With luck and dexterity it took me about an hour to put in a new string. Then the yards of photographic paper had to be developed in the dark room, hung up to dry, cut, mounted and labeled before the tracing could be interpreted.

Of course, if the wires (leads) had been wrongly hooked up to the patient's limbs, abnormalities could be introduced into the record that would cause errors in the interpretation.

Nowadays, the durable portable electrocardiograph weighs about ten pounds and it can be powered by transistor batteries. Its hot stylus writes on heat-sensitive moving paper, graphed for time intervals, and the significance of the record may be learned at once from that ticker tape as it piles up on the floor. However, human error in wrongly attaching the limb-leads can still vitiate the electrocardiographic diagnosis. Under that circumstance, analysis of the electrocardiogram even by a computer may provide an incorrect conclusion; the answer is no more reliable than the data.

Those pieces of ticker tape that the ECG machine, the child's heart, and I produced symbolized to me the frontiers of clinical research in cardiology. They lured me, I am sure, into that emerging specialty; in my fourth year at medical school it was the field of medicine toward which I inclined.

At home, my father the physician listened to our theoretical discussions of the new medical science. He asked questions but never intruded his views. He was fascinated by the electrocardiographic tracing with its line of peaks and valleys cast by the shadow of the Einthoven string. My father provoked me to think more precisely about its meaning when I tried to explain it to him. His quizzical mind and raised eyebrows made me realize how much I did not know. The quarter of a century since he had received his M.D. degree had produced a proliferation of medical knowledge with which he was determined to keep pace, and he was not too proud to learn from his children.

In retrospect, I took less interest in his old-world professional experience than he did in Ginny's and my new world of medical discovery. I appreciated his achievements more later when I held responsibility for people's lives and well-being, as he did then. The essence of clinical judgment is absorbed by the young physician through the example of practitioners and teachers of medicine.

My father was a great physician. I can not measure how much I gained at home during my medical-school years by exposure to his practical wisdom and specialized knowledge of physical medicine and rehabilitation. I was impressed when on August 31, 1947, he was awarded one of the first four honorary certificates of the newly organized American Board of Physical Medicine. What I specifically learned from him in that field had by then already redirected my interest into channels aimed at the relief of obstinate muscular pain.

While Ginny and I lived at home and went to classes at Cornell, our mother helped us organize many outings that we shared with our fellow students. Cousin Harriet and Cousin Jimmie Laidlaw made their estate on Long Island Sound at Sands Point available to us for picnics at all seasons. Some of the faculty came and helped us scoop up mussels in the shallow water at low tide and grill them over the fire to eat after a swim. When I spent the night at Bettina Warburg's home uptown—we often studied together—we hatched ideas not for new experiments but for the next winter sports weekend for members of our Class of 1926. Merryfield Farm at Sheffield was too far for a regular retreat from the city and we tried midwinter roughing it there only once. We would locate a cottage within a couple of hours' drive from New York where ten or twelve of us could stay, with my mother and sometimes my father to chaperone us. The cars—ours, Bettina's, and perhaps Irv Wright's—were always loaded with food prepared by my mother.

I remember one trip when Phil Armstrong—he was to be a professor of anatomy at the Syracuse University College of Medicine and also Director of the Marine Biological Laboratory at Woods Hole (where I visited him in 1963 from Hyannis Port)—absentmindedly took a different trail on Bear Mountain with all our broiled chicken in his knapsack. The rest of us went hungry for hours until we found him. One Thanksgiving weekend in that Hudson River mountain region, an unexpected snowstorm caught Roger Ogburn, of Greensboro, North Carolina, without boots or arctics. He hiked all day in the deep snow with his shoes and legs wrapped in the burlap bags that we tied and retied around them. At a cottage on Greenwood Lake in New Jersey, my mother and Sis Strunk were congenial nighthawks. Sis and her musician brother Ollie—he was to become head of the Music Department at Princeton—were occupying an apartment at 42 Fifth Avenue, a brownstone house that my mother had remodeled. Their father was William Strunk, Jr., Professor of English at Cornell University in Ithaca, and I had the pleasure of visiting in their home there. Before Sis died in 1949, she became coorganizer (under her married name, Dr. Catherine Amatruda) of the Gesell-Amatruda Child Clinic in New Haven. Sis was always a blithe spirit, and while everyone else in the cottage turned in for sleep, she and my mother sat up all night playing bridge with, I think, Lev Woodworth and Irv Graef. They were still at the game by daylight when I got up for breakfast. My mother was like that—as irrepressible as the rest of us.

Roz Brown, my classmate, and I spent an evening at a Broadway theater where Harry Houdini (he died in 1926) entertained a packed house with his incredible feats of magic and with an exposé of fake spiritualistic or "supernatural" phenomena. Between his acts, he stepped to the edge of the stage and invited four or five ladies to volunteer as participants. I ran down the aisle and up the steps into the limelight. Houdini sat with us close around a small table and explained to the audience that he would demonstrate how the Ouija Board was made to work. Leaning our elbows on the table, we were told to hold hands in a circle and each of us to place her right foot on top of her neighbor's left. The lights dimmed until the stage was in complete darkness. I held Houdini's hand and pressed my foot on his, while he kept on talking. Suddenly a bell rang underneath the table and the table itself tilted this way and that. When the lights went up, there was Houdini hopping barefoot around the stage, holding a bell with the toes of one foot. I still had my foot on his empty shoe and sock, and I was holding the hand of the person who sat just beyond his empty chair. Feeling sheepish, the amateurs filed back to their seats.

My father the magician looked knowing when I came home and recounted Houdini's magical tricks.

At medical school our extracurricular activities were not confined to recreation. In our second year, when the small Ithaca division that combined the last year at college with the first year of medical school joined the New York division, about a dozen of us formed an evening Journal Club. At each meeting after dinner, one student presented a scientific topic for discussion and we invited an interested member of the faculty. On our roster from the Class of 1926 was Milton Helpern, who was to become Chief Medical Examiner of the City of New York and Chairman of the Department of Forensic Medicine at the Post-Graduate Medical School of New York University. Our three Irvs were already scholars of medicine. Irving P. Graef would go later to the New York University-Bellevue Medical Center as Associate Professor of Clinical Medicine and to Bellevue Hospital as Pathologist. Irvine H. Page had started a career in brain chemistry before he entered medical school. He was to become Director of the Eli Lilly Clinic and Laboratory for Clinical Research and later, Director of Research of the Cleveland Clinic Foundation and Editor of *Modern Medicine*. Irving S. Wright would eventually be Clinical Professor of Medicine at the New York Hospital–Cornell Medical Center and consultant in cardiovascular disease to numerous scientific groups in this country and abroad, as well as President of the American Heart Association and President of the American College of Physicians. Our Journal Club also included Sis Strunk, Phil Armstrong, and two Normans. Norman S. Moore would achieve stature in student health care as Physician-in-Chief of the Cornell University Infirmary and Clinic, and Chairman of the Department of Clinical and Preventive Medicine of Cornell University at Ithaca, as well as President of the Medical Society of the State of New York. Norman H. Plummer would contribute to progress in occupational and preventive medicine and become Medical Director of the New York Telephone Company. Julius Chasnoff followed his drive toward clinical research at New York's Beth Israel Hospital and later as Associate Professor of Medicine at the New York Medical College. John S. Carman was probably the only member who pursued the dream of his future as he saw it in medical school: Jack was to go to the Christian Medical College Hospital in Vellore, South India. Roz—Roswell K. Brown—with his wife, Enid Crump of my sister's Class of 1925, embarked on a similar goal at the American University in Beirut, Lebanon, but after a few years they returned to the United States. They carried on in surgery and pediatrics at Buffalo, New York, until Roz accepted a post with the Committee on Trauma of the American College of Surgeons to attack the top priority problem of traffic accidents, and Roz and Enid moved to New York City. They visited me at the White House on November 18, 1963, as they were leaving for India, where they would see Jack Carman and his hospital in Vellore.

That second-year Journal Club fostered friendships that were based on mutual respect and intellectual honesty. It helped train us in the independent analysis of the fast-changing medical literature, and it developed skill in the defense of our convictions.

In the clinical years at medical school, it was my turn to ask questions of my father, the general practitioner. That relationship of apprentice and preceptor continued while I was a neophyte physician for two years in the New York Hospital and later after I entered private practice on my own, from my father's office. He could tell me what was not directly taught us in medical school: Precisely how does the doctor make the patient confident and comfortable while waiting for something to happen—for the results of laboratory tests and X-rays, or the specialist's opinion, for nature to cure the illness, or for a baby to arrive? My father was adept in caring for those vital needs of the whole patient.

My first encounter with complex medical situations in the home occurred during the obstetrics course in my fourth year. Five students at a time were assigned to live for two weeks in the Berwind Maternity Clinic, a four-story building on 103rd Street near Lexington Avenue in East Harlem. I elected an additional stint of two weeks. On the top floor were a couple of single rooms for the women medical students and a dormitory where the men slept. At night, whoever was on call for the next delivery answered the wall phone in the hall. On the ground floor were the clinic facilities, on the second floor a laboratory where the students did tests on blood and urine and often cooked something to eat over a Bunsen burner—no meals were provided. Also there were quarters for a small resident staff. During the day the obstetricians in training, with the assistance of the students and a couple of nurses, provided prenatal care for mothers who chose to come to the clinic; and if the patient's course of pregnancy was uncomplicated, one of the obstetricians supervised the delivery by one or two fourth-year medical students in the patient's tenement home, at any hour.

When word came to the clinic that one of its regular patients was in labor, two students went out together—unless the calls came so fast that only one of us was available. I did answer some calls alone. Well equipped with the heavy black bag, we made our way for several blocks, as a rule, to the street address. Day and night, the medical bag was a passport everywhere. Our flashlights guided us up the dark stairway to the specified floor and door. We knocked and at the same time announced in a loud voice, "The doctor, the doctor is here." The door, slightly ajar at first, opened wide.

That area of East Harlem was, and still is, regarded as one of New York's ugliest slums, and it has a high rate of muggings. Its population was mainly Negro with some Puerto Ricans and a few Irish and Italian families. "Metro North" of the recently created Department of Housing and Urban Redevelopment describes those tenements now as "filing cabinets for people," and indeed they were. An apartment with four bedrooms, a kitchen, and a toilet off its long, narrow hall was likely to house four families, each with several children in one room. We often had to prime the gas meter with a quarter in order to heat water on the stove for the work that we would have to do. When I arrived for my first delivery, the bedroom was lighted only by a kerosene lamp that looked like those at our Merryfield Farm. It put me at ease. The most squalid home where I went was that of a Negro janitor in a Negro apartment dwelling. A space for his family was crudely partitioned off from the coal bins, where his children played, and a cold-water spigot at the far end of the dark cellar supplied them with water.

Often we sat and waited by the hour for the mother's labor to end. We had plenty of time to think about our surroundings. At stated intervals we examined her and one of our team then went out to telephone the clinic and report progress to the staff physician there. That was the extent of the supervision that we received, unless we observed signs of impending trouble and asked him to come.

Late one night, Roz Brown and I were called to the quite pleasant apartment of a self-respecting Italian family. They had only one child and were eagerly expecting another, whom they had desired for several years. It was my turn to perform the delivery. My examination told me that the baby's position was unusual. I took Roz aside.

"Go quickly and phone. Tell them I think it's a face presentation and we'll need help. There's something wrong."

At that hour it was hard to find a telephone in the neighborhood, and before he returned, the baby was delivered. The overwrought father watched and his horrified eyes took in his child's six fingers on each hand, the malformed open skull and exposed brain. I shielded it from the mother's view. The defective infant was breathing, but could not live long. In that emergency I solemnly pronounced the words: "I baptize thee in the name of the Father and of the Son and of the Holy Ghost. Amen."

I made the sign of the Cross and the baby expired.

That act calmed the enraged father and hysterical mother. It was a heavy responsibility for a medical student. I felt easier when they began to ask me sensibly about the possibility of their having a deformed baby again if they had another child. One of the Berwind students had once delivered a dead baby and had been shot and killed by the disturbed father.

Although in my fourth year my stated preference was cardiology, I sampled as widely as I could my options within the spectrum of the medical school curriculum. For one month I took an elective in neurology with that indefatigable Scot Dr. Lewis Stevenson, who taught us neuropathology—we made intricate models of the central nervous system for him in the laboratory. In his search for rare neurological disorders I followed him—I was his sole student—around the city, from Harlem Hospital to Bellevue, to Welfare Hospital on the island in the East River. We photographed pathological specimens of nerve tissue and also living patients on the wards who exhibited abnormal gaits and bizarre movements, as in the dystonias, Parkinsonism, and other diseases of the brain and spinal cord. There was plenty of action in Dr. Stevenson's individualized system of teaching, and he permanently enhanced my interest in neuromuscular disorders.

Surgery was the clinical discipline for which I felt least suited. Nevertheless, or perhaps because of it, as a fourth-year student, during the summer I served as substitute intern for two weeks on the Second Surgical Division at Bellevue Hospital. That convinced me that I did not want to be a surgeon. The glare and heat of the operating room and the prolonged standing on its hard tile floor tired me excessively. But aside from those physical drawbacks, that specialty did not provide the opportunity for long-term personal care of the patient that appealed to me. My astonishment was unbounded when at graduation I learned my grade in our fourth-year course in surgery—an unheard-of 100. It made me wonder whether I recognized my own aptitudes.

Internship appointments were the big event in the spring of our final year at medical school. I applied to only one place, the New York Hospital. I had worked there for two weeks as substitute intern on the medical service when Dr. Evelyn Holt, Wellesley 1919, the hospital's first woman intern, took her vacation. I put all my eggs in one basket; to underestimate one's ability seemed to me as faulty as to overestimate it. (In the autumn of 1925, I had been elected to Alpha Omega Alpha, honorary medical society, on the basis of three years' work at Cornell, but I had no idea then that I ranked first in our class with respect to my academic average and that at graduation I would receive the Polk Memorial Prize for highest scholastic standing.) I wanted the highly prized two-year appointment to the Cornell Medical Division starting on either July 1, 1926, or January 1,

1927. The later date was my first choice—and I received it—because it would give me six months after graduation to travel abroad for pleasure with my mother and to attain some perspective on myself.

That medical service provided a broad training in an intimate-sized hospital. The Cornell Medical Division had three wards, one for men, one for women, and another for infants and children; experience in both pediatric and adult medicine was obtained. It provided six months of junior internship, then a term of four and a half months on the ambulance combined with six weeks in the pathology laboratory; next, six months as senior intern with duties equivalent to those of the present-day assistant resident; and finally, six months as House Physician, the chief resident in charge.

My main reason for applying to that teaching service was its chief, Dr. Lewis A. Conner, who had been for many years Chairman of Cornell's Department of Medicine. He was a strict disciplinarian and he ran the wards like a trim ship. Let no one be tardy at work or sloppy in appearance or in thinking, for the reprimand would be prompt and public. Dr. Conner was a master of the art, as well as of the science, of medicine. An outstanding cardiologist and astute clinician, he was foremost a humanitarian and he loved people. To him, treatment ranked on a par with diagnosis, and the House Physician was expected to arrange for proper follow-up care after the patient left the hospital. When we were medical students, Dr. Conner taught us: "Reassurance and encouragement are two therapeutic agents than which there are none other more important."

How well I must have listened to him was revealed by a letter written in 1961 by a former patient on our Ward L of the New York Hospital, when I was House Physician. She had hyperthyroidism and nearly thirty-five years later she wrote me:

> It was a very definite thrill to hear . . . that you are President Kennedy's personal physician. In the Summer of 1927, I entered the New York Hospital for a basal metabolism test—it was plus 45. The first time you came to see me you asked what was the matter—of course you knew. . . . Your laugh made me feel good. After three weeks in medical ward, [I was] operated on and after that, two weeks in surgical ward. I was scared; and you were wonderful to me. Dr. Travell, you came to see me every day and I have never forgotten you. Thanks in a great measure to you, I am in excellent health.

Sparing of speech, Dr. Conner had a vast capacity for listening. He heard between the words when a patient gave a medical history. I must have profited by Dr. Conner's example, for I was complimented years later when Dr. Harry Gold, Professor of Clinical Pharmacology at Cornell, said of me: "She has the art of listening. She listens until she understands not only what the patient says but what he is trying to say." [3]

Dr. Conner was so sympathetic toward the patient's view of things that he consented promptly when as House Physician I asked him one day: "Would it be all right, Dr. Conner, if I get some leeches in for Mr. Pozansky? [4] He believes they'll cure his terrible headaches. *We* haven't succeeded in stopping them—we haven't even found a cause."

"Where do you get leeches?" Dr. Conner's eyes twinkled under his stern, high forehead.

"Mr. Pozansky says his doctor—from the Lower East Side where he lives—will bring the right kind of leeches and apply them. The doctor can come on Saturday afternoon."

"All right, Dr. Travell."

I was using my Wellesley rule of thumb to obtain special permission before introducing an innovation.

Ward H knew all about the event in advance. On Saturday the doctor arrived during visiting hours with about a dozen neat small leeches in a bucket of water. They resembled those that I had disliked as a child swimming in the lakes of Nova Scotia. I had to leave Mr. Pozansky with the doctor and the leeches in the small "nurses' room" off the ward while I attended to a more urgent problem. When I came back, the leeches had attached themselves all over Mr. Pozansky's scalp. We fixed a wet towel loosely around his head.

Sunday morning when I came on the scene, the bloodsucking worms had gorged themselves to several times their original size. Like ticks, when satisfied they let go. But the scalp wounds caused by their teeth continued to bleed. We wrapped Mr. Pozansky's head in a fresh bath towel and as he paced up and down the ward, holding his head in his hands, the red stain spread through the white cloth. The nurse kept changing the towel. The leeches had inoculated the scalp with an anticoagulant substance, and, to my discomfiture, nothing that we had in the New York Hospital counteracted it. Tight pressure bandaging of his head might have stopped the leakage of blood but would have created headache. Mr. Pozansky had forgotten his head pain. He finally persuaded me to send for his doctor again, who was at home with leeches and who brought a powder that stopped the bleeding at once.

My foray into the ancient art of bloodletting may have been good psychosomatic treatment—that was probably why Dr. Conner approved it—

[3] Beverly Smith, Jr., "Doctor in the White House," *The Saturday Evening Post,* October 21, 1961, p. 70.
[4] Fictitious name.

but it did not raise my stature in the hospital and it spoiled my Sunday off.

An extra dividend of my internship at the New York Hospital was proximity to home. My craving for travel to new places had been temporarily satisfied during the four summers since Wellesley had given me my B.A. degree, and I was happy to live within a half-dozen short blocks from my parents. Ginny was not far away, either. She and Pop Weeks had been married in September, 1925, three months after she received her M.D., and they were living in Brooklyn Heights, across the river from downtown Manhattan. I was disappointed, however, that opportunities for the gay outings of our medical-school days were infrequent while I was interning.

On my vacation in the spring of 1927, I made one trip to Merryfield Farm, taking along Gilbert and Frances Dalldorf, both physicians. Gil was Assistant Pathologist at the New York Hospital, and he became a pioneer in the field of virology. He discovered the Coxsackie muscle virus that he named for the town of Coxsackie near Albany, New York, where he first isolated it in August, 1947. He was the first to show that a virus, the MM strain, could cause poliomyelitis in both mice and men. But in 1927, Gil and Frances had a European folding boat and I bought a similar one at Wanamaker's. My father and mother drove all three of us and the boats to our chilly Merryfield Farm. Near there we paddled for miles and miles on the river, where it loops back and forth across the valley between Sheffield and Canaan, Connecticut. Gil said, "We floated down the Housatonic in an unfolded sandwich," but I thought that we worked pretty hard.

Friendships wear well when they are built on sharing of work and play.

When I was on ambulance service at the hospital, on the Fourth of July, 1927, the sequel to a beach party at the Laidlaws' familiar haven at Sands Point was a near calamity for me. It caused me to be hospitalized as probably the first female patient on the male medical Ward H of the venerable New York Hospital. When I bent over to light a string of firecrackers on that July 4, someone threw a "torpedo" onto the brick terrace close to me and its explosion embedded gunpowder and gravel in my bare outstretched arm. Back at the hospital the next morning I consulted Dr. Mary Crawford, Chief of the Emergency Service, as to whether I needed protection against tetanus.

"You certainly should have tetanus antitoxin for that," she told me categorically. I knew the answer already. "Are you allergic to horse serum? Have you any allergies?"

"No allergies," I reported truthfully. "I never had horse serum, but I used to have a horse at the farm and I ride whenever I can. It doesn't bother me."

While Dr. Crawford was filling a syringe with the antitoxin, the ambulance bell sounded for me.

"There's my call—I'll get it when I get back."

I picked up my big medical bag and within seconds I was off in the "bus" that was parked in the driveway by the emergency entrance. If I had tarried for the "shot," in all likelihood I would not have returned from the ride alive.

When I had completed the ambulance call, I located Dr. Crawford again and she gave me the injection of tetanus antitoxin. As she did it in haste, the needle popped off the end of the syringe and part of the dose was lost.

"Clumsy of me—I'll get some more," she said.

"Thanks, it should be enough," I said and walked off. Chance had probably saved my life again.

I stepped into a waiting elevator and rode up two floors to Ward H. My eyes were itching and by the time I walked from the corridor into the ward they were swollen almost shut. I felt very peculiar.

Bill Gunter, senior intern on the Cornell medical service was standing by the nurse's desk. He took one look at me and ordered me into the nearest bed between two men patients. An orderly ran with two screens, one for each side; they were just flapping white curtains hung on a wooden frame. Bill ran with a syringe full of adrenalin and he gave me heroic doses. His presence on the ward, combined with his presence of mind, was my third lucky circumstance that day.

Presently, I was moved to the small, dark room that adjoined the twenty-bed open ward. That "nurses' room" was reserved for critically ill patients. I recall a blur of whispers, of injections, a blood pressure cuff on my right arm and stethoscope on my chest. I stared through the dingy window to a courtyard beyond the foot of my bed and at my fellow interns and several attending physicians. They crowded in to look at me. Their faces were anxious and solemn, so I shut my eyes.

"They think I'm going to die on their hands," I thought to myself, "but I don't."

Part of my mind concentrated on not scratching the violent itching that enveloped me all over, from my scalp and inside my ears to between my toes. I was a confluent mass of giant hives (urticaria). I lay perfectly still.

Another part of my mind concentrated on breathing. I was aware that

I had serious pulmonary difficulty. If I relaxed and restrained my coughing, I could coordinate the various muscles of respiration—chest muscles, diaphragm, and abdominal muscles. I knew that the will to live might determine the outcome. I thought about a friend who had been near drowning; he could easily have quit struggling to stay afloat and breathe, but his willpower kept him swimming and he was rescued. The life instinct must have been strong in us.

A third part of me contemplated dying. The process was neither painful nor frightening. The wrench would be to those whom I left behind. Images of my mother and father and Ginny flitted across the screen of my consciousness and momentarily I mourned for them.

Time passed and my father was in the room. I did not know how long he had been standing there. He appeared the calmest of all the doctors. I was beginning to feel better, except for vomiting and a splitting headache. "I'm all right, dear. Don't worry," I told him. I was glad that he had come.

My near-fatal reaction to horse serum was not a destructive, but rather a constructive experience for me. In the hospital and on the ambulance I was dealing with accidental and natural death in many forms. The dying who were conscious and could consider the impending course of events— some of whom survived to live again—had told me that imminent death was not fearsome to them. Now I knew for myself that what they said could be true. Almost none of them felt ready for death, yet living and dying merged easily and naturally into one state of being.

The medical emergency that had threatened me was grist for the milling of the young physician Janet Travell. Dr. Crawford, Dr. Conner, and the attending staff were dismayed by the unpredictability, the lack of warning of my violent, immediate reaction to a simple injection of tetanus horse antitoxin. Nothing like it had occurred before in the New York Hospital, and it was not then routine to make preliminary tests for hypersensitivity before administering such antitoxin. Under the direction of Dr. Arthur F. Coca, research immunologist and allergist, whose laboratory was located in the hospital adjoining the pathology department, I undertook to learn the physiological basis for my critical allergic response.

Questioning me carefully, Dr. Coca uncovered the history that in medical school I had indeed had two previous injections of horse serum in the form of diphtheria toxin-antitoxin, the solution then in use for immunization against that disease. I had forgotten about it and inadvertently I had misinformed Dr. Crawford. Dr. Coca believed that the amounts of foreign horse serum given me in those injections, though minute, were adequate to stimulate my long-term manufacture of antibodies against that highly antigenic material and to sensitize me to future doses of horse serum. He was right. I tested my blood serum for circulating precipitins to horse serum and the test was positive: a white layer of precipitate formed in the test tube at the junction of the two serums. My hypersensitivity was *acquired* by prior exposure and my reaction was truly anaphylactic.

In spite of my negative clinical history for allergic symptoms—asthma, hay fever, eczema, or drug intolerance—we investigated the possibility that I possessed also an *inherited* (atopic) allergic predisposition. Offhand, that seemed unlikely, especially since neither my parents nor my sister had any known allergies. But Dr. Coca wondered. He did skin tests on me for a variety of antigens such as pollens and animal danders. I showed no sign of allergy to horsehair mixtures but, to my surprise, my intradermal, intranasal, and ophthalmic tests were strongly positive to ragweed antigen in high dilution. Precipitins for ragweed were not present in my blood serum, but reagins were and they were accepted as evidence of an allergic inheritance.[5] I demonstrated the circulating reagins by a positive passive transfer test: local hypersensitivity (urticaria) to ragweed extract developed in the normal skin of a person not allergic to ragweed wherever I had previously injected intradermally a little of my own processed blood serum.

Similar tests for reagins in my mother's and father's blood were negative and failed to reveal a genetic source of my ragweed allergy. However, my mother's brother, George Davidson, and his children were severely afflicted with ragweed hay fever every summer. The specific gene was apparently recessive in my mother and reappeared in me in a masked form.

I was a new kind of allergic entity. To explain my lack of allergic symptoms in the face of the unequivocally positive tests, Dr. Coca postulated that a local tissue barrier in the healthy mucous membranes of my nose and bronchi and in the conjunctiva of my eyes prevented the ragweed pollen in the air from contacting the tissue cells that reacted to it, the antigen. He described "the interesting experience of Dr. Janet Travell" at length in his textbook,[6] but I think that he was still baffled by my freedom from symptoms during the ragweed season.

"Dr. Travell," he told me then, "if you live to a ripe age you will surely have asthma, and probably hay fever."

So far, his prediction has been wrong.

[5] William B. Sherman, "Types of Allergic Reactions," *Fundamentals of Modern Allergy,* Samuel J. Prigal, ed. (New York, McGraw-Hill, Inc., 1960), pp. 13–14.
[6] Arthur F. Coca, Matthew Walzer, and A. A. Thommen, *Allergy in Theory and Practice* (Springfield, Illinois, Charles C. Thomas, 1931), p. 82.

From my personal lesson in allergy at the New York Hospital I gained some knowledge of, and great respect for, the potential hazards of allergic reactions to therapeutic and other agents. When the safe bacterial tetanus toxoid (without foreign animal products) became available for immunization against tetanus, I made certain that members of my family and my patients were protected by it and kept their toxoid immunization up to date. Tetanus spores are everywhere—in the soil, street dirt, and house dust—and a scratch can kill you. One of every two persons who contracts lockjaw, even now, dies. But in World War II, owing to the military's insistence on tetanus toxoid, there were only twelve cases of tetanus among all our casualties. On the other hand, in our civilian population as recently as 1964 it was estimated that over two million doses of the dangerous tetanus horse antitoxin were being given annually to unprotected people, and 50,000 of that number caused allergic reactions. If young and old would universally avail themselves of the medical miracle of tetanus toxoid for the prevention of lockjaw, we should never have to give an emergency dose of tetanus antitoxin.[7]

On December 1, 1927, while I was on ambulance duty, distressed by what I saw of the city through the eyes of medicine, I wrote Jack Powell in North Carolina about my own wealth of riches and the smooth current of my life:

I've [not] had any great sorrows or regrets or unhappiness. A great deal has been given me and I have much to be thankful for: love, understanding from family and friends, an unusual amount of freedom without too great worry . . . health and a good inheritance of mind, opportunity and encouragement to study, travel—what more could one want as an endowment? Perhaps it's because I appreciate so much what I have that I feel so much sympathy for those who lack these gifts.

Sorrow was soon to pile up on me. On January 12, 1928, my grandfather Davidson died in Albany at the age of eighty-six after removal of the prostate gland under spinal anesthesia. Conscious throughout the surgery, he was happy to have his two physician granddaughters stand by him in the operating room. He had disapproved of our entering medical school at first, but he was proud of us then. On January 20, I wrote Jack what a fine gentleman my grandfather was and I meditated on how he lived after death:

[7] Although tetanus antitoxin has recently been prepared from the blood of tetanus-immune human subjects and now obviates the hazards of horse antitoxin, by the time the diagnosis of lockjaw has been made it may be too late for any antitoxin to save the victim of tetanus.

People of an older generation are a link with the past which lends stability and perspective to our younger years. Another thing I have discovered is the *influence* which those who are dead can exert on us to alter our actions. In little things I've caught myself thinking: "I can't do that—Grandpa wouldn't like it!" . . . In bigger things that influence might play an important role. It's a strange thing and worth thinking about. A strong and beautiful personality is a check, and a guide—even more so after death has apparently made it powerless.

My grandmother Davidson had died nine years earlier. My mother and her father had always felt close to each other—she was his surviving daughter. The dismantling of the old family home at 216 Lancaster Street was the toppling of a landmark for all of us and the task placed a strain on my mother. Ginny and I wished that we might have been more helpful. Ginny was expecting her first baby, and Ginger was born on March 9, 1928. I was tied to the New York Hospital.

Our house at 40 Fifth Avenue was sold in the spring of 1928 and it would disappear into a giant apartment complex built at that address. I was losing my home of college and medical-school years, but we still had Merryfield Farm as a psychological base and a refuge. The previous summer I had written Jack, as I was starting my vacation from the ambulance:

Tomorrow Mother and I leave for Sheffield, where I am longing to go. I am tired of pavements and automobile horns and blocked out glimpses of the sky. I want to sleep out under the stars and hear the crickets' chorus. "Peace" is a beautiful word, and I think it describes what there is at Sheffield.

On March 15, 1928, the first payment was made on the purchase of our new home at 9 West 16th Street opposite the old New York Hospital (it moved to 68th Street and York Avenue in 1932), and on July 17, my mother took final possession. Subsequently, when our furniture had to be moved out of 40 Fifth Avenue on October 1, the new house was not ready and our possessions were stored in a few of the large empty rooms. The extensive remodeling that my mother had planned was more complicated than building a new house. The brownstone stoop was removed and a marble floor laid in the ground-floor hall. The circular staircase was altered to make room for an elevator. New pipes and plumbing fixtures and a sprinkler system were installed. The kitchen was moved from the ground floor to the first-floor extension. The roof was lifted at the front to create a full story. The top two floors would be rented as apartments. Everything in my mother's main part of the house would match her dream of a beautiful home. Old Doric columns were placed by open arches in the dining room, and old Italian marble fireplaces replaced the plainer ones.

In the meantime my parents stayed with Ginny and Pop in Brooklyn Heights. As House Physician at the hospital, I was preoccupied with my responsibility for the wards of the First Medical Division. Whenever I could, I took time to run across 16th Street and to view with my mother the progress that was being made in renovating our new home. On Friday afternoon, October 26, 1928, she and I watched the workmen hang a large wall mirror in the dining room—the mirror was almost as high as the fourteen-foot ceiling. The house was cold, and I shivered in my white cotton uniform. My mother was wearing a coat. It was the last time that I saw her alive.

My father was starting to see patients downstairs in his new suite of offices on the ground floor, which had been finished. He and I talked briefly and I reported on the five cases of typhoid fever that I had on my wards. He had had typhoid fever himself. He had also cared for my mother's older sister Elizabeth in her last illness; he had fought a losing battle and she died of typhoid in New York six months after he and my mother were married. That day in October, I had to hurry back to the hospital because I wanted to be ready when Jack came to take me out for dinner.

He brought me back to the hospital at about ten o'clock that evening, and I checked for messages at the front information office.

"Call your sister in Brooklyn—it's urgent," Jimmie, the night superintendent, told me.

Jack and I stood together at the high desk while I gave the telephone number to the switchboard operator. Pop Weeks answered.

"It's your mother. Come right away," he said.

"Is she ill, Pop?"

"No." That was all he said. I understood.

Jack went with me on the subway; it was the quickest way to Brooklyn. My mother had had a heart attack shortly after dinner and she had died painlessly within half an hour. My father was there and he did everything that could have been done for her. It was a grievous duty for her husband, a physician, but a wonderful thing for my mother to be close to her loved ones at the end.

Now my father would have to face his life alone and to assume the joyless task of rebuilding our home out of the torn-up house at 9 West 16th Street. My mother had always attended to everything for us. My father put one arm around Ginny and one around me.

"We'll manage somehow," he said to us.

And he did. I could hear my mother's voice echo her cherished motto,

"A thing begun is half done." But it would be many months before my father and I occupied our new home.

For the first time in my life, I was homeless. My mother had given shelter to so many in search of a home that I could not grasp that reality.

Years later, I was moved to write a poem when I read Dr. Eric Mautner's account of his wanderings in Bolivia as an Austrian physician fleeing from Nazi persecution.[8] A refugee, he was looking for the place where he could make his home and where he could best serve in his profession. He did not find it in the Bolivian jungles. When he left there, his Indian aide told the doctor, "A home is a thing a man has. . . . It is there and he is there. I wouldn't know how to look for a home if I had to."

WITHOUT A HOME

Ages old refugees
With aching bones and calloused feet
Scale the walls, brave the seas.
They search for home on any street,
Home with doors, doors with keys.

My home? Home was destroyed.
Soul seared alone I saw it burn,
Stole off broken, devoid
Of hope I ever would return.
Where could *I* fear avoid?

Mother had been my home,
Her heart and arms a haven sure
Whenever I would roam
By rock fence, creek, barnyard, pasture
Under night's starry dome.

Heaven must be my home.
No peace is here. My mind still pores
On the thin ragged foam
Of life that breaks on hate-bound shores.
Gone's the safe port of home.

Faceless folk. Slow aimless
They lurk in shadow, led by fate,
Wed to wan weariness.
Hope starved, their hunger's fed with hate.
Who will serve them goodness?

[8] H. Eric Mautner, *Doctor in Bolivia* (Philadelphia and New York, Chilton Company, Book Division, 1960).

Wanderer, wake! You will win
By work the battle of rebirth.
Give of yourself—begin.
The homeless are your home on earth,
Their hearts will take you in.

I was at home in medicine, but medicine was not my home. I could give myself to my patients in my professional work, but few of them could share my inner life. I could not see my way clearly then. Working at the New York Hospital, I wrote my philosophy in a letter to Jack, who seemed to understand all my feelings:

I find that the less attention I give to the future the happier I am, because I am reasonably happy in the moment that is given me now. Outside of a general plan, a choice of direction, the road ahead is curving, with many hills, and rivers and bridges. I don't believe that God intended me to see it all straight ahead, and I am glad of it. For I am sure that I am not ready now for all that lies ahead, though later I may be better prepared. If I knew it all now, what a burden it would be! I should lie awake at night wondering, worrying. Isn't it really easier for us not to know?

My faith in the future was boundless.

CHAPTER 10

We Met
at a Dance

We met at a dance on February 22, 1927, on the Hotel Astor Roof where
the New York Southern Society was holding its annual white-tie ball. Jack
was a stag guest of his fellow Tar Heels, Mildred and Peter Lynch. He and
Peter had been at the University of North Carolina together and they had
shared an apartment in New York before Peter and Mildred were married.
My escort was a gay southerner, Frick Sutherland, a 1926 graduate of
Harvard Medical School and an intern on surgery at the New York Hospital where I was the junior medical intern on the Cornell service.

Although it was my "night off," I almost missed the party because of
the new insulin treatment for diabetes. That night on our Ward H, some
diabetics were in insulin shock and needed intravenous glucose to raise
their blood sugar, while other patients were admitted in diabetic coma
and were receiving massive doses of insulin to lower the blood sugar. The
emergency chemical tests for sugar that determined their treatment were
the job of the junior intern. We were never off duty when there was work
to be done, and it was a mad busy evening. Frick was free to leave earlier
than I. With my mind preoccupied and my muscles tired, I tried to back
out of the date, but some time after midnight we finally arrived in a sleet
storm at the Hotel Astor on Times Square.

Small details are vividly remembered when the milestones of life loom
suddenly before you. On that momentous night, I was wearing a silver
lace dress, short and straight line to the pale pink chiffon flounce at knee
level. I had bought the creation in Paris late that fall before I returned to

start my hospital internship after Christmas. My hair was cut for easy care and in the rush it had not had the attention that I wished. When Frick and I walked down the imposing high front steps of the hospital to a taxi, my evening shoes were soaked by the slush and they stuck a little to the floor as we danced. Peter and Mildred, who were my friends too, stopped at our table to introduce the debonair bachelor, Jack Powell.

Jack and I walked onto the crowded ballroom floor and I think that we danced together all evening. He led me with ease around all the other couples as if they were nonexistent. Indeed, for us they did not exist and we moved in a new world of our shared thoughts. Frick dropped out of mind until he took me back to the New York Hospital at 8 West 16th Street. My conscience did not bother me—he had lots of southern friends in town. You may not believe in love at first sight, but Jack and I fell in love on the dance floor that night. We have danced together through life ever since.

Jack was twenty-nine and I was twenty-five when we met on the Astor Roof. The trace of gray in his thick, black hair, his wide-spaced, dark eyes and his black eyebrows that met in the center above his aristocratic nose gave him a look of rare distinction. His manner combined the gallant chivalry of the Old South, the decorous dignity of the New York banker, and the romantic ardor of Old Spain. In 1919, he had gone from the University of North Carolina to work for the Overseas Division of the National City Bank in South America and he had lived for three years in Montevideo, Uruguay. He spoke fluent Spanish and he danced a beautiful tango. I knew southern men who were noted for their charm, but Jack was different. When he spoke or sang, his voice was like the music that he loved. Those were the days when the orchestra played, "Let Me Call You Sweetheart, I'm in Love with You."

Compactly built with broad shoulders, his trim figure of five feet ten inches possessed superlative coordination and grace. Nobody outdanced Jack. As we explored each other's young past—places, people, points of view, and preferences—I learned that Jack was an athlete of the first rank. At the University at Chapel Hill his prowess as pitcher for four years and captain for two years of the baseball team made him a campus hero. When his graduation approached, he received offers from the New York Giants, the Chicago White Sox, and the Philadelphia Nationals to play professional baseball. He chose a business career instead. Jack wished sometimes that he had had the fun of playing big league ball for a year or two, but at that time he was imbued with his southern family's pre-Civil War tradition that a gentleman devoted himself to an intellectual calling. His older Norfleet and Gordon relatives objected even to his playing amateur baseball in the summers of his prep-school and early college years.

*My Father, Willard Travell,
at three (center), and
his brothers Howard and
Winthrop, 1872.*

*Willard Travell, M.D.,
at his office. About 1909.*

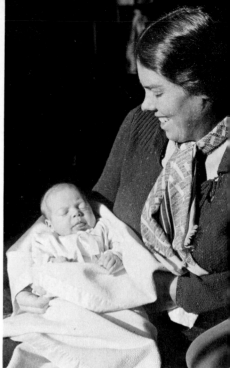

ABOVE LEFT: *My mother, Janet Davidson Travell,*
holding me (age: approximately one month).
ABOVE RIGHT: *I am holding my daughter, Janet,*
who is three weeks old
in this picture. LEFT: *My daughter,*
Virginia Powell Street, holding her one-month-old
baby, Janet Travell Street. RIGHT: *My daughter,*
Janet Powell (Gianna Pinci), in Madame
Butterfly, *holding her son, Mark Antony.*

ABOVE: *My sister, Virginia, and I in New York, 1908.* LEFT: *Janet and Virginia Travell, Wellesley College Doubles Champions.* RIGHT: *My mother and I at Merryfield Farm, 1924.*

June 6, 1929. Janet Travell Powell.

LEFT: *There's nothing to it really.*
BELOW LEFT: *"Pegasus."*
BELOW RIGHT: *"Ophelia Bump."*

ABOVE: *A dogsled in Hudson Bay, Canada.* LEFT: *Jack and Bobby Powell in boardwalk studio at Atlantic City.* RIGHT: *The New York Hospital electric ambulance.*

ABOVE: *Fort Knox, Kentucky*. LEFT: *Miss Janet G. Travell, M.D., Ambulance Surgeon, New York Hospital, 1927*. RIGHT: *In 1950, I demonstrated how to hold a syringe for one-handed muscle injection.*

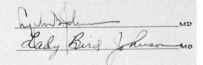

Drs. Johnson & Johnson & Johnson & Johnson
1600 PENNSYLVANIA AVENUE, N.W.
WASHINGTON, D.C.

Prescription for Happiness

℞ 1 large dose of Dr. Janet Travell
Take frequently
A sure cure for aches, pains,
occupational hazards, and general
complaints on and off whistle-stops,
in the White House and out.

Date March 25, 1965

Lyndon B. Johnson MD
Lady Bird Johnson MD

ABOVE: *Virginia, Jack, Janet and I in my office at the White House, 1961.* (Paul Schutzer — LIFE Magazine© Time Inc.)
RIGHT: *1955. Demonstrating the mock-up for Electra seat.* (George Silk — LIFE Magazine© Time Inc.)

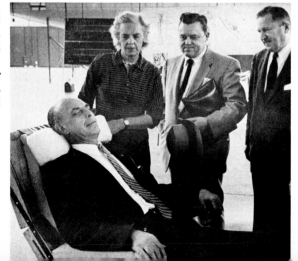

Janet and Virginia,
February, 1937.

LEFT: *Jack and I at*
Hartsdale, 1937.
BELOW: *My Father,*
the Magician, with
Virginia and Janet, 1938.

My picture of John Kennedy at Hyannis Port, 1957.

I photographed Senator Jack Kennedy, Jackie, and Joseph P. Kennedy. Palm Beach, 1957.

*I shot the President-elect catching a pass thrown
by his brother Teddy at Palm Beach, November 15, 1960.*

Caroline posed for me
at Palm Beach in 1961.

The Attorney General and his father
in the White House Rose Garden, 1961.

ABOVE: *Two of my grandchildren, Gordon Powell Street and Janet Travell Street, visited me in 1963.* BELOW: *The Powells and the Pincis on the South Lawn, 1963.*

Senator Barry and Peggy Goldwater posed for me at their Scottsdale, Arizona, home in 1960.

I took the picture of a station-platform crowd meeting the Lady Bird Special at Ahoskie, North Carolina, October, 1964.

In the President's Executive Office, 1961.

(Jacques Lowe)

War clouds hung over the men's colleges when at seventeen Jack entered the University of North Carolina in September, 1915. His brother, Junius Bishop Powell, was then a sophomore at Washington and Lee University; "Frenchy" left college to fight in France as a Second Lieutenant in the United States Army. At Chapel Hill Jack marched, drilled, and dug trenches with the SATC (Students' Army Training Corps). In the spring of 1918, his junior year, he enlisted in Naval Aviation and he was accepted that summer by the United States Navy. He was at home waiting to be called for training when the war ended on November 11. In January, he picked up the threads of university life again and although he had missed the first semester of his senior year, he graduated with his class in June, 1919.

Jack majored in English at college and had aspired to be a writer, I learned with admiration. He and Thomas C. Wolfe both belonged to two literary societies, Sigma Upsilon and Omega Delta, and although Tom Wolfe was a year behind Jack at the University, they had many classes together. I have wondered whether Tom Wolfe's prodigious talent discouraged Jack from his inclination toward the writer's profession. He told me how Tom devoured books as if he were starved for them, reading late and discussing them night after night, to the fatigue of his roommates. In English classes, Tom eloquently defended his points of view against the professor's, gesturing with his long, lean arms. During Jack's Commencement Week in 1919, the Carolina Playmakers produced Tom's tragedy *The Return of Buck Gavin,* and the author played the leading role that grew out of his boyhood life with the North Carolina mountaineers around Asheville. Jack was better informed than I concerning the literature, history, economics, and geography of the United States, and I loved to hear him talk about this country. He had an imaginative way of bringing past events and dull facts to life.

The Yackety Yack, the Class of 1919's yearbook, showed me later how distinguished a college man was John William Gordon Powell, born on December 26, 1897, in Roxobel, Bertie County, North Carolina. The book's picture of his home town shows a horse and buggy in front of the general store at the crossroads that constituted the little village. Roxobel's elementary school seemed so inadequate to Jack's mother that she set up a small school for her children, their cousins, and neighbors in the "office," a separate building on the plantation, and she brought teachers, who lived in her home. Before her marriage, Isa Cornelia Gordon had taught school at Maunch Chunk (renamed Jim Thorpe) near Scranton, Pennsylvania. Education was of paramount importance to her. Her ambition that her "children should amount to something" would have been satisfied had she lived to see her Jack graduate at Chapel Hill. That year he was President of the Athletic Association and President of the Pan-Hellenic Council of fraternities; he was a member of Zeta Psi. He was Captain of Varsity Baseball, Assistant Manager of Football, Business Manager of *The Yackety Yack,* and Commencement Ball Manager. Naturally, he had been Leader of the Junior Prom, active in a dance society known as the German Club, and honored by election to the Junior Order of the Gorgon's Head.

He was a member of the Student Cabinet and a member of the Athletic Council, on both of which Luther H. Hodges also served. Luther, who was to become Governor of North Carolina and Secretary of Commerce in President Kennedy's Cabinet, was Business Manager of Jack's winning baseball team, and he and Jack shared many interests. They were both elected to the Senior Order of the Golden Fleece, the University's top honor for outstanding leadership. Luther was President of their Senior Class and at Commencement Jack was elected 1919's Permanent Alumni President. Jack resigned from that office when we were married on June 6, 1929, in New York during his tenth reunion.

But all those honors did not explain why Jack was different. I had known other college "big shots" and none commanded the depth of feeling and respect that Jack did from me. Insofar as it went, *"The Yack"* was right when it highlighted his character: "Dignified? Very; but as genial, sincere, and well-liked as they make 'em." Tom Wolfe summed it up. In 1929, when Tom was teaching at New York University, he told a mutual college friend, "Jack was the finest gentleman I knew at Carolina."

After we met at the dance, Jack discreetly waited a few days before he telephoned me at the hospital for a date. I was obliged to decline, having come down with "la grippe." Was it the result of my wet shoes on the night of February 22? I thought that my excuse sounded lame, but Jack invited me for dinner and dancing the following week when Frenchy and Julia, his brother and sister-in-law, were coming to New York from Chicago. Surely I would be well by then and I promised to join them. My illness worsened and infection developed in my ears—"acute purulent otitis media." At the last moment, I had to call Jack and cancel our date. For better care, I moved from my room in the nurses' wing of the hospital to my home a few blocks away, where I spent miserable hours thinking that I would never hear from Jack again.

A couple of weeks later, undaunted, he did try to reach me at the New York Hospital and to his surprise I was at home, still ill. I had not been malingering. It was a month since our Washington's Birthday dance on the Astor Roof and a huge bunch of scarlet sweet peas with his card of sympathy revived my spirits. I wrote to him at his apartment around the corner at 121 West 11th Street:

March 23rd, 1927

Dear Jack:

You certainly have turned me the other cheek, when I was so inexcusably careless as to get sick and fall down on such a gorgeously planned party. . . . You repay me with a wealth of magnificent sweet peas. Do you call that vengeance? . . . There isn't a sweet pea anywhere that could hold up its head among these, not more than shoulder-high, anyway. Each one is exquisite, a princess of its kind—but all sweet peas remind me of princesses. They're like Cinderellas, they start growing the same as plain, low-brow, vegetable peas, until suddenly the old witch touches them and they blossom out fairy princesses. . . . They make this whole room bright and fragrant with their sunny smiles and laughter. . . . I do appreciate your sending them. I am convalescing rapidly, having had no out-of-town visitors but only horrid ears. . . . I wish you would come in to see your flowers before they fade. With many thanks,

Sincerely,
Bobby

It was my first letter to Jack.

That was the start of a spontaneous correspondence between us while his arduous courtship and my strenuous internship were combined. Jack knew how vital to my happiness was my two-year commitment to the New York Hospital, which had just begun. Then there were no married interns, men or women. It was not that I had a record to uphold as the second woman intern in the second oldest hospital in the United States. Medicine was an integral part of me and Jack had no intention of dismembering me. In that respect, he was different. He could wait, but he would never let the flame die.

Soon after I recovered from those middle-ear abscesses and resumed work, my six months' term as junior intern was cut short. I was suddenly catapulted up the ladder of duty to Ambulance Surgeon when one afternoon my immediate senior, Bill Gunter, was brought in off the ambulance on its stretcher. On the way to answer a call the New York Hospital "bus" had collided with a team of horses; the pole of the wagon penetrated its thin side and struck Bill in the neck. One of his cervical vertebrae was cracked in the accident; physician became patient. Bill was later to save my life, but he was through with riding the ambulance. As he was carried into the hospital, I picked up his bag and feeling unprepared I took the next call. I remember it well.

The bell clanged as we swung around the street corners to a small moving-picture theater on the west side of Irving Place south of Gramercy Park. A crowd was waiting in the front foyer where a man lay on a bench. My sense of relief shocked me when after making an examination all I had to do was to enter the diagnosis in my record book: DOA—"dead on arrival." The dead do not suffer. Our bell tolled a requiem as the ambulance pulled away from the curb and returned slowly to the emergency entrance of the New York Hospital on West 15th Street.

My life was topsy-turvy for the next nine months and I was sleepy most of the time. I filled out the rest of Bill's ambulance duty and then served my own six months on the bus. That included a respite of six weeks while I was assigned to the pathology laboratory. I rode more than a thousand calls in all, and Jack had a hard time catching up with me. My hours were day and night, around the clock.

The New York Hospital was responsible for a city ambulance district bounded by Fifth Avenue, the Hudson River, 14th Street and 42nd Street. It was a cross-section of New York, from the old Metropolitan Opera House to the slums of Hell's Kitchen only a few blocks away. My professional presence was welcomed on tugboats and ocean liners, in the old Waldorf Astoria Hotel's subterranean kitchens and maids' quarters under its dormered roof, in Bryant Park behind the New York Public Library, at warehouses along the New York Central Railroad tracks on 11th Avenue, throughout the furrier and garment-worker districts, in dime stores and big shops on Herald Square and Fifth Avenue. When ambulances of adjoining districts were all "out," we covered their territory, too.

On a substitute call for St. Vincent's Hospital to the south of our district, my bus driver became lost one day beyond Greenwich Village where 4th Street crosses 11th Street—normally they run parallel—and we were flagged by a policeman and excited people underneath a Sixth Avenue El station. We hurriedly climbed the steep steps to the elevated train platform and carried down an unconscious man in severe shock. He appeared moribund and he did not live to reach the hospital—a black mark for the Ambulance Surgeon. We had to take the body to the Bellevue Morgue and fill out special papers there. Back at last in the New York Hospital, I was entering my report in the big book at the front desk when the Superintendent of the hospital sent for me. Obviously, I had done something wrong.

"Dr. Travell, why didn't you complete the call that was given you? We had to send another ambulance. We received a serious complaint."

"But I did—I don't understand. The man died in the ambulance and I had to go to Bellevue. The call was out of our district and it took us longer to get there than it should. The delay would not have made any difference in the outcome, I'm certain."

The Superintendent and I were not on the same wave length and I was startled to discover that I had not reached the address that was my destination. In my green ignorance of the regulations, I had been lucky. The only time that the Ambulance Surgeon was permitted to pause or detour was when he was stopped to pick up someone critically ill.

Not every summons for the ambulance was urgent, by any means. On November 22, 1927, I wrote Jack in Charlotte, North Carolina, where he was to spend Thanksgiving with his sister, Dorothy Moore:

> This letter has been written under difficulties. I've had seven calls and it is three o'clock in the afternoon. I wish I could interrupt the interrupter. . . . I've been to a button factory, a lace factory where there were yards of thread forming a spidery network and completely filling several rooms [I thought of the Triangle Fire in 1911], a lithographing company, a packing house, a ribbon factory, a sewing machine sales office, and a dock at 26th Street. . . . Six of the seven were needless calls, chiefly hysterical [foreign] shop girls. . . . It is a little hard to carry on with any high ideal of service on a day like today, when one must deal with so many self-centered, unbalanced, and ignorant persons—it helps a great deal to have your good wishes.

Those less fortunate women, who lay screaming, kicking, and panting on the floors of the noisy factories, in their moment of hysteria achieved amnesia from their lot of monotony. I stopped their fits, but I did not fundamentally help them by ending their temporary release from reality. The Ambulance Surgeon was only a stopgap, and I transferred their frustrations to myself in writing to Jack.

Breaks in time while the empty bus was in transit allowed my thoughts to range. My days were never monotonous. In that same letter of Tuesday, November 22, I wrote Jack in a meditative mood about another kind of psychological stress that I had encountered on my calls. On the surface it appeared dissimilar, but actually it was similar to that of the nerve-strained sweatshop workers.

> One day, Friday I think, I had two cases of young men, both of whom came to the city for some unknown reason and lost their memory. They couldn't remember who they were or where they lived or why they were here, and begged me . . . to tell them the answers to these riddles to which they had lost the key. There was a complete

break in the continuity of their personalities, and it was very distressing to them. Their struggle was . . . an illustration of what we all suffer. . . . It seems that there is a universal urge to know the why and wherefore of our existence. Our own short lives are not enough, but we must weave them into the chain of infinity.

How often mankind tries to forget the crossing of yesterday with tomorrow, that is today, and then derives only distress from his self-induced amnesia.

The appointment of Ambulance Surgeon carried the rank then of Lieutenant in the Police Department of the City of New York. As his superior officer, I could always pick up a cop off his beat if I needed his help. The New York Hospital and the station house of the 7th Precinct on West 30th Street (now police headquarters for the 14th Precinct) were connected by a trunk telephone line and whichever received the call first notified the other. We were given two minutes to leave the hospital after the ambulance bell resounded throughout the halls, wards, and interns' quarters— everywhere, in fact, except in the nurses' wing where my room was located.

That location of my living quarters was the only drawback to being a woman that I encountered in my two years as intern, Ambulance Surgeon, and House Physician at the New York Hospital. The switchboard telephone operators had to call me in my room and relay the address of my ambulance call. When I was dog tired, I slept so soundly that sometimes I did not hear the phone ring beside my bed and a nurse had to be sent to shake me awake. Once I made the mistake of locking my door and I did not hear her banging on it.

A policeman on the scene of trouble usually requested the ambulance, but when the hospital was called directly, once in a great while we got there first. Then my bus driver and I sometimes had to break up marital combats or to push our way into the center of a street brawl. My badge of office was a military-style navy blue cap that was trimmed with gold braid and lettered in two lines above its black visor: "New York Hospital— Ambulance Surgeon." It gave me police authority, but I think that I hardly needed it. Everywhere I found that my smile, a confident manner, civility, and the double prestige of physician and womanhood, of which I took full advantage, opened the way among the toughest men. I had nothing to fear, unless it was my own inadequacy in a critical situation.

Cops and docs were partners in ambulance runs. I claimed no special prerogatives for myself. About midnight, without being called I made a routine stop at the 7th Precinct jail to give the "cokies"—a name first applied to cocaine users—an injection of morphine. I can still see the tortured faces of those drug addicts in separate cells as they held out their scarred arms through the bars and begged in singsong whines to be the first to receive the pain-relieving dole that would sustain them temporarily.

Those were the evil days of prohibition and cheap bootleg liquor, often poisonous with wood alcohol and other toxic products. The ambulance doctor was in constant demand late at night to determine whether the semiconscious man lying in a dark doorway and smelling of whiskey was probably drunk, or ill, or both. Coincidental illness or injury, like lobar pneumonia, brain concussion, or a broken bone could be masked by the depressant effects of alcohol. The patient on the sidewalk required an especially careful medical examination on the spot, and that was often not to his unruly liking. The cop and bus driver were my valuable allies then; they did more than hold my flashlight. If I judged the patient to be solely intoxicated and I delivered him to the city's overcrowded alcoholic wards at Bellevue Hospital, then that policeman had to make a report of the circumstances in court on his day off duty. That would be poor recompense for an ally. If I could, by means of ammonia inhalation, sober up the drunk enough to obtain his name and address and to see him walk, I might leave his recovery to nature. Then as the ambulance swung off for its next errand, the cop on the beat walked the inebriated man out of our district, perhaps to the downtown side of 14th Street, or down the stairs of a subway station onto a comfortable train for a long sleep en route to Brooklyn or the Bronx. Sometimes it was a vicious cycle and he came back to us later in the night.

Jack was not too happy about that kind of work for me. Those were not the "butter-and-egg" patrons of the expensive midtown speakeasies. Numerous and taxing as were those sordid ambulance calls, they had their lighter moments. On November 22, 1927, I wrote him:

> If you are keeping track of my schedule, you'll know that this is a second call day, a breathing space. . . . The [other] day . . . there was a man sitting in a drugstore, who complained of a "pain in his stummick." He sat because he was rather unsteady when he stood, and he reeked of alcohol. So I [said] in my most facetious manner: "What's the trouble? Have you been drinking hair tonic?" Thereupon the man raised his hat and hopefully remarked, "Do ye think it wad do me any good?" He was . . . *bald!*

On that Thanksgiving Day, November 25, I was on duty riding the bus. Possibly in response to Jack's protests, I altered the tenor of my ambulance tales.

Dear Jack;

Do you know this old saying, "If there were no sunshine, life would have no shadows?" I found it on an old New England drinking mug. . . . Dozens of things occur each day which I know would amuse and interest you, and I wish you were here at the time to enjoy them with me. Queer people on the streets, with strange shapes and faces and peculiar walks, others with fresh glad countenances and free strides—tinted clouds at the end of street-slits to the west and myriad lights in office buildings about Madison Square just at dusk—hysteria and courage and love and hate—these all whirl by as if in a kaleidoscope. Sometimes I feel like a spectator at a play, but it's more than that to me. I'd like to know your Southland. It sounds beautiful. . . . Must stop.

Bob

The New York Hospital bus of 1927 would be considered a vehicular oddity in any era. Its power was electric. Its ton or so of low-slung batteries beneath its high, boxed frame and its motorless, bumperless flat front gave it the pace and the face of a land tortoise. Uphill at full speed, it crawled at about five miles an hour—Murray Hill on Fifth Avenue was our steepest route. The clamor of its bell halted traffic long before we zigzagged around the waiting cars. We barely overtook the preoccupied pedestrians who hurried along in our direction past Altman's and Tiffany's stores. When Fifth Avenue was solid with automobiles, policemen's whistles shrilled at the blocked crossings. Then my impatient ambulance driver, Happy, would turn and say to me, "Watch it, Doc. We'll take the sidewalk."

I prepared myself for bumps as the bus mounted and dismounted the curbs at the end of each block. Shock absorbers were not standard equipment on that vehicle and its hard, rubber, solid tires did nothing to cushion the jolts. Happy liked to sneak along the sidewalk silently and then suddenly sound our gong close behind unsuspecting pedestrians. Scarcely believing their eyes, they jumped aside into doorways or into the street—startled marchers, secure, they thought, in the status quo.

"Happy, you ran too close to that man with the cane," I protested.

"I got the buttons off his overcoat, Doc," Happy claimed. He took pride in his marksmanship with the fenders.

On a downhill grade, the weight of our ambulance's electric batteries gave it added momentum and we made up time. When the pavements were slick with rain or sleet, I developed a fatalistic attitude, no matter what kind of a skid we made. I hooked my left arm through the looped strap, braced my back against one side of the bus and my feet against the other with my legs stretched out on the cross-seat at the open end, and I fixed my eyes steadily on the book that I was reading. Our drivers were alert and skillful, and I trusted them. On December 8, 1927, Jack may not have been entirely pleased by my report: "I am quite fond of Bill, my snappy little driver. . . . The streets are continually wet with melting snow, not clean wet, but greased with thick mud. The number of things we've missed are a caution. I have turned a complete circle three times, and today a circle and a half. . . . I am going to compose a song to the tune of, 'Skid me around again, Willie.' "

That kind of talk made my mother nervous. Roger Ogburn, my 1926 classmate at Cornell and an intern at Bellevue Hospital, was killed on July 25, 1927, when the Bellevue bus that he was riding collided with the Third Avenue El posts. The people of New York demanded speed of the city's ambulances.

I told Jack that in the sharp cold of December I was "so bundled up that it wouldn't have hurt me if I'd rolled off the back of the bus." As a matter of fact, I was more mortified than injured by my one accident while riding the bus. Our clumsy vehicle was proceeding north on Broadway at its top electric speed of twenty miles an hour when the left rear wheel above which I perched caught in the trolley track and was wrenched off. The wheel careened on ahead of us as the axle struck the pavement and pitched my feet higher than my head. I almost rolled off the seat into the street. The ambulance settled crazily sideways across both north- and south-bound trolley lines and created a traffic jam. It was the afternoon rush hour, at 30th Street just below Herald Square. In response to my driver's telephoned SOS, two more New York Hospital ambulances maneuvered their way to us, one to take me to my call and the other to repair or tow away the one in a state of collapse.

An ambulance on the run attracts little attention, but let it stop and within seconds a curious crowd gathers. Spectators packed in around us, everyone trying to see whatever the man in front saw.

"Three ambulances! It must be *some* catastrophe."

It took a squad of police to get us out of there.

Riots, explosions, holocausts, and other mass disasters only rarely required the simultaneous attendance of all our working ambulances. Two interns riding first and second call were able, if they did not tarry, to cover most of the emergencies in the New York Hospital's district. The reserve intern on third call hopefully slept all day and was off duty entirely that night.

During my many months on the ambulance, the only time when I might leave the hospital was from 7 P.M. to 7 A.M. every third night, unless I persuaded another intern to "hold me up" on the bus. Most of those free twelve hours were spent dining and dancing with Jack. He worried about my not getting enough sleep and insisted on bringing me back at a reasonable hour—one or two o'clock in the morning—because I started first call at 7 A.M. The strenuous first-call day ran until 7 P.M. and I might not have a chance to return to the hospital for hours at a stretch. We "called in" as soon as each emergency was taken care of and I often received another address then by telephone. When I wanted to eat lunch, I asked Mattie (Jo) Mathewson to trade his second call for my first call for a while. Teamwork made the hours bearable. The first-call day was followed by a second-call night from 7 P.M. to 7 A.M. and that by a second-call day, then a first-call night, each for twelve hours, so that we were on continuous first or second call for forty-eight hours. My uninterrupted sleeping time was one day in every seventy-two hours, with catnaps at night. It was a crazy schedule for our biological clocks.

We did not merely conduct a taxi service to the hospital. The majority of patients whom I saw on the ambulance were "treated and left." When I reduced an anterior dislocation of the shoulder on the scene or gave more than simple first aid, however, I expected to see the patient for follow-up care in the New York Hospital emergency service, conveniently located by the ambulance entrance on West 15th Street. The ambulance surgeons were in charge of that accident ward at night, from 10 P.M. until 7 A.M., and I liked to spend time working there between calls. It was routine for us to suture lacerations at the site of the accident and later, at the appropriate time, to remove the stitches ourselves when the patient came in to the emergency ward. If the sewing-up was too big a job to be done on the outside, but the victim was not hurt badly enough to be admitted to the hospital, I had the option of bringing him in on the ambulance and of working at the hospital under better conditions. One man, I recall, got in a razor fight and got the worst of it. He had ten clean slits, each six or eight inches long, in the skin of his chest and back. I brought him in to emergency and after giving him a sedative, I neatly repaired the two yards of damage with a hundred and twenty-three stitches. When a person swallowed poison, I was adept at washing out his stomach at the nearest drugstore or kitchen, before I transported him to the hospital; all that I needed for that, outside of my medical bag, was a pitcher of water and a basin.

The Ambulance Surgeon was also physician to the indigent ill, and the city reimbursed the New York Hospital in part for each ambulance run. At the discretion of the local cop, the ambulance doctor was called to tenement rooms and Skid Row lodging houses to examine adult or child acutely sick with fever, possibly due to pneumonia, diphtheria, secondary syphilis, a heart attack, acute appendicitis, intestinal obstruction, or any cause listed —or unlisted—in the textbook. Asthma, bleeding, and epileptic convulsions presented crucial problems in decision as to whether the patient should be hospitalized or not. Often no bed was available in the New York Hospital and then the patient would have to go to Bellevue. In that city hospital I have seen a ward for thirty persons when it was overloaded with sixty, lying in temporary cots in a double row down the center of the large room and in another row of cots against the walls behind the regular iron beds that were pushed toward the center. At Bellevue, no one in need of hospitalization could be turned away. Sometimes I preferred to treat the sick man and leave him in his own bed, even if the police officer had to put in another ambulance call for us later.

I take off my hat—my old ambulance cap—to the men of the New York police force with whom I worked on city streets and waterfronts, underground in subways and construction tunnels, in slums, prisons, and the backstairs of swank hotels. Although faced with instantaneous decisions and often with personal danger, those police officers usually managed to combine authority with humanity in helping the city Ambulance Surgeon serve the destitute, the dissolute, and the desperate.

Jack thought that every third night was a long time to wait to see me. Evenings when I rode second call, he sometimes came to the New York Hospital to catch me between ambulance trips. Then the night clerk in the front office gave me the key to the Board of Governors' big, high-ceilinged meeting room—the only place in the hospital that I discovered where Jack and I could be alone. Our strange trysting spot had the musty smell of a room shut from the sunlight and little used. Thick walls made it soundless, unless the phone rang for me. We sat in two of the highbacked old leather armchairs that were set in an orderly line close around the magnificent mahogany conference table. We talked in half whispers in the empty stillness. In wigs and robes the presidents of the Board of Governors, from the time when the New York Hospital was chartered in 1771 under the reign of King George III, looked down at us wisely from their portraits, which covered all the walls. We wondered what those early philanthropists would have thought of the new generation of doctors, including women, and of their ultramodern methods of treatment. In the days of the Revolution and the Civil War, the physician had little more to rely on than physic, opiate, quinine, bloodletting, and his gold-headed cane, but he was proficient in the art of medicine.

Jack listened patiently to my account of that day's drama on the bus; we had usually been dancing together only the night before. He seemed so much at home in the world of medicine that when a call came for me, a few times I let him ride with me on the ambulance to its destination. He joined the crowd to see me in action and to wait until I made my disposition of the case. He did not mind if he had to find his way back alone to his nearby apartment at 121 West 11th Street or perhaps to the New York Hospital.

"You handle yourself well in an emergency situation," he complimented me.

"The secret is always to do something, no matter how trivial, and no matter how helpless you feel at first," I told Jack. "That gives you time to think. You remember that you know more about the medical problem than anyone else there and that it is your responsibility."

Late one cold winter night, a rowdy gang was waiting for the ambulance to arrive in our district's toughest tenement neighborhood. The men had been drinking and were in a fighting humor; the couple of cops were having trouble keeping order. A drunken brawler lay on the sidewalk with his head covered with blood. I knelt on one knee on the pavement and made sure that it would be safe to move him, while the obstreperous crowd pressed close. It looked as if I might have more split heads to deal with. I led the way into the only lighted public place that was visible, a hole-in-the-wall restaurant a few doors down the street. The beaten-up victim staggered along behind, half supported and propelled by the officers. The brawny onlookers followed inside and blocked the doorway. To my dismay, I saw that the few small tables with white opaque glass tops would not hold the man's weight and that the floor was layered deep with sawdust. I set my medical bag on a chair, within reach.

"Lay him on the floor," I ordered.

I sat down in the sawdust and took his head in my lap. Those husky men's eyes were popping with surprise. Taking advantage of the moment of quiet, I handed each one an item from my Pandora's box that I would need to clean and sew up the scalp wound. I gave an open bottle of antiseptic solution to a sullen spectator who towered above me, and then swab sticks, sterile forceps, scissors, needle holder, gauze, and adhesive tape, around the circle.

"Hold it away from you—don't let it touch anything—and don't kick the sawdust," I instructed them as I allocated their roles.

Fascinated, my hastily organized team of helpers responded. They even tried to anticipate my next move as I cleaned the scalp, snipped off hair, blotted the blood, and passed the suture through the torn flesh, then tied and cut the thread before the next stitch. It was like a game in which I called the plays.

I changed those recalcitrant idlers into willing participants. They had something to do and they felt needed. They beamed with pleasure when I rewarded them with praise.

Jack and I were very congenial and we never ran out of conversation.

When we did not meet in the evening, he telephoned me, and we talked so long that the hospital switchboard operator often had to interrupt to give me an ambulance call. I think that Jack understood the world in which I grew up better than I did his. I had never seen the South and I could not hear enough about it from him.

Jack's early life on a cotton and peanut plantation in rural eastern North Carolina was very different from mine, yet in some ways they were alike. We both learned the peace of the country and also the intellectual stimulus of the city. When he was a boy, Jack's mother used to take him on the train to exciting events in Norfolk, Virginia, seventy-five miles away. His mother, like mine, played the piano and sang folk songs and lullabies to her children. Evenings at home, she accompanied his father, Edgar Powell, who played the violin. His classmate Frank Winston, later judge and Lieutenant Governor of the State, told how Jack's father had organized the first orchestra at the University of North Carolina and let him beat the drum. At home, neighbors came many nights to join Jack's parents in the music. A cousin, Eddie Bishop, brought his cymbals, drum, and harmonica and played them all at the same time. The cymbals he pedaled with his feet, he drummed with the sticks in his hands, and he moved his mouth along the harmonica, which was conveniently positioned in a rigid frame fixed around his neck. That orchestra fascinated Jack.

When Jack's sister Dorothy Elizabeth was born, on June 5, 1901, their widowed great-aunt, Fanny Bishop Jacobs (Mam), came to live with the family; she had no children of her own. Jack already had two older brothers, Edgar Gordon and Junius Bishop, and the boys adored their little sister. Like my own family, they were closeknit and reared in strong Scotch-English traditions. Their great-aunt Mam was born on January 12, 1844, when John Tyler was our tenth President of the United States, and she lived nearly a hundred years. She was a young woman during the Civil War; she told Jack, and later me, how she buried the family silver in the woods when the Yankee soldiers approached the area. Her father, William Bishop, told her about the Red Coats in the War of 1812 when the British came up Chesapeake Bay and burned the White House and the Capitol. Born on January 13, 1795, in Roxobel, where he lived until his death on January 27, 1863, William Bishop was a small boy during the Presidency of George Washington (1789 to 1797), and Mam quoted his first-hand accounts of the Republic's formative political years, as if they had occurred yesterday. That gave Jack a distinct advantage over me: he had a kind of speaking acquaintance with all the Presidents of the United States that I lacked.

A planter of the Old South, Jack's father was a fine-mannered country gentleman and one of the most respected, most universally loved men in that region. His word was to be trusted more than many a written contract. Robust and active, he covered his farms and the countryside on horseback. The shock was all the greater when in 1908 he died at forty-eight following a sinus operation in Norfolk, Virginia. Jack was only ten years old. Isa Gordon Powell became executrix of her husband's estate and manager of his two farms in Roxobel and Rich Square, which comprised 2,500 acres. Part of the land was subject to overflow by the Roanoke River. That created extra hazards in farming that were later inherited by Jack. Once, the river rose so high that the Coast Guard sent their boats from Norfolk to rescue the tenant farmers from roofs and treetops.

Born during the Civil War, on December 24, 1862, in Hertford, North Carolina, Jack's mother was beautiful, capable, and intelligent. Of strong Episcopal faith, she traveled to participate in Diocesan Convocations in the eastern part of the State. Her ideals of service led her to hope that Jack would join the ministry.

In October, 1911, calamity struck the family again. Gordon, the oldest son and her mainstay in operating the farms, was killed at nineteen by a train on the railroad crossing at Kelford, two miles from home. In October, 1964, during President Johnson's campaign for reelection, I took a picture of that crossing from the rear platform of the Lady Bird Special as the train hesitated there, and Mrs. Johnson, Lynda, Secretary Luther H. Hodges, and Jack waved to the waiting people, among whom stood many of his relatives and boyhood friends.

That autumn after Gordon's tragic death, his mother closed the house in Roxobel and went with Dorothy to the mountains of western North Carolina where Jack and Junius were at Christ School in Arden, near Asheville. They stayed until the Christmas holidays. Returning home with her children and a pet opossum in a box, on the four-hundred-mile train trip Jack's mother caught a bad cold. On January 15, 1912, she died of pneumonia at home under the care of her local physician. There were no miracle antibiotic drugs then. Junius had gone back to prep school, but Jack remained to help keep up the wood fires in the stove or fireplace that heated every room in the house, and he waited on his mother until the end. The night that she died, when she took a turn for the worse, he ran a quarter of a mile in the dark to get one of the tenants on the farm to drive the horse and buggy to town and fetch the doctor. At fourteen Jack was an orphan. He felt as if the end of the world had come.

Character may be strengthened or destroyed by such adversities, depending on its foundations. Maturity at an early age grew from the ruins of Jack's home and made him different.

Great-Aunt Mam and the three Powell orphans were given a home in

Roxobel by their Aunt Leila Powell and her husband, Thomas Spruill Norfleet, in the big house on their farm, another Roanoke River plantation. The
four Norfleet sons, Figuers, William, Edgar, and Eric, and their sister
Annie were older than Junius, Jack, and Dorothy, but they came to regard
each other as brothers and sisters. That second home provided love and
shelter for many years.

Junius and Jack were on their own at prep schools. For two years Jack
attended Warrenton High School, a boarding school seventy-five miles from
Roxobel, where he was well grounded in Latin and mathematics. He was
always popular, enjoyed school life, and even then he was a baseball hero.
He had one year at Randolph-Macon Academy in Bedford, Virginia, before
he entered the University of North Carolina in 1915. One summer he
earned money by making tires in a factory of the Goodyear Tire and Rubber Company in Akron, Ohio. If Jack had not been fully conditioned to hot
weather by the 100-degree summers of sea-level eastern Carolina, exposure
to the steam furnaces in which the rubber tires were cooked should have
built up his tolerance to heat. He can still play a cool game of tennis on
days so hot that they wilt younger men, and me.

Jack's sense of family responsibility expressed itself in unselfish devotion to his sister. Dorothy was three and a half years younger than he. At
sixteen, she went off to school, too, at St. Mary's School in Raleigh, for
three years. Her Great-Aunt Mam had been a student there before the Civil
War. Dorothy's brothers wanted her to enjoy the advantages of living in
New York, and she attended the Rayson School there for one year, 1920 to
1921. Jack gave her fatherly counsel from Montevideo when he had just
completed one year of his three-year overseas contract with the National
City Bank:

August 30, 1920

Dear Podge [her nickname]:
    Snipe [Junius] is having a hard time of it apparently. [He had in-
curred a severe back injury in France during World War I.] You must
try to keep him cheered up. . . . It is a great pity that we three being
so congenial cannot be nearer each other. However, in two more years
when you have finished school and he and I have enough business experience to be getting fair salaries, we shall get a home together where
we can be together and have some good times. We can have a house or
apartment near some city and reunite our broken up family since 1912.
Don't get any ideas about getting seriously in love yet Podge until
we have seen something of each other. . . . After you once leave
school things become much more serious and you lose all your care-
freeness along with most of your friends there. . . . You begin to
wonder what you will be doing 5 years and 10 years hence. . . . I

think that I have been fairly successful so far in my short business career of one year but I am only on the second rung. . . . I hope to have a responsible position in the bank before many more months and then I will have more of an opportunity to see if banking is my line. Remember Podge how much I think of you. . . .

Always,
Jack

On his return from South America in 1922, he declined to renew his National City Bank contract for another period abroad. He entered an allied field of finance and became secretary-treasurer of a firm that dealt in investment securities in Durham, North Carolina. He wanted to be close to Dorothy, who was living then in Roxobel with Great-Aunt Mam. He used to drive his car there from Durham on weekends.

When I first met Jack at the Southern Society ball, Dorothy was married and he had gone back to banking, with the Foreign Department of the Chase National Bank in Wall Street. But in November, 1927, while I was on ambulance service, he resigned from the Chase bank. He decided finally that banking was not his line—eight years after he had signed up for that career in college. In New York, his sedentary desk job was unrelieved by easy access to outdoor sports, and the lack of that activity was unnatural for him. In Uruguay and in North Carolina, the populations were less dense and while he worked there, he had been able to keep himself in top condition by regular golf, tennis, and swimming. That fall of 1927, Jack was half sick with a stubborn sinus infection that he had not been able to throw off. He wanted a vacation in a hot climate; he had in mind a quiet beach at Delray, Florida, on the ocean.

Late one afternoon before Thanksgiving, Jack came to our home at 40 Fifth Avenue to tell me a formal good-bye. We had tea by an open fire. We were in love, but we were a long way from making a commitment to each other concerning marriage. He did not know when he would return to New York. All he would say was that he intended to wait until he felt well again before deciding what to do next—but it would not be banking.

"Perhaps I ought to stay in North Carolina so that I could operate the farms better," he meditated. "New York is a fascinating place, but living here doesn't seem to agree with me—the air is not pure. You can take the boy out of the country, but you can't take the country out of the boy."

In Roxobel he visited his married Norfleet cousins and his Aunt Leila and Uncle Tom. He renewed his resiliency of spirit from them and from the acres of his boyhood home. He also attended to the extensive business of maintaining the family farms there that Junius, Dorothy, and he owned.

After their mother died in January, 1912, without a will, their properties had been managed by the Clerk of the County Court, W. L. Lyon, for about eleven years, until Jack returned from South America. Mr. Lyon did a fine caretaker's job for the three young heirs and the bales of cotton that he collected as rent for the farms paid for their educations. The orphans were financially independent.

Jack stayed away from New York for three and a half months that winter and they seemed like as many years to me. He traveled in the South that was strange to me, from Roxobel to Charlotte for Christmas with his sister Dorothy and her husband, Joe Erwin Moore—Great-Aunt Mam lived there with them—and then to Miami and Delray. After health-giving rest, sunshine, and exercise, he finally made the trip in reverse, reaching New York early in March. The long separation at a critical time of transition for both Jack and me dampened our romance for a while. On the other hand, the frequent letters that traveled between us favored the full expression of our feelings and helped each of us understand the other, as well as our own selves.

DISTANCE WAS A MIRROR

That day was different, when he wrote me.
His thoughts on paper flowed as though he spoke
Directly to me, freely. I could see
That I was diffident whenever he
In person showed me his heart to provoke
An answer. Reticent I need not be
By mail; then his warm touch could not evoke
The growing dissidence inside of me
Between my sense and love's captivity.
The words we wrote we never would revoke.

My letters to Jack were a diary of the slow change that took place in me as Jack won the battle against my exhausting schedule and my feeling of obligation for the years of training to serve in medicine that had been given me by the hospital, the medical college, and my parents. He had to erase, too, the image in my mind—a false image—of the gay southern blade who wore his heart lightly on his sleeve and to whose lips romantic words came easily. Jack had told me in fun how he used to "wear a fashionable dog-stick" in Montevideo. He and several of his buddies in the bank there organized a "Cane Club" and, I gathered, those "young Henglishmen" were in great demand by the lovely senoritas—although the duennas were very strict. Jack's popularity made him the life of many a holiday party in Buenos

Aires, one of the most alluring capitals of the world. As a member of the Uruguay tennis team, he played there in the "little Davis Cup" matches of the southern hemisphere.

For a long time I doubted my capacity to hold forever the love of so attractive, so amusing a man of the world as Jack. I never wanted to change him in any way, but I had to be sure that he knew me as I was and that he would not want to change me. I would have to make compromises between a home and a career, but my profession was bound to introduce complexities that required deep thought. I did not make Jack's courtship easy for him.

"Station B O B signing off," was the way I ended one of my letters to Jack soon after he left New York for Roxobel.

"BOB is a boy's name and you shouldn't use it. I don't like it," he wrote in reply.

Impishly, I added a postscript to my next letter: "P.S. I used to be a terrible 'tom-boy.' I can still climb mountains and rocky ledges and apple-trees, even if you will not have it so! Bob."

A serious protest from Jack followed. He loved mountains, too, but mannish women did not appeal to him. Apologetically I answered:

When I got your letter yesterday, I felt a little like the small boy who is scolded for something he hasn't done. . . . The meaning in a name can only be measured by the associations we have with it. . . . Now, Father has always spoken and written to me as Bob, and nothing else, and I have always loved him better than anything else in the world. So I suppose it has stood to me for comradeship and love and understanding. I rarely sign myself "Bob" to anyone else [I never did again to Jack]. . . . I think I wrote the P.S. about climbing mountains and trees just to be impudent, though it may be true. . . .

I used to wish that I were a boy, but as soon as I discovered how foolish all boys were, and how much wiser and really stronger girls were, I gave up this notion—long ago. To be masculine was the farthest thing from my ambition. . . .

For a girl to attempt to put on mannish airs is for her to warp her true personality. It isn't natural, and it isn't ever necessary, and I don't think it can be justified. . . .

Letters are so cold and inexpressive, compared with live words, that they may not say what we mean at all.

Always, Bobby

As soon as Jack received my explanation, he telephoned me from North Carolina. We had so much to talk about and so many things were left unsaid that his call spurred me to write immediately. He made me feel that he wanted to share every detail of my life.

December 8, 1927. The New York Hospital.

Dear Jack:

Your voice sounded so delightfully clear. . . . That call was worth a dozen letters. . . . This is a first call night [on the ambulance] . . . now they can keep me up until dawn and I shan't mind. . . .

I know you had a moon. . . . Last evening a big one played Peek-a-Boo with me behind the brilliantly lighted Metropolitan Tower, as I went chasing up and down Broadway. We rode all the way up to 49th Street and Broadway on one call, and the moving flashing colored lights, supreme achievements in advertising signs, gave me a never-failing thrill. Do you remember a tumbling, sea-green waterfall with spray rising above it—all in connection with Plumbing Fixtures? Then there was a man violently swinging a baseball bat around and around, way down on West 42nd Street. I needed you to tell me why he was acting up so. . . . I like [best] the bright arrows that flash into existence with light running from feather to point, and then disappear. They don't claim attention for themselves but always for something else, a green boot, or Chop Suey Restaurant, or what not. . . . A call—7th precinct.

Bobby

Riding the city ambulance through Times Square I felt a kinship to the running lurid light of the on-and-off arrows. Often I longed to vanish into darkness as they did, when I reached the "what not" of my destination. On December 17, when I had at last completed the long months on that service, I wrote Jack: "I had to persuade myself that I liked to ride the bus—I had to ride anyway. . . . And I'll tell you a secret—I'm terribly glad to be through with it. I don't like being spectacular—I always tried not to be. . . . Your letter just came by special delivery. . . . You did not know that you wrote me a birthday letter."

I did not know the date of Jack's birthday, either.

For the next six months I was senior intern on the wards of the Cornell Medical Division. My excitement in having responsibility for the continuing care of patients in the hospital overloaded my letters to Jack with people's illnesses, technical details, my sleepless nights and fatigue, yet withal my pride of accomplishment. I told him:

Oh, what a pile of work we've had in the last three days since I came back to the wards. . . . Two pneumonia cases came in. One was put under an oxygen tent, which I was supervising. It's like a steam furnace with a lot of valves, and an ice tank thrown in extra, and a man inside it. Quite a complication. I can't quite explain it, but I had to, to every intern in the hospital nearly, as it's a new piece of apparatus. . . . After riding around all day [on the bus] with my feet up, I suddenly find myself standing for long hours on stone floors, and running up and down long flights of stone stairs. It is very fatiguing.

Sunday evening. January 22, 1928

Dear Jack:

This afternoon things began to happen and being on duty all alone, I've been on the go every minute until now it is 10 P.M. . . . I am on the wards all day long, supervising dinner trays and medications, and giving treatments and answering questions, etc. The Senior really deals as much . . . with the patients as the House Physician does, and . . . a sense of accomplishment is a satisfying reward for long hours of work. I'd like to hold onto these days and turn the hands of the clock back. . . . Last night I went dancing . . . until two, and I tumbled into bed about three. . . . It would have been delightful if you could have been there and if we could have danced together. I was in the mood for dancing, and the music was irresistible, alluring, slow and full of rhythm.

That was not what Jack wanted to hear, in his absence.

Ward L is over-flowing. . . . It is a spooky place at night. There is one old lady who looks like a ghost—face white as a sheet, hair white for about three inches back from the face and rusty black beyond that. It is done up on top of her head with a few wild ends sticking out. She is quite unsettled in her mind, and in the semi-darkness, silently gets out of bed and tries to climb into bed with some other patient who wakes with a start and a loud scream.

Monday night, when I was on alone, a man was admitted to Ward H with a hemorrhage from an ulcer of the stomach, still bleeding. Another intern and I gave him a blood transfusion and he picked up wonderfully . . . and is at least out of danger. It is one of the dramatic . . . things in medicine when a man is snatched out of the grave, as it were.

If I were to tell you half how tired I am, you'd conclude the practice of medicine was very inefficient, at least for the practicee. There has been a succession of sleepless nights . . . and I've been fighting off a cold. . . . Please write me all about the birds and sunsets and clear water and the palm trees and green, soft golf course, and sunshine and blue sky so I may enjoy them in place of this cold grayness and dirty melting snow which fill the sky and streets.

Interested as Jack was in my doings, he had had an overdose of medicine with a capital *M*—I could see that later.

"You are killing yourself with work and you sound very officious. If I stay away a year until you are through in the hospital, I hope you'll have

learned there are other things, beautiful things we can enjoy together. . . .
Why don't you take vacation now and come here to Florida," he wrote
me.

I was studying for Part III of my National Board Examinations. My
answer to his concealed irritation with my absorption in medicine sounded
facetious to him:

> Please don't say I sound "officious." That's a terrible thing to be.
> There's simply lots to do. Do I *really* sound *officious?* I might be a
> year or so older when you return, but I can't imagine how I might
> change much otherwise. I *should* be wiser, but it doesn't always follow.
> . . . If I were to take a vacation now, I'm afraid the hospital would
> make it a permanent one. There could be nothing nicer than to take it
> in Florida. . . . I should so love to dip in the surf and lie on the
> sand and dream away the hours with you. . . . If it demands a year
> to complete your metamorphosis [from a banker], is the length of time
> of any significance? I read something about that in Marcus Aurelius—
> I've found it. He says: "Thou art not dissatisfied, I suppose, because
> thou weighest only so many litrae and not three hundred. Be not dis-
> satisfied then that thou must live only so many years and no more;
> for as thou art satisfied with the amount of substance which has been
> assigned to thee, so be content with the time." It seems it would be
> no more expedient for us to live to be Methuselahs than to look like
> the fat man in the circus. . . . There's my phone . . . so I'll mail
> this on the run.

Our correspondence exchanged our deep feeling for beauty and the spiritual values of life. Jack's poetic letters about love and life's meaning over-
flowed with personal warmth. My letters were spiced with only occasional
overtones of endearment. On December 26, 1927 (his birthday), I received
two letters from Jack and replied:

> Your letter of Christmas day was very sweet and understanding, as
> usual. . . . None of the real and genuine people I have known have
> made me feel more certain that they meant what they said, and also
> that they knew what they were saying, than have you. . . . I have
> so much faith in you. . . . You have showed yourself so plainly it
> is like looking down into a clear deep pool to the rock bottom on
> which lights and shadows are playing, cast by the ripples at the sur-
> face. . . . Your note written on the train came this afternoon—I
> didn't guess you hadn't heard from me in so long. [My letters missed
> Jack in transit between Roxobel and Charlotte and were forwarded.]
> . . . Dear Jack, of course I think of you, or I should not write you.
> . . . I look forward to your return, but would not urge your coming

until you are ready. . . . Don't hurry back to this busy, noisy cold city. . . . Do you think I don't miss you just because I don't say so?

On January 18, 1928: "Dear Jack: My radio is wonderful company, and you know how I love it. . . . Earlier there was some beautiful music —it sounded like the wind in the trees. You are right, music is a vital need. It expresses our emotions for us and . . . soothes our restless moods."

Across the back of that envelope Jack wrote, "My heart is a bleeding wound—music heals love." I saw it years later.

I continued:

You've been "feeding your soul" on the beauty of the ocean and the quiet of the country and so (as you say) you came nearer to God's peace and contentment that is lost in the complexity of the city, in a man-made environment. . . . On Sunday I got off in time to go to Communion Service at the Church of the Ascension. . . . I love the church with the beautiful La Farge painting, and the [sculptured] angels over the altar, and the two tall slender candles, and the deeply colored stained glass windows. It is beautiful to the eye . . . and sublime to your spirit. . . . I heard Dr. Fosdick preach on the radio this evening. His topic was built around the idea that "we don't have to make up our opinions, we have to make up our lives." Whatever we may say or think we believe, it is the direction we give to our lives at the deciding points, in love, and trouble, and sorrow, that counts. . . . On points of doctrine, the virgin birth or the Trinity, or on the nature of God, the creative force of the universe . . . I can't make up my mind, nor can I feel that it would affect my daily life directly if I could. Do you think so?

Jack replied: "I am not concerned about doctrine. The great things are simple and hard—purpose and faith and integrity, carrying a share of the world's responsibilities. . . . So, in the end old age may be the best time of life, unspoiled by regrets and sweetened by much wisdom and unafraid of the life after death. . . . I want to help you to find more beauty and to give more to life now."

A sheet of stationery inadvertently precipitated a misunderstanding between Jack and me. I had been writing to him on plain, personal letter paper or notepaper that carried only the address, "40 Fifth Avenue." On January 25 when he was in Delray, I happened to use business-style paper printed with the letterhead, "Dr. Janet G. Travell, 40 Fifth Avenue, New York City." There loomed in his lonesome mind a vision of my opening a medical practice at that address with my father and of my anchoring myself in New York, while he took second place. He insisted on being first, and he told me so.

I took Jack's reaction seriously and on February 2 I mailed him a hastily written discourse:

Dear Jack:

I've had this letter paper quite a long time. . . . It isn't news to you, is it, that the brief statement at the head of the sheet is a fact? . . . I'm afraid that I blossomed out as a doctor some time ago. Of course, more and more responsibility is attached to that as the months go on, and I'm trying to learn so that I'll be able to carry it, and do a little good instead of a lot of harm. An intelligent, conscientious doctor may be of some use. . . . Really, I am not playing a game, nor am I trying to make a name for myself. . . . I try to do as well and as promptly as possible each thing that is given me to do, and that makes for the greatest comfort of the people who are here as patients.

You'd be astonished how fond one can grow to be of . . . these people, babies, children, men and women in their prime, and old folks who look far backward as well as forward. Kindness toward them is an instinctive act, it isn't a thing one . . . comments on, but it's a predominating quality of most of the interns. Gratitude . . . on the part of the patients is not asked or expected—but it's often expressed —and brings satisfaction, though good medical results are the aim of our work. . . . You can't talk about the human side—it's too close. I've seen the whole staff of the hospital go into a state of depression on the death of some person who'd had a fighting spirit and for whom everyone had worked long and weary hours—and not a word said, just gloom.

It simply absorbs one. Perhaps you'd say we were "officious" at work. Yet we can't share our private lives with all these people. What would you have?

You haven't any notion how tired I can be, and yet feel contented. I'm not doing much outside the hospital. You know I'm on call for all the night work [seven nights a week]. Last night I was up until 3 . . . the night before until 2 A.M.—nearly every night something.

You're mistaken if you think it's a sacrifice. It's pure happiness. It doesn't represent all the happiness one asks from the world, by any means. . . .

I don't want to "impress you" . . . I hate shams and poses as much as you do. You know being a doctor is a part of me, I can't put it on or off like a dress. I might cover it up with something else, or it might wear off in time in the way one grows a new skin. . . .

I'm here in the maelstrom [of New York] . . . in the hubbub. There is a kind of peace gained from activity, like swimming with vigor through strong waves. Of course, it isn't *necessary* for anyone to live in any *particular* way [I was thinking of myself, as well as Jack, but he did not take it that way]. . . . If a young man's spirit feels confined by city walls and streets, and if his body craves country air and exercise, there isn't any reason why he should force himself to remain there. . . . Isn't it *what* one does and not *where* one does it that counts, Jack?

This is a long harangue, but you started me off on it. . . .

Dear Jack, distance, a few miles more or less, doesn't matter. It couldn't separate people. Only it seems such a *terribly* long time since I've seen you.

It is now 1:30 and I can try for a rest. I am too sleepy to read this over.

As always,
Bobby

I felt misunderstood, but "office hours" day and night clouded my judgment.

Jack was far from content with my arguments, and I could see that I had hurt him. I tried again on February 14, still using Dr. Janet G. Travell's stationery. He was on his way back to Charlotte.

Dear Jack:

I didn't answer your letter of Monday, the sixth, from Delray. I was so hurt and surprised by its sarcasm that I didn't know what to say, and besides there was a finality about its tone. . . . This morning a letter came mailed from Tampa, and apparently you did expect an answer. Now let me show you the situation here.

For the past year that you've known me, I've had to work frightfully hard, and under high nervous tension. I love to roam, to see new places, to be out of doors, just as you do. Instead I've been "cribbed, cabined and confined." I've been . . . living in one building—sleeping, eating and working under one roof. It isn't a natural or balanced existence, but for the experience and knowledge which can be concentrated in this time, I put up with it, with the expectation that I shall never have to do so again. . . . I can't help being moody and discouraged at times.

Now, when . . . I'm wondering why I'm not doing some of the happy and carefree things outside that I'd so love to do, you write and make fun of all this effort. Then having stepped on my toes, when I say Ouch, you jump on them hard with both feet. . . .

If sarcastic, my letter was unintentionally so, Jack, and I was astounded by its effect. I had a sense of failure, that I had been unable to create a strong enough bond of understanding for me, as well as for you, to be inconsistent and contradictory sometimes. . . .

In about ten more months, I shall start living again and will *take* time for the leisure which everyone needs. In the meantime, please be patient with me, Jack. You've scarcely ever known me away from this evil combination of city and hospital atmosphere. So you only half know me, really.

New York is a habit with me, nothing more, and perhaps a bad habit. I'm as fickle in my love for it as you are. . . . For the present, I happen to live here.

There isn't anything new in this letter. I think you knew all this before, but just forgot it for a while. Only don't be proud and haughty and cutting, because I'm not acquainted with that person, never met him before, and think he was just masquerading in your clothes.

Always,
Bobby

My previous letter of February 2 that had disturbed Jack was focused on what the role of Good Physician meant to me. Now I recognized that existence as incomplete—not balanced or natural. I reminded him of that other half of me that made a whole person, with whom he might some day find happiness and create a home anywhere that we chose to live. Jack's next letter revived me and on February 18, I sent him a special delivery to Charlotte:

Dear Jack:

There has been a fresh clean wind blowing here. . . . It came out of your letter and quite cleared the air. . . . I feel so gay I could dance all around the room even to a Symphony, now playing. . . . My radio is back. . . . I hooked up the new batteries, and Father has put in a new dial to tell me how much current I'm using, so I can't burn them out without knowing it. [Jack put a new dial on me to register the pace of my activities and he kept his eye on it always.]

Suppose we return to the more personal subject of ourselves, on which, Kind Sir, I should like to make a few remarks. I think we can sometimes know each other better through a misunderstanding, cleared away. If I hadn't felt that there was a mistake, I'd *never* have answered your last letter from Delray. . . . But to have written a letter like that, your sensitive and naturally kind and generous spirit must have been badly wounded, and I am very sorry if I was the cause. I'd never have troubled to say so if I hadn't understood the strain of the metamorphosis, O Caterpillar, and if I hadn't cared for the outcome.

Will you make a pact with me? We are both temperamentally like boilers; the steam is compressed until the pressure rises too high, and then there's an explosion unless there's an outlet valve. If you should feel hurt at some inadvertent act or word of mine, trust me enough to tell me about it, and I will guard against a second thoughtlessness. And I will try to do the same.

Being a woman, I cannot hope to understand you, or this spiritual harmony of our personalities—so I am told. I [am] . . . in a hopeless dilemma of being expected to do something I cannot be expected to do. It makes me feel like some impossible thing like the Cheshire Cat or a haunting dream or the fourth dimension. . . . You have put me in this dilemma, so will you kindly let me out? . . .

Your letter . . . answered several questions at the back of my mind, only half-formulated perhaps. . . . Yes, we'll dance and see new things and live—we'll feel perfectly free to be ourselves. We're not playing a game—at least if we do, we'll make up the rules for it together, as we go along. The agreement must be unanimous and only two votes are required to make it so. That should be easy, shouldn't it?

Always,
Bobby

Just a year after Jack and I had fallen in love at a dance, on February 22, 1928, he was in Roxobel on his way back to me. I wrote on that holiday:

So you're a bird of passage again, preceding all the other birds on their spring migrations. You should catch all the worms (including me). . . . Your last letters have restored the contact that was lost. . . . Now that you are on your way back, I can say how glad I am. . . . Every time I've wanted to see you, I've felt it was selfish of me even to wish you were here when your stay in the South was doing you so much good. . . . I am sure that any unhappy differences we may have felt will vanish into thin air when we can really talk in front of the fire, Jack. . . . We have a fundamental outlook and harmony of ideas. I think of you in connection with so many little things that I see and do that I know it must be so. It's late.

Good-night,
Bobby

The dusk of an early March afternoon masked the grime of New York's streets when Jack telephoned me at the hospital the moment he reached his apartment at 121 West 11th Street. So as to meet as quickly as possible, he would walk crosstown, then up the west side of Fifth Avenue and I would start down from 16th Street. On the Avenue between 13th and 14th Streets, before I was near enough to distinguish his face in the half light, I recognized him by his straight figure and easy walk among all the stooped and scurrying people. We spoke of little things as we walked arm in arm toward the brownstone house at 40 Fifth Avenue to sit by the fire. My Jack was different, for he loved me.

We were not yet ready to contemplate marriage. Jack had to establish himself in a new field of work. He formed a partnership in the import-export business with Latin America, which took advantage of his banking experience in those Spanish-speaking countries.

I had to live in the New York Hospital for nine more months, and I sorely needed a respite from my day-and-night duties there. Two months after Jack returned to New York, I attended my first medical meeting of national scope, and it was held in Washington. Although I found the scientific program exciting, I was not content to listen to investigators presenting their papers all day. Somehow, I found an entrée to events that were happening in the city. On May 3, 1928, I wrote a letter to Jack from the Hotel Grafton on Connecticut Avenue:

> Jack, dear:
> Today has been wonderful. We went in the morning to the [Potomac] Falls as I told you, great angry rushing boiling cascades of brown flood waters. The apple blossoms and dogwood are at their height and one could not walk in the woods without stepping on violets. . . . We had a picnic lunch (stylish kind) and grew very happily drowsy on fresh air and food. . . . Now, I have been holding back a surprise: . . . I went next to the reception for the fliers, with Surgeon General and Mrs. Ireland. I had my hand kissed by the Baron and the Major and shaken by the Irishman, all of whom are very homely. [Baron G. von Huenefeld with a crew of six on April 12 to 13 had performed the remarkable feat of flying nonstop across the ocean from Dublin to Labrador in thirty-seven hours.] I met Captain Maitland who flew to Hawaii and his navigator, the former being very tall and handsome and American looking. I never saw so many stars and medals and so much gold braid all congregated together before. General Ireland called for me himself, and can you imagine—I wasn't quite ready and had to keep a General waiting. . . . I shall go to some more meetings tomorrow. . . . Evelyn Holt [Wellesley 1919, Cornell medical school 1923, and the New York Hospital's first woman intern, just ahead of me] had to go back this morning, so I'm enjoying the suite alone now. I have a tree outside my window.

Trees on the main avenue of our capital city were a matter for comment.

That spring, my mother was involved in remodeling the house for our new home and my father's offices—40 Fifth Avenue had been sold. The process of moving would make new demands on me, especially since she was not well. Vacation was due me before I assumed the responsibilities of House Physician at the end of June. In May, after the medical meeting in Washington, my mother and I took a boat to Bermuda—the rest would do us both good. Now the tables were turned on Jack; he was hard at work in New York and I had time to think, not riding the ambulance through Times Square, but under a sunny sky to the sound of real sea-green water.

The only way to see that island then was by horse and buggy or on a bicycle. My mother had bicycled in Bermuda when she was young, but in 1928 her heart was aging and she was short of breath when she climbed stairs or walked uphill too fast. She took digitalis medication, and she was putting an elevator in the new house. Bicycling on the hard, level roads required relatively little physical effort, but most of Bermuda was hilly. I devised a plan that pleased my mother. I bought twenty or twenty-five feet of light manila rope and fastened our two bicycles together so that I could tow her up the hills, while she sat and rested. One end of the rope was tied to the frame underneath my bicycle's seat, and the other end to the handle-bar post of hers. When we coasted downhill or pedaled on the level, with one hand she wound the slack into the basket in front so that we could ride side by side. We dismounted on the steepest hills and I pushed both bicycles while she took her time walking up the grade. We thought it great sport and I jerked her off her bicycle only once.

Jack seemed to be with me every moment. On May 7, I wrote him in New York from the Hotel Frascati on the inlet at The Flatts, where I could dive from our bedroom balcony into the salt water:

Dear Jack:

Mother and I . . . bicycled all afternoon without disaster. The roads are of white limestone and quite level near the shores which some of them follow closely. Tomorrow . . . we may bike into St. Georges, eight or nine miles. . . . There is no twilight here . . . and the night is black in spite of bright starlight. There is no moon to-night. . . . I can send you no messages by him. So I'll have to write you this note instead to say, Good-evening and shall we go for a stroll in spite of the blackness and mystery of the night? There is a grounded freighter on a reef just off the inlet, thrashing around, sounding as though all devils were battering it to pieces. It . . . is eery, clattering and banging out there in the dark, but if you were here, I shouldn't be afraid. . . . So now Good-night, dear and Pleas-ant Dreams,

Bobby

The beautiful hours at Bermuda that week were empty without Jack. It was then that I came to terms with the fact that I needed his love as much as he wanted mine. So I was different, when my mother and I returned to New York on Monday, and it did not take Jack long to discover it. The very next day we were separated again; my mother and I drove to Merryfield

Farm for the balance of my two weeks of vacation. I sat there alone by the fire and wrote him:

May 16, 1928, Sheffield, Mass.

Dear:

You and I have been walking in a dream-cloud since those sweet moments that were Monday night. Time is so lamentably short for us. . . . I wish you were here beside me before the fire—you know there are no clocks or time at Sheffield.

Sheffield is always more beautiful than I remembered and its charm always fresh and new . . . with the young tender leaves on the trees as you imagined, and the grass startlingly green. There are plum, peach and cherry blossoms at their height—it is still early for apple blossoms —and there is a snowy white, soft flowering tree that grows wild in the woods, called the Shadbush. Violets and wood anemones grow in the moist and shady places. You see it is very early spring here.

This evening I got your letter at Mrs. Merriefield's . . . a very beautiful and dear letter, Jack. As I know you better, I appreciate more and more how fine and unselfish and understanding love can be. . . . All that you say about love, the love you would give and wish in return, is as true for me as for you. . . . I've never been in the habit of doing things by half measures, and I want to be able to love fully, intensely, happily.

Love grows slowly for me, though. Dear, you know that I do love you—I've told you so—but it is only a fraction of the love which I am capable of giving. . . . Sweetheart, all the time I am discovering that it is stronger and deeper than I knew. . . . Hours away from you lack a sparkle and zest which the hours we spend together possess. . . . When things interest and please me I immediately long to share them with you, and I know that we will see them from similar points of view, because our principles and beliefs, the rocks of our being, are alike. I know that I love to be near you, to let you hold me in your arms—Sweet Jack, isn't all this love?

It doesn't lessen my interest in things and people, but rather enhances it, and doesn't seem to absorb me as much as it broadens me. Should love do this?

I must put out the fire and go to bed—the room grows chilly. So Goodnight, dear, and I send you my love.

Bobby

I was a slow learner, but Jack was a patient teacher.

When my mother died suddenly of a heart attack in October, 1928, I learned what a comfort Jack was in time of sorrow. In December, my father and I transferred the urn that contained my mother's ashes to the Davidson family vault in the cemetery at Albany. He and I drove by to look at my mother's beloved Merryfield Farm and then went on to visit Evelyn Washburne Treanor and her family at Pittsfield. From there on December 20, 1928, I sent Jack a special delivery letter to New York:

> We reached the farm about three, where we surprised Roy at work hauling firewood. Then we surprised Mrs. Merriefield at the foot of the hill by our mid-winter call. . . .
>
> It seems no time at all since I was [here] in May, and so much has happened since. Then, I was just learning how much I loved you, Jack, and now I know: love is simply immeasurable. . . .
>
> Of course, I'll be back tomorrow and I'll see you then, but I wanted to send you just a little message to tell you that I love you.
>
> With all my love,
Bobby

By Christmas I would complete my hospital service and we were planning to be married.

"You were a citadel and I had a hard time storming it," Jack said.

The surrender was unconditional.

CHAPTER 11

Marriage and Medicine

I had the feeling that Jack and I were eloping. It was December 27, 1928, and we were aboard the overnight sleeper bound for Charlotte, North Carolina, from New York. Jack was taking his Yankee sweetheart south to meet his sister and we would spend the long New Year's weekend with Dorothy and her husband, Joe Moore, and Great-Aunt Mam who lived in their home. At last I would see for myself the fair Southland that Jack loved and I would sample North Carolina's vaunted hospitality. My excitement was a tonic.

My two years of voluntary confinement in the New York Hospital had ended just before Christmas. Then I moved into Ginny and Pop's small frame house at 72 Orange Street in Brooklyn Heights, that had been the kitchen of the old Hicks farm. It was already crowded; my father had been living there since my mother died in October and my niece, another Virginia Weeks, was nine months old. Jack joined us for Christmas dinner, which Ginny cooked—she was a wonderful cook, like my mother. There he and I decided to move our departure for Charlotte up a day to Thursday, December 27; we could not wait to set off together. He would send a telegram the next day to Dorothy in Roxobel where she, Mam, and Joe had driven for Christmas with the Norfleets, two hundred and fifty miles across the state.

Our arrival a day sooner than first planned would not matter to Dorothy, Jack was sure. They had been visiting in Roxobel for a week.

My struggle for time off duty when Jack and I could be together was over. In effect, we were starting a new life together at that moment. Both of us had already made most of the adjustments within ourselves that would allow us happily to combine marriage and medicine. We had learned to trust each other's love and understanding. We were not competing with each other in any way. Our companionship had grown and we had begun to share each other's friends.

In looking forward to our future together, each of us, without raising the issue, had made an important revision of attitude. I did not ask Jack to live with "office hours: day and night." He had made me see that neither satisfaction nor usefulness in medicine depended on that kind of service. I accepted a job starting January 1, 1929, with limited hours—no night work —and without the total responsibility of the practicing physician for the patient. I would be the Fellow on a collaborative clinical research project to attempt to answer the controversial question: What value has digitalis in the treatment of lobar pneumonia? [1]

The study was directed by Dr. Alfred E. Cohn of the Rockefeller Institute and was conducted by three university medical services—Cornell, New York University, and Columbia—on their ten wards at Bellevue Hospital. I would have two technical assistants and the latest model Einthoven string-galvanometer, compactly mounted on a table with rubber wheels. The investigation was broad in scope and appealed to me vastly; it would combine my basic interests in pharmacology and cardiology—in science and people.[2]

For his part, Jack relinquished his tentative idea of returning to North Carolina to live. He thought that it might not be possible for me to fulfill my potential for service there. He wanted to help me achieve that, not to hinder me. Also, he had discovered that he could work in New York, after all, yet lead the healthy active life that had been impossible when he was desk-tied at the Chase National Bank, with golf only on a Sunday at his club twenty-five miles from the city. Jack and I had found a way to enjoy outdoor exercise together for at least a short time nearly every day.

That summer of 1928, Jack and I used the old gravelly tennis court that the New York Hospital maintained in a vacant lot across from the hospital,

[1] John Wyckoff, Eugene F. DuBois, and I. Ogden Woodruff, "The Therapeutic Value of Digitalis in Pneumonia," *Journal of the American Medical Association*, Vol. 95 (1930), pp. 1243–1249.
[2] John Wyckoff, Harry Gold, and Janet Travell, "Importance of Differences in the Potency of Digitalis in Clinical Practice," *American Heart Journal*, Vol. 5 (1930), pp. 401–411; and Arthur De Graff and Janet Travell, "An Electrocardiographic Study of the Heart in Lobar Pneumonia," *Journal of Clinical Investigation*, Vol. 10 (1931), pp. 633–651.

between 14th and 15th Streets. It was wedged against two high loft buildings that were too close to the ragged chalk lines; the lack of standard space
did not detract from our fun or exercise. Our ball sometimes sailed over the
high board fence into the street and we peeked through a knothole to see
where it went. In tennis clothes I was still House Physician and accessible
for emergencies on my wards and for new admissions. A messenger could
always be sent for me, and I was skilled in fast changes of dress. Jack and I
and others on the house staff got up a game of doubles, or Jack and I played
singles until the moon rose over the two or three skinny ailanthus trees on
one side of the court.

Under those trees was an old-fashioned wood-slat swing, the kind with
two seats facing each other. On a hot summer evening we used to sit and
swing with our feet up on one seat. As a trysting place, disregarding dust
and traffic noises, we liked it better than the tomblike Board of Governors
room in the hospital.

Bridget, who took care of the doctors' small dining room, knew where
to find me. Night after night she came across 15th Street, opened the board
door in the fence with a key—we all had keys to its Yale lock—and complained: "Dr. Travell, I can't keep your dinner hot any longer—now come
on in. I've saved something special from the private side, for you and your
friend."

That all seemed a long time ago. To the soothing sound of wheels on
tracks, Jack and I sat together and talked while the porter made up the
berths for the night. Christmas travel was heavy and Jack had been lucky to
secure a lower for me at one end of the car and an upper berth for himself
at the other end. The conductor came through the train taking up tickets
and noticed the separate location of ours.

"I can put you folks up in a section if you don't mind moving back a
car," he volunteered.

We must have looked married.

"We'll stay where we are," Jack replied, without looking at me.

The train was due in Charlotte at noon. I primped in the ladies' lounge,
set my hat at the correct angle, dusted off my shoes, and inspected my
appearance in the full-length door mirror. Long before the train pulled into
the station I had put on my coat and gloves. I wanted Jack to be proud of
me.

He handed me down the high step and our eyes scanned the people who
were waving and scrambling across the tracks to meet arrivals. No one
spotted us.

"They must have been delayed. Let's go into the station," Jack suggested cheerfully.

Saying little, we sat on a high-backed, hard wooden bench in the waiting room. We watched the clock and flow of travelers.

"I'd better telephone the house," Jack said with less optimism. He was gone for several minutes—it always seemed like a long time when he was away from me.

"The house doesn't answer. They must be on their way." Half an hour had passed since we got off the train and Jack looked baffled. After a while he went back to the phone booth.

"I finally reached Maria Tucker. She has a key to the house—she's on her way here to get us."

Maria was an unmarried distant cousin, a generation older. She was much concerned about the lack of welcome for me by Jack's family. She had not heard from Dorothy and Joe. She drove us in her car to 1301 East Morehead Street. The red-brick house was set back from the broad avenue on a rise among tall, straight loblolly pines, so different from the white pine of the Berkshires. The scenery was wintry. Maria unlocked the front door and we stepped from bright sunlight into the living room, which was darkened by drawn drapes. The oil burner had been set on low and the house was cold. Jack pushed up the thermostat.

"So this is southern hospitality," I thought to myself.

We held a conference in the cheerless den. Joe had had the gas turned off during their absence and Jack called the gas company to get it turned on.

"If they don't show up, I'll come over for the night and chaperone you," Maria offered.

Jack telephoned the Norfleets in Roxobel. Yes, Dot, Joe, and Mam had left in the morning, but before Jack's telegram was delivered. The wire had taken more than twenty-four hours to get there via the railroad station in Kelford. They were not yet aware that we had changed our plans.

Maria fixed lunch for us at her house and loaned Jack her car. Feeling like conspirators, we bought steaks and other things for dinner. He calculated that his family would reach home by seven o'clock and we would have a hot meal ready for them.

"I wish I could get hold of Adlonia, Dorothy's cook," Jack meditated. "I used to know where she lived."

We drove around in the colored residential section of Charlotte and Jack inquired for her in several houses, without success. We were just driving off when Jack recognized Adlonia standing on a street corner, and she was glad to come with us.

The house was warm and lighted, a bright fire was burning in the fieldstone fireplace of the den and the cook was in the kitchen when at seven exactly we heard a car drive in at the rear of the house and Joe turned his key in the lock of the side door. Jack and I had stepped into the den, out of sight. I was uneasy. I looked at Joe's collection of guns on the wall above the fireplace; hunting and skeetshooting were his chief recreation. I wondered what went through his mind when he saw the lights on in the house—burglars? And how would Dorothy feel about having me, in a sense a stranger, enter her home in her absence?

Adlonia went quickly to meet them and Jack called a greeting as he stepped from our hiding place into the center hall. Dorothy leaned toward him, and whispered, as he told me much later, "Where's your wife?"

Like a good squaw, I appeared behind Jack. Dorothy's aplomb was complete. She kissed me, and said with rare warmth, "This is the nicest homecoming we ever had."

Dorothy's low-pitched voice had the husky quality of charm that I came later to associate with Jacqueline Kennedy's tone of speaking. Dorothy was littler than I had pictured and more beautiful. A dark brunette, she had wide-spaced brown eyes like Jack's, but in contrast with his deep tan her skin was as fair as a pink-tinted camellia. She shared with Jack a power of inner strength that made her durable in adversity—I was to see more of that in years to come. She moved like a dancer, on tiptoe. In fact, one of her ankles had been surgically fused in the tiptoe position and she balanced on the toes of her other foot, too. After multiple operations in Durham and Atlanta for a bad compound fracture of that ankle when she was thrown from a runaway horse in 1923, surgical stabilization of the joint had finally enabled her to walk. Joe had shown her constant love and attention during her long illness, and they were devoted to each other. They had been married four years. The pattern of Dorothy's life was greatly modified by that horseback accident, but she did not let her handicap disable her.

Dorothy and I were nearly the same age, but our worlds had been very different. From the start, in spite of my invasion of her privacy, mutual understanding and affection drew us together. As the years passed, even more than sisters we came to depend on each other in many ways. Dorothy was much like her brother, Jack.

Great-Aunt Mam was eighty-four and she was mortified that Jack's family had not been on hand to greet me. I had never met anyone like her. She was large of frame, taller than I, and she had not shrunk with age. She was as active as women twenty years younger, although she was lame and often leaned on a cane; it brought her offers of aid. She pretended to be deaf and to see poorly, but she heard what she wanted to hear and she could read without glasses. She was always misplacing them. Jack's respect for his elders, his chivalry toward women, and his special love for Mam were evident in his thoughtful solicitude for her every wish. He and Dorothy teased her constantly, but Jack's wit was never unkind. He brought her chocolates, which she devoured while he told her that candy was not good for her. Mam returned the teasing mischievously—she and my father were alike in that respect.

"Mam, you don't even remember what your husband looked like," Jack used to tell her. Dr. Jacobs, a physician, had been dead for forty years.

"Tut, tut, you silly boy," Mam replied coyly.

Mam found most old people dull. Like my father, she remained young because she kept up with the younger generations; she carried on a voluminous correspondence with the family. She filled a pretty candy box with letters that she had to answer, "so I can see and handle it every day," she said. She was well educated, as were most of Jack's women forebears, I learned. Mam read books constantly and she had a remarkable memory to the day of her death at nearly ninety-eight. On October 26, 1936, when she was ninety-two, she wrote Jack: "I've been reading 'Gone with the Wind'—a bad book, never ought to have been written." She must have changed her mind about it, however, for a couple of months later she wrote us. "I've read more trash than I believed I could, & now I'm just waiting for any other books that come along. . . . 'Gone with the Wind' was given me—think I enjoyed it with a few exceptions—[I hope] I never hear again of such people as 'Scarlette & Capt. Butler.' . . . Poor letter, but it's going, & write soon."

Mam knew from her own experience the plantation hazards and hardships of the Civil War, but she and Scarlett O'Hara had nothing in common.

It was only two months since my mother's sudden death and Jack had told Dorothy that we needed a quiet time. Charlotte was a sociable city, but we did not attend any of the New Year's parties. I was treated as a lady of leisure and breakfast was served me in bed. It was a welcome luxury. For dinner, Joe provided quail that he had shot in the corn and peanut fields at Roxobel, and I was introduced to water-ground corn meal and black-eyed peas—pretty fancy beans, I thought.

Dr. John Hill Tucker with his wife and Joe's uncles, Baxter and Wylie Moore, both doctors, dropped in to meet me. Jack could not escape from the aura of physicians. Dr. Wylie, a prominent surgeon, held the floor against most comers, and he flew his own airplane. He had interned at Bellevue Hospital in New York where he had acquired progressive attitudes. He was getting his patients up out of bed the day after an operation and sending them home in five days! Early ambulation was a heretical procedure then, but acceptable fifteen to twenty years later. We at Cornell's Department of Pharmacology helped make it so.[3]

Jack took me off for long walks in the piney woods, and the mild winter climate surprised me. We even played tennis out of doors at the country club. For us to have time to roam together without pressure of instant work was a foretaste of happiness.

After four days of bliss I took the sleeper to New York alone on Tuesday night, January 1. Jack returned by way of Roxobel and stopped off on business for several days in Virginia. On January 2, I came down out of the clouds. I went from Pennsylvania Station to Bellevue Hospital for my first day at work on the medical wards. It was strange how my scale of relative values had changed in a year. That night I wrote Jack in Roxobel:

> It seems a long time since we separated. . . . Each day when I don't see you seems like a day wasted. . . . The train was a half hour late, but it didn't matter. . . . Father was there to meet me, and took my bags and drove me to the hospital. . . . My boss [Dr. John Wyckoff] told me he would like to see me about once a week, and said a few more words and turned me loose. . . . I shall have to go to the hospital on Sunday morning, but not every Sunday. The work promises to be very interesting. . . . After all, I have two assistants and a *salary*. [Hospital interns and residents were not paid anything in those days.] Ginny stopped for me at the hospital about five this afternoon. This commuting from Brooklyn will be dreadful. I guess I'll go across the Brooklyn Bridge on foot or by trolley, and then catch the 2nd Ave. El to 23rd Street.

Ginny and Pop made me welcome in their little house. Although my "office hours" were daytime only, six or seven days a week, the mechanics of living were complicated. My father was busy in his office at 9 West 16th Street, but the reconstruction of the rest of the house that my mother had blueprinted was behind schedule. On September 29, 1928, four weeks before she died and while she was still occupying 40 Fifth Avenue, she instructed that the insurance on our old home be canceled as of October 5, when she would move out. She wrote in a letter:

> We thank you for the permit for use of oil burner furnace at 9 West 16 Street. The tank was placed in the ground today [underneath my father's front office] and should be in operation in a couple of weeks. We hope to have the passenger elevator . . . installed in about three weeks. . . . The alterations at 9 W. 16 St. were begun about Aug. 5th

[3] Cornell Conference on Therapy, "Use and Abuse of Bed Rest," *New York State Journal of Medicine*, Vol. 42 (April 1, 1944), pp. 724–730; reprinted in *Cornell Conferences on Therapy*, Vol. 1 (New York, The Macmillan Company, 1946), pp. 18–35.

and at the present slow rate are liable to continue two months longer.
. . . When the job is done we expect to have a very up to date house.

It was late spring of 1929 before our new home was ready enough for me and my father to camp out in it. We had to arrange the furniture and rugs and to unpack all my mother's household and personal possessions that had been stored there since October. I thought that I would never see the end of plaster dust; it crept into everything. If my father was down-hearted, he never showed that face to me.

The date for Jack's and my marriage could not be set until I had achieved some semblance of order in the house. On May 1, my father announced our engagement and *The New York Times* made it official. We were tentatively aiming at a June wedding. One evening early in May, in the midst of the endless packing boxes and trunks Jack and I telephoned my Uncle Sheldon, the bishop, in Chicago and he agreed to come east to marry us on Thursday night, June 6, at the Church of the Ascension. It was the only date that month that fitted his schedule.

Jack still had to decide where we would live. After talking with my father, he rented one of the newly created smaller apartments upstairs at 9 West 16th Street. I would keep house downstairs for my widowed father and, in a sense, my father would live with us. I would have to see to it that Jack was not overdosed again with medicine—with a capital *M*.

A bride, as a rule, fails to appreciate what her mother does for her in planning a big church wedding and a gala reception at home. I knew what was involved because I attended to the details myself with Jack's help. It is not often that the bridegroom participates to such an extent in the arrangements for his own wedding. It was a crash affair, getting the invitations engraved and lining up bridal attendants and ushers. The task of fitting dresses was not made easier by my choice of a rainbow wedding. Mrs. Edith Bates, Roswell Bates's widow and my mother's close friend, loaned me her train-length wedding veil of Belgian rosepoint lace, which was a family heirloom. Jack's brother Junius was his best man and Ginny, my matron of honor. Julia, Jack's sister-in-law, and Ginny helped us assemble the guest list and address envelopes. Dorothy was in the bridal party, of course, and at the rehearsal dinner on June 5, we surprised her with a cake and candles for her birthday.

Until the first of June I was carrying on the research program of the Digitalis-Pneumonia Study. I was also training my substitute for the month that I would be away on a honeymoon.

I wished many times then that Jack and I had really eloped on that New Year's trip to Charlotte. It was not the wedding that mattered to me, but our being together for the rest of our lives. My father wanted me to have the best of everything, and I was persuaded that the occasion would lift his spirits. I concluded in the end that the effort to bring our family and friends together was worthwhile and it made my father happy.

The wedding ceremony is a blur in my memory until Jack, holding his high silk hat, and I with my satin and lace train looped over my arm hurried from the church, under the awning, and across the sidewalk, into a sudden limelight of flashbulbs.

"Everybody happy?" was the caption under our picture as bride and groom in New York's *Daily News*. It was obvious that we were. When we settled back into the waiting limousine and I realized that we were married at last, it was the moment of deepest contentment in my life.

OUR LOVE WOULD STAND THE TEST OF TIME

My Jack was different: he married me.
He recognized better than I what sort
Of love was relevant to the full free
Union of our lives. Bitter jealousy
Had no home with us. I need not resort
To feuds of dominance since I could see
That I had his heart. He gave me support
To reach for excellence; hours I worked he
Did not resent—he held my heart, you see.
The love we wrought the years would not distort.

Nothing marred our honeymoon. Jack wanted to show me scenic spots in the Blue Ridge Mountains of western Virginia and in the Great Smokies of North Carolina, with long pauses in the small inns of his choice to dance, play tennis, and swim. He drove the convertible car at a leisurely speed so that I could breathe the fragrance of honeysuckle along the roadsides. He knew how much I loved to feel mountain air blow in my face, and we hardly ever put the top up. Its operation was not automatic. In a rain shower, Jack opened a big black umbrella that I held over both of us and we kept going. The upholstery was leather and the car's large trunk kept our luggage dry.

Between Blowing Rock and Asheville, North Carolina, we detoured from civilization to motor up Mount Mitchell and to sleep in a log cabin near the summit. From that highest peak east of the Rockies, with an elevation of 6,684 feet, we could see seven ranges fading with distance into paler and paler blues. The showy pink blossoms of mountain laurel that were packed in the open shade there took me by surprise; in mid-June that shrub had ended its flowering at lower altitudes. Momentarily I was homesick for

Merryfield Farm and the Berkshires where laurel would still be blooming.

Driving through the mountains in a thunderstorm, I remembered how cattle on the farm next to ours had been killed by lightning where they stood for shelter under the leafiest big tree in the field, and wrote:

WAR OF THE HEAVENS

Wild laurel blooms while thunder booms
On mountainsides, lightning the specter.
Laurel leaves shine beneath wet pine.
When Heavens war, Nature is victor.
Roll, thunder, echo to and fro, rain flowing
Ground blessing, and wind the dead trees felling, seed sowing.[4]

Under Jack's sophisticated and thoughtful guidance, getting to know North Carolina was enlightening for me. From beautiful High Hampton we drove east across the length of the state for a stopover in Charlotte with Mam, Dorothy, and Joe and then on to the "Free State of Bertie" where Jack's old home in Roxobel was situated and where most of his Norfleet relatives lived. They referred to Bertie County in that way because its geographical isolation between wide rivers without bridges had made its people unusually self-sufficient and independent, even for individualistic North Carolina. For many years, the only overland outlet from Bertie's plantations was through the funnel to the north between the Roanoke and Chowan Rivers that emptied into Albemarle Sound at the southerly end of the county. Bertie's hospitality was as much a tradition as its independence.

My first impression was astonishment to see its houses built on stilts—"brick underpinnings," Jack called them—without cellars. But I learned that Bertie's highest point of land was only eighty-eight feet above sea level and that every house had its own simple dug well. The gray sandy soil looked so poor to my New England eyes that I could hardly believe the wealth of cotton, peanuts, corn, soybeans, and tobacco that it supported. I watched for the boulders and crops of rocks of our Sheffield country, but there were none—only flat fields and tall open pine forests and strange shapes of cypress knees in the swamps.

Many of those roads on which we drove in eastern Carolina were constructed from the native sand mixed with red clay, and in the rain their surface became as slippery as ice. Then I knew why Jack was such a smooth driver. He rarely touched the brake with his foot for miles at a stretch and his skill at the wheel spoiled me for other chauffeurs. In fact, he spoiled me all the time.

4 With apologies to Lord Tennyson, "The Splendour Falls."

On our honeymoon, we stayed with Eric and Margaret Norfleet and Eric's hunting dogs in Jackson, the seat of Northampton County, which adjoins Bertie on the north. They entertained us lavishly. The Norfleets had decided in advance that Woodbourne, the old family home on the big farm, was not fancy enough for Jack's northern city bride. They changed their minds later, after they visited Merryfield Farm.

"Cup"—Jack's physician cousin, Edgar Powell Norfleet—came to Jackson and drove us the twenty miles through the countryside to Roxobel. On the way, I noticed some luscious blackberries growing within reach along the road.

"Do let's stop and pick some," I exclaimed, forgetting my city manners.

Cup pulled off the road. He and Jack made no move.

"I wouldn't do that," Jack said.

"Why not?"

"Chiggers," Cup said.

"What are they?" I asked blankly.

"Redbugs," Jack warned.

"Are they poisonous?"

"No, not exactly. But I wouldn't want you bitten by them," Jack advised.

"Who's afraid of redbugs then?"

If my mother had lived in Bertie County, she would have called me "buttheaded."

"You will be sorry," Jack said again.

Reluctantly they got out of the car and helped me pick a small box full of berries. Gentlemen they were, and polite, but I realized that their hearts were not in the task, as mine was.

That night I was abject with apologies when I saw the fiery welts on Jack's legs. Nor did Cup feel as warmly toward me the next day.

I learned about those Bertie chiggers by observation, not by experience. Apparently they too were polite, too polite to bite me. I had nary a welt.

From that time the family teasingly referred to me as: "Damn Yankee, Republican, and even the redbugs wouldn't bite her."

I loved them all, nevertheless, more and more as I knew them better.

Jack's Norfleet relatives were the kind of people about whom it was said: "Their word is as good as their written bond." For a man to keep his spoken word, he must be not only well intentioned, but also able to remember what it was that he said. A good memory is the essence of integrity.

I never met a family whose members were more diverse and yet more devoted and loyal to each other than Jack's kin. They depended on each other to share both large griefs and the little everyday pleasures of living.

Their minds seemed uncluttered by fruitless anxieties and a turmoil of decision making. That facet of character develops often in people who have strong convictions and who are close to nature. They lived each day for its present joys.

After Mam died, Dorothy wrote about her to Jack and me on May 15, 1942: "She got more out of life than anyone I knew and I realize now, more than ever, that it was because she enjoyed the small details of the lives of her loved ones."

When I became a wife, I had never kept house except in a tent and over a campfire. The arrangements at 9 West 16th Street seemed to me relatively simple. I inherited a young Irish sleep-in maid who used to call Ginny and me "the lassies" when she came green as Erin to work for my mother at 40 Fifth Avenue. Mrs. Margaret Donnelly was our long-time laundress and indispensable day worker, who had been with the family since I was a baby. There was also a cleaning man who had been employed by my mother, and for the house apartments a new janitor who lived down the block. My father's secretary-nurse spent the day in his downstairs suite of offices and she was welcome upstairs.

Jack, my father, and I ate dinner together, and sometimes breakfast, but Jack and I were out for lunch. He took the subway downtown to the Wall Street area, where the offices of his import-export firm, Whitfield and Powell, were located. I was at Bellevue Hospital all day. Jack now had two doctors on his hands. By mutual consent we made a rule: no medical shop talk at meals. I enforced it, and it became a habit for Jack and me throughout a lifetime of marriage and medicine.

My father was well taken care of in his home, and besides, the grandson of Hiram Pierce, the Forty-Niner, knew how to fend for himself. Ginny and Pop were near in Brooklyn, and Jack and I were free to go out of town anytime, work permitting.

Measured against my prior work load, my research duties at Bellevue Hospital were not taxing. The Digitalis-Pneumonia Study had been in progress for a year when I replaced the previous Fellow. All that I had to do was to make rounds on ten wards twice a day and examine the new patients admitted with a diagnosis of lobar pneumonia; to assign every other one of them to either a digitalis-treated or an untreated (control) group, according to the time of admission; to issue the digitalis leaf tablets in a small, round pillbox for each patient; to check the hour when each dose was given by the ward nurse, as she recorded it on a manila tag tied to the foot of the patient's bed—if the entry was not made, I tracked the nurse down to question her; to interpret the yards and yards of electrocardiograms that my two technicians took on the wards with the mobile

Einthoven string-galvanometer, at least one tracing daily on every patient, and that they developed in the photographic room; to observe the patients carefully for untoward side effects of digitalis; to record the clinical course for correlation with the bacteriologic type of pneumococcus and other laboratory data; to analyze the results with respect to the many biological variables—there were no IBM cards or computers to help me with the six thousand electrocardiograms taken on the eight hundred and thirty-five patients studied during the first two years; to write progress reports, which I presented to Dr. Alfred E. Cohn and his Committee for the three university services involved in the investigation; and to keep the patients, nurses, house staff, and attending physicians in a cooperative frame of mind. It was an excellent training in human relations.

The Digitalis-Pneumonia Study had been courageously and conscientiously conceived by physicians of broad scientific vision. The cherished dogma that digitalis, a "heart stimulant," was routinely beneficial in *all* cases of lobar pneumonia to them lacked a rational basis. I had no bias concerning the outcome. The attitude of the Bellevue medical staffs at first was: "Isn't it dreadful to withold a lifesaving drug from half our pneumonia patients!"

Toward the end of the study, I regularly encountered from the same hospital staffs the scathing comment: "How much longer are you going to poison half our pneumonia patients?"

The truth lay somewhere between those two points of view. The large collaborative investigation showed that the patient with a failing heart benefited from digitalis in the same way whether he had lobar pneumonia, or not. On the other hand, most of the patients in the series were not in heart failure. Moreover, the toxicity of digitalis was greatly increased by that infectious illness and the accepted full dosage of the drug, which we were using, was too large. Many of the patients were made worse by it. We learned that when signs of heart failure indicated a need for that medication during the course of lobar pneumonia, the drug had to be given with extra caution and in reduced amounts. Digitalis could both save life and kill.

During the summer months, few cases of lobar pneumonia were admitted to the hospital; the peak incidence was in late March or April. Jack and I were not content to remain city dwellers, but work prevented our ranging far. The West Side Tennis Club at Forest Hills offered us tennis, but its location was not as convenient as the old rough New York Hospital court off 15th Street that had saved the day for us the summer before. On weekends, we visited my Laidlaw cousins at Sands Point; Louise had been one of my bridesmaids. We built fires on their beach, swam in Long Island Sound, and played tennis on their courts. Mrs. Edith Bates made us feel at home in her guest house at Talcott Farms in Westfield, New Jersey, and she gave us guest memberships at her country clubs for tennis and swimming. My father often joined us.

Jack and I had itching feet; we loved to travel. Christmas of 1929 and the New Year found us with Tennessee friends, another couple, at Elbow Beach Hotel on the ocean front in Bermuda. It was a bride and groom's winter paradise. We relished the outdoor sports in a semitropical setting and the brilliant gaiety of our dancing nights, colored by spicy conversation about the Old South.

One basis for our congeniality was Jack's and my liking for each other's friends. Jack took kindly to my medical circle, particularly to Bettina Warburg, and she to him. She held a resident research appointment at the old Bloomingdale Hospital for Mental Diseases, now the Westchester Division, of the New York Hospital in White Plains. At her parents' estate in nearby Hartsdale, we met her to swim in the pool and to play tennis.

In the spring of 1930, Mr. and Mrs. Paul M. Warburg graciously gave us the use of a summer house on Inwood Avenue that backed up against their woods and gardens. We enjoyed that holiday home for several summers after the stock market crash of 1929 and subsequent depression. It was heaven for us. Without children in school we stretched the season from April to Thanksgiving. We acquired a small Ford coupé of my father's—he bought a new car—and we joined the ranks of New York's suburban commuters down Central and Jerome Avenues under the elevated tracks through the Bronx.

From then on, until Jack and I moved to Washington in 1961, I believe that I spent more hours in an automobile than in my living room. I put the time to good use, however, knitting, reading, or writing, while Jack drove. One day, years later, riding to my destination and thinking how that ant race contrasted with the leisure and pleasure of mountain roads where laurel bloomed, I scribbled on a pad in my lap:

THE POOR COMMUTER

Lo, they scurry from home, hurry
To work like ants. The poor commuter!
The traffic jams as cars he rams,
He needs for travel a computer.
Drive, commuter, ride to and fro, smile, knowing
How late the hour is growing, ever slowing, slowing.

Vacation was due Bettina that August. She and I cooked up schemes for a camping trip in the Adirondack Mountains—it seemed like the old days in medical school when I used to spend the night in her New York house and we planned outings. Betsy had a child's pup tent, triangular and tan, that she crawled into on her hands and knees to sleep. Jack and I borrowed Edith Bates's circular wigwam tent with a disjointable metal rod at the center. We could stand up in the middle of our tent. A canvas floor was stitched around the sides at the bottom, a netting covered the front slit and it was an elegant white.

Jack's enthusiasm for the trip did not equal Betsy's and mine. I knew about the redbugs and poisonous snakes in the South, but I prodded him: "Jack, darling, didn't you ever go roughing it as a boy *anywhere?*"

"Of course I did," he answered slyly. "When I was just a wee small tot, they put me on an ice cold pot, whether I wanted to or not."

"No, I mean really, Jack—outdoors."

"Oh, yes. There were the garden houses, one for ladies and one for gentlemen at the opposite ends of the garden. At Oakland our garden was a hundred yards long, big as a football field. The boxwood bushes were as high as your head. I used to rough it summer and winter."

Like my mother, Jack married into a camping family. Listening to the night's sonata, I could sleep between blankets on the ground, but Jack never became acclimated to roughing it. That summer, he insisted on sheets and air mattresses and we all had them. It seemed to me that the sheets were always cold and damp; when the sun shone, I spread them on rocks to dry. Whenever we broke camp and moved on, we had to let the air out of the mattresses so that we could roll and pack them in the car. Then Jack exercised his lung power blowing them up again while Bettina and I set up housekeeping in the new camp site.

Our Model A Ford was not large enough for the three of us and our fancy camping equipment so we borrowed my Uncle Warren's big Buick. He and Aunt Minnie had driven it across the continent from California and they wanted to leave it with us at Hartsdale while they embarked for Europe. It was just the thing for our camping trip. We loaded the fenders with tents and duffel bags, and every cranny was filled inside. In our old clothes we set off from the Warburg's palatial home.

One of Jack's troubles with sleeping out was his attraction for mosquitoes. Those northern insects liked me no better than the southern chiggers did; they did not bite me. But if one mosquito penetrated the defenses of our tent, Jack did not sleep until he had exterminated it. My curiosity was so aroused concerning the preferences of arthropoda for people that subsequently in the Department of Pharmacology at Cornell I carried out a research project with ticks. With the aid of the Rockefeller Institute staff at

Princeton, by flagging the New Jersey woods I caught jars full of those bloodsucking creatures and brought them back to the laboratory. I wanted to learn why some individuals repel insects and others attract them—it would have been nice to know.

The *Journal of the American Medical Association,* issue of April 18, 1966, published a symposium on that subject. In a paper entitled, "Factors That Attract and Repel Mosquitoes in Human Skin," the conclusion states: "We summarized our experiments to determine whether a person unattractive to the mosquito does, in fact, exist. It has been demonstrated with biting experiments . . . that variation in biological attractiveness occurs. The factors responsible for this variation are presently under study."

After thirty-six years, I would still like to know.

Jack was a connoisseur of coffee, ever since his South American years. He objected to our making that beverage with the brown water of Long Lake, in which we scaled and washed the fish that we caught. He said that it spoiled the taste of the coffee. On the other hand, I objected to his washing lettuce in the lake—in my medical view that was possibly unhealthy. We reconciled our differences and did it his way.

We had paddled our Adirondack guide boat laden with tents, gear, and supplies a long way up Long Lake, about eight miles from a store. At the end of our stay there we ran out of food. For our final meal in camp, a mess of lake fish went into one pot with all the leftovers of vegetables, flour, bacon fat, and bread to make a chowder—"slumgullion," Jack called it. Then we packed up, paddled out, and drove to the Loon Lake Hotel, where Betsy's parents were expecting us.

Jack and I exchanged our wigwam for a luxurious two-room cottage with a neat fireplace. We were back in civilization. Mr. Warburg, courtly and correct, had breakfast with Jack and me in the hotel dining room on the morning after our arrival. It was our first formal, or normal, meal in about two weeks. Our host was incredulous when he saw Jack devour every item listed on the table d'hôte menu: fruit, cereal, eggs, trout, pancakes, and a sirloin steak topped with French fried potatoes. I felt that Betsy's and my cooking had been a failure.

Mr. Warburg was not athletic, but he liked golf and he took Jack around the course for nine holes. Swinging a golf club was a refreshing change from paddling a boat and hauling spring water.

"Jack, I have only two shots—one is nip and one is tuck. They go this way and that," Mr. Warburg explained as they crisscrossed the fairway.

Knowing Bettina's family was a rare privilege for Jack and me. Mr. Warburg died the second winter after our visit to Loon Lake and we felt even closer to Mrs. Warburg. She used to call me her "banana twin." By choice she and I had both lived largely on bananas at one period of child-hood.

In the summer of 1931, Betsy and I took Jack on a second tenting tour that was even rougher. We drove from Yarmouth, where our boat docked, around the southern periphery of Nova Scotia to the Bras d'Or and back to the Bay of Fundy by way of the northern coast. It rained about once an hour. Jack and I had a convertible Chrysler then and we put its top up and down manually a dozen times a day. The sun never shone long enough to dry out the sheets. I never made a camper out of Jack.

Jack never made a golfer out of me. He bought me a set of clubs and he was an inspiring teacher. Some people excel in the sports in which the ball is stationary, but I did best with a moving target, as in tennis.

We never felt that we had to merge every facet of our existence outside of our careers in business and medicine. We could share some activities in the telling, not in the doing. Jack played golf without me and I rode horse-back without him.

In retrospect, I advise:

NIX ON TOGETHERNESS

Husbands and wives, listen—beware!
It is unwise to plan to share
All through your lives—daily, you swear—
Your exercise.

Home he arrives, ready to go.
Weary, Mom sighs, "Don't hurry so.
Johnny has hives—Doctor is slow."
So—down he lies.

Young Johnny thrives, now she is set.
Sun in disguise makes it a bet
Their tennis drives are stopped by wet
Rain from the skies.

If he survives, he goes alone.
Apologize? No, he's no drone.
He swims and dives—she must condone.
His health's her prize.

My father must have taken a lesson from our wedding, because he eloped. On August 14, 1930, he and Edith Bates slipped away to Kingston, New York, and were married. It happened while we were in the Adiron-dacks, and he was staying at the Lake Mohonk Mountain House. My mother, Ginny, and I used to visit there in the summers to be with Edith

Bates, her sister Grace, and Warner Van Norden. On the weekends, my father came by train from New York. When he was not on the tennis courts, he played endless games of chess with Warner.

My father the magician had kept his secret well and his remarriage was a surprise to Jack and me. Its impact on our lives was to extend our happiness, and Jack continued to be like a son to him. He came every day to see patients in his office at 9 West 16th Street, where Jack and I still lived. Edith and my father had twenty wonderful years together. Eventually, my step-family grew to be as close to me as blood kin.

On July 1, 1930, I became Instructor in Pharmacology at the Cornell University Medical College, a full-time teaching and research appointment. Until that date I was the Fellow on the collaborative Digitalis-Pneumonia Study. Questions had arisen concerning the pharmacology of digitalis compounds in the tablets of crude foxglove leaf that were administered to those pneumonia patients. I sought the answers from Dr. Robert A. Hatcher and Dr. Harry Gold, who had taught me that basic science six years earlier in Cornell's Loomis Laboratory across the street from Bellevue Hospital.

As the data accumulated, it was clear that on one medical service the digitalis-treated patients ran a stormier course, with clinical and electrocardiographic proof of greater digitalis toxicity, than did those on the other two university services. The one medical division had elected to use for the study a proprietary commercial preparation of digitalis leaf that was widely employed in the treatment of heart failure. The other two services approved a different specimen of the leaf, one that was purchased in bulk by the New York Tuberculosis and Health Association and distributed to its cardiac clinics. Both specimens of leaf were assayed biologically for physiological strength and the effective dose of digitalis was presumably the same for all the pneumonia patients.

In seeking an explanation for our observations on the Bellevue wards, Dr. Gold [5] carried out comparative bioassays of those two and other samples of digitalis leaf, using different methods on three species: the official frog method (subcutaneous injection) of the United States Pharmacopoeia, an intravenous method on the cat, and one by oral administration on patients with auricular fibrillation of heart disease, a clinical method that Dr. Gold devised. He showed that when assayed according to Federal law, the leaf with the intense toxic effects in the pneumonia study was mislabeled— its potency was stronger than the label stated. He demonstrated also that the official frog method was not consistently applicable to man; as digitalis leaf

[5] John Wyckoff and Harry Gold, "A Dangerous Preparation of Digitalis," *Journal of the American Medical Association*, Vol. 94 (March 1, 1930), p. 626.

aged, its strength changed by the frog method but remained constant with the passage of time for the human subject.

Criminal prosecution of the pharmaceutical company followed, and Dr. Gold testified at the trial on behalf of the manufacturer. Before a referee judge in court, the standard U.S. Pharmacopoeial bioassay of the suspected digitalis product was performed. Ranks of schoolchildren filled the spectator benches. Each frog was weighed on a long-arm balance, and then was injected with the calculated dose of digitalis solution. Precisely sixty minutes later the frog heart was observed for digitalis effects by the judge, Dr. Gold, the pharmacologist for the prosecution, and the legal counsel for both sides. A newspaper headline read, "Frogs Croak in Cause of Science."

The net result of the trial was that the manufacturer was found guilty of misbranding, but was fined only $500 and given a suspended jail sentence; the Federal law under which he was convicted was changed promptly—the cat superseded the frog in the official U.S.P. digitalis assay; and I went into pharmacology.

As a full-time member of the faculty, I taught second- and third-year medical students and carried on research with various drugs that interested me. I learned how much effort was required to prepare lecture material. Dr. Hatcher insisted that the level of teaching be directed at the superior student, the top percentile of the class. I was amazed by the wide span in learning capacity of that captive audience. One frequent impediment was a lack of facility with simple mental arithmetic, which the practicing physician must use constantly. The habit of visual thinking is frequently lost as childhood recedes. Another was a lack of training in logical thinking, in the ability to analyze variables and to distinguish a causal relationship from chance association of events. I concluded that an important guide to aptitude for the study of medicine was a liking for, and excellence in, mathematics.

Dr. Hatcher and Dr. Gold believed that the final examination in the pharmacology course should test not tricks of memorizing, but the ability to think in that complex scientific field. We permitted the students to bring to the three-hour examination their textbooks, lecture notes, and laboratory results. They might look up any facts that they needed, just as a doctor consults references in his office library. We devised questions to measure their grasp of pharmacological principles; at the examination we issued for analysis photographic records of unfamiliar experiments that we had done ourselves. In correcting those exam papers, we worked as hard as the students had in writing them.

The lecture course in pharmacology continued through the academic year, but our laboratory sessions extended over only twelve weeks, one trimester. During the other months, we all spread out our research equipment on the student desks in the big laboratory. In one corner was my old rolltop wooden desk, like my grandfather Davidson's at the bank twenty-five years earlier. The central heating system was inadequate and a gas floor-heater with a vertical grill over the open jets of flame helped keep us warm.

The Department of Pharmacology occupied the second floor of the Loomis Laboratory. On the floor above ours were the class preparation rooms of the Department of Bacteriology; all the sterile culture media were transported on hand trucks across 26th Street and up First Avenue to the main building of the medical school at 28th Street. Dr. Joshua E. Sweet's Department of Experimental Surgery was on the fourth floor. At that time, Charles A. Lindbergh, who had flown solo across the Atlantic Ocean in 1927, was working upstairs with Dr. Sweet and the chest surgeon Pol Corylloss on a germproof artificial heart that became known as the Lindbergh Pump. When Lindbergh was in our building, word got around that he was there and I ran up the two flights of worn steps—there was no elevator —to shake hands with him and stand near in the unpretentious experimental operating room. His tall, lean frame was stooped forward to let him watch the heart-pump that could be seen through a window sealed into the front of a dog's chest. If the old Loomis Laboratory was good enough for Lindbergh, it was good enough for me, I thought. It was the quality of the people working there that counted.

In the summer of 1932, when Cornell moved to the new towering white buildings at 1300 York Avenue, I would not entrust the department's delicate Einthoven string-galvanometer to a van. We lifted that precious electrocardiographic unit gently onto the cushioned back seat of Jack's and my convertible Chrysler with its top down. People in trucks and cars angrily honked their horns at me while I drove uptown at a speed of five miles an hour over the bumps of First Avenue.

In using the student laboratory of the old building on 26th Street, we had been exposed inevitably to each others' research in progress. Our fancy individual laboratories uptown had self-closing devices on the doors and they stayed shut most of the time. I propped my door to the hall open. The long corridors gave me a lonesome feeling. I missed the team play with scientific argument that clarified my thinking. Looking back to those days, I wrote:

TWO MINDS PLAY BALL

Ideas stall against a wall,
Tangled with facts and figures until
Two minds play ball across the hall.

Fresh concepts emerge then, doubts to still.
Toss, brains, toss the ball to and fro, provoking
Wisdom, words choking, new fitness of mind evoking.

The ceiling-high windows of my new corner room faced south and west; they overlooked the East River as far is the 59th Street-Queensboro Bridge. Sunlight streamed in with such intensity that I had to keep the long dark shades pulled all the way down until the sun set behind the Empire State Building, which had been completed in 1931. Then the magnificence of sunset colors distracted me. It took a long time to adapt to our new "ideal" environment.

In 1933, I was elected to membership in the American Society for Pharmacology and Experimental Therapeutics. Dr. Hatcher was its president in 1934 and he introduced me to the giants of pharmacology, particularly to his friend and adversary, Dr. Torald Sollmann. I was one of two women members of the Society then. Later, Jack attended many of the annual meetings with me, and my friends welcomed him as the "pharmacologist-by-marriage." Jack was expert at mixing medicine with marriage.

As the result of my research in the laboratory during the three academic years, July 1, 1930, to July 1, 1933, I was author or coauthor of nine studies in general pharmacology.[6] They dealt with the mechanism of action of digitalis, morphine and pseudomorphine, strychnine and antidotes to strychnine poisoning, with chemical tests for drugs known as alkaloids, and with uranium nephritis. I applied myself with enthusiasm to those and other fundamental problems.

Six of those papers were published jointly with Dr. Harry Gold. Working with him was a liberal education in style and techniques of writing. He believed that scientific articles should be not only lucid and accurate, but readable. In those days we had almost no secretarial help; the department secretary devoted her time to the chairman's needs and to class material.

---

[6] Harry Gold, Janet Travell, and Nathan Kwit, "Depression of the Vomiting Reflex by the Digitalis Bodies," *American Heart Journal*, Vol. 7 (1931), pp. 165–181; Janet Travell, "A Contribution to the Pharmacology of Pseudomorphine," *Journal of Pharmacology and Experimental Therapeutics*, Vol. 44 (1932), pp. 123–150; Janet Travell, "The Potassium Mercuric Iodide Reagents for Alkaloids," *Journal of the American Pharmaceutical Association*, Vol. 23 (1934), pp. 689–698; Walter Modell and Janet Travell, "The Role of Lipoid in the Renal Tubule of the Cat in Uranium Nephritis," *Anatomical Record*, Vol. 59 (1934), pp. 253–263; Harry Gold and Janet Travell, "Ethyl Alcohol and Strychnine Antagonism," *Journal of Pharmacology and Experimental Therapeutics*, Vol. 52 (1934), pp. 30–53; Janet Travell and Harry Gold, "Strychnine in Poisoning by Alcohol," *ibid.*, Vol. 52 (1934), pp. 345–354; Janet Travell and Harry Gold, "Ether and Strychnine Antagonism," *ibid.*, Vol. 52 (1934), pp. 259–274; Janet Travell and Harry Gold, "Mechanism of Action of Strychnine on Respiration," *ibid.*, Vol. 53 (1935), pp. 169–178; and Harry Gold and Janet Travell, "The Vaso-Depressor Effect of Strychnine after Ether, Alcohol, Barbital or Chloral," *Archives Internationale de Pharmacologie et de Thérapie*, Vol. 50 (1935), pp. 1–14.

When Harry and I wrote up our experimental results, I sat at an old type-writer and typed while he thought out loud. When his words paused, my fingers on the keys tried to anticipate what he was going to say and I completed his sentence. It is a wonder that we remained friends.

When President Kennedy announced my appointment to the White House, I was especially pleased when Harry Gold wrote in tribute to my work in the department: "I have rarely encountered a person with her capacity for collaboration. In all the 30 years which she served the Department of Pharmacology, I recall not a single instance of a break in friendly relation and cooperation with anyone." [7]

I was becoming firmly entrenched in that difficult and complex discipline of pharmacology. My faculty appointment gave me scientific opportunity, contact with the inquiring minds of medical students, academic freedom, and control of my extracurricular hours to spend them uninterruptedly with Jack. In many respects it was an ideal arrangement for me, but I was never fully satisfied with laboratory life. It seemed as though I had wandered a long way from the patient.

As a matter of fact, I was constantly exposed to the practice of medicine. Every day, my father came from his new home at 12 East 64th Street to the office that he kept at 9 West 16th Street, and he often stayed for dinner with Jack and me. Our big guest room served as a kind of convalescent home for members of the family. The New York Hospital had not yet moved uptown with the Cornell University Medical College. After hospitalization there for an operation or illness, it seemed natural to bring close relatives home to us for care and observation. They seemed to recover their normal strength faster than if they had stayed in a hospital bed or lounge chair; the modern convalescent care unit is built on the same plan.

In 1930, my Uncle Winthrop Travell was a guest in our home care facility. In 1931, after Jack and I returned from Nova Scotia, his sister came from Charlotte with a trained nurse, a school friend of hers from St. Mary's. They arrived after Labor Day and left just before Christmas; Dorothy was critically ill with infection from kidney stones that were finally removed at the New York Hospital. Her husband Joe at the same time was in a hospital in Charlotte recovering from serious injuries incurred in an automobile accident. In our home at 9 West 16th Street, we had staying with us, too, our springer spaniel Queenie and her puppy that we had given to Dorothy. After dinner, with a bright blaze in our guest-room fireplace, patient, nurse, and physician stretched out together on Jack's ancestral queen-sized bed while Jack read aloud to us. We followed the adventures of Sir Arthur

---

[7] McKeen Cattell, "Dr. Janet Travell: White House Physician," *Cornell University Medical College Alumni Bulletin,* Winter, 1961, p. 13.

Conan Doyle's Sherlock Holmes and his friend Watson. We laughed with Irvin S. Cobb, as he directed in his *A Laugh a Day Keeps the Doctor Away*. One or two of the dogs climbed onto the bed with us as members of the family and listened quietly. Convalescence was a merry affair.

On July 1, 1933, I began a year's leave of absence from the Department of Pharmacology, which was granted me because of pregnancy. In excellent health, I enjoyed my "time off" from the laboratory. Our first daughter, Janet Davidson Powell, was born in the new Lying-In Hospital division of the New York Hospital at ten minutes to midnight on December 16, 1933. She missed being born on my thirty-second birthday by only a few moments. Flaming plum pudding for Christmas dinner in my hospital room was served to the new mother and father. At the same time at 16th Street, Queenie presented us with nine handsome springer spaniel puppies, which grew up in and out of Janet's baby carriage.

With leisure time on my hands, I was not content to sit idly by with the baby in the wintry city of New York. Jack arranged to take vacation from the investment counsel firm Van Strum Financial Service—during the depression then business was slow. I would finally see the alluring land of Florida, which Jack had described to me in his letters when I was a New York Hospital intern. We started off in our cloth-topped convertible on February 9, 1934, and, ironically, that was the coldest day ever recorded by the New York weather bureau—it still is. I wrapped Janet, not yet eight weeks old, in a fur robe and covered her face with a thin, open-weave baby blanket to warm the air that she breathed. Jack's trust in my medical good sense was stretched to the limit. The roads were so icy and we stopped so often that we spent four nights in hotels between New York and Charlotte, where we picked up Dorothy for the rest of the trip south.

Riding with us in the car was not only baby Janet, but also an intelligent liver-colored springer spaniel champion, Papa Ben. In that pre-motel era, the combination of baby and dog created an unforeseen dilemma: the hotel that we thought good enough for Janet refused to accommodate a dog, and the one that rated low enough to accept Papa Ben, we judged not clean enough for the baby. In Lake Worth, Florida, Papa Ben more than made up for the trouble he caused us in transit. When we parked the baby in her basket under an umbrella on the beach and we all swam in the ocean, he never left her side. He was a perfect guardian and he took his turn swimming in the surf, too.

Well rested from the Florida trip, on April 15, 1934, I started work at Cornell on a half-time basis. My leave was not up—it ran until July 1—but the teaching staff was shorthanded and my research projects were waiting. Within a very short time, however, I realized that I was not ready to resume my full-time post in a couple of months. I astonished Dr. Hatcher by asking for another year's leave of absence. With some misgivings he finally urged the Executive Faculty to grant my request. It was refused. I resigned, with a light heart.

Dr. Hatcher and Harry Gold were bitterly disappointed that I was quitting the department and they conferred.

"Miss Travell"—Dr. Hatcher always called me that—"if we hold your position open and I do not look for an instructor to replace you, will you come back to us in a year?"

I promised that I would. He accepted my resignation.

Our second daughter, Virginia Gordon Powell, was born on March 22, 1935, also at the New York Hospital. She was adorable.

With two small babies, my predicament in returning to the laboratory had worsened. Virginia would be only three months old when my resignation expired. I had promised to return on July 1, 1935, and for a year the staff had done extra duty to hold my place. The fixed schedule of full-time teaching and research would give me no latitude for problems that were bound to arise with the children. I wanted greater flexibility and more time at home.

As soon as possible that spring, I talked the matter over with Dr. Hatcher.

"Dr. Hatcher, I've decided that I will have to go on a part-time plan. I'll work full-time throughout the laboratory course and most of the time I'll work harder than anyone else. But I want to be free to take a day off, or a week off, when it suits me or if the children are sick. It doesn't matter what my salary is—my conscience will be clear."

It was a bombshell. The New York Hospital–Cornell Medical Center had been converting to the full-time plan since the reorganization in 1932, and a number of the part-time clinical faculty had resigned. No one on the faculty of the basic science departments was part time. My request was nonsensical in the face of changing times, but it was granted.

My colleagues told me that I had ruined my future in medicine.

I remained on a "part-time" plan in Cornell's Department of Pharmacology for twenty-six years, until I received a "full-time" appointment to the White House in 1961. However, I gave the department the equivalent of full time on a half-time salary. Moreover, I learned the difference between full time and 100 percent of my time, as I gradually took on more jobs, including the private practice of medicine.

When I was asked how I managed to accomplish so much, Jack answered for me: "Ask her what she does between midnight and bedtime."

CHAPTER 12

We Were Four New Yorkers

It was January, 1938; Janet was just four and Virginia not quite three years old. At 9 West 16th Street, Sigrid, their warmhearted Norwegian nurse—she was a houseworker for my mother when I was a girl—had given them supper. They were bouncing around the living room, and they ran to hug "Mommy" when I ran up the short flight of steps from my father's office. After working at the pharmacology lab uptown, at the end of the day I had added on a patient with an acute attack of chest pain. I had my own portable electrocardiograph then. It was easy for me to take care of a few patients outside of my part-time hours at Cornell, since I did not incur any upkeep for the office and my father was glad to have me make use of it.

Jack was reading the *New York Sun,* the afternoon paper. Our springer spaniel, Gentleman Buppy, lay at his feet, warmed by the cannel-coal fire in the grate. Firelight played on the two caryatid columns carved in white marble that supported the shelf on their heads. My mother had moved that Italian mantel to 9 West 16th Street from the parlor of 42 Fifth Avenue when that house was demolished with our home next door.

"Daddy, Daddy," Ginia caught Jack's attention. "Why can't I eat bones? Gigi [Sigrid] says I can't. Why can Buppy eat bones?"

"Ginia, I'll tell you—it's simple. You've helped Gigi turn the meat grinder in the kitchen. Well, Buppy has a little machine inside him that goes, grr, grrrr, grrrr, and it grinds up the bones. You don't have a machine like that inside you, so you can't eat bones."

Virginia was satisfied with the explanation, but I was not.

199

"Ginia, Daddy is a joker. You know he's a joker. Buppy's stomach makes a juice, a kind of liquid—it looks like water. When you drop a bone into it, it dissolves—it disappears."

I was having difficulty—my words sounded less like scientific fact than like Gran's "disappearing magic." When the children were naughty, my magician father had a disconcerting trick of making their toys vanish before their eyes.

"No. Mommy is the joker," Ginia laughed and shook her head in disbelief.

I thought to myself, "Maybe Jack's version is closer to the truth than mine." Buppy's powerful teeth and jaws were what enabled him to eat bones; his gastric juice was not too different from Virginia's.

Jack entertained the children by the hour with his "make-believe" storytelling. His infinite patience was an asset, especially when they were tired or ill.

Janet and Virginia were healthy tots, but they had their share of fevers —nature's way of immunizing them against germs. When one of them was sick, I slept in their room. Jack was a light sleeper and often came to see if he could help—it is a hard thing to hear your child crying in misery or pain. Thinking of that universal suffering of worried mothers and fathers, I wrote:

℞ FOR PARENTS OF SICK CHILDREN

When you can not sleep
Don't count those countless sheep.
Set your feet to walk
On a path in the deep
Woods of your childhood,
Where you used to talk
With fairies bad and good.
There you used to talk,
And danced in the deep wood.

Hold your child's hot hands
And play on shifting sands
Of time. "Let's be frogs,"
Say, "Come, play by the ponds
Where we can share childhood,
In the muddy bogs
Where once alone I stood."
There deep in the bogs
The fairies understood.

My part-time jobs allowed me flexibility to share some special activity with Janet and Ginia every day. Our center of interest was not the kitchen: I had capable household help. In those depression years, our standard of living cost us more than Jack and I earned, and we drew on our capital. We regarded a sleep-in houseworker and a nurse not as extravagance, but as expenses essential to the children's care if I were to have freedom of mind for my professional work.

I could have found time to do more housework than I did, but I preferred to spend it in other ways with our children. When they were well, it was more important to me to give them affection and understanding than to concern myself with their physical care. They never had an "eating problem."

Whenever anyone told me about her pet, "I have to feed my dog every day because then he'll love me," I used to think of Buppy and reply: "I don't feed my dog and he adores me. He sticks to me like a burr all the time I'm home. I'm his playmate."

Neither were Jack and I obliged to "walk the dog." The small backyard at 9 West 16th Street had a door from the ground-floor laundry and a stairway to a porch off the first floor. An ailanthus tree with an attractive trunk grew in one corner. All we had to do was to open a door and let the dog out. When I exercised Buppy, I did it differently.

Our refrigerator in those days had no deep-freeze unit and we bought ice cream when we were ready to eat it. After an early supper, Janet, Ginia, and I all put on our roller skates and set off from 16th Street up Fifth Avenue to the drugstore in the Flatiron Building at 23rd Street. I held Buppy on a leash and he ran ahead—he exercised me. When we had purchased our ice cream, I rolled the open end of the paper bag so that Buppy could hold it with his teeth, and with his head high he carried it home. Our racing team did not let the ice cream melt, and Buppy always had his share. Whatever New Yorkers do seems natural, and we received hardly a stare or a smile.

The children became expert on their ball-bearing roller skates. When Ginia was four, I took moving pictures of her doing reverse turns and cutting backward circles on the smooth asphalt of Central Park's wide, hilly walks. The large roller skating area in that park opposite East 72nd Street attracted us and sometimes Jack drove us there in the car. He never took to roller skates, but he walked along with us. Afterward we visited the small Central Park Zoo at 64th Street and Fifth Avenue and then stopped to see Gran and Grandma Edie at 12 East 64th Street. Their brownstone home made a convenient headquarters for us.

One Sunday noon, the children and I skated from our house up Fifth Avenue among the after-church strollers and across 68th Street to the imposing buildings of Cornell University Medical College, a distance of nearly four miles. I wanted to check an experiment at the lab, and Janet and Virginia wanted to see the white mice and guinea pigs. Our roller skates were a mode of rapid transit, but that day we had enough of them. Jack chauffeured us home.

Gradually Jack acquired a New Yorker's tolerance of his wife's and daughters' unconventional activities. It was a wonder that with his background he accepted such behavior. He had grown up in the goldfish bowl of a very small village; as a young orphan on his own, he conformed to the proprieties of boarding school; after college, he was imbued with the decorum of the Latin American formal life; and he was engaged in the proper profession of banking and finance. His whimsical sense of humor and devotion to our happiness counterbalanced those influences and enabled him to share our irrepressible quest for adventure and for new knowledge.

Central Park's big lake at 59th Street provided us with ice-skating on a surprising number of days each winter. We laced up our skates in the chilly wooden shelter on the frozen shore of the lake. The colder the weather, the fewer the people out and the more room we had to race and practice figures of eight. Jack skated with us then, as smoothly as if he were dancing on a parquet floor. He steered me around the bumpy spots and we glided happily over the ice, arm locked in arm.

When our girls were toddlers, Sigrid used to push them in a wicker double stroller to the playground in Washington Square where I had played as a child and from which I had watched the Triangle Fire. Ginia was a large roly-poly baby with dimples, and Janet, petite. With their wide-set brown eyes and curly hair, in lookalike snowsuits or dresses they were mistaken for twins. They wished that they were twins; they were inseparable. They soon outgrew the Square and then Sigrid took them regularly to Central Park on the Fifth Avenue bus. In warm weather, I drove across town sometimes from the medical school to have a hamburger lunch with them on the terrace of the Zoo's cafeteria, which overlooked the sea lions' sunken pool. Those water mammals put on a good show.

Doolie (Julia) and Dotty Powell, Junius and Julia's children, lived uptown near the park. About the same age, the first cousins were an animated foursome on the big swings, slides, and seesaws. There were outcroppings of rock to climb. There were ponies to ride for a dime, and a real horse hitched to an old one-seater buggy to drive, and princely plunging steeds to sit astride on the musical merry-go-round. I did not hesitate to mount one for a whirl.

Our girls never tired of watching the animals outdoors at the Zoo. At the Museum of Natural History on the west side of Central Park, they were equally fascinated by the sculptured lions, deer, and water buffalo that Ed Sanford had caught in timeless motion on the façade of the new Roosevelt Memorial wing. I had seen the sculptor at work creating those friezes in his studio a few blocks to the south. A live bear had posed once as his model, and the elevator operator in the studio building promptly quit his job. He took unkindly to such passenger bears. Inside that museum wing, we learned about the fauna of other continents, mounted in their natural settings. We did not try to see all the exhibits at a single visit, but piecemeal. Small children focus on only one thing and they need time to wonder about it. We did not hurry Janet and Virginia.

In the Planetarium of the museum nearby, we observed the changing constellations of the automated heavens. Children in those formative preschool years absorb more from the leisurely exposure to natural science and art and history than they can express or their parents may realize.

The Metropolitan Museum of Art on the east side of Central Park was on our regular beat. The girls were fascinated by the shriveled Egyptian mummies in glass cases and by the pottery and tools of that ancient culture. The paintings of flat people and dogs on the walls of the imported Egyptian tombs appealed to the girls; they painted that way themselves, without regard for anatomy.

Yet Virginia knew even then about form and perspective. When she was four—she had just had her tonsils and adenoids out in May—she and I sat on a sandy beach in Old Greenwich, Connecticut. She was not allowed to go in the water. She amused herself by shaping the damp sand into objects that I did not recognize.

"Ginia, what's that you're making?" I asked.

"A city, Mommy."

"What are all those little bumps?"

"Houses. Can't you see?"

"Couldn't you make them bigger?" They were thimble sized.

"But, Mommy, they're so *far* away."

I should have known. The year before, she had seen how tiny the houses looked from a great height when she flew from the small airfield at Westfield, New Jersey. It was her first airplane ride. Sitting on Jack's lap in the open cockpit of a single-engined plane, she had leaned over the side to view the houses below, and the barns, pond, and lane of Talcott Farms. Edith, my stepmother, and her son Talcott Bates were both taking flying lessons at that airfield and they qualified as pilots. She would have bought a helicopter then, but on its demonstration flight a rotor broke and the 'copter remained stuck in a cornfield. Edith surprised me by her adventurous spirit—although I should have expected it in a native New Yorker—and Talcott inherited it. He was a student then at Cornell medical school and during World War II he volunteered as paratrooper-physician in the United States Navy, assigned to the Pacific Theater. Talcott was always the first to jump from the plane, ahead of his men.

Our girls never ran out of creative things to do together. A rainy day was not unwelcome. They loved to draw and color pictures. Ginia used up crayons and paper at a terrific rate. Modeling clay kept them occupied for hours, but it was hard on the furnishings. They had a large repertory of songs in English, French, Norwegian, and German that they had memorized naturally. With their pleasant voices they sang together while they built edifices with wooden blocks or whenever we drove around in the car. Janet begged for piano lessons for months; she would sit at my mother's Steinway, trying to compose music and picking out the notes for the pieces that she sang. When one of our children asked for something, Jack and I were likely to delay until we thought that she was old enough to cope with it. When Janet was six, she received her heart's desire: she started to study with a piano teacher uptown.

The piano did not interest Virginia then. She had little tendency to copy her older sister, nor Janet her younger one. Jack and I tried to recognize in each her individual talent and to encourage proficiency in it, not competition between them.

Broadway theaters drew us like magnets. Gilbert and Sullivan's *The Mikado* was the first show that we took the children to see, when they were four and six. We sat in the second row of the orchestra. They knew all the songs by heart and they sang them with the cast. Screen productions, like *Pinocchio, Snow White and the Seven Dwarfs,* and a rerun of Charlie Chaplin in *The Gold Rush,* were on our list, as well as the better Broadway musicals and light operas, like Jerome Kern's *Show Boat* and Victor Herbert's *The Red Mill.* Rodgers and Hammerstein's *Oklahoma* in 1943 was a favorite—Janet and Virginia saw it three times. Edvard Grieg's music from *The Song of Norway* permeated our home after we had enjoyed that show together in 1944. We stood in long lines outside the Radio City Music Hall for admission to the Christmas and Easter musical pageants and we all admired the precision dancing of the Rockettes. Comedy and drama, performances of Shakespeare's plays and such classics as *Cyrano de Bergerac* commanded our attendance.

New York's unlimited cultural opportunities introduced our youngsters to past and present worlds of artistic achievement and scientific adventure. Their excitement renewed Jack's and my enthusiasm as if we saw it all for the first time. The girls educated us. They were wonderful company and we never tired of being with them.

Everything seemed to be going our way. The mechanics of living functioned well for our family in New York. Jack and I were able to combine many advantages of that city in bringing up the children and in working at our professions. For those ten years, until 1944, Jack was Investment Analyst in the Wall Street firm of Cohû and Torrey, members of the New York Stock Exchange. He was in the center of the financial world and he liked his work. He analyzed economic trends and future prospects of stocks and bonds; he wrote reports and briefed the large staff of salesmen on current and new issues of securities. Lunch with his business associates was a productive affair, and cocktails or highballs in the middle of the day were not their custom. He was usually home by six o'clock and, aside from a wide range of reading matter, his evening hours were relatively free.

Jack adapted his spare time to my unpredictable schedule. After the children were asleep, in the evening we sometimes drove uptown to Cornell. He did his reading in my lab while I prepared for a class demonstration, conference, or lecture the next morning. That way, I could spend more daytime hours at home with Janet, Virginia, and my father.

Jack had his numerical figures and I had mine. We did not try to mingle them. My mixture of teaching at the medical school, laboratory research in general pharmacology, clinical investigation, and patient care made each day an exploration into the unknown. No one of my days turned out to be just like another; I never suffered from monotony.

In September, 1935, when Virginia was nearly six months old, I had resumed work as Instructor in Pharmacology, on a part-time basis by special dispensation of the Executive Faculty. That fall, I also started as visiting consultant on the cardiology service, of which Dr. Harry Gold was chief, at Sea View Hospital on Staten Island. In 1936, I received an appointment to that city hospital for tuberculosis, as Assistant Visiting Physician, and later as Associate Visiting Physician in Cardiology, without pay. One morning a week, a group of consultants drove there together. The "D.H." (Department of Hospitals) sign on our car gave us quick entry to the Staten Island ferry at Battery Park in Manhattan and at St. George's in the Borough of Richmond. We had the front spot on the big boat.

Even in winter's coldest winds, I and another energetic doctor—I never saw him wear overcoat or hat—marched around and around the outdoor upper deck. We made about ten laps in the five-mile crossing. We did not think then in terms of "physical fitness." We walked because we enjoyed it and because we wanted to watch the passing scenery of New York's downtown skyscrapers and the tugboats, barges, and ships in the harbor. The torch, that Liberty held high on her pedestal, a half mile across the water from the drab low buildings on Ellis Island, symbolized to me the opportunity for change and greatness that my country offered its immigrant citizens.

Our five-mile drive from the ferry slip at St. George's to Sea View Hospital took us past Silver Lake, where my father and I had fished when I was a small child. Thirty years later, apartment houses, stores, and filling stations lined our route, and I wondered whether any fish had survived civilization.

Dr. Gold had no difficulty in persuading me to come as a volunteer on Wednesday evenings, when I could, to his Cardiovascular Research Clinic at the Beth Israel Hospital on East 16th Street and Stuyvesant Square. It was not far from my house. After an early dinner with Virginia and Janet, from seven until nine or ten o'clock I examined clinic patients and participated in staff conferences.

In the fall of 1939, when Janet was not quite six, she entered first grade at the Friends Seminary on Rutherford Place between East 15th and 16th Streets. Its paved playground faced Stuyvesant Square. That year Virginia joined a play group that met mornings in Central Park, and the following September she also started first grade. Both the girls seemed happy at Friends, where the teaching was imaginative, thorough, and disciplined. Almost from the start, their courses included French and music. They sang in the choir. There were some foreign pupils in their classes and the school took pride in its liberal international outlook.

Virginia and Janet enjoyed their new independence and we did not discourage it. After a couple of years at Friends Seminary, we let them walk alone to school across 16th Street through Union Square, when they so desired. Otherwise, Sigrid escorted them. By then, Virginia had decided that she, too, wanted to play the piano and they went for lessons to East 50th Street. After school, together they boarded a Second Avenue uptown bus and walked crosstown to their teacher's studio. When their lessons were over, Jack or I brought them home and listened eagerly to their chatter about the day. We would not now consider it safe for them to go about New York alone at that age.

With less risk, we encouraged their self-reliance by letting them make small purchases for us. Walking or driving around the city with them, we would stop in front of a drugstore, or perhaps a delicatessen.

"Whose turn is it to go in?" we would ask.

The girls knew and one of them jumped up and down in anticipation.

"Ginia, we need a loaf of white bread. Here's a dollar. Be sure to add the change."

We waited outside. We were not cross if she returned with doughnuts and cookies, as well as bread. Nor were we impatient—we could have done the errand more quickly ourselves.

As children of six to ten years, Janet and Virginia were experienced shoppers. During the Christmas rush, in a Fifth Avenue "dimestore" they managed to attract the salesgirls' attention and to buy their gifts for the family. Even then, they were busy with their plans. If left to their own devices, they never had time enough for all that they thought up to do.

Schoolwork was their responsibility. When they had home assignments, Jack and I were careful not to distract them. Sometimes, we were able to help. When Ginia started arithmetic, the teacher at Friends school was baffled to know why about half her answers in addition were wrong.

"Sit down and let me see how you do it," I told her one day at home. "Add this column of numbers—now the next one."

I watched her. Sometimes she began by adding the right-hand column of digits and she "carried" to the left; sometimes she added the left-hand column first and "carried" to the right. She was "ambidextrous" in her visual orientation.

At 9 West 16th Street, my father liked to have Janet and Virginia help him with odd jobs around the house. Together they mended broken toys, china, and our furniture. The girls learned how to replace a broken windowpane or a washer in a leaky faucet. Gran patiently let the children use his electric drills and soldering iron while he supervised to prevent their harming themselves.

He encouraged their inventiveness. When I came home one rainy day, he had hung a rope swing in a wide, high doorway to the dining room. Standing on ladders, they had screwed two large metal eyes into the walnut door trim at the top, attached pulleys for the rope, and notched a board for the seat. If the swing traveled crooked, it struck the sides of the doorway; in the straight line, the girls' feet cleared the dining-room table. They took up the challenge of that new sport with enthusiasm and were soon swinging tandem, one sitting and one standing on the seat.

It was no wonder that years later Virginia's husband, Ed Street, wrote in a birthday greeting to my father:

A TOAST TO GRAN
ON HIS EIGHTY-FIFTH BIRTHDAY

Here's to Gran!
The father of the Clan.

Amid the hammers, saws and glue,
Axes, apples—old and new;
Up the ladder in a tree,

Hanging only by one knee;
With jokes for all and scrabble plenty,
Never *will* be over twenty.

We hail you on this happy day,
But can't write all we'd like to say.

So here's to Gran,
The grandest man,
The father of the Clan.

At the same time that Janet began school, in September, 1939, I started a two-year salaried Fellowship on the Arterial Disease Study, which was supported by the Josiah Macy, Jr. Foundation and which was conducted at the Cardiac Clinic of Beth Israel Hospital. As part of my work on that part-time job, I helped draw up with Dr. Gold comprehensive but simplified printed forms for recording clinical and laboratory observations on ambulatory cardiac patients. Those pages made it possible then, without computers, to obtain fairly uniform and accessible data from about sixty collaborating Cardiac Clinics[1] throughout the city. A carbon copy of the original record, written with a sharp indelible pencil, was detached from each clinic patient's chart and those copies were assembled in a central research office for mapping the natural history of chronic diseases, especially cardiovascular.[2] When a patient moved from one part of the city to another, he was not lost to the long-term study. The patient gained by the system, too, since his complete medical record in compact form was readily available to his new physicians in another clinic. So far as I know, the question of "invasion of privacy" was never an issue.

My small income from the Fellowship paid tuition for our girls' private schooling, in those early grades, but that was not the motive for my working at Beth Israel Hospital. Opportunity there was unlimited for research in heart disease and in the clinical pharmacology of cardiac drugs. When the Arterial Disease Study terminated in 1941, I received an appointment as Associate Physician to the Cardiovascular Research Unit, without salary. We followed our patients in the clinic and on the wards. I worked even harder then on the team of Cardiac Clinic physicians, whose encyclopedic minds were directed by Dr. Harry Gold's scientific vision and leadership.

While I was at the White House, I still retained that title "on leave" from Beth Israel Hospital. In 1964, when the Cardiovascular Research

---

[1] Of the New York Heart Association, also known then as the Heart Committee of the New York Tuberculosis and Health Association.
[2] Alfred Cohn and Claire Lingg, *The Burden of Diseases in the United States* (New York, Oxford University Press, 1950).

Unit ended its independent existence, I was pleased to continue on the Beth Israel staff as Associate Physician for Cardiovascular Diseases in the Department of Medicine. The hospital administration had been liberal in its financial support of research—X-rays, tests, and special examinations to bridge gaps in the physician's knowledge and patient's care. It was taken for granted that good research on the course and treatment of disease could not be done on human subjects without giving top priority to their welfare. The clinic patients in the district had shown a loyalty to the hospital second only to their devotion to the synagogue as a place of aid and consolation. The hospital social workers kept close contact with each patient's home situation, and they were largely responsible for the high order of clinic attendance without which the ultimate result in a long-range investigation would be unknown.

My skill as a cardiologist, augmented by the precision manual training of the pharmacologist, were called upon at an unexpected moment. In 1940, I was on my way by train to present a study [3] in clinical pharmacology at a meeting in New Orleans and I left New York in time to stop over in Charlotte with Dorothy and Joe. I wanted to see Jack's Great-Aunt Mam, too. She was ninety-six and she was confined to her room upstairs by arthritis. Her cousin, John Hill Tucker, the eye, ear, nose, and throat specialist whom I had met in 1928 on my first visit to North Carolina, was ill with a failing heart. It was suspected that he had a pericardial effusion and cardiac tamponade—fluid accumulating around the heart and constricting it.

Attempts to draw off fluid through the front, where the pericardium lies next to the chest wall, had failed to locate any fluid. When the doctors asked me to try, I could have declined, but I was deeply touched by John Hill's faith in the Yankee woman physician. I knew that the pericardial tap would be difficult, even hazardous, but his condition was desperate. In her clear fine handwriting, Mam wrote Jack about it:

March 13th, 1940

Dear Jack:—

Well, Bobby has been to see us & gone, left yesterday at noon. She made of herself quite a Heroine by performing an operation on John Tucker, that no Dr. in *this* town would do. And it was on the heart too. All the Tucker family are thrilled thru & thru. After it was over J. said he really felt better. I don't think Bobby knew whether it is a permanent improvement yet, but she was brave enough to do [it] . . . & by the request of his (John's) Dr. who has been going to see him twice every day for the last three months.

[3] Janet Travell, Oscar Bodansky, and Harry Gold, "Nicotine Excretion and the Role of Its Reabsorption from the Urinary Bladder as a Source of Nicotine Poisoning in Tobacco Smokers," *Federation Proceedings,* Vol. 69 (1940), p. 307.

I had elected to tap the pericardium by a posterior approach, inserting the needle on a long slant between the ribs close to the spine and just missing the lung. I was always handy with a needle and in class demonstrations at Cornell my touch was perfect in injecting drugs into the tiny veins of a rat. In addition, I possessed an excellent three-dimensional visual memory. I did not feel like a heroine—it was all in the day's work. It was New York that gave me a mantle of prestige.

I was equally moved by Mam's confidence when I convinced her that in spite of her ninety-six years and her rheumatic disability she could go down the stairs and up them again. Her letter of March 13 to Jack went on to tell about that excursion and how I coaxed her into it:

> Bobby was looking wonderfully well & really younger. . . . The arrangement of her hair makes the change in her looks [I had cut it]. But she is the same person every other way, & we love her as always. Do you realize I had not seen her in three years? . . . I must tell you I hadn't been downstairs last since July 15th & to my utter astonishment B. urged, persuaded, & insisted so much she could get me safely down I yielded, & she holding me, D. [Dorothy] & the nurse walking in front of us started down & there was no trouble at all & I spent the whole day down in the Den & it was the happiest day I'd seen in many —I felt I had gone on a nice visit. About six o'clock that evening, I asked to be taken to my room & we four started & I was landed safe in my room & chair & there was no accident at all & up to the present time, there has been no bad results whatever, but I haven't been down since. The weather has been bad & plenty of Ice on the top of the porch under my window. [Her rheumatism was always worse in damp weather.] I'll try to go down again, soon, if I feel I can. [She never did.] . . . D. said when she put B. on train, she found she could have some acquaintances as fellow travelers. . . . I didn't know you would be back in New York so soon after she left, but truly Jack I felt glad to know you would . . . the two girlies would miss you too much. . . . My love to you & kiss Babies for me.
>
> Mam

Mam lived for almost two more years, but I did not manage to see her again.

I presented a paper at a scientific meeting out of town about twice a year. Jack made an occasional trip on business for his firm and to oversee the Powell farms that were leased at Roxobel. We alternated our travel so that for sixteen years, from the time when Janet was born until her graduation from high school, he and I were never away from home simultaneously, unless the girls went with us.

Our jaunts to the country with Janet and Virginia were frequent. In the winter, on weekends we drove out of the city to visit Edith and my father at Talcott Farms in Westfield and we kept our belongings in a two-room guest house that was a second home to us. At intervals, we visited my Laidlaw cousins on Long Island Sound or stayed at the Gipsy Trail Club in Carmel, New York, in the Taconic range of mountains. I was a member, and we bunked in the lodge or rented a cottage for short periods. Our whole family took part in the winter sports. The steep toboggan slide that led across the ice of the big lake provided some spills and plenty of thrills, particularly after sundown. Literally and figuratively, we were always on the move.

Over long holidays, we drove as far as North Carolina, breaking the trip on the overnight Baltimore-Norfolk boat. At Roxobel, where we spent a number of Thanksgivings with Jack's assembled family, the girls enticed their cousins to ride the wise old farm mules Garfield and Sycamore. Some years later they named two of our automobiles in their memory. One car was a hand-me-down from Edith.

"It's bad enough to name that nice car of ours after a mule, but not after a *dead* mule," she protested.

A preferred vacation spot during the school season, at Easter and Columbus Day, Armistice Day and Washington's Birthday, was Atlantic City, where we stayed in a small family-style hotel. Coiled rope hung by the windows for escape in case of fire. Jack liked to stroll on the boardwalk or sit in the sun. The girls and I rode horseback at a canter on the hard sand, which was exposed at low tide for miles south into Ventnor. The impact of the horses' hooves was muted and softened so that we felt like Indians of old riding stealthily across the Western Plains. The horses liked to splash along in the thin edge of ocean foam as much as we did. When Virginia was four or five, a stable boy rode with her on another mount and controlled hers with a lead. She looked very little on a big horse, but she stuck to the saddle and soon learned to ride alone.

Janet and Ginia were truly horse crazy. We each had a particular steed that we chose to ride. Mine was a gaited pinto named Champ. We went out sometimes in the pouring rain, by special telephone arrangement with the stable man. Whenever we walked on the boardwalk past the Hamid Pier, we fed carrots and sugar lumps to our pets at their hitching stand. At the end of the afternoon, our girls—New York born and bred—were likely to sit astride their favorites while the string of mounts plowed through deep sand under the low boardwalk and then clattered at a trot through the paved city streets to the stables for the night. We never had a dull moment in Atlantic City.

Where to go each summer to get the children out of New York was a problem. Atlantic City did not attract us in those months—horses were kept off the beach from June to October. Merryfield Farm in Massachusetts was too far, except for a short period, since Jack and I had to remain within commuting distance of our work. The faculty members of the pharmacology department as a rule did not take "academic" vacations for the whole season. In fact, our research programs continued more actively than ever when classes were not in session. My own private practice from my father's office grew at a rapid rate. Inevitably, I was more and more intrigued by the obscure varieties of musculoskeletal pain that were referred to him for physiotherapeutic management. In 1940, at the invitation of Dr. Harold G. Wolff I began to see patients in the Neurology Clinic of the New York Hospital, and the next year I was appointed Physician to Out-Patients. That called for only one of my afternoons a week.

Our "summer" cottage on the Warburg estate in Westchester County solved our dilemma for several years. Before Janet and Virginia were able to walk, they bobbed around in the large pool there, tied into small rubber rings by means of tape harnesses that I devised. The fully inflated rings under their armpits lifted them well above the surface of the water.

"You'll never get those children out of their rings—they won't ever swim," pessimists predicted.

"They can't touch anywhere—the shallow end and the deep end are all the same to them. It's so hot, they want to go in the water," I said.

We heeded the warning, however. As Janet's and Virginia's dog paddles acquired propulsive strength and they learned to feel at home, to breathe, in the water, we blew less and less air into the rings. With diminishing support, the children were immersed lower and lower. The change was gradual, the way my father shaved off his beard—nobody noticed. Finally, like his small stubble, there remained only a bubble in the ring at the point of the chin.

All four of us were in the pool one July day when Janet was four and she announced: "I want to swim without my ring." It was her idea.

"I don't want mine eithe.." Ginia hastily pulled hers off and struck out from the underwater steps. Jack walked beside her while she swam across the pool without difficulty. She was three. From that moment, neither child ever used those props again.

Learning to swim like that, the girls never worried whether they were over their depth or if their feet could touch bottom. They swam without fear from boats, docks, sea walls, and diving floats.

"Summer" for us at Hartsdale lasted five or six months, from April into November—our girls were not yet of school age. Jack and I were 50 percent suburbanites and 50 percent New Yorkers. Those were transition years in which he and I both discovered that we could live twenty-five miles out in the country and yet work productively in the city. We were content.

After the Paul Warburg estate was sold, in 1939 we located a house on Lucas Point in Old Greenwich, Connecticut, that looked across six miles of open water to Long Island. A sea wall was so close to it that in storms the salt spray blew onto our open front porch. We slept well to the sound of the surging, slapping sea outside our windows. The family thrived there for two summers, and Janet and Virginia learned to love the beach.

Friends warned us of the dangers to our four- and five-year-olds in renting a place with a twelve-foot drop from the top of the sea wall to the rocks below at low tide and to six feet of swirling water at high tide. The children were sensible, surefooted, and obedient. Sigrid could not watch them all of the time, and they promised not to climb on the wall when they were outdoors alone. They never fell off.

For access to our beach at the foot of the wall, we bought a fourteen-foot wooden ladder and lowered it against the wall's sheer face. We had to remember to pull it up before the tide came in, or else high water would float it away. It lasted us the two summers. The sea grass growing in the sand between barnacle-covered rocks screened a mystery land of marine life—immobile starfish and mussels, scooting baby crabs and soft-shelled clams that squirted water at our approach. My father fished from the sea wall at night and a pail full of eels in salt water usually stood on our back porch, until we were ready to skin and eat them. The recipe for cooking our eels called for parboiling before frying the sections. Dipped in egg and bread crumbs, they were as tasty as fresh panfish.

Our springer spaniel Buppy learned to climb up the long ladder by hooking his paws over the round rungs, but going down, one of us had to carry him. He weighed forty pounds. When we forgot and left him behind on top, he backtracked around by the road to the Lucas Point private beach and swam across a stretch of water to join us. A sign beside the steps that led down to the sand warned, "No dogs allowed." Like the other dogs residing on Lucas Point, Buppy never learned to read. With his webbed toes, he had a powerful stroke in the water and he kept close to Janet and Virginia while they swam. When they took hold of his collar and floated, he towed them ashore.

To celebrate the Fourth of July, 1939, the Lucas Point community copied the New York World's Fair with an Aquacade. Our pair of girls led the procession of young people, who were lined up according to stature. I had made twin costumes of tangled seaweed caps and straight beach-grass skirts that masked Janet and Virginia's white wool trunks. They paraded down the long gangplank from the pier to a floating dock and they dove off together into deep water to the music of a Victrola in a rowboat. They swam arm over arm in unison, making a large circle around a buoy and back to the dock.

Hendrik Willem van Loon, the author, who had a house on Lucas Point, used to sit on a short bench on the high pier that led down to the landing float for boats. He watched the swarm of children swim. Virginia climbed up on the bench and startled him by jumping off the railing into the deep water fifteen feet below. She was small for her four years. As she plunged off over his shoulder, he turned to me and said: "Well. I call that prenatal bathing."

Hendrik van Loon was sitting on our porch and viewing the peaceful expanse of Long Island Sound—he loved the sea—the day that Germany invaded Poland on September 1, 1939. (He was a huge man. Teasingly, he had asked me to guess how much he weighed. When I underestimated his weight by sixty pounds, we became fast friends.) I remember the scene vividly at that awesome moment of history, and also another setting two days later when we heard on the radio that France and England had declared war on Germany to keep the terms of their treaty with Poland. In the calm of sundown that Sunday of the Labor Day holiday weekend, Bettina relaxed with us. We felt the change of seasons in the air, but masses of blooming petunias that I had planted still colored the bank by the porch and reflected the sunset clouds. Our generation had lived through the First World War and we were oppressed by the premonition that the United States would enter another war. Life would be rationed again.

In the meantime, Jack and I continued to sample suburban living around New York. The summer period was shorter for us since our girls had entered Friends school. For a couple of months in 1941, together with Ginny and Pop and the four Weeks cousins, we occupied Edith's guest cottages at Talcott Farms and swam in the pool at her country club in Westfield. Edith gave Ginny and me each two improved lots that had been part of her farm and she and my father hoped that we would build there. We held ours for years, but the twenty-five-mile commutation from there to New York was too arduous if we drove by way of the bottleneck Holland or Lincoln Tunnels under the Hudson River. The alternate route was by train to Jersey City and then ferry or Hudson Tube to Manhattan. We never seriously considered making Westfield our home.

After the attack on Pearl Harbor catapulted us into the war, Jack tried to enlist in the United States Navy. He was forty-four and he was rejected because of varicose veins—they have not caused him any trouble since.

In 1943, I was classified as "essential" to the war effort at Cornell. Teaching extended into a summer session, since most of the medical students were already inducted into the army or navy for the accelerated specialized training program. Jack and I decided to send Virginia and Janet away for two months that summer, not to a camp, but to a music school: Frank Bishop's Blue Spring Farm Summer School in the Pocono Mountains of Pennsylvania. Adults and children together went there to study piano. A granddaughter of Sir Winston Churchill's was a pupil then; she was a trifle younger than our eight-year-old Virginia. Daily piano lessons and recitals were mixed with hayrides, picnics, campfires, and swims in a pool that was fed by a mountain stream. Mrs. Bishop was French. If the children did not work an hour each day in the vegetable garden, they were not permitted to swim. Only French was spoken at meals, and the cuisine was as exotic as the language.

Janet and Virginia were not wholly disappointed when about halfway through the music school's season they came down with chickenpox and we received a telephone SOS from Mr. Bishop to take them home. To fill out the end of the summer, we rented rooms with kitchen privileges in a house in Old Greenwich. Because of war restrictions on gasoline for pleasure driving, we pedaled our bicycles to the beach and the railroad station.

The war year of 1944 found us back at Old Greenwich. We had made many friends there and we all loved that "Broken Bottle" private beach on Lucas Point. The house that we rented then was built on low land by a long, shallow arm of the Sound, on the opposite side of the point from our first house with the sea wall. From a rowboat, at low tide, we scooped large chowder clams out of the muck of the bay. Jack was in that house when a hurricane and its wind-driven high water hit the shores of Long Island Sound on September 14, 1944.

Except for the war, I doubt that we would have moved then out of New York, and Jack concurs. Our way of life there had great advantages. The Friends school suited Virginia and Janet; they had attended it for four and five years, respectively. My father spent part of the day with them at 9 West 16th Street. It was handy to have a doctor in the house, and his presence spared me a kind of anxiety that most mothers must experience. One day he ran a neat suture through Janet's eyebrow when she cut it in a fall and I did not even hear about it until I came home at the end of the afternoon. It was just an incident. Our house was convenient to the school, to Jack's and my places of work and to the countless fascinating events that we enjoyed in the city. The country was also accessible to us—until the war.

Suddenly, our long holiday travel and weekend outings by car were curtailed. I was less free to take time off with the children. I accepted many more private patients to try to do my share in meeting the shortage of civilian doctors. Then there were the summer sessions at the medical school.

The girls and I no longer went along when Jack made brief trips south on crowded trains to attend to the farms in Roxobel. Virginia unconsciously stated our problem—she was just seven—when she wrote him on April 12, 1942, from New York: "Dear Daddy, I miss you an offal lot. School is just wonderful. All we did today was play. . . . In our Weekly Reader there was a story about something very exciting. It was that the CIRCUS IS HERE. It is like the old fashion kind, exept extra special. I see signs up everywhere. Mummy is so bizzy, you know. . . . So when you come back, will you take us. Love From VIRGINIA POWELL."

At that season, we might have been in Atlantic City, except for the war. On Friday, October 9, 1942, Virginia wrote Jack again in North Carolina about our plans for the Columbus Day weekend and she gives a picture of Janet's and her life in New York:

Dear Daddy,
    I miss you. This weekend, Mummy may take us to the Bronx Zoo, and we may go to the Statau of Liberty. Janet told me, that in the Bronx Zoo, you can go in the cages and play with the tame animals like the rabbits. [They were thinking of my riding the sea tortoise and handling the snakes and gorilla once at the Bronx Zoo.] A friend of Grans came last night, a friend that Gran has'nt seen in about 40 years. He is an Officer, in the army. [People interested Ginia.] I still have the pencel you gave Janet and I in Sheffield. . . . I wish you were here. Janets got the stuffed-up-nose and sore throat that I have. Janet is going to take Mummys Boa Constricter Skin if Mummy can find it, and I am going to take the elephants tusk to school. [Those souvenirs of the African jungle were brought me from Liberia by my cousin Winthrop Travell.]

Love,
Virginia Powell

She knew that her Daddy wanted to hear all the news from home.

That August of 1944, when we were staying in Old Greenwich, an end to the war was not in sight. All four of us seemed suddenly to tire of New York. Packing the family's personal belongings and moving every spring and autumn loomed ahead of me as mountainous tasks. Indecision as to where we should spend the hot-weather months and the worry of finding good help in new places, since Sigrid had left us, seemed more than I could face each year. Lucia, our Dominican cook that summer, expressed her philosophy: "I can tell your fortune in your hand as well as them that gets paid for it, but why should I strain my brains?" As a cook, she was an artist.

Why, indeed, should I strain my brains with so many futile details of living?

In August, Jack was admitted to the New York Hospital for elective rectal surgery by Dr. Nelson W. (Pete) Cornell. When I returned to Old Greenwich late each day, the girls had written Jack letters that illustrated the charm and flexibility of their life there.

August 15, 1944

Dear Daddy,

I suppose you're in the hospital now. Janet and I were out in the field today catching butterflys. We caught about seven more. I wich you could see them all. It's about to rain. Oh, it is! It's poreing now. The wind is tereble. Lucia says it's a minor cyiclone. The lights just went out. I suppose it's raining in New York too.

With lots of love,
Virginia

P.S. Mummy hasn't come home yet.

August 18, 1944

Dear Daddy,

I am sending you my scrapbook. It is filled with jokes I cut out of the "Post." We just finished supper. Aunt Ginnie is out here. Janet and I went to visit the Maynards today. We dressed up and went swimming three times with them. . . . If you want to catch crabs, it's Lucus Beach. Get well soon.

Love,
Virginia

On the same day, Janet wrote:

Aug. 18, 1944

Dear Daddy,

I am sending you my scrapbook. It is full of pictures and writings about animals. I hope you will like it. . . . Today we caught six little crabs at Lucas Point. The kind you wanted to eat. One of them has his shell half on and half off. . . . How are you? I hope you have a nice nurse. Has Mummy ordered the alcohol rubs?

With much love,
Janet

On Lucas Point the girls met their friends casually at the beach or their homes, but in New York sociability was set in rigid molds. Janet and Virginia realized the difference.

"Mummy, when are we going to get a house in the country?" Janet asked me more than once. "I don't want to go back to New York. It's getting late—we'll have to go to school soon."

It *was* late. Jack and I discussed it while he recuperated for ten days in the hospital. We had considered such a move for years, but we were under the spell of New York. Besides, my father would miss us, especially the children, at 16th Street.

"I think that we'd all be better off if we could find a place close to New York with good public schools and some country around it," I told Jack. He was already convinced of that.

On his hospital rounds, Pete Cornell visited Jack once or twice a day. We asked him about the town in Westchester—Pelham—where he lived, and we questioned him about how he managed to practice surgery in New York and commute. We had no special friends in Pelham, but we had heard that its schools ranked high on the New York State list. Before Jack was discharged from the hospital on August 26, Pete gave us the name of a real-estate agent in Pelham. Chance changed the course of our lives.

When Jack and I arrived at the house in Old Greenwich on that Saturday of his hospital discharge, the girls greeted him with, "Daddy, when are we going to get a house in the country?"

Janet and Virginia pushed us to act. They were ten and nine then, and their votes counted. Jack was in no condition to look at houses, but on Monday, August 28, he telephoned the real-estate agent who agreed to meet me the next morning on a specified train at the Pelham railroad station. It was a stop on the local from Old Greenwich.

Optimistically, Jack and I decided to rent a house at once in Pelham, if I could find one suitable. We would try the experiment of suburban living for a year, or perhaps two.

Still, I had some misgivings. While commuting to New York, I would not be able to run in and out at home for a few extra minutes in the middle of the day. My housekeeping from a distance would be less efficient, especially without a Sigrid any longer to supervise it. But, I argued to myself, the girls were growing up and in many ways they were already as self-sufficient as adults.

Housekeeping was not the important thing. It was homemaking, and that depended on the team effort of the entire family. I knew that I could count on Janet's and Virginia's help, as well as Jack's.

CHAPTER 13

Follow Your Dream

Virginia balanced astride the rear rack of my bicycle while I pedaled it one mile to the Old Greenwich station to catch an early train. We were dressed to meet the real-estate agent in Pelham that Tuesday morning of August 29, 1944. Janet had overslept and we left her behind. Jack was asleep, too, recuperating from his operation.

We had not appreciated the rental situation during the war's prolonged housing shortage. We looked at the only house in town for rent and it did not fit our specifications. I felt acute disappointment. We would not get a house in Pelham, as we intended, after all.

"Would you consider buying a house?" the agent asked me. "There are a few for sale here."

"Oh, Mummy, let's do!" begged Virginia.

We had resolved to move out of New York. Was there any good reason why we should *not* buy a house? Otherwise, we might not make the move— time was short.

"We'll look at them," I said.

One of the houses that we inspected caught Virginia's fancy, and mine. Centrally located on a quiet street, it was within a short walking distance of the commuters' railroad station, bus stops, and the best elementary school. It perched on a high hill, well screened by white pine, hemlock, and large oaks. An upstairs porch was in the treetops. The house was solidly built of red tapestry brick on rock foundations and it had a tile roof. Money had not been spared in the details of its construction. A judge of Italian lineage had

219

added a heated sunporch extension with frescoed ceilings and walls. Rooms were generously proportioned; there were four bedrooms and three full baths upstairs and a maid's wing downstairs. They had all been freshly painted. The house was held by an estate, the price was reasonable, and it was vacant—"ready for occupancy."

It had been "for sale" and vacant for a whole year, I learned. I could guess why. It had no furnace, no stove, and no refrigerator. Those items were under strict wartime rationing; oil-burning furnaces were being converted to coal.

Our real-estate agent assured me that a joker in the regulations would permit us to install a new oil burner at once; the only circumstance in which a homeowner might obtain one was if there were no furnace at all. The agent could even supply us with a clock-thermostat to turn the heat on and off automatically. I was inclined to believe him. A secondhand range could surely be bought. We could manage with an old-fashioned icebox, if we must, like the one at Merryfield Farm. We were accustomed to living there without the niceties of electricity, and the austerity of war made such compromises acceptable.

But how about the hill and the thirty-five steps that led up to the front door? The rear of the lot had no access from a street, only beautiful rock ledges and a forest of trees. My father was seventy-five and still playing an active game of tennis, but not one of us was growing younger. I could picture those broad, curving cement steps covered with ice and snow in winter. The narrow garage was built underneath the thirty-five steps and a high terrace; its driveway, though short, was steep, with two right-angle turns. An inside flight of steps led up to the basement and another flight to the kitchen on the main floor. That would be the way to carry up groceries and to enter the house in the rain.

I wanted Jack to see the place as soon as possible, but he was still weak from ten days of hospital bed-rest and he would not appreciate the climb. I made an appointment to return in two days.

On Thursday, we used some of our precious basic ration of gasoline to drive to Pelham. Jack rested on the back seat of the car. The girls were elated at the prospect of moving—they had never changed homes before. The family voted unanimously to buy the house. We sat on the stairs and discussed the complexities of moving.

Five days from then, on the day after Labor Day, the schools would open. We drove past the Colonial elementary school and the imposing high school that also housed the "junior high." From the real-estate office, I telephoned my father at his office in New York. We had not seen him that week to tell him about our sudden shift in thinking—he might be upset by our leaving 16th Street.

"Dear, we're in Pelham and we're looking at a house to buy. Can you come right away? We want you to see it before we do anything," I said without preamble.

"I'll come. How do I get there?"

"Go to Grand Central, lower level. Take a New Haven train to Pelham. There's one every half hour. We'll meet you at the station."

"I'll leave right away and get the subway. I'll be at Grand Central in twelve minutes." His tone was matter of fact. It showed neither surprise nor disappointment, only interest.

At the house, my father inspected the quality of the pipes in the basement, looked for signs of termites, checked the roof for leaks, investigated the outside window trim for upkeep and lamented the absence of fruit trees. He did not comment on the steps.

"There's space on the side for a pear tree," he teased. "And if you cut down one of those oaks, you could have apples."

He added his "Yes" vote to ours, and took the train back to New York. At the real-estate office, Jack made an offer on the house. Our hearts had been won by its mountain seclusion.

Seven days later, on September 7, we dropped the girls off to start school. Jack made a down payment and signed the contract of sale. Subject to the search of title and final payment that was set for late October, Castle-Air was ours.

"We'd like to move right in," I said, as if there were nothing unusual about that. "We have a van lined up for September 14. The girls don't want to fall behind in the work at a new school."

Nobody moved into a house before the closing date, but the exigencies of war made it seem reasonable. The agent hesitated.

"I can't get you permission to move in by then. One of the trustees is away now."

"We'll take a chance on the title guarantee," I insisted. "Send for the permission—and forget us."

We had to move fast. We wanted our place in New York to be rented and ready for occupancy on October 1. I would soon be busy with teaching at the medical school. Jack could not help with sorting and packing our possessions since his new position with the Value Line Investment Survey required that he be on the job. My father was my right-hand man. At 9 West 16th Street, the movers loaded our things into the van on September 13 and unloaded them in Pelham the next morning. Some boxes of my mother's had not been opened since her death and we took them as they were. We never threw out any family treasures.

Luckily, I found a used kitchen range with six burners and a waist-level oven that was like new. Floor-level ovens that strain the back had become more popular. The stove was delivered on September 14 and it was connected the same day by the gas company. Two days later, through a local advertisement I bought a secondhand eight-cubic-foot refrigerator in Larchmont. By October 1, the new oil burner and thermostat had been installed.

Responsibility for a complete move had not fallen on me before. The training that I received was valuable when, in 1961, I suddenly left for Washington after seventeen years in our ideal Pelham home.

We slept in Old Greenwich throughout that week before moving day. Mornings, Jack and I drove five miles to Stamford and caught an early express to New York. Janet and Virginia rode their bicycles by themselves to the Old Greenwich station, took a local train, got off in Pelham, and walked to Colonial school. They returned in the same way in the afternoon. They thought it a lark.

Everything dovetailed in our plans except the weather on September 14. Our big pieces of furniture, including a grand piano, were carried from the van up those thirty-five steps during a downpour that totaled six inches of rain for the day. Jack was on hand for the dripping wet unloading and then he went to his office in midtown New York. Schools closed early, and Virginia and Janet appeared unexpectedly at the house.

The hurricane was in force late that afternoon. Trees in the churchyard across the street crashed in the terrific gusts. When we opened the front door a crack, the wind hurled it inward, wide open. The steady low-pitched roar of the hurricane was unlike any other sound that I have ever heard. To hear it better, we climbed the stairs to the attic and listened close under the roof. The house never trembled.

It was obviously unsafe to return to our Connecticut headquarters close to Long Island Sound—supposing that we could get there. We were marooned in our new home without telephone or radio and without anything to eat. Life was rationed, indeed, and the family's four books of blue, red, and green food stamps were in Old Greenwich. We would be hungry by morning.

In my raincoat and one of the girls' black slickers tied over my head by its sleeves, I set out in the storm to forage for whatever I could buy on the main street, another "Fifth Avenue." Janet and Virginia said that they were not afraid to be alone in the house. Navigating around fallen trees and leaning against the gale, I reached a market a long block away. My choice was limited; meats, butter, coffee, canned goods, sugar, and jams were on the war ration list. At least our stove was working and I bought eggs, cereal, and lima beans to cook and milk, bread, salt, and oranges.

I telephoned Jack in his office, but I could not dissuade him from taking a train out to Old Greenwich.

"It's Thursday, Lucia's day off," he said. "Buppy's shut up in the house —I can't leave him there like that. The car is sitting in the drive. I should be there to look after our things."

The children and I diverted ourselves by unrolling the large living-room rug and arranging the furniture and lamps. The floor had been too wet for the movers to finish that part of their job. We were sitting on the rug, feeling well settled if not well fed, when the lights went out. In the dark I located stubby candle ends in the sideboard and we melted the wax to stick them on saucers. We felt as unreal as actors on a strange stage with no script.

Wind velocity and the volume of its roar had increased and I worried about Jack in the old frame house down by the water. High tide would reach its crest past midnight. When the lights went out in Old Greenwich, he was unconcernedly taking a bath. Our landlord, who occupied a cottage nearby on lower ground, brought him candles and a flashlight.

"I'm leaving, the water's up to my steps," he told Jack. "I think you'll be all right here."

Neighbors came and took refuge in Jack's candle light when the rising water flooded their living room. They left in the early morning hours when the peak tide had ebbed. It reached only to our porch steps.

We were fortunate to escape harm. The 1945 *World Almanac* reported that the September 14 hurricane

swept the United States eastern ocean coast from Cape Hatteras to Maine. . . . The destroyer Warrington; two coast guard patrol craft, the Jackson and Bedloe; the Coast Guard lightship, Vineyard Sound; and the minesweeper YMS-409 sank with a total loss of 344 men, dead or missing. . . . Civilian losses approximated 40 to 50. The total damages along the coast were estimated at $25,000,000 for New England, Cape Cod and New Bedford . . . in New Jersey to the extent of $10,000,000. Hundreds of houses and thousands of trees were destroyed. Power and light poles, wires and phones were put out of commission.

We had been in the thick of it.

The following week, Jack, the girls, and I were eating dinner in our attractive new dining room in Pelham when the real-estate agent climbed the steps to see us.

"How are you getting on? I've brought you the note from the trustees," he said.

Jack read it aloud: "9-19-44. It is OK for Mr. Powell to move in right away—& at time of closing prorate expenses as of date he moves in."

We were happy to comply with that arrangement. Pelham was our home. The girls' dream of a house "in the country" had come true.

The challenge of the hurricane set the pitch for the day-and-night concerto of accomplishment performed by the family in our new suburban life.

The crescendo of three typewriters—Janet's, Ginia's, and mine—was heard upstairs in the evening. Both girls had stories and poems published. They carried on the family tradition of frequent letter writing. Ginia became a junior reporter for the Pelham newspaper, the *Pelham Sun,* editor of the school French paper and art editor of the *Pelican,* her high-school yearbook. She was a contributor to *Westchester Life* and *Dancing Youth.* She painted posters and designed scenery for school assemblies and for the Steffi Nossen modern-dance shows. For a couple of years on Saturday mornings, Jack drove her to Bronxville for a three-hour class in drawing and painting; most of the other students were adult professional artists.

Ginia began exhibiting her art work at an early age. *The Bronxville Reporter* of June 10, 1948 described only one painting: *"Pupils of Local Artist Exhibit Paintings at Bronxville Theatre. . . .* Of the younger artists, Virginia Powell of Pelham, twelve-years-old, was winner of the blue ribbon for her painting entered in the Pelham Women's Club Art Show this spring. The painting, that of a collie, a sagacious-eyed dog with a leonine fluff of hair at his neck, may be seen at the theatre . . . for the entire month of July."

Jack did his evening reading downstairs to the music of the radio or Victrola. In the morning before breakfast, Janet hurried to the piano—Virginia suggested that we ought to have two. They took piano lessons with the organist and choir master of Pelham's Christ Church; they went by train and foot to his studio in Mount Vernon.

"Do your girls make their beds before they go to school? Mine do their chores early," one mother said to me. She wondered how I managed with the housekeeping when I worked in the city all day.

"No, I don't expect them to do regular chores, because they make better use of their time. They know how to make beds already."

Janet and Virginia were actually expert and cooperative housekeepers. If Jack and I wanted to bring company home with us from New York, I telephoned the girls. By the time we arrived, they had put out the best table linen and dishes, arranged flowers, and put the house in A-1 order. We helped them with their parties, and they helped us with ours.

With our good-natured, but not always efficient live-in help, the children never came home to an empty house. Mrs. Donnelly commuted from Long Island City to do the laundry and cover the maid's time off. One afternoon when I came out from New York, I found our two girls visiting in the living room with nine high-school boys. After they left, I asked, "Please tell me, how do two of you entertain so many boys at once?"

"Don't you know, Mummy? We're noted for having the best food in Pelham," Ginia said.

Our monthly milk bill ran up to thirty and forty dollars, and the boys did not ask for beer. A special shelf in the butler's pantry was stocked with food for them all the time.

Planning our dinner each day was a game. I sat at breakfast with pad and pencil and directed: "Ginia, name a meat. Daddy, name a vegetable. Janet, another vegetable. Mummy, name the dessert."

The next morning, the order of choice rotated around the table. No one could complain if the food that they wanted was not served. I wrote down the menu and after a quick check of supplies in the kitchen I made a list and telephoned the order to the produce market. The memorandum was all that the maid needed. Except for an infrequent shopping spree on a Saturday, I economized on time by not standing in line at the supermarket.

We had planned well in the location of our home. I did not have to taxi the girls around, as many suburban mothers must do. Janet and Virginia were self-reliant. They walked or rode their bicycles, or if they wished, took the bus in bad weather. Every place was accessible in the residential town of Pelham that had a population of about 12,000 and was only a mile wide by three miles long—a wedge of land lying mainly between the Bronx, Mount Vernon, Bronxville, and New Rochelle. Most of the town's fathers were business and professional men who commuted to New York and there were no large estates in Pelham.

When our teen-agers obtained daytime junior driving licenses, they parked our second car every day outside the high school. Ginia especially did errands for everyone; she took class assignments to sick students, ran magazine copy to the printer, and taxied her coworkers on their extracurricular activities. Jack did the chauffeuring after dark; he knew all the streets and never got lost, as I did.

In Pelham, the Church of the Redeemer named Jack to its Vestry and he became Chairman of its Finance Committee. Janet and Virginia sang in its children's choir. He raised funds also for the Community Chest and the Red Cross. With his gift for people, he soon became acquainted with the neighbors in our area and with many of the town's residents. He served as a Director of the Pelham Men's Club. I joined the Manor Club, the women's club of Pelham, but I had no time to work for its worthwhile programs.

Janet and Virginia seemed to know everyone on the streets. Even Buppy knew his way around town. He used to call on our butcher in his shop and get his ration of meat trimmings directly.

After we settled in the suburbs, Jack and I regretfully gave up our long-standing individual memberships in the West Side Tennis Club at Forest Hills and I resigned from the Gipsy Trail Club in the Brewster hills. We did not require their diversions from the city any more. We had year-round country living at home and our hectic weekend travel in and out of New York ceased.

Our customary way of living, however, did not change fundamentally when we moved from city to suburb. Our social activities had not revolved around the cocktail circuit, and we never gave a large cocktail party either in New York or Pelham. We preferred to entertain at home dinners, usually with ten or twelve people of diverse backgrounds seated at one table. We made it a rule that our guest list include those of other professions, besides our physician friends.

The Pelham Country Club was a friendly, unostentatious place. Nearly all its members lived in Pelham. Our family membership provided convenient sports for all of us—tennis, golf, and pool swimming, which was particularly welcome on hot nights. Snack lunches were served to swimmers in bathing suits near the pool and our girls often spent the whole day outdoors at the club. They scored in diving competitions and in the marathon races. Tennis lessons improved their strokes and Ginia played on the Pelham tennis team in matches against neighboring towns of Westchester County. As a family we had many spirited doubles contests.

Nor were we laggards at the club dances and dinners in the evening on the outdoor terrace overlooking the tennis courts and illuminated pool.

We did not dream that Pelham had a shoreline on salt water, when we bought our house. As members of the Huguenot Yacht Club we took the club launch to primitive Pea Island, a dot on the map in the middle of Long Island Sound. There we swam in the buoyant clear tidal water, lay on the sand, fished, and cooked steaks over a charcoal fire—all within sight of the Empire State Building fourteen miles distant in midtown Manhattan.

Even the ocean surf at Jones Beach across Long Island was easier to reach from Pelham over the Whitestone Bridge than from traffic-snarled New York. Students at Memorial High School organized picnics there, in the senior year.

Exercise in the winter months was no problem for us. During the season of 1945 to 1946, the total snowfall in Pelham was about three feet and we were enchanted by our snow-laden evergreens, which made Castle-Air a continous fairyland. In the winter of 1947 to 1948, Jack became discouraged with shoveling our front steps; the official snowfall in Central Park totaled over five feet, the greatest yet recorded in a year in New York, and we got more in Pelham. The great blizzard of 1888 deposited twenty-one inches of snow on Central Park, but on December 26, 1947, Jack's fiftieth birthday, the heaviest single snowfall buried New York under more than twenty-six inches. The girls made a toboggan slide out of our S-curved thirty-five steps. It was the steepest hill in the area and children brought their metal trays to sit on and slide down it.

After the war ended in 1945, an indoor tennis court nearby in the U.S. Naval Armory at New Rochelle was booked for Saturday afternoons by Jack and Chet Froude. We met Chet through his daughter Joanie, a congenial friend of Virginia's at the Colonial school—children make many introductions for their parents in a new suburb. For the tennis I drove out directly from Cornell medical school and my partner was usually Boyd Lewis, an overseas war correspondent who had just returned to live in Pelham. When the Froudes moved away, "Coop" later became our regular fourth in the indoor doubles—Dr. Irving S. Cooper, the neurosurgeon whose home was also in Pelham. He was revolutionizing the treatment of Parkinson's disease, but medical science did not occupy our attention on the tennis court.

The Pelham Junior Skating Club reserved the large rink at Playland in Rye, New York, on Friday afternoons during the winter months. There was too much snow for outdoor skating. Our girls were members and I was on the Executive Committee. I kept my calendar free of late Friday appointments. One of my obligations as a committee member was to skate every week and help the younger learners. Ginia and Janet were easy to spot on the ice; Ginia wore a black velvet skating suit trimmed with red and Janet, a one-piece fitted suit of white wool that I had knitted. I had started at the bottom of the flared skirt with five hundred stitches on a round needle and I knitted it to her measure without a pattern.

I liked to knit in the car while Jack drove us in or out of New York, as he often did. My next opus was for him—a heavy cable-stitch sweater. As our grandchildren came along, I kept up the habit and made sweaters for them. When we moved to Washington and I stopped commuting, I stopped knitting.

Janet and Virginia kept us young. As they grew to be teen-agers, they still thought of us as being their age and they expected us to do what they did. In the fun houses at Playland Jack and I rode the roller coasters and fast merry-go-rounds with them. We climbed the steps to the top of the polished wood slide that was three or four stories high and we slid down together on squares of carpet. We ran through the revolving barrels and over the shaking bridges. We huddled at the center of a circular spinning turntable. When I was spun off on my back into the wooden trough around it, I climbed out over the low railing and momentarily sat on a short bench. I smiled briefly at the woman sitting on its other end.

"You seem to have discovered the secret of youth—I wish you'd tell me what it is," the young mother remarked. "I'm too tired to get on that thing. I can't keep up with *my* children." She looked ten years younger than my forty-plus age.

"I was born that way, I guess," I replied lightly.

Then I wondered. In a sense my answer was true—my parents had endowed me with energy by inheritance. But they had done more. They had developed in me a quality of endurance by exposing me as a child to a hardy life and by training me early in the efficient use of my muscles. Habitual economy of muscular effort had become a subconscious skill and it spared me fatigue.

Janet and Virginia starred in the performing arts from their first year at Colonial school. They played leading roles in dramatic and musical productions and in modern ballet. I was put to work making costumes for them. Our attic was a storehouse of capes, dresses, and hats from my mother's vintage of 1892 through my own flapper days.

One night when I came home, Virginia chattered so long on the telephone that I finally interrupted her.

"You shouldn't tie up the phone like that, Ginia. What on earth are you talking about?"

"Mummy, it's an emergency. We're rehearsing for assembly in the morning. The speaker just dropped out and they asked me to put on a skit for the program and Margie's writing a song and Rosemary's choreographing a dance and I'm calling the cast." She paused for breath. "We need some costumes. Do you think you could find the things in the attic?"

"Yes, of course. I'll look," I said meekly.

"I'll need breakfast early and could you please pick up some of the kids and take the things to school? We'll have to rehearse about seven."

She knew the answer. I had not missed a single school assembly program in which our girls took part. Those assemblies began at 8:30 A.M. on Wednesdays and I wrote the hour in my appointment book; I went in to New York an hour late. I could arrange the time because I spent that whole day in the pharmacology lab working on my research program. We had no classes scheduled and I did not see patients in the office at 9 West 16th Street. That evening, I had the Cardiac Clinic at Beth Israel Hospital, and I came home late.

In the spring of 1949, the Pelham Memorial and the Scarsdale High Schools exchanged assembly programs. About twenty Pelham students, boys and girls, were to put on several acts in the elegant Scarsdale school auditorium, which seated fourteen hundred. There would be a short play with special stage sets. Janet was to sing a solo, Gounod's "Ave Maria." Ginia and Marjory Schulhoff were to do a dance number. Three faculty men provided their cars and I was glad to help by driving ours the eight miles to Scarsdale. Our motorcade left Memorial High School at six-thirty that morning. Dee and Zella du Vigneaud, whose daughter Marilyn attended the Scarsdale High School—she was a close friend of Ginia's—sat with me during the show. I was the only Pelham parent at that important event in their children's lives.

The Pelham acts had previously received acclaim; the *Pelham Sun* reported the annual amateur talent competition that was held on the evening of February 19, 1949 at the Pelham Memorial High School:

> *Variety Entertainment By School Students*
> *Delights Big Audience. . . .*

The thirteen acts which were presented, all prepared and directed by students, had been selected from tryouts held a week previous. Prizes were awarded in four classifications: skits, singing, dancing and novelties, and piano selections. . . . Janet Powell won first prize singing "Ave Maria." . . . The first novelties prize was awarded to Marjory Schulhoff and Virginia Powell for a delightful dance fantasy telling the story of a boy and girl who meet at a carnival. This graceful pair demonstrated a professional quality in their work which predicted that they are certain to be heard from again and again in future dance presentations.

Ginia was in the ninth grade, Margie and Janet in the tenth. The dancers stole the show.

At the Scarsdale assembly, I was proud of our Pelham talent and of Janet's and Ginia's performances.

"Janet, I never heard you sing so well," I told her afterward.

"I never had such a big audience before, Mummy." Janet was a prima donna at heart, even then.

The dancers were, indeed, heard from again. Ginia, and Janet, too, learned modern dance techniques and choreography in Steffi Nossen's Teen-Age Dance Workshop of Pelham; it was a disciplined, hard-working group. Ginia, Janet, and three other Pelham dancers became troupers of Steffi's Master Class Concert Group. Ginia danced leading roles in productions of professional caliber that were given in the towns of Westchester County and in New York City. Janet danced smaller roles and sang.

The Master Class rehearsed on Saturdays in a big room at Steinway Hall on West 57th Street. It was a treat for me to drive them together to the city as far as the 57th Street crosstown bus that ended its run at York Avenue and East 72nd Street. Then, I put my car in the New York Hospital garage nearby on 70th Street. Later in the day I often drove to Steinway Hall to watch Steffi rehearse the girls in their leotards. I saw my favorite productions take form: Gordon Jenkins's "Manhattan Tower" in 1948, Hans Christian Andersen's story of "The Emperor's New Clothes," as composed by Douglas Moore, Kurt Weill's "Down in the Valley" in 1950, and "The Man on the Flying Trapeze," danced to the music of Robert Russell Bennett in 1951.

The story of those gay working hours was told in a ditty of twenty-six verses by Ginia and Marjory Schulhoff that was published in *Dancing Youth*. I have excerpted it:

REHEARSAL

Each Saturday morning
I'm off for New York,
Pack up my costume,
Prepared for hard work.

I reach Steinway Hall
At twelve twenty-five,
Jerk on my leotard
Feeling gay and alive.

I chat for a moment
With my friends all around,
Until Steffi says "Places!"
And we're there in a bound.

We practice the Fugue
For over an hour,
And then Steffi calls for
"MANHATTAN TOWER"!

When my turn comes 'round
I jump to be there,
Try hard to please Steffi
But she sighs in despair!

"Virginia, your leg . . .
Turn it out . . . just a bit!
And take off that skirt,
I can't think seeing it!"

"Girls, your timing is off,
Could you try it once more?
Try keeping together,
It was all right before."

I helped with the counting,
It's one, two, and then
Don't move on eight, nine,
On ten,—start again.

So on with remarks,
On with orders and praise,
"It's technique I want,
Not jellyfish!" she says.

You might call this bedlam,
Or an orderly mess,
But it's music and dancing . . .
Sometimes noisy—I confess.

But when rest time comes 'round
It's peaceful . . . serene,
Black leotards lounging . . .
Every one in a dream.

Jack and I followed the modern-dance troupe everywhere. We saw *Down in the Valley* in four different Westchester towns. Behind the scenes, Janet sang the soprano role of Jennie in the poignant ballads. "Don't mind the weather, so the wind don't blow" brought back memories of our moving day in the hurricane more than five years earlier. Our children had become young women.

For two years, 1948 and 1949, I was Cochairman—with Dorothy Reznikoff—of the Parents' Committee of Steffi's Pelham Workshop. Later, Mildred Talbot served as Steffi's Pelham Chairman. We saw more of her and Phil, her husband, when in 1961 President Kennedy appointed him Assistant Secretary of State for Near Eastern Affairs and we all moved to Washington. Those dance productions were outstanding community benefits for a college, or scholarship, fund or a Junior League project. The mothers and their more than a thousand daughters who worked each year with Steffi caught her zeal for fitness of character and for self-expression in the dance. Three of those dancing friends were chosen by Virginia to be bridesmaids in her wedding.

Although she had the natural ability and training for it, Ginia never expressed a desire to make dancing her career. She danced for the love of it. Through a chance circumstance, however, it may have interested her in sculpture, which became her major study toward her fine arts degree in 1956 from Cornell University.

One evening in the spring of 1949, I answered the telephone at home and a strange voice spoke.

"You don't know me—but have you a daughter who was a Christmas tree—in a dance program a few months ago? I never saw anyone stand perfectly still for so long." It was queer praise for a dancer.

"Yes, I do," I replied. Any mother would have been intrigued by that opening statement.

It had been my suggestion that Steffi hold a Christmas program in Pelham to give each of the very young students a chance to improvise a dance of her own. One was Santa Claus and she wanted to hang toys on a Christmas tree. There was no tree until Ginia took two long evergreen branches and posed with them in her outstretched arms.

"Your daughter has a magnificent head," the voice went on. "I'm Helen Beling and I'd like your daughter to pose as my model at an educational fair for Westchester County. I've been asked to demonstrate how a sculptor creates a head."

Virginia sat for thirty or forty minutes on a platform while her likeness was rapidly built in clay on an armature and the audience watched from a semicircle. Later, she visited Miss Beling's studio in New Rochelle and posed again for finishing touches on the sculpture.

Our maid told me dubiously, one day, "A lady called and said for Virginia to pick up her head." It sounded like a prank. But we still have our daughter with us in that static form.

At Cornell, Virginia also worked well with astonishing speed when she did a piece of finished sculpture in clay instead of a charcoal sketch each week in the two-and-a-half-hour life-drawing class.

The Pelham Memorial High School was cognizant of the special educational needs of the talented student.

"Janet has that priceless commodity, self-generated energy," Mr. Whipple, the Principal, told me.

When she was a ninth grader, her mathematics teacher asked me whether I would object to his letting her work at her own speed in algebra —she could move ahead faster than the class. After discussing it with Janet, Jack and I could not see any good reason why she should not.

Studying by herself in a corner of the room during math class, where her classmates were reciting problems that she had already done, she completed the first year of algebra in one term and took the New York State Board of Regents examination in it. Her grade was 94. For the second half of the math course she sat again by herself in a corner and finished second-year algebra; in June her Regents mark for the course was 99. As a tenth grader, she followed the same plan and completed two school years of geometry in one. The Board of Regents graded those examinations 100 and 100. Like my Uncle Warren Travell, Janet had a rare mathematical mind.

Janet seemed never to have any homework to do. She did extra reading and she took a book out of the library every few days. She was a fast reader and she remembered what she read.

"When do you do your homework, Janet?" I asked.

"In school, while the others recite or the teacher writes on the blackboard. Of course, I'm not supposed to."

"Can you pay attention like that? Do you think it's wise?"

"I can always think about two things at once. Can't you, Mummy?"

I agreed that I could—sometimes three or four.

Toward the end of tenth grade, her sophomore year in high school, she astonished us by saying, "I've just added up my credits and Mr. Whipple tells me that I can graduate next year. I've had four years of math. All I have to do is to take junior and senior English at the same time. I have to have four years of English for college."

When she telescoped her mathematics courses, it was farthest from our thoughts that she would skip a year of high school, but under the circumstances was there any good reason for her not to accelerate? She was certain that she could easily carry the extra course. She would be sixteen when she entered college.

She was promoted to the senior class and was graduated as its top student with a "four-year" average of 96, for the work that she had condensed into three.

Singing had long been Janet's dream. On March 19, 1947, when she was thirteen and in the eighth grade, she made her solo debut in the annual talent show. The one student from the junior high school who was selected in the tryouts, she sang "Ah, Sweet Mystery of Life." She learned it from a record and it was the only song that her classmate-accompanist could play. Janet was awarded "Honorable Mention." As a ninth grader, when she was still not fourteen, on December 12, 1947, she won first prize in the singing events at the high school with her rendition of "Cantique de Noël." Mr. Frederick Jagel of the Metropolitan Opera Company was one of the judges. She sang, too, as soloist with the high-school chorus in the gala concerts that were directed by the music department.

A new horizon opened for Janet when Jack took her, at the age of thirteen, to her first opera at the Metropolitan Opera in New York City. Lily Pons in *Lucia di Lammermoor* made a deep impression on her.

"I thought perhaps it would be boring," she wrote us later. "But I was entranced, mostly by the Mad Scene. It was like a beautiful effortless magical world and I wanted to be part of it. I wished I were the one on that stage."

Jack gave her that Lily Pons recording and she used to play it and try to sing with it. She was disappointed that she never could reach the high notes; she was not a coloratura soprano.

As parents, Jack and I were at a loss how to nurture our songbird. I made a nuisance of myself by asking people, "How can one recognize a good singing teacher?"

"Go to one of the teacher's recitals," someone finally told me. "If all his students sing alike, he's no good. If they all sing differently, he's a good voice teacher."

Diversity was the essential criterion. We did not find a teacher for her right away in Pelham.

For her ninth-grade term paper in career studies, Janet wrote about what it meant to be an opera singer. The project required each student to interview three people who were active in the chosen field. Janet talked with Mr. Jagel of the Met, who lived near us on Harmon Avenue, and with my mother's friend, Queena Mario, at her apartment in New York. Out of her long experience with singing at the Metropolitan Opera and with teaching the Opera Workshop at the Juilliard School of Music, her advice to Janet was not to start studying voice until she was at least sixteen, but to take lots of sports like tennis, swimming, and basketball.

"A strong healthy body is a prime requisite for a singer," she said. "You have to make the voice box—create the instrument—while you learn to play on it. You can easily damage it before you are physically mature, and then you can not buy a new one. Get the best musical education that you can, now."

Through the courtesy of my medical classmate Irving Wright, who was physician to the Met, Janet attended another opera there and went backstage between the acts to interview the star of her choice. To visit the dressing rooms and peek out onto the huge stage from the wings added a new dimension to Janet's interest. Her term paper was retained by the school as a model.

From those interviews, she had learned that the opera singer's career demanded the same order of hard work, study, and dedication as the profession of medicine.

"If Mummy can do it, I can," she said.

We arranged for Janet to study musical theory with Jane Peck, who was herself a concert singer, taught theory at the Juilliard School in New York and lived in Pelham. For that independent study Janet received two years' advanced standing in music by special examination when she entered college. And while she was in high school, she had helpful voice training from Mrs. Peck to keep her from getting into bad habits with all the singing that she was doing.

The unexpected decision that in June, 1949, Janet would become a senior rather than a junior caught her unprepared in the choice of a college. We had not taken her around to visit those that interested her. Her first preference was Oberlin in Ohio, which was noted for its music department. It was also the first college in the United States to accept women and Janet wanted a coeducational system. Time was short before colleges closed for the summer.

I canceled appointments. She and I flew early one morning to Cleveland, drove to Oberlin, and spent a night in the old inn there. We visited classes in session and saw the dormitories. Janet had the required auditions. Mrs. Stevenson, wife of the President of Oberlin College and a friend of Edith's since the time when she was Mrs. Roswell Bates, gave an evening reception for Janet at her home. The Dean of Women, the Head of the Department of Music, and others came to meet us. It was a delightful evening of piano music, and Janet, although she was only fifteen, sang with poise and maturity. I was satisfied that we had made up for the lost year.

"Didn't we have a wonderful time, Janet!" I said when we were on the plane homeward bound.

"Yes, Mummy. I'm so glad we went because now I know I don't want to go there."

"Then the trip was worthwhile," I said, barely concealing my surprise. "I'd be interested in your reasons."

"Well, I didn't know I'd have to eat breakfast with the boys—I wouldn't have my makeup on. But I guess I could get used to that. The trouble is that everyone there last night told me a different singing teacher I ought to have. When I get signed up for a course, I won't be able to change my voice teacher. There are six in the music department. How will I know beforehand which one is the best for me?"

"Sounds like a sensible reason," I agreed.

"I'll go to a college where I can take my voice lessons on the outside. And I'd rather be in the East, I think, but in the country. I don't want to be in a city, just near a city." She knew what she wanted then.

In the autumn, we started off again and Virginia and Jack went with us. Over the Armistice Day, November 11, long weekend, we drove to Ithaca to visit Cornell University, then to Merryfield Farm to spend a night in the cold house, and on to Mount Holyoke, Smith, Wellesley, and Radcliffe. On the way we had dinner with Willard Weeks, my nephew, a junior in Amherst College.

At Mount Holyoke Janet sang Schubert's "Ave Maria" and she was accompanied at the piano by the head of the music department in her home. At the end of the song, her accompanist wiped tears from her eyes, and said thoughtfully, "Janet, I advise you not to go to college. Start studying voice right away and spend your time singing."

Jack and I were nonplussed.

The day that we reached Wellesley, the fall colors were at their peak in the sunlight of Indian summer. We walked the wooded path around Lake Waban and paddled a canoe across its waters.

"Why didn't you tell me Wellesley was so beautiful, Mummy?" Janet asked.

I had leaned over backward not to influence her in favor of my mother's, my sister's, and my alma mater.

Janet went back to Queena Mario for advice. She heard Janet sing and we had tea together in her studio.

"You have a very pretty voice, Janet—a pleasing voice. Ten or fifteen years ago I would have told you not to take the time for college, but conditions are changing in the world. Very few of the singers with fine voices make the top," she reflected. "Brains are as important as a voice—you have both—and I think that a college education in music will be needed more and more for success as a singer."

"How old will I be when I have to stop singing?" Janet wanted to know.

"You have more time than you realize, Janet. Voices don't reach their maturity until much later than people think." She laughed. "If anyone were to figure it out, they'd find that my publicity has me graduating from high school at eleven or twelve years old. But it's a demanding career and if you're to have a happy married life, you'll need a very understanding husband."

She was fortunate in her own husband, Wilfred Pelletier, a conductor of the Met's orchestra.

Queena Mario did not express a preference for any college. Janet chose to go to Wellesley. There and in Boston she found the climate for music that she sought and a scholarly musician with whom she studied voice both at college and in town. He introduced her at the Longy School of Music in Cambridge where she sang with the Opera Workshop. She was elected to Phi Beta Kappa in her junior year at Wellesley and was graduated a Durant Scholar with honors and the Billings Prize in music.

As suburbanites in Pelham, none of us missed New York City because we had not really left New York City. With his office near Grand Central Station and only a thirty-three-minute train ride, Jack could come home for dinner and bring our teen-agers into town with him that same evening in ample time for me to meet them at the theater—I was often working late. Programs of concerts, plays, operas, and musical shows that Janet and Virginia attended piled up in their closets. We invited their young friends.

Virginia, with Margie Schulhoff as coauthor, described in *Dancing Youth* how Jack took us all in stride. In January, 1948,

Mrs. Powell and Mrs. Reznikoff hit upon a wonderful idea, a brainstorm! . . . With Steffi they planned a special party in New York City to see some popular musical hit with modern dancing [*Brigadoon*]. . . . A sharp wind whipped around the corners and blew the long ballerina skirts of the [Pelham] Workshop girls swirling around their legs. . . . Four of the Workshop-ers parents, Mrs. Powell, Mrs. Hazard, Mrs. Reppert and Mr. Powell, the only man among the 28 females, supervised the trip. . . . From Grand Central Station . . . they paraded up Fifth Avenue, across Rockefeller Plaza, of course stopping to watch the ice-skating, and uptown along Sixth Avenue [the Avenue of the Americas] and into the Ziegfeld Theater at 54th Street. Above the chatter of the girls could be heard: "Stay together!" . . . "Don't rush!" . . . "Keep up back there!" With Steffi [and her staff] they took up the whole front row of the balcony, the whole second row and part of the third. The girls were comfortably settled—after being sure to get a supply of candy, gum and lemonade—when the lights dimmed and the orchestra began to play . . . and the great heavy red curtain lifted from the floor. The girls relaxed in their seats to watch the play unfold. . . . The trip home even in the smoky commuters' train was fun. Everyone talked about the performance, the things each liked best. . . . I (Virginia) don't know about the others, but as soon as I got home . . . I ran upstairs three steps at a time, jumped into bed, pulled the blankets up under my chin and instantly fell asleep. I dreamed of a legendary little Scottish town, bright plaid kilts and whirling skirts, lovely singing, barefoot dancing, and a Scotch dialect that I will remember for a long long time!

The next morning, Jack's three "girls" were singing *Brigadoon* and whirling around the dining-room table. We settled, finally, for breakfast. Virginia looked meditatively at her sister and parents.

"I know I'm crazy. Janet's crazy," she announced. She studied me. "I guess Mommy's crazy, too."

Her eyes traveled to Jack. She shook her head. "Daddy's *not* crazy. But he understands us all."

Ginia was like him in that. She had a great gift of communicating with people, and that was a standard of excellence to her.

"It's all right for Janet to be first in her class, but I'll be second in mine. They don't like you so well if you're first, but it's all right to be second," she told me one day when she showed me her school grades. She liked being a bobby-soxer.

At her graduation from the Pelham Memorial High School Virginia ranked second in the class. She had made her contract, a feat perhaps more difficult to achieve than Janet's goal of intellectual perfection.

Years later, I was reminded of Virginia's comment when I told the Secretary of Commerce and former Governor of North Carolina, Luther Hodges, "North Carolina is my adopted state. I have come to think it's the finest state in the Union." I meant it.

"Oh—I'd never say that, Bobby," he deadpanned.

"No? What *would* you say, Luther?"

"I call it the second best state—then I never get into an argument."

One idiosyncrasy of his three girls that Jack tolerated was our habit of writing and reciting poetry—sometimes when he thought that we ought to be putting our time to other use.

Virginia loved dogs, like horses. After Buppy died, we got her a collie puppy. She read all of Albert P. Terhune's books about collies, and one of her early poems was about Lad. It was written when she was eight or nine:

LAD, A GREAT COLLIE

Lad was a great dog
Did always behave,
He slept in a corner
'Neath his piano "cave."

He was mated to Lady
What a temper had she.
Wolf was their puppy
A bad dog was he.

Wolf bit Lad, and kicked Lad
But never a word
From Laddie, Great Laddie,
Ever was heard.

Lad lived a long life
But his muzzle turned white.
His old legs stiffened
He could no longer fight.

All dogs age too soon
And soon Laddie died.
His big heart just stopped
He never cried.

Laddie you great dog
Who never was bad
Everyone knows you,
You great collie Lad.

Janet was partial to kittens and we usually housed both feline and canine pets. In the winter of 1945–1946, one of her poems was published in
the *Pel Mel,* the school publication that had a First Class Honor Rating by
the National Scholastic Press Association:

WHAT'CHA THINKIN', PUSSY?

What'cha thinkin', Pussy?
    Face so calm and wise.
Why'a winkin', Pussy?
    With your deep green eyes.

Thinkin' 'bout a butterfly
    Flyin' in the air
And when you made a jump for him
    He flew away from there?

Winkin' 'bout the time
    When you stole away my yarn
And when I went to look for it
    I found it in the barn?

Is that what'cha thinkin', Pussy?
    Face so calm and wise.
Is that why'a winkin', Pussy?
    With your deep, green eyes.

A couple of years later, Janet returned to the same theme:

PUSSY'S EYES

Have you ever looked into a pussy's eyes?
Seen how the light leaps up and dies?
Seen the deep mysterious fire
Flashing and glowing as though to inspire
One with thoughts from another world?
As if for moments one had seen unfurled
Thoughts from deep in a pussy's brain
And then they were covered quickly again.

In that period when she was about thirteen, Janet looked further into "another world":

DEATH

A silent phantom stealing down
Stopping at every village and town,
City and farm, near and far,
No one ever its pathway can bar.

A ghostlike figure, a shrouded form,
More frightening than the winter's storm,
A skeleton hand taking away
Somebody's loved one every day.

Cruel and harsh to those who love life,
Sharp and painful as the stab of a knife,
A parting from those whom they love best,
Leaving their bodies cold without zest.

To some, death is a happy thing
Setting the soul free to wing
Away to the place where our Father is
To belong to Him, be forever His.

For Jack's and my eighteenth wedding anniversary on June 6, 1947, Janet wrote in an opposite vein, about our example of married life together:

OUR ANNIVERSARY

When e'er our anniversary comes 'round,
I think that another year
Has passed, full of peace and joy and gladness
With all my loved ones dear.

I think of that day, oh, long, long ago,
When we were made man and wife,
To share all our fortunes, both good and bad,
And be each others for life.

Sleeping under the sky, Virginia knew the wind and stars at Merryfield Farm. When she was in high school at Pelham, she wrote:

NATURE AND CIVILIZATION

The wind that moans through city streets
And bites the powdered cheek,
That whips with glee the fashioned skirt
With jealous, laughing shriek,

Is a wind that loves its naughty pranks,
Like some lost urchin freak.

Yet the wind's soft, warming breath that blows
Caressing the verdant land,
Touching the forest creatures there
With gently brushing hand,
Is a wind whose power springs from Love—
As the breath of God was planned.

The stars that hang so high above
The cities' roofs and skies
Are hard-seen through the street lights' glare;
They watch with half closed eyes.
They watch the smog with scornful gaze
And flee before sunrise.

But the stars that lie above the fields
And woods and lakes of gray
Are soft and large as a puppy's eyes,
Only a treetop's height away;
When sunrise comes, they close their lids
And dream in Heaven all the day.

When I found those verses among her high-school papers, they reminded me of my own poem, "Sleeping Under Stars." [1]

The sea soothed Virginia, as it did me. In the spring of 1947 at Pelham, perhaps with nostalgia for Old Greenwich, she wrote:

AWAY TO THE SEA

Oh, to be free
Like the sea
Or a tree
Or a bee
Or a bird that flies in the air.

To be free
O'er the lea
By the sea
Just me
To have wings and never a care.

I would away
Never stay
Not a day

[1] Chapter IV, page 42.

On my way
To the ocean, my freedom is there.

In my flight
Through the night
Out of sight
To such height
On my way, with no troubles to bear.

But alas!
On the grass
Out of class
I pass
The time, eating a pear, that's where.

In 1953, when Virginia was a freshman at Cornell University by the shores of Lake Cayuga, she was still writing about the ocean—in a more sophisticated style:

RUNNABLE ROCK

We felt the wince of evasive sand
Under our feet as we walked that day
Where the sea was blocked by a headboard of rock—
A shiny slab of micaed gray—
Runnable, pocketing rock of the tide
That dared the tantrum sea at its side
To grind it away, grind it away.

We lay on our backs on the up-jutting rock,
Hot in the socket of gull swarming air,
Touching the mane of the lean dog beside us
Who quivered for hands on his salty-mixed hair;
Recalling ahead more winterly days
When the rocking horse sea would continue to graze
On the runnable rock, to grind it away.

The feel of the durable rock in those stanzas revealed the poet that Virginia was, as well as the sculptor that she would become. In 1953, she wrote also:

MARBLE

Going up,
I saw a man's mirrored image
in the glass-faced door
that blocked the stair, and for
a moment I was startled.

There had been no one in the museum but me.

I could see
him backed against the wall
looking straight ahead, and tall,
self-contained in waiting.

Yet there had been no one in the museum . . .

He swung away
as someone opened the glass door,
but there was no down-comer
on the stairs.

A wind blew through my spine.

I hurried out.
I knew the man still stood there (waiting
for the wind to blow the door)
as he had done for more
than centuries.

Janet and Virginia always counted on Daddy to understand.

Years later, during one of Washington's silent snowfalls, in mild exasperation because Jack seemed at the moment not to appreciate my own poetic efforts, I wrote:

DIALOGUE BETWEEN A POET
AND A PRAGMATIST

The cadence of cicadas ends
When night at last twilight transcends.
    "They're only locusts, I would say,
    They'll saw like jays another day."

The sequins of dark skies shimmer
Through breeze-etched leaves of summer.
    "Why, isn't that the milky way
    Just showing through the trees?—I'd say."

Like falling stars, silent fireflies
Gleam high, outshine the gala skies.
    "I call 'em lightnin' bugs, not stars,
    And watch 'em light up inside jars."

White winter's crystals, wind impelled,
In street lights shine, by warmth dispelled.
    "The blizzard's hard packed ice wont go
    Away; I shovel dirty snow."

The soundless drifting snowflakes are
The souls of fireflies from afar.
    "Reincarnation isn't so,
    As anybody ought to know."

Jack had the last word.

In September, 1944, when we moved from New York to our "house in the country," I dreamed that I might stay at home at least for holidays. My leisure time in Pelham that winter had been less than I had hoped, although I had resigned from the Sea View Hospital consultant staff and I had cut back on some of my other part-time activities. As Easter of 1945 approached, I was disturbed to hear Virginia talking with Janet about our going to Atlantic City on their vacation.

"Ginia, we decided not to go away this Easter, I thought. Don't you like our new home any more? You said you were crazy about it in Pelham."

"I am, Mummy. I like it so much I'd hate to get tired of it."

Just ten years old, she won the argument. Her logic was irrefutable, and we went to Atlantic City for a week to ride the horses on the ocean sands. And we went again at Easter for the next three years.

When we returned by train that Friday, April 6, 1945, my father met us at Pennsylvania Station and drove us to Pelham. Gasoline was more plentiful—victory for the Allies over Italy and Germany seemed near.

From Pelham we made few trips to Talcott Farms in Westfield, but Gran and Grandma Edie came often to visit us. On the children's birthdays, he mystified them with magic in our living room as he had in New York City. He enjoyed our new home and friends. When Edith took trips with her own children, he frequently stayed with us. He took special pleasure in our convenient year-round tennis.

"I don't see now why you didn't quit New York sooner—it was a good move," he told me. "I didn't realize that you could live like this and still work in town."

He and Edith attended many of the girls' singing and dancing programs in Westchester County. He had a strong feeling that the actor's profession, or that of any performing artist, was somehow incompatible with a happy normal existence. He knew the hardships that many had undergone on the Broadway stage. But like my grandfather Davidson, who objected to Ginny's and my studying medicine, my father was inordinately proud of his granddaughters' accomplishments then. He forgot his bias when Janet sang "Cantique de Noël" on December 18, 1949, as the soprano soloist with the high-school chorus at the Community Christmas Carol Singing of two thousand Pelhamites, which was sponsored by the Men's Club.

The recording of those carols was then broadcast by the town late in the afternoon during Christmas week near the railroad station to greet the weary commuters. Inside our home we could hear Janet's voice soaring above the village streets. It bridged a gap between his generation and hers.

After Edith died suddenly of a heart attack on September 20, 1950, while she and my father were traveling in California, he had a home available with us that he had already come to love. He never complained about our thirty-five steps.

One of our oaks, which my father had wanted to cut and replace with an apple tree, finally blew down in the November 25 hurricane of 1950. That Saturday, I left our convertible in the New York Hospital garage—its cloth top would not have reached Pelham intact—and I rode out with Dee du Vigneaud in his big Chrysler. We were standing in the front hall when "timber" crashed onto the roof of our house. The huge tree trunk made a horizontal bridge to the high ledge from which it was uprooted at the rear, and Virginia had a new thrill in walking it to the upstairs porch.

Our scary first night in the dark strange house during the disastrous hurricane of 1944 might have been worse for us, after all.

I never got around to planting that apple tree. In the years following the war, I became busier and busier. I allotted four afternoons a week for private practice in my father's office at 9 West 16th Street and I also saw patients at our home in Pelham. In the five years from 1944 to 1949, my income from that part-time source doubled; it rose from approximately $9,000 to $18,000. Although I was promoted in 1947 from Instructor to Assistant Professor, and in 1951 to Associate Professor of Clinical Pharmacology, my part-time teaching salary at Cornell did not change materially. Faculty salaries were not impressive. On the other hand, my research responsibilities there increased steadily. By 1951, as principal investigator I had a research budget of $21,500 a year at the medical school. My funds were derived mainly from the National Heart Institute of the National Institutes of Health and from the Josiah Macy, Jr. Foundation. With my own research staff, for both laboratory and clinical studies, the scope of my interests and my productivity expanded rapidly. Commensurately, I traveled farther and oftener to read papers, to demonstrate scientific exhibits at medical meetings, and to give invitation lectures.

"Office hours: day and night" was an understatement of my activities. After Janet's and my trip to Oberlin College in the summer of 1949, I stopped in Harry Gold's office at Cornell to worry him with my quandary.

"Harry, I can't go on expanding in all directions like this—what am I going to do? I should have more time at home. Maybe I ought to give up

teaching and all the research in New York and just open an office near
Pelham. I don't think I'd be happy to stop practice and go back on a full-
time plan after all these years."

"You can't cut off any one of your limbs, Bobby. You'll have to apply
tourniquets to them."

Still I worried whether Janet and Virginia felt neglected. We had wonderful fun together. I gave them my undivided attention in the time that we
could share—I could disconnect myself quickly from pending problems.

One Sunday at home, I handed Virginia an editorial to read in the
Westchester Medical Bulletin of August, 1949, about "Sex and Medicine."
The editor, while disagreeing strongly, quoted the conclusions of a recently
published sampling of opinion on women physicians. That poll "of Hospital
Chiefs of Staff [men] . . . on returns from about 100 whose identities are
mercifully unrevealed . . . included all the familiar criticisms. 'Women
doctors are emotionally unstable.' 'They talk too much.' 'They're always
on the defensive.' 'They get pregnant.' 'If she is married and childless . . .
she is frustrated . . . or if she raises a family . . . she is neglecting her
practice.' 'There's no hope for women in medicine.' "

The next day when I came home from New York, on my bed was Virginia's handwritten answer to the broadside against women physicians:

ARE THE CHILDREN OF WOMEN DOCTORS NEGLECTED?

I am the daughter of a woman doctor, and I couldn't say that I have
been neglected during one of my fourteen years, or my sister during
any of her fifteen. Nor can I say that our mother neglects her practice. The truth is, she practices on us. She turns us into guinea pigs
with as much loving care as the housewife changes milk and flour into
a cake. If any one is neglected in our family, it's Daddy, but he is
Pappa Guinea Pig when he is needed.

I suppose we have turned out to be almost normal children, despite what some people think is a great barrier to contend with. Although, sometimes I wonder. I've learned to dislike bubble gum because it is "bad for my jaws" and murder mysteries on the radio
because "they poison my mind," and I admit my friends sometimes
get annoyed when I say, "You'll get a stiff neck sitting like that," but
they forgive me because I'm a doctor's daughter. I get stuffed with
huge pills for the slightest ache or pain, but I can go barefoot and
step on all the rusty nails I want because Mom will fix me up! And I
guess I go to as many dances and picnics, and talk on the phone as
long as any average teen-age girl.

I admit we aren't "Mamma's little pets" like some—who I think
see too much of their parents and become pampered babies who never

grow up. We are on our own most of the time, we have much more freedom than most, and I guess we learn responsibility earlier, but I'm not complaining! I don't feel neglected!

And we are one up on most children. Mom takes vacations from her work, not from us, and we go along on those Family Honeymoons.

In answer to the question, "Do I wish Mom was not a doctor?" I say, Don't be silly! I wouldn't change places with anybody on earth. I like being a guinea pig! Virginia Powell, September 13, 1949.

"It's a beautiful piece of writing, Ginia," I said. "And it makes me very happy. Would you care to send it off to the editor of the *Bulletin?*"

She mailed it, exactly as it was written, and it was published in the editorial section. [2]

Soon afterward, Jack and I were talking with friends at home and one of them said, "If I had my life to live over, I wouldn't be doing any of the things that I am now."

"No? What would you be doing, Bill?" I asked.

"I'd be swimming and fishing off the beaches of Honolulu."

"That's a lovely pastime, but you wouldn't enjoy it for longer than two months if you had nothing else to do," I predicted. "If I had my life to live over again, I'd do it exactly the same—except that I would like one more hour a day with the children."

Janet was playing the piano in the alcove off the living room and I did not realize that she heard me. Without interrupting the movement of her fingers on the keyboard, she leaned toward us and called to me in a tone of alarm.

"That's fine for you, Mummy, but I don't have one more hour in the day."

A senior in high school, she was as busy as I. The girls would soon be away in college and our "family honeymoons" would end.

I never made that wish again.

[2] Virginia Powell, "Are the Children of Women Doctors Neglected?" *Westchester Medical Bulletin,* Vol. 17 (November, 1949), pp. 29 and 39.

CHAPTER 14

My Standard of Comfort Was Raised

Those were radiant days for walking on the boardwalk that second week of June, 1949, when the American Medical Association convened in Atlantic City, New Jersey. On my way from the Convention Hall I encountered one of my father's New York friends in physical medicine, Dr. Richard Kovacs, and his wife. They were strolling along with a tall man who was a stranger to me. Dr. Kovacs formally introduced me to Dr. W. S. C. Copeman, the British rheumatologist, whose 1948 *Textbook of Rheumatic Diseases* stood on my bookshelf.

Dr. Copeman stared down at me as if he were wearing a monocle. His laconic drawl took me by surprise: "O-oh! Doctor Travell. So-o, you're the Trigger Queen."

I was complimented by the title. He was not calling me a "pistol packin' mama." He was indicating that he knew about my mapping of uncharted patterns of pain referred from "trigger areas" in the voluntary muscles of the skeleton. The missing key to many painful states of the skeletal muscles was, I had observed, that the patient felt pain in the target, or reference zone, often at a considerable distance from the spot in a muscle where pain originated. A knowledge of the specific referred pain patterns of individual muscles could help pinpoint the trigger area.

The incident was memorable to me as an indicator of my progress in studying skeletal muscle pain, and in talking and writing about its mechanisms and management. It was ten years since a chance combination of circumstances had diverted my interest in that direction.

The tenor of my professional life changed when I assumed a part-time academic position at the medical school after Virginia was born in 1935. I was able then to follow my dream as a physician in ways that had been impossible under the restrictions of my full-time appointment in a preclinical science department. In my "spare time" I developed a small private practice from my father's office in the building where we lived in New York. I began to view medicine from my father's perspective.

His unchanging concern for all aspects of a patient's care led him to describe himself then as a family doctor and only "part specialist" in physical medicine. But his advanced knowledge of electrotherapy brought to his office people with stubborn pain, some of whom were referred to him as a last resort by his orthopedic friends. The old Toepler-Holtz static machine performed nobly in his hands for relief of neuritis, "neuralgias," muscular strains, bursitis, and protracted disability following fractures and joint immobilization. His techniques were not taught us in medical school, but his therapeutic results in that heterogeneous group of painful conditions impressed me at times as only short of miraculous. Explanations for its benefits, as well as the mere operation of that static machine, intrigued me, much as the Einthoven string-galvanometer had challenged me as a medical student.

My father's inventive mind devised original hookups for the Toepler-Holtz machine's static electricity. He wired the swinging arm of a metronome in series with the patient, so as to create an interrupted rhythmic discharge with surging intensity that could be applied through a metal plate to any region of the body. In 1923, he described the "static surge" and stated: "It is fully as vigorous as the sinusoidal current. . . . When used upon the abdomen a working of the muscles is readily secured which is conspicuously massive, deeply penetrating, and decidedly agreeable." [1]

In those obscure clinical entities that responded to my father's treatment, the common denominator for pain appeared to be persistent spasm of the skeletal muscles. His use of the static machine first alerted me to the crippling consequences of muscle spasm, a functional disorder of the motor system that accounts for half the weight of the human body.

In 1941, I assisted my father in writing a second article to amplify his original observations and to extend their underlying theory.[2] We concluded:

[1] J. Willard Travell, "The Static Wire Brush Discharge and the Static Surge," *American Journal of Electrotherapeutics and Radiology,* Vol. 41 (1923), pp. 6–9.
[2] Willard Travell and Janet Travell, "Modifications and Effects of the Static Surge and of the Wire-Brush Discharge," *Archives of Physical Therapy,* Vol. 22 (August, 1941), pp. 486–489.

The static surge produces vigorous exercise of muscles. . . . The effect of alternate muscular contraction and relaxation obtained in this way is probably analogous to that of voluntary, rhythmic muscle work which has been shown experimentally by Barcroft and Millen (1939) to increase blood flow through muscles, in contrast to the effect of sustained contraction which decreases blood flow. . . . Evidence suggests that this increase in blood flow is not due solely to mechanical factors [pumping blood through soft-walled veins], but is, in part at least, caused by the liberation of a vasodilating substance in contracting muscles.

The nature of vasodilator metabolites released by working muscle is still under investigation. I do not doubt, however, that the static surge augmented circulation in the electrically stimulated muscles, if for no other reason than that muscular contraction generates heat, and warming a muscle, as by immersing a limb in hot water, eventually increases local blood flow to carry off the excess calories (heat). That, incidentally, can partly explain the value of a "warm-up" before strenuous exercise of cold muscles.

I was exposed to my father's enthusiastic practice of medicine at a critical time. Personal experience is a great teacher, and while I was championing static electricity as a therapeutic agent—a far cry from pharmacology—I was a beneficiary of its effects. I developed a severely painful right shoulder and arm, and the static surge gave me periodic relief of the steady ache that often prevented my sleeping. In spite of the convenient treatment, the pain became so disturbing that for most of 1940 I decided to forego tennis —but not work. At thirty-eight, I was not wise enough to slow my pace.

Overuse of my muscles in longhand writing and in precise laboratory procedures was at the root of my shoulder-arm pain. Besides teaching the class and directing special research projects for our pharmacology students, I was carrying on laboratory experiments with Dr. Harry Gold that required our giving injections of nicotine around the clock. We took turns with the day and night shifts in the lab. In the same period, basic questions arose concerning the absorption of nicotine and other potent alkaloids, and I pursued the answers energetically.[3] I continued to accumulate data during my

[3] Janet Travell, "The Absorption of Alkaloids from the Stomach," *Federation Proceedings*, (1938), p. 37; "The Influence of the Hydrogen Ion Concentration on the Absorption of Alkaloids from the Stomach," *Journal of Pharmacology and Experimental Therapeutics*, Vol. 69 (1940), pp. 21–33; "Influence of pH on Absorption of Nicotine from Urinary Bladder and Subcutaneous Tissues," *Proceedings of the Society for Experimental Biology and Medicine*, Vol. 45 (1940), pp. 552–556; Janet Travell, Oscar Bodansky, and Harry Gold, "Nicotine Excretion and the Role of Its Reabsorption from the Urinary Bladder as a Source of Nicotine Poisoning in Tobacco Smokers," *Journal of Pharmacology and Experimental Therapeutics*, Vol. 69 (1940), p. 307; and Janet Travell, "The Absorption of Nicotine from Various Sites," *Annals of the New York Academy of Sciences*, Vol. 90 (1960), pp. 13–30.

twenty-one years of demonstrating variables in nicotine absorption to the pharmacology class, and I finally summarized my observations at a New York Academy of Sciences Symposium in March, 1960.

My curiosity was originally sparked by a 1933 report in the *Journal of the American Medical Association* about a man who vomited and collapsed while he was sitting on a park bench wet with an insecticide solution that had been sprayed on the trees overhead. Taken by ambulance to Bellevue Hospital, he recovered by virtue of the tincture of time and without a diagnosis. Preparing to leave the hospital, he put on his clothes again and promptly had a second attack. The poison that had soaked into the seat of his pants was identified then as nicotine and the spray as a 40 percent aqueous nicotine solution that was alkaline. It was also shown that 40 percent nicotine in an acid solution was relatively unabsorbed through the skin, and therefore much less toxic on contact. Both nicotine sprays were in use as insecticides.

My subsequent studies showed that, like the skin, the internal surfaces of the body absorb such compounds as nicotine rapidly from a slightly alkaline aqueous solution, but very slowly when it is slightly acid. The former fact was known, but the latter was not. Morphine, for instance, is absorbed from the mouth because the saliva is usually alkaline. It does not pass through the stomach wall when a tablet is swallowed; absorption is delayed by gastric acidity until the material reaches the alkaline medium of the small intestine. The retarding influence of gastric hydrochloric acid on absorption from the stomach is nullified, however, by ethyl alcohol in concentrations of 20 to 25 percent, so that some drugs taken with a cocktail may produce unexpectedly intense effects.

The unexplored wilderness of pharmacology and the excitement of discovery drove me. In those early years of my part-time plan at Cornell, Harry Gold, Walter Modell, and I tied off coronary arteries in cats so as to study drug effects in the healing stages of acute myocardial infarction.[4] Our results matched my prior observations at Bellevue Hospital, where patients with lobar pneumonia had shown a decreased tolerance to digitalis. Likewise, in experimental myocardial infarction digitalis became more toxic.

[4] Harry Gold, Janet Travell, and Walter Modell, "The Effect of Theophylline with Ethylenediamine (Aminophylline) on the Course of Cardiac Infarction Following Experimental Coronary Occlusion," *American Heart Journal*, Vol. 14 (1937), pp. 284–296; Janet Travell, Harry Gold, and Walter Modell, "The Effect of Experimental Cardiac Infarction on the Response to Digitalis," *Archives of Internal Medicine*, Vol. 61 (1938), pp. 184–197; Harry Gold, Walter Modell, and Janet Travell, "The Influence of the Size of Cardiac Infarcts upon the Electrocardiogram," *American Heart Journal*, Vol. 15 (1938), pp. 77–83; and Janet Travell, Harry Gold, and Walter Modell, "The Blood Pressure and the Size of a Cardiac Infarct," *American Heart Journal*, Vol. 15 (1938), pp. 448–451.

We should not have been surprised that in normal and diseased states the effect of the drug was quantitatively different.

It was no wonder that my overworked right arm continued to hurt. Poking around at night on the muscles over my shoulder blade, trying to give some "do-it-yourself" massage, I was astonished to touch sore spots that intensified, or reproduced my pain, as though I had turned on an electric switch. It was my first introduction to the enigmatic trigger area. No nerve existed, I knew, to connect those firing spots directly with my arm. I was baffled, but I did not discard the observation on the grounds that I could not explain it.

Soon afterward, in relation to our Cardiac Clinic at Beth Israel Hospital I read a scientific article by two University of Pennsylvania internists, published in 1936 and entitled, "Persistent Pain in the Shoulder Region Following Myocardial Infarction." [5] As an incidental finding, the authors mentioned that two of their patients had "a so-called 'trigger zone' in the scapular region, pressure over which caused great increase in pain. . . . [One man] discovered that pressure over the upper portion of the scapula produced a pain which radiated to the left shoulder, down the left arm and up the left side of the neck." They had listened to the patient, and I was not imagining what I felt, after all. They also noted what I had already concluded, that "treatment was singularly ineffective."

In that era of prolonged bed-rest and immobility, acute myocardial infarction was complicated in 10 to 20 percent of cases by the sequel of an intractable shoulder-arm pain syndrome. It was a problem that made life unendurable to the patient.

The Cardiac Consultation Service at Sea View, the city hospital for tuberculosis on Staten Island to which I was appointed in 1936, supplied the conditions that crystallized my emerging interest in muscular pain. Most patients there had life-threatening pulmonary disease, but some of them complained more about devastating pain in their shoulders and arms than about their major illness. When I examined them by systematic palpation of the scapula and chest muscles, I easily uncovered the presence of trigger areas. I knew what to look for. The curiosity of the medical resident, Dr. Myron Herman, was stimulated.

On October 4, 1940, I gave Dr. Herman a short list of references that would serve as a basis for initiating treatment of our hospital patients by local injection of the intramuscular trigger areas with procaine (Novocain). On the list was a diagnostic study by Arthur Steindler and J. Vernon

[5] Joseph Edeiken and Charles C. Wolferth, "Persistent Pain in the Shoulder Region Following Myocardial Infarction," *American Journal of Medical Sciences,* Vol. 191 (1936), pp. 201–210.

Luck at the University of Iowa (the *Journal of the American Medical Association,* January 8, 1938)—and another one by Steindler in 1940—in which they described their "procaine test" for allocating the source of back pain with sciatic radiation either to tender spots in the soft tissues or to the spine. In fine print, one case report indicated that the test apparently cured the patient's pain. That scientific paper first alerted me to the potentially lasting benefits of the transient local anesthetic action of procaine when injected into trigger areas in the skeletal muscles.

That therapeutic procedure was less well known in the United States then than in England, France, Australia, and other countries. On my list, too, was Dr. J. H. Kellgren's article in the February 12, 1938, issue of the *British Medical Journal,* entitled, "A Preliminary Account of Referred Pains Arising from Muscle." He reported first, that tender spots in the muscles gave rise to referred pain (pain mediated by an altered excitatory state in the central nervous system) and secondly, that injection of those spots with procaine solution resulted in spectacular relief of the referred pain. One of his patients had shoulder-arm pain with trigger areas at locations that resembled mine and those of our long-suffering group at Sea View Hospital. In conclusion Kellgren stated the crux of the problem of clinical application:

> The injection of local anesthetics is of course a well known therapeutic procedure which has claimed occasional successes in these complaints.
> . . . The uncertain results obtained with such local therapy are not surprising when one considers that without an accurate knowledge of muscular pains the therapy must often be applied to areas of referred pain and tenderness instead of to the source of pain. It remains to be seen how much a further knowledge of muscular pain will help in the treatment of these very difficult cases.[6]

I took my cue from J. H. Kellgren.

With Harry Gold's approval—he was chief of the Cardiac Consultation Service—we selected patients with painful shoulder syndromes and I asked Dr. Herman to inject their trigger areas with procaine when he had ample time. With due care, it was a safe procedure. He was not as optimistic as I about the outcome, but with that technique he secured prompt and lasting pain relief, return of the normal range of motion at the shoulder joint, and some very grateful patients. From the viewpoint of study, the long hospitalization for chronic disease at Sea View was favorable to our observation of the end results of therapy.

My father took a keen delight in hearing about the progress of my work

[6] John H. Kellgren, "A Preliminary Account of Referred Pains Arising from Muscle," *British Medical Journal,* Vol. 1 (February 12, 1938), p. 326.

there. It was not long before he used the new procedure to rid me of my own nagging pain. If comfort could be restored so easily in that way, I determined to broaden the distribution of that healing knowledge among physicians.

In 1941, I extended my study of referred skeletal muscle pain to include patients at Beth Israel Hospital. That study was made feasible by a windfall in the person of Dr. Seymour H. Rinzler. He joined me as a volunteer full-time associate at both Sea View and Beth Israel Hospitals and in the Department of Pharmacology at Cornell. Having just completed his internship at Bellevue Hospital, he needed a year of research to qualify for the American Board specialty examinations in internal medicine.

Although we were strangers at the start, our relationship thrived. Interrupted only by Seymour's Army service abroad during World War II, it continued until I left New York for Washington in 1961. His industry, persevering curiosity, and knowledge of the medical literature contributed largely to my research output and to my pleasure in it. We worked with the same enthusiasm when we had no special financial support as when I was principal investigator under grants from the National Heart Institute (1950–1957) and from the Josiah Macy, Jr Foundation (1952–1958). Our last two scientific papers appeared in 1960.[7] We had collaborated then in twenty-four publications concerning various aspects of muscular pain, cardiovascular disorders, and the pharmacology of cardiac drugs.

Our first paper dealt with procaine infiltration of trigger areas as a means of treating pain and disability of the shoulder and arm.[8] It was accepted for the program of the American Medical Association in June, 1942, and I was to present it before the Section of Experimental Medicine and Therapeutics in Atlantic City. In March, 1942, as a trial run I reported our excellent clinical results of treatment at a research meeting of the New York Heart Association [9] in the New York Academy of Medicine. Criticism was more favorable than I had anticipated.

At the end of the evening, the President (Chairman) of the New York

[7] Dorothy Karp, Seymour H. Rinzler, and Janet Travell, "Effect of Ergometrine (Ergonovine) on the Isolated Atherosclerotic Heart of the Cholesterol-fed Rabbit," *British Journal of Pharmacology*, Vol. 15 (1960), pp. 333–444; and Janet Travell, Seymour H. Rinzler, and Dorothy Karp, "Cardiac Effects of Nicotine in the Rabbit with Experimental Coronary Atherosclerosis," *Annals of the New York Academy of Sciences*, Vol. 90 (1960), pp. 290–301.

[8] Janet Travell, Seymour H. Rinzler, and Myron Herman, "Pain and Disability of the Shoulder and Arm: Treatment by Intramuscular Infiltration with Procaine Hydrochloride," *Journal of the American Medical Association*, Vol. 120 (October 10, 1942), pp. 417–422.

[9] Known until March, 1944, as the Heart Committee of the New York Tuberculosis and Health Association.

Heart Association, Dr. Edwin P. Maynard who lived in Brooklyn, drove me home to 9 West 16th Street. As we rode down Fifth Avenue in his car, we discussed the enigma of how a short-acting local anesthetic like procaine could conceivably produce any permanent effect.

"Not so long ago," Dr. Maynard reflected, "a physician in this city claimed he was curing people with Novocain, and we kicked him out of the County Medical Society."

We were silent for several blocks while I digested his remark.

"Maybe it wasn't so much what he said as how he said it that was wrong," I surmised hopefully.

"That's right—it all came out in the newspapers first," Dr. Maynard replied.

Soon after our investigation had been published in the *Journal of the American Medical Association,* I received a telephone request for an interview about it that would appear as a feature in the *New York Journal-American* newspaper. Naturally, I refused. It was politely suggested to me that the story would be printed anyway and I might wish to ensure its accuracy. The Public Relations Department at the New York Hospital–Cornell Medical Center advised me to check the text of the story and then send it for review to Dr. Iago Galdston at the New York Academy of Medicine, who handled such matters of medical ethics.

The manuscript, written by a columnist of King Features Syndicate, described "the almost epidemic outbreak of shoulder pains in the last few years" and proceeded to give a sober exposition of our article in the *Journal of the American Medical Association.* I particularly liked the choice of quotations: " 'The maximum point of tenderness was located with precision. . . . "Blind" injection in the hope of infiltrating a trigger point by mere chance is usually ineffective. . . . Referred pain was often induced momentarily [by the needle] and was helpful in demonstrating the accuracy of injection.' "

The full-page feature in the "Saturday Tabloid" Home Section of December 12, 1942, carried the approved conservative text under the inch-high headline: "HELL, RIGHT FROM THE SHOULDER." One-third of the newspaper page was occupied by two eye-catching illustrations. In one, a horned and hairy, long-tailed devil with a saturnine expression hauled on a paunchy magnate's arm; the magnate was yelling, "Help! It's that Imp again, tying shoulder muscles into a knot." The other cartoon pictured an oversized woman angel with an "M.D." bag, who was standing on a cloud and giving an injection into the bare shoulder of a little man with a blissful smile. The caption explained: "Now medical science comes through with new hope for thousands of sufferers from muscular shoulder and arm pains, in the form of procaine injections into . . . the 'trigger and pressure zones,' like the 'touch of an angel.' "

No patient had ever implied that about my probing fingers and needle.

The large, mounted page proof of the newspaper version and the original drawings were sent to me by the editors, to mollify me, I did not doubt. However, unknown to them I had it framed and hung in the office at 9 West 16th Street, where it provided many laughs. To my surprise, I received not a single adverse criticism to disturb my peace of mind, and I remained in good professional standing.

After the war, when Dr. Foster Kennedy came to me for treatment of his painful shoulder some years before he died in 1952, I felt that I had reached the summit of professional achievement and recognition. He had been my Professor of Neurology at Cornell medical school, and he stood out as a giant among our great teachers there. With British eloquence, he was outspoken on the philosophical issues of medicine. Sitting in my quiet office, he took a broad view of my work in muscular pain.

"It sometimes happens that a person writes one scientific paper and it changes the entire course of his life," he told me. "I think that your study of shoulder pain in the *Journal of the American Medical Association* will prove to be that kind of a paper."

Foster Kennedy did not live to know how correct was his prediction, but I had occasion to remember his words.

Ideologically, the trigger mechanism boomeranged and I became its target. It bombarded me with riddles, and I set out to seek their solutions like Stephen Leacock's legendary general, who mounted his horse and rode off in all directions.

The first question was: What is the nature of the trigger area in the skeletal musculature?

I wanted to see what it looked like under a microscope. I arranged with several patients to have a muscle biopsy done under local anesthesia of the skin only, so that the hyperirritable trigger area could be positively identified by the referred pain induced during its excision. Normal skeletal muscle was known to be relatively insensitive to needling or cutting, although its chemical stimulation—for example, by injection of concentrated (hypertonic) salt solution—set off briefly its predictable pattern of referred pain. Microscopic examination of the biopsied tissue was unrewarding in that no pathological changes were seen. The abnormality at the trigger area must be pathophysiological in nature—not cellular, but molecular. Electronmicroscopy, when applied to the study of trigger areas, may yet reveal the nature of the molecular disorder at that site.

From watching the surgical biopsy procedure, I learned that merely touching or lifting the fascial covering of the muscle at the trigger area, or pinching the fibrous sheaths within the muscle mass, instantly caused pain in the reference zone. We modified our terminology, therefore, and began to talk about "myofascial" pain so as to include both the red contractile and the white fibrous elements of skeletal muscle.[10]

The myofascial trigger area was clearly a link in a self-sustaining cycle of noxious nerve impulses between the central nervous system and the peripheral structures. The principles of cybernetics, or feedback, by which the modern computer functions, are better understood now than they were a quarter of a century ago. However, it was evident to us then that muscles have a long memory and that they can maintain themselves indefinitely in a steady state of spasm until the automatic control circuit is broken. By means of electromyography, we did eventually show that the trigger area is a high-frequency, electrically discharging focus.[11] Its firing, when amplified, sounds like the barrage of a machine gun.

The next question was: Precisely how does a fleeting interruption of the peripheral arc by a local anesthetic permanently extinguish the discharging focus, the trigger area?

Dr. Audrie L. Bobb, a former Sea View Hospital resident (1941–1942), and I tried to separate the effects on the trigger area of (1) the procaine, (2) the fluid injected, and (3) the multiple punctures by the needle. We treated patients with acute ankle and knee sprains that showed easily accessible trigger areas in joint capsules and ligaments and adjacent muscle tendons—all composed of fibrous connective tissue.[12] Military surgeons and others had reported success with the local anesthetic injection of

[10] Janet Travell and Seymour H. Rinzler, "The Myofascial Genesis of Pain: A Scientific Exhibit," *Postgraduate Medicine*, Vol. 11 (1952), pp. 425–434; and Janet Travell, "Pain Mechanisms in Connective Tissue," *Connective Tissues: Transactions of the Second Conference* (New York, Josiah Macy, Jr. Foundation, 1952), pp. 86–125.
[11] Virginia D. Weeks and Janet Travell, "How to Give Painless Injections," *A.M.A. Scientific Exhibits Volume 1957* (New York, Grune and Stratton, 1957), pp. 318–322; "How to Give Painless Injections," *Abstracts of the Tenth Annual Scientific Assembly 1958* (Kansas City, Mo., American Academy of General Practice, 1958), pp. 17–19; and Janet Travell, "Symposium on the Mechanism and Management of Pain Syndromes," *Proceedings of the Rudolf Virchow Medical Society* of the City of New York (New York, S. Karger, 1959), Vol. XVI 1957, pp. 128–136.
[12] Janet Travell and Audrie L. Bobb, "Mechanism of Relief of Pain in Sprains by Local Injection Technics," *Federation Proceedings*, Vol. 6 (1947), p. 378; and Janet Travell, "Basis for the Multiple Uses of Local Block of Somatic Trigger Areas," *Mississippi Valley Medical Journal*, Vol. 71 (1949), pp. 13–21.

sprained joints. In our hands, likewise, the procedure promptly enabled the patient to bear weight on the injured joint and to walk without pain; a reasonable amount of activity continued to be possible afterward. But instead of injecting the procaine solution diffusely, as others had done, we aimed our needle at the few exquisitely tender spots that we could identify within the swollen, black-and-blue region of the sprain. True trigger areas, those small spots evoked a spread of pain thoughout the joint. In some patients, we eliminated the procaine and infiltrated plain salt solution (in physiological strength) into the trigger areas; saline solution proved effective. In one elderly woman who was bedridden by a severe ankle sprain— we took color pictures of her ankle—we hit each trigger area with a hypodermic needle attached to an empty syringe; we used a rapid peppering motion in the same manner as when injecting a solution. That dry-needling worked too.

Later, we mounted those color photographs on a chart that was part of our scientific exhibit at the 1947 Annual Meeting of the American Medical Association in Atlantic City.[13] It was five years since I had presented our shoulder-pain study there. In the meantime, we had accumulated data on about seven hundred patients with pain referred from myofascial (somatic) trigger areas. The dry-needling experiments, first in sprains and then in acute muscle spasm, were relatively recent, and I had "strained my brains" to come up with a variety of physiological explanations for the efficacy of that procedure in eliminating trigger areas. In 1947, I had set forth several theories in a final manuscript that I brought with me to Atlantic City, ready for mailing. I never mailed it.

Dr. William K. Livingston, the neurosurgeon whose book *Pain Mechanisms* (1943) had encouraged me to pursue my own observations, stopped at our exhibit booth soon after it opened. We had lunch together that Sunday, and he read my manuscript. I was eager for his comment.

"If I were you, I wouldn't publish it," he advised, handing it back to me. "Your theories are speculations—you haven't proved one of them."

"That wasn't the purpose of the paper—there aren't enough facts to establish a theory. Don't I have the right to speculate?"

"Yes, you do," he agreed. "But all your theories can't be true. People will remember about your work only that you were wrong."

I appreciated his criticism—it was a mark of friendship—and I took it to heart. Thereafter, I never deliberately built an edifice of ideas that ex-

[13] Janet Travell, Seymour H. Rinzler, Audrie L. Bobb, Nolton H. Bigelow, and Lawrence L. Hanlon, "Somatic Pain Syndromes: Abstract of Scientific Exhibit," *Journal of the American Medical Association*, Vol. 134 (May 3, 1947), p. 62.

tended beyond the supporting data, and no scientific paper that I submitted was turned down by an editor.

If the suggestion was made that I shorten an article, it seemed reasonable to me. Once, however, a medical editor asked me to "compress" my submitted paper, and I did literally just that: I put the wrinkled pages of my manuscript through our laboratory mounting press. They came out neatly ironed and I returned them to the editor with a polite note saying that I had complied with his request. He was satisfied and published the paper as it was.

Our reports about dry-needling brought as visitors to my Cornell laboratory some foreign advocates of acupuncture, the ancient Chinese practice that attempted to cure disease by introducing needles into the skin at specified points of the body. One line of their points was for liver disease, one for heart disease, and so on. So far as I could learn, the concept of myofascial trigger areas as sources of referred pain was not a part of their thinking. Nevertheless, Sir William Osler had stated in his textbook of medicine that acupuncture was a valuable procedure: "For lumbago acupuncture is, in acute cases, the most efficient treatment. Needles of from three to four inches in length (ordinary bonnet-needles,[14] sterilized, will do) are thrust into the lumbar muscles at the seat of pain, and withdrawn after five or ten minutes. In many instances the relief is immediate, and I can corroborate fully the statements [about] this practice, as to its extraordinary and prompt efficacy in many instances." [15] That wise clinician was alleviating the symptom of pain and was not attempting to cure a disease.

At Cornell, an acupuncturist from Indochina described to me his method of painless placement of a series of fine short needles in the skin— he showed me his gold box of little needles—and his procedure was totally unlike our technique of hitting a trigger area and causing an explosion of pain in the reference zone. We conversed in French.

"Who taught you your points?" he asked me.

"Nobody," I replied. "I taught myself."

"*C'est impossible!*" he exclaimed. "How could you teach yourself your points?"

"By examining the patient." To me, it was a logical method.

"But I don't understand." He gesticulated with expressive hands.

"How did you learn your points?" I asked in turn.

"I have charts, from a thousand years. But of course I know them by

14 Ladies' hatpins.
15 William Osler, *The Principles and Practice of Medicine,* 8th ed. (New York, D. Appleton and Company, 1912), p. 1131.

heart." He showed me his Chinese book of beautifully drawn plates, page after page.

"Don't you examine the patient?" I puzzled.

"Certainly not," he said indignantly. "I know the points already. And besides, I wouldn't have time."

I felt that we were truly at opposite poles and a thousand years apart.

Another question followed naturally from the observations that we had reported on the mechanism of myofascial pain relief: If saline solution and dry-needling are effective, is there any advantage in using procaine for the attack on trigger areas?

We learned that there was indeed. The patient could easily tell the difference in the intensity and duration of the referred pain evoked by those procedures. Without the local anesthetic, the treatment was so painful that it was unendurable to some people. Procaine has a long record of safety in clinical usage, and it was well tolerated by most of our patients. We finally selected a procaine (hydrochloride) concentration of 0.5 percent in physiological salt solution as one that moderated the immediate pain of hitting the trigger area and yet gave rise to a minimum of transient side effects of the drug.

It was my conviction—one that would be difficult to prove statistically—that procaine enhanced not only the comfort, but also the efficacy of our injection techniques directed at trigger areas. Procaine is a versatile drug with useful pharmacological actions besides the best-known one of sensory nerve block. It has central analgesic effects and has been injected intravenously to lessen the pain of childbirth. It causes vasodilatation locally, at sites of injection. It blocks the generation of abnormal impulses in the heart and is employed (as procainamide) to terminate certain rapid cardiac arrhythmias. Like curare, a drug that is utilized to produce profound skeletal muscle relaxation during surgery under general anesthesia, procaine interrupts the flow of nerve impulses across the myoneural junction, the ending of each motor nerve on its skeletal muscle fiber. Partial curarization blocks high-frequency discharges that may serve to maintain feedback cycles. Furthermore, the curarelike effect of procaine has been observed with very low concentrations, of the order of 0.01 percent, when injected into the artery feeding a particular muscle.

Added together, those pharmacological actions of procaine might well aid the process of stretching a muscle in chronic spasm and of restoring its normal resting length.

On the cardiovascular services at Beth Israel Hospital, Seymour Rinzler and I inevitably encountered patients with chest pain and trigger areas in related muscles in whom we were not sure of the source of the noxious impulses that activated the myofascial feedback. Were those trigger areas reflexly connected with the patient's coronary artery disease and ischemia of heart muscle, or were they simply the result of coincidental skeletal muscle strain?

We hoped to find that procaine injection into trigger areas could be used as a therapeutic test to exclude the heart as a cause of pain. However, as early as 1943 we concluded that the treatment stopped both noncardiac myalgias and true cardiac pain of coronary insufficiency. I was surprised to learn that even the pain of classical myocardial infarction, which had not responded to demerol or morphine, might be relieved at once by the local procaine infiltration. It was clear that success with the procedure did not rule out a heart attack as the initiating event in the protracted cycle of pain-spasm-pain.

Our results would not have surprised me if I had thoroughly scanned the medical literature. About fifteen years earlier (1928), another Cornell pharmacology-trained investigator, Soma Weiss, working with David Davis at Bellevue Hospital had stopped acute coronary pain by injecting procaine solution diffusely into the superficial tissues of the chest wall overlying the heart—its somatic reference zone. They had similarly relieved pain due to acute disorders of other internal organs—appendicitis and distention of the gall bladder or ureter by stones. The therapeutic worth of their observations became buried, however, in the ensuing controversy about the neurological mechanisms involved: In what manner could nerve impulses from somatic reference zones contribute to perception of visceral pain, and by what anatomical pathways might they travel?

Bill Livingston had given me good advice, indeed.

I never rushed into print. In 1946, after Seymour returned from overseas, we published our preliminary report on the subject.[16] In June, 1947, he presented our results in a larger series of cardiac patients at the annual meeting of the American Heart Association in Atlantic City; David Davis discussed them. Our paper was entitled "Therapy Directed at the Somatic Component of Cardiac Pain," [17] and it provoked attention and protest.

In both those accounts, we reported the unlikely clinical finding that pain from the heart was sometimes dramatically terminated not only by procaine infiltration of appropriate trigger areas, but also by a brief application of a chilling spray to the skin in the regions where pain was felt. Our curiosity had been spurred by Hans Kraus's article (1941) on the treat-

[16] Janet Travell, and Seymour H. Rinzler, "Relief of Cardiac Pain by Local Block of Somatic Trigger Areas," *Proceedings of the Society for Experimental Biology and Medicine,* Vol. 63 (1946), pp. 480–482.
[17] Seymour H. Rinzler and Janet Travell, *American Heart Journal,* Vol. 35 (1948), pp. 248–268.

ment of joint sprains and muscle injuries with ethyl chloride spray, which he described as surface anesthesia for relief of painful motion.[18]

One day in my laboratory at Cornell, Seymour had remarked, "We ought to try that ethyl chloride spray—it doesn't make much sense to me. Maybe we could set up a study and see for ourselves what it does."

"Good idea," I agreed. "But in theory, it's no stranger than that a little procaine in the right spot can stop muscle spasm that's gone on for months and years."

"What sort of problem should we try it in?"

Seymour's questions often stimulated my mind to action. I had not thought about such a project, but with sudden insight I replied, "Seymour, when you're making rounds at Beth Israel, use it on the next patient you see with a typical attack of acute coronary thrombosis and a lot of pain."

"Why—do you think it would do anything for that kind of pain? And where would I apply it?" he puzzled.

"Spray a little on wherever the pain is. You can't do harm if you don't freeze the skin and make blisters. It may not do a thing—but try it."

I did not want to prejudice him in favor of the test; I knew well that the clinical trial of a therapeutic agent was subject to the potent influence of subconscious bias. One of my eminent colleagues had told me that I could not trust my own clinical observations because unfortunately I had "a therapeutic personality."

Seymour's lack of enthusiasm for ethyl chloride spray had vanished by the next day when he telephoned me at 9 West 16th Street.

"It works!" he reported excitedly. "What made you expect it to?"

In simplified terms, my thinking was that if cooling the skin blocked a feedback that helped maintain painful muscle spasm, and if noxious stimuli from the heart were reinforced by feedback from skeletal muscles in spasm so as to be perceived as pain, then the answer was predictable. The mechanism of action of the spray was not a matter of refrigeration anesthesia of injured musculoskeletal structures.

I was reassured when I received a letter dated March 6, 1948, from my hard critic, Bill Livingston, in Portland, Oregon:

> I have just read the article that you and Dr. Rinzler wrote for the Feb. issue of the American Heart Journal [on the somatic component of cardiac pain]—and was delighted with it. . . . I don't agree with all your interpretations but that is of minor importance—I thoroughly approve of the data you submit and your handling of it. I'm sure you are on the right track, and that your work will be a stimulus to the

[18] Hans Kraus, "The Use of Surface Anesthesia in the Treatment of Painful Motion," *Journal of the American Medical Association,* Vol. 116 (1941), pp. 2582–2587.

clinician as well as to furthering our insight into this whole subject of pain.

More important to me than general acceptance of my published work was the support of McKeen Cattell, Chairman of our Cornell Department of Pharmacology until 1956, and of Harry Gold. They encouraged me in planning experimental programs and they gave me security to pursue my divergent ideas. McKeen, I sometimes thought, was like the good voice teacher whose pupils all sang differently—so many styles of scientific investigation were being used by members of his department.

My father was quick to apply a new medical concept. In 1949 at the age of seventy-nine, when he recognized the onset of his third heart attack—acute myocardial infarction—he took a bottle of ethyl chloride from his medical bag and sprayed his chest with it. One minute of spraying stopped his severe substernal pain—no analgesic drug was needed. At the same time, he put himself to bed in his home at 12 East 64th Street and asked his cardiologist, Harry Gold, to come as soon as possible.

It gave my father special pleasure when I published a paper, "Early Relief of Chest Pain by Ethyl Chloride Spray in Acute Coronary Thrombosis," [19] which was based on his well-documented case record.

For control of chest pain, the simple procedure of eliminating myofascial trigger areas by an external spray—even if it needed to be repeated, I thought—was preferable to giving a potent analgesic drug, like morphine, that often had adverse side effects in the person with a heart attack. Moreover, we obtained some evidence that trigger areas at certain sites in the chest muscles contributed to a feedback responsible for paroxysmal disorders of cardiac rhythm—a serious complication in acute myocardial infarction.

In heart disease, pain is deleterious to the circulation. For example, noncardiac pain may cause spasm of the coronary arteries and so impair blood flow to heart muscle. I had been one of several subjects for a study of Harry Gold's (1943) in which severe somatic pain, produced by tightening a metal band around the head, resulted in electrocardiographic (T-wave) changes. We found that in laboratory findings, as well as clinical features, the chest pain of somatic origin could mimic that of ischemic heart disease, and vice versa.

Seymour and I sometimes encountered the objection: If you don't know what kind of pain you are treating, you shouldn't treat it until you know the diagnosis. We did not agree. In a paper on the resemblance of pain syndromes of the chest muscles to effort angina and myocardial infarction, and

[19] Janet Travell, *Circulation*, Vol. 3 (1951), pp. 120–124.

their relief by local block (local procaine infiltration and ethyl chloride spray), we concluded: "In our opinion local block therapy is indicated for the relief of chest pain whether the somatic manifestations are believed to be skeletal or visceral in origin, and even when there is so much evidence in support of both etiologies that the primary cause of pain cannot be positively determined." [20]

Skeptics still contended that the patients with heart disease whom we made comfortable by local block therapy had only simulated cardiac pain. We needed a safe procedure that would consistently induce an unquestionable attack of pain from the heart, like angina of effort, so that we could study our local methods' efficacy in blocking the somatic feedback of cardiac pain.

Eventually, Seymour suggested that we make use of the ergonovine test for coronary insufficiency that Dr. Isidore Stein had described during the war (1944). In the person with a normal heart the drug produced no circulatory effects. However, when injected intravenously in resting patients who complained of effort angina but had a 12-lead normal electrocardiogram, ergonovine reproduced at rest the pain that appeared regularly on walking. It caused not only pain, but also electrocardiographic changes typical of inadequacy of coronary blood flow to heart muscle. The drug-induced pain and electrocardiographic abnormalities were both quickly reversed to normal by a tablet of nitroglycerin placed under the tongue. Since such a nitrite dilates the coronary arteries, that objective response was taken to indicate that the seat of the disturbance after ergonovine injection was in the heart itself. Subsequently, we confirmed the coronary-dilator action of nitroglycerin directly by perfusion of both normal and atherosclerotic rabbit hearts.

We interested Isidore Stein at the Brooklyn Veterans Administration Hospital in our question as to whether ergonovine angina could be relieved by applying a vapocoolant spray to the regions where pain developed during the test. Joint publication followed.[21] In his patients and with his two-channel electrocardiographic set-up at the Veterans Administration Hospital, we found that applying ethyl chloride spray briefly to a region rendered

[20] Janet Travell and Seymour H. Rinzler, "Pain Syndromes of the Chest Muscles; Resemblance to Effort Angina and Myocardial Infarction, and Relief by Local Block," *Canadian Medical Association Journal,* Vol. 59 (1948), pp. 333–338.

[21] Seymour H. Rinzler, Isidore Stein, Hyman Bakst, Joseph Weinstein, Robert Gittler, and Janet Travell, "Blocking Effect of Ethyl Chloride Spray on Cardiac Pain Induced by Ergonovine," *Proceedings of the Society for Experimental Biology and Medicine,* Vol. 85 (1954), pp. 329–333; Isidore Stein, Seymour H. Rinzler, Hyman Bakst, Joseph Weinstein, Robert Gittler, and Janet Travell, "Cardiac Pain in Man: Blocking Effect of Ethyl Chloride Spray on the Angina of Ergonovine," *Bulletin of the New York Academy of Medicine,* Vol. 30 (1954), p. 318.

painful by ergonovine stopped the pain in that particular area almost at once—faster than the nitroglycerin did. As the pain reference zones of the heart were sprayed in turn—specific areas for each patient in the chest, neck, upper back, or arm—pain stopped there, too. Electrocardiographic changes, however, that had appeared with the ergonovine angina, lasted throughout the pain-free state secured by the spray until we elected to terminate them by sublingual nitroglycerin. Under those circumstances, pain did not parallel the electrocardiographic signs of coronary insufficiency. The situation was analogous to the "silent" attack of acute myocardial infarction that was known to occur occasionally without any pain whatsoever.

That dissociation between subjective and objective evidences of coronary insufficiency, brought about by use of a vapocoolant spray in the ergonovine tests, gave me a clue to our next procedure.

"Seymour," I said, as he and I discussed the results, "in the next patient with a positive ergonovine test, when you run a duplicate test apply the spray to the pain areas *before* the ergonovine is injected. Maybe it will prevent the pain altogether."

He sprayed ethyl chloride over the patient's known pain reference areas (the angina of exercise matched the angina of ergonovine) for about two minutes just prior to drug injection, covering the skin once or twice with the moving spray, without frosting or freezing. It worked, too: pain either did not occur at all, or else its onset was delayed for several minutes. But the identical electrocardiographic depression of the S-T segment appeared at the same time interval after drug injection as in the ergonovine test without spray; and again the change seen in the tracing persisted until reversed by the nitrite. By prespraying with ethyl chloride and giving nitroglycerin as soon as the running electrocardiogram became abnormal, we uniformly made the patient as comfortable after ergonovine as after a control injection of physiologic salt solution. We had unwittingly devised what was probably the first painless clinical test for coronary insufficiency.

Those dramatic clinical results with the Stein ergonovine test led Seymour and me into a pharmacological morass. We had stated cautiously: "It is reasonable to infer that the angina of ergonovine depends on a coronary vasoconstrictor mechanism." But then, when questioned we could not find that ergonovine effects had ever been studied by perfusion of the coronary arterial tree with direct measurement of coronary blood flow. In fact, indirect experimental evidence in animals indicated that ergonovine dilated the coronary arteries—the opposite of what we had postulated. Under the circumstances, how could we be sure that we were dealing with relief of *cardiac* pain?

We were convinced that if ergonovine enhanced the coronary circulation, it did so only for *normal* coronary arteries, and that it reduced the circulation in an *atherosclerotic* coronary system. Our concept was heretical, since drugs employed therapeutically to dilate the coronary vessels in cardiac patients were tested pharmacologically then on the normal hearts of animals.

Our pharmacology laboratory was not equipped to study experimental atherosclerosis—a long-range elaborate undertaking that was usually carried out in rabbits fed a high-cholesterol diet for months. In about a year, however, we published in *Science,* a journal devoted to new scientific discoveries, a preliminary report on "Detection of Coronary Atherosclerosis in the Living Animal by the Ergonovine Stress Test." [22] Before that, the only known way to determine whether an animal had coronary atherosclerosis was by an autopsy. The galley proof of our paper came to the medical college while I lay in bed at home with my neck in a steel collar, and Jack brought the pages to me in Pelham for checking.

To test our hypothesis as to how ergonovine caused chest pain, we had carried out experiments on borrowed atherosclerotic rabbits, in a strange laboratory about forty miles from New York, and with a special electrocardiograph loaned us for the day. Dee du Vigneaud, Chairman of our Department of Biochemistry, had introduced me to Dr. Herald Cox, who placed at my disposal the facilities of the Lederle Laboratories' Division of Viral and Richettsial Research in Pearl River, New York. At stated intervals cholesterol-fed rabbits (and normal controls) were being sacrificed there for pathological estimation of the degree of atherosclerosis, and the results would not be affected by our giving the animals a few intravenous doses of ergonovine while we recorded drug effects, if any, on the electrocardiogram. We knew that in normals—both rabbit and man—the drug produced no electrocardiographic abnormalities, and we hoped to observe changes comparable for rabbit and man in the presence of coronary atherosclerosis.

Once a month or oftener, Seymour and I and two members of my technical staff piled our equipment into a car and drove across the Hudson River and through New Jersey to Pearl River. Since a rabbit's heart rate is very fast, 300 or 350 beats per minute, for accurate recording of the form of its electrocardiogram we picked up at the Sanborn Company's New York office their demonstrator model of a portable twin-beam electrocardiograph with photographic paper and a speed-changer. It was the only machine of

[22] Seymour H. Rinzler, Janet Travell, and Dorothy Karp, "Detection of Coronary Atherosclerosis in the Living Animal by the Ergonovine Stress Test," *Science,* Vol. 121 (June 24, 1955), pp. 900–902; Seymour H. Rinzler, Janet Travell, Dorothy Karp, and Diana Charleson, "Detection of Coronary Atherosclerosis in the Living Rabbit by the Ergonovine Stress Test," *American Journal of Physiology,* Vol. 184 (1956), pp. 605–612.

its kind that we could find in New York to borrow. We took along also our direct-writing two-channel Visocardiette and ran the tracings in duplicate to see whether its slight mechanical lag would obscure any effects of ergonovine. Our last trip to Pearl River was on December 22, 1954, in the midst of the Lederle Laboratories' staff Christmas party. Some rabbits, then nearly six months on the cholesterol diet, had far-advanced atherosclerosis and I was afraid that they would not live for us to complete the serial tests after the holidays.

The courtesy of Dr. Herald Cox afforded us truly "blindfold" conditions for our investigation. We did not know which of the animals presented to us for testing had been fed the high-cholesterol diet and which the regular control diet. When we analyzed our yards and yards of paper tracings, we were able to divide the rabbits into two groups: ergonovine-negative and ergonovine-positive. Later, we compared our electrocardiographic interpretations with the pathology found in the coronary arteries. All rabbits without coronary atherosclerosis or myocardial damage had negative ergonovine tests, whereas all rabbits with occlusive lesions in the lining of the small coronary arteries—similar to the process that occurs in the human heart—had myocardial damage and showed electrocardiographic effects of ergonovine that were the counterpart of those similarly induced in patients with both effort and ergonovine angina.

We still had not established that ergonovine constricted the coronary arteries when they were atherosclerotic, although our thirty-four rabbits at Pearl River had shown a perfect correlation between advanced coronary atherosclerosis and ergonovine-induced electrocardiographic changes. But in that animal with intact circulatory and nervous systems, those changes might conceivably have been secondary to ergonovine effects on organs or tissues other than the heart.

We undertook to learn techniques for perfusing drugs through the coronary system of the rabbit heart removed from the body. Pessimists warned us that we would never succeed in getting a heart diseased by atherosclerosis to beat in the Langendorff perfusion chamber—it had not been done before. Optimistically, I arranged with McKeen Cattell to set up our own rabbit colony in the Department of Pharmacology, and we used our ergonovine test to tell us that coronary atherosclerosis had developed during the course of high-cholesterol feeding. The isolated atherosclerotic heart did beat for hours of perfusion with drugs through its coronary vessels, and a flowmeter measured directly the flow volume that changed only with changes in the caliber of those arteries. We found [23] that under appropriate

[23] Dorothy Karp, Mario Penna, Seymour H. Rinzler, and Janet Travell, "Effects of Ergonovine on the Heart," *Journal of Pharmacology and Experimental Therapeutics,*

conditions ergonovine usually increased coronary flow in the normal isolated heart but that it had predominantly the opposite effect in the atherosclerotic. The flow reduction on the average was regarded as sufficient, in the presence of myocardial damage, to cause characteristic abnormalities in the electrocardiogram.

Our experiments proved beyond doubt that normal and atherosclerotic coronary arteries might react differently to a given drug. That finding created headaches for the pharmaceutical industry in the screening of coronary dilator compounds on animals for therapeutic use in man.

Ten years after our first report in 1946 about the relief of cardiac pain by ethyl chloride spray, we had emerged from the pharmacological bog into which we had fallen in our research. We had finally confirmed in animals the inference that was basic to our empirical clinical results. Our conclusion was sound that impulses from the heart's somatic reference zones were essential under some circumstances to the perception of cardiac pain.

We could not resist further expeditions, however, while we had the team and equipment for exploration. Assisted by two medical students, Fred Flatow and Mary Amatruda, who was the daughter of my medical classmate Sis Strunk, we studied the effects of some other drugs by perfusion of isolated rabbit hearts. Vincent—Dee—du Vigneaud's purified vasopressin, a hormone of the pituitary gland, impaired the coronary flow profoundly in both normal and diseased hearts, presumably by a direct action on the muscular arterial wall.

The response to nicotine, on the other hand, differed quantitatively with the state of the coronary arteries.[24] In the normal isolated heart, that drug caused a brief drop in coronary flow followed by a rise. But when atherosclerosis was present, the same doses of nicotine produced a more prolonged reduction in flow without any subsequent increase. It required a dose of nicotine ten times larger than that for the normal heart in order to cause an occasional secondary rise in flow for the diseased heart, even though the response to nitroglycerin showed that the atherosclerotic coro-

Vol. 116 (1956), p. 34; Dorothy Karp, Janet Travell, and Seymour H. Rinzler, "Ergonovine and Vasopressin Effects on the Isolated Heart of the Rabbit with Coronary Atherosclerosis," *Abstract of Communications, XXth International Physiological Congress* (Brussels, Belgium, 1956), p. 482; Dorothy Karp, Seymour H. Rinzler, and Janet Travell, "Effects of Ergometrine (Ergonovine) on the Isolated Atherosclerotic Heart of the Cholesterol-fed Rabbit," *British Journal of Pharmacology*, Vol. 15 (1960), pp. 333–344.
[24] Janet Travell, Dorothy Karp, and Seymour H. Rinzler, "Nicotine Effects on Normal and Atherosclerotic Rabbit Hearts," *Federation Proceedings*, Vol. 16 (1957), p. 341; Janet Travell, Seymour H. Rinzler, and Dorothy Karp, "Cardiac Effects of Nicotine in the Rabbit with Experimental Coronary Atherosclerosis," *Annals of the New York Academy of Sciences*, Vol. 90 (1960), pp. 290–301.

nary arteries still had the capacity to dilate. The difference in nicotine effects on normal and atherosclerotic isolated coronary circulations was attributed to the fact that nicotine exerts those effects indirectly by releasing stored norepinephrine from depots and that the intracardiac stores of norepinephrine are depleted in atherosclerotic disease.

I felt scientifically rewarded when the Advisory Committee to the Surgeon General of the Public Health Service, Luther L. Terry, included our nicotine study as evidence for the cardiovascular hazards of smoking.[25]

During that decade, my clinical interest in the relief of musculoskeletal pain associated with myofascial trigger areas had not flagged. In the beginning, at the Sea View tuberculosis hospital I was told by the staff that the painful shoulder-girdle spasm was "reflex from the lung, of course." On the Beth Israel cardiac service, it "came from the heart," and when no organic disease was found in the patient, the pain was "psychosomatic."

There was some truth in each ready-made judgment. Those somatic pain syndromes, which looked clinically alike to me, were always due to a combination of causes. In medical school I had been taught that according to the "unitary concept" of disease a patient's symptoms and abnormal physical signs must all be explained on the basis of a single overall cause. It is a concept that still prevails. I relinquished it quickly at Sea View Hospital, where the victims whom I saw had trouble simultaneously in at least two major systems—pulmonary tuberculosis and perhaps inadequate kidney function or heart failure due to long-standing high blood pressure. At the same time, the inactivity of bed-rest, often with immobility after chest surgery, was the chief causal factor in the painful spasm of shoulder, neck, and chest muscles, as was lack of movement likewise in the person kept in bed because of acute myocardial infarction.

In 1946 at a Cornell conference on rational therapeutics, I called attention to the high proportion of people with acute coronary thrombosis who developed "a painful or frozen shoulder syndrome. . . . It is likely that one of the most important factors in the development of this syndrome is the complete immobilization of the shoulders which is usually enforced in the patient with an acute infarct who is confined flat on his back in bed. I believe that regular, gentle, active motion of the upper extremities would do much to prevent the appearance of muscle spasm in these cases." [26]

My analysis was correct. With the introduction of arm exercises and early chair-rest, the refractory condition that used to make it impossible for

[25] *Smoking and Health,* U.S. Department of Health, Education and Welfare, Public Health Service Publication No. 1103 (1963), p. 318.
[26] Janet Travell, "Use and Abuse of Bed Rest," *New York State Journal of Medicine,* Vol. 44 (1944), p. 727: reprinted in *Cornell Conferences on Therapy,* Vol. 1 (New York, The Macmillan Company, 1946), p. 26.

the patient to turn over in bed unassisted became relatively infrequent as a post-infarction sequel. The main cause was mechanical.

When the onset of a somatic pain syndrome coincided with severe emotional stress, so that it was said to be psychosomatic, I found again that a major factor in the perpetuation of skeletal muscle spasm was always a mechanical one. The circumstances that precipitated the painful disorder of muscle were different from the combination of conditions that kept it going. Even in "psychogenic rheumatism," it was the mechanical cause that the doctor often overlooked and that retarded recovery.

The steady deep-seated pain of skeletal muscle spasm, like a continuing cramp, destroys sleep, limits movement, and jeopardizes income from work. The "tension" that it creates aggravates the painful spasm—they are not the same thing. The person who is "tense" tends habitually to contract his muscles, but they can still be relaxed by an effort of the will—both are positive acts. Spasm is a local biochemical disorder within a muscle in which the shortened section resists stretching and can not be relaxed voluntarily.

That unremitting pain was sometimes so devastating to the patient that I called it not psychosomatic, but somapsychotic disease. He might remark to me, "My shoulder"—or "my back is driving me crazy—I'm afraid I'm losing my mind." And when hope of obtaining relief was lost, that kind of pain had been known to drive a man to suicide.

Unraveling the sources of repetitive mechanical strain in the patient's daily activities required time-consuming detective work that I liked because it challenged my ingenuity. There was the young woman who slipped and sprained her knee while playing tennis; treatment of the joint had consisted of immobilization by a heavy plaster cast for two months. Her attitude was complicated by the fact that her husband was a physician. The regimen that I instituted for her with local-injection treatment of the knee muscles and regular but not excessive movement—it included the use of a rocking chair —brought about improvement, but the range of knee motion tended to regress in each week's interval between by treatments. During a month's winter vacation free of home responsibility and the care of a baby born not long before the injury, she played tennis and her knee did not bother her. Within a short period after her return to New York, the joint again became painful and stiff. Surely, her symptoms must be psychosomatic, she was told. At that point, I uncovered the new fact that each day she knelt on the hard bathroom floor, balancing with her knee muscles for about fifteen minutes while she bathed her baby in the tub. She had discarded the infant's folding rubber bathstand soon after I first saw her, I learned. I asked her to sit on a stool and bathe the baby in the sink, and then her residual knee problem cleared up rapidly with a little more treatment. The continuing stress that had reactivated trigger mechanisms and renewed the muscle spasm was primarily mechanical, after all. But its nature was different from the mechanical event that had caused the strain in the first place.

Painful spasm of the neck muscles proved especially responsive to the application of a vapocoolant spray during passive stretching movements, perhaps because the mobile arrangement of bones, intervertebral disks, and ligaments in the neck permits the muscles to be stretched fully and because they are not ordinarily overtaxed by heavy weight-bearing.[27] To that chilling and stretching method of treatment I applied the term, "instant traction."

In those pain syndromes of the neck muscles—often precipitated by end-to-end auto collisions—a perpetuating factor of constant postural strain was obvious to me in the nearsighted person without correction by glasses who unconsciously projected his neck forward in the effort to see clearly. Such malpositioning of the neck also resulted from too short a focal length of reading glasses, or a weak reading light beside a bed, or too thick a bed pillow, or from placing copy off at the side of a typewriter. A clue to the causes of daily mechanical strain might be hard to uncover, however.

I remember a New York executive who returned from a business trip abroad with an attack of acute neck pain that resisted various sorts of therapy, including mine. On the transatlantic flight from New York, he had slept on the plane with his neck in a strained position and exposed to a cold ventilating draft. But I did not discover right away that on his European trip he had converted from spectacles to contact lenses. One day he told me, "When I sit at my desk in the office, I get a reflection on my contact lenses from the overhead lights—I never noticed it before I got them. I keep tilting my head to avoid it. Could that have anything to do with why my neck doesn't get well?"

"Indeed it could," I answered. "But when did you get your new lenses? Or were new lighting fixtures put in your office?"

The lights had not been altered, but he had changed his bifocal visual

[27] Janet Travell, "Rapid Relief of Acute 'Stiff Neck' by Ethyl Chloride Spray," *Journal of the American Medical Women's Association*, Vol. 4 (1949), pp 89–95; "Ethyl Chloride Spray for Painful Muscle Spasm," *Archives of Physical Medicine*, Vol. 33 (1952), pp. 291–298; "Relief of Pain by Ethyl Chloride Spray," *New York State Journal of Medicine*, Vol. 52 (1952), pp. 1550–1558; republished in *Cornell Conferences on Therapy*, Vol. 5 (New York, The Macmillan Company, 1952), pp. 164–185; "Temporomandibular Joint Pain Referred from Muscles of the Head and Neck," *Journal of Prosthetic Dentistry*, Vol. 10 (1960), pp. 745–763.

correction to contact lenses soon after the onset of his neck pain; as bifo-
cals, they could only be obtained then abroad. He insisted that he could not
do without them, and I wondered about his attachment to them.

"You are not vain, and you don't appear on a stage or TV. Why must
you wear contacts?" I protested.

"Dr. Travell, I got tired of not being able to see when I walked in the
woods in the rain," he explained apologetically.

I understood his reason perfectly—I walked in the rain, too. He sent to
Europe for bifocal contact lenses that were *tinted* to eliminate glare, and his
neck muscles recovered.

"Why am I so tired? All I do is housework," was a question that the
housewife with painful muscles raised. I heard it so many times that I published an article entitled "Six Ways to Make Housework Lighter," or "Use
and Abuse of the Muscles in Housework." [28] I formulated some simple rules
for efficient body mechanics that might enable the housewife to do the
physically heavy job of housework without excessive fatigue or serious
harm to the muscles.

My directions to the housewife were:

1) Vary your tasks each day so as not to overuse any one group of
muscles in repetitive work, like ironing for hours at a stretch. Especially,
don't combine too many jobs that involve bending and stooping; they place
a heavy load on the low back muscles. Don't even try to do all the mending
at one long sitting, or to finish a piece of needlepoint in a hurry. One patient
of mine—a man—strained his finger muscles in his hobby of fitting and
gluing together delicate ship models. To achieve variety of movement, you
will have to scramble your housework.

2) Slow your working pace to a speed no faster than your muscles will
tolerate. Fatigue of any one of your muscles is the warning signal—learn to
pay attention to them. Most housewives rush to finish, but they can afford
to spend a little longer on the necessary work around a house. They can not
afford muscle injury.

3) Cultivate a rhythm of movement. It discourages the prolonged fixed
contraction that tires a muscle, and it encourages pauses during which the
working muscles fill up with new blood and fresh fuel. Do your housework
as if you were dancing—music helps. Once on a television show, I had fun
demonstrating that rhythmic technique while I brushed a sofa with a whisk-
broom and swept a floor.

4) Take short rests frequently. After every hour or less of housework,

[28] Janet Travell, *Today's Woman*, February, 1950, pp. 38–39, 67–70; "Use and Abuse
of the Muscles in Housework," *Journal of the American Medical Women's Association,* Vol. 18 (1963), pp. 159–162.

lie down to rest for a couple of minutes, if only on the floor. The antigravity muscles of the neck and back that hold you erect do not relax fully unless your body is supported in a nearly horizontal position. Such momentary breaks are taken naturally by a hunting dog; he runs for a while, flops briefly on the ground and then goes on again. Muscles regain their energy faster if you don't drive them to a state of exhaustion in which some essential chemical reserve seems to be used up. As in heart muscle failure, it may take a long time to restore the reserve.

5) Don't sit too long in one position. At a movie or the theater, move around in your seat. At intervals, turn your head from side to side and rotate your shoulder blades. At long formal dinners, straighten your knees periodically under the table—first one and then the other, pulling your foot up at the same time. When you drive far, pull off the road every hour and walk around your car two or three times. That doesn't take long. At home, you can sit in a rocker. Its constantly changing position prevents resting muscles (electrically silent) from building up the tension (electrical activity) that inevitably occurs when you stay motionless for several minutes up to a half hour, as electromyographic studies have shown.[29]

6) Don't try to lift a heavy piece of furniture by yourself, or to carry large awkward things that extend the lever length of your arms; the extra leverage multiplies the weight transmitted to your low back muscles. Keep the load close to your body, and just before you lift it, raise your head smartly and look up. That tightens the long spinal muscles and prepares your back for the load.

If those principles of cost-efficiency are applied to muscle function in housework, the gain may not be in neater housekeeping, but it will show in happier homemaking.

"I feel a hundred years old," was another complaint that I heard from young women with chronic muscle stiffness. They learned to live with it because pain was minimal—only discomfort. That aging sense of the body's resistance to moving was often due to a residue of muscle spasm from old strains and injuries years before. I demonstrated that muscle shortening around those "stiff joints" caused the limited motion, because my eliminating latent trigger areas in the affected muscles restored mobility; there was nothing wrong with the joints. The patient was unaware of the existence of the "silent" abnormal foci that I disclosed in the muscles on physical examination. When I stimulated them mechanically by deep palpation or contact of a needle, they resurrected the pain of past injury.

[29] Arne J. S. Lundervold, "Electromyographic Investigations During Sedentary Work, Especially Typewriting," *British Journal of Physical Medicine,* Vol. 14 (February, 1951), pp. 32–36.

Nor were men immune to that hangover of stiffness in muscles that had not regained their full length after strain, either by overwork for a period of time (microtrauma) or overstretching during sudden momentary force (gross trauma).

In my medical practice the men who came with musculoskeletal complaints were not as ready as the women, I think, to settle for less than optimal health. They constantly and constructively sought ways to improve their physical condition. In 1943, an athletic man in his forties had a severely painful right shoulder as his main trouble; he had hurt it in a fall while he was skiing three years earlier. When I had relieved that disabling pain, one day he asked me to examine his leg.

"I pulled a muscle in my calf on a tennis court years ago. I had to limp for a while, and ever since it stiffens when I run. Would you take a look—maybe you could do something for it?"

Then we shifted from his calf, which had lost its stiffness after treatment of the dormant trigger areas, to a tender toe that had been broken a long time before, and then to his left elbow, which he had lamed once—it bothered him only when he played the violin—and on to other regions that had not recovered entirely from old trauma.

"Your complaints now seem pretty minor to me," I told him. "Your shoulder has been better for quite a while—we're not working on that any more—and I'm not sure that it's really necessary to treat all these other things."

"Oh yes, Dr. Travell—it is," he assured me. "These things slow me up—I was beginning to feel old. Since I met you, my standard of comfort has been raised."

I conceded that he was right in his heightened expectation of top performance from his muscles. I had raised his standard of comfort, and he had raised mine for all my patients.

Twenty-five years later, he is still playing vigorous tennis.

Clinically latent trigger areas not only reduce the pleasure and benefits of exercise, but they offer a threat to a person's total stamina under stress. In periods of emotional crisis and physical strain, they are likely to reactivate the subthreshold feedback and to set off a full-blown attack of crippling muscle spasm. It became clear to me that the accumulated myofascial trigger areas of a lifetime curtail activity in advancing years and that they account, directly or indirectly, for some of the physiological deterioration of old age.

In the spring of 1960, I discussed that concept before the Academy of General Practice at the University of Utah in Salt Lake City, under the title,

"Geriatric Aspects of Myofascial Trigger Mechanisms." I concluded my talk with the summary:

(1) When spasm of skeletal muscles develops as the result of diverse stresses, it is likely to long outlast the precipitating causes.

(2) Many elderly patients with disability thought to be due to arthritis suffer from chronic pain and stiffness mediated by latent trigger mechanisms in the skeletal muscles.

(3) Rehabilitation may be accomplished and mobility restored if the responsive trigger areas are extinguished by local procaine infiltration and/or vapocoolant spray, together with movement to achieve full muscle length.

(4) Local therapy must be applied to trigger areas, the sources of pain and dysfunction, rather than to reference zones where the patient complains of symptoms.

(5) Motivation to maintain normal muscle length by subsequent daily activity is essential to lasting benefit from local treatment of the muscles.

(6) The old-fashioned porch rocker, or its equivalent, encourages mobility in the elderly sedentary patient.

My oldest patient was ninety-one when I first saw her. Her son took me to her home in northern New England in mid-winter after she had strained her neck and shoulder muscles in writing Christmas notes and tying up packages. The response of her painful muscles to a vapocoolant spray—like that of my other elderly patients—was as good as in people half her age. She became a centenarian without a recurrence of that muscular pain, but I credit the excellent result to her daughter, a nurse, whom I instructed in the continuing use of the spray.

I did not let my patients handle ethyl chloride, a dangerous volatile liquid that is flammable, explosive in certain concentrations of air, and capable of rapidly inducing general anesthesia when the vapor is inhaled. I knew that when used locally for muscular pain, ethyl chloride was acting not as a drug, but only as cold in a bottle—a physical agent in a pharmacological package. I wanted to find a safe nontoxic substitute with comparable cooling effects for medical use in the relief of pain.

One day, my secretary in the office at 9 West 16th Street interrupted me when I was with a patient.

"There's a man from a drug company who wants to talk with you about . . ."

"Tell him I'm sorry, I haven't time," I cut her short.

Presently she returned. "The gentleman is still here. He's been waiting an hour."

"What gentleman?" I asked.

"It's Mr. Gebauer, president of the company that makes all that ethyl chloride you buy."

Mr. Charles L. Gebauer and I became friends. He was a chemist who had an altruistic view of life and some fifty years' experience with manufacturing and marketing ethyl chloride for prescription use. He wanted to know what I was doing with so much of his product and he became interested in my search for an ideal vapocoolant spray. In 1951, when I attended a meeting of the Federation of American Societies for Experimental Biology in Cleveland, Ohio, I visited his chemical plant there. The fine glass nozzles of the ethyl chloride spray bottles were drawn from heated glass tubing and calibrated by hand; it was an unusual craft.

That day I persuaded Mr. Gebauer to make a modest grant to Cornell University Medical College in support of my research in the Department of Pharmacology on how the cold sprays acted to relieve pain. With the money, I obtained an eight-channel Speedomax for recording temperatures simultaneously from several sites in deep muscle and superficial tissues. "Max's" writing device whirled every two seconds and inked a point in a different color for each channel. It traveled so fast over the foot-wide moving graph paper, to keep up with the rapidly changing skin temperatures during sweeps with the vapocoolant spray, that its plotting of data was more exciting to watch than a horse race.

"Max" enabled me to measure objectively some physiological effects of volatile mixtures of halogenated hydrocarbons[30] that cooled by rapid evaporation at body temperatures. Their properties had been extensively investigated because they were used as household refrigerants and propellants in insecticide spray dispensers. They were known to be nonflammable, nonexplosive, and virtually nontoxic. For the purpose of relieving pain associated with myofascial trigger mechanism, the kind of nozzle was important, we found. One that delivered a jet stream for spot cooling was more effective than a diffuse mist. The nozzle-opener had also to be handy to operate, and it ought not to drip the spray liquid on the fingers or they might become frozen.

Eventually, the Gebauer Chemical Company marketed for medical distribution the mixture that I had selected,[31] dispensed in a handy bottle with a satisfactory calibrated spray nozzle. I had no financial interest in the product and so felt free to urge its wider application in clinical medicine.[32]

[30] Known under such trade names as Freon and Genetron.

[31] The trade name is "Fluori-methane Spray," and the label adds, "Calibrated Nozzle —For Relief of Painful Muscle Spasm."

[32] Janet Travell, "Factors Affecting Pain of Injection," *Journal of the American Medical Association,* Vol. 158 (1955), pp. 368–371; Virginia D. Weeks and Janet Travell,

The vapocoolant sprays introduced me to new places, new friends, and new concepts. I was invited by Dr. Frank Fremont-Smith and the Chairman, Dr. John H. Talbott, to become a member of the Josiah Macy, Jr. Foundation's series of six annual conferences on "Cold Injury"—the physiology of cold exposure and cold adaptation. The conferences were unusual in that most of the participants were military men of the United States and Canada, and that some meetings were held in geographical cold spots in midwinter.

On February 22, 1954, Captain Chekaluk, the British Queen's crack pilot of the Royal Canadian Air Force set down our small plane, which carried nineteen Cold Injury conference members, on the single runway at Fort Churchill in north central Canada at the latitude of the subarctic circle. Measured in wind chill, a combined index of air temperature and wind velocity, Churchill on Hudson Bay was the coldest spot—after Thule, Greenland—on the North American continent. We had been issued cold-weather clothing by the Canadian Defense Research Board—our hosts—before our flight of a thousand miles north from Winnipeg. In the subzero temperatures of the severest period of winter, the endless snowy tundra below our plane looked inhospitable, and we applauded when our wheels—not skis—touched down on the ice in a thirty-mile crosswind that blew off the frozen expanse of Hudson Bay.

As a New Englander accustomed to the high-peaked housetops built to shed the blizzard's snow, I looked with astonishment at the completely flat roofs on the long, low buildings of the Canadian Defense Research Laboratories where we stayed. They were clear of snow. I inquired how a flat roof could serve in that climate.

"We never lose a snowflake," I was told. "From October to May not one ever melts and the wind blows them away."

As far as the eye could see, drifted snow created Lilliputian mountain ranges of peaks and valleys.

The first afternoon following the conference session, John Talbott and I put on our arctic gear—he wanted to photograph the sunset—and we stumbled along the shore of the frozen bay. We leaned into the wind and bent the stiff wire around our parka hoods so as to leave only a slit opening for the eyes. When I slipped and fell on the ice, I was so clumsy that I could

"How to Give Painless Injections," *A.M.A. Scientific Exhibits Volume, 1957* (New York, Grune & Stratton, 1957), pp. 318–322; Virginia D. Weeks and Janet Travell, *Abstracts of the Tenth Annual Assembly, American Academy of General Practice, Dallas, Texas, March, 1958* (Kansas City, Mo., American Academy of General Practice, 1958), pp. 17–19; Janet Travell, "Temporomandibular Joint Pain Referred from Muscles of the Head and Neck," *Journal of Prosthetic Dentistry*, Vol. 10 (1960), pp. 745–763.

hardly get up. On returning to the base, we were reprimanded like naughty children.

"It's not safe to go down by the shore late in the day. That's when the polar bears come out."

One afternoon, Dr. Irené Ferrer and I started to walk a short distance outdoors to the small hospital, but the intensely cold air that we breathed drove us back to detour around through connecting buildings. We wandered into a ward—the medical attendants were all having tea—and we smiled at a patient. She did not speak English. The identifying card on the foot of her bed informed us: "Lady Eskimo pregnant."

All three facts were obvious.

At dinner I asked the wife of one of the Canadian officers who was stationed there for two years, "What do you do for outdoor exercise here in the winter?"

"I never go out of doors," was the astonished and astonishing reply. "The children sometimes go over to the sports arena to ice skate in the indoor rink."

"It must be a pleasant relief when the summer comes," I made conversation.

"Everyone who can takes leave in the summer. You can't stand the mosquitoes," she said.

Thinking as a housewife rather than as a scientist, I asked the officer's wife, "How do you dispose of garbage here—incinerate it?"

"No, garbage from the base is carted out to the bay where the Eskimos wait with their dog teams. They carry it off on their sleds. In downtown Churchill, it's just tossed out the back door—it freezes before it hits the ground. When the spring thaw comes, trucks go around and pick it up."

When we were riding in a heated bus to nearby Churchill, behind the houses in town I saw those garbage mounds, already one story high and shaped like a large haycock.

There were only a few miles of roads, but still there were automobiles. Generally they wore out in one season, because it was customary to leave the engines running all winter, day and night, or else they could not be restarted.

The Canadian base was an outpost of civilization, but the buildings were a showplace of what can be accomplished in arctic regions to provide comfort in housing. They were well heated, if not overheated, and there was hot running water in the bathrooms. Water was pumped from the bottom of a deep lake, heated, and conveyed to the base in large overhead pipes. Like the engines, the water ran continuously, circulating through the insulated conduits to prevent freezing.

I was learning about life in the arctic.

Even the symbols of Christianity were modified by the culture of the glacial north. Over the altar in the little church on the base, a painting of the Ascension showed at each side of the risen Christ a fur-clad man driving his team of huskies over fluffy clouds. In Churchill, the soul rose to heaven on a dogsled.

In that primitive land of the ice age, the Eskimo relied on the husky for hauling loads and for transportation. That canine breed is not far removed from the wolf, and the wild dog knows instinctively when his paws will incur cold injury. He can not be driven to leave the region of the igloo when the outside temperature drops to 60 degrees below zero. Man in his clothing had no such built-in gauge.

Much as I love dogs, I knew better than to try to make friends with the huskies, but as soon as an Eskimo offered me a ride, I climbed into his dogsled with Ren Ferrer, who was walking with me on one of our warmer days—only minus 10 degrees. I should say "dogsledge," I suppose, because it had no runners. My proprioceptive memory recalls that as the team mushed ahead I felt every bump in the rough ice through the flat, pliable bottom, which curled up in front like a toboggan. A thin, frozen mist filled the air, and we elected not to ride far.

Another vehicle that I tried out for the first time was a military tank on the driving range, a broad, rough snowfield. In the tank's dark interior I felt as cold and isolated as if I were in a tomb. More than four years later at the last Cold Injury conference in Fort Knox, my sensations were quite different when I rode in the open turret of a tank with Dr. Orr Reynolds of the United States Department of Defense. In the dusty Kentucky sunshine and warm breeze, I tied a pale blue scarf around my short hair to keep it from my eyes—its color matched my summer dress. With trepidation I even piloted one of those huge monsters down a road in a procession of tanks there at the U.S. Army Armor Center. Studying the controls around me, alone inside the vehicle, I was alarmed to see this notice: "If red light comes on, read instructions in drawer."

I had worked on a classified defense project concerning the positioning of a gunner in a tank for most efficient use of his muscles, and I was particularly eager to evaluate operational posture. That defense job had incidentally facilitated my security clearance for the trip to Fort Churchill. An investigator for the New York Ordnance District of the Department of the Army had visited my medical office at 9 West 16th Street, and he had asked me in some confusion, "I don't understand—what is it you make in your plant here?"

"Ideas," I had replied.

I was still pursuing those ideas.

On Hudson Bay our field trips to inspect tents and snow-block shelters made me wonder how any man could have energy to fight for survival under arctic conditions and at the same time to wage war against an enemy. Man had learned how to take his warm environment with him, but he still had to work outside in frigid air.

Dr. Paul Siple, explorer of the antarctic ice cap for the Office of Research and Development of the Department of the Army in Washington, was a member of our Cold Injury panel. In July, 1958, at Fort Knox he made graphic [33] his wintering over with eighteen men in the Amundsen-Scott IGY South Pole station—elevation about nine thousand feet with a never-ceasing wind. During the winter's six months of darkness, the minimum temperature there averaged $-73°$ F., and the absolute minimum was $-102°$ F. Frostbite and illness were minimal until the arrival of visitors caused an epidemic of respiratory infections; but the visitors were ill, too. When the temperature was in the -90s, two men well adapted to the cold and dressed in twenty-six and a half pounds of clothing remained out of doors, ambling around in the dark for three to four hours with no great discomfort, without shivering, and with a drop of only $1°$ F. in body temperature. The bridge of the nose had a tendency to freeze; the men wore no face masks.

Man's ingenuity and his adaptability to new geophysical conditions gave promise that the species of Homo sapiens might extend his locus of existence on the earth, and even to outer space. He might conceivably become a hibernating mammal, I thought, like the rat that acquired the capacity to raise its body temperature up to normal after it had been frozen solid on several occasions a few days apart. I saw moving pictures of those experiments that were presented at our fourth Cold Injury conference in November, 1955, by Dr. Audrey Smith of the National Institute for Medical Research in London.

In Alaska at our next meeting, Dr. Alan C. Burton, the Canadian biophysicist from the University of Western Ontario, expressed my unspoken speculations on acclimatization when he told the group: [34]

"We should not neglect the classical literature on this subject. Though the scientific details may not be as well controlled and reported as we would like, there is a well known report of an actual case of hypothermia in a human, and it might even be true hibernation. It is told in a poem entitled,

[33] Paul A. Siple, "Living on the South Polar Ice Cap," *Cold Injury: Transactions of the Sixth Conference, July 6–10, 1958* (New York, Josiah Macy, Jr. Foundation, 1960), pp. 89–115.
[34] Alan C. Burton, *Cold Injury: Transactions of the Fifth Conference, March 10–15, 1957* (New York, Josiah Macy, Jr. Foundation, 1958), pp. 128–130.

'The Cremation of Sam McGee' by Robert W. Service . . . about 1900."
I have excerpted from Dr. Burton's reading of that poem.

Now Sam McGee was from Tennessee, where the cotton blooms and
   blows.
Why he left his home in the South to roam 'round the Pole, God only
   knows.
He was always cold, but the land of gold seemed to hold him like a
   spell;
Though he'd often say in his homely way that "he'd sooner be in hell."
On a Christmas Day we were mushing our way over the Dawson trail.
Talk of your cold! through the parka's fold it stabbed like a driven
   nail.
If our eyes we'd close, then the lashes froze till sometimes we couldn't
   see;
It wasn't much fun, but the only one to whimper was Sam McGee . . .
He turned to me, and "Cap," says he, "I'll cash in this trip, I guess;
And if I do, I'm asking you that you won't refuse my last request . . .
Yet 'tain't being dead—it's my awful dread of the icy grave that pains.
So I want you to swear that, foul or fair, you'll cremate my last re-
   mains." . . .
He crouched on the sleigh, and he raved all day of his home in Ten-
   nessee;
And before nightfall a corpse was all that was left of Sam McGee. . . .
Some planks I tore from the cabin floor, and I lit the boiler fire.
Some coal I found that was lying around, and I heaped the fuel higher.
The flames just soared, and the furnace roared—such a blaze you sel-
   dom see.
And I burrowed a hole in the glowing coal, and I stuffed in Sam Mc-
   Gee. . . .
I was sick with dread, but I bravely said, "I'll just take a peep inside.
I guess he's cooked, and it's time I looked"; then the door I opened
   wide.
And there sat Sam, looking cool and calm, in the heart of the furnace
   roar;
And he wore a smile you could see a mile; and he said, "Please close
   that door.
It's fine in here, but I greatly fear you'll let in the cold and storm—
Since I left Plumtree, down in Tennessee, it's the first time I've been
   warm."

   The chief factor in producing acclimatization to cold, I learned, was
prior exposure to extreme cold. Adaptation depended on general metabolic
changes and also on local tissue phenomena. For example, in Hans Selye's
laboratory, it had been shown that injuring a rabbit's foot by heat reduced

the amount of damage caused by a second burn. Dr. Frederick A. Fuhrman of the Department of Physiology at the Stanford University School of Medicine reported to us that cold exposure of a rabbit's toes protected them against a considerable degree of subsequent freezing.[35] Damage by heat also conferred tissue protection against later experimental frostbite. The tissue itself must have been altered locally in some nonspecific way.

The crossed adaptation between heat and cold may have helped poor Sam McGee!

Those experiments made me see added significance in my own observations under conditions in which tissue damage was absent. In patients I had found that brief local cold, in the form of a vapocoolant spray lightly applied to the same region at intervals during some weeks, reduced the perception of cold in that area for a long time afterward. People were surprised —and spoke of it spontaneously—that the spray felt much less cold on the previously cold-exposed skin than elsewhere in the body. Clearly, the neurophysiological effects of the vapocoolant spray—both local and central, probably—were not as evanescent as generally supposed. It must be pertinent to the mechanism of the spray's clinical efficacy that pain and temperature sensations travel over the same nerve pathways to the same higher centers of the brain.

In many of our conference sessions, I was outclassed by the technical knowledge and long experience of the multidisciplinary experts in cold injury. Sometimes I became lost in the welter of graphs and figures that were presented, but I listened with concentration. I absorbed information and conflicting points of view in the free-for-all interchanges. My self-confidence was bolstered when at one point in the discussion Alan Burton remarked epigrammatically. "Often the truth is confusing."

Oversimplification is a curse to the scientist.

When the fifth conference of the series met for a week in March, 1957, at the Arctic Aeromedical Laboratory of Ladd Air Force Base near Fairbanks, time was arranged for me to hold a clinic at the base hospital. Members of the conference and hospital staff attended, together with medical officers who were visiting from other Alaskan Air Force bases. Brigadier General John Copenhaver, Medical Corps, Alaskan Air Command, had come from Elmendorf Air Force Base. I was in my element when I could show on patients with skeletal muscle pain syndromes the effect of minute doses of "cold in a bottle."

[35] Frederick A. Fuhrman, "Changes in Cellular Metabolism Following Experimental Cold Injury," *Cold Injury: Transactions of the Fourth Conference, November 7–9, 1955* (New York, Josiah Macy, Jr. Foundation, 1956), pp. 153–172.

My first problem was to get the patient to relax. Just as pinching the upper lip at the right second can stop a sneeze, so can general muscular tension inhibit the vapocoolant's reflex blocking of feedback from trigger areas, an effect that permits "instant traction"—stretching during spraying. I started the clinic by asking that a comfortable armchair be brought for the patient, a Negro airman with a very painful and "frozen" shoulder of several weeks' duration. He was nervous. Facing all that Air Force brass was bad enough without adding a strange woman doctor with strong probing fingers. It was essential to successful treatment that I gain his confidence.

It was an old story to me to find the trigger areas responsible for referred pain, test the shoulder motion, explain the underlying theory to the group and demonstrate the special technique of rhythmic interrupted spraying combined with passive stretching. But every patient was different. My basic assets in such teaching clinics were that I liked people and that I could stand in their shoes.

My second problem usually was to displace from the minds of my listeners some preconceived ideas; I found it difficult to implant a new concept when I had first to eradicate an old one. I felt like Alan Burton when he told one of our Cold Injury participants, "I am trying to rearrange your prejudices."

The belief was prevalent then, even in physical medicine, that heat was good for muscle spasm and cold was bad for it. That view was held even though in 1941 George D. Gammon and Isaac Starr had shown that the on and off application of ice was the most effective of the counterirritants tested, including heat, for relieving superficial and deep pain.[36] Before the safe fluoromethane cooling spray became available, I sometimes asked my patients to try that simple procedure at home. In later years, "ice massage" acquired status under the name of "cryokinetics."

Immediate success with cold for painful muscle spasm depended mainly on two variables in the technique of application: periodicity and dose. The strong sensory input needed to block feedback from trigger areas resulted from make-and-break stimulation and the steeply changing gradients of skin temperature during the spray's evaporation—I graphed the curves with our multichannel Speedomax. The mechanism of action of the vapocoolant sprays was neurogenic, but that did not imply a lowering of surface temperature to the threshold level for refrigeration anesthesia of nerve fibers. Nor did we observe any change in the deeper muscle temperatures while the

[36] George D. Gammon, and Isaac Starr, "Studies on the Relief of Pain by Counterirritation," *Journal of Clinical Investigation,* Vol. 20 (1941), pp. 13–20.

pain of ischemic muscle contraction was alleviated by the vapocoolant and while the circulation was occluded by a blood pressure cuff.[37] Hence, reflex redistribution of blood could not account for the therapeutic effect.

At Ladd Air Force Base my clinical demonstration was so impressive that I was asked to see more patients the next day. When the Cold Injury conference ended and we prepared to leave for Seattle on our MATS flight, General Copenhaver said to me, "Dr. Travell, you have saved the government enough money to pay for the conference."

By attacking the hangover of myofascial trigger areas, I found it relatively easy to obtain immediate improvement in such well-conditioned patients as the young men of the Air Force. The challenge lay in uncovering the elusive reasons for long-term therapeutic failures: incomplete recovery or recurrence. In fresh injuries, feedback mediated by trigger areas theoretically served a useful function: muscle spasm provided a warning signal of pain and prevented excess movement in the damaged structures. After healing, however, spasm often failed to subside and its pain became harmful—nature overdid the job of protective splinting. Frank Fremont-Smith called the myofascial trigger mechanism then a "misfitting of adaptation."

I concluded that concrete causes must exist for the intangible "misfitting of adaptation," and that they should be amenable to correction. One important environmental source of mechanical stress was obvious to me in our chairs and seating of many sorts. Early in my medical practice, I recognized prolonged sitting in unfortunately designed chairs as a perilous activity, and one of our most tiring. In 1948, at a Cornell Conference on Therapy concerning the management of painful muscle spasm, I reported that to reduce "the daily burden on the muscles . . . we often find it necessary to redesign the patient's furniture both at home and in the office, especially chairs, in order to provide proper support for the framework of the body. . . . Seating facilities should be so designed that, as the muscles relax and the body tends to sag, correct posture is maintained by the chair [not by muscle work]; muscle fatigue and joint strain are thus avoided." [38]

In November, 1955, the fourth Cold Injury conference met in Princeton, New Jersey. While a stenotypist recorded every word, for about seven hours a day we sat around a conference table in ancient mahogany diningroom chairs. They had vertical backs, and a seat height about eighteen inches from the floor, and no armrests. They were the kind of "maiden

[37] Janet Travell and Seymour H. Rinzler, "Influence of Ethyl Chloride Spray on Deep Pain and Ischemic Contraction of Skeletal Muscle," *Federation Proceedings,* Vol. 8 (1949), p. 339.
[38] Janet Travell, "Treatment of Painful Disorders of Skeletal Muscle," *New York State Journal of Medicine,* Vol. 48 (September 15, 1948), p. 2054; reprinted in *Cornell Conferences on Therapy,* Vol. 4 (New York, The Macmillan Company, 1951), p. 263.

aunt" chairs that I had condemned during my Brearley School days and that I had hopefully predicted would be nonexistent in three hundred years —there was still time for their disappearance. At Princeton, I sat sideways on the old black leather seat in order to rest my toes on a rung of my neighbor's chair; my feet barely reached the floor. Everyone fidgeted— and not from disinterest in the discussion. At intervals, members stood up to rest and leaned against the wall of the room.

During the proceedings, Frank Fremont-Smith, the Macy Foundation's Medical Director, passed a note around the table to me.

"What can be done about these chairs?" it read.

"Throw them out—get new ones," I scribbled.

His question was natural since I had listed nine common faults of most household chairs in an article for a recent issue of *House Beautiful* magazine (October, 1955). They were: no support for your low back; armrests too high; too scooped a backrest in its upper portion; backrest nearly vertical; backrest short, failing to support your upper back; jackknifing effect at hips and knees; high front edge of the seat, shutting down the circulation in your legs; seat bottom soft in the center, creating a bucket effect and placing the load on the outer side of your thighs, rather than on bony points in the buttocks; wrong-sized chair for you.

For the benefit of the *House Beautiful* editor, I had illustrated each of those faults with a small sketch in the margin of the manuscript that I submitted. I was surprised to see them, with added curls and frills, interspersed throughout the printed text. I realized then how often I found myself drawing when I was making notes. Traveling, I put in my purse a carpenter's folding two-foot rule and an architect's devil-level so that I could measure and sketch the different seats in which I sat.

When thirty new armchairs appeared at the next Princeton conference —I was not there to witness the reaction—an eminent physiologist commented to Frank, "Tell Dr. Travell that I thank her from the heart of my bottom."

His standard of comfort had been raised.

Those chairs were my best contribution to the Macy Foundation conferences. As a result, Frank asked me to prepare a paper for reading at a 1956 conference on the management of small conferences in Eastbourne, England. The title that I chose was "The Importance of Sitting Comfortably," and the text for my subject was the old proverb: "The mind can absorb no more than the seat can endure."

Discomfort and distraction go hand in hand.

My work in industrial seating design started because I criticized my friends' and patients' chairs. I pulled so many apart and remade them to fit a given purpose and person that in 1943 Mr. Murray Graham, Executive Vice-President of R. H. Macy and Company, asked me to go to the store and talk with Mr. Charles S. Shaughnessy, the Vice-President in charge of Macy's furniture department. I called his office and made an appointment. When I arrived, he greeted me coldly.

"What do you want, Dr. Travell? I only have a few minutes."

"Nothing," I replied, feeling at a loss. "Mr. Graham suggested that I come in and talk with you about how chairs should be designed." I looked around his office. "See that one over there—if you took the back off and just turned it around, the horizontal curve in the upper part would be convex forward and it would give better support at shoulder level. It would be a novel idea."

Mr. Shaughnessy contemplated me with a surprised expression. "My father was a furniture manufacturer in New England. He always wanted to build a chair like that, but he never did."

I had hit the jackpot.

"Is there a chair in the store like what I have in mind?" I asked.

"No, not exactly. Let's see—there is one . . ." and he sent someone to bring it. Soon we were studying a variety of chairs brought from the retail floor; we matched the seat of one to the back of another, placed books under the front or rear chair legs to change the seat level, and argued about angles and slopes and dimensions. A couple of hours passed.

"I wish it weren't war time," he said at last. "We can't bring out any new designs now, but I'd like to keep in touch with you."

A few months later, Mr. Shaughnessy telephoned my office downtown and asked whether he might give my name to an industrial designer, Henry Dreyfuss. "He asked if I knew anybody with fresh ideas in seating, and I thought of you, Dr. Travell."

Shortly afterward, Mr. Dreyfuss called me about a seating project for a Consolidated Vultee airplane, the Convair. It sounded interesting, I told him. Actually I had dreamed about how such seats should be built for comfort.

"What experience have you had in industrial seating?" he asked.

"Not any," I replied.

"What could you contribute to the project?"

"I can only say that I would be willing to think about it, Mr. Dreyfuss," I replied.

On that basis, I met with him and his associates in his New York office, which overlooked Central Park. Then on May 17, 1944, in a letter to him I outlined my professional qualifications for the work. I enclosed reprints of two scientific articles that I had published in relation to the problem of pain due to muscle strain and dysfunction. I mentioned my several talks on painful muscular disorders, given for medical groups. I listed my professional appointments in pharmacology, cardiology, and medicine (neurology). I added hopefully that I had served as Consultant for the Council of Pharmacy and Chemistry of the American Medical Association.

Henry Dreyfuss accepted my heterogeneous qualifications, but they were not as dissimilar to his requirements as might appear. The processes of logical thinking and of testing a hypothesis were alike whether one dealt with the action of a drug, the illness of a patient, or the comfort of an airplane seat. He and his engineering associates approached the problems of industrial design with the same spirit and insight as did the top scientific investigators in medical research whom I was privileged to know. Man's welfare was the central theme and common denominator.

My association with Henry Dreyfuss as Medical Consultant in Seating led me into a new world of technology and environmental preventive medicine. To many a practicing physician, medicine is a holding operation and he is constantly reminded that no matter how hard he works death is inevitable. Those experts in design and engineering held a philosophy that was refreshing to me: "It takes just a little longer to accomplish the impossible," I was told.

Over the years, I assisted Henry Dreyfuss in the essential project of revising dynamic and static body measurements for the average-sized man and woman, as well as for adults at the extremes of stature size.[39] I had criticized existing anthropometric standards so effectively that Henry Dreyfuss wrote on the flyleaf, referring to the new charts and diagrams shown at the front and back of his book,[40] "For Janet—The beginning and end is your fault. Henry 1957." Those body measurements were basic to things designed for people's use.

Adventures in industrial seating with Henry Dreyfuss [41] took me far afield, where I studied and outlined specifications for truck seats, plumbing fixtures, telephone operators' seats, and consoles, bicycles, recline seats for Lockheed Aircraft's new turbojet Electra, and seats on John Deere tractors. We were constantly testing our design concepts in experimental models. With other volunteer subjects, I rode a Rube Goldberg test bicycle-frame with variable positioning of the seat, handlebars, and pedals. I sat in an adjustable wooden mock-up of our Electra seat in a hangar at Burbank, Cali-

[39] Henry Dreyfuss, *The Measure of Man: Human Factors in Design* (New York, Whitney Library of Design, 1960).

[40] Henry Dreyfuss, *Industrial Design: A Pictorial Accounting 1929–1957* (New York and California, Henry Dreyfuss, 1957).

[41] Henry Dreyfuss, *Designing for People:* New Edition (New York, Paragraphic Books, Grossman Publishers, 1967).

fornia. *Life* magazine's photographers pictured me there as I demonstrated a dumbbell-shaped, or butterfly pillow.[42] We recommended that support for the neck and head, but it was not adopted. My marginal notation made then opposite the recline range of the backrest states: "You can't eat at 18 degrees." I had much to learn.

Unusual situations confronted me when I flew to Deere and Company's headquarters and factories. My first night in Moline, Illinois, I inquired what time we should meet in the morning. The answer was, "I know you Easterners like to sleep late—how about seven thirty?"

At that hour the next morning, I breakfasted with half a dozen engineers, all but one of whom were strangers to me. They had already been at work in their offices.

What should the well-dressed woman doctor wear in midwinter to drive tractors over a measured course of Iowa corn rows and ditches, and then to go directly to lunch with the company officials and chief engineers? Fifteen years ago, pants were not accepted as indoor female apparel in the Midwest, but I wore them.

I had never driven a tractor before. I had spent hours studying tractor operations in motion-picture film sent to New York, and before I left home I sketched my idea of an ideal tractor seat, for safety, comfort, and mobility. It was close to the design finally approved. But when I drove the big tractor down the field at a snail's pace, for a while theory and practice seemed far apart.

I was proud of the end product of my happy collaboration with Deere and Company's research and development team and with Henry Dreyfuss and his associates. When our seat was finally unveiled on a new line of John Deere tractors at the introductory show in Dallas, Texas, on August 30, 1960, I was told that one demonstration used a lanky tall Texan and a short fat boy to emphasize the quick adjustability of the tractor seat to accommodate operators comfortably.

In that period of time, I was meeting with Presidential candidate John F. Kennedy in New York. From the start of the tractor seat project in January, 1953, I had stipulated that my name not be used in connection with any advertising, and my wishes were meticulously respected. I was a dark horse in tractor seat design.

Designing chairs for use in offices and homes still intrigued me. In the fall of 1951, Mr. Shaughnessy suggested me as a speaker for the Home Fashions League, a nonprofit women's organization, and I jumped at the opportunity to express my ideas to designers, manufacturers, and distributors of home furnishings. The speakers were grouped on that program as

[42] October 24, 1955, pp. 36–37.

"Challengers" and "Responders"—I was in the former category. I discussed anatomical principles of support, with pictures of live subjects and skeletons seated in chairs and auditorium seats. I referred to physiological and postural studies of the circulation, skeletal muscles, and other supporting structures of the body. I was not complimentary to chairs currently styled by some well-known designers. I used the name-brand chairs in which the speakers sat on the platform as an example of stupidity in design, at least as far as comfort was concerned.

My "responder" brushed off my presentation as "pseudoscience." However, I felt justified in my remarks when we rose at the end of the evening and I saw the chairman of the panel pick up the Manhattan telephone directory that she had been sitting on. She knew from experience the discomfort of those seats.

Ed Street, our architect son-in-law, and I designed a bentwood armchair and we had it custom made in a small furniture shop in New York. Ed styled it in handsome modern lines, and I supplied the data for body support adjusted to pivotal points of joint motion. The same chair accommodated comfortably either a person as short as five feet four inches or one as tall as six feet four inches.

Virginia posed in the chair as one of our subjects—her stature was five feet four inches—and we took a series of pictures in a clinic waiting area of the New York Hospital. From them, I had lantern slides made that I showed frequently in lectures—I liked to see our photogenic daughter on the screen.

Ed and I were tempted then to create a Travell-Street line of "Work-at-Rest" chairs. Enthusiastically I went to talk about it with Mr. Shaughnessy in Bronxville, where he had retired. Afterward, on December 17, 1955— my birthday, which I spent in Palm Beach with Senator and Mrs. John F. Kennedy—he wrote me a letter stating seven reasons why I should *not* undertake the manufacturing of chairs. I listened to his advice.

Henry Dreyfuss was urging me to spend more time in his New York office, but I decided to stick to what I knew the most about and liked the best—people and the profession of medicine.

Dysfunction of joints locked slightly out of position was another mechanical source of skeletal muscle spasm. First, when I was a medical student living at home, and later, when a New York Hospital intern, my father was my preceptor in some techniques of manipulation—the passive movement of joints through their normal range of motion. To him, that kind of therapy was an integral part of physical medicine; he left no facet of that discipline unexplored. I learned from him that in the appropriate condition and with proper safeguards the benefits of manipulation in musculoskeletal pain might be significant, and I used my father's techniques effectively. I was aware of the dangers of manipulation when excessive force was applied and when the patient was wrongly selected without adequate diagnostic studies to rule out fracture, fragility (osteoporosis), infection, tumor, and other defects of bone and joints. My high degree of kinesthetic dexterity undoubtedly contributed to the success that I had with manipulative methods.

I made it a policy to take my scientific observations to headquarters in the field. On September 2, 1941, with some trepidation I read a paper [43] on sacroiliac joint manipulation at the annual meeting of the American Congress of Physical Medicine in Washington. My father was senior author. We quoted the orthopedist, Dr. H. C. Pitkin, who had said in 1937, "Manipulative surgery is a therapeutic waif of lowly origin whose infancy and childhood have been shielded from the light of reason by a congenital veil of empiricism and quackery." [44]

My father and I had no thought of curing infectious illness or remote internal disease by joint manipulation, as the theory of some healing cultists claimed for it. In the United States manipulative methods were held in wide disrepute, and it seemed a pity to us that our profession failed generally to recognize when legitimate musculoskeletal indications existed for that form of treatment. My conviction was strengthened when I met Sir Morton Smart, the British specialist in physical medicine, whose titles included that of Manipulative Surgeon to His Majesty the King.[45]

In spite of an excursion into a world of taboos, my professional survival was aided by several favorable circumstances: my father's stature in physical medicine, my own scientific standing in pharmacology, and the encouragement of McKeen Cattell, my chief in that department, to publish our data on manipulation. Cardiologist and pharmacologist, I had truly become a hybrid.

Openmindedness toward the results of manipulation fortunately existed in this country among medical innovators. During the Second World War, sixteen thousand copies of our article on sacroiliac manipulation were reprinted by the Josiah Macy, Jr. Foundation and were distributed to military medical installations by authorization of the Surgeon General, U.S. Army. One copy reached a Cornell medical classmate of mine while he was

[43] Willard Travell and Janet Travell, "Technic for Reduction and Ambulatory Treatment of Sacroiliac Displacement," Archives of Physical Therapy, Vol. 23 (1942), pp. 222–232.
[44] H. C. Pitkin, "Sacrarthrogenetic Telalgia: A Plan for Treatment," Journal of Bone and Joint Surgery, Vol. 19 (1937), p. 169.
[45] Sir Morton Smart, "Manipulation," Archives of Physical Medicine, Vol. 27 (1946), p. 730.

a patient in a military hospital in Asia, and ten years later he thanked me for having rehabilitated him then from a back injury.

Nevertheless, our report did not make much of a dent in the medical profession. In the winter of 1945–1946 during my father's long convalescence from an acute myocardial infarction, he and I wrote a second paper on low back pain that combined principles of joint manipulation and procaine injection of myofascial trigger areas.[46] That effort cheered him immensely, and it may well have contributed to his total recovery from serious illness at the age of seventy-five. In that article we were pleased to reproduce an illustration of our "corkscrew maneuver" for sacroiliac manipulation, which Dr. William Bierman of New York's Mount Sinai Hospital had published in 1944 in his treatise *Physical Medicine in General Practice*.[47] We had arrived—in the textbook. However, the fulfillment of our objective —acceptance by physicians of the special, although limited, usefulness of manipulative therapy—was still far distant.

A common built-in stress on our skeletal muscles is the seesaw movement that results when a person's legs are unequal in length. More than twenty years ago, measurements were made by means of a standing X-ray technique on a thousand young men in the United States Army, and it was found that 77 percent of the subjects had a difference in length of the lower extremities.[48] On the average, it amounted to about one-quarter of an inch (seven millimeters). Textbooks recognize that a larger difference—a half inch or more—is one cause of low back pain. The tilting of the pelvis and sacrum with compensatory side-to-side curvature of the spine (scoliosis) distorts structures in the sacroiliac and lumbar regions.

In my clinical laboratory of patients with myofascial pain syndromes, I learned that quite a small disparity in leg length, as little as one-eighth of an inch sometimes, produced enough seesaw motion to prevent a musculoskeletal strain from getting well, although initially another kind of stress had set off the attack.

As a child's seesaw travels up and down, it is easily seen that near its central support the arc of excursion is smaller than at the ends of the board. Similarly, for the standing adult person a quarter-inch difference in the level of the more centrally located hip joints swings the tips of the shoulders

[46] Janet Travell and Willard Travell, "Therapy of Low Back Pain by Manipulation and of Referred Pain in the Lower Extremity by Procaine Infiltration," *Archives of Physical Medicine,* Vol. 27 (1946), pp. 537–547.
[47] (New York, Paul B. Hoeber, 1944), pp. 442–443.
[48] Weaver A. Rush and Howard A. Steiner, "A Study of Lower Extremity Length Inequality," *American Journal of Roentgenology and Radium Therapy,* Vol. 56 (1946), pp. 616–623.

so far that one sags about an inch below the other. That small inequality in leg length may not cause trouble when muscles are in condition, but it can play a major role in the persistence of symptoms after an injury not only to the low back, but also to the neck.

A heel lift commensurate with the bony discrepancy may alter an individual's stance and outlook on life, I noted. That observation prompted me to write in a geometric vein:

POINT OF VIEW

Against the sea
The sky
Is slanted.

Or can it be
It's I
That's canted?

In the neck, the sternomastoid muscles take the brunt of an uncorrected difference in leg length. Extending diagonally around the sides of the neck from the mastoid process and back of the skull to the sternum and clavicle in front, those paired muscles overwork in attempting to counteract the seesaw motion of the chest and shoulders.[49] That mechanical wear and tear on the sternomastoids is enhanced when a tight shirt collar binds them and impairs their circulation; the pressure of the collar may precipitate acute symptoms by activating latent trigger areas.

To my mind, the sternomastoid is the most intriguing muscle in the body. I discovered [50] that in addition to setting off referred pain in the head and face, it apparently transmits proprioceptive nerve impulses that inform the brain of the position of the head and body in surrounding space. When trigger areas and abnormal tension develop in a particular part of the muscle—its clavicular division—the deranged sensory input conflicts with information from the eyes relayed to the balancing centers of the brain. Then,

[49] Janet Travell, "Mechanical Headache," *Headache,* Vol. 7 (1967), pp. 23–29.
[50] Janet Travell, "Pain Mechanisms in Connective Tissue," *Connective Tissues: Transactions of the Second Conference, May 24–25, 1951, New York* (New York, Josiah Macy, Jr. Foundation, 1952), pp. 111–112; "Referred Pain from Skeletal Muscle. I. Pectoralis Major Syndrome of Breast Pain and Soreness. II. Sternomastoid Syndrome of Headache and Dizziness," *New York State Journal of Medicine,* Vol. 55 (1955), pp. 331–340; Virginia D. Weeks and Janet Travell, "Postural Vertigo Due to Trigger Areas in the Sternocleidomastoid Muscle," *Journal of Pediatrics,* Vol. 47 (1955), pp. 315–327; Janet Travell, "Symposium on the Mechanism and Management of Pain Syndromes," *Proceedings of the Rudolf Virchow Medical Society of the City of New York,* Vol. 16, 1957 (New York, S. Karger, 1959), pp. 128–136; "Temporomandibular Joint Pain Referred from Muscles of the Head and Neck," *Journal of Prosthetic Dentistry,* Vol. 10 (1960), pp. 745–763.

whenever head movement changes the antigravity load on the sternomastoids, as in looking up or raising the head to turn over in bed, the person experiences a lightheaded form of dizziness best described by the Old South's phrase "a swimmin' in the head." It is a frightful feeling, worse than hard pain.

The victim of such sternomastoid trigger mechanisms also suffers from poor equilibrium and false sensations that the body is leaning or that the walls are tilting. On walking he veers involuntarily, as if drunk, bumping into furniture and doorjambs. When he is asked to heft two identical objects, one in each hand simultaneously, the one on the side of the sternomastoid spasm (if unilateral) feels lighter to him; the brain underestimates its weight. On bending over he may pitch onto his nose; the muscular contraction reflexly set in motion to oppose the pull of gravity is insufficient. He feels, and is, canted.

When postural dizziness and imbalance are due to a sternomastoid etiology, it is astonishing to witness how procaine infiltration of trigger areas in that muscle's clavicular division may at once reverse the clinical picture and restore the patient's equilibrium and weight appreciation. He is no longer canted.

To sustain the benefit of local treatment, for the time being overwork of the sternomastoid muscles must be prevented—as caused, for example, by the long leg–short leg disparity, or too short a focal length of reading vision, or unaccustomed overhead activity, like painting a ceiling or hanging drapes. One elderly gentleman aggravated a sternomastoid strain by merely standing and watching the painters do over the ceilings of his large apartment.

In aviation medicine, "pilot's vertigo"—illusions of body attitude and movement known as "spatial disorientation"—is an important cause of those major airplane crashes that are attributable to human factors; one survey by the United States Air Force found the incidence of disorientation to be as high as 25 percent.[51] In some cases, it was blamed largely on disturbed neck-muscle reflexes due to the pilot's angling his head to watch cockpit controls placed overhead or at the side, especially during turbulent flight. No neck muscle was specifically designated as the source of proprioceptive disorientation, but the load in that type of repetitive movement would fall mainly on the sternomastoids.

During an acute attack of sternomastoid postural dizziness, a person suddenly cannot drive his car. It veers, too. The operator's brain misjudges the amount of force that he applies to the steering wheel, and try as he may,

[51] James B. Nuttall, "The Problem of Spatial Disorientation," *Journal of the American Medical Association,* Vol. 166 (1958), pp. 431–438.

he can not keep the automobile moving in a straight line. While I was at Fort Knox in 1958 for the Cold Injury conference, I outlined a project to evaluate the influence of sternomastoid trigger areas, latent or clinically active, on the capacity to control a motor vehicle. The performance of blindfold drivers on the test auto-track there was to be correlated with the incidence of palpable spasm and trigger areas in the sternomastoid muscles as disclosed by physical examination. I heard no more about it after the conference ended. Sternomastoid trigger mechanisms are still, I believe, an undocumented factor in traffic accidents.

My niece, Ginger—Dr. Virginia Davidson Weeks—assisted me in research on the sternomastoid symptom complex of headache and dizziness. She was a Postdoctorate Fellow of the Muscular Dystrophy Associations of America—it was not a case of nepotism under my grant from the National Heart Institute of the Public Health Service. She held a joint appointment in the Department of Pediatrics under Dr. Samuel Z. Levine and in the Department of Pharmacology at the New York Hospital–Cornell Medical Center.

In that period, Ginger and I prepared a scientific exhibit on "How to Give Painless Injections," [52] which was a by-product of my years of dealing with peoples' pain. We wanted to obviate one psychological deterrent to medical care, fear of the needleprick. We quoted an old limerick:

> There was a Faith Healer from Deal
> Who said, "Although pain isn't real,
> When I sit on a pin
> And it punctures the skin,
> I dislike what I fancy I feel."

I had laid the groundwork for our exhibit in my report on "Factors Affecting Pain of Injection," [53] which I gave in October, 1954, at a New York meeting of the Parenteral Drug Association. I asked the audience for a show of hands as to how many had never had any injection of a medicine, vaccine, or test material; only one person raised his hand. And 90 percent indicated that they dreaded the next hypodermic. I stated then: "Fear of the needle is usually acquired in childhood. The psychic trauma . . . produced in this way undoubtedly creates obstacles to good doctor-patient re-

[52] Virginia D. Weeks and Janet Travell, *A.M.A. Scientific Exhibits Volume 1957* (New York, Grune and Stratton, 1957), pp. 318–322; *Abstracts of the Tenth Annual Assembly, American Academy of General Practice, Dallas, Texas, March, 1958* (Kansas City, Mo., American Academy of General Practice, 1958), pp. 17–19.
[53] Janet Travell, "Factors Affecting Pain of Injection," *Journal of the American Medical Association,* Vol. 158 (June 4, 1955), pp. 368–371.

lationships, essential diagnostic procedures and even life-saving therapy."

People suffering myofascial pain were in a special category. They tolerated painful muscle injections because they perceived prompt and measurable benefit. Hitting the myofascial trigger areas accurately with a needle was bearable also because it reproduced the patient's complaint of deep pain and thus, it was appreciated as reaching the origin of the difficulty. Penetrating the skin, the defensive covering of the body, was another matter. The psychological reaction to the sharp needleprick was often out of proportion to the hurt. It seemed important to me to make that part of the treatment more comfortable for the patient.

When infiltrating trigger areas, I made a practice of spraying the site, just before I inserted the needle, with enough of the vapocoolant to induce brief refrigeration anesthesia, but not enough to frost or injure the skin. That pleased the grown-ups.

When Ginger applied the technique to infants, however, she found that the cold shock of the spray startled and frightened them as much as the needle pain. I suggested then that she spray a sterile cotton ball, instead of the skin, and lay it gently against the spot. Evaporation of the coolant from the fluffy ball achieved the same degree of chilling, but more gradually, and the babies made no outcry.

We investigated several variations of the technique, recording surface temperatures for sprayed gauze squares as well as cotton, and using both ethyl chloride and fluoromethane sprays. We carried out bacteriological studies that showed the vapocoolant liquids to be sterile as sprayed from our dispenser, although they were not antiseptic for bacteria on the skin. Since the cotton ball remained wet for several minutes, we recommended to the allergist doing a series of skin tests on a patient in rapid succession that the sprayed ball be moved along from one cleansed spot to another. We found that such momentary chilling of the skin did not prevent the histamine wheal typical of the local allergic response.

Our vapocoolant spray technique was a handy and inexpensive way of eliminating pricking skin pain; it did not necessitate any special syringe or size of needle for painless injection. Incidentally, it materially reduced the discomfort of drawing blood from a vein. For intramuscular injection, the rules that we formulated included the placement of a nonirritant solution in a spot that was not tender to firm palpation, so as to avoid activating latent trigger areas.

In April, 1956, Ginger and I demonstrated how to give painless injections for the scientific program of the Cornell Medical College Alumni Reunion. With superior showmanship we inserted sterile hypodermic needles into the skeptical medical students and graduates who held out their arms to be punctured. The surprised verdict was, "I didn't feel a thing—I wouldn't have believed it!"

The following June, we displayed our exhibit in the New York Coliseum at the annual meeting of the American Medical Association, Section of Pediatrics. The Academy of General Practice invited us to show it again in Dallas, Texas, for its 1958 Annual Assembly. Ginger could not leave her new home at Lake Placid then, but Jack helped me and my Cornell secretary, Peggy Freund, install our big charts in Exhibit Booth Number A-1. We had a favored location in the new Civic Auditorium. Dallas gave the visiting physicians an elaborate welcome, while Jack played golf in Fort Worth with his former baseball coach at the University of North Carolina, Bill Lourcey.

From Dallas we flew to visit our daughter Janet and her husband, James R. McAlee, at Houston. They had lived there since 1955, when Jim was graduated *magna cum laude* from Harvard Law School in the same month that Janet received her Bachelor of Arts degree from Wellesley College—Durant Scholar, Phi Beta Kappa, with honors and the Billings Prize in music. They had taken up residence in Texas. Jack and I were beginning to feel like Texans.

In Houston, our small grandson, Richie, greeted me plaintively, "Grandma, couldn't you give me my next shot? The doctor here hurts me."

He was used to our painless injections. I had raised his standard of comfort.

The New York Hospital School of Nursing asked Ginger and me to write detailed rules for eliminating injection pain, to be used in instructing student nurses and in hospital procedure. While taking part in a field health project on a Navajo Indian reservation, one of our New York Hospital nurses had reported success with our vapocoolant technique, which she had introduced into the health clinic there. It really worked.

Ginger's brother, Dr. Willard Travell Weeks, told us when he was stationed on U.S. Public Health Service duty in the outpost Pribilof Islands of Alaska that our vapocoolant method eliminated a certain hesitancy of Eskimo mothers to bring their babies to him for immunizations. He was the only doctor in the region. Relieving the mother's apprehension for her child's feelings was a bonus of "painless injection."

The cotton ball wetted with vapocoolant liquid served equally well on a skittish horse and a baby. I interested several veterinarians in the procedure. The method failed, however, in the dolphin—the mammal. Dr. John C. Lilly telephoned me in 1961 from the Communications Research Institute in Miami, Florida; we were strangers, but he had heard of our efforts to minimize injection pain. He said that the friendly bottle-nosed dolphin sulked and sometimes fasted for days after he had to give it an injection—penicillin, perhaps. He was concerned for fear that the psychological needle trauma would interfere with his studies of two-way communication between species—especially if the trauma were needless. I explained the vapocoolant spray procedure to him and he tried it. Apparently, the layer of cold water on the dolphin's skin, which was an inch thick with fat, made the spray ineffective as a cutaneous analgesic.

For painless injection in the marine mammal, I then proposed the application of an absorbable "surface" anesthetic in a special base that was miscible with both water and fat. That procedure prevented the sensitive dolphin from feeling pricking skin pain. In 1967, when Jack and I visited the Communications Research Institute's exciting laboratory for the second time—the dolphins had made us all friends—John Lilly was still employing that local anesthetic mixture for giving them painless injections.

I admit that I have a missionary's zeal for converting to painless techniques everyone in the health services. That enthusiasm may be the result of my own dread of injections as a child.

I was an old hand at making scientific exhibits. In 1944, my first experience was in sketching the Department of Pharmacology's exhibit on the pharmacodynamics of digitalis for the annual meeting of the American Medical Association. It received a Certificate of Merit for Correlation and Presentation of Facts derived from experimental studies by members of our department. Subsequently, with the help of my collaborators in pain research I assembled several exhibits on the mechanism of referred muscle pain and its management. Seymour Rinzler and I demonstrated our most widely quoted one, "The Myofascial Genesis of Pain," [54] at meetings of such diverse societies as the Federation of American Societies for Experimental Biology (1951); the American Medical Association, Section of Experimental Medicine and Therapeutics (1951); and the Academy of General Practice (1952). At the last of those, held in Atlantic City, a professional Tele-Clinic sound film[55] pictured me in action applying the vapocoolant spray and injecting trigger areas in my educated subject, Ginger Weeks. In the movie and in our exhibit booth, I demonstrated also on an electrified hollow leg. Light exploded in the reference zone of the foot when I pressed a button at the trigger area higher up in the leg. Treatment was aimed at the source of pain, rather than where it was felt, and I explained the basic importance of the referred pain patterns of skeletal muscle

[54] Janet Travell and Seymour H. Rinzler, "The Myofascial Genesis of Pain: A Scientific Exhibit," *Postgraduate Medicine*, Vol. 11 (May, 1952), pp. 425–434.
[55] Sponsored by the Wyeth Laboratories.

that were constant from person to person for a given site of origin. The rubberized ankle joint of the model could be moved through a normal range of motion to show also passive stretching of the muscles in relation to local procaine infiltration and vapocoolant spraying.

The hours that I spent with strangers who visited our scientific exhibit booths were invaluable to me. I can not measure how much I learned about two-way communication between people. My approach was to discover quickly what pegs of knowledge the inquirer had in his mind so that I could hang my facts on them. I had less difficulty in trying to rearrange his prejudices when what I offered sounded not new but vaguely familiar to my listener.

It was hard work. Instead of the usual low chairs, I placed in our exhibit booths a couple of high stools so that I could perch and talk at eye-to-eye level. The comfort of sitting retarded the onset of mental fatigue.

The condensed pictorial approach to the presentation of scientific data appealed to me. It was a kind of discipline in some ways like writing a poem. Working at home of an evening, I would say to Jack, "Oh dear, I have space for just thirty letters to nail down this idea"—or it might be, "twelve syllables to express an emotion."

In 1952, our neighbor in Pelham, William A. Lydgate, who was an associate in a New York public relations firm, proposed that he and I write a medical cartoon strip. He was versed in popular medical writing, and after dinner we sometimes discussed advances in medicine.

Our "Today's Family Doctor" cartoon strip was a new frontier. With little expectation of approval, I sent a format of the first one—on diabetes, "Are You One in a Million?" [56]—to Dr. Iago Galdston at the New York Academy of Medicine. He returned it with an enthusiastic letter. Bill Lydgate remarked to me, with a trace of envy, "Bobby, you're the only person I know ever to draw blood from a galdstone."

On May 12, 1953, the diabetes specialist Dr. Edward Tolstoi wrote to compliment me on the cartoon strip and to question a detail of my theory: "Dear Janet: I think what you are doing is a good job, appropriate and to the point. The only point that I may challenge is that 'excess sugar in her blood fattens the baby'—because some of our women have large babies ante-dating their diabetes by 5 and 10 years, and yet the blood sugars are normal. . . . Sincerely, Ed."

I take advantage now of the opportunity to correct that error.

Bill and I prepared one cartoon series on trichinosis that was an outgrowth of my preoccupation with the causes of skeletal muscle pain. It was

[56] Janet Travell and William A. Lydgate, "Today's Family Doctor: Are You One in a Million?" *Today's Family*, May 1953, p. 79.

not published, but I had a lantern slide made of the completed drawings and script, omitting names of the authors. I used it in lecturing to our medical students about the pharmacology of drugs employed in parasitic infestations of the intestinal tract. That visual aid always obtained a laugh, but the students remembered its lesson.

Fifteen years later, it is still unfortunately a fact that in the United States our naked-eye inspection of pork for trichina is inadequate. One hog with microscopic trichina cysts alive in its muscles may infect a lot of consumers.

Most people recognize that eating rare pork may cause trichinosis, yet they may do it and incur the risk of contracting that serious disease. In my experience, a big obstacle to preventive medicine in practice is getting a person to do what he knows is good for his health.

One of my elderly patients, whose gall bladder condition caused pain whenever he ate fried or fatty foods, came to my office with a long face. "I had a dreadful attack of pain," he reported.

"You ate fried potatoes?" I guessed.

"You *know* I can't eat fried potatoes," he countered with a wry smile.

"Yes, but do *you* know it? Just why did you eat them?" I asked.

"The cook gives them to me."

"Are you afraid of your cook? Tell her not to."

"She doesn't know any other way to fix them," he rationalized.

I wrote on a prescription pad, "℞ Mashed, creamed, diced, riced, boiled, baked, scalloped potatoes—NO FRIED POTATOES." I directed him, "Give that to your cook."

At his next visit when I asked for an interval report, his face grew long again. He was silent.

"Now, what's the matter? Did you eat fried potatoes anyway?"

"No, I didn't," he answered dolefully. "The trouble is, I *like* fried potatoes."

I could handle such problems in the logistics of living. Getting patients to understand the importance of my specific medical advice was only a part of my job. I had to ensure that each item was feasible, and then I had to remove it from the realm of daily decision making. That technique was particularly helpful in the case of urban dwellers who lacked regular exercise. To the busy executive with access to a swimming pool but "no time to use it," I would say, "Do you mind if I call up your secretary?" She put it in his schedule, and he swam.

For the housewife who liked to swim but would not plan for it, I located a pool—often at the Y.W.C.A. or at a Y.M.C.A. with special swimming hours for women—and I saw to it that she joined. But that was not enough.

An arrangement had to be devised for a friend to sign up with her; she would keep a commitment to someone else, but not to herself.

Sometimes I used that trick on myself. When Janet and Virginia attended school in Pelham, I took time on a weekday to ice-skate at Playland in Rye because I had an obligation to them and to the other children in the skating club. Of course, ice-skating was no hardship for me. I had loved it since my sister and I started out on double runners and skated with our parents on the big lake in Central Park.

I made a point of learning what kind of exercise each of my patients enjoyed. As a rule, they had developed skill in whatever activity they preferred, and its coordinated smooth movement was most likely to benefit their muscles. Once, I utilized the principle of pleasurable exercise to rehabilitate a woman who had had a brain tumor removed in the New York Hospital. For months there, in the department of occupational therapy she had been unproductively chasing a hypothetical rabbit on the racetrack of the weaving loom or the sewing machine. I discovered that she was a golfer, and I asked her to send for her putter. I rolled up the Oriental hall runner in our home at Pelham, borrowed Jack's indoor practice cup, and set up a putting "green" in her uncarpeted hospital room. Soon she sent for a second putter so that she could compete with the interns who flocked to her room. Later, she attributed her long-delayed muscular recovery largely to the putting games that she played with them.

As long as people were ill or in pain, they made the effort to follow their doctors' instructions, I observed, but after recovery from the acute episode they often tolerated the second-rate state of average health. Unfortunately, "average" and "normal" were frequently equated with respect to the indices of health. When I lectured my patients on the subject, they defended themselves with the questions:

"Doesn't everyone get up tired in the morning?"

"Why wouldn't I expect my feet to hurt? They've been doing it ever since I remember."

"Don't most people have backache a lot of the time?"

"I've been chilly all my life. Isn't it just my nature?"

"I'm told I'm a tense person, so my neck muscles should hurt, shouldn't they?"

They had not complained about these things to their doctors. I persuaded them that they would receive the best possible medical care only if they expected their human machines to run at top efficiency. Educating patients in the quality of first-rate health required extra effort on my part, but I was not satisfied to let "good enough" alone and I raised their standard of well-being.

Usually there were answers to the challenges of discomfort and fatigue. In ferreting out evidence for contributory conditions in persistent muscular pain, I often spent a couple of hours in taking a medical history at a patient's first visit. In one solid session, as long as necessary, I was able to think in depth about the problem and to come up with solutions in a way that would have been impossible if I had fragmented the same amount of time into several visits. I focused not only on the ever-present mechanical sources of strain, but also on the nutritional, metabolic, infectious, allergic, and emotional factors in painful stress disorders of the skeletal muscles.

In 1961, after I left New York for Washington, I was complimented when a former patient, Hayes B. Jacobs, wrote about my approach to his problem of "sciatica" and low back pain:

> She took my history—the most complete one any doctor ever asked for. . . . She took out a red pencil, and began making marks on printed diagrams outlining the human figure. . . . She soon had diagrammatic records of the pain from its first occurrence through all its various manifestations. She studied the X-rays, the reports from my doctor, and from the hospital. . . . With everything spread out over the top of her desk, she . . . pondered it all, as concentratedly as if in a trance.[57]

For such a process of assembling and interpreting data, the patient must sit comfortably. Hayes Jacobs implied that I might be "a bit unorthodox." I had collected an assortment—he called it a "hodgepodge"—of chairs to suit people of different sizes and shapes, and to demonstrate good points and faults of chairs when used for various purposes. In our office waiting room, my father's mahogany Morris chair with a movable back occupied a place beside a North Carolina, natural-blond porch rocker. Three modern-styled armchairs were identical except that I had had the legs of two of them cut down for testing three different seat heights in the same design.

A motley group of footstools stood around—high, low, adjustable. There was an old milking stool from Massachusetts. There were models of the sloped "gout footstool" of old England. There was even a rocking footstool to match the rocking chair.

An unusual item that my father installed in the office was a "cobbler's table." It was equipped with leather insoles, sponge rubber, moleskin, and felt, and with scissors and glue, for remodeling patients' shoes. The Venus de Milo build of foot with the second toe as the longest one—or more importantly for weight-bearing, with the second metatarsal bone in the foot

[57] Hayes B. Jacobs, "The President's Doctor, Before Election," *Esquire,* November, 1961, pp. 94 and 96.

longer than the first (big toe) metatarsal bone—transmitted mechanical stress to the ankle, knee, and hip joints and to their muscles. We had first learned about that congenital foot disorder, and how to correct it by padding the shoe, when Dr. Dudley J. Morton of Columbia University's Presbyterian Medical School discussed the subject before the Medical Society of the County of Kings, Section of Physical Therapy.[58] The date was October 29, 1942, and it was a rainy night when my father and I drove out to Ocean Parkway in Brooklyn. I had had a long day, and Dr. Morton's lesson did not impress me then. My father drilled it into me.

That evening I was the next speaker on the program. I was enthusiastic about my own topic, "The Treatment of Somatic Pain by Intramuscular Infiltration with Procaine." Seymour Rinzler also narrated a motion picture that we had filmed to show the local procaine technique and its results in our Beth Israel Hospital patients who had painful shoulder syndromes with restricted movement. We had taken turns running the camera and treating the patients. The hospital room where we worked was so small that to obtain perspective we had to shoot film through the doorway of the adjoining bathroom. Seymour had our twenty-minute silent movie professionally titled and captioned. It cost little, but it had made a hit that June of 1942 at the annual session of the Americal Medical Association in Atlantic City. It pictured one patient who could not raise his hand high enough to touch his nose just before we treated him and who a few minutes later swung his arm in wide circles above his head. We called that victorious scene, "Waving the American Flag." That was not unfashionable during the war.

As the years passed, my father's and my office, distinctive for its comfort, its handsome walnut paneling, and absence of chrome, represented a merger of his long practical experience and inventive thinking with my enthusiasm for the new frontiers of medical science. He was in his eighties in the 1950 decade when patients of all walks in life, but with the common complaint of insufferable pain, flocked to 9 West 16th Street. I was proud that many workers in medical fields came there for help—physicians, nurses, dentists, scientists, and medical students. There were patients of many faiths and races, and they traveled to New York from many countries.

I wished that I spoke a dozen languages. A Chinese gentleman once brought along several of his friends as interpreters, none of whom spoke enough English for me to take his medical history. We resorted to signs and pictures. A deaf-mute presented a similar obstacle to communication, but I managed. Without any history at all, I could usually examine the patient for trigger areas in the muscles, and knowing their individual patterns of re-

[58] Dudley J. Morton, *The Human Foot, Its Evolution, Physiology and Functional Disorders* (New York, Columbia University Press, 1935), pp. 179–186.

ferred pain I could diagram the regions where I concluded that he felt his pain. At a teaching clinic, in that way I sometimes deliberately tested the reliability of the "eyes in the tips of my fingers," and my deductions mystified strangers, both physicians and patients.

As a consultant, I traveled far and wide to treat people with muscular pain. Those invitations gave me a welcome opportunity to educate doctors in methods for its rapid relief and long-range management. In 1951, I flew to Seville, Spain, on a Constellation named "Undaunted," to see what I could do for the acute back pain of a former patient whose home was in Venezuela. Her physician and I could not communicate in words, for he spoke only Spanish and it was foreign to me, but each morning for a couple of weeks I walked a few blocks to his home and watched him at work in his ground-floor office. The melody of roosters crowing on the roof was funneled down to us through a sky-covered patio inside the house. At 8 P.M. in the "afternoon," he would come for me at the Hotel Alfonso XIII and we would pick up his children at school to taxi them home in his little car. Then he would courteously sip an apértif with me at a little round table at a café on the sidewalk. When our mutual patient was better, she and I rode together in an open carriage through the narrow streets of the ancient Moorish city to visit the churches. Gipsy children ran alongside.

Jack would have loved Spain, but he kept my promise to take Virginia to Bermuda for her Easter vacation that year.

Washington was in my orbit of office hours. In November of 1954, I flew there from New York for an overnight stay in consultation with the orthopedic surgeon, Dr. Eugene de Savitsch, who had been a Russian émigré.[59] Only Jack knew that my plans included a visit with General Snyder, Personal Physician to President Eisenhower, in his medical office at the White House. That morning, with ordinary vanity I decided that my hat and gloves had a used look, not good enough for the occasion. Walking along Connecticut Avenue near the Mayflower Hotel, I bought new ones in a store that had just opened at nine o'clock. To my surprise, my taxi was admitted without delay through the great iron gates on Pennsylvania Avenue and we drove to the North Portico. In 1961, I discovered how simple it was to clear a visitor for entrance to the White House.

General Snyder's courteous welcome and comfortable informality—we were two physicians—seemed at variance with the stiff potted palms in the corridor and with the straight military bearing of his aides. I was at ease, since I had no medical responsibility there. Looking out through his barred window, I felt rather sorry for General Snyder. What a difficult and isolated

[59] Eugene de Savitsch, *In Search of Complications: An Autobiography* (London, Andre Deutsch Limited, 1958).

spot in which to practice medicine, I thought, compared with my busy office and academic milieu.

A few years later when I sat in his place, a young physician wrote me that he would like to come to the White House to watch my techniques of treatment. I replied: "I regret to tell you that my patients here do not lend themselves to observation."

CHAPTER 15

My First Visit to North Ocean Boulevard

On December 14, 1955, the telephone rang in my office at 9 West 16th Street. It was Senator Kennedy. Would I fly down and spend the weekend with him and Jackie in Palm Beach before the family arrived for Christmas? He could get me on a flight Friday afternoon, December 16.

Without hesitating, I replied that I would be delighted. At the same time, I thought rather ruefully about the Christmas party that Friday evening at the New York Hospital when the medical house staff would put on a show with takeoffs on the faculty. Saturday, December 17, was my fifty-fourth birthday. That night my sister was giving a reception for my favorite niece, Ginger Weeks, who was to be married two weeks later. There would be a birthday cake for me.

My husband would understand. If he felt disappointment, he would not show it. My trip was not a casual Florida holiday.

My flight was scheduled to leave La Guardia Airport at 4:55 P.M., but it was delayed by a winter storm. In Philadelphia our plane developed mechanical trouble, and from the airport there I telephoned Jackie in Palm Beach. How much later the flight would be was uncertain—I would take a taxi to the house when I arrived.

It was approaching 3 A.M. when our wheels touched down at the "West Palm" airport, ten hours after I had boarded the plane at La Guardia and about six hours late. I located a taxi and learned that it was eight or ten miles to 1095 North Ocean Boulevard, the home of Mr. Joseph P. Kennedy. The driver assured me that he could find the house.

No one was abroad at that hour; street lights were sparse and house numbers invisible. I could hear the surf as we drove along close to the ocean. After a while the taxi slowed and the cabbie remarked, "I guess I must have passed it."

He turned his cab around and headed back, then circled again and stopped in front of a forbidding solid wooden door that was set in a high stucco wall. There was no bell and no number.

"Are you sure this is the house?" I asked.

"Well, not for sure, but I think so," he said dubiously. He set my bags in the road.

I raised the antique iron latch and pushed. The heavy door opened. I looked straight ahead into a long, cloistered walkway, roofed above, closed on the right by a stucco wall and bordered on the left by a colonnade that disclosed dim vistas of a tropical garden. Wall brackets on the right lighted the passage.

The driver picked up my suitcases and followed me. Our footsteps echoed in the night stillness. At its far end the cloistered walk turned ninety degrees to the left and brought us to a flight of stone steps. High above, we made out the large bulk of a dark house.

We climbed the steps and emerged onto a broad patio that was enclosed on three sides by the main house and its two wings. In a corner of the patio the fronds of a palm tree rattled eerily in the breeze and I shivered in unison. A small steplight over a doorway cast strange shadows. I looked around, listening intently. I tried the doorknob and opened the door a crack.

"I feel like a housebreaker," I whispered, "but the light is on and the door unlocked. They must be expecting someone. Let's go in."

The taxi driver looked as though he wanted to run, but he stepped inside after me and deposited my bags in the entrance hall. From it a circular staircase led upstairs. On each side of the hall a spacious room vanished into darkness. In the one at my right I distinguished a grand piano; across the center of the room the back of a large sofa faced us. My eyes searched the hall table for a note. There was none.

"Please don't leave me yet," I said softly.

Suddenly, like a jack-in-the-box, a startled face appeared above the back of the sofa. It was Jackie, twenty-six but looking sixteen.

"Oh, Dr. Travell, I'm so sorry—I must have fallen asleep. What time is it? You must have had a dreadful trip. It was good of you to come."

Slowly she got up from the sofa and hobbled toward me, her hand outstretched. Her right foot and leg were encased to the knee in a plaster walking cast. She answered my gaze.

"I broke my ankle playing touch football a month ago," she said casually. She smiled a warm welcome. "You must want something to eat."

I paid off the taxi driver. Despite my protest, she led me through the long dining room to the big kitchen. She set out ice cream and angel food cake and fresh orange juice from the refrigerators, and dishes and silver from the cabinets. We sat at the kitchen table and talked while I ate.

Limping along, Jackie guided me up the staircase to my room on the second floor. She apologized because the bathroom connected with another bedroom.

"But there's nobody in it," she assured me. "Breakfast is any time, so sleep as late as you like."

In the distance I heard her tap, tap, tap, like Long John Silver with a wooden leg, down the uncarpeted stone steps as she proceeded to a bedroom on the ground floor.

I scarcely knew Jacqueline Kennedy then. Her thoughtfulness for my comfort and appreciation of my coming, in spite of the predawn hour, were gracious and genuine beyond the obligation of a hostess. They expressed to me her deep concern for her husband.

I was not then aware of Mr. and Mrs. Joseph P. Kennedy's generous hospitality to their many friends and the numerous friends of their children. When the bedrooms in the main house were all occupied, there was still the "children's wing" over the kitchen. A surprise was soon in store for me.

As I relaxed gratefully between the smooth sheets, in a matter of seconds I was sound asleep. It seemed only a moment later that a lilting voice recalled me.

"Wake up, wake up, it's morning, the bright sun is shining, the blue ocean's calling, it's morning, wake up!" the voice sang.

I could not remember where I was. I opened my eyes. The bathroom door stood ajar and a laughing Irish lass in a flowing nightgown was dancing around my room like a whirling dervish. I sat up in bed and the apparition gave a small scream.

"Oh, I thought you were Edith!" Edith, it turned out, had been stranded by the bad weather and never arrived at the house.

Explanations followed. My intruder's flight from the west had been delayed even longer than mine from New York. After her all-night trip she was so bedraggled that the taxi driver took her to the servant's entrance of the Kennedy house. When she walked up the back steps, the kitchen maid looked at her and asked, "You're the new cook?"

"I'm a house guest," she replied. She was familiar with the place and its informal ways and she located an empty bedroom upstairs. It was barely 7 A.M. and she was ready for bed when she remembered that Edith was to have come the evening before for an overnight stop. We laughed over the trials of travel; she had been up all night and I had had little sleep. She told me, too, how people came and went in that big house—I did not see her again.

On one of my subsequent visits to 1095 North Ocean Boulevard, when I again made an unexpectedly late arrival, I was wiser. The chauffeur met me at the West Palm Beach Airport. As we drove along by the ocean, I asked him, "Dave, I suppose all the family will be asleep when we get to the house. How will I know which room I'm to use?"

"They said whatever bedroom was empty, they'd drop a towel outside the door."

When we tiptoed upstairs, we found a white bath towel lying on the floor in the hall and we understood the signal.

That morning of December 17, I was the last to show for breakfast. Senator Kennedy had already had a swim in the pool. Under a cloudless sky and shielded from the wind off the ocean, he was soaking up the sun within a partially sunken enclosure built at one end of the pool. The "bullpen's" boarded walls had no roof, but inside there was a telephone. The instrument was often set on the top board where it could be reached from either inside or outside the enclosure and the Senator kept it in nearly constant use.

I wandered barefoot across the lawn of deep, springy Bermuda grass to the jutting prow of a high sea wall. I gazed down on the blended blues and greens of a lace-edged, gentle ocean. In the sunlight its surface was set with flashing diamonds. I descended a flight of stone steps to a doorway cut in the massive wall. The door opened onto a wooden walkway wet with spray that clung to the smooth face of the retaining concrete. The frame walk turned back from the prow toward the dry, soft sand and its steps led me onto the steeply sloping beach.

Dropping my towel on the sand, I glanced at the myriad shells that fringed the foam, and I plunged into the ocean. The water was surprisingly warm. Instantly, I was in another world, the world of sea creatures, far from the dark December city of New York. The buoyancy of salt water, the lift and fall of ocean swells—Virginia called it "the rocking horse sea"— and the sound of the busy surf erased the pattern of my daily life.

My host and his beautiful bride of two years had that health-giving world to hold forever. What forces drove him to leave it for the ravages of politics? After all his pain and suffering, had he not fought his share of his country's battles?

In the afternoon, we talked beside the pool with our voices pitched against the now familiar rattle of palm fronds. Senator Kennedy had been at my office earlier in December and things were going well then with his chronic back problem. That August and September of 1955, only a few months after I had first seen him on the Memorial Day weekend, he had traveled in Europe. On the day that he returned, October 11, he came to my office again in New York and he reported that he had not been obliged to use his crutches on his trip abroad. I had been concerned about him when *The New York Times* of September 22, 1955, pictured him standing and leaning on his crutches at a private audience with Pope Pius XII. I asked the Senator about that episode.

A slow smile at the corners of his eyes signaled that he was about to poke fun at himself. The flash of a grin followed, as he said, "I used the crutches then only because I couldn't kneel gracefully."

At the same time, he admitted that his back was more uncomfortable than it had been when he left the country on August 5. He would arrange to come to my office every week or so for treatment of his long-standing muscle spasm, which was the residue of old injuries. In eight of the weeks throughout the late fall, he managed to leave Washington to see me, usually on a Monday or Tuesday, or perhaps on a Friday. His plans were subject to last-minute revision and he was apologetic whenever he had to change an appointment. His first order of business was his health, but it had to dovetail with the Senate's duties. I knew that his schedule was not under his control and I made mine conform to his.

He had looked forward to the Christmas respite in Florida, but I learned that a spell of damp, cold weather had plagued him there. The sea was uninviting for swimming and he had contented himself with long walks beside his beloved ocean on the steep, sandy beach. His back was bothering him again.

First, I checked his shoes for the left heel lift that I had prescribed earlier in 1955 for all his shoes, to correct the inequality in the length of his lower extremities. His beach sandals at Palm Beach lacked that correction because of the difficulty in modifying that kind of footwear. Most of the time, he had been walking barefoot there around the house, by the pool, and on the beach. His disparity in leg length created an abnormal seesaw motion in the sacroiliac and lumbosacral regions with each step, and was a potential source of low back pain. I advised him to use only those beach shoes to which a heel lift could be added—sneakers, for example—and to avoid going barefoot.

I pointed out to him that walking on sand involved very heavy muscular effort, and I emphasized the special kind of strain that is placed on the back when a person walks on a surface sloped sideways like that beach. Such a slant makes one leg function as if longer than the other, tilting the sacrum and pelvis and producing a curvature of the spine that makes the muscles work at a mechanical disadvantage. Senator Kennedy agreed to eliminate that activity in the future.

On the other hand, I assured him that he had the capacity to swim in the ocean if he desired, provided that the surf was not rough. He had spent a large part of the previous winter there at his father's house while he was convalescing from two operations on his back, but more than a year had elapsed since he had had a swim in the sea.

"It's more invigorating to swim in the ocean than in a pool," I said. "The water is alive and it moves you. It creates a helpful variety of both active and passive motion in a way that still water never does. It's like riding a horse."

He raised the question of the temperature of the water.

"The water is not too cold for you. I tried it myself this morning."

He was ready to go. Within seconds, we had crossed the lawn and were descending the steps through the sea wall to the beach. One of my most cherished memories is of that swim in the ocean together. The brilliance of his pleasure surpassed the sparkle of the afternoon sun on the waves.

In December the sun sets early. Dinner by candlelight was served to the three of us, grouped around one end of the shining mahogany table at which twenty places might have been set. Then we settled in the living room for the evening, equipped with newspapers and magazines, books and television.

We sat within the circle of light from tall, dark-shaded table lamps. Jackie selected an upholstered armchair. I slipped my shoes off and tucked my feet underneath me as I sat on the deep sofa on which she had been sleeping while she awaited my late arrival early that morning. From its place against the wall Senator Kennedy brought up a straight firm-seated chair and he set it beside his wife's.

I felt the deep currents of understanding that flowed steadily between them. The shadows in the dimly lit, huge room—symbolic I thought of the shadow of illness in their lives—seemed to draw them close together inside the circle of light. I was not an intruder.

Jackie asked me a few questions about the program that I had outlined to her husband. She loved to walk on the beach with him.

"Do you mind if I turn on the TV," the Senator interrupted—and promptly did so.

At an appropriate pause in the program, I asked to be excused to telephone New York, explaining that my sister was having a party and I could catch my husband there then. In apology, I murmured something about his expecting to hear from me on my birthday; the end of the explanation slipped out before I could check myself. When I returned from telephoning, Jackie was gone from the room. A few minutes later, she hobbled back on her walking cast from the ground-floor wing of the house and she handed me a white cardboard box.

"Jack and I want to wish you a happy birthday," she said. Then she added in her soft, low voice, "I'm sorry I don't have any pretty paper and ribbon to wrap it."

"If we'd known, we would have had a cake and candles for you." Senator Kennedy made me feel that that would have been a special pleasure.

In mixed embarrassment and appreciation, I opened the box. It contained a handsome evening purse; I felt sure that Jackie had just brought it from Europe. Its deep blue velvet was bordered with gold leather and lined with cream-colored silk. On the flap of the bag were circles of fine gold filigree, each edged around with a ring of blue and gold beads and brilliant stones. It was the most beautiful purse that I ever owned. Now our daughter Janet treasures that generous impromptu gift of the Kennedys as a special heirloom.

After we had been sitting for quite a while that evening, Senator Kennedy inquired why chairs were so uncomfortable. His only really comfortable one, he said, was the rocker that he had asked me to order for his Senate office. He had liked it the first time that he came to see me at 9 West 16th Street with Dr. Ephraim Shorr. He wondered whether I should not design a chair to fit him.

As a starting basis for that, I needed to know which chairs in the house he found relatively comfortable and which immediately uncomfortable. He sat briefly in various ones in the living room and dining room while I studied his seated positions and the dimensions and angles of the chairs. I carried with us books of several thicknesses and I occasionally raised the chair legs at the front or at the back to increase the seat height from the floor or to modify the pitch of the seat and backrest. I picked up a ruled pad and made quick sketches and notes as the Senator tested the chairs. The hour grew late.

"Tomorrow," I suggested, "let me measure your own dimensions that are pertinent to designing a special chair for you. And I can improve the comfort of one of these armchairs that is nearly right for you already."

The next morning I made those measurements while Senator Kennedy sat by the pool reading the Sunday newspapers, shifting his position as I directed. I recorded my observations on another page of the pad, according to a profile graph that I had drawn for handy reference.

That Sunday morning, Evelyn, the competent housemaid, helped me layer a pile of outdated magazines beneath the loose seat cushion of an upholstered armchair. They served two purposes, to make the seat bottom firmer and also higher at the rear; that leveled its backward slope almost to the horizontal. I warned Evelyn not to let anyone disturb those magazines when cleaning the furniture.

The Senator knew of my interest in seating design, since I was active then in two major industrial projects in that field. In July and early in September of 1955, I had flown to the Midwest to advise on comfort and safety factors in tractor-seat design. Later in September, I had gone to California to evaluate our seat mock-ups for a new propjet-engine airplane. He had seen some of that work featured in a recent issue of *Life* magazine. The demands of my part-time commitments, together with the even greater demands on Senator Kennedy's time, prevented my designing a truly comfortable chair for him then.

Time passed. It was not until I came to the White House with President Kennedy in 1961 that I had an opportunity to provide him with the consistently good seating that reduces muscular fatigue and strain. He asked me to tackle this problem for his Executive Office, the Cabinet room, the boats that he often used—the *Honey Fitz,* the *Patrick J.,* and the *Marlin*—his helicopters, and Air Force One, the bubble-top presidential limousine, and his personal home furnishings. Success in chair design was made possible by the carpenter's and upholsterer's shops in the White House, together with the accessibility of the President for quick testing of experimental models. My detailed notes, hastily handwritten on December 17 and 18, 1955, in Palm Beach, more than five years later provided the basic formula for optimal "sittability" of the President's chairs.

Before my first visit to 1095 North Ocean Boulevard, I had seen Senator Kennedy only in a transient medical atmosphere—either at the New York Hospital, my office, or in August before he flew to Europe, at the Waldorf Towers. With his wife, in the natural setting of his father's home by the ocean, I saw new aspects of his character. He wanted to shield her from anxiety for his welfare—he was thirty-eight, twelve years older than his young wife.

"It's best if you don't go into my medical problems with Jackie," he smilingly advised me that Sunday. "I don't want her to think she married either an old man or a cripple."

I respected his wishes.

Until that summer of 1955, and even through the fall, for a long time he had been fighting the erosion of his time and energy by pain. He had learned the discipline of disability and he had to relearn the freedom of mobility. In Florida that December, he recovered his trust in his health. He could swim in the ocean again. When he had an ache in his back, he understood that mechanical causes contributed to it and that they could be corrected. The prospect of chronic ill health need not hamper him in his high purposes.

CHAPTER 16

Campaign Years

The year of 1956 brought personal sorrow to the young Senator, Jack Kennedy. After a period of excellent health over Christmas and that New Year in Palm Beach, he came to my office on Friday morning, January 6. We were talking together when the intercom buzzer rang. My secretary had instructions to defer telephone calls—he never had a moment to spare.

"I'm sorry to interrupt—maybe it's for you," I said. I listened to the message with shock and dismay.

"Senator, I have bad news for you," I told him with lagging words. "It's Eph Shorr. That call was to tell me that he dropped dead a short while ago. He was at breakfast—there was no warning."

I had lost one of my closest professional and personal friends, from whom I learned constantly. The Senator had lost his trusted physician who had battled for the Senator's life during two operations on his back in the winter of 1954–1955 at our Hospital for Special Surgery. Dr. Shorr had masterminded the management of his adrenal insufficiency, a field of medicine that had suddenly become a jungle of new developments. Cortisone had been introduced in 1950 and hydrocortisone in 1952. They were the chief hormones of the adrenal cortex and Eph Shorr was in the forefront of their clinical application.

We sat silently. The Senator bowed his head for a couple of minutes. We each had our own thoughts of what the loss would mean; I knew that Eph Shorr's contributions to medical science would never die. The Senator raised his head and sighed deeply.

314

"A wonderful man—" was all that he said. He showed little emotion, not because he felt it lightly, but because he felt so deeply.

By a coincidence, Eph had been with us when we first met at 9 West 16th Street eight months earlier and we were together there at the time of his death. Later, I realized that Jack Kennedy was Eph Shorr's finest gift to society.

"Where do we go from here?" the Senator asked me, with a tinge of desolation in his tone.

"If you wish, Gene Cohen could take over. You already know him," I replied.

Dr. Eugene J. Cohen was on Dr. Shorr's endocrinology staff at the New York Hospital and had substituted for him during the summer months when Eph was vacationing at Martha's Vineyard. All three of us had worked together on the Senator's medical problems.

I arranged for Senator Kennedy to be admitted to the hospital again for a general review by Dr. Cohen at the end of the following week. I requested a room for him on the fifteenth floor where he had been a patient, because the nurses in charge were the same as before and would not be strange to him. He had no need of special duty nursing. I also designated a room for him on a particular side of the tall steel building since the television reception was better on that exposure. By a coincidence, he was admitted again to Room 1502, the one that he had occupied the previous May.

On Friday, January 13, 1956, at 5 P.M., a memorial service was held for Dr. Ephraim Shorr in the main auditorium of the Cornell University Medical College. It was an hour when the medical students and most of the staff were free to come. At Senator Kennedy's request, an attendant brought him through the long bare corridors from his hospital room, a distance of two city blocks, to the medical school building. My husband and I were sitting in the auditorium's hard uncomfortable pews. Just as the service began, I saw the Senator's chair pushed into the room; a wheelchair was a requirement when patients moved around the hospital. He was wearing the regular gray cotton hospital robe and slippers. Hardly anyone noticed the slim young man where he sat inconspicuously behind the end wall of the lowest tier of seats.

After the service, I dismissed the Senator's attendant and I wheeled him to my laboratory in the Department of Pharmacology, which was located on the same floor of the medical school as the auditorium. He wanted to see everything that related to my research studies on the basic mechanisms of musculoskeletal pain. In his grasp of essential scientific principles he was an intellectual giant.

Then I took the Senator in his chair back to his room, while he gave the wheels an occasional turn with his hands to speed the ride. As planned, I discharged him. He dressed and left the hospital immediately. He had tarried to pay tribute to Dr. Shorr.

In 1957, when the Shorr Memorial Fellowship Fund was organized as a means of helping able young physicians develop in the study of endocrinology, I mentioned it to Senator Kennedy. Later in the year, his father personally brought me at 16th Street a check in five figures as a contribution to that memorial for Dr. Shorr. I had first met Mr. Joseph P. Kennedy in November, 1956.

"We thought that it would give you pleasure to hand the check in at the hospital," he told me.

It was a characteristically thoughtful gesture, and it did indeed give me great pleasure.

The gift to the fund was made in the name of Joseph P. Kennedy, Jr., who was killed in the war, and the donation was not publicized.

In 1956, Senator Jack Kennedy was back in harness, making up for lost time. In those campaign years before he announced his candidacy for the Presidential nomination in January, 1960, he served in the United States Senate as Chairman of its Subcommittee on Labor, as a member of the Foreign Relations, Labor, and Public Welfare Committees, and of Senator McClellan's Select Committee to Investigate Improper Activities in the Labor and Management Field.

In April, 1956, hearings were being held on a bill that he introduced with Senator Lister Hill to establish a National Library of Medicine in order to facilitate medical research and to ensure the greatest possible benefits from it. That Kennedy-Hill bill was endorsed by the American Medical Association, the American Dental Association, the American Hospital Association, and other organizations. Senator Kennedy had also been active in securing passage by Congress of appropriations for nationwide medical research that was under jurisdiction of the National Institutes of Health. He was the darling of the doctors then.

That year he campaigned for Democratic candidates who would be up for reelection in November, 1956, mainly in the East and South. On April 30, he spoke in my city at a Joint Conference of Postal Employees of Greater New York and Northern New Jersey. He emphasized the "obligation of Congress to deal fairly with postal workers because they don't have the right to strike." Before his speech that day, he came by to see me at my office.

The Senator was constantly on the move. I saw him only at long intervals of four to eight weeks during the first half of 1956, but he kept in touch with me by telephone.

I was on the move, too, making quick swings to lecture not only in the metropolitan New York area, but also throughout the country. Like Jack Kennedy, I had multidisciplinary interests. On March 16, 1956, after attending a morning symposium on the pharmacology of nicotine in the city, I took a train from Grand Central to meet my husband in Pelham. He drove me in a blizzard to the Austen Riggs Center in Stockbridge, Massachusetts, where I gave an evening seminar on "Psychogenic Stress and Myofascial Pain"—in other words, "Tension: Mind and Muscle"—at the invitation of Dr. David Rapaport, formerly Director of Research at the Menninger Clinic, where I had lectured to the staff in 1950. The snowdrifts piled so high that the New Haven trains did not run and the roads in to nearby Merryfield Farm were impassable, but my incredibly expert driver dodged the stranded cars and we reached Stockbridge on time.

On March 23, a week later, I flew to the University of Kansas Medical Center and participated in teaching a postgraduate course on "The Heart: Recent Advances in Diagnosis and Treatment" for practitioners in the State of Kansas. Likewise on the panel was a young physician-scientist, Lawrence E. Lamb, who was helping to build the first School of Aerospace Medicine in San Antonio, Texas. Larry and I became friends on the spot.

On April 23, a month later, I was in Texas. In the morning, I was the guest lecturer on the Orthopedic Section of the Texas State Medical Association at its annual meeting in Galveston. My topic was "The Management of Skeletal Muscle Pain." I was impressed by the dearth of women physicians in the audience and on the program of that surgical specialty. In the afternoon, I lectured on the same subject for the Department of Physical Medicine of the Veterans Administration Hospital at the Houston Medical Center.

When I looked over the scientific program of the Texas State Medical Association meeting in Galveston, I saw that Dr. Sara M. Jordan of the Lahey Clinic was a speaker on another Section, and I met with her after her talk. We had exchanged medical reports on Senator Jack Kennedy, and I knew in what high esteem he held her. She was from Boston and I from New York, but it did not seem odd to either of us to discuss our mutual patient from Washington in Texas—medical meetings were like that.

I took advantage of that lecture trip to spend one day with our daughter Janet and her family at her home in Houston.

Early in May, at Cornell I lectured to our second-year medical students on the metabolism of bone as a living tissue. In the spring term, fortunately the laboratory sessions in pharmacology had ended and each of us in the department had only an occasional class lecture to give. Research, however, moved full speed ahead. On May 25, at a joint scientific session of the

Society for Experimental Biology and Medicine with the New York Academy of Medicine, I reported the differing effects of a drug, ergonovine, on the normal and on the atherosclerotic heart—a basic study in clinical pharmacology.

My mobile pattern of activity trained me in how to compress time and detail into an organized design. It speeded up my rate of thinking. That, in turn, in all probability accelerates metabolic processes and augments physical stamina. The converse is expressed in the old saying, "An idle mind digs a grave for the body."

In June, 1956, our daughter Virginia Powell Street received a Bachelor of Fine Arts degree from the College of Architecture of Cornell University. Jack and I attended her commencement at Ithaca, where she and Mary Amatruda, daughter of my Cornell medical classmate Sis Strunk, led the parade as Marshalls for the women students. Ginia had been elected in her sophomore year to Alpha Alpha Gamma, the national women's honorary society in architecture and fine arts. At graduation, for her sculpture she received the Faculty Award in Fine Art for Professional Promise, a special prize not given every year. Ed, her architect husband, was as proud of "Dina" as were her parents.

Both our daughters were married and graduated from college. Jack and I felt free to plan an extended trip to Europe. I was scheduled to read scientific papers at the International Rheumatology Congress in Aix-les-Bains, France, and at the International Physiological Congress in Brussels; and I was invited to conduct a clinic for the Department of Physical Medicine and Rehabilitation of the West London Hospital in England. We would take a beach vacation in seclusion from tourists in the picturesque cliff town of Positano on the Amalfi Drive in southern Italy. We would be abroad for seven weeks.

Senator Kennedy came to my office shortly before we were to leave the United States on June 25. I had discussed those plans with him in mid-May and I would not have gone on the trip if his back had not shown satisfactory recovery. I had cautioned him then against overoptimism, which might in that stage lead to overuse of the muscles and a fresh strain of the back. He was still not on a full exercise program. It was with a sense of uneasiness that I read press reports of his thirty-ninth birthday party (May 29) when two thousand friends gathered to honor him "for his recent recovery from surgery resulting from wounds suffered during World War II." Jack and I returned from Europe on Thursday, August 9. The next day, Senator Kennedy checked in with me at 9 West 16th Street on his way to the Democratic National Convention, which opened in Chicago on August 13. During the summer, his back had been relatively comfortable.

For the rest of August, I worked intensively in New York, catching up
with my patients' problems. Weekends, Jack and I drove to Merryfield
Farm, where our two daughters and their husbands, with Janet's small son
Richie, were vacationing.

New sorrow and political disappointment had descended on Senator Kennedy when he and I met again on September 11, 1956. In Chicago
he had lost the Vice-Presidential nomination to Senator Kefauver by only
thirty-eight and a half votes short of a majority. Then while he was in
Europe on a deferred holiday his first child was born two months prematurely, a stillbirth, and he hurried back to Jackie. As he stood tall, straight,
and thin in my office I expressed my sympathy in their bereavement.

"Jackie got too excited at the Convention," he said ruefully. "It was all
my fault for losing."

Then I congratulated him on *not* having won that close race. I told him
that in my opinion his back had not been tested long enough to know
whether it was ready to stand the strain of a national candidacy or the
vicissitudes of the Vice Presidency if he were elected. He was a man who
always wanted to know the facts.

"Senator, you weren't *really* disappointed when you lost the nomination,
were you? I was afraid you were going to win."

"Yes, I was," he said with conviction. Then he added reflectively, "But
I learned that it should be as easy to get the nomination for President as for
Vice President. Until then, I thought I would have to work first toward the
Vice Presidency."

From that date, he discussed freely with me the potential of his health
in relation to the stringent responsibilities of the Presidency.

I glimpsed from time to time how much of the happiness of his private
life he would have to renounce in order to assume that enormous public
burden. One day in my office I asked him, "Why under the sun does anyone
in good sense want to be President of the United States?"

Senator Kennedy leaned forward in his chair like a racehorse at the
starting gate. His whole self seemed poised behind eyes that shone with an
inner fire.

"I think it is the most interesting job in the world," he said.

"Eventually, I believe your health will not handicap you in that job, if
you want it," was my judgment.

If his intent was to test his back and to erase any reservations that I
might have had about his stamina under stress, he could not have set out on
a more strenuous program. In the six weeks before Election Day, with Ted
Sorensen [1] he traveled some thirty thousand miles by commercial airline

[1] Theodore C. Sorensen, *Kennedy* (New York, Harper & Row, 1965), p. 100.

and small chartered plane; in twenty-four states he made more than 150 campaign speeches and appearances for the Stevenson-Kefauver ticket. That wear and tear did not cause a recurrence of back trouble.

By January, 1957, Jack Kennedy was widely discussed as a front runner for the Democratic Presidential nomination, and the state of his back, whether good or bad, was newsworthy. That year, he found time for golf, usually nine holes, and he enjoyed it immensely. In April, when my husband and I were vacationing in Palm Beach with our family, the Senator even played tennis with me—doubles—on his father's court at 1095 North Ocean Boulevard. From that January until early September, his back gave him no real cause for complaint. He traveled to make speeches that were sandwiched between Senate roll calls and hearings. To protect his low back on the arduous schedule he wore a canvas inelastic support, something like a polo belt that he referred to as his "brace," or occasionally as his "corset." When he might have to sit for a long time, he sometimes added a wide elastic bandage on top of it.

Suddenly in mid-September, 1957, a painful point of redness appeared in the midline operative scar of the lumbar spine fusion (1954), which had been complicated by secondary staphylococcal infection. He had some fever. I hospitalized him for wide incision of the soft tissue abscess by Dr. Preston A. Wade; drainage was accomplished under general anesthesia. Bacteriologic studies, directed by Dr. David E. Rogers, whose special field was infectious diseases, again incriminated the staphylococcus; a search for tuberculosis bacilli, including guinea pig inoculation, was negative. Senator Kennedy's X-rays of the lower spine then showed the scarring compatible with his previous three operations (1944, 1954, and 1955) and the secondary infection. The appearance was what might be called "a mess," but when seen in a single set of X-rays, such defects do not tell the whole story. The sequence of X-ray pictures, taken over the period of years in which I observed him, showed the same defects and therefore indicated an old inactive condition.

Healing of his incision occurred satisfactorily on a three weeks' course of antibiotic therapy. The New York press noted Jack Kennedy's stay in the hospital, but it received small comment because his disability was brief.

Soon after his hospital discharge he went to Hyannis Port, and a few days later he called me to ask if I would fly up to see him. I talked with his physician on the Cape and I learned nothing to create alarm. I was puzzled. Mr. Joseph P. Kennedy telephoned me—he was anxious and upset about his son's health.

"Maybe Jack should stop torturing himself and he should call the whole thing off. Do you think he can make it? There are plenty of other things for him to do—and there's Jackie," he said. He was devoted to his daughter-in-law.

On her doctor's order she was leading a secluded life and staying close to the New York Hospital where Caroline would be born that November. Extra precautions were being taken because the year before an emergency cesarean section had been done in an effort to save the first baby. Jackie was not with her husband in Hyannis Port.

"Mr. Kennedy, I'll be glad to go and see Jack—let me try to discover what's wrong before anything's decided," I told the Senator's father.

The next morning I had a bumpy ride on a small chartered plane. When I arrived at the big house in "the Compound," Senator Kennedy and Ted Sorensen were walking together outdoors on the macadam driveway by the shore of Nantucket Sound, and I watched them from the high front porch.

The color of the water matched the gray sky. A thin fog floated in the air; it was damp and cold. The Senator's hair was ruffled by the wind. He was wearing a sky blue sweater and carrying a contrasting yellow pad of legal-length paper. He moved without obvious restriction as he walked along and as he climbed the flight of steps to the porch. He perched naturally on the railing to talk.

When I examined him in his room, I was still baffled as to why he was seriously discouraged about the long-range view of his health. I looked out through the window into the gray mist; it was a leaden view. I felt chilly, sitting there, and I sensed a stiffness in my muscles.

"I don't feel great," he said.

"Senator, what you need right now is a long soak in a hot bath." It was not much to offer him, I thought to myself.

"Oh, I couldn't do that," he replied sharply.

"Why not?" I was surprised. I knew that relaxing in hot water always rested him, and he depended on it.

"Not with that big hole in my back. I haven't been in a tub since I entered the hospital."

"But, Senator, you don't *have* a hole in your back! The abscess is practically healed—there's hardly any discoloration on the gauze," I said in astonishment. I showed him the four-by-four-inch square.

Then I realized what was wrong. The physician on the Cape had changed the gauze each day and had reported to Dr. Wade in New York. At no time, either there or in the hospital, had the Senator actually seen the condition of his back beneath the taped-down dressing. He did not have a moment to waste and he concentrated on reading while the doctor did that mechanical job. The Senator carried in his mind the depressing recollection of the gaping wound that failed to heal after the 1954 spinal fusion—with both a bone graft and a metal plate—until months later when the plate was removed. Final closure of the wound after that difficult reconstructive surgery occurred not long before Dr. Ephraim Shorr first telephoned me about Jack Kennedy in April, 1955.

With the change of locale from New York to Massachusetts and with several doctors sharing responsibility, no one had remembered to tell him when the time came for him to resume his customary hot tub baths. A defect in communication was his trouble. I should have rectified it sooner, but I did not have the facts.

The Senator's eyes began to twinkle.

"I couldn't use soap, could I?"

"Of course you can," I answered seriously. "Wait—I'll get Dr. Wade on the phone."

It was about noon on a Saturday and I located the surgeon at the Piping Rock Club in Locust Valley, Long Island, where he played golf. I explained the situation to him.

"Let me put the Senator on—he's right here—and let him ask you directly about the soap," I said. Dr. Wade added his OK to mine.

On that damp, cold, gray day, a hot bath was a welcome prescription.

After lunch at the house, the Senator and I went over his schedule for the next five weeks—there was scarcely a free hour for rest—and I tried to use a red pencil on it, without success. A couple of days later he was in Canada; on October 8, he spoke at the University of New Brunswick in Fredericton about ways to ease tensions and achieve understanding on basic issues between the United States and Canada. On October 10, he addressed some ten thousand delegates to a teachers' convention in Baltimore, Maryland, on the subject of the Federal Government's responsibility to enact a school aid program without delay. And so it went. Senator John F. Kennedy was back in harness, and running. He was a man in a hurry.

After recovery from that acute episode late in 1957, his back performed better than in many years. It was not again an important clinical problem for him until he reinjured it in May, 1961, by his overenthusiastic use of a shovel in a tree-planting ceremony. He told me then that he had become so accustomed to not thinking about his back that he "forgot to take care."

We do not know what accounted for his flare-up of infection localized to the old operative scar that September of 1957; but a recent study offers new evidence that under the stress of surgery an allergic reaction to the suture material used may explain a high proportion of postoperative secondary infections.[2]

---

[2] Lindsay C. Getzen and George A. Jansen, "Correlation Between Allergy to Suture

Senator Kennedy was well aware that he was highly allergic to dogs. In the *Daily Mirror* of April 2, 1956, a Washington columnist, George Dixon, reported an interview with the glamorous Jacqueline Lee Bouvier Kennedy: "Throughout the interview, Mrs. Kennedy nursed a small Siamese kitten, explaining she had gotten a cat because the senator is allergic to dogs."

One problem that could not be coped with adequately during the campaign years was that extreme allergy to dogs, because he was constantly on the move. However, I was able to arrange for the Senator to have hypersensivity tests by Dr. Paul F. de Gara in New York. They disclosed a marked reaction not only to dog dander, but also to cats and house dust. A mixed vaccine for hyposensitization was prepared, but his schedule precluded its administration then. It became my unhappy duty later to banish a pet cat—not the Siamese—from his Washington household. When he had a permanent base at the White House, I sampled his new environment—the living quarters on the second floor of the Mansion—and I sent Dr. de Gara a shoebox full of freshly vacuumed dust from which an autogenous environmental vaccine was made. A long course of injections of the vaccine, over a couple of years, apparently made the President more tolerant of exposure to the dogs that he loved.

In 1958, Jack Kennedy was up for reelection to the United States Senate against President Eisenhower's tide of popularity. His weekends were spent crisscrossing the state of Massachusetts. During the week he worked in Washington and crisscrossed the nation. His wife was campaigning with him then. In that period, he was described by one columnist as "a slender slat with an awning of tousled brown hair . . . handsome, clean-cut, warm and friendly, with an air of candor and forthrightness." [3] In *The New York Times* of October 10, 1958, James Reston headlined:

Kennedy Looks to 1960. . . . He looked a little self-conscious today riding down the main street of Parkersburg West Virginia in a scarlet Cadillac convertible with his attractive young wife . . . in a parade with a Democratic donkey and the Parkersburg High School band, especially since few people on main street seemed to know who he was. . . . On the platform Senator Kennedy made his points with an assurance he did not have two years ago and with a clarity and brevity not usual in political oratory. He has an excellent New England voice: cultivated, yet strong and full of vitality.

His old record of ill health was not featured in the newspapers then, nor in 1959. I saw him at long intervals, but he telephoned me from anywhere

---

Material and Postoperative Wound Infections," *Surgery*, Vol. 60 (October, 1966), pp. 824–826.
[3] Bruce Biossat, *New York World-Telegram and Sun*, October 8, 1958.

in the country when he had some medical matter on his mind. I could be reached night and day, even at the beauty parlor in the Nurses' Residence, which had a New York Hospital extension. The first time that he asked me for a full medical statement concerning his health was in connection with a biography that James MacGregor Burns was writing about him. My report addressed to Senator Kennedy was dated July 21, 1959, and it was my understanding that my name would not be published in connection with my statement. Senator Kennedy respected my wishes. That book was the first relatively accurate publicized account of his health background that I know of. [4]

On April 1, 1960, I was disturbed to read in *The New York Times* about a new campaign hazard that Senator Kennedy encountered while he was handshaking his way down the main street of Oconomowoc, Wisconsin. "When he extended his hand to take that of . . . a registered nurse at the Wilkinson Clinic, she asked him when he had had his last polio shot. The Massachusetts Senator, who is competing against Senator Hubert H. Humphrey of Minnesota in the Wisconsin Presidential primary next Tuesday, said he had had two shots three years ago. . . . [She] pulled him into the clinic and told him to roll up his sleeve. In a flash he had his third shot."

The following day, Saturday, I wrote him at the Senate Office Building in Washington:

April 2, 1960

Dear Senator Kennedy:
In the New York Times yesterday I read about your impromptu polio shot given by a nurse in Oconomowoc, Wisconsin. I quite understand the situation in which you found yourself placed.

In view of the publicity, I am writing because someone may raise a question as to whether you had been careless in not having kept up your Salk polio shots, or your doctors negligent in not seeing to it that you received them.

All you need to say is that you are over forty now. The Salk vaccine has not been generally advocated for persons over forty years of age. I recall your asking me about this a couple of years ago, and I told you that further polio shots were not necessary.

If the newspaper account is correct, the nurse is open to criticism for giving you an injection of Salk vaccine without a doctor's order.

The directions for administering the Salk vaccine include a caution in giving it to anyone who may be allergic to eggs. Reactions can

[4] *John Kennedy: A Political Profile* (New York, Harcourt, Brace & Company, 1959), pp. 30, 53, 54, 62, 101, 131, and 156–161.

occur since in preparing the vaccine the virus is grown in egg media.
With all good wishes and regards,

Sincerely,
Janet Travell, M.D.

His youthful appearance may have created that hazard.

During Senator Kennedy's 1960 campaigns in the Presidential primaries of seven states, his allergies to inhalant antigens may well have contributed to his "speaker's" laryngitis. In West Virginia—the voting was on May 10—in order to avert prolonged hoarseness his nose and throat specialist, Dr. Anne M. Belcher of the New York Hospital staff, ordered him not to talk, not even to whisper, until he was better.

He was a completely cooperative patient. For that period of time, he was mute. He scribbled directions and messages on a pad. An aide read his speeches while he stood by on the platform. I have one of his handwritten notes, which he issued to the crowd at the height of the West Virginia campaign. It reads: "Sorry—I have lost my voice—but I would appreciate your vote anyway—thanks! John Kennedy."

In one city, a local ear, nose, and throat man examined the Senator's throat. When I asked what the doctor had found and done for him, Jack Kennedy scrawled on his memo pad only the words, "He is an ass."

The Senator did not hesitate to knock the medical profession to me, if he thought that he had reason to. I did not always agree with him and I sometimes pointed out that I was not fully informed of the findings. I appreciated all the more his telephoning me on May 11 from Washington to thank me for my long-distance advice during that West Virginia primary.

The dedication of young doctors impressed him; he recognized the rigors of their long hours. At the hospital one morning, I thought that the assistant resident had done a sloppy job of changing the dressing on the Senator's back.

"Senator, who did that, Dr. R———?" I asked with a frown and an irritated tone.

"Yes." The Senator looked away from me and said persuasively, "He was in the operating room all night, Doctor—don't say anything."

He was more concerned about that young man than about himself. I wondered how I could have forgotten what it meant to be a house physician on duty day and night.

Jack Kennedy took special steps to prevent a breakdown of his voice when he became a Presidential candidate. A speech therapist on the campaign trail aided him with voice placement and projection. That, together with better amplifying equipment for broadcasting at airports and other outdoor gatherings, eased the unending strain on his vocal cords.

Although Senator Kennedy had asked me not to leave the United States in 1960 while he was campaigning for the Presidency, I saw him professionally then only three times, early and late in May and in mid-August, on account of his upper respiratory problems. On a hot Sunday afternoon, August 14, after Senator Kennedy had visited with Mrs. Eleanor Roosevelt in Hyde Park, Dr. Belcher and I saw him together in New York for treatment of one of his rare attacks of sinusitis. We met in a midtown radiologist's office where technicians joined us to provide X-ray and other diagnostic services, including blood chemistries for an endocrinologic checkup. His back needed no attention in 1960.

At appropriate intervals, he had examinations by the endocrinologist Dr. Eugene J. Cohen, who relayed the results to me. I was the central clearinghouse for the medical records. The Senator had one such health survey by Dr. Cohen on a holiday, February 22, in New York while I was in Hawaii.

By flying to Honolulu I did not consider that technically I had broken my promise to the Senator not to leave the country that year. He agreed that the opportunity was irresistible for me to discuss the treatment of painful disorders of the skeletal muscles in a series of lectures and clinics for the Hawaiian Medical Group, the Straub Clinic, and the Honolulu Orthopedic Society, which met at Tripler Army Hospital. Besides, my husband and I were invited to stay with our New York Republican friends, Mr. and Mrs. Gayer G. Dominick, in their new Japanese-style home on secluded Kahala Beach. (They were both dead when Mrs. Jacqueline Kennedy rented that house for her 1966 holiday in Hawaii.)

The practice of medicine, in my mind, was a nonpolitical profession. So it was to Senator Kennedy. In the spring of 1958, when I was visiting our daughter Janet in Houston, I received the following memorandum from my secretary in the office at 9 West 16th Street:

> Mrs. Coerver, secretary to Senator Barry Goldwater (Arizona), phoned for an appointment for him. . . . Senator Kennedy referred him. His number is Capitol 4–3121, Ext. 3824. I told her you were in Texas. . . . Mrs. Lincoln also phoned this morning for Senator Kennedy. . . . I gave her your address and phone number. She said she did not think he would bother you. The Senator's phone number in Washington is Capitol 4–3121, Ext. 4544. It is the same number as Senator Goldwater's, but different extensions.

It was the central switchboard number for the Senate Office Building, in which they both had offices.

The Academy of General Practice had asked me to read a paper before its Utah Chapter in Salt Lake City on April 22, 1960, and I found it convenient at that time to accept another invitation to lecture in Phoenix, Arizona, on April 25. I visited old friends in Phoenix from the New York suburban area—also Republicans—and they drove me to call on Senator and Mrs. Barry Goldwater in their hilltop home, which blended with the arid desert near Scottsdale. But that year the Arizona desert was in bloom, incredibly beautiful in its pastel shades of yellow and green. The color pictures that I took then delighted Senator Goldwater, the expert photographer. I loaned him my negatives.

In August, 1960, when Senator Goldwater flew from the Republican National Convention in Chicago to see me, it surprised him that *The New York Times* published an item about his coming to New York to "see Senator Kennedy's doctor"—he told the press that it was a personal matter. Nor did it seem unusual to me that both those Senators consulted the same physician.

The year of 1960 was a traveling one for me. Prior to Election Day on November 8, I journeyed nearly thirty thousand miles in making eighteen quick professional trips out of New York, mainly to lecture. Four of my trips were for the Joseph P. Kennedy Jr. Foundation to universities that were expanding their research in mental retardation. I was a member of the Kennedy Foundation's scientific advisory committee, known as the Corporation Visiting Committee.

I went prepared for all sorts of eventualities. At one place, the foundation's committee members stayed in a country motel that had an attractive swimming pool. I had packed a bathing suit and Mrs. Eunice Shriver had none. In off moments between all-day conferences she and I took turns wearing it, still wet. Sargent Shriver inquired how I happened to know enough to bring it.

"I called your secretary in Chicago," I said. "You probably didn't ask her."

We were both enthusiasts for physical fitness, but I had outdone him that time.

Speculation concerning Senator John F. Kennedy's "Addison's disease" did not come up as a hot political issue until July, 1960, in the second week before the Democratic National Convention in Los Angeles. Neither he, nor his physicians, had made a secret of his adrenal insufficiency.

A year earlier, he had told me that the status of his health was a matter of some discussion in the campaign when he had asked me for my first medical statement. On July 21, 1959, I wrote him:

Senator Kennedy incurred an injury to his back in 1939, and reinjured it in 1943 during the war. He had a disc operation in 1944 and a spinal fusion in October, 1954. After the fusion, he had some back pain

which disappeared under further treatment. . . . His back is entirely
well. Senator Kennedy is physically very active. He swims regularly.
When time permits, he plays tennis and golf. He carries his nearly two
year old daughter on his shoulder without thought of his back.

In 1943, when the PT boat which he commanded was blown up,
he was subjected to extraordinarily severe stress in a terrific ordeal of
swimming to rescue his men. This, together perhaps with subsequent
malaria, resulted in a depletion of adrenal function from which he is
now rehabilitated.

Concerning the question of Addison's disease, which has been
raised. This disease was described by Thomas Addison in 1855 and is
characterized by a bluish discoloration of the mucous membranes of
the mouth and permanent deep pigmentation or tanning of the skin.
Pigmentation appears early and it is the most striking physical sign of
the disease. Senator Kennedy has never had any abnormal pigmentation of the skin or mucous membranes; it would be readily visible.

Senator Kennedy has tremendous physical stamina. He has above-
average resistance to infections, such as influenza. The outstanding
vigor with which he meets an incredibly demanding schedule, often
seven days a week and with the briefest of vacations (only once as long
as two consecutive weeks in the past four years), is clear evidence of
his fine physique and remarkable vitality.

After an interview with Senator Kennedy in the summer of 1959, James
MacGregor Burns gave a true summary of the facts in his political profile: [5]

While Kennedy's adrenal insufficiency might well be diagnosed by some
doctors as a mild case of Addison's disease, it was not diagnosed as the
classic type of Addison's disease, which is due to tuberculosis. Other
conditions, often not known, can cause inadequate functioning of the
adrenal glands. As in Kennedy's case, this can be fully controlled by
medication taken by mouth and requires a routine endocrinologic
checkup as a part of regular physical examinations once or twice a
year.

His back has, however, continued to give Kennedy trouble. He
tried a number of treatments without much improvement. In the fall
[spring] of 1955, he encountered a New York City doctor who specialized in the use of novocain to treat muscular spasm. Injections of
novocain, according to Kennedy, relax the spasm and permit blood to
flow in: otherwise his muscles might stay in spasm for years and gradually stiffen. According to this doctor . . . today "his back is entirely
well."

[5] *Ibid.,* pp. 156–160.

Burns then quoted correctly from my memorandum of July 21, 1959, to Senator Kennedy. At that time, his back had recovered in a satisfactory measure; the aftermath of trauma and infection had turned out well. That did not preclude the possibility that he might strain his back again at any time.

The Senator understood his situation. Burns went on to say: "Kennedy feels, however, that no statements will put the rumors to rest. They are inherent in a campaign situation. The best way he finds to answer them is by keeping up his strenuous physical schedule. Anyone interested in his condition, he says, can try the pace of his next barnstorming tour."

Many observers did just that and found it exhausting. One wrote: "His schedule is enough to wear down a six-day bike racer. His day usually starts at dawn and carries on until the small hours of the following morning." [6]

Confusion in people's minds about "Addison's disease" was inevitable because the meaning of that diagnosis was changing during the decade 1950–1960. The name had implied a virtual absence of adrenocortical function, but it was becoming a loose term that included all grades of functional insufficiency of the adrenal cortex, no matter how mild. Thus, even two physicians might be thinking of different conditions when they said "Addison's disease." The name was no longer limited to the classic disease that had been progressive, fatal, uninfluenced by any form of treatment, and associated, as a rule, with tuberculous destruction of both adrenal glands and often with tuberculosis of other organs or the spine.

After cortisone became available in 1950, biochemists identified a spectrum of other corticosteroid hormones that are made by the cortical cells (outer layers) of the adrenal glands. Those new physiological tools led to precise recognition of partial adrenal insufficiency and to hope for rehabilitation by replacement therapy. The situation was analogous to the introduction of the hormone insulin for diabetes. Thus, the outlook as well as the terminology of the fatal disease described by Addison was changing in the 1950 decade.

In a book published in 1950, Dr. George W. Thorn, endocrinologist at Harvard, charted the approximate five-year mortality rate for his series of patients with Addison's disease:[7] Prior to 1930 and before any specific therapy, it was 90 percent; from 1930 to 1937, when treatment consisted essentially of a high salt, low potassium diet, it was 78 percent; and from

[6] Beverly Smith, Jr., "The Prospects of Senator Kennedy," *The Saturday Evening Post,* January 23, 1960, p. 27.
[7] George W. Thorn, "Metabolic and Endocrine Disorders," *Principles of Internal Medicine,* T. R. Harrison, ed. (Philadelphia, Blakiston, 1950), Part IV, p. 598.

1938 to 1946, when extracts of the whole adrenal cortex and imperfect hormone replacement were available, one of every two patients with Addison's disease died within the five-year period of observation. The diagnosis then was likely to be a death sentence.

Suddenly, before our eyes one of the great miracles of medicine happened. From 1950 to 1955, with the advent of oral preparations of new corticosteroid adrenal hormones, optimal replacement of the deficiency and a normal life span became possible for the first time. Surgeons then did not hesitate to remove both adrenal glands completely for treatment of hypertension and for suppression of some cancers. Women of childbearing age, whose atrophied adrenal glands secreted no cortical hormones, were enabled by replacement therapy to have normal children, even though pregnancy represents perhaps the heaviest metabolic load on the body.

Senator Kennedy was the beneficiary of the discovery of adrenal hormones that was achieved by basic medical research. The timing of their clinical application was right for him. He was a man of destiny.

On October 22, 1959, at his request I forwarded to Senator Kennedy a succinct statement by Dr. Cohen and myself about the current view of adrenal insufficiency. At that time, my enthusiasm for recent developments in adrenal physiology made me wish that the new knowledge could be disseminated more rapidly to the general practitioner and to the public. When the Senator was in my office, I urged that something be done about the widespread ignorance on the subject.

"Senator, I think a series of reviews in the medical journals and popular magazines should be written right away. People don't realize how the outlook has changed in Addison's disease," I said.

"But I don't have it, Doctor."

"That's right, Senator. You don't have classical Addison's disease. But the language is changing, too, and doctors disagree maybe because they aren't talking about the same thing."

"Doctor, you'll never educate all those Republicans," Senator Kennedy answered tartly.

I dropped the subject, but not my desire to clarify a remarkable course of events in medical history.

In New York, a few days after he won the Oregon primary vote on May 20, 1960, I tucked a piece of paper into the pocket of his white shirt.

"That's my telephone number at the farm—I'll be there over the Memorial Day weekend," I told him.

"Don't give it to me—I'll only lose it," he objected. He did not look at the paper.

"But it's not listed in my name. You wouldn't be able to reach me without it, Senator."

"What town is it?" he asked.

"Sheffield, Massachusetts."

He concentrated on my answer. It was all he needed—he knew every town and village in the state of Massachusetts.

I did not hear from him that last weekend in May, nor did I see him again before I started my vacation a month later at Merryfield Farm.

Our hill was not as remote from world affairs as it used to be, I thought. On Monday, the Fourth of July, we watched Senator Kennedy on a nation-wide television broadcast from the Hotel Roosevelt in New York when he answered former President Truman's charge that at forty-three he was too young to serve in the White House. It tickled me to hear Jack Kennedy declare that "the White House needs a young man of strength, health, and vigor."

The family was finishing supper that holiday Monday when the telephone rang in our dining room. It was Sargent Shriver, asking for Dr. Travell.

"Yes, I'm on, Sarge, but this is a party line," I interrupted quickly. "Give me your number—I'll go down the road and call you back."

In the dusk I hurried down the dirt road to the du Vigneauds' house. They gave me the privacy of their one-party line and I reached Sargent Shriver in Hyannis Port.

"You're a hard person to find," he said. "Jack finally told us to call the Sheriff in Sheffield—he'd know where you were."

Jack Kennedy guessed right. The Sheriff, Dwight Ford, had grown up on the farm that adjoined ours on Crow Hill in the days when I rode Maggie across the hayfields to visit the neighbors. I marveled that with all the large issues confronting him prior to the Convention, Jack Kennedy remembered that detail—the name of my Massachusetts village.

I was told over the telephone that at a news conference in Los Angeles supporters of Senator Johnson had raised the question: Is Kennedy fit?

"It's that rumor about Addison's disease," Sargent Shriver continued. "They claimed he's living on drugs—cortisone. Bobby replied that he doesn't have Addison's disease and he doesn't take cortisone."

"Well, that's right," I said. "Jack hasn't taken cortisone in years. Of course, he does take some relatives of cortisone, but in the way he uses them, in physiological doses, they're not *drugs*. Bobby can say that those hormones are natural constituents of the body and they're given prophylactically to make up for some deficiency of his adrenals when he's under stress. Jack feels so well that his doctors are not inclined to stop them now."

"Would you mind talking with Bobby at the headquarters out there?"

Robert Kennedy explained the situation further.

"Doctor, Jack wants to release your last medical report but it won't mean anything without your name and Dr. Cohen's. They're saying out here that Jack can't have qualified physicians if he won't name them."

"It's OK to use my name," I volunteered.

"Will you call Dr. Cohen? We have to have his consent. It's urgent—Jack wants the statement issued in time for tomorrow's papers, along with the charges. But he won't do it without your permissions, he says."

Before leaving New York on summer holidays, Gene Cohen and I together had drawn up that medical statement and had both signed it on June 11, 1960, in my office at Cornell medical school. It was written on my office stationery and I forwarded it to Senator Kennedy. It ended with a restriction that our names were not to be publicized in connection with it. Gene was adamant on that point.

I understood why he felt that way; publicity could only complicate our lives. We were in agreement that the practice of medicine is best kept separate from politics. A year earlier, I had withheld my own name from publication as a source for John Kennedy's medical history in Burns's biography about him; in that book I remained an unnamed "New York physician."

On the other hand, I believed that the doctor's obligation to a patient takes precedence over personal considerations—so did Gene Cohen—and I had changed my attitude in the spring of 1960. After returning from Hawaii, at Senator Kennedy's request I discussed his health on March 4 with Jack Anderson for an article that he was writing about the leading Presidential candidates.[8] I did not prohibit publication of my name and he attributed his source material to "Kennedy's physician, Dr. Janet Travell."

A couple of weeks later, I filled out and signed a questionnaire about Senator Kennedy's health for Ruth Winter, Science Editor of the *Newark Star-Ledger,* and as time went on, I spoke with other members of the press when the Senator requested it.

From Sheffield, I telephoned Gene Cohen at his vacation hideout.

"Gene, in Los Angeles they're calling Senator Kennedy's doctors a couple of quacks because he refuses to reveal our names to the press. He has to issue a statement about his health. Are we afraid to back up what we sent him last month?" I asked.

8 "The Candidates—How Healthy Are They?" *Parade,* April 10, 1960, pp. 4–5.

"No, of course not, Bobby."

"Then please call Senator Kennedy right away—I'll give you his number where he is now—and tell him you're willing to release your name with our statement. He has my permission already."

When I talked with Senator Kennedy about fifteen minutes later, his way had been cleared of that roadblock.

That Monday night—still the Fourth of July—at 10 P.M. California time, the Kennedy campaign headquarters issued our joint medical bulletin with our signatures.

The next day, newspapers throughout the country featured controversy and alarm over the state of health of the Presidential candidates:

"Now It Seems Democrats' Race Is to the Healthiest."

"Kennedy Still in the Running."

"If Addison's Disease Hits." A physician at the Peter Bent Brigham Hospital in Boston "said Senator Kennedy had nothing to worry about if he has the disease. He said victims could live as normally and as long as other people and that treatment consisted mainly in taking two or three pills a day."

Mrs. India Edwards, Cochairman of the Citizens for Johnson National Committee, who sparked the blast about Kennedy's health, was quoted as having said: "Senator Kennedy, who appears so healthy that it's almost illegal, is really not a well man. . . . If it weren't for cortisone, Senator Kennedy wouldn't be alive. Many doctors have told me about it. . . . I object to this muscle flexing about his youth as if he were in better health than anybody else."

In another newspaper story: "Addison's Disease Can Be Fatal . . . unless treated medically. . . . The most widely used medication for Addison's disease is cortisone and hydrocortisone, according to a Columbia Presbyterian Medical Center spokesman."

One columnist stated:

the medical report [was] . . . issued in the name of Dr. Eugene J. Cohen and Dr. Janet Travell, of 9 W. 16 St. New York . . . two Greenwich Village physicians. . . . The report added: "Your health is excellent. Your vitality, endurance and resistance to infection are above average. Your ability to handle an exhausting work load is unquestionably superior. . . . With respect to the old problem of adrenal insufficiency, as late as December, 1958, when you had a general check up with a specific test of adrenal function, the result showed that your adrenal glands do function." [9]

[9] David Wise, "Now It Seems Democrats' Race Is to the Healthiest," New York *Herald Tribune,* June 6, 1960, pp. 1, 6.

At a nationally televised news conference on July 5, the day after India Edwards's attack on Jack Kennedy's health, Senator Johnson formally announced his candidacy for the Democratic Presidential nomination and he cooled the campaign health issue. He recalled, as the press noted, that he and Senator Kennedy had "both had some health troubles . . . but both were tough enough. . . . Kennedy's travels around the country in campaigning for the nomination show he is fit, Johnson said. 'So far as I am aware all the candidates are in good health,' he said." Senator Johnson did not mention Addison's disease.

I listened to that televised press conference on July 5 with Gene Cohen in New York and at its close I said, "There is the logical Vice-Presidential running mate for Kennedy. What's more, Johnson will accept the second spot on the ticket. He said 'No,' but he meant 'Yes.' "

Senator Kennedy's health did not come up again as a serious issue in the 1960 campaign.

After the Democratic Convention in Los Angeles I wanted to know candidate Kennedy as a public speaker at firsthand. Of course, I watched him in his debates with Vice President Nixon and in other appearances on the television screen, but I had heard him speak in person from a public platform only once.

On December 6, 1957, he had addressed a group of New York Hospital student nurses during lunch hour in the lecture hall of the Nurses' Residence. His coming was not announced to the medical college or hospital staffs, but the Senator spoke to me about it in advance. His daughter Caroline and her mother had not yet been discharged from the New York Hospital.

"Doctor, what do you think I should talk about for the nurses?" he asked me. I was flattered.

"Ways to make nursing education more attractive are being studied here. The trend is to hold some joint conferences for medical students and student nurses. There is one Commencement exercise for the graduating nurses and doctors in June now . . ." I thought that he might like to be oriented in regard to special programs at our medical center.

"I think I'll stick to what I know," he replied with a grin.

On the way to hear Senator Kennedy speak that day, I happened to meet Marilyn du Vigneaud in the medical school corridor—she was a medical student—and I took her with me. He discussed foreign relations and labor legislation and he brought those topics alive. I was impressed with how much informative material he condensed into a few minutes, without boring his audience. He did not talk down to those young women.

My first opportunity to hear candidate Kennedy deliver a campaign address was on Columbus Day, 1960, at the Waldorf-Astoria Hotel in New York. I secured a special pass from Mrs. Evelyn Lincoln to admit me to that full-scale morning session of the National Council of Women. Candidate Nixon was their speaker in the afternoon.

When I arrived, not long before Kennedy, every seat in the ballroom was taken. I entered at the front by the stage and a spot was found for me across the room in the midst of TV cameras on stepladders, cables, flood-lights, and men with earphones fastened over their heads. I sat only a few feet from the speaker's lectern. Being in the center of that kind of commotion was new to me.

Jack Kennedy spoke without notes. His appearance of well-being and his easy command of his subject measured up to what I had expected. The spontaneous appreciation of his listeners expressed itself in repeated bursts of applause. He seemed to be enjoying the occasion as much as anyone else.

At the conclusion of his speech, during the final applause, I tried to leave ahead of the crowd through the same door by which I had entered. Everyone was standing and shouting as I walked across the wide ballroom between the stage and the front row of spectators. Suddenly I was trapped. Candidate Kennedy—as I learned later was his custom—crossed the room, too, on the platform, descended the steps at its far end and headed back in my direction on the floor level. He was shaking hands with everybody in the first row. My retreat was blocked and as he approached me, I stepped back into the front receiving line. I found myself standing between Mayor Robert Wagner and another dignitary of the City of New York.

Jack Kennedy shook hands with Mayor Wagner, and then he came to me. We shook hands also.

"Dr. Travell! What *on earth* are you doing here?" he asked in astonishment. I was definitely out of context.

"I came to hear you speak, Senator," I replied.

We never mentioned that encounter when we met again.

Early that month, in response to a telephone call from John J. Hooker, Jr., Director of Professional Groups, John F. Kennedy for President, I had agreed to serve on the National Committee of Doctors for Kennedy. I was in sympathy with his goals for medical education, research, and medical care for the aged. I believed that Senator Kennedy was sincere in his stated views against socialized medicine and for the individual's right of free choice of a physician.

I did not make much progress in changing the political opinions of my Republican colleagues in New York, but I tried.

"If only you knew Senator Kennedy, if you could meet him and talk with him, you would feel differently," I told some of my doctor friends at the New York Hospital. "Have you ever read his statements on medical care for the aged under Social Security?—you're not quoting him correctly."

I carried reports of his views in my versatile purse, which doubled as a medical bag in miniature. The emotional bias among those educated leading citizens distressed me. I was reminded of my mother's saying that intolerance is the hardest thing to tolerate.

Shortly before the election, a pro-Kennedy New York Hospital physician gave a cocktail party at his home for members of the hospital staff. Afterward, our host could not wait to tell me about an incident that occurred at the reception. Looking across the room toward me, the wife of one of the doctors asked him, "Isn't that Senator Kennedy's doctor over there?"

"Yes, it is," he replied. "Wouldn't you like to meet her?"

"Certainly not!" the lady answered indignantly and turned her back.

She would have been surprised to know that, not long before, my medical skill had made it possible for a patient of mine, who supported candidate Nixon, to introduce President Eisenhower at a big Republican rally. Without my help and encouragement she could not have met her commitment to appear on the platform. I derived a vicarious satisfaction from doing the best job that I could for my patients—without regard to the political consequences.

As my father used to say, when he instructed Ginny and me in our tennis strokes, "Forehand or backhand, always follow through."

Jack Kennedy would have agreed.

On October 18, 1959, my father had a stroke and he was hospitalized for two months at the New York Hospital. Then, with nursing around the clock he came home to Pelham with us. After ninety years of vigorous activity, he could not walk unassisted. His spirit made his illness easier for the family to accept.

His mind remained alert, and his speech, vision, and hearing were not impaired by that vascular accident to the base of the brain. He read constantly. He carried on a regular correspondence with his friends and family, who were not of his generation. On November 23, 1959, from the George F. Baker Pavilion of the hospital, he wrote our daughter in Nashville: "Dear Virginia—Many thanks for the socks which are perfect—and for your good wishes. I find myself suddenly writing with ease,—before I can swallow well or talk much or walk—legs bad and all muscles weak. Brain always clear even during the first few hours. Lots of love Gran"

On May 8, 1960, he wrote her from Pelham: "Dear Ginia: It is good to receive your letters but your handwriting is becoming habitually deplorable. . . . Later May 9, 1960. I believe I owe you a 50% apology. Today in looking over some of your letters to me I did not find a single bad word. Your letter which started this diatribe was your last to your father, which he let me read. But please do not hurry when writing letters to anyone. All well here but me. Love Gran."

He cut out the word in Jack's letter and sent it back to her. It was undecipherable.

At Christmas, 1959, his tennis-playing friends Katie and Franz Stone sent my father an electric blender to mash solid foods—he still had some difficulty in swallowing. He wrote them:

Bedridden at 34 Harmon Ave, Pelham N Y

Dear Katie and Franz:

What a wonderful present Santa Claus has brought me with your name attached. I thank you de tout mon couer [sic]. I have found that after spending a total of seven weeks in a hospital because I could not stand or walk, it is one thing to say "Hurrah! you are home,"—and quite a different one to "WALK." . . . All my food must be eaten PUREED,—some job for the cook. I have said Santa Claus is for the Children Class, which for the time being I have joined. I thank you for recognizing the fact. . . .

Cordially yours,

GRAN—Willard Travell

Jack and I bought my father a remote-control portable television set and he followed the campaign issues with partisan interest. In spite of his age and disability he remained young at heart and flexible in his opinions. In religion, he was a Presbyterian and in politics, an independent Republican. He had lived for years in the "silk stocking" Republican district of Manhattan. Yet his conviction that Senator Kennedy would best achieve social progress in medicine and in other human needs led my father to vote for the Kennedy-Johnson ticket by absentee ballot well in advance of Election Day on November 8. He was a frontiersman still.

We celebrated my father's ninety-first birthday (November 5, 1960) at the home of Boyd and Hazel Lewis in Pelham. Jack's and my contribution to the rather large gathering was to be the birthday cake. Jack said that he would like to get it and he would take it over to Hazel.

When we brought my father to the party, the ample cake reposed on the dining-room table. Its white icing was bordered with Irish green sugar roses. Across its center the greeting in large block letters read: JOHN F. KENNEDY FOR PRESIDENT.

Jack had bought it at a cake sale of the Pelham Democratic Headquarters. My father was delighted with its birthday message. As he reclined in a chaise longue, he was wearing a "Vote for Kennedy" campaign button that was four inches in diameter.

After the election, my father and I reminisced about the qualities of the man that made John Fitzgerald Kennedy President of the United States.

"Senator Jack Kennedy is the only man I've ever known who impressed me as having the capacity to be President. And with luck and timing, I believe he will be," I had remarked in 1956.

My father recalled how at our 9 West 16th Street office, our secretary one day escorted Senator Kennedy to the front door as he was leaving. She returned startled and stirred; he had taken an interest in her.

"He asked me how I liked my job," she gasped.

"Well, what did you say?" I laughed.

"I told him I liked it fine."

On one occasion, I attempted to learn from Senator Kennedy whether a new masseur whom I had sent him was satisfactory.

"Senator, what kind of a reaction did you have to the massage?" I was not prepared for his reply.

"Doctor, do you know how many children Mr. P——— has?"

"I'm sorry—I don't."

"Five. Do you know what he earns in a week?"

"No. I'm afraid I don't. Senator, how did you like the massage?" I persisted.

"Do you realize that he won't be able to educate his children on what he makes?" His worry for the man was genuine.

It was as if I had not spoken. His intense absorption in his line of thought caused him to ignore my query. His questions were more important than mine, I concluded, and I tuned myself to Senator Kennedy's concern for the people around him.

A young lawyer came to interview the Senator in my presence. I was not surprised when the questioner turned out to be the one who was interviewed. The Senator quizzed him.

"What's the most you can hope to earn in your profession if you stay in that small city and continue along the line you're going now? Have you figured the total cost of your children's education? What else could you do to increase your income? What is it you want out of your work?"

Senator Kennedy provoked that bright young man to think and to plan more intelligently for his future.

Nothing escaped Jack Kennedy's attention. One day he spoke to me about a laboratory technician: "I feel so sorry for Miss G————. Did you know that she itches? Isn't there something you could do about it?"

I had not noticed it, although it was, in a sense, my concern.

Senator Kennedy cared for working people, not merely in the abstract, but as individuals. He was always putting himself in their shoes. He could project himself into their lives because he was by nature a worker and because he was endowed with a remarkable capacity to feel deeply.

He had an abiding faith in the spark of divinity and in the intrinsic goodness of people. Mr. Kennedy, the Senator's father, once told me: "I believe there isn't a person on earth whom Jack dislikes. He sees some good in everyone. He's like his mother in that."

Although Senator Kennedy indefatigably pursued nothing less than excellence for himself and his associates, he seemed to me to be surprisingly tolerant of mediocrity. His manner never patronized those who had fewer advantages than he; he met people on their own levels. But appropriate status symbols, like a scarlet Cadillac convertible in a campaign parade, were important to him.

My niece Dr. Ginger Weeks one day offered him a ride uptown from 9 West 16th Street in her sixteen-year-old Chrysler, which had been turned out to pasture for a while at Merryfield Farm. My father had bought it before the war; our girls had driven it to the Pelham Memorial High School; it had been Janet's transportation when she attended Wellesley College; and finally we brought it to New York for Ginger to use while she worked in pediatrics at the New York Hospital–Cornell Medical Center. It was an educated car, but its blue paint was faded, running board rusted, and upholstery ragged. Senator Kennedy settled himself gaily in the front seat.

"Where would you like to go?" Ginger asked him.

"To the 21 Club, on West 52nd Street."

He invited Ginger to join him there at lunch with his other guests, and she did. The doorman at the Club parked the inelegant car. Whatever the circumstances, Senator Kennedy never lost the air of innate dignity that was the product of personal reserve, self-respect, style, and a distaste for ostentation.

Jack Kennedy's concept of humanity, its struggles and satisfactions, was built on first-hand data about people that he correlated and stored in his prodigious mind. As I saw the process of his thinking, he did not start with a theory and then find cases and illustrations to prove it. His was the method of observing and classifying a wide representative sample, which enables one to arrive at scientifically valid deductions.

The man who had become President-elect was different, not only in his passionate concern about the welfare of the individual, but also in his tire-less drive to do something about it. Although he was optimistic about the future of freedom and democracy, wishful thinking was not a habit of his mind.

"Illusion is a curse," he told me once.

I thought then that he was referring to a false hope for the recovery of his health, but his statement held true also of the threats to our nation's existence that he envisioned in the Cold War.

With those events in mind, when my father and I looked back over the five years that Senator Kennedy and I had traveled together, I wrote a poem:

ILLUSION

On summer porches lolling, we daydream.
A storm is forming for another day
As silent as sheet lightning far away,
Its movement subtle as the eel's upstream
At night in darkness, scavenger supreme
That feeds on death in bottom's muck. We say,
"The sun lies golden on the fresh mown hay,
It can not rain next day,"—or so we dream.

Prosperity will not be reaped by dopes
Who lack foresight against adversity.
Why do we not bale up the hay today?
Security will not be won by hopes
Nor earth made safe for man's diversity
Where laissez-faire's the credo: "Let's delay."

Jack Kennedy had few illusions.

Decision and action came easily to him, perhaps because he saw the road ahead so clearly. But he retained the capacity to change his direction, if necessary, in a changing world of technology and social science.

I quoted the words of Tabori to my father, that greatness depends on the perfect cooperation of instinct and reason: "All human action is self-expression. Nobody can give something that is not within himself. . . . There are people in whom instinct and thought are completely merged: then we have a genius, a human being who can express his human qualities completely. This is possible only if a man does not use thought to cover his instincts but uses it rather for the most perfect expression." [10]

Such a man was John F. Kennedy.

[10] Paul Tabori, *The Natural Science of Stupidity* (New York, Chilton Company Book Division, 1959), pp. 3–4.

CHAPTER 17

The President-elect

On Thursday, November 10, 1960, two days after the election, President-elect Kennedy telephoned me from Hyannis Port and asked me to join him in Palm Beach. He would fly to Florida on the weekend. Would I come down on Monday? Thinking of my teaching schedule and my practice I hesitated before answering, "I'll try, Senator—I'll see what I can do."

"If you will stick by me, I will make you notorious," was his quick rejoinder. He won his point.

It was Tuesday, November 15, before I could get away. My patients had to be satisfied and their appointments changed without an explanation of my plans. Then, too, I was scheduled to lecture to our pharmacology class of second-year medical students at Cornell on Saturday morning, November 12, and again on Wednesday, November 16. I arranged to exchange my Wednesday lecture hour with someone else in the department and to fly Tuesday to West Palm Beach; I was due to arrive in ample time for lunch.

My plane was an hour late. Someone from the Kennedy household met it at the airport and I was soon settled in the back seat of a convertible car with the top down. The bright Florida sunshine, warm air, and semitropical flowers and foliage refreshed me after my flight from New York City's gray November. I was enjoying the ride immensely. The car picked up speed on the long bridge across Lake Worth and the wind whipped my hair into my eyes—that year I was letting my short bob grow out. I pulled a silk scarf out of my purse and fighting the wind I finally managed to tie it, pirate style, tight around my head.

When the car stopped at Mr. Joseph P. Kennedy's residence on North Ocean Boulevard, police patrols were parked in front and a crowd watched from across the street. The solid wooden door in the high stucco wall was shut. I made my first acquaintance with the Secret Service agents who checked all comers. Cleared to enter, I was scrutinized inside the door by another agent, who sat with a telephone beside him. Someone went ahead of me with my bags and I proceeded along the familiar cloistered walkway that suddenly now seemed unfriendly, different. At the end of the cloister I made the right-angle turn to the left, emerged into the open and climbed the few steps to the broad patio. There a long glass-topped table unexpectedly confronted me, around which a number of guests were seated for lunch. At its near end sat President-elect Kennedy.

I stood stock still and started to untie the scarf around my head. My baggage was disappearing into the house across the patio. The President-elect jumped up, shook my hand, and escorted me to the empty place at his right.

"Sit right down," he said. "We've been waiting lunch for you."

"I'm so sorry the plane was late," I apologized. "Perhaps I should go in and fix my hair—the wind blew it in the open car."

"No. no. You're fine," he insisted. "I want you to meet Governor Ribicoff."

Governor Abraham Ribicoff of Connecticut sat at my right. The conversation between him and his host continued from the point where it had been interrupted, while I tried to compose myself. I thought how my mother used to look at me when my dress was in disarray, shake her head and say, "Oh well, no one will notice on a galloping horse."

But now for the moment I had stopped galloping.

Everyone wore sports attire after what under ordinary circumstances might have been a lazy morning spent in and around the swimming pool. However, I surmised that Governor Ribicoff was there to discuss an appointment in the new cabinet, perhaps Secretary of Health, Education and Welfare. As the talk revolved around health and medicine I took part in the discussion and forgot both my confusion and my appearance.

After lunch I went upstairs to my room—I was given his mother's room —while the President-elect and the Governor conferred and then played a quick round of nine holes of golf. During the campaign, Senator Kennedy had not had time for golf for many weeks, and he was in fine spirits. On his return from the golf course he came up the stairs, paused to call to me in my room and ask if I had everything I wanted, and then he walked on to the end of the hall to his father's room, which he was occupying.

Soon I went downstairs with my camera in hand. I walked through the large living room and stood for a while by the pool just outside. No one was visible except the Secret Service sentries. I came inside and sat at a small desk in a corner of the living room opposite the piano and near the hall. I was busy writing a letter when the President-elect descended the circular staircase; he was wearing sport shirt, swimming trunks, and beach slippers. As he turned toward me on his way to the pool, he was intercepted by Evelyn, the executive maid.

"Telephone, sir," she said.

"I'll take it in the kitchen." Swiftly he crossed the hall and the dining room and he vanished through a swinging door to the kitchen. I knew that just inside those doors was a wall phone and in that part of the house it was his nearest telephone instrument. He used it often, perhaps because he preferred to stand for a brief conversation. Besides, he felt at home in the kitchen.

I resumed my writing. Almost at once Governor Ribicoff, in a business suit, came from the guest wing on the ground floor, crossed the living room, and set his suitcase in the hall. He stood there indecisively, then returned to the living room and leaned against the piano. He looked at his wristwatch.

"Do you know where the President is?" he asked me.

"Yes, he's in the kitchen telephoning."

The Governor glanced at his watch again. "What does one do, miss one's plane or leave without saying good-bye to the President?" He meditated on his dilemma, standing motionless and leaning back against the piano with one foot crossed in front of the other.

"I wouldn't do either. I'd go into the kitchen," I replied. "But he should be coming back soon, he had on his swimming trunks."

The Governor of Connecticut smiled a wry smile and said dryly, "How does one take leave of a President who is talking on the telephone and wearing swimming trunks?"

He made no move. The seconds ticked by, but he never shifted his position against the piano. I marveled at his balanced stance. The words popped out before I could check them, "You are one man who will never have ulcers."

He laughed, and at that moment the President-elect came out of the kitchen.

At that time Kennedy told the press that he would announce his first Cabinet appointment on December 1, and he did so from his Georgetown house in Washington; he named Governor Ribicoff Secretary of Health, Education and Welfare.

More than four years later, on March 3, 1965, when Abe Ribicoff was a United States Senator, I attended the unveiling of his portrait at a ceremony in the auditorium of the Department of Health, Education and Welfare. President Johnson told how one of his aides had asked him if he would speak at a hanging. "That depends on who is to be hung," he said. President Johnson was there to pay high tribute to Ribicoff's services to the country as Secretary of HEW.

Then Senator Ribicoff recounted the circumstances under which Kennedy had appointed him to the Cabinet on November 15, 1960, at Palm Beach. It was the first of the Cabinet appointments and he had been given his choice. When he asked for HEW, the President-elect was surprised. Kennedy enlarged on the complex responsibilities of that department and warned that its services concerned a greater number of Americans than any other governmental department. Senator Ribicoff quoted the President-elect as saying then, "That is one office in which you can never win."

Sitting in that auditorium I thought with nostalgia, "I was there." My mind raced back to that luncheon when we sat together on the patio in the midday sunshine and eagerly anticipated the future.

Senator Ribicoff looked down from the speaker's platform, paused in his remarks and as if by mental telepathy said, "Dr. Janet Travell is in the audience and she was there that day in Palm Beach. She told me then that I would never have ulcers. And," he added with a smile, "I never have."

Although he wore twenty different hats each day and ran 110 separate programs as Secretary of HEW, he said, he had not regretted his choice.

After Governor Ribicoff left the house on North Ocean Boulevard for the West Palm Beach Airport that momentous day in November, 1960, I went outdoors again and stood on the little patio beside the front lawn. The green of the grass had been yellowed by the salt spray of autumn storms, but the wind-bent trunks of the tall palms were changeless, as was the everlasting deep blue of the ocean beyond the white sea wall.

I found the President-elect passing a football with his brother, Teddy. He saw me standing near and with spontaneity unaltered by the election he asked me if I wanted a picture. I had hardly opened and set my camera when he exclaimed, "Get ready—here's one for the record!"

The President-elect started running toward me and my lens caught him in midair as he jumped with arms outstretched to receive the football that had been thrown ahead of him. He caught it cleanly. In 1961 I gave him a framed enlargement of that picture and he placed it proudly on his desk in the Executive Office of the White House.

I shared, too, in some events that John F. Kennedy could not control. A week after the November, 1960, election, the President-elect and I were sitting in his room in Palm Beach when the telephone beside him rang. He answered it. It was his father calling from Hyannis Port about the annual family reunion at Thanksgiving; they were expecting Jack in Hyannis Port the following weekend. Bobby and Teddy would be in Mexico. As the President-elect hung up the receiver, he said ruefully, "Why didn't someone tell me when Thanksgiving is! I can't go—appointments have been made here for my whole weekend and I can't change them." Circumstances did change them, however.

He looked at me dubiously. "I could pick up Jackie in Washington and we could fly to the Cape for Thanksgiving Day."

I could see how much he hated to disappoint his father and mother, and I knew also how precarious had been Jackie's pregnancies. I begged him not to consider such a trip for her. He toyed with the idea.

"The baby won't be due for another month. We would never be more than an hour away from a hospital—in Boston, or New York, or Washington," he argued, as much with himself as with me.

"It isn't that simple," I said. "There's the problem of the obstetrician—and a hospital room. The risks of such an emergency are too great. Besides, Jackie has confidence in Dr. Walsh."

"All right. I'll fly up and spend Thanksgiving with her and Caroline in Washington." Then he added, "I'll have to be back here that night. Can't you come down for the weekend? Fly to Washington Thursday afternoon and join me on the *Caroline.*" So it was arranged.

Later I wondered whether my fortuitous presence and protest that evening in Palm Beach might not have made a difference in John Jr.'s survival.

On that 1960 Thanksgiving Day, I was at Butler Aviation's Terminal in Washington in ample time to board the *Caroline,* the Kennedy's two-engined Convair. While waiting for the President-elect to arrive, I visited with Peter Lisagor, the only member of the White House Press Corps whom I knew personally. The *Caroline* was airborne after 8 P.M. for a smooth four-hour flight. Part of the time I sat in the forward lounge with Mrs. Evelyn Lincoln, and part of it I spent with the President-elect in his private compartment, where he worked and relaxed most of the way. Once or twice he walked back through the plane to speak with the "pool" of reporters. We landed at West Palm Beach well after midnight. As the plane neared the airfield, he had been alerted by radio that an important telephone message awaited him on the ground. While the landing steps of the Convair were being lowered the President-elect stood at the exit door, and as it opened he was handed a piece of paper. I stood behind him and he turned to me. He said tersely, "Come in the airport with me, Doctor—I'm going to phone. Jackie's gone to the hospital. I may need you."

The Secret Service agents made a path for him through the pushing crowd of exuberant well-wishers, whom he scarcely noticed, and I had to be agile to keep close to him. In the office of Mr. Woodward, the local Manager of Eastern Airlines, a telephone line was being held open and the President-elect spoke at once with a nurse in the Georgetown University Hospital. She was downstairs and did not know that his son had been born by cesarean section at 12:22 A.M., just as the *Caroline* was landing. He told me, "Jackie's in the operating room having the baby—I'm going back."

He spoke with the agents about his changing for the return flight to the chartered DC-6 press plane because it was faster than the *Caroline*. Then he said to me, "Doctor, I want you to go out to the house here. Bobby and Teddy are expecting me—you can be helpful to them."

I watched him walk onto the airstrip and mount the steps to the press plane that had left Washington after the *Caroline* and had landed before it. After momentary indecision I followed him. I squeezed myself along the crowded aisle to the forward compartment where he was sitting in an aisle seat. "Senator, are you sure that I couldn't help you in some way? I'd be glad to go back with you," I said.

"I think you can be helpful at the house. Come up to Washington tomorrow."

I made my way again slowly through the rear compartment and off the plane. In the commotion nobody paid any attention to me. I located my suitcase and I was lucky to find a late taxi.

The time was approaching 1 A.M. when my taxi stopped in front of Mr. Joseph P. Kennedy's home on North Ocean Boulevard. Unlike five years earlier, when I made my first middle of the night visit there, the street was brightly lighted. Now I knew the house well, but the Secret Service agent stationed outside did not know me. I explained who I was but my name was not on the list of those who had been expected with the President-elect. Now no door stood on the latch for me.

"Either Bob Kennedy or Ted Kennedy can vouch for me," I said patiently to the agent. "And you had better wake them up because they will be wakened soon anyway."

I simply would not go away. Finally, I heard a telephone ringing distantly within the house as the agent consulted with someone inside. Soon Teddy Kennedy came down the long cloistered walkway to the street entrance and he welcomed me warmly in spite of his surprised and sleepy look.

Inside the house, I explained what had happened as Teddy led me upstairs. He and Joan and Bobby and Ethel had been away in Acapulco, Mexico, on a vacation after the pressures of the campaign and the election. They were all awake now and they fired questions at me: "Do you know what hospital Jackie is in?" and "Do you know her obstetrician? Maybe you can reach him."

From my room, where we were sitting on the bed and chairs, I put in a call to the hospital, explained who and where I was, and I asked to be connected with the operating room. In a moment I was talking with Dr. John W. Walsh in the anteroom to the surgery. He told me that he had just completed the operation and that the baby boy weighed six pounds, three ounces. Mother and son were all right.

Teddy said that he would get a message to his brother Jack. It was shortly after one o'clock and he asked me if I knew what time the press plane had left West Palm Beach. I did not know, because I had not waited for its takeoff, but it was reported later that it departed at 12:50 A.M.

"Never mind," said Teddy, "I'll get a radio message through to him. I'll start at Palm Beach and work on up the line if the plane is out of range."

At 1:15 A.M. the message relayed from the West Palm Beach Airport reached the President-elect while he was flying north at thirteen thousand feet over the Florida coastline. The cheers that greeted the announcement over the plane's loudspeaker resounded around the world. It was the first child to be born to a President-elect. As the news was flashed, I thought of Paul Revere on his midnight ride.

By coincidence, I was on the scene for the birth of John F. Kennedy's three children, Caroline, John, and Patrick. I was in New York City when Caroline was born at the New York Hospital on the date elected for the necessary cesarean section, November 27, 1957. On that evening, in a blinding snowstorm I drove Senator Kennedy from his and Jackie's temporary apartment at 1035 Park Avenue in my new Mercury Turnpike Cruiser to see his wife and daughter in the hospital. During the ride he was fascinated by the back window that went up and down, electrically operated—then an innovation in car design. I met him with the Auchinclosses at the New York Hospital the following afternoon, Thanksgiving Day.

On August 7, 1963, when Jackie went by helicopter from their summer house on Squaw Island in Hyannis Port to Otis Air Force Hospital for the premature birth of Patrick, she asked me to remain at the house to take telephone calls and relay the news. I was the person to give President Kennedy, who was at the White House, first-hand information about the events that transpired at the hospital.

That November 25, 1960, when John Jr. was born, the remnant at the Kennedy villa in Palm Beach prepared to leave. The Secret Service detail, leftover staff, and reporters and I obtained seats on a Northeast Airlines flight that made a special stop for us in West Palm Beach and that landed at Washington's National Airport early in the evening. I wrote our daughter Virginia Street from the plane that when I boarded it my hair was still damp from a late-afternoon swim in the ocean and that I dangled a wet suit in my bathing cap from one finger. I told her, "Otherwise, I'm decorum itself. . . ." The President-elect's golf clubs and several suitcases packed with his clothing were checked on my ticket, since he had invited me to spend the night at his Georgetown home. His long-time chauffeur Muggsey met me. Muggsey drove out onto the airstrip beside the plane so that things could be loaded without delay directly into the station wagon. Alas, one bag could not be found to match the baggage checks that I held. I had little or no idea what the President-elect's luggage looked like. In the darkness of the airfield, the airline personnel spread all the contents of the hold out on the ground under the plane's wings while they and Muggsey and Secret Service men went from piece to piece with flashlights, examining the stubs. Finally, one suitcase was located from which the baggage check had been torn off and that proved to be the missing number.

I arrived at 3307 "N" Street in Northwest Washington at about 9 P.M. AND THE HOUSE WAS SILENT. The night before, the President-elect had been up nearly all night. It was after 4 A.M. when he had seen Jackie and glimpsed the baby briefly at the hospital. It was 4:35 A.M. when from the sidewalk of his home he had given the press his son's name, "John F. Kennedy, Jr." I thought that he might have gone to sleep early, but he was reading in his room. He seemed glad to see me. He talked about how the baby was doing in the incubator and I gave him news of his family in Palm Beach.

As I was leaving for my room a half flight down at the rear, he said, "Would you like to see the baby? Ride with me to the hospital in the morning."

Fame was born to me as an unwanted child on that Saturday, November 26, 1960, when I went with President-elect Kennedy to the Georgetown University Hospital to see his day-old son. I was practically unknown to the press when he and I and Pierre Salinger stepped through the front doorway of his home into a blaze of photographic fire. Police, reporters, and Secret

Service men filled the street and spectators spilled off the crowded side-walks. For a moment the President-elect stood and smiled at the top of the steps before we started for the waiting car. I hastily looked down at my feet, and the floppy brim of a black velvet hat hid my eyes. That Associated Press Wirephoto of us together alerted the public to an unrecognized role that I had played on the medical scene. In the New York *Sunday News* of November 27, 1960, Robert Thompson reported: "Accompanying Kennedy to the hospital . . . was his personal physician and long time friend, Dr. Janet Travell of New York."

The President-elect marched me along with him through the hospital corridors, which were lined with photographers, visitors, nurses, and other members of the hospital staff. While he disappeared into his wife's room, I saw baby John Jr. kicking in his incubator and I chatted with the pediatricians. I believe that I was the third caller to visit John Jr. in the hospital nursery, after his father and his grandmother, Mrs. Auchincloss.

It occurred to me months later that the President-elect had wanted to observe my reactions to the limelight of publicity, as well as to give me the pleasure of seeing the baby. He would have fully anticipated that his invitation to ride with him to the Georgetown University Hospital would project my name before the public.

Earlier in November, during my twenty-four hours in Palm Beach a week after the election, I had tried to elude a similar exposure. On the afternoon of November 16, my return flight to New York was due to leave soon after his flight to the LBJ Ranch in Texas. He asked me to ride in his car from his father's house on North Ocean Boulevard to the "West Palm" airport. It was a slow triumphal drive for him and for me it was the first motorcade view of those cheering crowds that always stood waiting patiently for him to pass. We drove through a gate onto the airstrip close to his chartered jet. As he got out on the right side of the car and faced the cameras, I opened the left rear door and ducked out on that side. I turned and walked quickly away. Just when I thought that I had concealed myself among the people who were gathered inside the airfield's wire fence, the reporters and the President-elect were upon me. Smiling mischievously, he drew me out of the crowd and took my arm. "I wondered what happened to you. I didn't tell you good-bye," he said.

Still holding my arm, he walked with me back to the steps of his plane while the photographers, snapping pictures, ran backward in front of us. As he mounted the steps with the pack concentrated on him, I walked hastily toward the terminal building and secluded myself behind a parked flight of landing steps within the airfield fence. Out of sight I sat on the bottom step to wait for the departure of his jet. A reporter appeared from around the corner and asked, pad in hand, "Why did Mr. Kennedy go over and pick you out of the crowd?"

"I rode over with him to the airport," I said ambiguously.

"I didn't see you. Where did you get in his car?"

"At the house," I said truthfully.

"What were you doing at the house?"

"I was staying there."

"Why were you there? How long were you there?"

"I was a house guest."

"Oh yes? Who *are* you?"

"I'm a friend of the family." That was a true statement, too.

"How long have you known the Kennedys?"

"Several years."

"What's your name?"

"Powell. Mrs. Powell," I answered promptly.

"You're from Boston?"

"No, New York."

The reporter turned away in disbelief and disgust, with the parting shot, "Well, all I can say is, you must be a *very* good friend of the family."

I thought how my father had a way of telling the truth so that sometimes nobody believed him. An account of my presence with "Senator" Kennedy at the airport that day was, to my knowledge, never printed. The press corps went along with him to Texas and they had ample copy there.

Back within the solid shelter of his Georgetown house after visiting John Jr. in the hospital, I told the President-elect how much I appreciated his taking me with him to see the baby. "And I should go on to New York now. You don't need me here and I will only be underfoot."

He would not hear of my leaving. "Stay another night, Doctor. You were expecting to spend this weekend in Florida so you don't have anything else planned."

Mrs. Lincoln came to work at the house that morning, and she and I ate lunch together, served on trays upstairs while the President-elect had guests in the dining room. When she had gone home, I sat at the electric typewriter, which had the familiar Kennedy blue ribbon, and wrote a note to our daughter Virginia Street in Nashville, Tennessee: "Caroline here is just three. . . . I told Caroline that I had heard she had a baby brother. She replied, 'I don't have him yet.' She has a 'hot rod,' as she calls it, that she rides around the hall, living room and dining room. It has a motor in it that responds to the foot pedals. She was wearing overalls, and is just like other little tomboys of the same age."

When the dining room was emptied of luncheon guests, I went through it into the garden, which was enclosed by a high board fence. A wooden door opened onto an alley at the rear. I talked with the Secret Service agent in the garden and learned that I could walk to the street unobserved by way of the narrow alley, which turned a corner to the left. By a devious route, I reached Wisconsin Avenue and paused in the Georgetown Pharmacy at the corner of "O" Street. There I bought a copy of the Washington *Evening Star*. I was startled to see my picture with President-elect Kennedy on the front page. Georgetown was quaint but crowded and noisy, I thought. Sightseers in cars and buses wanted to drive through "N" Street past the Kennedy residence and traffic was stalled. I did not imagine that before the summer a house five doors down the block would become my home, that our car would be parked every night in the same alley and that my husband and I would breakfast and dine in our own little garden beneath one of the biggest trees in that part of town. It was the tree-shaded alley that won us to Georgetown; mockingbirds sang there early in the morning.

Before dinner, President-elect Kennedy and I settled in his living room with a large supply of the day's newspapers. We were alone. Dinner was served to us there on trays. I sat on the sofa with a low coffee table in front of me. A telephone on a small table beside his armchair demanded so much of his attention that I thought he could not enjoy the delicious meal. I told him that anyone would get indigestion talking and eating at once like that. I persuaded George Thomas, his valet, to set the instrument on the floor behind his chair as far away as the cord would allow and to switch the calls to the pantry until dinner was over. Later I asked George how he made out with my telephone ruse after I had gone, and he said, "Not so good."

On an inside page of the *Evening Star* I noticed a report of a speech that Senator Barry Goldwater had made the day before at the annual meeting of the National Interfraternity Conference in Los Angeles. I started reading the news item aloud: "In his speech he called the fraternity system 'a bastion of American strength.' . . . Senator Goldwater . . . says that 'where fraternities are not allowed, Communism flourishes.' " The President-elect located the Associated Press article next to Jackie's picture on page A-3 and he quickly scanned it. It went on: "He [Senator Goldwater] singled out Harvard University yesterday as a seat of learning which, he said, is a non-fraternity institution which permits Communist and Socialist philosophies to breed what he called a faithless generation. . . . There was no immediate comment at Harvard University."

The President-elect sighed. "He's such a likable man—if only he didn't have such strange ideas." Senator Kennedy had introduced him to me the year before and we shared a warm regard for Barry Goldwater, the man.

During 1960, as a member of the Scientific Advisory Committee of the

Joseph P. Kennedy Jr. Foundation, of which Jack Kennedy was a director, I had made several trips in connection with the foundation's research grants to alleviate mental retardation. Until that evening at his home, I had not had an opportunity to tell him my impressions of those visits to medical centers, which were advancing basic research in the causes of mental retardation. I was always amazed at his ability to penetrate to the heart of a complex scientific problem and to frame precisely the essential question that had been skirted in discussion.

He turned to another subject close to his heart, the great need in America for medical insurance that was prepaid under Social Security because most people did not have the foresight or, more often, the ability to provide that protection for themselves. He believed absolutely in the individual's right of free choice of a physician.

"I will tell you one thing," he said with a sideways look at me, "I do not intend to change my doctors."

That was his first direct expression to me of his intent concerning his own medical care during the Presidency.

"We will always do everything we can for you, Senator," I replied.

He had been playing golf regularly in Palm Beach and he had played again that Saturday afternoon at the Burning Tree Club. Earlier in the day, I had seen him lift Caroline and carry her piggyback on his shoulders around the "N" Street house. We spoke about how well his back had withstood the strains of his campaign travel—standing endlessly, sitting in utilitarian folding chairs, speaking and parading in all weathers, shaking hands constantly, sleeping short hours in all shapes of beds, and eating at irregular times. Paraphrasing the adage "It's not the work but the worry," he remarked, "It wasn't the work, it was those chicken dinners!"

The ten days in Palm Beach since election had rested him. He had been underweight. With the benefits of health-giving Florida sunshine, a regular routine in one location, food prepared to his taste, and the free-moving exercise of golf and swimming, he soon regained the lost pounds. His stamina, like his back, had not been impaired by the wear and tear of campaigning. Dr. Eugene J. Cohen had flown with me from New York to Palm Beach on November 15, and he, too, had been pleased then by the President-elect's general health.

On November 26, that Saturday when the "Senator" and I were having dinner at his home in Washington, he had no urgent medical problem, but he mentioned a discomfort that he was having in his right shoulder. He blamed it on all the handshaking, although he took special care to avoid such strain. When he stood in a receiving line he had a way of using his right and left hands alternately that spared the right arm and gave it a momentary pause to relax between handshakes. Tentatively I suggested that when he shot the deer at the LBJ Ranch the week before, the gun might have kicked him in the shoulder, but he pooh-poohed that explanation. Whatever the cause, it got better with simple conservative treatment. Nevertheless, in 1961, 1962, and 1963, as the opening of the baseball season approached, in pursuit of excellence he asked me to check the condition of his right shoulder muscles a few days before he was to throw out the first ball at the opening game between the Washington Senators and the visiting American League team.

Before I left Washington the next morning, President-elect Kennedy said, "Doctor, you were cheated out of your time in Florida. You should come back for a rest this weekend. We'll make it this trip."

On Friday evening, December 2, I joined him again on the *Caroline*. When we landed at the West Palm Beach Airport, in the light of television floodlamps and camera flashbulbs the real Caroline held the spotlight as she descended the plane's steps with her "Daddy." Stephen and Jean Kennedy Smith had also accompanied him on the flight. Without attracting attention, I rode to the Kennedy home in another waiting car.

On Saturday morning, December 3, I was at the "Temporary White House" by the ocean when the second appointment to the new Cabinet was announced: Governor Luther H. Hodges of North Carolina was named Secretary of Commerce. It gave me special pleasure to be there because he was an old friend of ours and a classmate of my husband's at the University of North Carolina, Class of 1919. Storms were sweeping the Eastern Seaboard and Governor Hodges had taken a sleeper to Palm Beach Friday night to avoid the uncertainties of flying in bad weather. On the train he read a letter from my husband that had reached him just before he left the Governor's Mansion in Raleigh. Rumors of his Cabinet appointment had appeared in the newspapers and the letter told him of my whereabouts.

I had had a breakfast tray upstairs so that I would not encounter the reporters and photographers who had assembled early, but the Governor's train was quite late. I was in my room on the second floor—Mrs. Rose Kennedy's room—when I heard the President-elect calling, "Doctor, Doctor, come quickly, come quickly!" As he spoke, he was running up the steps of the circular staircase.

Dressed in a long Hawaiian muumuu, and barefoot, I dashed into the hall, disturbed to know what could be wrong.

"Come right away—a friend of yours is here."

I followed him, as I was, down the stairs and through the long dining room. At its far end Luther Hodges stepped from the library to give me a warm greeting while the President-elect stood by, beaming. Then they

retired to the study to confer on the business at hand. The informality of
that "White House" household behind the scenes and the gaiety of the
President-elect's outlook during those days of crucial decisions were typ-
ified by that meeting.

Later in the morning, a press conference was held on the outdoor patio
under a gray sky. The *Miami News* of December 3 reported the event:
"The two leaders conferred for about 25 minutes before they walked out
onto the patio and Kennedy made his announcement. Green fronds of a
coconut palm thrashed overhead in a high wind blowing off the white-
capped sea as the two men stood beneath the tree in a semitropical setting
and spoke of another major step in the formation of the new administration. Threatening clouds scudded overhead but rain, which had been intermittent earlier in the morning, held off for the impromptu ceremony."

High above the microphones and television cameras and alongside that
noisy patio palm was a second-floor recessed balcony; its railing and iron-
work grill were twined with vines. From there Jean Kennedy Smith and I
together heard the President-elect's formal announcement and the reply of
the future Secretary of Commerce as they appeared in business suits and
spoke with deep concern about the economy of the nation. Jean was standing and leaning out over the railing to hear and see better, while I knelt on
the cement floor of the balcony and peeked through the large green leaves.
As the wide-ranging discussion continued, I grew tired of kneeling and I
settled gradually until I was lying on the balcony floor with my chin
propped on one hand and my face against the leafy screen.

After the press conference I put on my bathing suit and made my way
across the front lawn, on the other side of the house from the patio. A
Secret Service agent opened the locked door in the seawall for me so that I
could swim in the ocean. I did not feel alone under the watchful eye of the
outpost at the top of the massive wall. The air was cold, in the upper sixties,
and the water was warm by comparison. The surf was rough, but beyond the
breakers the rhythmic lift of the swells was as exhilarating as a ride on a
cantering horse. "Seas up to 12 feet in the Gulfstream," the *Miami News*
reported that day. Returning to the house I met Governor Hodges still in his
business suit and standing a short distance from the pool where Caroline
and her father and others were in swimming.

"What's the matter, Luther?" I asked. "Don't you want to swim?"

"I don't care much for pools, Bobby," he answered. "How do you get
to the ocean from here?"

Quickly he put on his bathing trunks in a downstairs guest room while I
waited in the wind in my wet suit. I escorted him down the steps in the great
seawall and onto the sandy beach. I pointed out where the underwater

rocks were located. Out beyond the breakers together we bobbed up and down riding the choppy waves and we talked as fast as two old school pals for about forty-five minutes. In two weeks I would be fifty-nine and Luther Hodges was sixty-two. We were the oldest representatives of the New Frontier there that day.

The President-elect loved to swim in the ocean, but he went in the pool with Caroline; she greatly missed her mother, who was still in the hospital.

On December 4, I wrote our daughter Virginia: "The sea at sunset is particularly grand. The sky lends color to the spray off the breakers and to the palm fronds. I just came in from a late swim in the surf. . . . I have become Caroline's special playmate. She comes to my room, tries on my jewelry, powders her nose—her father calls her 'Button Nose Kennedy.' " Later it became just "Buttons," but then I thought sympathetically of my own upturned nose, which I had so disliked when I was the same age as Caroline.

Saturday night, after Governor Hodges's appointment and his departure, President-elect Kennedy, Steve and Jean Smith, Mr. and Mrs. Earl E. T. Smith, Senator George Smathers, and I dined in the long dining room. There was lighthearted banter in retrospect about the recent campaign in various parts of the country. The conversation turned gaily to future events. Kennedy was to meet President Eisenhower at the White House on the coming Tuesday, December 6. An honor guard and fanfare would be staged as a ceremonious welcome for him. Someone suggested that Jack should hold a rehearsal. Quickly he rose from his seat at the head of the table and with mock solemnity took up a position at the end of the room.

"Let's see," he deliberated. "I'll be wearing my hat when I drive up to the north entrance of the White House. No, I'll be carrying my hat in my left hand. I'll go up the steps and he'll be waiting for me at the top. He'll say to me, 'Good morning, Mr. Kee-nedy.' "

The President-elect paused and in an aside to his appreciative small audience he said plaintively, "Why does he always call me Kee-nedy?"

He went on with the rehearsal, gesturing in his most dignified manner. "I'll hold my hat at my side. I'll bow a little, we'll shake hands and I'll say to him, 'Good morning, Mr. Eee-senhower.' "

His sense of the comical never failed him when the time was right for it.

The rollicking mood of the evening continued as we gathered outdoors for a movie. The patio that was the scene of the morning's press conference held a huge screen against the far wall of the house. Facing it, comfortable chairs and chaises occupied the place of the microphones and cameras.

Under the brilliant stars and to the steady accompaniment of the breaking surf, we watched the great ocean in action in a Navy tale about *The Wackiest Ship in the Army.*

Sunday and Monday, the next two days, were so beautiful that they should have warmed the hearts of every Floridian. I did not know it then, but on Sunday, December 4, President-elect Kennedy telephoned Dean Rusk at a conference in Williamsburg. On December 8 in Washington, he met for the first time both Dean Rusk and Robert S. McNamara and the following week he announced their respective appointments as Secretary of State and Secretary of Defense. The selection of his Cabinet was completed on December 17 when he designated J. Edward Day as Postmaster General.

Before we left Palm Beach on the *Caroline* at about 6 P.M. that Monday, December 5, while we were sitting by the pool in a quiet moment the President-elect abruptly said to me, "I don't know what the medical setup is at the White House—maybe I won't even need a full-time physician. You could come down from New York every week or so to see me, Doctor. You don't want to spend all your time looking down people's throats at their tonsils, do you?"

"I will do whatever seems best for you, Senator."

"Well, I shall have to wait until I get to Washington," he said thoughtfully.

I never raised a question about any plan that he might have for me when he became President. He had weightier and more urgent matters to decide concerning his new administration's arsenal of personnel and policies. I would have to make my own decisions.

On December 7, back in New York, I wrote to the National Board of Medical Examiners, of which I was a Diplomate, requesting the necessary application forms for certification of licensure in the District of Columbia. It was clear to me that under any circumstances I would need a D.C. license. As it was, if I became involved in a patient's care outside of New York State, where I was licensed to practice medicine, I functioned as a consultant through the courtesy of the local physicians. I had followed that accepted procedure even in foreign countries. But such a consultation basis would not serve should the President wish me to assume the responsibility for his medical care. I did not believe that I would quit New York and move to Washington, but I concluded that I should become a part of the District of Columbia's medical community.

On December 20, the National Board of Medical Examiners replied and instructed me to write to the District of Columbia for the application forms. The letter reached me on December 27 with the Christmas mail. I learned that the District would request from the National Board office a transcript of my grades, also the questions asked me in the basic sciences (Part I of those examinations taken in 1928), and my answers, if available. If they did not show a satisfactory knowledge of the basic sciences, the District could refuse licensure. That did not worry me because I knew that I had taken "honors" in Part I of those countrywide tests. With the help of Peggy Freund, my secretary at the Medical College, I managed to assemble promptly the necessary data about my education and medical career: a transcript of my Cornell University medical-school grades for four years, certification of my two-year internship by the New York Hospital, curriculum vitae, bibliography, two endorsements of moral character (with establishment of the high professional character of my endorsers), and a covering letter from the Chairman of the Department of Medicine of the New York Hospital–Cornell Medical Center. On January 9, all these were ready, together with the completed D.C. application form, my check, and a recent photograph, postcard size. Without the knowledge of the President-elect I obtained my D.C. medical license in my own right.

I got it done just in time. On January 11, partly to satisfy the Secret Service, I met President-elect Kennedy at his suite in the Carlyle Hotel in New York and I went with him again on the *Caroline* to Palm Beach, to remain there until we returned to Washington on Tuesday, January 17, for the Inaugural events. That time I stayed at the Palm Beach Towers. At the invitation of the President-elect my husband came from New York to join me. I did not see New York again until late on January 23. Then I spent one day in my 9 West 16th Street office before I flew back to Washington to continue in the role that I had already been playing unannounced for a long time.

The heaviest load of my teaching duties at the medical school fortunately came in the first trimester of the school year and that ended well before Christmas. Decisions concerning future professional commitments to speak at meetings were deferred. In November and December, 1960, I was faced with the dilemma of adequately caring for my patients while silently allowing my schedule to be disrupted by the top priority of the President-elect. After that Thanksgiving weekend I instructed my office secretary not to accept new patients until the middle of February, 1961. I declared a two months' vacation for myself. Our daughters were coming for Christmas, then we were going to Florida in January and to Washington for Inauguration week. The Associated Press picture of me with President-elect Kennedy on the steps of his Georgetown house the day after Thanksgiving surprised my patients but it explained my absences from the office. My referred type of practice simplified the continuation of my patients' care since they had their own physicians. Before I left for Palm Beach in January, I was able to find a solution for most of the acute medical problems that had brought them to me.

On Saturday, January 21, 1961, I was perhaps the President's first appointment in the Executive Office in the White House. On the flight from Palm Beach in the *Caroline* earlier in the week, he had asked me to see him in his office "the first thing the morning after Inauguration." I inquired what time he wished me to be there.

"Eight o'clock," he said.

I was dubious about that early hour after the late Inaugural Balls on Friday night, but he was there. We stood in the center of the Oval Office in the West Wing of the White House and we talked briefly about Jackie and the bitter cold weather. Then he said, "I would like very much to have you here, Doctor. Would you be happy?"

"Yes, I would. I never was afraid of change."

"What would Mr. Powell do? Would he like to live in Washington?" His concern for my husband's interests and for our joint happiness was characteristic.

"We have discussed it. My husband has always liked Washington. He could carry on his business easily from here."

"You could finish your medical book." He smiled broadly. He knew how busy I had been and how little progress I was making with it. "Fine. We will look into it and see what the situation is. Come back on Monday morning, Doctor."

Although I had tried to anticipate the improbable event that I would move to Washington, it was not easy to leave my appreciative patients and to close my office on short notice when on Monday, January 23, I received my White House appointment from President Kennedy in the Executive Office.

We had gone a long way on the journey that we started together in May, 1955.

CHAPTER 18

He Had
a Rendezvous

President Kennedy was a master of the economy of time. He made every second count. He moved fast. When he walked, I had to trot to keep up with his long stride. He knew how to end a conversation or a conference. In his Senate office, beside the desks of his staff there were no chairs for visitors; that discouraged tarrying. In the Executive Office at the White House, the President would sometimes rise from behind his desk to greet a caller and then stand in the center of the circular room while they talked, drifting slowly toward the paneled exit door. Suddenly the door would open, the President extended his hand and the visitor was outside the room. In the days when he was a Senator, he kept handy a card for long-winded friends that he could produce and lay silently in their line of vision; on it was written one word, SCRAM. He had little time in proportion to his goals.

President Kennedy appreciated the value of time more than any other person I ever knew, and he saved many precious moments in order to spend them wisely on play and relaxation. Time was not wasted when he wound up a toy for John or ran to a second-floor window with Caroline to watch the "Big Bird," the helicopter, alight on the south lawn of the White House. He considered a daily swim in the White House pool essential to his health. His train of intense thought paused momentarily while he listened to music, watched a movie or a play, or read poetry.

On October 26, 1963, President Kennedy expressed his need, and that of the human race, for renewal of the spirit through the arts when he said at Amherst College: "When power leads man towards arrogance, poetry reminds him of his limitations. When power narrows the areas of man's concern, poetry reminds him of the richness and diversity of his existence. When power corrupts, poetry cleanses. For art establishes the basic human truth which must serve as the touchstone of our judgment."

Within an incredibly short span of time after that address at Amherst College, I heard Fredric March read from the late President Kennedy's favorite poems, which had been selected by his widow. One was Alan Seeger's "I Have a Rendezvous with Death":

> It may be he shall take my hand
> And lead me into his dark land
> And close my eyes and quench my breath—
> It may be I shall pass him still.
> I have a rendezvous with Death
> On some scarred slope of battered hill.
>
> . . .
>
> And I to my pledged word am true,
> I shall not fail that rendezvous.

In retrospect, those haunting lines might be construed to have held a sinister meaning in the mind of our youngest President, then in the prime years of his life. But he had met death face to face so often that he accepted without dread the prospect of dying on any day—today, tomorrow, a year from tomorrow. With both fatalism and optimism President Kennedy anticipated his own death.

In his 1960 campaign speeches, Senator Kennedy quoted more than once words that he attributed to Abraham Lincoln a hundred years earlier during *his* 1860 campaign for the Presidency:

> I know there is a God
> And that he hates injustice.
> I see the storm coming,
> And I know that His hand is in it.
> If He has a place and a part for me,
> I believe that I am ready.

When John F. Kennedy took the oath of office on January 20, 1961, he was the thirty-fourth man to become President of the United States. Of the thirty-three men who achieved the Presidency before him, three were killed by assassins' bullets while in office. A fanatic wounded Theodore Roosevelt with a shot in the chest when he was no longer President and was campaigning for reelection. Many other attempts to assassinate the President of the United States have failed. Four Presidents died in office because of illness and one, Woodrow Wilson, became seriously disabled by a stroke during his second term but lived several years afterward.

Thus, when Senator Kennedy became President-elect in November, 1960, eight of the thirty-three men who preceded him, or approximately one of every four Presidents, had been fatally stricken during the Presidency. President-elect Kennedy knew well the high mortality rate for Presidents of the United States.

I had not given the hazard of assassination much thought until I flew from New York to Palm Beach on Tuesday, November 15, 1960, one week after Election Day. Then I saw the changes that the Secret Service had made in the Kennedys' ocean-front home since my last visit there.

I occupied Mrs. Rose Kennedy's gracious room on the second floor of the house. Its French doors opened onto an uncovered balcony that overlooked the lawn, the seawall, and the first line of surf, where it broke far out on a sandbar. The balcony was nearly level with the tops of the leaning palms, and from it I surveyed the intrusions that had been wrought to assure the security of the President-elect. Partly screened by shrubbery, a sentry was stationed at the south end of the seawall. A telephone instrument was installed on the wall close beside him. Black telephone cables extended across the lawn of Bermuda grass, wound around the sides of the house and down the flight of steps to the now closed and locked door in the massive retaining wall. The sandy beach could be reached from the house only through that doorway.

But the palms brought home to me most vividly the power of the Secret Service and the essential need for protection by that agency. The graceful fronds that had hung from the crown of each tree had been lopped off, and only a small cluster stood up stiff and straight at the center. The surviving fronds reminded me of the worn-out feathers of an old duster, and the long, curved tree trunk, of its warped handle. The desecration of beauty was all the more conspicuous against the backdrop of full-topped palms on the neighboring estate to the south beyond the high dividing wall. The ancient trees that had been bent by ocean gales were easy to climb; a child could run halfway up them. Now, no man could hide in their tops and peer into the upstairs rooms. The skeleton palms testified to the peril in which the President of the United States lives.

At that point in time, John F. Kennedy must have felt the force of that danger with heightened awareness. One afternoon in November while we sat by the pool under a sunlit Florida sky, he asked me abruptly, "What do you think of the rule that for the last hundred years every President of the United States elected in a year divisible by twenty died in office?"

I replied that I did not know about the rule.

Quickly he named the Presidents and the years of their election, "William H. Harrison 1840, Lincoln 1860, Garfield 1880, McKinley 1900, Harding 1920, and Roosevelt 1940."

"You don't really believe such a coincidence can continue," I protested. "The odds against it are too great, and you are not superstitious."

He looked at me quizzically, silently.

Fantastically improbable, that twenty-year historical rule held true in 1960 for the seventh time. Astrologers might say that our youngest President had lived under a bizarre and threatening combination of the stars.

Those were lonely days of decision for the President-elect at the "Temporary White House" in Palm Beach. He made brief trips to see Jackie, who remained in Washington awaiting the arrival of the baby on Thanksgiving Day. In December, while she and John Jr. were still there in the Georgetown University Hospital, I traveled with the President-elect and his staff on the Kennedy family plane, the *Caroline,* back to Palm Beach. Again I stayed at his father's home on North Ocean Boulevard.

One evening, we were discussing some practical aspects of his health, in particular, the wisdom of having a physician travel with him constantly after his inauguration as President. He questioned whether that would be a necessary routine and strongly resisted the idea. Senator Kennedy as candidate had not felt the need for such medical protection during the recent rigorous campaigning, and there was no law that required it for the President.

I argued that the American people wanted their President to have that kind of health insurance, even though it was never used. I predicted that the political implications of past illness, an issue that had arisen during his campaign, would no longer be pertinent when he ran for a second term. The excellence of his health record as President would have put to rest any doubt concerning it four years hence.

My prediction proved correct. During his one thousand days as President, he missed one full day, June 22, 1961, from his office on account of an acute infectious illness. Earlier that month following his European trip, on crutches once more, he had gone to Palm Beach for a long weekend to recuperate from the low back strain incurred in the tree planting ceremony at Ottawa on May 16, 1961. During his slow recovery from that new injury, he carried on "business as usual" at the White House. At the time of his death, his health was at optimal efficiency for the performance of the functions of the Presidency.

But when we talked that evening in December, 1960, his mood was quite different. The time was about ten o'clock, and the glow of two small table lamps illuminated his father's corner room on the second floor, where we were sitting. He had moved upstairs from his own familiar bedroom on the ground floor. The front casement window that overlooked the lawn and Secret Service posts was curtained by closed drapes. The other casement window was wide open and it framed a panorama of stars. The night air was still, and the sound of the surf filled the room. Without speaking, he gazed for a long time through the open window to the horizon beyond the sea. Then he said, as if to himself, "Why should I worry about a second term? My wife will have a pension and my children will be well cared for."

The impact of his words echoed through the cliffs and valleys of my mind. There by the rhythmic ocean, in the absence of his wife and in the face of great new responsibilities, the young President-elect expressed a passing tide of melancholy. Or did there remain deep in his mind a current of conviction that he would not survive the Presidency? If so, it did not deter him from action but rather, it drove him.

Jacqueline Kennedy said, "The poignancy of men dying young always moved my husband." Kennedy himself wrote about his older brother Joe that "his life, though denied its future promise, had . . . the completeness of perfection," and he cited Solomon: "Having fulfilled his course in a short time, he fulfilled long years." [1]

Meditating on those events, after November 22, 1963, I wrote a sonnet that I like to think might have made President Kennedy smile:

A LONG LIFE SPAN
IS NOT SYNONYMOUS WITH GREATNESS

A great white bear, monarch of polar ice,
Lithe in life, sniffs the frozen air. The stain
Of his heart's blood spreads red where he is slain
By hunters' bullets. There his length they slice
While huskies wait first share and men cast dice
To see whose romping children will have lain
Upon the great bearskin. Aged bears strain
Against disdain, slide away under ice.

Magnificent tall timber in its prime
Is cut and crashes down with rending sound,
To be preserved in human homes and hearts.
An old tree ages, falls, rots in the slime
Of putrid swamp, a soft forgotten mound.
In years great, greatness with decay departs.

[1] Theodore C. Sorensen, *Kennedy* (New York, Harper & Row, 1965), p. 751.

At the Warren Commission's hearings, Kenneth O'Donnell told how President Kennedy happened to say on the morning of his death, "If anybody really wanted to shoot the President of the United States . . . all one had to do was get a high building some day with a telescopic rifle, and there was nothing anybody could do to defend against such an attempt on the President's life." [2] Kennedy had often spoken casually of how easy it would be to kill the President if a demented person were willing to sacrifice his own life to accomplish it. In the setting of violence and agitation that were then at their peak in Dallas, President Kennedy's description of the precise mode of his own death a few hours later followed logically from the discussion of the functions of the Secret Service on such a trip. His remark need not to be interpreted as a premonition of death on that particular day.

The shadow of death hung over Jack Kennedy all his life, said Cardinal Cushing of Boston. As President, he knew the precariousness of life because of the frequent encounters that he had had with death, and his disregard of personal danger stemmed in part from that knowledge. Once, unexpectedly, I had occasion to see that shadow in his eyes.

On a Saturday in March, 1961, the President asked me to go to Glen Ora with him the next morning after church.

"Shall I meet you at the church or at the White House?" I asked.

"Meet me at the bridge under the golden lions," was his enigmatic reply.

The golden lions turned out to be the gilded statues of rearing horses on high pedestals at the entrance to the Arlington Memorial Bridge by the Lincoln Memorial. At the estimated time of his arrival there, I waited in a White House car that was parked on the Lincoln Memorial Circle where he would pass. My driver sat half turned so that he could see the Presidential and Secret Service cars as they approached.

"Here they come!" he said as he put our car into motion. We were gaining momentum to fall in line behind the President's car when it suddenly braked and stopped short just in front of us. An agent jumped out and ran back to me.

"Dr. Travell, the President wants you to ride with him."

President Kennedy was alone in the back. I sat at his left. He was reading the Sunday newspapers and he offered me one. He continued to read, but I was more preoccupied with the two-lane high-crowned road and the slow-moving Sunday traffic than I was with the news. At one point, the Secret Service lead car passed a sedan that was going in our direction, but the President's car had to drop back in line and could not pass because of

[2] *The Witnesses,* compiled by the Editors of *The New York Times* (New York, McGraw-Hill, Inc., 1965), pp. 81–82.

oncoming traffic. I observed the people in the sedan a few feet ahead of us; a boy on the back seat was holding a rather large motion-picture camera against the back window, and its lens pointed at the President.

At the slowing of our speed, the President glanced up from his newspaper directly into the eye of the camera. Instantly his muscles tensed.

"It's only a child with a movie camera," I said.

He took a deep breath and said, as he resumed reading, "I will not live in fear. What will be, must be."

Thomas F. Pendel, who served as Door-Keeper at the White House for more than thirty-six years, from November, 1864, during the Civil War, when Lincoln was President, until September, 1901, when McKinley was shot and Theodore Roosevelt became President, wrote in simple words of wisdom:

> The first Sabbath . . . we were on duty at the White House, we were in a little waiting room on the right-hand side of the stairs. . . . This was a favorite stairway of Mr. Lincoln's. . . . When Mr. Lincoln came into the room he said, "Which one of you gentlemen will take a walk with me as far as Secretary Stanton's house?" . . . I immediately arose and said, "Mr. President, I will walk with you." . . . After we had passed out of the front door and were still on the main portico, but out of the hearing of any one, the President said to me, "I have received a great many threatening letters, but I have no fear of them." I said, "Mr. President, *because a man does not fear a thing is no reason why it should not occur.*" [Italics mine.] He replied, "That is a fact."
>
> After we got off the portico, going east, I said, "Mr. President, *there has been many a good, brave man who has lost his life simply because he did not fear.*" [Italics mine.] Then he remarked in a thoughtful way, "That is so; that is so." [3]

Pendel helped with the White House funeral arrangements of three assassinated Presidents, Lincoln, Garfield, and McKinley. He described the grief of the nation's First Lady—Mrs. Garfield—which could not be assuaged; [4] and the lamentation of the throngs who came to honor murdered President Lincoln for the last time as his casket lay in state and his funeral procession traveled by train from Washington across the United States to the chosen place of burial. Pendel accompanied Lincoln's body on "the train decked with sombre trappings." [5] The final march of that great President

[3] *Thirty-six Years in the White House* (Washington, The Neale Publishing Company, 1902), pp. 12–14.
[4] *Ibid.*, p. 111.
[5] *Ibid.*, pp. 45–50.

lasted about three weeks and mournful processions of his "remains" were held in the cities of Washington, Baltimore, Philadelphia, New York, Albany, Buffalo, Indianapolis, Chicago, and Springfield, Illinois.

Concerning the assassins, Pendel wrote, "In the case of the late lamented Lincoln, the infamous crime . . . occurred at a time when there was some excuse for unbridled passion [the Civil War]. The shooting of President Garfield can be traced to no other cause than the wild act of a man either surcharged with malice or crazed by his own misfortune." [6] In conclusion, he said, "I hope I shall never live to see again what I have seen during the last thirty-seven years in the White House, as I have been on duty there when the three great tragedies of our country were enacted." [7]

Jacqueline Kennedy met sorrow in the quiet of her room in the same manner as in the eyes of the world. When the three days of President John F. Kennedy's funeral ceremonies were over, one morning upstairs in the White House, she said to me, "I have peace in my heart and hatred for no one."

On December 3, three days before she moved out of the White House, Jackie stopped in my ground-floor office. It was 6:30 P.M., and she remembered that she wanted to see the Huntley-Brinkley evening news report. I turned on my television set. We sat together on the pale green sofa that President Truman had used in the Oval Office upstairs, and we watched the awarding of a medal to Clint Hill, her Secret Service agent, for his courageous action in climbing into the Presidential car to protect her immediately after the assassination in Dallas. The next item of news was an interview in Texas with Mrs. Oswald, the mother of President Kennedy's presumed assassin.

I glanced uneasily at Jackie; I wished that I could have spared her reliving that tragic event. She was watching Mrs. Oswald intently, and she spoke in a voice vibrant with warmth of feeling, "I feel so sorry for her. She's such a nice looking woman."

An unknown poet wrote, "Shadows speak not of darkness but of the golden light that cast them; . . . memories are only the bright dreams of today moved into yesterday by tomorrow. Build new bright dreams that you may have golden memories." [8]

In 1965, two years after the assassination of President Kennedy, I translated into words some of my own golden memories of him and I wrote a poem about his rendezvous:

[6] *Ibid.*, pp. 105–106.
[7] *Ibid.*, p. 167.
[8] *Plantation Health,* Nils P. Larsen, M.D., ed. Vol. XXII (January, 1957), p. 22.

IN MEMORIAM

November 22, 1963

He had a rendezvous with greatness here.
A flaming meteor, he came to light
The deep abysses of this mortal sphere,
Illuminate men's minds and souls to fight
Life's vices: bigotry, greed, malice, fear.
In his noontime of the year.

He had a rendezvous with life to steer
The ship of earth to wondrous ports of brave
New beauty, music, hope that children dear
May live with love immortal past the grave,
In harbors arched by rainbows tier on tier.
In his noontime of the year.

He had a rendezvous with duty clear,
Courage instilled by mother, father proud
To see his star ascend. Now on his bier
His flag becomes a shroud. Their heads are bowed,
Their knees are bent on ground grown hard and sere.
In the fulltime of their year.

He had a rendezvous with death to hear
The bells of heaven chime, "Peace, rest in peace."
Again a star in space far and yet so near,
Eternal light, he guides mankind's release
From self; the tryst with death men will revere.
In the noontime of this sphere.

CHAPTER 19

Safe Haven

When I flew back to Washington from Pelham early on Wednesday, January 25, 1961, I arrived just in time to surprise Pierre Salinger at a press briefing while he was announcing my appointment by the President. I had spent less than forty-eight hours in New York closing my office and my laboratory at the medical school and caring for our daughter Janet, who had had her impacted wisdom teeth excised on Monday, January 23, at the New York Hospital. She remained in the hospital for five days, and even there the press questioned her about her mother's appointment.

I soon discovered that to work in the White House as a Presidential appointee was unlike any other conceivable job. President Kennedy chose aides for their ability to meet new situations—people who had shown that they were willing to try out new ideas and not afraid to make personal sacrifices. When one of his newly appointed assistants asked how he could prepare himself for his White House post, the President replied, "You can't—there isn't anything else like it."

I had to learn for myself the conditions and regulations that limited the duties of the Personal Physician to the President. I found a wide latitude in their interpretation. Reassuring and wise in his guidance, Lt. General Leonard D. Heaton, Surgeon General of the United States Army, came promptly for lunch with me at the White House Staff Mess, and he proved a warm friend during my years in Washington. I became acquainted, too, with the retiring Surgeon General of the United States Navy, Rear Admiral

Bartholomew W. Hogan, and with Rear Admiral Edward C. Kenney, who was sworn in to that command on February 14. Their welcome and their assistance to me, the civilian woman White House Physician, were unbounded.

President Kennedy gave me few directives regarding my duties. His first one, shortly after my appointment, was: "Do not make any commitment that, if I am ill, I will use any particular hospital. Remember that I am Commander in Chief of all the Services."

His second order to me was brief: "Never make a statement on Medicare."

That implied to me that the political aspects of medicine were outside the sphere of my activities in the White House. Indeed, I had plenty to do without that kind of involvement. When opponents or proponents of special health legislation called me to say that they could not find a statement of mine on an issue, I replied, "That is correct. And if you ever see one, you will know that I did not make it."

Public interest in the past and present health of President Kennedy gave rise to a stream of questions that were directed to me by mail, telephone, and from the White House Press Office. Often I referred my reply to the President for his reaction. Ordinarily, he was easily accessible to me and I never had difficulty in communicating with him. One day, I asked him with whom he would wish me to consult if he himself were not available and if I were in doubt concerning the appropriateness of my answer about his health.

"Ted Sorensen is the only person here who is fully informed about my health," he told me. "Discuss it with nobody else."

President Kennedy instructed me early on one more point: "Do not be in a hurry to choose an assistant."

In view of the urgent health needs of the White House personnel in that period of hectic readjustment, blizzards, and winter's epidemic of respiratory illness, I could not heed that for long. Colonel Walter R. Tkach, Medical Corps of the United States Air Force, had served for eight years as the Assistant White House Physician during President's Eisenhower's two terms. Not intending it as a complaint but as a matter of course, he told me that he had not had as much as a week's leave in that time. Yet, in view of the transitional vacuum in health services, he offered to remain on voluntary duty in the White House Dispensary for another week until I could arrange for help. It was my first example of the dedication that I came to know was typical of the White House staff who toiled around the clock for the President.

My mind was relieved when on February 1, 1961, by arrangement with Rear Admiral Bartholomew W. Hogan, Surgeon General of the United States Navy, President Kennedy announced the appointment of Captain George G. Burkley, U.S. Navy Medical Corps, as "Assistant White House Physician to Dr. Janet Travell and Director of the White House Dispensary." He replaced Dr. Tkach. Dr. Burkley was fifty-eight and I, fifty-nine. He was my logical choice because he had traveled on President Eisenhower's overseas tour in December, 1959; he was already cleared for duty at Camp David, the Presidential retreat, and at the White House. At the time of his appointment, he was Commanding Officer of the U.S. Naval Dispensary in Washington, and before that he was Chief of Medicine in the U.S. Naval Hospitals at Portsmouth, Virginia; at Newport, Rhode Island; Memphis, Tennessee; and at Charleston, South Carolina. Travel with the Chief Executive was arduous and George Burkley served many long hours with good humor and devotion to the high calling of medicine.

Before returning to New York on Monday, January 23, I talked at length with Dr. Tkach's staff in the Dispensary and I offered to retain them in their positions, if they wished to stay. Mrs. Genevieve R. Herrell, a civilian nurse with a sunny disposition who had carried her share of the work load since former President Truman was in office, elected to remain, and she is still there. Master Sergeant Philip Sidmore, now a Colonel in the United States Army, continued for a while to be in charge of our clinical laboratory.

Major General Howard McC. Snyder, Personal Physician to former President Eisenhower, had left the White House by Inauguration Day, with his personal staff and equipment. His three rooms, which were to become my medical offices, were entered through a single door opposite the President's elevator on the long ground-floor corridor in the Mansion. A White House guard sat outside in the hall and had the key. I inspected the suite after my appointment had been decided by President Kennedy on Monday morning. Those empty rooms with bare green walls and magenta carpeting marked by the weight of furniture looked very different from what I remembered when General Snyder had invited me to call on him there in the White House more than six years earlier.

My medical duties at the White House actually began before my official appointment. During the Inaugural week, I had called each day at 3307 "N" Street to see what I might do for President-elect and Mrs. Kennedy. She had flown that week from Palm Beach to the home that they were quitting in Georgetown, and she had left the children in Florida. It was a week of hardship for a young woman who was still recuperating from major surgery —the cesarean section—and whose premature baby was just eight weeks old. The creation of her wardrobe for the Inaugural events, and its hours of fitting, took their toll. In addition, Inauguration Day was moving day for her.

The Hotel Shoreham was our headquarters; Janet had flown from Italy, and Virginia and Ed Street, from Nashville, Tennessee. We had official invitations and tickets to everything and the exhilaration of President Kennedy's Inauguration kept us on the move. In spite of the blizzard, we managed to get to all the Inaugural events, because of Jack's skillful driving. The girls were guests of Mr. Joseph P. Kennedy at the party for the Inaugural Gala's cast at Paul Young's Restaurant, which the President-elect attended in the small hours of the morning.

Thursday, in the snowstorm, I was unexpectedly the recipient of a farm truck and driver. I had telephoned my old friend Orr E. Reynolds, then Director of Research in the Office of Science, Department of Defense, and his secretary said that he was flying in from Europe that morning. When I called back, he invited me to lunch. I was to let him know shortly where to meet me. At noon I phoned again.

"I'm free now, Orr. Can you pick me up soon at 3307 'N' Street in Georgetown?"

A long silence preceded his answer: "Last night I slept on the plane in the suit I'm wearing. I'm driving my old pickup truck from the farm. I parked it two weeks ago at the airport when I left—it's pretty disreputable. Bobby, are you sure you want me to come for you at that address?"

"Yes, it'll be fine," I said promptly. "When you arrive at the house, give your name to the man outside—I'll have you cleared."

The block was crowded with Inaugural sightseers, press, and police. The street was closed to traffic, but Orr's muddy farm vehicle was admitted. He parked across the street from the Kennedy house. When I emerged onto the front steps, where I had appeared with the President-elect eight weeks earlier after John Jr. was born, Orr shielded me from the cameras as we crossed the street. Somehow, part of the story leaked out.[1]

Orr helped me up the high step into his large truck, which he used to haul horses. I felt at home in it. He and I had ridden together last in military tanks and amphibian vehicles at the United States Army Armor Center in Fort Knox, Kentucky, during July, 1958.

"Where to first, Bobby?" Orr asked amiably.

"To the Shoreham, please. I couldn't reach Jack by phone—I'll leave a message at the desk before we go to lunch."

[1] Shirley Thomas, *Men of Space* (Philadelphia, Chilton Books, 1963), Vol. VI, pp. 146–147.

In the snowstorm, Orr pulled into the line of limousines under the Shoreham's porte cochere. An expressionless doorman handed me down, in my fur coat, from my high perch in the truck as if he did it every day.

That afternoon, in the wind, Jack and I plowed on foot through deep snowdrifts for the long block from the Shoreham to the Sheraton-Park Hotel, where we attended the reception in honor of the governors of the states and special distinguished guests. Nothing dampened our spirits, but we wished for Orr's cartage.

After the Inauguration ceremony at the Capitol, during the parade I made my first official call in the White House. Jackie had asked me to watch when she left the open-air President's box and to follow her soon afterward. It would be unwise for her to sit through the entire Inaugural parade in that bitter cold—the temperature was in the low twenties and the wind was frigid. I sat with my family on the frozen spectators' wooden bleachers next to the Presidential viewing stand.

At about four o'clock, I received a signal from the Secret Service. Jack stood on a bench that served as a seat and I stepped in his clasped hands, as if I were mounting a horse. He boosted me onto the top of the high board fence that isolated the Chief Executive's area, and the agents helped me land on the other side. It was not the most dignified of entrances, but my pride was unruffled. I walked through the box, bowing to the President's family and special guests; he was preoccupied with salutes from the paraders. I descended the steps on the far side to reach the temporary wooden walkway to the White House. The music of the marching bands retreated in the distance.

Walking alone across the North Grounds I felt the beauty and the awe of the President's Mansion as I never had before. In the winter's setting sun long, straight shadows of great tree trunks slanted across an unbroken surface of snow that leveled the ground. The fountain had disappeared. A dark line of old boxwood bushes demarcated the whiteness of the walls from the snow's matching white. Lights inside the building gleamed orange. Above the peaked cornice over the majestic columns, the Stars and Stripes stood straight out in the wind, bright and brave in its colors.

In that momentous instant of history, I had a premonition of change in my life. I stood there reflecting on the extraordinary events that had brought me from an office on 16th Street in New York City to 16th Street and Pennsylvania Avenue in Washington.

The spell of the moment was fragile. Upstairs, when I entered the Queen's Suite on the second floor, where the new First Lady was resting, the topsy-turvy confusion of her moving day greeted me. Partly unpacked suitcases filled the small study, and her personal maid, Providencia Paredes, was busy bringing order out of chaos.

"Provie, where did you put Mrs. Kennedy's heating pad?" I inquired optimistically. "She needs it."

"I don't know." Provie concentrated on the question. "Oh, I remember now—we left it in Georgetown. It was plugged in under the bed."

"Can we send for it?"

"The house is all shut up. I don't know who has a key," Provie replied.

"Isn't there a heating pad in the White House?" I asked.

We telephoned the housekeeper. There was not.

"Then we'll have to order one from a drugstore," I concluded.

A White House car made a long detour around the parading units and executed my first prescription in the White House.

When I took charge in my White House office on January 25, my immediate need was for a secretary who knew the ropes. My telephone rang constantly. Congratulatory telegrams, flowers, and visitors arrived. On the afternoon of my appointment, the Correspondence Section of the White House "loaned" me pretty Martha Gorber—new people from outside could not be engaged on short notice because of the need for top security clearance. Martha was a whiz at her work and she made mine easier in countless ways. She was still with me when I left the staff in 1965.

In the midst of the first day's turmoil, I sat down at my temporary plain desk and wrote a longhand letter: "Dear Father: My first letter from this address should go to you since you are responsible for my being here. I feel like Cinderella! I have a big job to do here and will do my best to carry the responsibility. I won't see you as often as I'd like, but I can talk with you on the telephone, and I'll come up to New York at intervals. Keep well. Much love, Bobby."

In reply, he wrote me:

Dear Bobby;

Writing you is good and well deserved by you, of whom I am as proud as if you were president. The fact is that I expect you in the field of medicine to stand at the head of a change as important . . . as was (1) the change when homeopathy became unpopular, (2) or they found that sick people could not all be cured by a few drugs like quinine, strychnine, digitalis, etc. or (3) all quickly by an antibiotic. We are just emerging from the antibiotic stage. There are some good things about each stage: none add to homeopathy as much as your discovery that pain, both acute and chronic, exists as you explain, from simple far-distant points of trouble which . . . often fail to attract attention as a primary source of trouble. . . . So try to remember that I think of you as one of medicine's leaders. . . . Even so everyone needs sleep—please be careful as to that.

Lots of love & congratulation,
Father

He gave me too much credit, but I understood his bias.

My White House appointment brought him great pleasure and he told people, "Now I know why I lived so long."

He was content. In March, 1961, from a nursing home three miles from our Pelham house he wrote to Dr. Rudolf W. Hack in San Bernardino:

> Dear Rudy:
>   I am busy overtime daily examining & filing away my correspondence & hoping to find time to write a bit. Bobby's good luck in happening to have as a patient the new President . . . she richly deserved. . . . I have wonderful care, day & night—I can not stand alone at all. I am comfortable—good appetite, no regular pain—a good bed—visitors welcome. I may live to 100 years.
>
> Again to you my affection,
Willard T.

Several years before his stroke, when he was in vigorous health, my father wrote his own obituary and gave it to my secretary to keep. To him that act was like making a will—it would save someone trouble. At ninety-one he loved life and he was looking toward his future years on earth.

Within a week after the announcement that a woman was the new Personal Physician to the President, Virginia flew back from Nashville and Janet came from the New York Hospital with Jack, in order to comply with Pierre Salinger's request that *Life* magazine be permitted to do a feature article about our family.[2] Paul Schutzer,[3] *Life*'s fine photographer, and Gail Cameron followed me around for several days. That was the first of a series of interviews that the White House Press Office requested me to arrange.

One day, I told President Kennedy that all the publicity about my appointment made my work more difficult and made me vulnerable to criticism.

"Don't pay any attention to it, Doctor," he advised.

When I overreacted to that tidal wave by finally refusing to talk with any representative of the news media about anything, Merriman Smith

---

[2] "A Lady Doctor in the White House," February 17, 1961, pp. 37–40.
[3] Paul Schutzer was killed in action on June 6, 1967, while he was riding an Israeli half-track in the Sinai Desert.

wrote: "Dr. Travell has become such a recluse that some people think she has left the White House."

Furnishing my White House offices was made easy by Mrs. Jacqueline Kennedy. She suggested that I use whatever pieces I liked that were in the White House storerooms. I selected tables and lamps, a desk that Mrs. Eisenhower had had, and a sofa with two high-backed matching armchairs. That set, upholstered in pale green satin with a pattern of gold medallions and stars, I discovered later had stood in the Oval Room on the second floor of the Mansion when Mr. Truman was President.[4] From my New York office I brought the rocking chair, slipcovered in green, my portable electric typewriter, and my tape recorder.

The walls and ceiling of my private office and its anteroom were painted in the off-white shade that Mrs. Kennedy had introduced in the White House. The lovely old window drapes were remade and rehung. Neutral carpeting was installed in all three rooms. Virginia's paintings hung on the walls, and a sculptured wheeling horse that she had made stood on a table. Its motion was often admired.

Over my desk, photographed in color, President Kennedy's smiling face was framed. Early in February, 1961, I had watched him inscribe it rapidly in the Executive Office before he handed it to me:

For Dr. Travell—Who made the smile possible—With affectionate regards

John Kennedy

That spring, Vice Admiral Joel T. Boone, Medical Corps of the United States Navy, Retired, visited my redecorated offices. For eleven years he had been assigned as physician in attendance on four Presidents at the White House and I especially appreciated his comments. On May 5, 1961, he wrote me:

Dear Dr. Travell:

Again I wish to congratulate you on the new look you have provided the medical facilities in the White House. . . . You have created a most attractive atmosphere . . . with utilitarian elements well arranged but not overly conspicuous. Your color schemes are pleasing to the eye and your selection of furnishings becoming to a very unique and specialized office. . . . It pleased me to . . . [know] of the President's evident pride in it.

Where my husband and I lived was a minor matter for the moment. Unlike many of the Presidential appointees who moved to Washington almost

[4] Amy La Follette Jensen, *The White House and Its Thirty-three Families* (New York, McGraw-Hill, Inc., 1962), p. 260.

overnight, we had no children at home to be considered. For the first three weeks, I stayed at the quiet old Sheraton-Carlton Hotel near the White House; Jack spent most of that time in New York. Then we sublet a furnished apartment by the month at the Potomac Plaza in Foggy Bottom. It was my first experience with apartment living, and we began hunting for a house to lease at once.

On July 1, we moved into a three-story unfurnished residence at 3319 "N" Street in Georgetown. It had a lovely small garden and beyond the brick wall we could hear the water falling in Benjamin Bradlee's fountain next door. A mockingbird sang in the top of our big tree and we were happy there.

We camped out. We intended to move our furniture down and to rent our house in Pelham after July 1, but we delayed on account of my father. We thought that dismantling our place—his home—which was near his pleasant private nursing home in New Rochelle would destroy a kind of anchor in his life that he needed. Jack was like a son to him. He spent part of nearly every week in Pelham and I went there at long intervals.

Jack's office was in New York, too. He was Vice President of Trainer, Wortham & Company, Investment Counselors, and he became the firm's Washington representative. Commuting back and forth between the two cities, he sometimes loaded our car with patio furniture, lamps, dishes, pots, and linens for our new Georgetown residence. The transition was in many ways more wearing on Jack than on me.

It did not disturb me that I slept on a camp cot and kept my clothes in a borrowed bureau, nor that the dining room held only a folding metal table and eight folding chairs. The thirty-two-foot-long narrow parlor was empty except for new wall-to-wall carpeting; our grand piano, which Janet had left with friends in Washington when in 1960 she moved from there to Italy; two straight chairs; and a large air-conditioning unit that Jack had had installed. I was too busy to entertain friends.

In August, 1961, the situation changed. My father's condition had gradually worsened, and I told President Kennedy that I ought to see him on the coming weekend. I suggested that Dr. Burkley go on the usual trip to the Cape. I did not mention to the President what my sister and the nurses had told me—that my father was failing fast and wanted to see me once more before he died.

After President Kennedy left for Hyannis Port, on Friday evening I flew to New York. I spent Saturday with my father in New Rochelle. Early Sunday morning, the President telephoned me at Pelham. He asked whether I could conveniently fly to Hyannis Port and be at his house in "the Compound" late that afternoon.

"Yes, Mr. President, I'm sure I can," I replied, not knowing how I would accomplish it. Then I obtained a reservation on a one o'clock flight from La Guardia Airport.

Hastily I packed my bag, and Jack and I drove the three miles to the nursing home. After a while, I broke the news to my father that I would have to fly shortly to Hyannis Port.

"When will you be back?" he asked quietly.

"As soon as I can, dear," I answered matter-of-factly. Farewell was brief.

It was six-thirty or seven o'clock when my visit with the President ended. I decided not to try to fly back to New York that Sunday evening. Summer travel from the Cape was heavy, and besides, the President wanted me to return with him to Washington. In a quandary, I telephoned our house in Pelham, but there was no answer. It was supper time at the nursing home, a poor hour to call. I walked alone through the Kennedy Compound to the beach in front of Mr. Joseph P. Kennedy's big house. A cold wind was blowing and the water was choppy, but I knew that the salt water of the bay would feel warmer than the air.

The Secret Service agent in the sentry booth watched me. "Dr. Travell! You wouldn't go in swimming now," he protested.

He was wearing a winter parka with a fur-trimmed hood.

I dropped my towel on the chilling sand and I swam a distance out. Floating on my back in the buoyant waves as if I were swinging in a hammock, I could see the whole expanse of sunset that domed the sea. Clouds on the horizon were tinted at first with the orange-red of flames. Then color slowly spread over the entire sky, changing to the hue of crimson roses and finally to the deep ruby red of late twilight.

Red was my father's favorite color, I thought. He loved red neckties, a red hunting cap, and in his hip pocket a red bandanna handkerchief. When I wore a new dress and asked him how he liked it, he cocked one eyebrow and studied me attentively.

"Why didn't you buy a red one?" he would ask.

His favorite sweater was one that I had given him when I was at Wellesley College. Maroon red, coat style, he wore it for about forty years, even to the year of his death. He never required something new to make him happy; it was hard to think of a thing he wanted for his birthday or at Christmas. Worldly possessions were not important to him.

He cared little for flowers, except red roses. Other flowers reminded him of funerals, he used to say. When my mother's coffin rested in the nave of the beautiful Church of the Ascension in New York, it was completely draped in a tapestry of American Beauty roses. My mother would have wished that, because she loved flowers above every other material thing. Those dozens and dozens of deep red roses at her funeral are still fresh in my memory.

It was about eight o'clock when I came out of the water. At that hour my father suffered a sudden heart attack. Jack and Ginny were with him. Although he lingered until the morning, his spirit was already in the sunset.

He died on Monday, August 14, while I was flying with the President on Air Force One back to Washington. When news of my father's death reached President Kennedy at the White House, he sent for me. He expressed his deep sympathy.

"I never would have asked you to come to the Cape if I had known. Why didn't you tell me your father was so ill?" he asked.

"I think my father would not have wanted me to."

I did not feel that life was unfair to me.

Jack and I promptly sold our house in Pelham. We decided that it was too large for us then. Nor could we again face daily commuting between suburbia and New York. Nor would we live in the city itself.

On September 21, the moving van from Pelham unloaded our furniture at 3319 "N" Street, Northwest. Our camping days in Georgetown had come to an end.

Our transition was over, and New York was no longer the center of the universe to us. Washington and the White House had changed Jack and me.

CHAPTER 20

Office Hours: Day and Night

Time at the White House flowed like a great river in flood, without academic cycles, without vacations or seasons. Only a stream of crises marked its passage. In the long range view, I felt as though I were living without a clock, the way we did on vacations at Merryfield Farm. At both the White House and the farm, meeting a personal schedule was unimportant to me, and to my understanding husband. The number of invitations were legion, but I was good at saying no.

In the short-term view, every moment was precious for what could be accomplished in that small increment of time. The White House Physician had to work at maximum speed, yet without the sense of hurry that mars efficiency. Nor should the ever-present sense of history and awe for the Presidency be allowed to intrude itself in the making of sound medical judgments.

After six months of service in the White House, when I had weathered some Presidential medical storms, I told in a telephone interview about my reactions to them: "When you take a job, you already have worried about responsibility and accepted it. From then on, you just do the best you can. . . . You're so busy doing things and figuring out certain technical aspects of what needs to be done that you don't wonder about the Presidency." [1]

Sometimes it seemed as if I were practicing medicine in Grand Central Station, on the run or perhaps at its central information booth.

The White House held the challenge of the unexpected and the un-

[1] Robert Thompson, "Capital Circus," New York *Daily News*, June 29, 1961, p. 4.

known in medicine. I was always preparing for trouble, beyond the ordinary meaning of the term "preventive medicine."

In 1961, I insisted at first that Dr. Burkley, the Assistant White House Physician, ride in the Secret Service car directly behind President Kennedy's when he drove with a visiting head of state in a parade through Washington. The Secret Service objected that there was not room in their car for him.

"He has to sit with his feet on a Tommy gun," I was told. "Besides, if anything happened, we'd take off like a bat out of hell for the nearest hospital."

"It's just possible that a doctor could save the President's life on the ride," I argued, knowing at the same time that the Secret Service agents were trained in first aid emergency measures. As it turned out, on the motorcade in Dallas no physician could have changed the outcome.

President Kennedy finally overruled me.

"Doctors have better use for their time than to follow me around," he told me.

"We have nothing more important to do than to protect your health, Mr. President," I disagreed.

Within the Mansion where my office was situated, in spite of the thousands who toured the reception rooms above on the first floor, the controlled quiet gave me the feeling that I was living inside the eye of a hurricane. My friends from the "outside" who came to call on me used to remark, "Where is everyone? I imagined there would be a great bustle going on here."

They were not aware that I was constantly informed as to the whereabouts of the President—whether he was in his office, in the gardens, upstairs, or perhaps in the indoor swimming pool. When he intended to walk through the corridor past my door, three buzzes sounded. For Mrs. Kennedy, two buzzes rang. The Mansion was their home and I made certain that they did not unexpectedly encounter my visitors in the halls. That area was ordinarily off limits for reporters, in an attempt to maintain privacy for the children.

Members of the press were to spend a day—Thursday, March 16, 1961 —in the White House watching President Kennedy at work. My day there began, as usual, at about eight o'clock, when an official car brought me to my ground-floor office. The guard in the hall opened the door for me—I usually arrived before my secretary or my Navy nurse. I glanced through my stack of unopened mail. When I received a call from George Thomas, the President's valet, I took the elevator upstairs to see the President in his bedroom, where he was finishing breakfast and visiting with Caroline. I entertained her while the telephone interrupted. General Ted Clifton had already been in to brief him on the night's events.

According to my view, March 16 was not the usual "Day with Kennedy" that the press reported it to be. That morning, playing with Caroline he had struck his forehead against the corner of a table and it had cut an inch-long gash above his left eyebrow. As a temporary expedient, I drew the edges of the wound together with narrow strips of adhesive tape, each about a millimeter wide, until a time could be arranged in his schedule for a plastic surgeon to suture it. Meanwhile, the conspicuous dressing did not improve the President's always correct appearance. It was scarcely in harmony with the morning coat and striped trousers that he wore later to the noon reception at the State Department, where Jackie accompanied him to commemorate the Centennial of Italian Unification.

The President, Caroline, and I descended in the elevator together. As they stepped off into the hall on the ground floor, they blinked in the sudden glare of flashbulbs. Reporters and cameramen were lined up waiting.

It was one of the few times that I saw President Kennedy angry. He had not expected to meet newsmen in the Mansion, or he would not have brought Caroline down with him. With a sweep of his arm, he pushed her back into the elevator where I stood out of sight.

"Doctor, take her back to Miss Shaw," he said tersely.

Then he turned and faced the group with a smile. After all, it was not their fault that they had taken him by surprise.

Caroline burst into tears and he paused to console her. She often went with her Daddy in the morning along the covered walk by the rose garden; as they passed my office, walking hand in hand, he sometimes called to me to come with them so that I could escort her "home." That day, Caroline was bitterly disappointed that he left her behind. When the elevator took us to the second floor, she ran and hid sobbing under a sofa in the hall, as any three-year-old might do.

At one o'clock, I took Captain Joseph R. Connelly of the Bethesda U.S. Naval Hospital upstairs to the President's room. He quickly sutured the laceration with several hidden (subcuticular) stitches. A few days later he removed them. In the interim, Dr. Connelly or I changed the dressing daily. Despite its White House aura, the incident reminded me of my long months on ambulance and hospital emergency duty in New York.

On that day when the press followed President Kennedy wherever he went on official affairs, the patch above his eye was featured in the pictures. Before he finally left the Executive Office at about 8 P.M., a reporter asked him whether it had been a typical day.

"No," the President replied with a smile. "It was one of the easier days."

Another feature that evolved from that day's surveillance was an Associated Press story by Marvin L. Arrowsmith about the Executive Office rocking chair. He telephoned on March 20 to ask me a few questions about it and I answered them, as I had before for other members of the press. But his column in the March 21 Washington *Evening Star* was accompanied by a picture of President Kennedy sitting in his plain porch rocker during a conference on March 16 with Vice President Johnson and Secretary McNamara. That story, one might say, "broke" the rocking chair—it rocked the world.

The prevailing impression then, at least among the more sophisticated, was that rocking chairs had been relegated to attics and to porches of resort hotels. For example, in 1960 *The New York Times* published an obituary and eulogy for the rocker by a New Englander who remembered "when chairs were made to live in, not just sit on" and who stated: "Granny's Old Rocking Chair may be considered a gone goose. . . . The American people don't want to rock. . . . What's the matter with us, anyway?" [2]

The writer was mistaken—they did want to rock. My mail quickly convinced me of that. Within a few days after Arrowsmith's article appeared, I received some five hundred letters about rockers, and the number addressed to the White House eventually ran into the thousands. Some people asked questions, mainly as to where they could obtain a chair like the President's, but many wrote just to say how much they enjoyed reading about his chair and to tell me how glad they were that I approved of rockers.

I was glad to hear another physician's voice raised in December, 1960, to champion the physiological virtues of the rocking chair. A general practitioner in Ontario, Canada, advocated its use as an antidote to the common effects of inactivity and he noted in a British medical journal: "For the benefit of readers unfamiliar with North American civilization, it should be understood—Hollywood and glossy magazines notwithstanding—that in many urban and rural areas of America . . . rocking chairs are a familiar item in many homes, and far more common than in Europe." [3]

I was never one of the crowd who had discarded our heritage of the rocking chair. When I came to the White House in 1961, I had been prescribing for a quarter of a century a well-proportioned firm-seated porch rocker with head-high support as an adjunct to the management of

[2] John Gould, "A Lament for the Rocking Chair," *The New York Times Magazine,* April 24, 1960, pp. 12 and 96.
[3] R. C. Swan, "The Therapeutic Value of the Rocking Chair," *The Lancet,* Vol. 2 (December 31, 1960), p. 1441.

musculoskeletal pain. A New York lawyer, whose homes and Wall Street office each contained one of those unpretentious chairs, wrote a letter on December 9, 1941: "Dear Dr. Travell: In the midst of the thick and ever thickening gloom in connection with the Japanese war, I have one bright ray of light to contribute, and that is the enclosed suggestion to your patients who, like myself, have invested in Bloomingdale rockers. Sincerely yours, Henry Root Stern."

The accompanying cartoon showed a chair with two sets of curved wooden rockers, one pair underneath in the usual position and another pair inverted overhead on top of the high backrest. The furniture salesman was saying to a little old lady, ". . . And why not a rocking chair in which you can turn somersaults?"

Mr. Stern's North Carolina oak rocking chair of 1941 vintage was identical in make and design with the one that Senator John F. Kennedy found comfortable when he first came to my New York office in the spring of 1955. He was already using one in his Senate office when I selected it that year to illustrate an article [4] for *House Beautiful,* but neither my magazine article nor his chair made headlines then. They had to wait until both his and my office rockers traveled to the White House.

Things that seem natural in an ordinary setting take on extraordinary aspects against the backdrop of the White House. The intense focus of the press spotlights small details in the lives of its occupants because the American people are avid for every scrap of information about the President and his family. That interest is fundamentally an expression of the personal identification that men, women, and even children in our democracy feel for their elected Chief Executive. It is a healthy thing.

Take the rocking chair, for example. A widow in her sixties wrote me on March 24, 1961: "Dear Dr. Travell: This is the first time in my whole life that I have ever written to a dignitary of any kind, but I saw President Kennedy sitting in that old fashioned rocking chair. . . . The truth is, I have one that looks almost exactly like it. Everybody teases me about it, calls me old fashioned . . . but I would not trade it for any other chair in the world. I rest so good in it. Now, I can class myself with our good President, ha!"

A letter about the therapeutic benefits of the old rocker was typical of many that I received: "Dear Doctor: My rocking chair is over eighty years old and I have rocking chairs all over my home upstairs and downstairs I

[4] Janet Travell, "Chairs Are a Personal Thing," *House Beautiful,* October, 1955, pp. 190–193; reprinted as "How to Choose a Chair," *ibid.,* July, 1961, pp. 80–83; condensed, "Ladies and Gentlemen, Be Seated—Properly," *Reader's Digest,* August, 1961, pp. 159–162.

don't ever sit in any other kind of a chair as I would be utterly uncomfortable. The rocking chair does all you said and helps my back so much that I just had to write and tell you the good you are doing people all over the world."

The thoughts of the elderly, as expressed in their letters to me, were summed up in a poem written by a man, Charles Marion French, in 1955 when he was one hundred and three years old:

THE OLD ROCKING CHAIR

Your gentle tipping to and fro
Gives our blood a youthful glow,
Heals our soreness, cheers the heart,
Keeps our minds and thoughts alert,
Makes us glad you so behave
That in your arms a place we crave.
We recommend to your good care
All who come from everywhere.
May God's blessing on you rest,
As you serve guest after guest.

Rocking chairs, I was informed, were in use around a formal dining-room table, in the kitchen, and as standard equipment in hospital nurseries. I myself sat in one to typewrite.

Well-wishers offered to give President Kennedy their favorite rocking chairs. In reply, I had to point out that not all styles of rockers were equally comfortable and that not all of them were of a size to fit a man six feet tall.

Not all the mail praised his rocking chair. Forgetting that he was President of all these United States, protesters wrote that he ought to use one manufactured in Massachusetts, instead of North Carolina. Some people did not admire the one that he had, in spite of its new look given by cushions slipcovered to match the decor of the Executive Office.

A registered nurse described her handsome upholstered antique to me and then went on:

. . . I hope you won't take exception to what I am about to say. While I am sure that the President's chair *is* comfortable, somehow it just does not look distinguished enough for our darling President. While I would not sell my chair—I love it too much—I would give it to President Kennedy. . . . I believe that the President would love it and as Caroline bless her heart would say—"My daddy can take his shoes off and do nothing!" I might whisper to her, "While daddy *appears* to be doing nothing, he is thinking an awful lot"—with the burden of the whole world on his capable shoulders. I surely wish I could tell her I *love* her little rag doll—guess it's because I never had one when I was little. . . . Please tell her mother and daddy not to be concerned over her little antics or capers creeping into the newspapers—please don't deny us that. A child is neither Republican or Democrat, just a precious bit of love.

The power of the press and the appetite of the public converted the rocking chair almost overnight into an emblem of the Kennedy administration. Ted Sorensen explained it in this manner: After the tree planting ceremony in Ottawa, Canada, in May, 1961, when the President aggravated the old injury to his back, "more fit than ever in every other way, a picture of health and vitality, he was still plagued by his aching back. . . . More rockers were acquired, becoming a nationally recognized symbol of the traditional values, reflective patience and practical informality prevailing in the White House." [5]

President Kennedy knew the importance of sitting comfortably. To me, his sturdy rocking chair in the White House expressed his dedication to the principle of freedom for each individual, which is the real heritage of our country. It was a sign of his right to choose a way of life, or a chair, for himself, and by implication, of his right to choose a personal physician, in this case one who happened to have provided him with that simple device for seated comfort.

Besides the furnishings that provide external support for the framework of the body, I scrutinized other aspects of environmental health in the White House.

In the bitter weather and blizzards that marked the 1961 Inauguration, the high-ceilinged rooms were penetrated by chill drafts. The President said that the Executive Office was cold, although the heating system was operating at full capacity. One noon when he had gone to lunch, I investigated. I stood in the open doorway between his office and Mrs. Evelyn Lincoln's, which also connected with the Cabinet Room. A cold wind whipped past me as if a window were open and a sheaf of letters blew off her desk onto the floor.

Playing a game of "Cold, colder, colder . . ." I moved around the President's Oval Room. The windows were shut and well sealed. At the wide fireplace between the two sofas, I located the source of the wintry blasts. The damper in the chimney must be open. Mrs. Lincoln said that she would send for the engineer.

"Nonsense," I replied, "I'll close it myself right now."

[5] Theodore C. Sorensen, *Kennedy* (New York, Harper & Row, 1965), p. 368.

Stooping down, I reached up under the waist-high front of the fireplace and found the handle that operated the big iron damper. It dropped down into place, showering me with soot. At that point, I was happy to let the engineer close the damper in the fireplace in the Cabinet Room, which I had found to be also standing open.

I asked Mrs. Lincoln to write a notice that the damper must be opened before a fire was started and I placed the card on the logs laid ready to light in the President's office. The warning remained there, unchanged, for a period of years.

When President and Mrs. Kennedy moved into the White House on Inauguration Day, they occupied the Lincoln Room and the Queen's Suite. They stayed in those temporary historic quarters for a couple of months while their personal rooms at the opposite end of the second floor were being redecorated to their taste. The work progressed slowly because the children's rooms had to be made ready also and because the number of painters with security clearance was limited.

In those first days, I remember how the central ventilating system made the fireplaces upstairs smoke—the windows were never supposed to be opened. Smoke somehow traveled by back drafts even into my offices two floors below. One morning, I went upstairs to see what was wrong; the stubborn fire in the Lincoln Room was pouring smoke out of the fireplace. George Thomas managed to raise the long windows at floor level and let in a freezing current of air while I stuffed burning newspapers up inside the chimney. We finally succeeded in reversing the direction of the draft, but the fire only made the room colder because we had to leave the windows open.

The radiant warmth and glow of an open fire would have been a pleasure, but after a few attempts the President gave it up. In the evening after dinner, when his family stayed at Glen Ora and I stopped to see him upstairs, he was sitting by himself in a cheerless room with a handcart stacked with books beside him—his *Profiles in Courage*. As he wrote page-long personal inscriptions to his friends and supporters, he balanced each copy on his knee. It bothered me to watch him.

To make his task easier, I provided him with a felt-covered board that rested across the arms of his chair. One side of the rectangle was cut out in a semicircle to fit close to him and to give him elbow and arm support at the right height. It was the first of several such writing boards that were made according to my patterns in the carpenter shop of the White House.

Like the rocking chair, the semicircular cutout board was a sensible device that my patients had enjoyed for years. It ensured writing comfort and reduced fatigue—it was actually a form of preventive medicine.

In the upheaval of her life to the milieu of the White House, Jackie had to be given time to regain her full vitality. On January 27, 1961, I issued a statement to the Press Office concerning the need for curtailment of her social activities:

> It is two months today since Mrs. Kennedy underwent major surgery. She has recuperated better than was to be expected in view of the strain that circumstances have understandably placed on her. Any woman should know the effort involved in packing her belongings and moving from one house to another. In addition, moving day was Inauguration Day. Mrs. Kennedy has been advised that complete convalescence will be accomplished sooner if her activities continue to be somewhat restricted for the present.

She and Caroline and John spent as much time as possible at their nearby country retreat in Middleburg, Virginia, during the redecoration of the family living quarters in the White House. That included the practical addition of a kitchen on the second floor adjacent to the family dining room and the preparing of a suite of rooms for the children and their nurse across the hall from their parents' room. In that period, the Kennedys' "home" was alive with workmen and their ladders.

In the bleak wintry months after his Inauguration, President Kennedy was not enthusiastic about the White House pool. Its close humid air and still water contrasted unfavorably with the ocean at Palm Beach and with his father's palm-encircled pool, where breezes off the sea rippled its salt water. He had just left there as President-elect. He did not return to Florida until his first flight in Air Force One for Easter in April, 1961.

At the White House, a loudspeaker was placed in the pool area so that his favorite music could be piped from a record player in the nearby gymnasium, but it did not charm him to swim often, then. Absorbed in his new responsibilities, he preferred to take short breaks for exercise. He would step out of the Executive Office into the biting cold and alone walk briskly around the circle of the South Grounds on the driveway, which was cleared of snow. Sometimes I saw him from my office window above the snowbanks, as he walked past wearing an overcoat but hatless.

He invited a few members of the White House staff to use the fifty-by-fifteen-foot pool and I swam in it occasionally when the First Family was at Glen Ora.

That summer, after President Kennedy had strained his back in May on the trip to Canada, the need for conditioning of his muscles was evident. While he was in Hyannis Port, the mood of the pool was wonderfully transformed through the thoughtfulness and generosity of the President's father. Mr. Joseph P. Kennedy commissioned Bernard Lamotte to decorate three of the walls with a continuous mural showing scenes from the Virgin Islands.

Mr. Lamotte first prepared small panels, which he copied on a large scale onto the high walls. For his record, I photographed those models in the rose garden. Sometimes he came in his artist's smock to rest in my cool air-conditioned office.

The fourth wall of the pool enclosure was entirely covered with large mirrors, which created perspective and a far horizon. Subtle new lighting with variable intensity control magnified the beauty of the tropical colors and gave a mystical quality to the music. The only jarring note was the ubiquitous telephone set by the water's edge.

After that, President Kennedy derived pleasure and benefit from the pool, where Caroline was likely to join him before lunch. He often swam twice a day. Swimming was coordinated with a series of exercises and massage. Our two Navy Chiefs were physiotherapists on call in the Dispensary to render him service at any hour. In the gymnasium, they supervised the President's individualized exercise program, which was directed by the New York physiatrist, Dr. Hans Kraus. It helped him greatly. I had known Dr. Kraus for years, through a mutual interest in the relief of painful muscle spasm by vapocoolant sprays, and I first asked him to see President Kennedy late in the summer of 1961 at Hyannis Port.

The small gym that opened into the pool's dressing rooms was likewise given a new decor. A corridor was built later from it to the glassed-in ground-floor entry to the Mansion so that after swimming the President was not obliged to walk outdoors on the covered walk along the Rose Garden.

When I came to the White House, the gym was cluttered with a variety of electrical apparatus for physiotherapy and more space was needed in the West Wing Dispensary for its proper use. A room was needed, too, where such diagnostic tests as measurement of basal metabolism and the electrocardiogram could be conducted. Furthermore, the White House had no equipment for X-ray examination. At my request, a room that was used by the news clipping service and that adjoined the waiting room to the Dispensary was allocated to the medical department. Screened massage tables and X-ray apparatus were installed in it. X-ray photography required a darkroom. For that purpose I secured part of a large closet off the basement hall, which housed the Presidential flags. One end was partitioned off and a door was cut to connect it with the Dispensary on the other side of the closet. The new setup functioned well.

Those structural changes that I initiated extended the scope and efficiency of the White House medical facility. Its staff of eight consisted of two physicians, two Navy Chief Corpsmen (Master Chief Hendrix was also a registered nurse), a technician, the civilian nurse in the Dispensary, the Navy nurse in my office, and my secretary. My resources for the care of the President and his family, as well as of his official family in the White House —the Vice President, members of the Cabinet, the Subcabinet, and Presidential aides and assistants—included any military and civilian consultants, as well as technical medical experts, whom I wished to call upon, anywhere.

Strangers unacquainted with the ways of Washington used to ask me if I lived in the White House—I did not—but there was a time when that was true of the White House Physician.[6] President Buchanan (1857–1861) gave his friend Dr. Jonathan M. Foltz a room in the White House, and thus, about a hundred years ago Dr. Foltz became the first physician regularly on duty in the Mansion. Dr. Cary Grayson likewise lived in the White House before he married, when he was assigned by the Surgeon General of the Navy as President Woodrow Wilson's physician.[7] Later, Dr. Grayson stayed there for long periods when the President was ill and his wife laughingly called him a visitor under his own roof.

Soon after my appointment as President Kennedy's Personal Physician, Rear Admiral Joel T. Boone, U.S. Navy, Retired, told me how the official post of White House Physician had evolved. He had served four Presidents. When a young Navy officer, he was first assigned as a physician to the White House in April, 1922, during President Harding's short term of office. J. T. Boone's signature is included as one of the physicians who attended him in his last illness before his death on August 2, 1923, in San Francisco.[8] Boone's assignment was continued through the Presidency of Calvin Coolidge. In those two Administrations, both an Army and a Navy physician served at the White House in the category of military aides to the President. The Commander in Chief was not limited in his choice of such aides.

It was President Hoover who secured legislation that officially constituted the post of "White House Physician" and that recognized the need for systematic "in-house" medical care of the President of the United States. Public Law No. 89–71st Congress (S. 2515), effective March 6, 1929 (retroactive), did not specify a requirement that the President must appoint a White House Physician, nor that the appointee to that position must be a military officer. It provided "that the officer of the Medical Corps, United

[6] Ross T. McIntire and George Creel, *White House Physician* (New York, G. P. Putnam's Sons, 1946), pp. 55–72.
[7] Cary T. Grayson, *Woodrow Wilson: An Intimate Memoir,* Cary T. Grayson, Jr., ed. (New York, Holt, Rinehart and Winston, 1960), p. x.
[8] R. L. Wilbur and C. M. Cooper, "President Harding's Last Illness: Official Bulletins of Attending Physicians," *Journal of the American Medical Association,* Vol. 81 (August 18, 1923), p. 603.

States Army, or of the Medical Corps, United States Navy, below the rank of colonel or captain, respectively, who is now, or hereafter may be, assigned to duty as physician to the White House, shall have the temporary rank and the pay and allowances of a colonel . . . or of a captain . . . while so serving."

The present law [9] reflects a revision so as to include the Medical Corps of the United States Air Force, since that branch of the services was not in existence then.

Admiral Boone wrote me on February 4, 1961:

For approximately eleven years I was . . . in attendance on Presidents and their personal and official families, and [I was] the first physician to be benefitted by Public Law No. 89–71st Congress (S. 2515), as approved April 4, 1930, which, by statute for the first time, established the position and provided the title of Physician to the White House. President Hoover . . . [also made] possible the creation of an office for the Physician to the White House within the White House proper. Until his Administration . . . there was only a medicine bag in use, to be supplemented . . . by a part of a linen closet in the hallway on the second floor of the White House as a makeshift provision for medicines, dressings and sundry medical and surgical supplies. Upon President Hoover . . . taking up residence in the White House, he directed me, as his physician, to select a suitable room for an office. When he saw it he determined forthwith that two rooms would be a necessary requirement.

Dr. Boone told me that he chose for his private office in the Mansion a room on the ground floor directly across the hall from the President's elevator, which was known as the "pool room." In my era it was used by the Secret Service agents and was called the "map room." To connect Dr. Boone's office and treatment room, a doorway was drilled in the thick wall between them. His treatment room was my private office. My treatment room adjoining had been a servants' dining room when he was at the White House.

Admiral Boone brought great dedication to his long public career in medicine. During my first days at the White House he gave me insight into my responsibilities there. His letter to me of February 4, 1961 continued:

I hope, Doctor, you will enjoy thoroughly your new life of vital service to our country in a position of transcendent responsibility only second in importance to the Presidency because you will be the one to keep him fit and physically and mentally well so that he can carry on his incomparable tasks in this volatile world. . . . You will be faced with

[9] United States Code, Section 744, Title 10, p. 1150 (Public Law 70A Stat. I, enacted August 10, 1956).

serious demanding obligations; however, you will be a most privileged person in your profession. I found the White House to be a house of joy, sorrow and tragedy. It always has been such.

And, I think, it will always be so.

President Franklin Roosevelt did not bring a physician with him to the White House and Rear Admiral Boone remained on duty there for a few weeks after Inauguration Day (until March 30, 1933). Dr. McIntire, an eye, ear, nose, and throat surgeon in the U.S. Naval Hospital at Bethesda, reports in his memoirs that his surprise appointment as White House Physician came through Rear Admiral Cary Grayson, a personal friend of President Roosevelt's. When Dr. McIntire demurred about his qualifications, Admiral Grayson told him, "The President is as strong as a horse [although a victim of infantile paralysis] with the exception of a chronic sinus condition that makes him susceptible to colds. That's where you come in." [10]

Dr. McIntire wrote about his duties, "The job is to *keep* [the President] well, to *guard* him against illness, and that entails daily observation and constant watchfulness." [11] As White House Physician, he saw President Roosevelt each morning in his bedroom and in the late afternoon before his therapeutic hour in the White House pool, which had been built for him by popular subscription. At the same time, Dr. McIntire served as chief of the eye, ear, nose, and throat section in the National Naval Medical Center until in 1938 the President appointed him Surgeon General of the Navy. Then Rear Admiral McIntire stated: "At the height of the war, the Medical Department of the Navy, which came under my direction, was made up of 175,000 doctors, dentists, nurses, and hospital corpsmen, 52 general hospitals, and 278 mobile hospitals all over the world." [12]

President Roosevelt belittled the need for having a physician travel with him, but Dr. McIntire usually went along. The President referred to his doctor as a "hitchhiker," just for the ride.[13]

Not until after President Eisenhower's illnesses and at Dr. Howard McC. Snyder's insistence did it become the custom for a physician to travel with the President. It was still an issue during President Kennedy's Administration.

Aside from the primary concern for the health of the President and his immediate family, each White House Physician has shaped that office according to his inclination and professional training and in line with the directives of his sole chief, the President.

[10] Ross T. McIntire and George Creel, *White House Physician*, p. 57.
[11] *Ibid.*
[12] *Ibid.*, p. 64.
[13] *Ibid.*, p. 73.

General Wallace H. Graham, White House Physician to President Truman for nearly eight years, and I had in common, in spite of different professional backgrounds, similar broad interests in medical research and teaching as well as in the personal care of the individual patient. When he left the White House in 1953 at the age of forty-two, Major General Graham, Medical Corps of the United States Air Force, Active Reserve, continued his career as a civilian surgeon. In a letter to me on January 29, 1967, he commented on his tour of duty in the White House:

> This was extremely interesting and pleasant for several reasons; the main one, however, was knowing the fine and interesting people whom it was a pleasure . . . to aid. I never met an undesirable character in the White House. . . . My duties were ramified with such a multiplicity of tasks: teaching at the University [George Washington University School of Medicine], full time duty at Walter Reed Hospital [Chief, Section of Surgery], special missions for the President, domestic and to other countries, establishment of a clinic at the White House, and the early morning and evening hours at the White House in my offices and clinic. . . . I had written different medical articles that were published while [I was] there. . . . President Truman was really a tremendous individual with whom to work. . . . He was not enthusiastic about everyone from the cellar to the stars writing his individual concepts in an authoritative manner. . . . I never went further than gathering material for the subject of physicians in this particular position. Perhaps some day I may get to this, but my practice certainly allows no time now.

Mrs. Graham and two of their children visited me at the White House in 1961, and Dr. Ross McIntire's widow came with her daughter, Mrs. Wilson, in 1962.

The Dispensary, which Dr. Graham started, had grown with the changing panorama of medicine and with the increasing trend for private business, labor unions, and Federal Government agencies to provide on-the-job diagnostic and emergency medical services for their personnel. The people who worked in the White House and its extension, the Executive Office Building, included Secret Service agents, White House police, drivers of the White House cars, the White House Press Corps, the ushers in the Mansion, maids and household workmen, telephone switchboard operators, Mrs. Kennedy's social, press, and correspondence staffs and those of the business and transportation offices in the East Wing of the White House, the special assistants to the President and their secretaries, and the Vice President's staff in his Executive Office Building offices. In the wintry first part of 1961, the Dispensary handled about six hundred visits per month.

The members of our medical department worked long hours and had few idle moments.

The high privilege that I felt in serving as White House Physician was expressed by a young lady of twelve in a letter to me not long after my appointment by President Kennedy: "Dear Dr. Travell, I want to be a child's specialist. I want to help children who need my help. And maybe I'll be able to meet the President and maybe will be his child's physician. This may be a dream but me being a doctor is not. I'm not writing to you for nothing, but to tell you you're a very lucky doctor."

Her dream had almost come true for a pioneer woman pediatrician in the last century. After President Kennedy had broken the tradition of a military man as White House Physician, the story was told of Dr. Anna Easton Lake whom President Grover Cleveland appointed in 1893 as a physician at the White House for his daughter, a victim of cerebral palsy.[14] As Dr. Lake was packing to go to Washington in that position, she was suddenly disabled by a stroke that ended her work in providing free medical care for impoverished crippled children in Baltimore.

The White House physicians must have been hardy. Although in this country doctors as a group do not live as long as the general population, I do not recall that one of them died while attached to the White House or had to leave that position because of illness.

During the four years and two months that I was White House Physician to two Presidents and their families, I missed only one day from my office on account of illness. Although my health was not a problem, I took the precautions of having thorough medical checkups and of taking a sensible dose of regular exercise.

Tennis was convenient to me all the year round, either indoors or out. Washington was a tennis town and my husband had a way of ferreting out the players. He made it easy for me; when I sometimes showed inertia, he overcame it, saying "Come on—I have a game all set up for you."

That sport made friends for us in our new locale. Soon after my appointment by the President, we obtained the use of an indoor court at Pooks Hill. Jack arranged weekend doubles among a group of enthusiasts that included Tish Baldrige, Ted Sorensen, Mike Feldman, Walt Rostow, Frank Keppel, Anne Jones and her son, Boisfeuillet Jr., Mac and Mary Bundy, the Arthur Schlesingers, Dr. Peter Bing of the White House Office of Science, the Reverend Leslie Glenn, and Bob and Peggy LeBaron.

On a Saturday afternoon early in 1964, President Johnson reached me by telephone at the indoor court in Pooks Hill.

[14] Nancy Hoover, "Dr. Anna Easton Lake," *Journal of the American Medical Women's Association,* Vol. 17 (November, 1962), pp. 906–907.

"What are *you* doing on a tennis court, Doctor Travell?" he teased. "Don't you know you're too old for that?"

"I'm running Mike Feldman around, Mr. President," I explained.

Jack and I preferred the popular courts outdoors at the St. Albans School for Boys, but on a weekend we sometimes played on the one that was hidden inside the shrubbery of the White House South Grounds. The patches of shade from the overhanging old trees made for poor visibility, and its hard surface tired our feet.

It was not a hardship when President Kennedy suggested in March, 1961, that for his six-day Easter trip to Florida his office would find me a secluded motel directly on the beach, where I would be accessible to him. Mr. and Mrs. John W. G. Powell registered there and Jack rented a red convertible car. We enjoyed relative privacy. Aside from my visits at the commodious Michael Paul home on North Ocean Boulevard, where the President and his family were staying, I relaxed on the sand in the sun, "on call." The independent arrangement proved satisfactory and we obtained similar accommodations in Palm Beach over the Christmas holidays. A "White House telephone" was connected to the security switchboard from our housekeeping apartment by the ocean.

During the spring of 1960, Mr. Joseph P. Kennedy and I were talking one morning in his New York apartment at 277 Park Avenue when his wife, Mrs. Rose Kennedy, came in from the next room. His face showed amazement as he stared at her.

"Where are you going?" he asked. "You can't go out looking like that."

She was dressed as if for a subteen fashion advertisement. Her black curls peeped out from under an enormous silk kerchief that was tied under her chin. Its point hung nearly to her waist. The gaily flowered silk square surmounted a flaming red wool coat, straight line, full length, buttoned up, and cut for the Junior Miss, size nine. Only the loafers and bobbysocks were missing.

"I'm going to Boston to see my mother. No one will recognize me," she replied with a saucy smile and a tilt of her head.

Her disguise was perfect. As she departed for the airport, the step of that mother of nine matched her attire.

From that event I learned a lesson. When I was at Palm Beach with President Kennedy and I wanted to move around incognito, I drove our bright convertible with the top down, in full sight. I tied a gay scarf over my head, tucked my gray hair under it and wore my sunglasses.

To test the effectiveness of that ensemble, one day I whirled the car off North Ocean Boulevard and drove through the gates of the Paul house without pausing. I looked straight ahead and without a wave or smile of acknowledgment I passed the police guards and Secret Service agent who were stationed at the entrance. Before I had gone far on the curving pebbled driveway screened by palms and semitropical shrubs, I was met by other agents running from the house. With a gasp of surprise, one of them said, "Why, it's Dr. Travell! They didn't recognize you at the gate."

There are some advantages in being a woman.

John Kennedy's first Christmas as President was saddened by his father's stroke on December 19, 1961, in Palm Beach. Mr. Joseph P. Kennedy's niece had called me at the White House that day when he showed signs of illness and I telephoned the President at once in the Executive Office.

President Kennedy came over to the Mansion and sat by my desk while we consulted by long-distance phone with the doctors in St. Mary's Hospital where his father had been taken by ambulance. Mr. Kennedy had suffered a cerebral vascular accident with paralysis and loss of speech. The outlook was grave. I called Dr. William T. Foley, a New York Hospital cardiovascular specialist, and the President asked him to leave at once for Palm Beach to see his father.

As the President and I sat there in my office, tragedy drew us closer.

I knew Mr. Kennedy—"the Ambassador"—well. I admired his brain power and open-mindedness, his directness, his loyalty and anonymous generosity to people in trouble or in need. He never forgot a friend, nor an enemy either, for that matter. His restless energy would make invalidism hard for him to bear—he had always succeeded in achieving his goals. At seventy-three, could he conquer that disability?

I recalled that a year earlier in November and December of 1960, when John F. Kennedy was President-elect and I was flying back and forth between New York and Palm Beach, I stopped more than once to see the Ambassador at his Park Avenue apartment. He was always eager for firsthand personal news of his son.

"How did you find Jack, Doctor?" he would ask. "How did Jack look? How is his weight? What did he say?"

I glimpsed the wall then that success had built between them. I was a bridge across it.

"Mr. Kennedy," I remarked one day, half in jest, "you weren't at the Convention in Los Angeles when Jack got the nomination—when he made his acceptance speech. And I didn't see you on TV after he won the election. I hope you'll be at his Inauguration!"

His eyes filled with tears.

"The country has gained a President, and I have lost a son," he said in a haunting tone.

That December, 1961, in a sense, the son had lost his father.

When I went to St. Mary's Hospital in Palm Beach to talk with the team of physicians and to see Mr. Kennedy, although he could not speak, he gripped my hand to show his pleasure at my being there. The other doctors were strangers to him.

On Christmas Eve, Mr. Kennedy's condition became critical. The President went back to the hospital at 11 P.M. and stayed there for an hour. Shortly after midnight, he telephoned me at the motel to discuss his father's illness. It was not surprising that his back was bothering him somewhat, in view of the extra strain and fatigue—standing, waiting, and sitting in hospital chairs, like any patient's anxious relative. He asked me to come to the Paul house in the morning to examine him. He suggested that it would be wise for Dr. Preston Wade to fly to Palm Beach and to give him another checkup.

I reached Dr. Wade. He was snowed in and would arrive on the second day.

On Christmas morning, I happened to read the newspapers early. To my bewilderment, I was headlined on the front page:

DR. TRAVELL QUITTING AS KENNEDY'S DOCTOR

Dr. Janet Travell, first woman ever to serve as a President's official White House physician, is resigning . . . the Washington Post learned last night. Dr. Travell could not be reached for comment. She is vacationing with her husband in Palm Beach, Fla., apparently in an unofficial capacity. . . . Friends of Dr. Travell here [Washington] last night were surprised at the disclosure. She has not even hinted at leaving. . . . Dr. Travell's family did not know her reason for being in Palm Beach this week [Virginia and Janet had learned discretion], although she and her husband have had a long-standing date to meet one of their daughters there for a family vacation upon her return from Europe. [Both our girls were in Tennessee and joined us in Palm Beach after Christmas, according to plan.] . . . There is only speculation about her reason for leaving. . . . Regular White House observers have noticed a restlessness in Dr. Travell. . . . Some sources conjectured that the President felt, because of his relative youth, he did not need constant [medical] attention.

After nearly a year in the White House, I was still sufficiently naïve to be surprised by such "conjectural journalism," a term that President Woodrow Wilson used with ire in connection with the Washington correspondents.

The meaning of Christmas—hope for the world—was in my mind that December 25 when I saw President Kennedy in his bedroom. His manner of greeting me was not unusual. We went straight to the matter of his problems.

I thought to myself that he had enough worries without my presenting him with one more situation for decision. Finally, I produced the front page of the *Washington Post* and handed it to him.

"I read this morning that I'm resigning," I said. "Mr. President, I will do anything I can for you as long as you wish. But I am ready to leave at a moment's notice, if that is your pleasure."

"I don't want you to leave. If I do, *I* will let you know," he replied.

He stepped to the door and called down the hall, "Pierre, Pierre—come in here."

When Pierre Salinger joined us, the President spoke to him as if they were continuing a conversation.

"That story about Dr. Travell—deny it completely. And you can announce that she has arranged for Dr. Wade to fly down and give me a year-end checkup."

On December 26, the newspapers carried more headlines about me. The *Miami Herald* announced: "Dr. Travell To Resign? . . . In Palm Beach, Press Secretary Pierre Salinger said: 'There is nothing to the report.' Asked whether that meant Dr. Travell was staying on indefinitely, Salinger said that was the case."

The New York *Herald Tribune* of the same date reported:

> The elder Mr. Kennedy underwent an emergency tracheotomy Sunday [Christmas Eve] when he had difficulty in breathing after pneumonia developed. At 12:30 p. m. [Monday, Christmas day], White House press secretary Pierre Salinger issued this bulletin: "Ambassador Kennedy's condition remains serious. . . . His fever . . . has subsided. His doctors are encouraged." . . . Dr. Preston Wade, a New York back specialist will give the President a year-end medical check-up here today in company with Dr. Janet Travell, the President's personal physician. Mr. Salinger denied a report published yesterday . . . that Dr. Travell was resigning. He said it was completely untrue.

The President never did "let me know," and I took it for granted that he meant what he had said.

There was one disadvantage to being a woman, I found, and that was having the correct attire for every occasion when I traveled with the President. On April 14, 1961, Mary Ann Pardue, Washington correspondent for the *Dallas Times-Herald,* surmised: "When President Kennedy leaves for his Paris conference with President Charles de Gaulle on May 31, a very important member of his entourage will be a silver-haired, soft-spoken woman, whose small brown bag undoubtedly will receive especially careful handling among the mountains of luggage that will accompany President and Mrs. Kennedy on their first trip outside the country. . . . The woman is Dr. Janet Travell. . . ."

There was more to my luggage than a medical bag. I started off on that European summit trip by flying to Hyannis Port on Air Force One for the Memorial Day weekend. The President and members of his family stayed in his father's big home on the shore and I occupied his mother's charming room,[15] which had an upstairs porch, like her room at Palm Beach. I took along my beach wear and naturally, I used it. It went with me to Europe.

For the family dinner on May 28 in celebration of the President's forty-fourth birthday the next day I needed a stylish sports dress. I sat on his right at the long table where Ted Sorensen and I had lunched together on the bleak gray day in October, 1958. On that evening in May, the dining room was bright with candlelight and merriment, with confidence in meeting the challenges ahead.

When I flew with the Presidential party to New York, my husband met me at the airport and we had a few hours together. It would have been wise for me to shop and replenish my wardrobe, but I wanted to spend the time with my father in his nursing home at New Rochelle. He was as excited about my overseas trip as if he were going himself.

Then Jack drove me to the Carlyle Hotel in New York. Carrying my heavy medical bag, which I always kept close to me, I joined the President and Mrs. Kennedy for the motorcade from the city and the overnight flight on Air Force One to Orly International Airport outside Paris. There, on May 31, the Chief Executive of the United States and his party were welcomed with military honors.

It had not occurred to me that as a physician I would need a long evening dress—I did not pack one. But I was also in residence at the Palais des Affaires Étrangères on the Quai d'Orsay, and I was invited to some official functions. Staying in that palace were President and Mrs. Kennedy, and also Secretary Rusk, Special Assistants McGeorge Bundy and Kenneth O'Donnell, Air Force Aide Colonel Godfrey McHugh, Dave Powers, Tish Baldrige, and Mrs. Evelyn Lincoln. We were treated like royalty, even to the best of hairdressers.

From Paris on June 1, I wrote a note: "Dear Father; That was a short visit that I had with you, but half a loaf is better than no loaf at all. This is a whirlwind life. The only thing in slow motion is eating. . . . The food is delicious. So far, I have had all my meals in this palatial guest house

[15] Mrs. Rose Kennedy had already left for Europe and would meet the President in Paris.

of the French Government, but tonight I expect to go to a State banquet at Versailles. . . . Keep well. I'll be back soon. Lots of love, Bobby."

The state dinner "en l'honneur de Son Excellence Monsieur JOHN F. KENNEDY Président des États-Unis d'Amérique," given on June 1 by "LE GÉNÉRAL DE GAULLE Président de la République Française," at the glittering "Château de Versailles" was to be a gala affair. It would be followed by a ballet, "Soirée offerte au Théâtre Louis XV," which is a part of the Palace.

I consulted Tish Baldrige. I told her that I could not go that evening because I had nothing to wear. Inches taller than I, she loaned me one of her long formals. I "lifted" it at the shoulders with a few stitches—I knew how to improvise with a needle.

At the reception that preceded the white-tie banquet for some eight hundred people, the Presidents of both countries and their First Ladies— the French called Jackie "la Présidente Jacqui"—formed a receiving line of four in the center of a long salon. A military aide in dress uniform and decorations stood with a megaphone in the wide doorway and he boomed forth the guests' names as they entered, singly or in couples. The announcer waited until they had shaken hands before he admitted the next. It was a dramatic unhurried procession across a wide stage—only there was no audience.

As I swept into the salon alone, in Tish's sapphire-blue flowing chiffon gown and my high hairdo, the aide asked me: "Quel nom, s'il vous plaît?"

"Mrs. Powell," I replied.

"Madame Pow-éll," reverberated from the megaphone.

President Kennedy's eyes sparkled mischievously as he solemnly shook my hand.

"How are *you* feeling tonight?" he said.

Already dressed for the evening, I had asked him that question an hour earlier in his room at the Quai d'Orsay. My "office hours" were whenever I could catch him.

Janet and our grandson Richie—Richard Gordon McAlee—arrived the next morning by sleeper from Milan. I had not seen them in four months— Janet was studying voice in Italy—and I telegraphed her from the Quai d'Orsay. We spent most of that day visiting in my room at the Palais des Affaires Étrangères, and they were invited to have lunch at the single large table that accommodated the staff and members of the American Embassy who had business there.

Afterward, we three stood in a doorway of the wide hall on the second floor of the Palace to watch for President Kennedy when he came from a luncheon with the European press. He would not pass directly by us, but we would be able to see him before he turned off to enter the parlor that adjoined the Presidential bedrooms. Meanwhile, we talked informally with Secretary Rusk—he was waiting, too. When the President strode in, accompanied by a group of people, he recognized Janet and Richie in the distance. He detoured swiftly to shake hands with our small boy and to welcome our daughter. It was like him to give pleasure and proud memories by such a thoughtful act.

Upstairs in my room I put in a call over the trunk line to Martha, my secretary, in Washington. The telephone was identified only as "White House Paris." Within seconds, she answered.

"Dr. Travell, I have Mr. Powell on your other line," she said. "Wait —I'll have the operator switch the call."

Jack had dropped a dime in the slot of a public telephone at National Airport in Washington on his way to visit Virginia in Nashville. Suddenly he found himself talking with me in Paris, and then with Richie and Janet— all for ten cents. Anything could happen at the White House.

After the three-day state visit, I left with the President for Vienna. Across my mind's eye drifted afterimages of huge French and American flags intermingled on the Place de la Concorde, of gendarmes at attention as the Presidential cortège crept past the cheering thousands of ecstatic French citizens, and of the splendor of France's ceremonial welcome to America's young le Président and la Présidente, handsome and beautiful beyond compare.

Vienna was chill and gray when Air Force One—with its military insignia painted over—landed at Schwechat Airport on Saturday morning, June 3. A thin rain was falling and the temperature was in the mid-fifties. It was the lunch hour when we left the airport to drive into Vienna. The highway and streets were lined with people whose drab weary faces matched their rain wear and working clothes. Black umbrellas dotted the crowd. Flags and banners that might have brightened the scene were scarce.

As President and Mrs. Kennedy's limousine passed at a slow speed, the spectators snouted and waved. Then almost at once they lapsed into a curious watching silence.

"They have stood and waited so long in the rain, they're disappointed that the show is so short," I thought to myself. "Perhaps I can wake the spectators."

I was riding about a dozen cars behind the front of the motorcade. I rolled down the rear window beside me so that I could lean out and see ahead along the curb. I picked out groups of people who were more responsive than most of the crowd and when my car drew alongside of them, I flicked my gaily colored scarf rapidly back and forth outside the window.

At the same time, I looked directly into the eyes of the bystanders, holding their gaze briefly. The effect was electric: they came alive again. Their lassitude had been dissipated momentarily by the unknown American lady who smiled at them. Then they lapsed into immobility, as if a ripple had passed over a still lake.

That evening, "Frau Dr. Janet Travell" was invited to the dinner and ballet at the "Schloss Schönbrunn," a gala social function given by Dr. Schärf, the Austrian President, "für Herrn Kennedy, Präsident der Vereinigten Staaten von Amerika, und Ministerpräsident der Sowjetunion, Nikita Sergejewitsch Chruschtschow." The program of entertainment was printed in German, English, and Russian, in that order. In the enormous Palace, the guests moved five times. We assembled in a salon and were served drinks while the top officials of the three countries gathered separately. Then we were presented to the receiving line and proceeded into the "grossen Galerie" for dinner. Coffee was served to everyone in another room. Finally, we were seated for the ballet, which was accompanied by the Viennese Philharmonic Orchestra.

The next morning I wrote a letter to Janet in Milan:

Dear Janet:
    I never in my wildest dreams thought that I would sit at dinner with Khrushchev! Last night I went to the Grand Salle just before eight, in my new yellow short formal that you saw in Paris. It was a "black tie" affair—the Russians wore business suits, of course. There were 250 people seated mostly at tables of six in the brilliantly lighted ballroom. Tables were festive with roses and carnations—no candles as at Versailles. For each two Austrians, one Russian and one American were invited. . . . Before the dinner started, there was a stand-around period, in which fruit juice (pineapple) and vermouth were served.

The procedure for the receiving line was as speedy in Vienna as it had been stately at Versailles. About a dozen people stood in the line, including Mrs. Rose Kennedy. A narrow strip of carpet was laid from door to door about fifteen feet from them, for the guests to traverse. My account to Janet continued:

Everyone filed through a room past a receiving line, but only bowed and didn't shake hands. It moved right along. At the end, those in line filed in last to sit at the center table in the big room. . . . One thing that impressed me about Khrushchev was how short he is—not much over five feet, perhaps. . . . In the drawing room for coffee, President and Mrs. Kennedy, Chairman and Mrs. Khrushchev, sat on a long velvet sofa with everyone milling around, leaning over the back of the sofa and shaking hands. [A coffee table was placed in front of them.] Khrushchev couldn't have been comfortable. His back couldn't reach the backrest, and the seat was too high off the floor. He jumped up and stood . . . at every opportunity. Mrs. Khrushchev never stood up if she could help it, and then very slowly. She walks ponderously. . . . I couldn't help thinking how uncomfortable Chairman K. must be in all the palatial and modern furniture at meetings and conferences. That must make him very irritable.

Our President K. . . . looked his magnetic best. Jackie was radiant.

During the coffee hour I stood only a few feet from their sofa, but I did not intrude on their conversation. I moved around the salon talking with the mixed international representatives. Nearly everyone spoke excellent English. Mrs. Eunice Shriver introduced me to the Russian diplomat, Andrei Gromyko. I turned aside while they laughed over a personal joke. Afterward, I asked Eunice if she might tell me what was said.

"Oh, yes. He asked me if my brother, the President, was hard to live with, and I said he was. Very hard to live with. Mr. Gromyko said, 'I hadn't noticed it.' "

My detailed account to Janet on June 4 continued:

After coffee we moved into another salon with little gilt chairs on three sides of a square and the orchestra on the fourth. [The ballet dancers performed in the center, almost brushing those in the front rows.] I sat about 25 feet from Khrushchev [in the second row on one side] where I could watch the expressions and gestures of those in the VIP row. Khrushchev clapped in a restrained manner—slow rhythm, hands very slightly cupped and never separated by more than 1 to 2 inches. He held them in his lap. He only used his fingertips for contact. His wife let her hands hang down at her side and applauded gently. President Kennedy held his hands well out and up, and clapped vigorously and fast. . . . More later.

Love,
Mummy

That day in Vienna, I noticed that when official pictures were taken outside, Khrushchev was usually standing one step higher than President Kennedy on a flight of steps and their eyes were on a level. When they stood on even ground, the top of Khrushchev's bald head reached up to the point of President Kennedy's chin. Sitting together on the sofa, by comparison the Russian Chairman appeared taller than he was because he perched stiffly on its hard front edge.

At Hyannis Port later in the summer of 1961, thinking of the gain in personal communication between the leaders of the U.S.A. and the U.S.S.R. that had been made at that summit conference, I suggested to President Kennedy that he might wish to send Chairman Khrushchev a rocker. If not, he might let me design a chair to fit him.

"Khrushchev might be easier to deal with if he could sit more comfortably," I said.

"We have enough to do without that," was the quick rejoinder. The Berlin Wall was being built—the President was not amused.

Flying back to the United States on June 4, 1961, I wrote to my father: "Last night I had dinner with Khrushchev in the palace at Vienna and two evenings before with de Gaulle at Versailles. . . . Tonight I will be in Nashville, by-passing London. It's no wonder that you can't keep up with my itinerary. I am . . . on the march with history."

Prior to the European trip, at President Kennedy's request, I had agreed to deliver the commencement address on June 5 at the Meharry Medical College in Nashville, Tennessee. After flying over Greenland and changing planes at New York's Idlewild Airport, my flight reached Nashville at 3 A.M. on the day when I was to speak, in the afternoon.

Taking into account the seven-hour time difference, I had been twenty-six hours in transit from Vienna to Nashville. Fortunately, my long-standing pattern of office hours day and night had demolished my biological clock. Jet travel across that many time zones did not disturb me.

Before I went to Europe with President Kennedy, I was offered a medical writer from the National Institutes of Health to help in preparing my commencement address. Busy as I was, I preferred to do my own thinking.

I wanted to express in my words what it is that distinguishes the medical professions from all others and that draws physicians together regardless of their race, nationality, or creed.

To those young graduates of Meharry Medical College I said:

It is a pleasure to tell you that President Kennedy . . . asked me to extend his best wishes to you on this important occasion. As a physician, I am here in my own right to welcome you into the healing professions. There are bonds between us . . . that time and distance and changing circumstances can never erase. The degree that each of you has earned, and received today, is an unseen force . . . that converts strangers, who may not even speak the same language, into colleagues and confrères almost at once.

During your stay in this 85-year-old Medical College of fine tradition and high academic standards, you young men and women dedicated to medicine, nursing and dentistry have shared hard work and exposure to human suffering, and have tasted the exhilarating experi-

ence of healing the sick. You have done this in common with thousands
of other young women and men who are now receiving similar degrees throughout the world. All these are your friends.

What is the nature of the ties that draw us so close—more so than
for any other occupation or profession? . . . Foremost is mutual respect. No profession sets for itself such high standards of intellectual
achievement and at the same time devotion to human welfare as do
medicine and its partner professions. The foundation of mutual respect in our medical world is intelligence. . . . Another basis for our
universal kinship is our common goal, the betterment of mankind in all
lands. . . .

But, you might object, other professions have man's welfare as their
ultimate objective. The engineers . . . those engaged in agricultural
production and development would do away with malnutrition, that is
of global proportions.

Such professions differ fundamentally from ours in that they lack
the personal responsibility of a physician for his patient. We deal not
with man's well-being in the abstract, but with the life and death of
people known to us for their strengths and weaknesses, their success
and their sorrows. We are privileged with insight into the souls of
men.

But, you say, so are the ministers of religion who guide the way
toward a better world through the brotherhood of man and faith in
God. This profession, too, entails personal relationships and responsibility.

In the medical sciences, our real uniqueness lies in the fact that we
often hold in our hands the specific tools for alleviating pain and illness, immediately, personally, directly. This power to relieve suffering must be nurtured with humility, and never tarnished by jealousy,
avarice, laziness or disinterest on our part. . . .

It has been said that medicine is the only profession that consistently works to put itself out of business. If its goal, the conquest
of disease, were achieved, what then would there be left for us to do?

The challenges of the future for medicine lie in the possibilities of
modifying the behavioral patterns of the human race for the good of
Society. . . . The behavioral science of the future is indeed already on
the doorstep of the present.

June 5 was a kaleidoscopic day. Dr. Harold D. West, President of
Meharry Medical College, and I gave a television broadcast. There were
newspaper interviews with picture-taking at Virginia and Ed's home. It was
tantalizing for me to have only about an hour with our two- and four-year-
old grandchildren, Janet and Gordon Street. At a reception I met the officers, trustees, and faculty of the medical college. Mayor Ben West pre-

sented me with a Key to the City of Nashville, and the outdoor commencement exercises followed in ninety-degree heat.

A swim in Victor S. Johnson's pool—he was Chairman of the Meharry
Board—and a steak cookout ended the evening. I had left for Europe via
Hyannis Port nearly two weeks before, and I still had a bathing suit in my
bag.

Early the next morning I was flying to Washington. President Kennedy
was on his way back from London after dining on June 5 with Queen Elizabeth at Buckingham Palace.

"Gina" Street, prize-winning sculptor and painter, "explained" me reflectively in her press interview in Nashville:

> Dr. Travell [Mummy] thrives on the hectic schedule. . . . She's in
> fantastic health and believes in vitamins and exercise for everyone. She
> plays tennis, swims, rides horseback. She's always been very busy and
> very happy whether in lecturing or in writing a book. . . . Life [at
> home] was never boring. . . . We were urged to be creative, do some-
> thing useful and develop our own interests. A great many doctors and
> professional people used to come home discussing medicine and sci-
> ence, something like the latest rocket design or Nobel Prizes. . . .
> Dr. Travell is casual, dresses quickly and will never learn the intri-
> cacies of diplomatic protocol. She also has a green thumb and saves
> coffee grounds and old egg shells for prize ferns.[16]

It was a true profile of me.

In amplification of what Virginia said then, I might quote from a letter
that I wrote from the White House to a twelve-year-old Boy Scout:

> Taking care of a President requires constant attention to the preven-
> tive aspects of medicine . . . because the President does not have
> time to be ill. Neither does the physician who is responsible for the
> President's well-being. Physical fitness is built by habits of living from
> youth all the way through the "golden years" of advancing age. What
> the Boy Scouts' organization is doing for you, and you in turn for it,
> will go a long way toward ensuring you a vigorous healthy body and a
> sound disciplined mind. Taking care of a President's health involves
> long hours of work and lots of detail—but so does any job that is worth
> doing.

Preventive medicine at the White House involved so many details of
daily living that my secretary once laughingly referred to my office as "the
miscellaneous department." On our European trip in 1961, President Kennedy's back comfort and also his allergies required him to use his own

[16] Julie Hollabaugh, "Dr. Travell Here Tomorrow," *The Nashville Tennessean*, June 3,
1961, p. 6.

pillows and mattress—a matter for some comment abroad. Special mattresses without inner springs had been made up to provide the extra firm support that he liked and to fit the different-sized beds that he used at Glen Ora, Camp David, and Hyannis Port, as well as on Air Force One and in the White House. The outlandish story, published in August, 1962, that the President's mattresses were manufactured only out of the imported tails of white Argentine horses was false; his allergy to horse dander precluded the use of any horsehair in his mattresses.

President Kennedy made me aware of his interest in my medical activities and of his concern for my continuing professional growth.

Shortly after I came to the White House, I received a formal invitation to join the faculty of the Department of Medicine as Associate Clinical Professor at the George Washington University School of Medicine. Not knowing then what the demands of my office would be, I deferred replying to that welcome opportunity. About a week later, President Kennedy remarked, "Doctor, have you accepted that appointment at George Washington University yet? You should do it right away. You should align yourself with academic medicine in Washington."

That was the President's fourth and last directive to me.

As a member of the faculty, I attended with special pleasure the outdoor ceremonies on May 3, 1961, when Dr. Thomas H. Carroll was installed as President of George Washington University and President Kennedy received an Honorary Doctorate of Laws. In the morning sunshine, John F. Kennedy received an ovation when he closed his address with the remarks: "I am particularly glad to be here today when we are witnessing the swearing-in of a new President. Many years ago, as most of you know, at Harvard University somebody came around and asked for President Lowell. They said, 'He's in Washington seeing Mr. Taft.' I know that some other day, when they are asking for the President of your University, they will say that he is over at the White House seeing Mr. Kennedy."

My own relationship with George Washington University School of Medicine and Hospital could not have proved happier.

President Kennedy wanted me to teach physicians my special skills for rapid relief of skeletal muscle pain that had benefited him and the many people whom he had sent to me as patients. With his approval, I accepted invitations to lecture and to give clinical demonstrations whenever it was feasible. In the vicinity of Washington, I talked to many groups—hospital staffs and medical students—that included the U.S. Naval Hospital in Bethesda, the Clinical Center of the National Institutes of Health, George Washington and Georgetown University Hospitals, Mount Alto Veterans Administration Hospital, Casualty Hospital, the National Orthopaedic and

Rehabilitation Hospital in Arlington, the University of Maryland Medical College in Baltimore, and the Women's Medical Society of the District of Columbia.

At intervals, I traveled to more distant universities, at Iowa City, Buffalo, and Chicago, and to military hospitals. As Special Consultant to the United States Air Force, Office of the Surgeon General, I participated in teaching programs at the Wilford Hall Hospital of Lackland Air Force Base, Texas, at Travis Air Force Base in California and Otis Air Force Base on Cape Cod. In each of three years, I taught at the School of Aerospace Medicine of the Aerospace Medical Division, Brooks Air Force Base, Texas, where I renewed my friendship with Lawrence E. Lamb, M.D., Chief of the Aerospace Medical Sciences Division. Besides my formal lectures, in clinics patients with stubborn pain problems were presented to me for examination and treatment. I like to think that I was able to keep flying a few key pilots who might otherwise have been grounded.

Soon after I came to the White House, at President Kennedy's request I held an interview with the editors of *U. S. News & World Report*.[17] President Kennedy urged me to present my observations directly to the public with the aim, I thought, of also informing physicians about my research in painful muscle spasm lasting long after the injury or overexercise that caused it.

Dr. Walter Tkach, on my first day in the Dispensary, had warned me about the volume of mail that the White House Physician had to handle. If the object of that interview was to alert people to my work, I can only conclude that it was eminently successful. I was deluged by a flood of letters from sufferers with maladies of all sorts. Many were obviously not in the category of musculoskeletal pain that I had been discussing. I could not answer the hundreds of letters promptly. In the interim, I sent a general reply to the editor of the magazine, in which I stated:

1. Procaine injection of the muscles is not a "cure-all," as I clearly indicated in the interview. For this treatment to be effective, it must be used in the condition for which it was intended.

2. Treatment of the muscles will not cure multiple sclerosis, amyotrophic lateral sclerosis, scoliosis, rheumatoid arthritis or a multitude of other neurological and structural disorders.

3. For me to recommend a doctor for anyone when I have no real knowledge of the diagnosis, would be folly. . . .

4. The best way to obtain continuity of medical care is for your own physician to make the appropriate referral. In the long run, you

17 "Kennedy's Doctor Tells How to Relieve Aches and Pains," February 20, 1961, pp. 66–71.

will do better to stay with your own doctors who are struggling to achieve the best possible result and are well acquainted with your problem. My advice is to continue to have confidence in them.[18]

Before I mailed my "Letter to the Editor," I showed the draft to President Kennedy. He picked up a pencil from his executive desk and crossed out my fifth point, which dealt with the scope of my duties at the White House. In its place, he wrote at the bottom of the page: "I believe that most doctors are becoming more aware of the problems connected with muscle spasm—and more concerned with effective treatment of them."

His revision was to the point. It was one more example of his lively interest in my scientific contribution to medicine and also of his ability to highlight in simple words the crux of a problem.

The discouragement of strangers—young and old—who wrote about their pain and disability distressed me. I would have liked to advise many of them, but my uninformed meddling would not have helped them. I gladly corresponded with their doctors who desired it. I never tired of the challenge presented by the real clinical problems of painful muscle spasm.

Complexities in the diagnosis and treatment of painful stress disorders of the skeletal musculature begin to be apparent if one considers how many words can be made from twenty-six letters of the alphabet. The parts of the human body are moved by more than *seven hundred* muscles, and the combinations of muscular strains that can be created by internal and external forces are infinite. In addition, each person may be imagined as representing a different language, or dialect.

President Kennedy's confidence in my ability to thread the maze of overlapping pain patterns of the muscles prompted him to request that I see members of the hard-working White House staff and people there on political business or as guests, who had pain of clinical consequence. He would call me himself, saying, "Doctor, *do* something about it."

Such an order from the President delighted me. Seeing patients was the breath of my medical existence.

The President was likely to follow up on the result himself. Sometimes he sent me copies of pertinent correspondence. I made it a rule to tell him what provision I had arranged for future care by the patient's own physician.

With respect to my services, the President made no distinction between Republicans and Democrats.

The day before I came to Washington for the official announcement of

[18] "A Letter From the President's Doctor," *ibid.*, March 13, 1961, p. 16.

my appointment on January 25 by Pierre Salinger, Senator Barry Goldwater consulted me in New York. His was my last appointment in that office. When he was questioned about me, the Associated Press quoted him as commenting: "I certainly hope Jack's kind to me and lets her treat me once in a while. . . . [I] visited her in New York this week without learning she was about to get the White House appointment. . . . I told her I hoped to see her soon again but she was a little indefinite—I thought she was going to be busy writing a book. I was pleasantly surprised when I read she had been appointed White House physician."

On reading that statement some years later, my husband remarked dryly, "Writing a book excuses everything."

When Senator Goldwater wrote to President Kennedy on February 24, 1961, the President sent me a copy of the letter:

Dear Mr. President:

For a time I thought you had developed a new way to get rid of this particular Republican, the method being to monopolize the services of Dr. Travell, but yesterday she called and told me of your personal interest, and I cannot begin to thank you enough for this.

You will probably do many fine things in your life, but I doubt that you will ever do anything finer for the American people than you have done in bringing this remarkable woman to their attention. I recall that you said it was your desire to do this, and now that you have done it you should be very proud. I am willing to bet you think, as I do at times, that the sweetness and graciousness of this lady does as much for our aching muscles as her chills and needles.

My best wishes to you always,
Barry

Two years later, a comment was made within the White House that President Kennedy was recruiting me to improve relations between the Executive Branch and Congress. That remark was prompted by a letter from Congressman William S. Moorhead on April 29, 1963, a copy of which the President sent to me:

Dear Mr. President:

Just about every newspaper in the country has felt free to make comments or suggestions for the improvement of relationships between the Executive and the Congress. Therefore, a comment by a Member of Congress might not be out of order.

My suggestion does not involve any increase in the budget or personnel, because right now in the White House organization, there is the answer, and it isn't my friend, Larry O'Brien, or any of his equally able associates. No, I refer to one who, as I know from personal experience, can treat a Congressman with the kindness of a Florence Nightingale combined with the authoritarianism of General DeGaulle over the Chamber of Deputies.

It has been alleged that on occasion arm twisting is the proper technique for the handling of Congress. As an erstwhile sufferer from tennis elbow, I recommend one who uses Novocain before she twists the arm of a Member of Congress, making the whole process painless and effective. She has even added strength to my backbone, which is a good, if dangerous, thing for a politician.

My sincere thanks to you for letting me see my candidate—your own—the incomparable—Dr. Janet Travell.

Respectfully yours,
Bill

P.S.: By the appropriate use of felt shoe pads, Dr. Travell can correct a tendency to lean too far to the left or to the right. The potential political results from the application of this technique stagger the imagination.

Bill

According to Congressman Moorhead's deductions in his P.S., since President Kennedy's left leg was a trifle shorter, the heel lift that I prescribed must have leaned him toward the right—but not beyond the center.

I am glad to say that my efforts with the Congress established an excellent relationship between the Attending Physician to the United States Capitol, Rear Admiral George W. Calver, and myself.

Many people had an idea that I had nothing to do but sit around and wait for the President to get sick. My mail piled up, to be answered in free moments, and I did it like knitting. I dictated replies to Martha, attached longhand memoranda to letters, talked into the microphone of my dictating machine, and typed drafts of more complicated answers on my small portable electric typewriter. The perspective into people's minds that the correspondence provided fascinated me.

One day early in 1963, my secretary asked me, "Dr. Travell, do you realize how much mail goes out of this office every day?"

"No, I have no idea," I said.

"You are putting out about a thousand letters a month," she told me.

Much of my mail dealt with questions, advice, and comments about the President's health. Strangers who had met John F. Kennedy in his younger days wrote to tell me their impressions of him and to commend him as President. An especially poignant letter, dated February 17, 1961, came from a manufacturing chemist, Mr. Ernest W. Rose, Sr.:

Dear Dr. Travell:

Sixteen years ago this month, Mrs. Rose and I were guests at the Camel Back Inn, in Arizona. At that time, President Kennedy was also a guest at the Inn. Our table in the dining room was right next to Mr. Kennedy's. We saw him every day for a month. He evidently was trying to recover from shock. He had just been dismissed from service . . . after his ship was sunk by the Japs.

At that time, little did we dream that this ill, sad and lonely young man would be President of the United States. More power to him. It is the most ardent wish of the Rose family that with your help President Kennedy may have continued health, happiness and success.

My office was at a crossroads of traffic in the White House. After my staff went home at the end of the afternoon, I waited for President Kennedy to leave the Executive Office in the West Wing and come over to the Mansion, at about 8 P.M. He usually paused to step inside my room, where a table lamp illuminated my day's collection of scientific reading matter. When there were items of special interest, I left the pages open to catch his eye—an editorial in *Science,* a review in *The Pharos* of Alpha Omega Alpha, Honor Medical Society, or perhaps the reprint of a medical article.

"Doctor, do you mind if I take this with me?" he would inquire without lifting his gaze from the page.

One day he borrowed my autographed copy of Nobel Laureate Wendell Stanley's new book on the nature of viruses,[19] and I asked my friend, the author, to send another for the President. When it came, George Thomas and I located the book on the President's bedside table and I substituted his copy for mine.

My protean taste for the new frontiers of science provided a handy accessory library for the President.

Occasionally, I showed him an entertaining letter about himself. With a smile, he would tuck it in his pocket and say, "I'll answer that one."

Like her father, Caroline had a habit of dropping in—at a run—to see what was on my reading table. She could not read yet, but I kept a file of magazines for her that were illustrated with color pictures of horses, birds, and strange creatures in their natural settings.

"Dr. Travell, can I have this to show my Mommy?" she would ask politely.

"Of course, Caroline, take it along." One day, flipping the pages I remarked, "There's a particular picture in this you would like."

[19] Wendell M. Stanley and Evans G. Valens, *Viruses and the Nature of Life* (New York, E. P. Dutton & Co., 1961).

"Don't show it to me," Caroline said as she took the magazine out of my hands. "I want to be surprised when my Mommy shows it to me."

Trailing behind Caroline came John. He made a beeline for the telephone that he could just reach on the desk. He picked up the receiver and immediately started telling his Daddy something. John seemed to think that his father was connected with that black instrument. The White House operators must have understood and put John's calls through.

John liked to look at the handsome smiling color photograph of President Kennedy above my desk. He would jump up and down pointing both hands at it.

"Tocter Tarbell, there's my Dadee, there's my Dadee!" he would repeat.

Caroline sometimes brought in a playmate and asked, "Dr. Travell, can we see the Neanderthal man?"

She was fascinated by a small model of the skeleton and reconstructed figure of primitive man that President Kennedy had given me at his birthday party in 1961 at Hyannis Port.

"Is he a bad guy?" Caroline asked me once as she studied the Neanderthal man.

"No, Caroline, not really," I replied. "He just never had the advantages of an education—he never went to school like you. And he was born without much brain to think with. You see how little of his head there is above his eyebrows."

I turned to Martha sitting at her desk. "Look at Martha and you'll see the difference. She has a lot above her eyebrows."

Quickly Caroline raised her hand to her forehead and asked, "How much do I have above my eyebrows?"

"Plenty," I replied.

Caroline always noticed colors.

"Have you any other color dresses?" she would ask, regarding me seriously.

She liked to show me her dresses hanging in the closet and she named their different shades. Pink was her favorite.

When Caroline and John came into the Mansion through the Diplomatic Reception Room on the ground floor, their dogs—Charlie, the Welsh terrier, and Clipper, the German shepherd—often raced down the hall and reached my room first. Charlie usually landed in my lap. In the quiet of the evening, sometimes a huge black furry head slowly appeared around my half-open door. Then Brumus the Great would place his nose in my hand and settle down to wait for his master. I knew that Bobby Kennedy, the Attorney General, was in the building when his gigantic Newfoundland came to visit me. Dogs were not allowed in the living quarters on the second floor.

Physical fitness programs, good and bad, were the mode. For exercise, when I had been sitting too long in my office, I could have relied on simply jogging in place beside my desk, but it was more fun to jump rope. Scientific study had demonstrated that five minutes of rope skipping a day improved the physical condition of untrained subjects within a relatively short period.[20] I kept several jump ropes handy and my nurse, my secretary, and I were known to have shut the doors and taken turns skipping rope in my inside treatment room.

The long, carpeted hall outside my door would have been a temptation to any rope-skipper. One evening when all was still, to the amusement of the White House guard, I turned my rope and jumped it at a run down the hall's length. Just as I started back from the far end of the soft red carpet, Caroline, John, and Miss Shaw entered unexpectedly after a late outing. I was caught. Caroline ran alongside me with envy and delight. Afterward, she would rush up to me at embarrassing moments and request loudly: "Dr. Travell, please, I want to see you jump rope down the hall again."

Although I knew the benefits of regular exercise on many indices of health, I recognized also that sporadic bursts of strenuous exercise could be as harmful as physical inactivity. Both the abuse and proper use of exercise were the theme of an article written with Dave Lewis in which we stated:

> In the United States we have become . . . victims of the demand for excelling in sports. The goal should be physical excellence, achieved through sports. . . . A thoroughly healthy nation depends on a solid "middle-class" of athletes who never win a championship but who, on the other hand, have skills just adequate to enjoy whatever sport they pursue. . . .
>
> One of the fundamental health problems facing our nation today is that of getting our young people to develop proper exercise habits, so that their muscles are trained for sturdy use in later life. Another problem is getting ourselves to keep those muscles exercised and healthy when later life arrives. . . .
>
> Variety is the key to getting the right kind of exercise. . . . If you specialize in only one kind, there is the likelihood of overworking one set [of muscles] and not giving the remainder enough work. . . . Keep your exercising well within the bounds of your energy. . . . The best guide is to stop when you begin to tire—don't wait until you are exhausted. . . . Not all varieties are equally good for everybody, and

[20] D. Merritt Jones, Chadwick Squires, and Kaare Rodahl, "Effect of Rope Skipping on Physical Work Capacity," *The Research Quarterly*, Vol. 33 (May, 1962), pp. 236–238.

there are times—too soon after eating or during recovery from [infectious illness]—when strenuous activity of any kind should be avoided. . . . Coordinating exercise, which is designed to develop agility, rather than conditioning exercise, designed to develop sheer muscle power, will stand you in good stead as life becomes more sedentary. . . .

"The physical vigor of our citizens is one of America's most precious resources," wrote John F. Kennedy. . . .

It is my task to remind the President of his admonition.[21]

Meditating on my federalized existence, in a lighter vein I wrote a series of verses about:

HOW THEY GOT PHYSICAL FITNESS

I. THE HEN

> The hen sat to brood,
> Sultry was her mood.
> Her exercise was scratching lice,
> Her coop was overrun with mice,
> Food did not suffice.
>
> More room for living,
> Air-conditioning,
> Ratproof kitchen she would entice
> From FHA—and some device
> For home exercise.
>
> Reborn a housewife,
> She ran in this life
> So hard, by housework so driven,
> Each night she wished she were a hen
> In a coop again.

(FHA—*Federal Housing Administration,* an agency that has the power to condemn land and buildings and to plan and finance new housing developments.)

II. THE CLAM

> The clam in the sand
> Took himself in hand
> His fitness program to revise
> And locomotion to devise
> Before his demise.

[21] Janet G. Travell and David D. Lewis, "Fit to Be President," *Sports Illustrated,* April 3, 1961, pp. 8–9.

Sedentary, soft,
The clam edged aloft.
His magic dinner, we surmise,
Was DNA; to his surprise
Mobile did he rise.

With other turtles
On now he hurtles.
His legs as oars work at the sides,
A rudder steers the rear besides,
His shell skims the tides.

(DNA—*Deoxyribonucleic acid,* a molecule of the gene that determines hereditary characteristics of man and animals; the mutation and origin of new species depend on rearrangements within the DNA molecule.)

III. THAT CAMEL

The clumsy camel
Was slow in travel,
Resented his odd lot that he
Was laid out by—it's clear to see—
A large Committee.

This Panel's mad plans
The public now pans.
The camel sought an Agency
Called GSA. Who could foresee
What changes would be!

They cut off his humps
And streamlined his rumps,
Made him a steed of equine grace
Who wins the fifty mile free race,
Pegasus of space.

(GSA—*General Services Administration,* the Federal agency that supervises the design, construction, and maintenance of Federal buildings and their equipment, including garages and means of transportation.)

IV. HOMO SAPIENS

The man in his cage
Chinned himself in rage.
All day he labored to deduce
A clever ruse, some way abstruse
His weight to reduce.

Hearings he arranged,
Science so deranged

That he was able to seduce
The FDA; got by abuse
LSD for use.

He resigned manhood
And resumed apehood,
As per the drug's effects adverse.
Now evolution in reverse
Spares him from the hearse.

(FDA—*Food and Drug Administration,* a Federal agency that controls, with respect to safety and clinical effectiveness, the manufacture, labeling, and distribution of drugs and therapeutic devices for human beings.

LSD—*Lysergic acid diethylamide,* a drug with unusual psychological effects, transient or permanent; it causes a dissociation of the personality from reality, hallucinations, or a state of exaggerated imagination.)

The windows of my offices were barred and sometimes I felt momentarily as though I were the Homo sapiens living in a cage.

Close outside my window, a child's rope swing with a wood seat hung from the old magnolia tree that bore white waxen flowers in the spring. Starlings roosted in the trees of the White House grounds, and I took the precaution of having samples of soil underneath tested for the presence of fungi, such as histoplasmosis, that can cause disease in man.

Across the driveway, Caroline and John's playhouse, jungle gym, and slide were erected where their father in the Executive Office could watch them at play. When John fell and knocked out a front tooth there, I notified Dr. Edward B. Broocks, the pediatrician, and I arranged for a dentist to come to the White House. On the floor below my suite in the Mansion was a fully equipped dental office.

From my desk I could see the helicopters land and take off on the south lawn. But usually I stepped outdoors to join the welcoming group of personnel whenever visiting heads of government arrived at the White House. Then, the helicopters landed farther away beyond the fountains. There the whirling rotors would not whip the national flags presented by the honor guard, nor disarrange the hair of the ladies who stood in the receiving line on the red carpet laid across the green to a platform for speeches. Opposite the microphones, reporters and photographers lined up to wait in a roped-off section on the grass.

I marveled at the precision of President Kennedy's official welcome to visiting dignitaries. His timing was perfect. At the exact instant, he strode from the West Wing along the circular drive to the South Portico awning, where they stepped from limousines that drove them the short distance from the helicopters. I felt the march of history as I heard the ceremonial guns boom salutes and as I watched the procession of foreign representatives who came to meet our young President—Sukarno of Indonesia; Fanfani, Premier of Italy; Prime Minister Macmillan of the United Kingdom; Chancellor Adenauer of West Germany; and many more. The outdoor arrival ceremony for Marshal Josip Broz Tito of Yugoslavia was held on October 17, 1963, and I met the alert Mrs. Broz in the Mansion afterward.

A year earlier, on a Friday—October 19—President Kennedy was leaving on a trip West. At my office window, through the low-hanging branches of the magnolia I watched him walk briskly from the West Wing across the lawn to "Chopper Number One." The usual retinue of aides and Secret Service agents trailed behind him. They boarded the helicopter and I waited to see the steps drawn up, the door closed, and the "big bird," as Caroline called it, fly past the Washington Monument.

Instead, the President unexpectedly reappeared in the doorway and descended the steps alone.

"How unusual," I thought. Then I saw why.

Jackie, her hair wild in the gale of the rotors, was running from the South Portico across the grass. She met him almost at the foot of the helicopter steps and she reached up with her arms. They stood motionless in an embrace for many seconds. Then she returned under the awning and he was away.

Perhaps no one else noted that rare demonstration of affection. A few days later in the publicized hours of the Cuban missile crisis, I remembered it. I thought on its deep significance—the unbreakable bond of love between them that showed clearest in times of trouble.

The next morning, news flashes reported:

The President is ill. A cold, a fever, force cancellation of his trip. He is returning home at once from Chicago to rest.

That Saturday, I stood at my office window again and watched the helicopter land just outside. The President entered the Mansion through the South Portico and the Diplomatic Reception Room. He passed my door on the ground floor and before he entered the elevator, he spoke to me.

"I'll see you in a few minutes, Doctor."

I picked up the telephone in my inner office. Standing with my back to the door, I was receiving a report from Dr. Burkley, who had gone on the flight West. Suddenly, I was startled to see the President standing in the room a few feet away. In mid-sentence I dropped the receiver on its hook and moved nearer to him. I searched his face for signs of illness.

He spoke softly, gently.

"Don't be worried about me," he said.

His face was set, but his eyes smiled. I smiled in return.

No other word was spoken. He turned and hurried on to the Executive Office. We had communicated many things in the language of silence and I knew that there was no need to question his health. His concern for me had stilled my anxiety about him.

While I was at the White House, that was the only occasion when the "diplomatic illness" was utilized. It was classed as the "uncommon cold."

I was delighted when Jackie and the President early in 1963 asked me to devote myself to her care in collaboration with Dr. John W. Walsh, her obstetrician, and to be with her until after the birth of their third child in September. The secret of the pregnancy was well kept until the planned announcement in April at Palm Beach.

In some respects our consultations and communications reminded me of a James Bond intrigue. I smiled to myself when I read Dr. Ross T. McIntire's argument that the White House Physician should be a military man and not a civilian. He wrote: "Through long-established custom it is the habit of presidents to select either an Army or a Navy doctor . . . [as] the medico who will look after their well-being. There are many good reasons for naming a member of the service. These men are officers as well as physicians, and being subject to the iron discipline of the armed services, they can be counted on to keep a close mouth about what they see and hear." [22] He implied that a civilian doctor could not.

His other reasons were that the civilian who might serve as White House Physician would not "find much of a private practice on his return," and that the "fees of a civilian doctor would have to come out of the chief executive's own pocket." He was in error on all three counts.

The selection of Walter Reed Army Medical Center as her hospital was Jackie's, not her physicians'. Since she would spend the summer months at Hyannis Port, a medical facility in that area had to be alerted in case of an emergency Cesarean section. In the late spring, Dr. Walsh and I flew together to the Cape and made a tour of three hospitals. We concluded that Otis Air Force Hospital provided the best combination of medical service, security, and accessibility. It was a happy choice. In spite of the sad loss of the premature infant, Jackie called it the most pleasant hospital in which she had ever been a patient. That she said so was a credit to the Air Force personnel at the hospital and to the foresight of Surgeon General Richard L. Bohannon.

Members of the press were unreasonable and unkind, I thought, in their

[22] Ross T. McIntire and George Creel *White House Physician*, p. 58.

jibes about the simple preparation of a hospital wing, Building 3703, at Otis Air Force Base. The one-story frame building that resembled the air base barracks had been readied after the 1960 election for President Kennedy's use as an office or as a hospital while he stayed at Hyannis Port. The Kennedy children had been moved there for safety in September when a hurricane threatened Cape Cod, and Air Force VIPs had occasionally used the suite. That July, the walls were washed and a standard incubator placed in a room designated as the nursery. A mobile dishwasher was rolled into the diet kitchen from another part of the hospital, an inexpensive garbage disposal unit installed, and new dishes were purchased. Window air-conditioners were rented because security could not be assured if the ground level windows were open. A steel mesh screen was placed over the window of the bedroom for the President. The two-year-old furnishings looked like new.

On July 24, the *New York Journal-American* carried a "Combined Wire Service" news item:

BUILD SPECIAL WING FOR JACKIE

Elaborate facilities have been set up for Mrs. Jacqueline Kennedy to have her baby next month at Otis Air Force Base, Mass., it was learned last night. A special wing has been prepared at the Cape Cod base, 18 miles from Hyannisport, at a cost of more than $12,000. It includes such features as bulletproof windows and an adjacent room reserved for the President. The suite is being held on a standby basis by Mrs. Kennedy's obstetrician, Dr. John W. Walsh, and White House physician, Dr. Janet Travell. . . . The specially built wing of the Otis AFB Hospital was reported to contain seven or eight rooms, connected by a corridor to the main hospital building. It is 100 feet from the delivery room.

Columnists took up the story and on July 27, one of them wrote in the New York *Daily News:*

Jacqueline Kennedy . . . will celebrate her 34th birthday in Hyannis Port, Mass., presumably unaware of the exercise in confusion in Washington this week over where her third child will be born [as if anyone could predict!] . . . It is understandable that there should be some befuddlement among the palace guard over such details as to whether Otis Air Force Base Hospital on Cape Cod had refurbished an eight-room maternity suite to the tune of $5,000 for Mrs. Kennedy's use. In the middle of the muddle was the President's press secretary, Pierre Salinger. He stoutly maintained that he knew nothing of any switch in plans [there had been none] and that Mrs. Kennedy would go to the Walter Reed Army Medical Center. . . . If the word was a little late in getting to Pierre, he can take comfort in the fact that Cleveland's secretary was not even informed of the . . . birth of baby Esther until two hours after the event. Even in that day the press was annoyed at this delay in getting the news. . . . It is a matter of coincidence, of course, that Mrs. Cleveland also awaited the birth of a baby at Cape Cod with her doctor . . . also spending the summer at Buzzard's Bay, then accompanying the family back to Washington in time for her confinement.

We hoped that history would repeat itself, in that respect.

President Kennedy telephoned me on the White House line in my quarters at Otis Air Force Base—Building 110—which I occupied off and on from June until mid-September when we left for Newport.

"Doctor, what exactly was done up there?" he asked me.

"Nothing more than your office knows about, Mr. President," I replied. "Except maybe some construction in the operating room—the delivery room—the Air Force moved up the timetable—to improve the electrical grounding for explosive anesthetics. And the air-conditioner had to be serviced through the operating room—then the room couldn't be used for twenty-four hours. Stretchers had to travel outdoors in an open corridor, and that was glassed in. I don't see how they did without it up here in the winter."

President Kennedy wanted to know the facts. He was bothered by the needless gunfire from the press, I thought, and it must have taken a toll.

His relations with the news media and with Congress were not entirely harmonious in those months. On August 23, when the President's request for foreign aid authorization was being pared down, just before flying to the Cape he defended the need for those funds in a nationally televised address from the Fish Room of the White House. When he reached Squaw Island that afternoon, he called me and I saw him in his room upstairs.

"It's time for Huntley-Brinkley—do you mind if I turn on the TV?" he said to me.

That newscast showed excerpts from his own broadcast a few hours earlier, in which he prodded the lectern repeatedly with his right index finger. The news commentators referred to "the President's angry words."

President Kennedy watched the screen intently to the end of the program while I studied his face. He made no comment as he flicked off the switch by remote control.

"Mr. President, were you really as angry as they said you were?" I inquired.

"Not angry—frustrated," he answered with a little smile.

I was not bored or lonesome living "on the flight line" at Otis Air Force

Base that summer. I was kept busy seeing patients in the hospital in consultation with the Air Force physicians. After Jackie was discharged to Squaw Island on August 14, I gave two clinical seminars for the medical staff—on August 16 and September 6. I returned again in May, 1964, to give the spring "dining-in lecture" for the Otis Hospital staff and local physicians in that region of Cape Cod.

From the Fourth of July, President Kennedy flew to Hyannis Port every weekend that summer. I saw him regularly at the roomy house on Squaw Island and I never felt closer to him.

On August 7, from the Secret Service trailer back of the house at Squaw Island, I informed the President at the White House that Jackie was on her way to Otis Hospital. In a second conversation with him, I gave him a report from Dr. Walsh as preparations were being made to proceed with the emergency cesarean section.

"Mr. President, don't worry, Jackie will be all right."

"How about the baby?" his voice was anxious on the telephone.

"Fifty-fifty, Mr. President," I replied.

"I'm coming up as fast as I can."

When it was decided that Patrick Bouvier Kennedy's serious breathing difficulty might be eased by the hyperbaric chamber (oxygen under pressure) in the Children's Hospital Medical Center at Boston and preparations were being made to move him there from Otis, the President spoke to me, aside.

"Take a car and go to the house now, so that you will be there when I arrive. I'll leave shortly."

At Squaw Island I was told that the President was not expected—he was on his way to Boston.

"I believe I'll wait a while, anyway," I said. I did not have long to wait for him.

President Kennedy wanted to tell Caroline and John about their new brother and to explain to them himself the danger that lay ahead, I thought. The President asked me searching questions about the problems of prematurity and hyaline membrane disease. My briefing may have helped him in his understanding of the medical decisions in which he, as a father, participated.

Two days later after Patrick's death early that morning, President Kennedy returned from Boston to Otis Hospital. He thanked the team of doctors in a way that lifted our saddened hearts. Again he quietly asked me to precede him to the house so as to be there when he came. I left by the rear entrance of the wing, made my way through the hospital to my Air Force car, and bypassed members of the press on duty at the front of the building. They did not see me come or go.

Building 3703 was a beehive of activity. Gifts for baby Patrick, flowers, and congratulations had given place to condolences and the gathering of the family to mourn.

Caroline and John in their matter-of-fact way made it easier to accept the loss of the brother whom they had never seen. The next day at the house, Caroline came up to me where I sat on a low chair and she looked me in the eye. She spoke with her father's directness.

"Why did Patrick die?"

"Because he was not strong enough to live on this earth and the angels in heaven wanted him," I replied.

She walked on without a word, apparently satisfied.

That summer of 1963, I felt that President Kennedy had changed in an intangible personal way. People remarked that he was "more relaxed." At sunset, he often played nine holes of golf, or less, with Jackie beside him on the picturesque hilly course of the Hyannis Port club. He was bursting with vigor and he enjoyed the outdoor exercise, but he seemed aloof from the game, uninvolved in its competitions. The sport did not absorb him then.

Cruises on the *Honey Fitz,* with lunch on board and swimming at anchor in the salt water of Nantucket Sound, refreshed him and provided time for reflection. I thought of an article that he had written in 1956, entitled "What My Illness Taught Me." He said: "I would not wish to exaggerate the compensation of being ill. It is better by far to be well. But . . . we seldom realize, until we are laid up in bed, how little 'leisure time' we have. . . . When we are not busy at work, we are busy at play, or busy traveling, or busy enjoying our families, or even busy loafing or sleeping. We just don't have enough time, we think—until suddenly we find that we have nothing but time." [23]

He had come more and more to appreciate leisure. He did not squander time, and energy, on overexercise.

President Kennedy was forty when Caroline was born in 1957. The demands of public life and of campaigning had kept him out of contact with her life for much of the time until they moved into the White House. That summer in Hyannis Port, John was still a baby but she was five and a half, and mature for those years. Abruptly, she had become good company for her father—winsome, gay, intelligent. Being Caroline's father had made him different.

His intimate friend, Ben Bradlee, wrote: "John Kennedy loved his chil-

[23] John F. Kennedy, *The American Weekly,* April 29, 1956, p. 7.

dren with a light that lit up his world . . . and he lit up the hearts of all who saw them enjoy each other." [24]

John F. Kennedy would have made an outstanding physician. He appreciated both the science and the art of medicine. In spite of personal experience with the inadequacy of medical knowledge, he still expected the best from members of the profession and he was delighted when he encountered it. That day when Patrick died, the President went out of his way to tell me what a fine man Dr. Samuel Z. Levine was—our chief of pediatrics at the New York Hospital–Cornell Medical Center, who had flown to Boston to advise on the treatment of the baby's hyaline membrane disease.

On December 7, 1961, President Kennedy sent a filmed greeting to the New York Hospital–Cornell Medical Center's dinner for "Medical Progress" at the Waldorf-Astoria in New York. I was present. As his picture appeared on the screen, his voice and words filled the room:

The New York Hospital–Cornell Medical Center, which we salute tonight . . . has had a long and useful life, stretching all the way back to the early days of our Revolution. . . . This institution has combined, almost from its beginning, great emphasis on research and on medical development, and also emphasis on training men and women to serve the people, not only here but in all parts of the globe. I am very much aware of what this Center has done. . . .

The federal government has played an important part in sustaining research in this Center and other centers—but it has done so through a happy union of the private and the public. The research has been under the encouragement of the federal government—but entirely under private control.

I spoke about a year ago about what we could all do for our country. I can think of no more important work, or satisfying work, than the work in which you are engaged tonight—supporting this great institution—making it able to meet the great challenges that are coming in the days to come. As long as we have dedicated citizenry who are willing to bear this type of burden—who do not seek to have all of these matters sustained by the national government—so long will freedom be maintained in medicine, and in all other kinds of human endeavor.

So, I strongly support this work. . . . It is a matter of personal interest because our first child was born in this Center, and we know something of the dedicated work of so many men and women who have spent their lives to help other people. This is our chance to help this

[24] Benjamin Bradlee, "He Had That Special Grace . . ." *Newsweek,* December 2, 1963, p. 38; *That Special Grace* (New York, J. B. Lippincott Company, 1964).

Center. In helping this Center now, we help a people who stretch to the other end of the world.

I often said that medicine and politics are alike in many respects. Neither is an exact science. Both depend on the art of compromise, compromise between what is ideal and what is feasible. The risks in a course of action must be balanced against its possible gain. Alternative procedures must be constantly weighed with changing circumstances. The illusion that a different course of action will be necessarily better afflicts both professions. The methods of problem solving and decision making are similar because both deal with imponderable human factors. In practice, medicine and politics are pragmatic professions. They are dominated by today's crises that may obscure the basic long-range goals of better health, on the one hand, and a better world to live in, on the other.

In 1962, President Kennedy analyzed the qualities of leadership that are essential for the Presidency. They are also requirements for the great physician. John F. Kennedy concluded, in an open letter to a youth who might some day be President of the United States:

> The first lesson of the Presidency is that it is impossible to foretell the precise nature of the problems that will confront you or the specific skills and capacities those problems will demand. . . . And when you assume the Presidency you too will face problems, difficulties, crises and challenges which no one can foresee. . . .
>
> Most difficult to consciously pursue is an understanding of the people you will lead. . . . And the final measure of your Administration will, in large measure, rest on how well you respond to their inward hopes while leading them to new horizons of ambition and achievement. . . .
>
> The most important qualities of leadership are best embodied in that most towering of American Presidents, Lincoln: a combination of humility and self-confidence, inner resolution and energy, which gives a President the capacity to listen to others, to be aware of his own limitations and . . . to act his own mature and unbiased judgment. . . .
>
> Many of our outstanding Presidents . . . have had a deep sense of history. For of all the disciplines, the study of the folly and achievements of man is best calculated to help develop the critical sense of what is permanent and meaningful amid the mass of superficial and transient events that engulf the Presidency. And it is on this sense, more than any other, that great leadership depends.[25]

[25] John F. Kennedy, "To an Unknown Youth Somewhere in America. How to Prepare for the Presidency," *Parade*, September 23, 1962, pp. 6–7.

CHAPTER 21

Transition in the White House

The White House was quiet that November weekend, except for John and Caroline. On Thursday morning, I had seen President and Mrs. Kennedy upstairs in the Mansion before they departed for San Antonio, Texas, by helicopter from the White House lawn. Then I left to meet Jack at the Supreme Court and to hear a case argued, at the invitation of Justice Arthur Goldberg. It was my first visit to the Chambers.

The afternoon before, Jack and I had attended the White House Reception for the Judiciary, a crowded affair. President and Mrs. Kennedy had gone out of their way, as they briefly greeted the guests, to shake hands with us and with Dr. and Mrs. John Walsh where we stood chatting together. During the reception, Jack and I had talked also with Arthur and Dorothy Goldberg.

I regretted that I did not see Arthur then as often as I had when he was Secretary of Labor in the Cabinet. A few of President Kennedy's appointees had moved on in the three years since I had traveled to Palm Beach with the President-elect and John was born. I was becoming an old-timer at the White House, I thought; how fast one adjusts to a new way of life.

After being away from Washington for part of 1963, in view of the President's good health I wondered whether my full-time services were needed there any longer. I had raised the question in a note for President Kennedy's consideration. On the evening before the Texas trip, General Ted Clifton, his chief Military Aide, telephoned me at home: the President wanted me to know before he left that I was not to consider leaving the

White House. Fine—I had only brought up the question. I would relax on the weekend.

On Friday two of my Washington friends came for an early lunch with me in the White House Staff Mess. Dr. Robert A. Aldrich, for two years Director of the new National Institute of Child Health and Human Development, was returning to his academic post as chief of pediatrics in the University of Washington School of Medicine at Seattle. Bob had to leave promptly, but Don S. Wenger, Brigadier General in the Medical Corps of the United States Air Force, tarried to talk. A Texan, Don and I had traveled together to the School of Aerospace Medicine at Brooks Air Force Base in San Antonio when I had lectured there as Special Consultant for the Surgeon General of the Air Force. My last trip that May was my third teaching tour in San Antonio.

President Kennedy took a lively interest in what I learned there about research in space medicine. Only the day before, November 21, he had dedicated the new buildings of the Aerospace Medicine school, by arrangement with Vice President Johnson, Chairman of the National Aeronautics and Space Council.

It was John F. Kennedy's last official address.

Don and I were walking back to my office after lunch when Rusty (Elmer M.) Young, White House master of floral table art,[1] rushed up to us in the corridor of the Mansion.

"Dr. Travell, did you hear that the President was shot? Do you know if—maybe it isn't true?" he said excitedly.

We hurried into my office. Martha at her desk knew nothing about it. I turned on the television, and the first report was confirmed. The news worsened. Don stayed until the final bulletin. The country had lost its President.

The journey had ended that John F. Kennedy and I had started together eight and a half years earlier. They had passed as an instant in the infinite span of time.

The seeming futility of human endeavor overwhelmed me at first as I thought back over those years of effort that ultimately brought us both to the White House. If we had never met, might his destiny have been different?

The Secret Service had not been able to circumvent our American President's folly of courage, which ignored the danger in public exposure. In my first reaction of helplessness on November 22, I could not grasp the numb-

[1] Mr. Young's floral arrangements are pictured in Ruth Montgomery's book *Flowers at the White House* (New York, M. Barrows and Company, 1967).

ing fact of the assassination, but deep in my consciousness I realized that I had expected it. I did not feel the shock of surprise.

John F. Kennedy had accepted the personal risks of the Presidency knowingly and fatalistically. Should I feel bitter if his death were so ordained? His struggle to make the world better for mankind could not have been in vain; his vitality and vision would never die.

In my White House office I had sat on former President Truman's sofa and had watched President Kennedy's televised press conferences at the State Department—I had not missed a single one. I had stood there at his special lectern, in a sense, in his shoes. He had asked me to improve its construction and I had modified it to suit it to his stance and best reading distance. I remembered all that, and also how members of the housekeeping staff in the Mansion used to come into my office for those special occasions. The White House guard in the corridor could not leave his post and he stood in my doorway to listen. I turned up the volume of my TV set so that he could hear the President's crisp words, even if he could not see the crinkling smile at the corners of the President's eyes.

There is still work to be done to move America forward, I thought. He would have wished me to do everything that I could for our new President. Lyndon Johnson was the man whom he had chosen and trusted, and he would have wanted us all to support him then.

I did not have long for grieving retrospection. From where I sat in my inner office, regarding the smiling photograph on the wall, I suddenly heard Senator Ted Kennedy's familiar voice speaking to Martha in the anteroom. His inflections had the same timbre as both his brothers' voices; they were so much alike that I was startled.

"May I use the phone?"

He had already lifted the receiver and was talking when I stepped to the door.

"Please come inside, Ted," I interrupted. "It will be more private."

We shook hands briefly, and I added, "I just spoke with Eunice—she's on her way here." She had telephoned me.

Ted went into my office and I closed the door so that he could continue the conversation alone. Other words were not spoken between us.

Eunice Kennedy Shriver arrived shortly afterward, and then separately, Bobby Kennedy and Sargent Shriver. I escorted them into my large treatment room, which had a sofa and comfortable chairs, and they met together with controlled emotion.

Three telephone lines through the White House switchboard with four intercom instruments and a Signal Corps security line served my suite of offices. My secretary and Betty Chapowicki, my nurse, placed calls for them and my lines were kept busy. During the overloading of Washington's telephone system that day, the White House gave priority to the Kennedy family's need to communicate and to make decisions about the postmortem examination and the funeral.

On that afternoon of November 22, White House aides came and went in my office to express their sympathy and shock, and to assist with plans for the ceremonial tributes that the world's heads of state and the citizens of our nation would attend. I saw no hysteria, no need for sedatives—only a tense attitude that the right things must be done to honor the immortal dead.

From my window I watched Eunice and Ted board a helicopter on the White House South Lawn to fly by Air Force jet to Hyannis Port. Their mother and invalid father were staying there late in the season, until after the Kennedys gathered for the traditional Thanksgiving dinner in the large home by the shore. I recalled the Thanksgivings that I had spent in Hyannis Port in 1961 and 1962, and I pondered on life's moments of sudden change.

On the second floor of the Mansion, Caroline and John were cloistered with Miss Shaw, their nurse. I asked the Secret Service agent in the map room next to mine whether the children were aware of their father's death and he replied, "Probably not."

He told me that riding in a car that afternoon Caroline had perhaps heard a fragment of a broadcast about the Dallas shooting, but the radio had been turned off quickly. Miss Shaw knew of the ultimate tragedy.

I could not face Caroline or John. My nurse had a sphinxlike control of her features, and I sent her upstairs to do what she could for Miss Shaw, who was at the breaking point under the burden of silence.

In the West Wing, the Presidential office was being dismantled. During the night, I walked from the Mansion past the shadowy Rose Garden, and I saw the familiar mementos being trundled away. By Saturday morning, the Oval Room was bare of furniture, books, and the paintings of ships. Only the blood-red new rug remained that Jacqueline Kennedy had planned for her husband's return. He never used it. It was a piece in the mosaic of life and death.

The White House had the empty feeling of a tomb. It consoled me somewhat that the Kennedy family felt at home in my office and that they had made use of it that day.

When people throughout the country described their reactions in that period, they were likely to tell me, "I was glued to the TV for days."

By contrast, I realized that I had not had time to sit by the television; I was busy. That black Friday evening, at Pam Turnure's request I remained in my office. Mrs. Kennedy wished me to be there, she said. Dr. John Walsh had gone out to Andrews airfield to meet her when Air Force One landed. The new President and his staff would come to the White House, and that was where I belonged.

Those who had work to do that night did it. The government could not be ruled by sentimentality.

While the Presidential plane was flying from Texas in the afternoon, without instructions I telephoned Dr. J. Willis Hurst in Atlanta—he was Chief of Medicine at the Emory University School of Medicine there and he had been Vice President Johnson's personal physician. I located Willis at a medical meeting in a New York hotel and I sent him a message to stop off in Washington that evening, instead of returning directly to Atlanta as he planned. He went straight to The Elms, the Johnsons' home, and although no emergency arose to require his presence, he spent the night there. We met the next day at the White House.

In retrospect, the transition within me took place when I assumed the responsibility for President Johnson of bringing Willis Hurst to Washington.

René, the chef with the high white cap, thoughtfully brought me supper on a tray, as he had often done when I was on duty in my office during an official dinner or social function in the evening at the White House. Otherwise, I would not have remembered to eat. Dr. Joseph English, physician to the Peace Corps, stood by in the East Room with the group who were erecting the catafalque for the casket and were pinning sheer black cloth in folds over the long gold draperies and around the three great crystal chandeliers. In the night, Joe came downstairs to my office for medicines, for simple complaints like a headache or indigestion. White House staff members of all ranks dropped in to see me, mainly to talk. There were no serious medical problems.

At intervals I received telephone reports from the National Naval Medical Center in Bethesda. The hour-to-hour delays in the anticipated arrival of the late President in his coffin seemed interminable. After 4 A.M., when I walked out into the North Grounds by way of the dark drive from the West Wing, I felt blinded by the flood of white light that was reflected from the gleaming walls of the Mansion. Brilliantly illuminated were men of the honor guard in their blue dress uniforms, standing motionless in a half circle along the driveway in front of the North Portico, waiting for their hero to enter the Northwest Gate on his last trip home. Spotlighted against the great dark trees, the Commander in Chief's final review of his honor guard seemed as unreal as tragedy played on a stage.

During the next three days, I paid solemn tribute to John F. Kennedy as his casket lay in state in the East Room of the White House, in the Rotunda of the Capitol during the eulogies by representatives of the Congress and Judiciary, and at the low Mass requiem in St. Matthew's Cathedral. The nonconformity of General Charles de Gaulle, when he continued to stand after the mourning congregation sat down, sticks in my mind like a burr. From the Cathedral, Jack and I rode together in the cortège behind the horse-drawn caisson that took an hour to reach Arlington National Cemetery. The flag that covered John F. Kennedy in his casket was folded and handed to his widow, the "eternal flame" was lighted, and a single bugler sounded "Taps" over the grave. Only then did I begin to appreciate the finality and enormity of our loss.

As was the custom with a change of Administration, I sent a letter of resignation at once to President Johnson. He accepted it in January, 1964. Jack and I started looking for a house to buy in the metropolitan area of Washington—I would not need to live as near as possible to the White House. The books in my office were packed in boxes ready to leave on February 1, but the Press Office did not make an announcement of my scheduled departure. Before that date, the President asked me to come upstairs to his room, and he persuaded me to stay.

I telephoned Jack to let him know the change in plans. It was the only time that I nearly lost my husband. His unprotesting patience with my day-and-night office hours was exhausted, but he said: "I understand—you can't refuse the President now."

On February 13, the announcement by Pierre Salinger, the President's Press Secretary, was reported:

> President Johnson has asked the White House medical team of Dr. Janet Travell and Rear Admiral George G. Burkley, U.S. Navy physician, to continue in their joint assignment to handle medical problems at the Executive Mansion. Both Dr. Travell and Dr. Burkley bear the title of "a Physician to the President." Both have offices at the White House and are on call around the clock. So far, both have been called upon to serve members of the Johnson family as well as White House staff. The President has not been ill since he has been in office. But when he was Vice President, he consulted Dr. Travell on occasion.

I first met Lyndon Johnson in January, 1961, at Palm Beach when he came as Vice President-elect to confer with John F. Kennedy at the big house on North Ocean Boulevard. I was curious about this man who had figured conspicuously in the campaign, first as Senator Kennedy's political opponent and then as his political partner. The new Vice President was sitting beside the pool, apparently in deep preoccupation with his thoughts.

His physical bulk was greater than I had expected and I was surprised by his appearance of youthful power. After all, he was only fifty-two.

He had little to say as my husband and I were introduced to him. We were walking back from a cool swim in the ocean surf; he was fully dressed. From a lounge chair he squinted up at me against the sun above the palms. He gave no sign that he recognized my name as that of a "Greenwich Village" doctor who had signed Senator Kennedy's publicized health reports. Jack and I went on quickly, and near the dressing rooms we met Franklin and James Roosevelt who had been swimming in the pool.

At the time of the assassination, even inside the White House few appreciated that I had come to know all four members of the LBJ family while I served there with President Kennedy. One day in the spring of 1963, Jackie stepped off the elevator opposite my open office door just as the Vice President was telling me good-bye. She greeted him warmly and paused while he walked down the hall to the Diplomatic Reception Room.

"I didn't know you were seeing the Vice President—I'm so glad," she told me with obvious regard for him.

My office was not a fish bowl after all, I thought with satisfaction. During the first half of 1963, before I went to Hyannis Port with Jackie, the Vice President made a habit of stopping to see me when he had a few minutes to spare in the White House. He could stretch out to rest on the long sofa-bed in my treatment room and he could talk on the telephone at the same time. If he desired background music, our piped-in system supplied an unobtrusive flow of sound without interruption by commercials. My office was a small oasis of peace in the center of the hurricane.

Lyndon Johnson was pleased that Lady Bird, Lynda, and Lucy had each chosen to see me professionally. He relished telling me of their accomplishments, especially Lucy's talent for writing poetry. He did not have to talk politics to me, and I did not want anything from him.

"Doctor, if I stopped being Vice President, I couldn't come in to see you whenever I pleased," he said once, teasingly.

At that time, there were rumors of his being dropped from the Democratic ticket for 1964.

The Vice President invited me to see his stately Senate office. He led me down the private stairway to the platform where he presided over the Senate and he asked me to try out his chair behind the imposing desk. I looked across the empty seats and aisles of the Senate Chamber and transposed myself mentally to the First Lady's box in the similar Chamber of the House of Representatives, from which Jack and I had heard President Kennedy deliver his State of the Union message to a joint session of Congress on January 30, 1961. A few surprised tourists in the spectator galleries watched the Vice President guide me around the Senate floor to point out where various Senators sat, in particular Margaret Chase Smith and Maurine Neuberger. He would like to see more women in national politics, he said.

The Vice President discovered what he had long suspected, that his seated comfort could be improved by the simple structural modifications of his chairs that I suggested. When I was at The Elms, he asked me to obtain for him several rocking chairs, for his home in Washington and for the LBJ Ranch in Texas. His preference for a partially reclining position made desirable both a sloped footstool and a suitable headrest. I secured a soft, round pillow for neck support and attached it at the right level of his chair.

Early in 1963 I did not guess that the year-end sudden transition in the White House would include the migration there of those rocking chairs with their brown homespun-style cushions. Rocking-chair history had repeated itself.

Late in June of 1963, Jack and I were happy to attend the family reception at The Elms when beautiful Lynda's brief engagement to Navy Lieutenant Bernie Rosenbach was disclosed. I had become very fond of both the Johnson girls. At fifteen, Lucy,[2] in a long ruffled dress, was enjoying the party hugely and she scarcely stopped dancing on the outdoor platform. It was then that I made acquaintance with Senator Hubert Humphrey's talent for the dance.

I was at Hyannis Port on September 2, 1963, when the Vice President, Mrs. Johnson, and Lynda started off from Otis Air Force Base on their goodwill trip to five Scandinavian countries. While Vice President Johnson went by helicopter to Squaw Island to consult with President Kennedy, Lady Bird and Lynda were given a tour of the Base and "Jackie's" recent hospital building; Jack and I rode in the car with them. The Vice President had invited us to the dinner that night in the Officers' Club at which he was host for Colonel and Mrs. Walters, Air Force officers, Liz Carpenter, Bess Abell, and others of the working staff.

Before midnight that evening, Jack and I followed the Vice-Presidential party to the crowded plane and went on board. It was not merely a social farewell. In view of the size of the group and the long arduous nature of the overseas trip, I had suggested to the Vice President that my Navy nurse at the White House go along—the Johnsons knew her already. She might be helpful to their physician friend whom I had just met, and, in any case, she could double as a secretary.

No conflict was created in my mind, either then or subsequently, by the fact that I served in a professional capacity at the same time to both the

[2] In the spring of 1964, she changed the spelling of her name to "Luci."

Kennedy and Johnson families. Nor was it a difficult decision for me to make that I should remain as White House Physician to President Johnson; and I did not regret it.

During February, 1964, the President spoke to me one day in my office.

"I understand that you are seeing Mrs. Kennedy regularly. I want you to do everything you can for her," he said with emphasis.

The President's concern for her was like an echo from a year earlier. The scene and the lines were similar, but the performers had exchanged roles.

I had used my own judgment in continuing to give Jacqueline Kennedy medical supervision while she lived in Washington. After she moved out of the White House two weeks following the assassination, I stopped often to see her in Georgetown, first in the W. Averell Harriman residence at 3038 "N" Street and later in her new home across the street at 3017.

Since Jack and I lived only a short distance away at 3319 "N" Street, it was convenient for me to call on her early in the morning en route to my office or sometimes later if I came home for lunch. But the frequent transitions between my past and present White House years were not easy for me emotionally.

In her new house, during early February of 1964 I watched with heartbreak the placing of furniture and the unpacking of china and personal treasures that Jackie and her husband had shared. Most of those possessions had been put in storage when they moved into the White House from their last Georgetown home at 3307 "N" Street.

Jackie hoped to find peace in Washington with her children and her memories. But tourists stared up at her house at all hours, from the sidewalk across the street and from the creeping sight-seeing buses. They hoped for a glimpse of the idolized figure of the young widow, and she patiently smiled at them.

However, on her account I resented their scrutiny whenever I hurried up or down the long flight of steps from the street to her front door—there was no rear entrance to the house. The curious onlookers could not have watched me with more rapt attention if I had been a clown in the circus. The White House had ensured a measure of privacy, of sanctuary, that was gone forever from Jacqueline Kennedy's life.

At my office in the White House, I saw the same pressures of publicity being applied to the new young occupants of the White House. Lynda had loved her freshman year at the University of Texas in Austin. But on December 20, 1963, when she was a sophomore, the Washington *Evening Star* reported her changed status: "Pickets marched in front of Lynda Bird Johnson's University of Texas dormitory last night to protest the university's alleged segregation policy. A spokesman for the marchers said the action was not intended as a personal reflection on the President's 19-year-old daughter."

After the assassination, almost overnight, Lynda had become a political extension of her father. The metamorphosis must have been a shock to her. In January, 1964, she and Warrie Lynn Smith, her college roommate from San Antonio, transferred to George Washington University, and she found relative freedom inside the White House.

Circumstances in some ways made the transition to "daughter of the President" easier for Luci than for Lynda. Black-haired, blue-eyed Luci was younger and she did not change schools. A high-school junior in bobby socks and saddle shoes at the National Cathedral School for Girls in Washington, she brought with her into the White House the same merry crowd of friends who had enlivened The Elms. Lynda's classmates at the Cathedral School had scattered to various colleges and states.

Sixteen-year-old Luci had a kind of independence that I admired. She sat beside my office desk one day—February 20, 1964—and she "doodled" with a pencil on a memo pad while we talked. She studied the pad and pushed it toward me.

"How do you like it?" she asked.

She had written again and again, "Luci" and "Luci Johnson."

"I'm changing my name—I always wanted to," she explained—and it was so announced by Liz Carpenter, Mrs. Johnson's Press Secretary.

A new name is part of her transition to the White House, I thought. She does not acquire a new title like her father, or even like her mother, the new First Lady, but her responsibilities and her life will be changed as much as theirs. It had already been changed, in fact.

Only a few months earlier in September, 1963, I had arranged for Lucy to see me at the White House when I flew down from Otis Air Force Base with President Kennedy on Air Force One—as I occasionally did that summer for a couple of days' work in my office. Lucy came then to the West Executive Avenue entrance opposite her father's office in the Executive Office Building, and she gave her name to the White House guard inside the door. He refused to admit her.

"Don't try to kid me," he told her. "The Vice President's daughter is in Europe."

Ruefully, Lucy related the incident to me and said, "The man didn't know the Vice President has *two* daughters!"

Warrie and Lynda elected the same courses at George Washington University, and they were inseparable. Away from her own family and her old friends, Warrie had been catapulted into a unique world for which she was less well prepared than were the daughters of the Vice President, but she retained an unselfish resiliency of mood and a sense of fun that caused her to be greatly missed when she returned home in June of 1964.

The girls had long outgrown their pediatricians, but I was not through with the problems of childhood's contagious diseases in the White House. Caroline came down with chickenpox on January 26 in the Harriman house, and after the expected interval John followed suit in mid-February. When I called at their new home on "N" Street, John was sitting tucked in his mother's bed. He pulled up his pajama sleeve to show me his arm.

"Tocter Tarbell, do you want to see my chicken pops?" he asked proudly.

He could not see the pocks on his face.

The children were not really ill and Dr. Broocks took care of them, but chickenpox in Jackie's house presented me with a dilemma. As soon as possible after she moved across "N" Street on February 1, President and Mrs. Johnson, the Cabinet, and a few other members of the government planned a ceremonial call on Jacqueline Kennedy to present a gift for her new home and to pay tribute to her late husband. I knew that some of the official group had no record of ever having had chickenpox; and in adults that disease is likely to cause serious illness. It may even be fatal.

Through personal diplomacy between Mrs. Johnson and myself, the new Administration's formal visit to the former First Lady was delayed until February 26—after the chickenpox.

Like the Kennedy children, Lynda, Luci, and Warrie brought the gaiety of youth to the home behind the scenes in the White House. They had not been there long when they discovered my jump ropes. To the fast beat of Luci's portable record player in the red-carpeted corridor outside my office, she and Warrie staged an impromptu exhibition of tandem rope skipping that would have won first prize in a talent show.

Only a few weeks earlier, on that carpet outside my door Caroline's schoolmates used to gather, waiting with their teacher, Miss Grimes—waiting for President Kennedy to come down in the elevator. He spoke their names and joked with them, as he passed, and then they rode up to the solarium on the third floor. After-images of those mornings still blurred my vision.

Warrie could hardly wait for her first big snowfall. It arrived on Lincoln's Birthday. Then she went out to play in the fresh fluffy stuff, with "Him" and "Her," the new canine tenants of the White House grounds. The beagles' tails just showed above the drifts. Sedate little Pushinka, daughter of the Russian space bitch and gift to Mrs. Jacqueline Kennedy from Chairman Khrushchev, had never cared much for the snow; she had moved on, too.

On February 14, two days after that blizzard, Jack and I received a lacy Valentine. At the center of its large heart was a snapshot of laughing Warrie covered to the chin by the white snow, which was a scarce commodity in her homeland of southern Texas. Warrie's artistic creations added to the decor of many a party of young folk at the White House.

My mind drifted back to the previous winter when Caroline was lost in the South Grounds in another blizzard. It was dark, about seven o'clock, and her Secret Service agent had gone off duty after she went upstairs for the night. No one expected Caroline to come down again. But when her young supper guest was picked up in a car at the South Portico, Caroline followed her friend out under the awning to see her leave. As the car drove off, in her frilly dress and patent leather pumps Caroline chased it down the drive at a run. She disappeared into the invisible world of wind-driven snowflakes. A frantic search located her, minus a shoe, inside the iron fence near the Ellipse. She did not even catch cold—hardiness begins young.

On February 12, 1964—Lincoln's Birthday—I wrote Virginia in Nashville:

Dear Ginia;

Something that I had never seen before occurred this morning on the South Lawn here, which Janet and Gordon would have enjoyed. On the unbroken snow about a foot deep, two helicopters landed stirring up a cloud of snow in the gale from the rotors, which blotted out the bright sun and drove everyone in the receiving line for cover. At the same time, great piles of snow on the thick magnolia leaves of the tree outside my window, where I snugly watched, were whirled in all directions. Sir Douglas-Home, Prime Minister of the United Kingdom, was . . . safely ensconced inside Chopper No. 1 [as it landed]. The welcoming speeches were held under the North Portico. A guard of honor carrying the flags of all fifty of our states, and a variety of others, lined the circular driveway. . . . The air was very zippy, 20°. The ladies wore mink, and hats. [I walked outdoors to join the group of welcoming White House staff.]

Besides the helicopter landing on the snowfield, I saw something else quite new in the last three years. That was the President ushering everyone into the elevator ahead of him, including Mr. Duke [Chief of Protocol] and Mr. [McGeorge] Bundy, as well as the visiting Britishers. It has been a rule of protocol that the President of the United States precedes everyone, except a visiting Head of State, and Mr. Kennedy adhered to that rule. Only once did President Kennedy say to me at the elevator, "After you," and that seemed like an inadvertent reversion to old habits. It always appeared right and fitting that President Kennedy should step forward and lead the way, with everyone running to keep up with his long fast stride.

I think that President Johnson does not walk so fast, but he dances more. Last evening we attended the White House Diplomatic Reception, at which he danced all evening. . . . Daddy and I stayed on the dance floor to the end, among many others. . . . Yes, I danced with the President, too—he cut in on Daddy [with a tap on the shoulder and a "Do you mind?"]. Daddy had a whirl with Warrie Lynn Smith. . . .

Love,
Mummy

Of different generations and backgrounds, Jacqueline Kennedy and Lady Bird Johnson were alike in their search for solitude to offset the battering impact of the political stage. They drew strength from nature—one from the winds of the sea and the other from the live oaks and land of Texas. Each wife merged her life with her husband's to serve best his needs as she saw them. Each mother deeply loved her children and concerned herself with their full growth. As individuals in their own right, both worked industriously and effectively for selected objectives that enhanced the human values and the beauty of life on this planet.

The two First Ladies differed legitimately in their interest in the scientific disciplines. Mrs. Kennedy rarely sponsored events of that kind; she left that phase of activity to her husband.

Mrs. Johnson's genuine concern for better medical training and services first impressed me when the Vice President's wife and I attended a tea on March 9, 1961, at the Washington home of Mrs. Homer Ferguson, Chairman of the National Board of the Woman's Medical College of Pennsylvania. I had accepted an invitation to become the first physician member of the Board and I was the guest of honor. In June, 1961, at Philadelphia, the Woman's Medical College conferred on me the Honorary Doctorate of Medical Sciences. Four years later, as the President's wife, Mrs. Johnson graciously assumed the Honorary Chairmanship of that National Board, whose women members represented all fifty states of our Union.

Her encouragement of qualified young women to study medicine was a mutual interest that, among other things, drew me to her. I learned to admire her ease and directness of manner, her common sense and quiet energy, which endless demands never seemed to exhaust. I understood her zest for work—I was a "doer," too.

Mrs. Johnson not only enjoyed the beauty of flowers, but also liked working to make them grow. After she came to the White House, she was quoted as saying, "I like being real tired from getting the last weed out of the zinnia bed." [3]

I felt that way myself about gardening and raising flowers. But I used to wonder, as I walked through the fields at Merryfield Farm, how a wildflower made the transition to a weed. In the mood of the moment, I wrote a poem about my favorite weed, which flowered in places where cultivated beauties died:

THE DANDELION EXPLOSION

Give me a dandelion weed
With blooms as soft as nylon blends,
With stem to suck and curl its ends
By point of tongue. In winds it bends
But never breaks; unlike a reed.
Disdained and lovely is my weed.

My backyard lot displays a breed
Of yellow polka dots on green
Fabric flagrantly flung to screen
The shabbiness beneath, between
The fragrant flowers that exceed
My dreams of beauty. They're a weed!

The dandelion takes no heed
To keep its population down.
With pride it bears its fragile crown
Fashioned of fairest lightest down
And lets the wind disperse its seed.
Untamed and lusty is that weed.

My analyst will pluck each weed
That bravely grows within my brain—
He says. But nought will then remain,
I fear, in barren ground my rain
Of tears to water. Weeds I need.
Unnamed and sturdy grows thought's weed.

I remembered how at eighty-six Robert Frost, the great American poet, with the sun in his eyes recited his lines at John F. Kennedy's Inauguration as President:

The land was ours before we were the land's . . .
Something we were withholding made us weak
Until we found out that it was ourselves

[3] Ruth Montgomery, *Mrs. LBJ* (New York, Holt, Rinehart and Winston, 1964), p. 199.

We were withholding from our land of living,
And forthwith found salvation in surrender . . .

Lyndon Johnson brought to the Presidency a great love of the land, which most Americans shared with him—except those who were hopelessly city-bound. In his zest for productivity, he told the nation to be thankful for freedom and its harvest of blessings. He appealed to the people's conscience and their faith in God. With harder work, they would have more affluence to divide among those who were less fortunate.

John Kennedy loved life and humanity. He cared how each person surmounted disability and survived disaster. He was more at home on the ocean than in a forest. He had a zest for creativity, and he spurred young and old to achieve beyond their expectations. From the platform of the Democratic National Convention on July 16, 1960, he told the American people:

> The world is changing. The old era is ending. The old ways will not do . . . we stand today on the edge of a New Frontier—a frontier of unknown opportunities and perils. . . . Woodrow Wilson's New Freedom promised our nation a new political and economic framework. Franklin Roosevelt's New Deal promised security and succor to those in need. But the New Frontier of which I speak is not a set of promises—it is a set of challenges. It sums up, not what I intend to offer the American people, but what I intend to ask of them. It . . . holds out the promise of more sacrifice instead of more security.[4]

In my days of transition in the White House, I seemed to have lost a sense of the urgency of those challenges. Later, I regained it on the campaign trail with Lady Bird Johnson. Writing in retrospect, I gave expression to my quandary of mind in a poem:

HORIZONS OF SEA AND LAND

He who plows the furrows of the ocean,
Must turn a tiller tugging in his hand.
Unlike the tiller of the earth's stable land,
The sailor braces against the motion
Of ever restless seas. Hot emotion
Has no place in his decision to stand
Against the gale. Coolness and daring and
Skill will bring him to new lands of Goshen.
He steers his ship by stars. Idealist,
The clean-etched navigator of the seas

---

[4] Theodore H. White, *The Making of a President 1960* (New York, Atheneum Publishers, 1961), p. 177.

Envisions endless space beyond the moon;
He dreams to tread the skies. Yet realist,
He prepares for the storms that he foresees
Are coming, always coming soon, too soon.

He who plants crops, breeds stock and plods through soil,
Must wait for fertile earth to warm, to sun,
To water what his long day's work has done.
Cloudbursts and hail the planter's temper roil.
In rain his boots bear mud, his mark of toil,
Unlike bare white sand by the blue ocean.
He loves the fields that once his forebears won;
Now *he* slaves nature's wily ways to foil.
The men who plow the ground are united
By faith in fruition, by the challenge
Of disaster that may render barren
Their native land. The stranger benighted
Is unwelcome; the herd will avenge
On aliens the threat of the foreign.

Wise country folk are the seat of justice.
On lonesome plains ancient ways of barter
Still provide today's coin of the farmer—
A hog, a steer, a cake or a service—
And his bond is the same as his promise.
Individualist each, his neighbor
Is both his ally and competitor.
Farming is not a trade for the novice.
The sea man knows that there are real rainbows
On his horizon with a wealth of gold.
The landsman knows that want follows plenty;
Drought or flood, he is tethered by his long rows.
Who knows which man at last will better mold
Our country for peace and prosperity?

CHAPTER 22

New Spectacles

The White House matures not only the man who becomes President of the United States, but also every person privileged to work there. While I was stationed in that eye of the hurricane, my mind was preoccupied with current and impending crises, whether or not they were related directly to my medical duties. As the days rushed along, I did not pause to contemplate the growth that was taking place in my unconscious attitudes. Suddenly, out of the cloud of the assassination I became aware of the transition in my outlook from a largely personal concern for the individual to a broader sense of national responsibility.

I was, in a sense, shocked awake. On April 20, 1964, I flew with Mrs. Johnson to Cleveland, Ohio, where she visited low-cost public housing for six hundred "geriactive" occupants, most of whom received Social Security or Old-Age Assistance. Staffed by the nearby Lutheran Hospital and supported jointly by Federal, city, and private funds, a diagnostic Well-Elderly Clinic was being opened in the Golden Age Riverview Center. It was an innovation in preventive medicine for the aged.

Prior to the trip, Liz Carpenter, the First Lady's Press Secretary, had asked me to prepare material for briefing reporters about the health of the elderly. Such participation—presenting general medical information to the press—was an agreeable role that as White House Physician I had not played before.

I did my homework. In the Washington *Evening Star* of April 6, a column caught my eye about the twenty-one thousand centenarians in the Soviet Union—1 per 11,000 of the population, I calculated. As expected, the lowest proportion of centenarians was among city dwellers. But my curiosity was aroused by the statement that more than half of those who had reached one hundred years or more lived in the very high mountains.

I speculated that, contrary to general assumption, the lower concentration of oxygen in the air at high altitudes might be a *favorable* factor in longevity. It was known, of course, that in rarefied atmospheres the human body compensates by manufacturing extra amounts of oxygen-carrying hemoglobin and red blood cells. But at sea level, elderly men who were healthy had less free oxygen in their blood than did young healthy men. [1] My novel notion of a relationship between longevity and chronic hypoxia— a limited deficiency of free oxygen in the tissues—was crystallized by Dr. Larry Lamb's studies at the School of Aerospace Medicine.[2] His ingenious experiments on chair-rest and bed-rest in young men had just demonstrated that hypoxia prevented some of the undesirable effects of inactivity that had been noted in space flights. I would hear more about that new research when I flew to lecture again at the School of Aerospace Medicine, soon after the Cleveland trip.

From the Bureau of the Census I had obtained statistics for the elderly, particularly those whose ages were eighty-five years or more. For the year ending July 1, 1963, the proportion of centenarians in the United States was 1 per 16,000 of our population. Women greatly outnumbered men, and I pondered on the reasons for that sex difference in survival.

At 7:45 A.M. that April morning, with figures in mind and medical bag in hand I boarded United Air Lines flight 771 from National Airport. In the front section of the Viscount plane were Mrs. Johnson; Mrs. Marie McGuire, Commissioner of the Public Housing Administration; Mrs. Anne Celebrezze, wife of the Secretary of Health, Education and Welfare; Liz Carpenter; and myself—a company of women-doers. Liz sat on my right by the window and Mrs. Johnson sat at my left across the aisle. In the row behind us were the Secret Service agents and back of them, members of the press.

We flew at fourteen thousand feet in turbulent air and we kept our seat belts fastened. Once or twice I saw lightning flash between clouds. Liz nervously watched the fog outside; I had not realized before how much she dreaded flying. Later, during the 1964 campaign, on our Lady Bird Special

---

[1] James E. Birren, Robert N. Butler, Samuel W. Greenhouse, Louis Sokoloff, and Marian R. Yarrow, eds., *Human Aging: A Biological and Behavioral Study* (Washington, D.C., U.S. Government Printing Office, 1963), pp. 63–64.
[2] Lawrence E. Lamb, "Hypoxia—An Anti-deconditioning Factor for Manned Space Flight," *Aerospace Medicine,* Vol. 36 (1965), p. 97–100.

flying whistle-stop, paraphrasing a Goldwater-for-President slogan she remarked, with a straight face and fright in her eyes, "You know in your heart the Wright brothers were wrong."

After an hour's rough flying, Liz suggested that I lean out into the aisle and try to talk with the reporters toward the rear. I could not make myself heard over the high seat backs and above the noise of propjet engines. If our stewardesses managed to walk in the aisle, surely I could stand and hold onto a seat while I discoursed. I unlatched my safety belt, stepped back a row and presented my statistics. Pencils flew over notebooks, and questions were fired at me. Within days, Frances Lewine's Associated Press column was mailed to me by friends and strangers throughout the country. On April 22, the *New York World-Telegram and Sun* carried her story:

MOM OUTLIVES DAD
BECAUSE SHE'S BUSY DOING THE CHORES.

White House physician Dr. Janet Travell believes women live longer than men nowadays because "a woman never retires. She keeps on doing the things she's been accustomed to doing all her life," Dr. Travell notes. The ever-present chores of housekeeping, the dusting and cleaning up, may be what's behind the longevity of the ladies, Dr. Travell said. "In the older age groups women keep much more active than men." . . . Dr. Travell evidenced a longtime interest in the study of geriatrics. She said that . . . she's always been interested in muscular problems and this is a big part of the disability of the aged. She believes, with many other doctors, that keeping mobile and keeping going plays a large part in keeping people living longer. . . . Armed with Census Bureau reports, she called attention to these facts: There are now 18 million Americans 65 or over and more than one million over 85; 12,000 are over 100 years of age. In the 95 to 99 bracket, there are twice as many women as men . . . as of the latest 1963 count; . . . age 90 to 94: 71,686 men to 126,292 women; age 85 to 89: 295,289 men to 457,102 women. . . . Although Dr. Travell is 62, an age when many persons start to talk about retiring, she has no such plans. . . . [She] has just a bit of advice, too: "Never lose your enthusiasm and your drive."

I never got to the subject of hypoxia. While I was speaking, a sudden flash of intense blue-white light illumined the cabin. At the same instant, I felt a physical impact against the soles of my feet, as if a sledgehammer had struck the floorboards directly underneath. "A piece of the plane came loose," I said to myself. "Lightning—not a bomb. If it had been a bomb, we wouldn't still be flying."

A stewardess walked from the rear of the plane. "We have a lot of static around a plane in an electrical storm like this," she told the excited passengers.

"Static! Nonsense," was the consensus.

Bruce Biossat of Newspaper Enterprise Association's Washington Bureau had a window seat on the left side of the plane, and he told me later: "I saw a burst of flame, not exactly a ball of fire, at the tip of the wing—I was looking right at it. It was orange-colored, with a bluish tinge—maybe a reflection from the thick cloud we were in. And I heard a loud report like a pistol shot at close range. It was a very unusual sound around an airplane."

I walked forward to my seat and fastened the safety belt. Liz hid her eyes against my shoulder. I tried to reassure her.

"There's nothing to worry about now, Liz—lightning never strikes twice in the same place," I joked.

Liz lifted her head and looked at me without a smile. We were coming down for a landing, and her thoughts were with the press.

"Dr. Travell, can you give me some pills for my newsgirls?"

"It depends on what they need, Liz. Do you want something to pep them up, or calm them down?"

I spoke like a pharmacologist interested in specificity of drug effect. Liz laughed.

Standing on the airstrip in the rain before 10 A.M., Mrs. Johnson graciously acknowledged a large bouquet of roses and greetings from the city of Cleveland. Her poise was perfect.

Thunderstorms plagued our movements all day. By afternoon the weather was so bad that a plane could not bring Mrs. Jerrie Mock, the first woman to fly solo around the world, from Columbus to the Cleveland Airport for a 3 P.M. reception for the First Lady.

Mrs. Johnson had met a tough schedule of speeches and receiving lines, and she did not want any more rough flying that day. At four o'clock she elected to motor back to Washington—365 miles. Traveling in several cars and escorted by state troopers, our party paused for a hasty supper at a Howard Johnson's restaurant on the turnpike near Wexford, Pennsylvania. While we all ate in an alcove room, candid camera shots were taken. From the pay phone Mrs. Johnson spoke with the President in the White House.

On leaving the restaurant, I went back to get my coat from a rack, and I overheard the Howard Johnson waitresses talking. One exclaimed, "Imagine all that fuss and bother for the boss's wife!"

Mrs. Johnson, Liz, and I relaxed then in the back of the borrowed limousine, half reclining on bed pillows loaned by the Cleveland Airport

Motel. It was good to be on the ground, and our mood was gay in spite of the steady rain.

"It's a long while since I've eaten a hamburger on the road like that," Mrs. Johnson said laughing.

She had told reporters that indeed she was scared by the lightning. Discussing the episode twelve hours later on the trip, she said: "Dr. Travell, when I looked across at you, I was glad to see you smiling and comforting Liz. Were you really not afraid?"

"No, I really wasn't," I replied.

In the darkness our car rolled smoothly along the highway. She questioned me further, "Tell me, do you have greater faith, or perhaps better sense, than I do?"

"Neither. It just doesn't help to be afraid."

My answer was inadequate. Later, I reasoned that even in the air I was occupied with what I could do for others, because that was inherent in my medical training. Besides, my mother and father had conditioned me as a child not to fear the lightning storms.

Jack, however, was jolted when at our house on "N" Street he heard a newscaster announce briefly that the First Lady's plane had been hit by lightning. Jack quickly telephoned the White House.

A spokesman for United Air Lines was quoted as saying that when we landed at Cleveland our Viscount showed evidence of two separate lightning strikes, one on each side of the plane. I had been in error when I assured Liz that lightning never strikes the same spot twice. The damage was minor. I took the matter more seriously when within the year the Civil Aeronautics Board for the first time ascribed lightning as the cause of an airplane crash—the explosion of a Pan American jet near Baltimore. All aboard were lost.

My interest in the broad problems of health care for the aged led me to obtain a follow-up on the Riverview Well-Elderly Clinic three years after our ceremonial visit. Dr. Myron August, my Cornell medical classmate, had been the Clinic's Director when it opened, and on November 6, 1967, he wrote to me about its progress:

> As to Riverview . . . the project is no longer supported by the Federal Government. The local City Health Department . . . has maintained it on a reduced scale. I . . . act in an advisory capacity only. It is essentially now a nursing project. Because of the absence of support we have abridged the [disease] screening phase . . . [but] we have amassed interesting statistics on the 640 people . . . who have voluntarily joined the clinic—90% of the occupants. A second major

aspect is a referral system which we have developed to get these people into the proper medical hands. . . . A number of physicians [specialists] . . . have volunteered to see them at reduced rates. . . . Those who cannot afford even these small fees are referred to four large hospital out-patient services in close proximity. . . . The number of . . . people admitted to hospitals has been almost identical, 13%, each year. In the first six months of this year there were 3046 referrals of all types, from dentists to neurosurgeons. This referral system now . . . almost functions automatically. A third major aspect has been nursing care and this has been tremendously successful because . . . the nurse in charge and her two assistants, both practical nurses . . . have sympathy, understanding, devotion, ability and personality. . . . In addition to taking the electrocardiograms, the audiometer readings, the histories and [other tests], they advise and counsel the residents. . . . In the Lutheran Hospital . . . which, if you recall, is just across the street . . . I spend most of my working hours . . . and [the nurse in charge] and I have almost daily conferences. . . . In short, I feel that this has been a valuable community service.

I was especially pleased to learn that at the Well-Elderly Clinic the nurses were given the full responsibility for which they were qualified.

My recollections of the elderly in their high-rise buildings, of mud in their unfinished approaches, of the Texas roses that Mrs. Johnson received on her stops, blended with memories of our precarious travel, took form in a poem:

THE EARTHY

The fragrance of nature is not
Alone aroma from the rose,
But pungency of soil in hot
Summer, cool when I press my nose
Against it. Scent of seasoned rot—
Past years' dead leaves that were our woes—
Remains with me although my lot
Is city blocks where nothing grows.
Still, aging trees nurture my plot
Where finally I may repose
And smell the ground's bouquet—the spot
Where timelessly I'll dream and doze.

The lively, well-dressed old people whom we met at the Riverview Golden Age Center contrasted with the millions of the elderly in our country who were carrying on their existence under less fortunate circumstances of loneliness and illness in the absence of good medical and loving care.

I thought of the time when I was a medical student and I discovered that my visual acuity was poor. The microscope taught me that I could not see what was on the glass slide, and I had my vision checked. One clear frosty evening, riding on the upper deck of a Fifth Avenue bus I put on my new eyeglasses and I saw the stars overhead for the first time. To my amazement, rays of light really radiated outward from each one; all my life I had thought it merely an artist's custom to picture the stars that way. No one had told me otherwise, and I did not question my blurred view, which was like a Corot painting. When I suddenly perceived every individual star more clearly, the entire heavens became more brilliant. That new vision of the whole did not detract from my appreciation of its separate units. In Washington, I acquired a new kind of spectacles.

They improved my vision not merely for the vistas of medicine, but also for the peaks and valleys of the world at large. Through White House prestige, Jack and I joined the mixed diplomatic scene in Washington. In that climate my certainty grew that understanding and tolerance of other people's cultures constitute the basis for peace on earth.

During my White House years, I was freed from the necessity of constantly studying the scientific literature for my research programs, and I reverted to previous habits of omnivorous nonpurposeful reading. Biographies, books of political analysis, and, in particular, poetry appealed to me. I was deeply moved by meeting Carl Sandburg when President Johnson invited him to the White House.

On the emotional tidal wave of violent change that followed November 22, 1963, my old tendency to express a mood in verse reappeared. As Archibald Macleish wrote,

> A poem should be motionless in time
> As the moon climbs

In the early summer days of 1964, the Democratic National Convention and Presidential campaign loomed ahead. There was an uneasy restlessness in the air, as if we were waiting for the starting bell of a race to sound. I knew that I needed a vacation. In the soft May mornings, Jack and I breakfasted under the tree in our small garden back of the house on "N" Street. We would sit there sipping coffee until the black White House car pulled up in the alley at the rear and waited to take me to my office. Tongue in cheek, we called it the paddy wagon, and my destination, the White Jail. One June morning, in fun I wrote a ballad:

LAMENT ON WORKING
IN THE WHITE HOUSE

Sad, sad is the day
When the paddy wagon comes
To take me away
From my alley home that hums.

I sit in my cell
In a mansion known to bards,
Where great folks must dwell
In a prison manned by guards.

I pore in my cell,
Scanning words at record pace,
Listen for the bell.
Three buzzes sets the guards a-race.

My window is barred
From the fife and drum, gun smoke,
Red rug on greensward.
Sitting is the prisoner's yoke.

A bird flashes past
In the sun of heaven's blue sky,
Its flight free as fast.
If I may not run, I die.

It was truly dark in the corridor past my office when nearly all the lights were turned off in the evening. The guard stationed near my door told me, "They ought to give us silhouette lessons—I can't recognize anyone coming down the hall."

One night after three bells announced the approach of the President through the darkened passage, he walked by my office with John L. Lewis, and his guest was heard to say, "Mr. President, it looks like a mine tunnel to me."

Late in June, my vacation materialized. I was invited to help open that season's *The Lost Colony,* the outdoor pageant of the first American settlers on Roanoke Island, North Carolina; Secretary of Commerce Luther Hodges introduced me on the stage. In a cottage loaned by Jack's Norfleet cousins, on a wild stretch of beach at nearby Nags Head, we were joined by Virginia, Ed, and our grandchildren, Gordon and Janet Street.

My awareness of new meaning in the simple things that I saw was sharpened by the steady sound of the surf's rhythms. The wind off the ocean blew the swings where the children played, and it pulled at the beachwear drying behind the cottages. It lifted up the kites that Janet and Gordon held as they ran along the hard sand. I wrote about those timeless images:

TO AND FRO

A wild wind flings the children's swings,
Fast emptied at the crack of lightning,
Hung at armyard in the courtyard,
Shroud of clouds the youngsters frightening.
Jerk, swings, jerk to and fro, in the gale tangling,
Ropes slackening, tautening, the seat hanging, dangling.

The clothes entwine pinned on the line,
High winds a crazy quilt preparing—
Slim jeans, broad shirt, thin slip, trim skirt,
Each garment greater antics daring.
Flap, laundry, flap to and fro, sleeves embracing,
Skirt twisting, pants kneeling, blouse falling, grass defacing.

The weaving kites rise light to heights
As twine binds them to tautened fingers.
Aimless their flight, never from sight,
They charm us while the sunset lingers.
So swing to and fro, on the soft wind winging
And rising, dipping, to our hearts enchantment bringing.

My writing poems amused my family, and it entertained me. It was an exercise in orderly imagination that I undertook for the pleasure of it. It was also a natural outgrowth of my lifetime fascination with words, which the stimulation of Washington's wit and style encouraged. In the frame of poetical expression, although dangerously self-revealing, I even tried to explain the elusive need to write poetry. On December 31, 1964, I stayed at home, baby-sitting for our one-year-old grandson Mark Antony, while Jack escorted Janet and her second husband, Captain Vinicio Pinci of the Italian Air Force, to a New Year's Eve rendition of operatic arias. It was Vinicio's second visit to Washington since he and Janet were married on October 11, 1962, in Rome. Looking into the open fire in the living room of our Georgetown house, that evening I composed a sonnet:

THE PHOENIX OF POETRY

A poem is a window of the soul.
It opens, not wide, but enough to blow
Aside the curtains of the mind and show
Inside the glow of love that makes man whole.

The gales of his emotion have ripped off
The poet's pride, his bias, let in light
From the sky and flooded him with insight
Immortal; as a twister lifts a roof.

Wind, rain, hail lash him. Flames chase the storm.
From ashes of emotion arises
The phoenix of poetry, in attire
Of simple singing words that transform
Her by the mind's subtle swift surprises
Into a torch to set men's souls afire.

CHAPTER 23

Contemporary Years

It took us a year to find our "house in the country" within the heart of the District of Columbia. Jack and I realized the attrition caused by our daily travel for seventeen years between the concrete of New York and the forested suburb where we lived, and we agreed that we would never become commuters again. Nor did we wish to retire to a farm. But we tired of city living, even in quaint old Georgetown. In the spring of 1965, we exchanged our dark row house and the traffic noise of "N" Street for a residence not far distant in a high, wooded section of Northwest Washington—Wesley Heights.

Jack's specifications for our new home were simple: a sunny well-built house on a quiet street with trees, hot-water heating system, a library, and a garage. Mine were more complicated. I desired a house on a hill—the foremost requisite was the hill. I required a ground-floor wing that would serve as my medical office. I wanted a large room upstairs where I could write in isolation and in juxtaposition to my research files. My medical writing on musculoskeletal pain had been interrupted for too long, and I had decided to write my autobiography.

Without special aid we might not have found our present home. Jack had looked at a hundred houses in Washington and I had looked at one of those—none fulfilled all our criteria—when we met Mrs. Jeane Dixon whose crystal ball was lengendary. Her husband was in the real-estate business, and she showed us through the house that she had chosen for us.

"The vibrations are right for you," she told us earnestly. "If you do not buy this house, I will buy it myself and I will hold it for you until you do."

It fitted us exactly, and we purchased it as soon as possible. Without its serene setting this book might not have been written.

With my new spectacles I saw more clearly than ever the natural beauty of our world. The land dropped away steeply on two sides of the house, and from the elevation of our windows we looked off into vistas of trees—dogwood, hemlock and pine, oak, and flowering tulip. They were tall trees in which the wind sighed. Our bedroom opened onto an uncovered upstairs porch, and it became a feeding station for the wild birds. They soon trusted us and came to our window sills for tasty bits; when the supply ran out, they all but tapped on the glass panes to attract our attention inside. With head cocked to turn one bright eye, they watched us curiously. "They feel sorry for us," Jack said. "They think we're in a cage."

It was a long time since I had heard the early chorus of the bustling birds, and I reveled in it:

DECIBELS OF DAWN

As red and friendly as a Valentine,
And not more subtle either, comes my guest,
The cardinal, at dawn. Safe in the pine
By my bedroom he rouses from her rest
His lady with staccato call: "Come, dine
At window sill on sunflower seeds, lest
The greedy jays and squirrels first align
Themselves against us. Fluffing feathered chest,
Red-crested he pecks fast. By my design
He wakens me likewise to see the best
Half-hour of day, the dawning. Then, sunshine
Outlines no shadows. Sounds that thought arrest
Are silent still—the rattle, bang and whine
Of garbage trucks upon our hill—that test
My equanimity. My Valentine
Thanks me; his decibels do not molest.

Moving day into our chalet on the highest plateau of Cathedral Avenue coincided by chance with moving day from my White House office—March 31, 1965. A few days earlier at a farewell reception in the Oval Room on the second floor of the White House, President and Mrs. Johnson presented me with a framed "Prescription for Happiness" that stated at the top, "OFFICE HOURS Day & Night." That indeed had been my life, and my happiness was founded on hard work.

The year that I stayed on at the White House with President Johnson might have been termed "Office Hours in Orbit." My orbital duties, which had begun with Mrs. Johnson's electrifying flight to Cleveland and her motorized return to Washington, gained velocity during the 1964 political campaign—at the Democratic National Convention in Atlantic City, on the Lady Bird Special train and plane, at the LBJ Ranch—and finally, during the Inauguration of Lyndon Baines Johnson on January 20, 1965, as thirty-sixth President of the United States. From my vantage point within the White House and as Chairman of the Medical Care Committee of the 1965 Inaugural Committee, I had an unrestricted view of the massive problems involved in assuring security for the President and governmental family and in providing health protection—housing, food, and emergency medical care —for the thousands of visitors and official guests at the Inaugural events. I am grateful to President Johnson for that additional year—it was one of the most challenging of my life.

After my 1,527 days in the White House, Jack's and my deceleration and reentry into a commonplace atmosphere was not precipitous. Having chosen to live in Washington and having made friends in both the Kennedy and Johnson Administrations, we remained on the current scene.

Those who traveled with Mrs. Johnson on the Lady Bird Special train began to hold reunions almost as soon as its "crew" and hostesses had returned to Washington. Those parties kept us "turned on" throughout the ensuing year. As whistle-stoppers, like astronauts after orbit, we were bound together by an intense shared experience that had been self-limited in space and time. The mood had been set by Mrs. Johnson, whose style was a reflection of her character—tolerant, concerned, clear-sighted, energetic, and gay.

Incongruous details of those reunions recur in my memory. On October 21, 1964, in Georgetown's City Tavern, the Women's National Press Club assembled representatives of Presidential whistle-stop campaigns from Al Smith's and Franklin D. Roosevelt's to Barry Goldwater's and Lyndon Johnson's. As Jack and I were leaving the Tavern after a hilarious evening, I reached into the basket of a "Goldwater Girl" and I lifted a handful of uninflated rubber balloons. They came to light again when we were moving to Wesley Heights and our belongings were being carried out of 3319 "N" Street into the van. Benjamin Bradlee's small son Dino wandered in from his house next door to watch the fascinating confusion. From an open carton box he pulled out a large Lady Bird Special campaign button that pictured a saucy train zigzagging across it. He admired it and I gave it to him. He ran home with it and quickly returned. Dino's next draw from the box produced a Goldwater balloon, and I blew it up for him.

"Why do you have *that?*" he asked me accusingly.

I had a hard time explaining. His father was then an editor of *News-*

week magazine, and I wondered how much of a credibility gap in my record as a Democrat the incident might create.

On April 21, 1965, the engine of a diminutive Lady Bird Special train, which had been the State of Georgia's float in the Inaugural Parade, was parked at "Joe and Laura Moran's Depot" on California Street in Washington. Train Commander Joe's invitation to whistle-stop veterans read: "Come as your favorite Whistle Stop Character—maybe yourself. The Chief of Police estimates the crowd will be 500,000. . . ." Liz Carpenter hung a stethoscope around her neck and pinned a name tag on her dress that identified her as "Dr. Travell." I put on my old Ambulance Surgeon cap, reminiscent of those days in New York when with the authority of police lieutenant I handled emergencies out of my large black medical bag. It was my first sampling of official power.

Day and night, on the Lady Bird Special campaign train I had been physician, nurse, and pharmacist for the 250 people who were housed and fed in the nineteen cars—Mrs. Johnson, Lynda or Luci, VIPs, White House staffers, and about 150 reporters and photographers. During the four-day journey, about half of that train population and a few of the 1,600 short-haul local guests who rode between whistle-stops required my medical attention.

"Dr. Travell dispensed more drugs than I did press releases," energetic Liz Carpenter remarked. In addition to my medical bag, I took aboard so many boxes of supplies—with their contents neatly listed—that I could hardly step into my small sleeping compartment. Reporters wrote about their occupational hazards in whistle-stopping: "Everything developed from high blood pressure and a laryngitis epidemic to sprained ankles and cinders in the eyes." Not everything, I thought—hypokinesia was not one of their complaints. Appreciatively, they dubbed me "the heroine of the Whistle Stop tour." In the intervening years, I have not lost my regard for those hard-working and hardy friends.

Scenes change fast in Washington. On the day after that April reunion at the Morans' home, when the yellow tulips were in bloom, Jack and I attended the dedication of the formal Jacqueline Kennedy Garden of the White House. It had been a vision of John F. Kennedy's that was fulfilled through Mrs. Johnson's efforts. From there, we left in our car for the Golden Triangle Hotel in Norfolk to be with Luci for the ceremonies that saluted her coronation as Queen of the 1965 NATO Azalea Festival. The season was so late that potted flowering azaleas were banked in the garden, and the wind off the reflecting lake was bitter cold where Jack and I sat four rows behind President and Mrs. Johnson. Unobserved, Jack bent low, crept forward, and slipped my fur stole around her shoulders. As the newly crowned Queen's mother departed for Air Force One, she rolled up the fur piece and passed it to me like a football quarterback on the run.

Jack and I kept step with Luci and her attendants, the fourteen Princesses who represented the countries of the North Atlantic Treaty Organization. At the final luncheon in the Officers' Club of the U.S. Naval Station, Jack was seated at Luci's right. She was always thoughtful of him; whenever she sent me a picture of herself, she inscribed it to us both. She had an educated heart.

The "generation gap" did not afflict Jack and me in our attitudes toward those who were either older or younger than ourselves. Perhaps that was because we grew up with the rebels of the flapper era in the decade following World War I. In Wellesley College I wore my daytime dresses at the accepted ankle length, but I was receptive to change, and by the time I finished medical school their hemlines were above my knees. The miniskirt charms me now by reminding me of my own youth. The frug, watusi, and what-have-you revive happy memories of my dancing the Charleston across Europe, from London to Karlovci in Serbia on the Danube. In 1926, as a fledgling doctor I traveled in a third-class railroad carriage for three days with forty students, representatives of Great Britain and her Dominions at an International Student Service conference. When we left London's Waterloo Station, they were all strangers to me except Eleanora Iredale, leader of the delegation, and she had invited me on short notice to "come along."

On the train in 1926, those reserved British students elected me their mascot and christened me "Miss America." That gave me the privilege of sleeping overhead in a luggage rack that resembled a feed trough for farm animals. At night, the others—eight women and thirty-two men—spread out newspapers, removed their shoes, and lay down on the wooden bench seats or on the floor of the unpartitioned car. I dispelled their image of the "soft American," which prevailed in Europe even then.

As I looked back from the Lady Bird Special, its hardships were dwarfed by that earlier adventurous train ride. However, the gaiety of my contemporary heart had not diminished. Between whistle-stops, Luci taught me the modern dances and I taught her the Charleston, practicing in a quiet corner of the family dining area as we rolled along the tracks ahead of the crowded Hospitality Car. I knew that I had spanned our generations when Luci told Jack later, "Dr. Travell will do anything."

I, in turn, concluded that Luci could do anything to which she applied her boundless energy. Whistle-stopping at seventeen, as a public speaker she displayed singular talent for communicating with people in the mass. When she was offered aid in preparing a speech on the train, she would reply, "No, thank you. I know what I want to say and when the time comes, I'll find the words."

Luci used no notes, nor did she memorize phrases. For as long as she spoke, her spontaneous words stilled the restless tired crowds to motionless silence. From the rear platform of the train or in auditoriums, few veteran campaigners held such command of the same audiences. Watching her I thought, "If the time arrives when a woman may be President of the United States, Luci will have the qualifications."

Capable, lovable Luci's public image was sometimes clouded by her mixing merriment with seriousness, nonconformity with convention. Jack and I were impressed anew by the contrasts in her personality when in August, 1966, we attended her wedding and reception, which were distinguished by pageantry, magnificence, reverence, and simplicity of spirit.

In my own way, with divided loyalty I spanned the widening gulf between members of the Johnson and Kennedy political forces. On May 27, 1967, at the invitation of the Kennedy family Jack and I attended the christening of the aircraft carrier USS John F. Kennedy. If the late President had lived, it would have been two days before his fiftieth birthday. We flew from Washington to Newport News on Air Force One with President Johnson. Sitting in his private compartment, we enjoyed his reminiscences about Luci in the White House. In a moment's respite from national crises he speculated, like any prospective grandfather, about the arrival and future of his first grandchild.

The Presidential motorcade brought us to the platform erected beneath the bow of the towering ship. Its height from keel to mast equalled that of a twenty-three-story building, and it cast a cold shadow over us. Jack and I had chairs by the steps up to the christening stage near Ted and Joan Kennedy, where we could watch left-handed Caroline splash champagne against the curving prow. Then the aircraft carrier with its great American flag slid slowly down the inclined ways toward the sea that John Kennedy loved, and its shadow passed from us. Warmth of sunshine suddenly dissipated the chill in the atmosphere.

That beginning contrasted with an ending that Jack and I witnessed also. The "Mother Ship" Caroline, the Kennedy Convair of the 1960 campaign, was presented on November 17, 1967, to the Smithsonian Institution at Washington's National Airport. I was glad that the hardy little plane had a final historical home. The reception for the Caroline's friends was not a melancholy one, for the vital presence of Jack Kennedy pervaded her. Although the aircraft carrier named for him would never know his step, the men to serve on the USS John F. Kennedy would think and feel differently because he had lived.

That November, the fourth anniversary of his assassination, I listened to the televised comments and noted my reaction in a few sentences. In them I found a poem:

FOUR YEARS LATER

From whatever fragments
Of reality
The myth of John F. Kennedy
Has been fabricated,
The fact of the myth is real.
It exists, it lives.
The myth now inspires men
Because John F. Kennedy,
The man, inspired them then.
The myth wields power
Because of the man.
In the ultimate,
The myth is the man.

In our new nonofficial setting in Washington, I rewove threads in the fabric of my professional life. My White House years had disconnected me from the absorbing routine of scientific investigation, and I did not resume that phase of my activities.

The creative energy that I had formerly expended on medical research —and that involved writing—I was content to divert into my autobiography—and that involved research. To me, the quality of challenge was similar. Both sorts of original thinking require staying power, since a successful conclusion in each is marked by long periods when nothing seems to be happening. Having faith in the ultimate truth, I had learned to take one step at a time. There was another similarity. To Jack's dismay, I reverted to my old habit of driving my brain through thorny terrain during the unclocked hours "between midnight and bedtime."

When President Kennedy asked me to come to the White House, I told him that change did not disturb me. In my contemporary transition, I did not sense any inner conflict growing from the fact that this book occupied me to the exclusion of a research program. My shift in focus from scientific to literary writing made me pleasantly aware that not all the doors had closed behind me regarding my choices for action.

Past the retirement age of sixty-five, I feel that I am in the middle of my life. And with work space in our hillside home, flexibility in my new schedule has given Jack and me more time together—yet still not enough.

It did not surprise me to find that there is a basic conflict between reflective writing and practicing medicine. Imaginative composition needs blocks of uninterrupted time for ideas to emerge. On the other hand, to a patient the prompt availability of his doctor is perhaps the most important facet of their relationship. It is an essential difference between the family physician and many specialists.

My patients held priority over the story of my life—they had to come first. I could not give them half measure. To extricate myself from the dilemma of time, regretfully I limited my clinical responsibility by sharply curtailing the number of new patients whom I accepted.

Having an office in our home helped. The arrangement made me constantly available, and yet spared me the demands of running a medical establishment as I had done in New York. Washington is a mecca of medicine, and in my consultant practice I did not lack for associates to provide the team health care that is necessary in this complex era of medical science.

It was unthinkable that I should retire from the practice of medicine because I had reached the "retirement" age. My excitement had not faded in seeing people respond to that healing art, and my years as a clinician had never been monotonous. No two persons have identical fingerprints, and the medical conundrums presented by patients are as infinitely varied. Among my friends who practiced medicine, I did not know a bored physician.

In the laboratory likewise, it was always immediately satisfying to observe experiments unfold—although arduous to give meaning to the data for publication. Writing is the hardest work that I know, and my autobiography took precedence, except for one paper[1] that was a sequel to my last one on myofascial pain[2] before I left New York for the White House.

Next to writing, the systematic teaching of classes is the most exacting. In my contemporary existence, I have taught students only as a visiting lecturer in pharmacology at various medical schools. But I use my pharmacologic training and knowledge[3] constantly in caring for patients.

When I visited the Woman's Medical College of Pennsylvania in Philadelphia, in the college hall I saw again Clara Hill's bas-relief of the "Woman Physician," for which I had posed as a girl. I had come a long way since then, beyond the scope of my wildest dreams.

In building a professional career, one proceeds step by step, not looking back to the bottom of the staircase. It comes as a surprise, if not something

[1] Janet Travell, "Mechanical Headache," *Headache*, Vol. 7 (1967), pp. 23–29.
[2] Janet Travell, "Temporomandibular Joint Pain Referred from Muscles of the Head and Neck," *Journal of Prosthetic Dentistry*, Vol. 10 (1960), pp. 745–763.
[3] Janet Travell, "Assessment of Drugs for Therapeutic Efficacy," *American Journal of Physical Medicine*, Vol. 34 (1955), pp. 129–140.

of a shock, suddenly to find oneself on a high plateau of achievement with new vistas stretching ahead. One goal that I still pursue is to increase the physician's diagnostic acumen and therapeutic skill in the relief of pain. Another goal is to enhance the stature of the investigator-physician, the practitioner who is trained in the basic sciences through participation in creative research. He brings the principles of scientific investigation to the analysis of the individual patient's problems, and he also brings the insight of the family physician to the biological vagaries of the laboratory.

In this contemporary period in Washington, I have found time to lecture to medical societies on my favorite topic, referred skeletal muscle pain and its management. Invitations to speak in Jack's home state have been especially welcome.

In May, 1965, in the Governor's Mansion at Raleigh it was a novel experience for me to talk on the subject of general health to the Sir Walter Cabinet of distinguished North Carolina women, who were state officials or married to legislators or members of the Council of State. In the Tar Heel audience were wives of four of North Carolina's governors, and as guests, Jack's sister from Charlotte and his sister-in-law, Julia Manning Powell, of Raleigh.

Too many of us, I said, put up with only average health. Even in the highest walks of life, we may suffer from a state described about 150 years ago by Dr. James Johnson, Physician Extraordinary to the King of England: "A condition of body and mind, intermediate between sickness and health . . . that WEAR AND TEAR of the living machine . . . which results from over-strenuous exertion of the intellectual faculties . . . conducted in bad air and anxiety of mind. . . . It makes much work for the doctor ultimately, if not for the undertakers." [4]

The perspective of history teaches that Dr. Johnson's "wear and tear of civilized life, caused by chafing tides of human existence," is not new. As a White House Physician, I had a kindred feeling for him. One enemy of the Great Society is fatigue, not disease.

When I hear people casually discuss the health of our Presidents and enumerate their lesser or greater ailments, I recall all my father's diseases and also his long lifetime of high-quality performance in his profession. He was not disabled by having had severe typhoid fever, diphtheria, scarlet fever, and acute poliomyelitis with partial paralysis of eye muscles that later

[4] James Johnson, M.D., *Change of Air or the Pursuit of Health and Recreation: Illustrating the Beneficial Influence of Bodily Exercise—Change of Scene—Pure Air and Temporary Relaxation in Sickness and in Health*, 4th ed., with additions (London, S. Highley, 1838), pp. 1–3.

required corrective surgery; by Paget's disease of the spine and pelvis, fortunately arrested before it progressed to the bones of the skull; radiation burns of his hands, acquired in his pioneering application of X-ray; Type III lobar pneumonia; three serious heart attacks—acute myocardial infarctions; diabetes and occlusive arteriosclerosis so advanced that pulses were absent in his feet. In his eighties, the only disability that really troubled him was his "seeing double" sometimes when he was playing tennis. Then he would alibi with a mischievous smile, "I hit the wrong ball." His energy and enthusiasm were boundless, and he never seemed to tire. He was a happy person.

It is obvious that our potential for optimal health depends not alone on the pathology of disease, but on the fiber of our personalities.

One of my father's dreams for medical progress was realized in part when the North American Academy of Manipulative Medicine was founded in 1965 by physicians of Canada and the United States. At its second annual meeting in 1967, Dr. John Mennell took office as its President and I became President-elect. John and I had each acquired an interest and capability in manipulation from our respective physician-fathers. By coincidence, nearly twenty years earlier they had been mentioned in separate editorials on the same page of the *Archives of Physical Medicine*.[5] One editorial noted that the new American Board of Physical Medicine had "bestowed honorary membership on four living pioneers" in the field—one was Dr. J. Willard Travell of New York. The other editorial concerned itself with Dr. James Mennell, the visiting British author and teacher of systematic manipulative procedures, and it stated: "While he is with us [in this country], we should take advantage of his special skills and experiences to develop further the science and art of joint manipulation."

The Mennell-Travell team of the young North American Academy of Manipulative Medicine has a heritage to fulfill. We hope that Victor Hugo's words will ring true for it: "Stronger than all the armies is the idea whose time has come."

Not all the presentations were technical at the medical meetings that I attended. The 1966 opening session of the American Medical Association in Chicago's new convention hall featured *Sing-Out '66*, a production sponsored by Moral Re-Armament. I was stirred by the patriotic music and by the young performers' zeal for sharing their American ideal of democracy with their own restless generation. Subconsciously influenced by them, perhaps, I wrote verses for our elder generations to read while rocking the hours away:

[5] Vol. 35 (1947), p. 726.

ROCKING-CHAIR SING-OUT

When you start aging
Don't just drop out raging.
When you retire,
So you'll do nothing?
Well, you can't do nothing
For long.

When you quit marching,
Just resting and watching
Won't keep your fire
Glowing and burning
If your mind's not turning—
Not long.

When I sit rocking
Then I keep on thinking—
Never do tire.
I'm with the living
While I keep on singing
A song.

I'll sing-out, giving
As long as I'm living.
No angel choir
For you is singing—
It's you I'm bringing
My song.

It's you I'm mocking
For I'll still be rocking
When you expire.
Where you're now tearing
No halo you're wearing
Along.

You can't stop living!
It's not late for giving.
Love's not for hire
So start in loving—
Dough's not worth the shoving—
Belong.

The seasons now have completed three full cycles for Jack and me in
our Cathedral Avenue home. Each year our tall trees have signaled time's
passage by their fluttering poplar-leaf shadows on gray bark, by acorns fall-

ing on our slate roof and by the piling of snow upon wide-reaching horizontal limbs so that the squirrels run upside down along the bottom surface of those aerial bridges. I told in a poem the pictorial story of the months on our forested hill:

SEASONS ON CATHEDRAL AVENUE

The tracery of tree limbs bare of leaves
Is flawless tapestry that autumn weaves.
Their geometric arches lace on high;
Head bare, I stand beneath the woven sky.
Just as a short-cropped haircut is to me,
Are leafless lightened branches to a tree.

The mystery of winter's drifting snow
Blots out black lines of boughs now sagging low.
The weight of white is like the hoary hair
Of age that bends us with its wear and tear.
But when the spring removes that fitted wig,
New greenery of leaves will mask each twig.

My flower gardens at Cathedral Avenue are peopled with our friends. There are flat-topped lavender and white Japanese iris, offshoots of clumps that Mrs. Nina Warburg, Bettina's mother, gave me thirty years ago in her Hartsdale garden. I planted them at Merryfield Farm and from the original clumps, grown large, I brought them to our contemporary hill. Saffron "Fashion" roses bloom on bushes that Dr. and Mrs. Eugene F. DuBois— our Cornell physiologist of calorimeter fame—gave me for my garden in Pelham. Then the plants lived and flowered for four years in pots set in dirt behind our Georgetown house, and now they thrive in their more permanent setting. A "Peace" rose from Jeane Dixon blooms nearby, and next to that, the imperishable white "John F. Kennedy" rose. In a favored spot are white star chrysanthemums from President Kennedy's Rose Garden—the petals become tinged with red as they age. In 1962, the White House gardener said that some small plants were not good enough for the Rose Garden and he set them in the car for me. They lived in the garden of our house on "N" Street, near Senator Jack Kennedy's home, and they live now on Cathedral Avenue.

Nothing dies in our garden—unless it is the aphids that the birds eat. Near my insect-free hybrid rosebushes, I encourage old-fashioned rambler roses to grow, and I do not cut back their sprawling branches. All summer, their luscious long stems and young green leaves are covered with aphids, but I spray them with no chemicals. Looking at them with an editorial eye, Bob Gutwillig remarked one day, "I never saw decoy rosebushes before."

Over the years, many patients transported to my New York office roots, slips, and seeds of their favorite plants. Now, in their flowering descendants I recognize the faces of those friends. Sometimes, when I sighed and wished for more time to work in my Pelham garden, Jack used to say to me, "Don't fret, your patients are your flowers." In truth, I thought, they are interchangeable.

Prized among the new generation of shrubs and perennials that have moved from our hill in Sheffield to the District of Columbia is an offspring of the double-petaled giant syringa that my mother planted at Merryfield Farm fifty years ago. As she taught me, I created a new one by layering a branch with longitudinal slits in its bark under a stone and then disconnecting it after a couple of years. The successful gardener is a patient person.

From Jack's East Carolina country we brought sturdy cowslips, and in the shade of our dogwood trees their delicate yellow blooms are a curiosity in Washington. Margaret Norfleet dug them for us in her garden in Jackson, North Carolina, and she said that the plants had a long lineage in her home state of Virginia. Those southern cowslips probably outancestor any other perennials in our garden, even the ones of Massachusetts stock.

A gardener learns to control overpopulation, to avoid waste and to conserve the soil by means of household organic fertilizers. Janet, at her new home in the outskirts of Milan, remembers my gardening lessons. For different kinds of plants she knows the value of wood ashes, coffee grounds, egg shells, leafbone compost, and the needles of pine and spruce. On Cathedral Avenue, I still feed my azaleas our Christmas tree—and our neighbors' castoffs—after making firewood of the trunk and heavy branches. This winter, I knew that Virginia had joined the clan of thrifty gardeners when she told me, "I asked the people around us for their Christmas trees—I want to plant a lot of azaleas in the spring." She and Ed had a new home in Nashville.

My vision in college of achieving happiness while I combined the profession of medicine with homemaking would not have come to pass without Jack—the special kind of husband who believed in my work and was resourceful with the children. That was the theme of my speech to the reuning classes at Wellesley in June, 1967, forty-five years after my graduation there. I had learned meanwhile that behind a successful woman in any profession usually stands a man.

In high school Janet estimated her capability to have both the home and operatic career that she wanted. She said. "If Mummy can manage, I can too."

At Milan with Richie, where she went in 1960 to study voice, her road as a singer was steep. Fluent in Italian, she did part-time work as an interpreter; she liked mental gymnastics. After she married Vinicio, his pride in her and her musical sensibility sustained her in auditioning, learning operatic roles, singing in concerts and on the Italian national radio (RAI). A study grant was awarded to her by the Martha Baird Rockefeller Fund for Music. By 1967, mother of three boys, as "Gianna Pinci" her success in opera in Italy had been assured.

That autumn at the Eliseo theater in Rome, Janet's three-year-old son Mark Antony played the part of Butterfly's child with her. Born on October 17, 1963, and christened Marcantonio Giovanni Severo Pinci after his Italian grandfather, he was a blue-eyed, curly-blond Botticelli cherub when he made his stage debut with his beautiful brunette mother. Janet wrote us: "M.A. was adorable. He did everything he had been told to—called out Mamma . . . kowtowed to the consul, stayed still to be blindfolded and till the very end. Then he took all the curtain calls with me and bowed like a professional."

About his wife's performance at the Eliseo theater, Vinicio wrote us proudly: "Last night Gianna sang Madama Butterfly and it was a hit success. She received much applause and the audience requested encore after the very famous aria, 'un bel di vedremo.' The impressario said she is a great actress. . . . I was very nervous. . . . She did beautifully: a 'trionph.' "

In Washington Jack and I wanted a place that might still be "home" to our girls and our grandchildren. At Christmas of 1964, they had filled all crannies of our quaint Georgetown house. Mark Antony crossed the ocean with his parents, and Richie came from Milan, too. Virginia brought Gordon and my namesake, Janet Travell Street, from Nashville for the family reunion. One evening to the sound of caroling music, we walked together— Vinicio carried Mark Antony—along the path between lighted evergreens for a close view of the enormous Christmas tree that the President had lighted on the Ellipse. That Yuletide spectacle marked a time of fulfillment. The exterior of the White House had been freshly painted. In front on Pennsylvania Avenue the spectator stands were being constructed out of massive lumber for President Johnson's Inaugural Parade. I would soon leave my White House post.

When Richie flew alone from Europe during his school holidays, his international education and travel gave him maturity. At fourteen he went with Jack and me to a reception where he held an animated conversation with Walter Lippmann. Afterward, the columnist asked us, "Does that boy get along as well with his own generation as he does with ours?"

Richie did, indeed. In Milan, he danced, played school basketball, and rode his small motorcycle with the other boys to camp out on the beaches.

of our relatives eventually visited us. My sister, whose husb
two weeks before the 1960 Democratic National Conventi
e from her busy pediatric practice for trips to Washington. S.
ten while her daughter, Dr. Elinor E. Weeks, lived in Georgetow.
rked for a year at the Children's Hospital. All four of Ginny's and
children obtained doctorates—Ginger, Willard, and Elinor in medi-
and Sheldon in education from Harvard University.

ur home offered a comfortable headquarters for friends, too. When
du Vigneauds visited us—Dee received an honorary Doctor of Science
m George Washington University, with which I enjoy affiliation in the
partment of Medicine—he remarked thoughtfully, "Your house has dig-
ty, charm, and livability—a rare combination." Jack and I like it best of
he places where we have lived.

Before our marriage, I had told him, "I am as fickle in my love for New
York as you are." We never missed that megalopolis.

Our teenage grandson Richie—Richard McAlee—recently viewed that
overpopulated city in a poem that he wrote in the spirit of his student
generation:

THE LONELY CITY

Cliffs of glass rise bleak and bare
Towards the silent empty heights,
Into chill and blighted air,
Buoyed by noise and blinding lights.

Milling figures crowd the street,
Grope, but know not what they seek;
Chaos rings from rushing feet,
Drowns the sound of those who speak.

Furrowed faces, hard as stone,
Walk in silence, frown and stare—
Among the millions, yet alone;
Few are there who dare to care.

Death and darkness can but sear
Men so far and yet so near.

Unlike New York, Washington is a friendly city. It impressed me by a
kind of leisurely courtesy to which I had been unaccustomed in New York.
One wintry night, as we were leaving Constitution Hall after a National
Symphony concert, our host's car had a flat tire. It had Pennsylvania license
plates; he worked temporarily in Washington. A policeman walked over to
get us moving and to clear up the traffic jam, and our host asked him apologetically, "Is there a filling station around here with a mechanic?"

Janet, Vinicio, and their children
beautiful shores of the Mediterran.
to do.

In late January, 1966, Janet pres.
and Italian songs at the Phillips Collect.
nine-month-old baby, Valerio Ottaviano,
home acquired a crib. The day that Valeri.
March—Jack and I took final possession o.
Jeane Dixon. As I was leaving my office to m.
saying to my secretary, "Martha, be on the lo.
today we'll have another grandchild in Italy." At
proposed a toast to our new grandchild's arrival.
cablegram was already on the way to tell us that Val.
world a month early. Jeane Dixon said that I was psych.

No one predicted the full force of the blizzard that
ington with near-zero temperatures on January 29, 1966.
in decades," sixteen inches had fallen by the day of Janet
drifts blocked the streets and shut down airports. Schools c
ment workers were excused, police cars transported doctors to
Post Office was unable to deliver the mail, and the White House
scheduled dinner that night—but Janet's song recital and the
afterward on our hill went on. Jack shoveled out our car and I tac.
steps. Janet calmly vocalized at our piano, in spite of telephones ringi.
Valerio, in a playpen, singing with his mother. Jack taxied her accompa.
the help for our party, and stranded guests who hiked part way in sn.
boots and dinner jackets, or long dresses tucked inside slacks. My sister i.
Brooklyn, with characteristic determination and foresight, went out to La
Guardia Airport and waited until she got on a through flight to the deep
South that let her off in Washington. When we arrived in the Phillips Gal-
lery, there was Ginny sitting and knitting. Boyd and Hazel Lewis had come
from Pelham before the storm, and about a hundred of our more recent
friends overcame the obstacles of the weather. Only the young in heart
continue to make such friends, I thought.

The next day, the Washington *Evening Star* reported that in spite of the
blizzard at Janet Pinci's recital "the audience was one of the dressiest of the
season. . . . Her stunning appearance, rare musicianship, and beautifully
controlled singing made the recital a three-fold pleasure. Difficult music is
her forte. . . . Her voice has a huskiness of great allure. She resembles
Dorothy Kirsten in sound and has the same skill in bringing mood and
drama. The treasures of her program were the contemporary Italian songs.
. . . She has great gifts and must be heard in more frequent recitals."

"None open at this hour," the Negro officer answered. "That's tough on a night like this and you all dressed up. If you'll wait until the cars pull away, I'll change it for you. I'd hate for your trip to be spoiled."

Imposing in helmet and orange overvest, he knelt in the snow and replaced the flat with the spare. To him we were tourists in his fair city. Jack obtained his name, and from the White House I wrote a letter of appreciation to his precinct chief.

Our contemporary years in Washington have restored my appreciation of our cities as the central unit of American culture. Although the District of Columbia has a superstructure of commuting Federal workers and millions of tourists yearly, it is still not a large city. Its parks provide oases for wild life, even snakes and, recently, rabid foxes within a couple of miles of our house. Living in Washington has reminded me that "urban" and "megalopolitan" are not synonymous. It has made me increasingly aware, too, of the civic art museums with instruction in the graphic arts, symphony orchestras, small opera companies, repertory theaters, and music festivals in the cities throughout the United States.

No doubt, my excitement in this country's cultural explosion has been enhanced by Janet's career as a singer and Virginia's as an artist. Under the name Gina Street, her sculpture and painting have been widely exhibited in museums and galleries. She is also enlarging her contribution to the community by teaching art to children at the Ensworth School. Jack and I have a "Gianna" and a "Gina," two daughters who from early childhood shared their talents with their parents. The miles can not now separate us.

Busy, cheerful people tend to be healthier than the idle and unhappy. As the age of automation becomes the age of leisure, with a lengthening life span, the menace of creatively empty hours for the elderly will be met largely by involvement in the arts. And to be available, the resources for that must be widely distributed in our smaller cities. But participation in the arts should not wait until retirement. We must start by educating the young for leisure.

When Virginia was six years old, her fingers already possessed the sensitivity of perception that is the basis of the sculptor's three-dimensional memory. When she and Janet were six and seven, Jack and I took them to a one-ring circus in Great Barrington where I persuaded the trainer to let them ride, with some older girls, on the bare back of an elephant. Recently, I asked Virginia whether she rode over the tail or on the head of the elephant and she replied, "I must have been in front because I remember holding on to the ears—I was surprised how thin they were."

Ours was never a family of spectators. In August of 1967, our youngest grandchild, Edward Hunt Street, Jr., born September 24, 1966, found barefoot freedom on our bumpy lawn at Merryfield Farm. Scattered objects stimulated Hunt to endless activity—croquet mallets and balls, a horseshoe set with rope rings, and, best of all, an imaginative toddler's bench that my nephew Sheldon Weeks had built for his children there. It had a flight of three shallow steps guarded by railings, up one side and down the other, and it had brass handles to rattle and turn, hinged lids that opened into compartments to be stuffed with grass and twigs, and round holes in which to stick the fingers. For Hunt there were no fences at the farm, nor were there any for his brother and sister, Gordon and Janet.

No traffic passed the old farmhouse then. Our dirt road was closed and barricaded by the town of Sheffield's Selectmen. Both the approaches to our hill were impassable after fifty-five inches of rainfall in seven months, as compared with the region's annual average of thirty-seven inches. Virginia commented, "Our road looks like the beach when the tide goes out." Polliwogs hatched in its drainage ditches.

Merryfield Farm was a magnet that drew our younger generations as it did Ginny and me. With their three children, a cat, and a dog, Ed and Virginia had driven a thousand miles from Tennessee in two days, only to arrive in a rainstorm after dark at the southerly "Road Closed" sign. That morning they had visited Niagara Falls, and they had seen enough water. With a quarter of a mile left to go, they moved the barricade and drove through a washout. Their car stuck in the mud in front of the dark and empty house. Jack and I were driving from Washington and we made a similar decision about the northerly road block. With a flashlight we explored steep, rutted Crow Hill. Water was rushing across the road above an old-fashioned Thank-you-Ma'am, and we filled in the stream bed to make tracks for the wheels with rocks that we scooped from the bank on each side. The car had to go through—it carried all the food for the weekend. Spinning and sliding, our pretty white "Doll" made it "safe home."

It was as if the clock had been turned back to another late rainy night in 1932 when Jack, Pop Weeks, and I drove from New York to the farm and our heavy Chrysler became mired near the bottom of the hill. During the intervening years, the trees overhead had grown taller, but the road in the rain was the same. While Jack and Pop tried to dig the car out, I had stumbled along in the ruts up the hill to the house—my bare feet found the way through the pitch darkness. I removed the chains from my father's car, without waking him, slung their heavy weight around my shoulders and walked back down the hill. We had shut our springer spaniel in the car, to keep him and it dry and clean. When at last we got in, wet and muddy, we found that "Papa Ben" had eaten our cooked ham. We knew the joys and sorrows of traveling with a dog.

The hill in Sheffield preserved the pioneering spirit in us and in our neighbors. Marilyn du Vigneaud and her husband, Barry Brown, drove that August of 1967 from Rochester, New York, bringing their two small children and behind the car, in a trailer, their two riding horses. They made it, too.

Hunt took kindly to his first horseback ride in front of his mother on her petite mare, while I rode beside them on Retz who had grown big and wise in horses' ways—he was king in the field then. Eight-year-old Janet rode him bareback, as if she were part of him, on all-day "saddle trips" with the group—perhaps to swim and picnic at Umpachene Falls. I stayed at home to watch Hunt and to keep my typewriter keys moving. Our hill and its riding trails still satisfied me. I kept them open with clippers and axe.

Gordon, who was ten, sometimes baby-sat with me. I selected items to read to him about space and science in *The New York Times,* and his sharp questions often provoked me to think in depth. One day after I had combed the pages and set the newspaper aside, he asked, "How's the war going, Grandma?"

"Not so well, Gordon."

"What's the trouble, Grandma?"

"We don't have enough allies," I replied. Friends were perhaps a nation's, or a person's, most important assets, I thought.

I realized that I had avoided news about the Vietnam war, whereas he accepted it with matter-of-fact concern. At Merryfield Farm I had been not much older than Gordon when World War I engulfed Europe in 1914, and the fighting had seemed equally remote to me then, as it did to him. Wars rose against the land and receded like the ocean tides, and on the shores laughing children continued to build sand castles that the waves would erase.

Poetry was my castle in the sand, I mused. Playing with Gordon's Siamese kitten from Tennessee, I had typed off these lines that tickled him:

ANDREW IN SHEFFIELD

Dandy Andy,
Personality Plus,
Sweet as candy,
Meow—hear how he can cuss.

Fine 'n dandy,
Andrew the Siamese,
Always handy,
Prrr, prrr—how he loves to tease.

Buckskin, black nose,
Andrew Street the Second,
Tail high he goes,
Kitten tummy still rotund.

Mittens on paws—
Andy Kitten the Plus—
They cover his claws.
Plus he is and not minus.

Handsome Andy,
Personality Plus,
Lo the Dandy,
See how proud; he struts for us.

No one ever lacked for exciting things to do at the farm. It was a great event when one of the horses had to be shod. When I was a girl, I used to ride Maggie down to the blacksmith shop in the village of Sheffield, where Clarence Martin worked in his leather apron at a forge and anvil. Great showers of sparks flew up when he pounded the red-hot iron to bend and fit it. I can still smell the pungent odor of the scorched horny hoof. In our grandchildren's day, half a century later, Clarence Martin still had his shop but he drove a small smithie's truck up the hill to us. Horseshoes came in many sizes and he easily pounded the cold alloy metal into the shape that he wanted. Holding the hoof between his knees against his old leather apron, he would look up at the circle of captivated faces and philosophize about horses he had known.

Gordon and Janet spent as many hours at the farm catching frogs and salamanders as I had catching butterflies. While Jack and I were in Europe in 1956, Ginny arranged to have a bulldozer scoop out a huge hole for a pond. It was a year of severe drought, and the swamp that had once been an ice pond was dry for the first time in our memory. On my return from abroad, Willard Weeks was showing me and a neighbor the empty excavation, and I was amused to hear my nephew issue the invitation, "Come and fish here next summer." Only a trickle of water from our spring reached the house then, but my father bought the biggest electric hot-water heater that he and Jack could find in Great Barrington, to replace our rusty old forty-gallon tank. The new one was so heavy that the pantry floor had to be shored up to carry its weight. My father and Willard were optimists; they had faith in the future and time proved them right. After ten years of drought, in the rains of 1967 the last of the trout with which Willard had stocked the pond washed across our dirt road and swam downstream. The new eighty-gallon tank had become barely big enough to supply the hot water needed by Ginny's and my enlarging families and their friends.

In retrospect I have asked myself: What is the combination, the mystique, that has kept alive for all these years the spirit with which my mother endowed Merryfield Farm? The place has, of course, freedom from clocks, schedules, and cocktail parties. Clearly, there is closeness to nature, and the healthy fatigue of physical activity. There is time for parents to join in the fun of their children, time to read books and draw pictures, to watch the sunset and to sing on the porch by the light of the old Japanese candle-lanterns. There are bonfires on the lawn at night, brilliant stars and cool mountain air—at an altitude of 1,100 feet perhaps even a small degree of hypoxia.

But those ingredients are to be found in many vacation resorts and by themselves they are not enough. The essence of the enduring combination is the forward-looking productivity of a farm, which my father recognized. There will always be another, and a better season. Our fields are fertilized, plowed, planted, and the harvest reaped through the industry of our neighbors, but we share in the responsibility. Our horses are not merely ridden; they are lovingly brushed, petted, and fed each day by the children. The genie of the house has been my sister to whom, like my mother, an unkind thought or ill word is unknown. Thanks to her, we have flowers that bloom, plumbing that works, a roof on the house and paint on its walls. For every generation Merryfield Farm is an adventure in learning, peace and friendship.

In my lifetime, the dark shadow of hallucinatory drugs has not passed over the farm. Young people must build new worlds for themselves, but as they join the next older generation their point of view inevitably shifts from nonconformity to the perspective of experience. Drugs such as LSD can damage the mind and block that normal process of maturing. They constitute a new imponderable and destructive force on the present scene.

I have wished that each young person who is in the dilemma of choosing his path through the complexities of life could know the hazard of trying those drugs "just for kicks." He may become enmeshed in their trap and never escape from being an emotional cripple. The psychological disability that results is painful beyond all physical injury.

In Sheffield I thought about the blessings of our interlude there, and I had time to write:

ODE TO POETRY, 1967 MODEL

The language of suffering
Is the language of poetry,
Its syllables buffering
Dreams from pain of reality,

> Its images offering
> Drugless trips, painless fantasies.
>
> Who has need of LSD
> When he gets kicks from poetry?
>
> The drumbeats of poetry
> Drive off specters of stuttering
> Teachers steeped in bigotry;
> Bury in music moldering
> Preachers of idolatry
> Duped by their own dull muttering.
>
> Swing it, sing it! Poetry
> Can turn you on and set you free.

Our world is not inevitably "going to pot." Our grandchildren and great-grandchildren will find new frontiers to explore, and they will build a new quality of life, far beyond our vision of today.

Both the folly and achievements of mankind were told over a hundred years ago by Henry Wadsworth Longfellow, when in 1864 during our Civil War he wrote about the "Christmas Bells":

. . .

> And in despair I bowed my head;
> "There is no peace on earth," I said;
> "For hate is strong
> And mocks the song
> Of peace on earth, good-will to men!"
>
> Then pealed the bells more loud and deep:
> "God is not dead; nor doth he sleep!
> The wrong shall fail,
> The right prevail,
> With peace on earth, good-will to men."

Young people of all countries will continue to hope and work for peace on earth, as they have for centuries. They will find the strength to face new threats of war and nuclear destruction, so long as the older generations do not lose faith in them and so long as the fiber of our family life is preserved.

One of my finest compliments was a remark of McGeorge Bundy's that I overheard. Mac ran up our steps at Cathedral Avenue and handed Jack a book with the words, "Please give this to your bride."

I am proudest of that title.

On a New Year's evening in our contemporary home, I wrote a greeting to my husband:

A HAPPY NEW YEAR!

Ring in the new New Year,
My dear, the old one ring out.
Each year on year we hear
Ourselves jubilantly shout,
"Happy New Year, my dear!"

In the gardens of love
We two have walked hand in hand
Spanned by rainbows above.
Sun sets; still we understand
The language of the dove.

Swift the stream of life flows
As rapids plunge us onward.
Now the river broadens, slows.
We look not back, but forward
Toward the sea in repose.

Moon's wake of golden hue
Stretches to infinity,
Calm, glorious to view,
Gateway to eternity.
Happy New Year to you!

Bibliography of Writings
by the Author

SCIENTIFIC PAPERS

(with JEANETTE A. BEHRE) "Effect of Insulin on the Rate of Fermentation of Glucose by Yeast," *Proceedings of the Society for Experimental Biology and Medicine,* XXI (1924), 478–79.

(with JOHN WYCKOFF and HARRY GOLD) "Importance of Differences in the Potency of Digitalis in Clinical Practice," *American Heart Journal,* V (1930), 401–11.

(with ARTHUR C. DE GRAFF and J. ALLEN YAGER) "An Electrocardiographic Study of the Heart in Lobar Pneumonia," *Journal of Clinical Investigation,* X (1931), 633–51.

(with HARRY GOLD and NATHAN KWIT) "The Depression of the Vomiting Mechanism by Digitalis," *Proceedings of the Society for Experimental Biology and Medicine,* XXIX (1931), 66–68.

(———) "Depression of the Vomiting Reflex by the Digitalis Bodies," *American Heart Journal,* VII (1931), 165–81.

"A Contribution to the Pharmacology of Pseudomorphine," *Journal of Pharmacology and Experimental Therapeutics,* XLIV (1932), 123–50.

(with WALTER MODELL) "The Role of the Lipoid in the Renal Tubule of the Cat in Uranium Nephritis," *Anatomical Record,* LIX (1934), 253–63.

"The Potassium Mercuric Iodide Reagents for Alkaloids," *Journal of the American Pharmaceutical Association,* XXIII (1934), 689–98.

(with HARRY GOLD) "Ethyl Alcohol and Strychnine Antagonism," *Journal of Pharmacology and Experimental Therapeautics.,* LII (1934), 30–53.

(———) "Ether and Strychnine Antagonism," *ibid.,* LII (1934), 259–74.

(———) "Strychnine in Poisoning by Alcohol," *ibid.,* LII (1934), 345–54.

(———) "Mechanism of Action of Strychnine on Respiration," *ibid.,* LIII (1935), 169–78.

(———) "The Vaso-Depressor Effect of Strychnine after Ether, Alcohol, Barbital or Chloral," *Archives Internationale de Pharmacodynamie et de Thérapie,* L (1935), 1–14.

474

(with HARRY GOLD and WALTER MODELL) "The Effect of Theophylline with Ethylenediamine (Aminophylline) on the Course of Cardiac Infarction Following Experimental Coronary Occlusion," *American Heart Journal*, XIV (1937), 284–96.

(———) "The Effect of Experimental Cardiac Infarction on the Response to Digitalis," *Archives of Internal Medicine*, LXI (1938), 184–97.

(———) "The Influence of the Size of Cardiac Infarcts upon the Electrocardiogram," *American Heart Journal*, XV (1938), 77–83.

(———) "The Blood Pressure and the Size of a Cardiac Infarct," *ibid.*, XV (1938), 448–51.

"The Absorption of Alkaloids from the Stomach," *Journal of Pharmacology and Experimental Therapeutics*, LXIII (1938), 37.

"The Influence of the Hydrogen Ion Concentration on the Absorption of Alkaloids from the Stomach," *ibid.*, LXIX (1940), 21–33.

(with OSCAR BODANSKY and HARRY GOLD) "Nicotine Excretion and the Role of Its Reabsorption from the Urinary Bladder as a Source of Nicotine Poisoning in Tobacco Smokers," *ibid.*, LXIX (1940), 307.

"Influence of pH on Absorption of Nicotine from Urinary Bladder and Subcutaneous Tissues," *Proceedings of the Society for Experimental Biology and Medicine*, XLV (1940), 552–56.

"Some Recent Advances in Hypnosis and Sedation," in *Medical Clinics of North America* (Philadelphia, W. B. Saunders Company, 1940), XXIV, 603–11.

(with HARRY GOLD) "Studies on the Absorption of Some Digitalis Preparations from the Gastrointestinal Tract in the Cat and Man," *Journal of Pharmacology and Experimental Therapeutics*, LXXII (1941), 41.

(with WILLARD TRAVELL) "Modifications and Effects of the Static Surge and of the Static Wire-Brush Discharge," *Archives of Physical Therapy*, XXII (1941), 486–89.

(———) "Technic for Reduction and Ambulatory Treatment of Sacroiliac Manipulation," *ibid.*, XXIII (1942), 222–32.

(with SEYMOUR H. RINZLER and MYRON HERMAN) "Pain and Disability of the Shoulder and Arm. Treatment by Intramuscular Infiltration with Procaine Hydrochloride," *Journal of the American Medical Association*, CXX (1942), 417–22.

(with HARRY GOLD, NATHANIEL T. KWIT, and MC KEEN CATTELL) "Studies on Purified Digitalis Glycosides: IV. The Single Dose Method of Digitalization by Digitoxin," *ibid.*, CXIX (1942), 928–32.

(with HARRY GOLD, WALTER MODELL, and OSCAR AUERBACH) "A Study of Cardiac Hemorrhages Caused by the Digitalis Glycosides," *Federation Proceedings*, I (1942), 170.

(with THEODORE T. FOX and LEONARD MOLOFSKY) "Action of Digitalis on Conduction in the Syndrome of Short P-R Interval and Prolonged QRS Complex," *Archives of Internal Medicine*, LXXI (1943), 206–18.

(with SEYMOUR H. RINZLER and HELEN CIVIN) "The Oscillometric Index," *ibid.*, LXXIII (1944), 241–47.

(with CHARLES BERRY and NOLTON BIGELOW) "Effects of Referred Somatic Pain on Structures in the Reference Zone," *Federation Proceedings*, III (1944), 49.

(with NOLTON H. BIGELOW) "Referred Somatic Pain Does Not Follow a Simple 'Segmental' Pattern," *ibid.*, V (1946), 106.

(with WILLARD TRAVELL) "Therapy of Low Back Pain by Manipulation and of

Referred Pain in the Lower Extremity by Procaine Infiltration," *Archives of Physical Medicine*, XXVII (1946), 537–47.

(with SEYMOUR H. RINZLER) "Relief of Cardiac Pain by Local Block of Somatic Trigger Areas," *Proceedings of the Society for Experimental Biology and Medicine*, LXIII (1946), 480–82.

(———) "The Electrocardiographic Diagnosis of Acute Myocardial Infarction in the Presence of the Wolff Parkinson White Syndrome," *American Journal of Medicine*, III (1947), 106–12.

(with NOLTON H. BIGELOW) "Role of Somatic Trigger Areas in the Patterns of Hysteria," *Psychosomatic Medicine*, IX (1947), 353–63.

(with AUDRIE L. BOBB) "Mechanism of Relief of Pain in Sprains by Local Injection Technics," *Federation Proceedings*, VI (1947), 378.

(with SEYMOUR H. RINZLER) "Therapy Directed at the Somatic Component of Cardiac Pain," *American Heart Journal*, XXXV (1948), 248–68.

(———) "Pain Syndromes of the Chest Muscles: Resemblance to Effort Angina and Myocardial Infarction, and Relief by Local Block," *Canadian Medical Association Journal*, LIX (1948), 333–38.

"Basis for the Multiple Uses of Local Block of Somatic Trigger Areas," *Mississippi Valley Medical Journal*, LXXI (1949), 13–21.

"Rapid Relief of Acute 'Stiff Neck' by Ethyl Chloride Spray," *Journal of the American Medical Women's Association*, IV (1949), 89–95.

(with SEYMOUR H. RINZLER) "Influence of Ethyl Chloride Spray on Deep Pain and Ischemic Contraction of Skeletal Muscle," *Federation Proceedings*, VIII (1949), 339.

"Discussion of Paper on Diagnosis and Treatment of Mechanical Backache by George S. Phalen," *Journal of the American Medical Association*, CXLI (1949), 448.

(with SEYMOUR H. RINZLER, HYMAN BAKST, ZACHARY H. BENJAMIN, and AUDRIE L. BOBB) "Failure of Alpha Tocopherol to Influence Chest Pain in Patients with Heart Disease," *Federation Proceedings*, VIII (1949), 328.

(———) "Comparison of Effects of Alpha Tocopherol and a Matching Placebo on Chest Pain in Patients with Heart Disease," *Annals of the New York Academy of Sciences*, LII (1949), 345–53.

(———) "Failure of Alpha Tocopherol to Influence Chest Pain in Patients with Heart Disease," *Circulation*, I (1950), 288–93.

(with LAWRENCE W. HANLON, N. CHANDLER FOOT, and SEYMOUR H. RINZLER) "Pathological Muscle Changes Produced in Guinea Pigs by Deficiency of Antistiffness Factors and Effect of Ergostanyl Acetate," *Federation Proceedings*, IX (1950), 282.

(with THEODORE GREINER, HARRY GOLD, MC KEEN CATTELL, HYMAN BAKST, SEYMOUR H. RINZLER, ZACHARY H. BENJAMIN, LEON J. WARSHAW, AUDRIE L. BOBB, NATHANIEL T. KWIT, WALTER MODELL, HAROLD H. ROTHENDLER, CHARLES R. MESSELOFF, and MILTON L. KRAMER) "A Method for the Evaluation of the Effects of Drugs on Cardiac Pain in Patients with Angina of Effort. A Study of Khellin (Visammin)," *American Journal of Medicine*, IX (1950), 143–55.

"The Adductor Longus Syndrome. A Cause of Groin Pain; Its Treatment by Local Block of Trigger Areas (Procaine Infiltration and Ethyl Chloride Spray)," *Bulletin of the New York Academy of Medicine*, XXVI (1950), 284.

"Discussion of Paper on Myofascial Pain by Ralph L. Gorrell," *Journal of the American Medical Association,* CXLII (1950), 561.

"Early Relief of Chest Pain by Ethyl Chloride Spray in Acute Coronary Thrombosis. Case Report," *Circulation,* III (1951), 120–24.

(with IRENE KOPROWSKA, BARBARA B. HIRSCH, and SEYMOUR H. RINZLER)"Effect of Ethyl Chloride Spray on Thermal Burns," *Journal of Pharmacology and Experimental Therapeutics,* CI (1951), 36.

"Ethyl Chloride Spray for Painful Muscle Spasm," *Archives of Physical Medicine,* XXXIII (1952), 291–98.

(with SEWARD J. BAKER and BARBARA B. HIRSCH) "Myofascial Component of Intermittent Claudication," *Federation Proceedings,* XI (1952), 164.

"Pain Mechanisms in Connective Tissue," in *Connective Tissues. Transactions of the Second Conference,* 1951 (New York, Josiah Macy, Jr. Foundation, 1952), pp. 86–125.

(with SEYMOUR H. RINZLER) "The Myofascial Genesis of Pain. A Scientific Exhibit," *Postgraduate Medicine,* XI (1952), 425–34.

(with SEYMOUR H. RINZLER, HYMAN BAKST, ZACHARY H. BENJAMIN, ROBERT L. ROSENTHAL, SIDNEY ROSENFELD, and BARBARA B. HIRSCH) "Effect of Heparin in Effort Angina," *American Journal of Medicine,* XIV (1953), 438–47.

"Pharmacology of Stimulant Laxatives," *Annals of the New York Academy of Sciences,* LIX (1954), 416–25.

(with SEYMOUR H. RINZLER, ISIDORE STEIN, HYMAN BAKST, JOSEPH WEINSTEIN, and ROBERT GITTLER) "Blocking Effect of Ethyl Chloride Spray on Cardiac Pain Induced by Ergonovine," *Proceedings of the Society for Experimental Biology and Medicine,* LXXXV (1954), 329–33.

(————) "Cardiac Pain in Man: Blocking Effect of Ethyl Chloride Spray on the Angina of Ergonovine," *Bulletin of the New York Academy of Medicine,* XXX (1954), 318.

"Assessment of Drugs for Therapeutic Efficacy," *American Journal of Physical Medicine,* XXXIV (1955), 129–40.

"Referred Pain from Skeletal Muscle. I. Pectoralis Major Syndrome of Breast Pain and Soreness; II. Sternomastoid Syndrome of Headache and Dizziness," *New York State Journal of Medicine,* LV (1955), 331–40.

(with VIRGINIA D. WEEKS) "Postural Vertigo due to Trigger Areas in the Sternocleidomastoid Muscle," *Journal of Pediatrics,* XLVII (1955), 315–27.

"Factors Affecting Pain of Injection," *Journal of the American Medical Association,* CLVIII (1955), 368–71. (Translation: "Factores que Affectan el Dolor de la Inyección," *El Dia Médico* (Buenos Aires), November 14, 1955, pp. 2760–64.)

(with SEYMOUR H. RINZLER and DOROTHY KARP) "Detection of Coronary Atherosclerosis in the Living Animal by the Ergonovine Stress Test," *Science,* CXXI (1955), 900–902.

(with SEYMOUR H. RINZLER, DOROTHY KARP, and DIANA CHARLESON) "Detection of Coronary Atherosclerosis in the Living Rabbit by the Ergonovine Stress Test," *American Journal of Physiology,* CLXXXIV (1956), 605–12.

(with DOROTHY KARP, MARIO PENNA, and SEYMOUR H. RINZLER) "Effects of Ergonovine on the Heart," *Journal of Pharmacology and Experimental Therepeutics,* CXVI (1956), 34.

(with DOROTHY KARP and SEYMOUR H. RINZLER) "Ergonovine and Vasopressin

Effects on the Isolated Heart of the Rabbit with Coronary Atherosclerosis," in *Abstract of Communications. XXth Physiological Congress,* Brussels, 1956, p. 482.

(———) "The Ergonovine Test Detects Coronary Atherosclerosis in the Living Rabbit, *ibid.,* p. 765.

(———) "Nicotine Effects on Normal and Atherosclerotic Rabbit Hearts," *Federation Proceedings,* XVI (1957), 341.

(with VIRGINIA D. WEEKS) "How to Give Painless Injections," in *A.M.A. Scientific Exhibits,* 1957 (New York, Grune & Stratton, 1957), pp. 318–22.

(———) "How to Give Painless Injections," in *Abstracts of the Tenth Annual Assembly, American Academy of General Practice,* Dallas, Texas, March, 1958 (Kansas City, Mo., American Academy of General Practice, 1958), pp. 17–19.

"Symposium on the Mechanism and Management of Pain Syndromes," in *Proceedings, Rudolf Virchow Medical Society in the City of New York, 1957* (Basel, S. Karger, 1959), XVI, 128–36.

(with DOROTHY KARP and SEYMOUR H. RINZLER) "Effect of Ergometrine (Ergonovine) on the Isolated Atherosclerotic Heart of the Cholesterol-fed Rabbit," *British Journal of Pharmacology,* XV (1960), 333–44.

"The Absorption of Nicotine from Various Sites," *Annals of the New York Academy of Sciences,* XC (1960), 13–30.

(with SEYMOUR H. RINZLER and DOROTHY KARP) "Cardiac Effects of Nicotine in the Rabbit with Experimental Coronary Atherosclerosis," *ibid.,* XC (1960), 290–301.

"Temporomandibular Joint Pain Referred from Muscles of the Head and Neck," *Journal of Prosthetic Dentistry,* X (1960), 745–63.

"Mechanical Headache," *Headache,* VII (1967), 23–29.

MISCELLANEOUS ARTICLES

"Six Ways to Make Housework Lighter," *Today's Woman,* February, 1950.

"Don't Argue When He Wants to Exercise," *ibid.,* September, 1950.

(with ADA C. REID and MARY P. CLAPP) "Housework and the Physician-Mother," *Journal of the American Medical Women's Association,* VIII (February, 1953), 63–64.

(with WILLIAM A. LYDGATE) "Today's Family Doctor—Are *You* One in a Million?" (cartoon strip), *Today's Family,* May, 1953, p. 79.

"Doctor, Wife and Mother," *Wellesley Alumnae Magazine,* November, 1953, pp. 13–14.

"Chairs Are a Personal Thing," *House Beautiful,* October, 1955, pp. 190–93; reprinted, "How to Choose a Chair," *ibid.,* July, 1961, pp. 80–83, 104–105; condensed, "Ladies and Gentlemen, Be Seated—Properly," *Reader's Digest,* August, 1961, pp. 159–62.

"How to Relieve Aches and Pains," (interview), *U.S. News & World Report,* February 20, 1961, pp. 66–71; condensed, "Why We Have Aches and Pains —And What to Do About Them," *Reader's Digest,* May, 1961, pp. 91–95; condensed, "Muscular Aches and Pains," in *Our Human Body. Its Wonders and Care* (Pleasantville, N.Y., Reader's Digest Association, 1962), pp. 198–202.

Letter to the Editor, *U.S. News & World Report,* March 13, 1961, p. 16.

(with DAVID D. LEWIS) "Fit to Be President," *Sports Illustrated,* April 3, 1961, pp. 57–58; reprinted, "Fit to Be President," *Scouting,* October, 1961, pp. 8–9.

"Use and Abuse of the Muscles in Housework," *Journal of the American Medical Women's Association,* XVIII (February, 1963), 159–62.

"How Fitness Begins," in *Fitness for the Whole Family* (Garden City, N.Y., Doubleday & Company, 1964), pp. 55–57.

CONFERENCES TO WHICH THE AUTHOR CONTRIBUTED

Cornell Conferences on Therapy, Departments of Pharmacology and Medicine

"Evaluation of Drugs Used in the Treatment of Syphilis," *Journal of the American Medical Association,* CXII (1939), 2415 ff.

"The Use of Anthelmintics," *ibid.,* CXIII (1939), 410 ff.

"Treatment of Poisoning," *ibid.,* CXIII (1939), pp. 493 ff.; republished in *Cornell Conferences on Therapy,* I (New York, Macmillan Company, 1946), 266–294.

"Routes of Administration of Drugs," *Journal of the American Medical Association,* CXIV (1940), 1447 ff.

"Treatment of Pneumonia," *New York State Journal of Medicine,* XLI (1941), 276 ff.

"Management of Constipation," *ibid.,* XLI (1941), pp. 1959 ff.

"Treatment of Some Intestinal Infestations," *ibid.,* XLII (1942), 443 ff.; republished in *Cornell Conferences on Therapy,* I (1946), 224–45.

"Use and Abuse of Bed Rest," *New York State Journal of Medicine,* XLIV (1944), 724 ff.; republished in *Cornell Conferences on Therapy,* I (1946), 18–35.

"Management of Pain Due to Muscle Spasm," *New York State Journal of Medicine,* XLV (1945), 2085 ff.; republished in *Cornell Conferences on Therapy,* III (1949), 202–33.

"The Rational Use of Cathartic Agents," Part I, *New York State Journal of Medicine,* XLVII (1947), 387 ff.; Part II, *ibid.,* pp. 504 ff.; republished in *Cornell Conferences on Therapy,* III (1949), 275–303.

"Treatment of Some Chronic Muscular Diseases," *American Journal of Medicine,* II (1947), 630 ff.; republished in *Cornell Conferences on Therapy,* V (1952), 138–63.

"Treatment of Painful Disorders of Skeletal Muscle," *New York State Journal of Medicine,* XLVIII (1948), 2050 ff.; republished in *Cornell Conferences on Therapy,* IV (1951), 253–79.

"Relief of Pain by Ethyl Chloride Spray," *New York State Journal of Medicine,* LII (1952), 1550 ff.; republished in *Cornell Conferences on Therapy,* V (1952), 164–85.

Conferences of the Josiah Macy, Jr. Foundation, New York

Connective Tissues. Transactions of the Second Conference, May 24–25, 1951, New York. Charles Ragan, ed. New York, Josiah Macy, Jr. Foundation, 1952.

Id., the Third Conference, February 14–15, 1952, New York. Charles Ragan, ed. New York, Josiah Macy, Jr. Foundation, 1952.

Id., the Fourth Conference, February 18–20, 1953, Princeton, New Jersey. Charles Ragan, ed. New York, Josiah Macy, Jr. Foundation, 1953.

Id., the Fifth Conference, February 8–10, 1954, Princeton, New Jersey. Charles Ragan, ed. New York, Josiah Macy, Jr. Foundation, 1954.

Cold Injury. Transactions of the Second Conference, November 20–21, 1952, New York. M. Irené Ferrer, ed. New York, Josiah Macy, Jr. Foundation, 1954.

Id., the Third Conference, February 22–25, 1954, Fort Churchill, Manitoba, Canada. M. Irené Ferrer, ed. New York, Josiah Macy, Jr. Foundation, 1955.

Id., the Fourth Conference, November 7–9, 1955, Princeton, New Jersey. M. Irené Ferrer, ed. New York, Josiah Macy, Jr. Foundation, 1956.

Id., the Fifth Conference, March 10–15, 1957, Arctic Aeromedical Laboratory, Ladd Air Force Base, Alaska. M. Irené Ferrer, ed. New York, Josiah Macy, Jr. Foundation, 1958.

Id., the Sixth Conference, July 6–10, 1958, U.S. Army Medical Research Laboratory, Fort Knox, Kentucky. Steven M. Horvath, ed. New York, Josiah Macy, Jr. Foundation, 1960.

White House Conference on Health. *Proceedings of the White House Conference on Health,* November 3–4, 1965. Washington, D.C., U.S. Department of Health, Education and Welfare, pp. 171 and 488.

Index

481